STANDARD HANDBOOK
FOR SECRETARIES

Standard Handbook
for Secretaries

BY

LOIS IRENE HUTCHINSON

SIXTH EDITION

McGRAW-HILL BOOK COMPANY, INC.

New York   *Toronto*   *London*

1952

STANDARD HANDBOOK FOR SECRETARIES
Copyright, 1936, 1939, 1941, 1944, 1947, 1950
by the
McGRAW-HILL BOOK COMPANY, INC.

In this edition, the section on *Postal Information,* has been thoroughly revised, and the latest postal rates are included.

New **cable and express rates** are also included, as well as new **patent, trade-mark, and copyright fees and information.**

Recent **Civil Service and American Foreign Service information** is given; and the new setup of **Government offices** under 1949 reorganization is shown.

IV

PUBLISHED BY THE McGRAW-HILL BOOK COMPANY, INC.

Printed in the United States of America by The Maple Press Co., York, Pa.

AUTHORITIES CONSULTED

Dictionaries

Funk & Wagnalls New Standard Dictionary of the English Language, Funk & Wagnalls Company, New York.
(Excerpt from Funk & Wagnalls Practical Standard Dictionary reprinted by permission from the Editor and the Publishers.)

The Oxford English Dictionary, The Clarendon Press, Oxford.

The Shorter Oxford English Dictionary, The Clarendon Press, Oxford.

Webster's New International Dictionary, G. & C. Merriam Company, Springfield, Massachusetts.
(Excerpts from Webster's Collegiate Dictionary reprinted by permission from the Publishers.)

English Handbooks

Fowler: "A Dictionary of Modern English Usage", The Clarendon Press, Oxford.
(Excerpts reprinted by permission from the Publishers.)

Fowler: "The King's English", The Clarendon Press, Oxford.
(Excerpts reprinted by permission from the Publishers.)

Hall: "English Usage", Scott, Foresman and Company, Chicago.

Hill: "Beginnings of Rhetoric and Composition", American Book Company, New York.

Hill: "The Principles of Rhetoric", Harper & Brothers, New York.

House and Harman: "Handbook of Correct English", Longmans, Green and Co., New York.
(Excerpt reprinted by permission from the Publishers.)

Jespersen: "Essentials of English Grammar", Henry Holt and Company, New York.

Kittredge and Arnold: "The Mother Tongue", Ginn and Company, Boston.

Leonard: "Current English Usage", prepared for The National Council of Teachers of English, Chicago.
(Excerpt reprinted by permission from the Publishers.)

O'London, John: "Is It Good English?", G. P. Putnam's Sons, New York.
(Excerpt reprinted by permission from the Author and the Publishers.)

Sonnenschein: "A New English Grammar", The Clarendon Press, Oxford.

Vizetelly: "How to Use English", Funk & Wagnalls Company, New York.
(Excerpts reprinted by permission from the Author and the Publishers.)

Wendell, Barrett: "English Composition", Charles Scribner's Sons, New York.
(Excerpt reprinted by permission from the Publishers.)

Woolley and Scott: "College Handbook of Composition", D. C. Heath and Company, Boston.

Stylebooks

Ives: "Text, Type, and Style: A Compendium of Atlantic Usage", Little, Brown & Company, Boston.
(Excerpts reprinted by permission from the Publishers.)

AUTHORITIES CONSULTED

Summey: "Modern Punctuation", Oxford University Press, New York.

"The New York Times Style Book", New York.

The University of Chicago Press: "A Manual of Style", Chicago.

"United States Government Printing Office Style Manual", Washington, D.C.
(Excerpts reprinted by permission from the Public Printer.)

Banking and Finance

American Institute of Banking: "Banking Fundamentals", New York.

"Crowell's Dictionary of Business and Finance", Thomas Y. Crowell Company, New York.

Harr and Harris: "Banking Theory and Practice", McGraw-Hill Book Company, Inc., New York.

Munn: "Encyclopedia of Banking and Finance", The Bankers Publishing Company, New York.

"Tate's Modern Cambist", Spalding (Editor), The Bankers Publishing Company, New York.

Law

Ballentine: "Law Dictionary", The Lawyers Co-Operative Publishing Company, Rochester, New York.

"Bouvier's Law Dictionary", Baldwin's Century Edition, Banks-Baldwin Law Publishing Company, Cleveland.
(Excerpts reprinted by permission from the Publishers.)

"Corpus Juris: The Whole Body of the Law", The American Law Book Co., New York.

"The Martindale-Hubbell Law Directory", Martindale-Hubbell, Inc., Summit, N.J.

Accounting

Daniels: "Corporation Financial Statements", University of Michigan, Ann Arbor.

Finney: "Principles of Accounting", Prentice-Hall, Inc., New York.

"Accountants' Handbook", Paton (Editor), The Ronald Press Company, New York

Prickett and Mikesell: "Introduction to Accounting", The Macmillan Company, New York.

Printing

Freshwater and Bastien: "Pitman's Dictionary of Advertising and Printing", Sir Isaac Pitman & Sons, Ltd., London.

Insurance

Crobaugh: "Handbook of Insurance", Prentice-Hall, Inc., New York.

Government Publications

"Congressional Directory", Government Printing Office, Washington, D.C.

"United States Official Postal Guide", Government Printing Office, Washington, D.C.

AUTHORITIES CONSULTED

United States Government booklets and pamphlets on different subjects, as referred to in the text.

Miscellaneous Publications

The New York Times, The New York Times Company, New York.

The Saturday Evening Post, The Curtis Publishing Company, Philadelphia.

The Wall Street Journal, Dow Jones & Company, Inc., New York.

The World Almanac, New York World-Telegram, New York.

Whitaker's Almanack, J. Whitaker and Sons, Ltd., London.

United States Government Offices
(Washington, D.C.)

Bureau of Foreign and Domestic Commerce.

Civil Service Commission.

Copyright Office.

Department of State.

Federal Reserve Board.

Government Printing Office.

Library of Congress.

National Bureau of Standards.

Navy Department.

Patent Office.

Post Office Department.

Treasury Department.

Defense Department.

Business Organizations

American Institute of Banking, New York.
(Mr. Richard W. Hill, National Secretary.)

Railway Express Agency, Inc.

San Francisco Stock Exchange.

Santa Fe Railway Lines, Chicago.

The Pacific Telephone and Telegraph Company, San Francisco.

The Western Union Telegraph Company.

American Cable & Radio Corporation

CONTENTS

ix

CONTENTS

ENGLISH

"TO make your meaning clear—that is the secret of good punctuation, good usage, good speech, and good writing!"

> Ruth Mary Weeks, in the Foreword to "Current English Usage", by S. A. Leonard, for The National Council of Teachers of English, Chicago.

"MY point of view is that, in everyday life, good English follows clear thinking rather than that system of rules called Grammar which youth loathes and maturity forgets."

> —John O'London (Wilfred Whitten), "Is It Good English?"

Terms Used in Classification of Words

❖

archaic	antiquated
colloquial	informal, or conversational
commercial	used in business
dialectal	used in certain dialects or local forms of the language
idiomatic	following no definite rule, as certain expressions characteristic of the language
illiterate	used in uneducated speech
obsolete	no longer used
provincial	used in certain districts or provinces; hence not general
slang	coarse or grotesque

ITALICS, throughout this book, signify words that are incorrect or incorrectly used.

❖

ENGLISH

To determine what is right:

Analyze the sentence structure.

By elimination or substitution of words, or completion of unfinished sentences, test the correctness of the whole.

In a single sentence everything should agree—should be in accord. In testing sentences remember that there is a reason—not necessarily a rule, but a reason—for grammatical construction.

The Fifteen Most Common Errors

1. Pronouns incorrectly used.
2. Singular verbs with plural subjects, and vice versa.
3. Tenses of verbs mixed.
4. Collective nouns confused.
5. Possessives, especially of plural nouns, incorrectly formed.
6. Double negatives formed.
7. Foreign plurals unrecognized.
   The misuse of:
8. **Don't** for **doesn't.**
9. **Like** for **as** or **as if.**
10. **Set** for **sit.**
11. **Lay** for **lie.**
12. **Raise** for **rise.**
13. **Affect** for **effect.**
14. **Only** (placement of).
15. **Can** for **may.**

WORDS MISUSED

a   used before all consonant sounds, including h when sounded.

an   used before all vowel sounds, except long u.

Consonant Sounds	Vowel Sounds
a hotel	an honorary degree
a historical event	an honest opinion
a hilarious parade	an hour
a heroic effort	an heir
a humble opinion	an herb
a hysterical action	**Long U Sound**
a hundred tons	a unit
a habitual thing	a unique method
a humorous tale	a union
a oneness	a unanimous decision
a one-day period (in the word "one"	a eulogy
o has a w sound)	a uniform

3

Note: Some publishers and writers use "an" before a sounded h, if the first syllable of the word is not accented, which accounts for "an historical novel", "an hotel", "an Herculean task", etc. British writers sometimes use "an" before a long u sound, as "an union", "an eulogy", etc. But these uses are not general, and authorities favor the clear-cut distinction first above given.

above
above-mentioned } In commercial phrases these words are often used as nouns.
above-named

   ...in accordance with the above.
   ...any of the above-mentioned may be signed. } as nouns
   ...the above facts.
   ...the above-mentioned data. } as adjectives

all is commonly used without "of", as in

   ...all the time that we were there.
   Practically all the judges are...
   We counted all the people.

all of them is commonly used instead of "they all" or "them all".
all of us is commonly used instead of "we all" or "us all".
   (In fact, the "all of" phrases sometimes convey a meaning different from the other phrases.)

   Send it to all of them. (OR: them all)
   All of them are involved. (OR: They all)
   All of us are needed for that job. (OR: We all)
   They meant all of us. (OR: us all)

alone means "by itself" or "solitary". Do not use it in the "not only" phrase.

   They not *alone* sold the property but took... (USE: only)

The placement of "alone" affects the meaning of a sentence.

   Alone, he solved the problem. (without company)
   He alone solved the problem. (no one else)
   He solved the problem *alone*.
      ("Alone" is ambiguous here. Better to re-place it, or use "only".)
   The plates specified cost, alone, 11¢ a pound. (by themselves)
   The building alone cost $100,000. (NOT: cost $100,000 *alone*)
   ...for that, they alone are to blame. (no one else)
   ...for that alone they are to blame. (nothing else)

Commas should occasionally be used to clarify the meaning.

   ...and the rambling adobe where he lived in Monterey alone remains.
   CLEARER: ...where he lived in Monterey, alone remains.

amid   **amidst** } Since there is no difference in meaning between
among **amongst** } these word forms, the shorter and more modern
while   **whilst** } form is to be preferred.

4

and should not be used when "but" is intended in an idea of "on the contrary", "on the other hand", etc.

but expresses contrast or opposition, either faintly or emphatically, whereas "and" does not.

> They said they were mailing the check, *and* we have heard nothing since. (USE: but)
> Some people do that *and* they should not be imitated. (USE: but)

and is frequently omitted before the last word in a series, being replaced by a comma. This device is not approved by some good authorities, but still it is seen in many publications.

> They are interested in no past, no present, no future, but rather in the tradition...
> If our aim had been numbers, size, riches, then whatever...

and/or is a commercialism, used especially in the law of the land.

> ...transmitting and/or receiving radio communications.—Radio Act.
> ...secured by warehouse receipts, and/or shipping documents..., and/or mortgages, and/or such other collateral...—Federal Reserve Act.

A subject composed of singular nouns connected by "and/or" may be considered singular or plural, according to the meaning of the sentence.

> Robert B. Logan and/or James T. Hanna **are** hereby appointed my **executors.**
> (meaning that both are to act; or either one is to act if the other is not living, or is incapacitated)
> All loss and/or damage is to be paid for by the carrier.
> (one or the other, and possibly both)

any is used idiomatically in the following sentences, the word "other" being understood. (In formal writings, "other" should be used.)

> Their workmanship is better than any we have seen.
> (FOR THE CORRECT:...than any other we have seen.)
> They are stronger than any concern in the field.
> (FOR THE CORRECT:...than any other concern in the field.)

any may represent an indefinite quantity (large or small).
all represents a definite quantity (the whole).

> Send us any [letters] that you receive.
> Send us all [the letters] you have received.

"Best of All" and "Best of Any". When the whole quantity is available for comparison, "all" should be used. When only an indefinite or unknown quantity is available, "any" may be used.

> He is the **best** pilot of **all** on our lines.
> Our planes are held to be the **fastest** of **all** nations.
> Pick the **best** of **any** suggestions that are submitted.
> He is the **most** promising of **any** of the candidates who are likely to be proposed.
> COMMON USAGE: { Last month was the **best** for **any** February since 1930.
> The total is the **largest** for **any** comparable period.
> Naturally the advertiser wants the **strongest** market offered by **any** newspaper.

5

CONFUSED:

> He is the **youngest** of **any** college *president.* (FOR: of all college presidents OR: of any of the college presidents OR: is younger than any other college president)
>
> It was the **best** of **all** *year's earning* since 1928. (FOR: best of all years' earnings [poor construction] BETTER: of all yearly earnings OR: best year's earning of all since 1928)

anything like a usual, though rather homely phrase.

They won't receive anything like its value.

appreciate is often left unfinished. It usually takes an object.

(Also, supposedly, it requires no modifiers, because it represents in itself a fullness of gratitude, or esteem, sensibility, etc. But such words as "fully", "greatly", "deeply", and "very much", have been used with it for so long a time—to express degrees of appreciation—that it is doubtful whether they will be abandoned now.)

UNFINISHED: We shall appreciate ∧ if you will do that. ("it" omitted)
(One would not write "We shall enjoy if you will... ")
MODIFIED: We **fully** appreciate your position.

apt suggests a habitual or natural tendency—an aptitude.
likely suggests a probable tendency—a likelihood.
liable suggests an unfavorable tendency—a liability.

They are apt to do it. (it is their habit)
They are likely to succeed. (it is probable)
They are liable to fail. (an unfavorable possibility)

around **round** "Round", without an apostrophe, is interchangeable with "around" in American usage; but "round" is preferred in British usage.

the year round   a round-the-world flight
the wheels turn round   all round the town

"All-round" is generally preferred to "all-around", although the latter may be used.

an all-round scholar   gives economy all round
an all-round machine   guesswork all round
a square deal all around (colloquial)

as...as usually used with positive statements.
so...as usually used with negative or emphatic statements.

As far as we know, they are reliable. (positive)
They are not so reliable as we thought. (negative)
EMPHATIC: They even went so far as to ridicule the idea.
It will be agreeable so long as the final terms...
...and stimulate so far as possible the new trade.

as far as... so far as... These expressions, to be grammatically correct, should not be left unfinished in sentences. But in commercial writings, the complementary words, "is concerned", "concerns", "goes", etc., are often omitted and supposedly understood.

6

UNFINISHED: So far as reducing the payments, we would not consider...
BETTER: So far as reducing the payments **is concerned,** we would...
UNFINISHED: The work is at a standstill as far as obtaining permission to rebuild.
BETTER: The work is at a standstill **as far as concerns** obtaining permission to rebuild.
UNFINISHED: Conditions will be changed as far as working overtime with no extra pay.
BETTER: Conditions will be changed **as far as they concern** working overtime with no extra pay.
OR: ...**as far as** working overtime with no extra pay **is concerned.**

as per is a commercialism for "in accordance with", as in the phrase "as per shipping instructions". But it should be kept in its place among abbreviations.

as regards is a commonplace expression meaning "concerning".

as to Do not overwork this phrase. It is properly used to introduce an inverted clause or phrase; or to introduce something that is **especially indefinite.**

As to that, we cannot say.

To avoid the constant use of "as to" substitute "regarding", "concerning", "about", "of", etc. Sometimes "as to" may even be omitted, to the sentence's advantage.

The question is *as to* the employment or nonemployment... (BETTER: The question concerns...)
We cannot plan so long as we are uncertain *as to* what will be done. (USE: about)
Contracts should not be so phrased as to permit a moment's doubt *as to* the correct meaning. (USE: about)
(The first "as" belongs to "so" and not to "to permit".)
A controversy arose *as to* whom the money should be paid.
(Another "to" is needed at the end to complete the sentence. It would be better to write: A controversy arose regarding the one to whom the money should be paid.)
This is usually the test *as to* whether or not a venture is ... (USE: of)

"As to" is commonly used before "whether", although it is not always necessary.

USUAL: Opinion is divided as to whether both cities are...
UNNECESSARY: We are undecided *as to* whether to increase or decrease our selling organization.
UNNECESSARY: They give little consideration *as to* whether or not a law is just. ("As" may be omitted.)

"As to" is often superfluous in other constructions.

UNNECESSARY: *As to* who would file suit was the question.
UNNECESSARY: We have no means of judging *as to* the wisdom of that.

at least is like "alone" and "only" in that its placement in a sentence can affect the meaning.

7

One should be sent at least.   (ambiguous)
One should at least be sent.   (if nothing else is done)
At least one should be sent.   (if no more)

between   should be followed by words that represent two or more things.

> between times (NOT: between *time*)
> NOT: between the *organization*
> BUT: between the members of the organization

If two things are clearly indicated by modifying words (as with "the" before each), a singular word may follow "between"—although plurals are often used in such constructions.

> There is a difference between the European and the American **system.**
> (OFTEN: ...between the European and American **systems.**)
> ...the struggle between the Democratic and the Republican **Party.**
> (OFTEN: ...between the Democratic and Republican **Parties.**)
> ...the interval between the red and the green **light.**

If possessives are used, which tend to join rather than separate the ideas, a plural word is used.

> ...an agreement between his and my attorneys. (BETTER THAN: attorney)
> ...the street between Morrow's and our buildings was not paved. (BETTER THAN: between Morrow's and our building)
> ...effected a settlement between Hildreth's and Newcomb's clients. (NOT: client)
> Note: A better arrangement in many such sentences is to move the noun forward, as "between the European **system** and the American", "between Morrow's **building** and ours".
> Or repeat the noun, as "between the World **War** and the Civil **War**".

between each
between every
   Phrases such as "between each item" and "between every building" are regarded by some as incorrect, because "each" and "every" can refer to only one thing. However, authority now sanctions similar phrases; and such phrases have been used by the best writers for hundreds of years: Shakespeare, Goldsmith, Coleridge, Scott, Dickens, etc.

If it is necessary to be wholly correct, one might use "and the next", as "between each item and the next", etc.

between...and   is the correct combination, not "between...*or*", nor "between...*to*".

> between right **and** wrong (NOT: between right *or* wrong)
> between three **and** four hours (NOT: *to* nor: *or*)
> The decision is between a feast **and** a famine. (NOT: between *either* a feast *or* a famine)
> NOT: ...between 11 p.m. *to* midnight (USE: and)
> NOT: It is the difference between performing the analysis in four steps *or* in eight steps. (USE: and)

both   introduces two things; and if two things are clearly indicated by modifying adjectives (as with "the" before each), a singular

8

word may follow "both"; but more often a plural is used to agree with the rest of the sentence, especially if possessives are involved, which tend to join rather than separate the ideas.

...in both the common and the civil **law.**
Both the Panama and the Suez **Canal** are built...
(OFTEN: Both the Panama and Suez **Canals** are built...)
The consul appealed to both the **Ministers** of War and of Navy.
Both Washington's and Lincoln's **birthdays** occur in February.   (NOT: *birthday*)
Note: For rearrangement of such sentences, see note under "between" on p. ?

both   refers to two things collectively (sometimes to two groups).
each   refers to two or more things individually.
either   refers to two things selectively—one or the other.

INCORRECT: There is a road on *both sides* of the river.
(One road could not be on both sides.)
CORRECT: There are **roads** on **both sides** of the river.
There is a **road** on **each side** of the river.
There is a **road** on **either side** of the river.
("Either" in this sense is not commonly used; "each" is preferable.)

both...and   is the correct combination, not "both...*or*", nor "both... *as well as*".

It will profit both the giver and the receiver.   (NOT: both the giver *as well as* the receiver)

Theoretically, the small words **following** "both", such as "the". "to", "for", etc., should be repeated after "and"; but practically, this is not always done.

...both **for** the one and **for** the other.
OR: ...for both the one and the other.
...both **in** theory and **in** practice.
OR: ...in both theory and practice.
...both **the** incoming and **the** outgoing.

both of...   The "of" is often dropped before nouns, but is used before pronouns (although not always before pronouns acting as modifiers).   The "of" adds a degree of emphasis.

BEFORE NOUNS	BEFORE PRONOUNS AS MODIFIERS	BEFORE PRONOUNS
both men, or	both these men, or	both of these
both the men, or	both of these men	both of us
both of the men	both his partners	both of you men

due to...   should modify nouns ("due" being an adjective).
owing to...   may modify either nouns or verbs (the phrase "owing to" having become a compound preposition).
But the above distinction is being overridden in practically all fields of business writing.   The following sentences illustrate the correct uses (and the complexity of the situation):

9

The change was due to a reorganization.
   ("Due" modifies "change".)
Owing to a reorganization, the change was made.
   ("Owing to..." modifies "was made".)
It is a common error due to ignorance.
   ("Due" modifies "error".)

TEST: Substitute "attributed to" for "due to". If correct, then "due to" is correct. If not, use "owing to".

each other   is used with regard to two.
one another   is used with regard to more than two.
   This is a general distinction and may be varied.

If two stations interfere with each other... (RATHER THAN: with one another)
...the waves of radiation cancel one another. (RATHER THAN: each other)

either............**or**
neither..........**nor**
not.......**or (or nor)**
no........**or (or nor)** } Correct combinations.
never.....**or (or nor)**
nothing...**or (or nor)**
none......**or (or nor)**

Either...or.   Attempt to make the phrases balance after "either" and "or".

NOT: These loans must either come from the Government or banks.
BUT: These loans must come **either from the Government or from banks.**
   ("Must come" belongs to both parts, and therefore should stand before the "either".)
NOT: ...if they should make some move either toward helping or hindering us.
BUT: ...if they should make some move toward **either helping us or hindering us.** ("Toward" belongs to both parts.)
NOT: He will fail either to rise higher there, or will seek other employment.
BUT: He **either will fail...or will seek...**
NOT: The rules are either being deliberately disregarded or the people have overlooked...
BUT: **Either the rules are...or the people have...**

Neither...nor.   "Neither" always takes "nor", never "*or*".

NOT: ...neither to the north *or* the south.
BUT: ...neither to the north nor to the south.

(See also Subjects, p. 73.)

Either...*nor* (incorrect combination).   "Either" never takes "nor" even when a negative occurs before the combination.

NOT: It depends upon the man—not **either** the reputation of the firm *nor* the general prospects.
   (Use "or" to agree with "either" which introduced it.)
NOT: They are not to be used **either** for this *nor* for that. (USE: or)

Not, No, Never, Nothing, None...or (or nor).   Where the negative force of the first word carries over, use "or"; that is, where the sentence

10

construction remains the same, and the same negative could be applied to each part.

> They need **never** trade, **or** correspond, **or** even exchange courtesies with us.
> (never trade, never correspond, never exchange)
> He did **nothing** that was good **or** that was particularly bad.
> (nothing that was good, nothing that was bad)
> It occurred to **nobody** to obtain a sketch of the proceedings **or** even a summary.
> (to nobody to obtain a sketch or a summary)

Where the negative force is cut off and needs renewal, use "nor"; that is, where the sentence construction changes, and the same negative could not be applied to each part.

> He thinks **nothing** of his misfortunes, **nor** does he talk about them.
> It came about with **no** fanfare; **nor** was it received with any particular rejoicing

"Nor" is sometimes used after these negatives for particular emphasis —even when the negative force carries over.

> ...a very great technician—**nothing** more **nor** less.
> We will **not** argue **nor** plead with them.
> It will **not** be worth while to pursue the matter further, **nor** to explain it.

even   The placement of this word in a sentence has much to do with the meaning.

> Even he could solve the problem.   (as dull as he was)
> He could even solve the problem.   (as well as do other things)
> He could solve even the problem.   (as well as other things)
> They were asked even to read the documents.   (as well as to do other things)
> They were asked to read even the documents.   (as well as other things)
> They were even ordered to read the documents.   (as well as being ordered to do other things)

Avoid placing "even" at the end of a sentence, if in that position it could be misinterpreted.

> NOT CLEAR: They were asked to read the documents even.
> (This sentence would have to depend on other sentences to clarify its meaning.)

ever so often   means very often.
every so often   means at different times.   (Regarded as idiomatic.)
every now and then ⎫
every once in a while ⎬ Colloquialisms for "occasionally".
every now and again ⎭
more often than not   is a common expression.

first two
last two   These expressions are preferable to "the *two first* pages", or "rows", etc., or "the *three last* pages", or "rows", etc. There could scarcely be two first pages or rows—just one first page or row.

> NOT: ...as regards the *two last* items.
> BUT: ...as regards the last two items.

11

former⎰ These words should be used only when two things are referred
latter ⎱ to. When three or more things are involved, the references
should be "first" and "last".

> NOT: France, England, Italy, and America will sign the pact if the *former*
> will agree to...
> USE: ...if France will agree... OR: ...if the first country will agree...

good deal⎰ These are good, practical phrases, used by many authorities,
great deal⎱ and listed as "colloquial" by only a few.

> A great deal of time is lost...
> We have tested it a good deal.
> They contain a great deal of information.

hardly...when ⎞ These are the correct combinations, not "hardly...
scarcely...when ⎬ *than*", nor "scarcely...*than*", nor "no sooner...
no sooner...than⎠ *when*".

> **Hardly** had the turning point come **when** (NOT: *than*) a new issue
> arose.
> or: **No sooner** had the turning point come **than** (NOT: *when*) a new issue
> arose.

hence ⎛ These words imply "from" within themselves and do not
thence ⎨ need it as an introduction; but it is often used with them,
whence ⎝ as "from hence", "from thence", and "from whence".
Such usage is considered "established".

how ever   "How ever did you get here?"⎞
what ever   "What ever can it mean?" ⎟ Provincialisms; "ever" mean-
who ever   "Who ever can it be?"   ⎬ ing "in the world".
where ever   "Where ever shall we end?"⎠

Note that in the above constructions "how ever", etc., are separate
words. The closed forms, "however", etc., have different meanings,
and are of course in good usage. Also, "ever" may follow "what" or
"who" in sentences like:

> No one knows what ever came of it.
> Who ever heard of such a thing?

if ⎰ These words are interchangeable; but when followed by "or",
whether⎱ or "or not", "whether" should be used instead of "if".

> They asked **whether** (NOT: *if*) their order would be delayed **or** shipped at once.
> We do not know whether we can meet their price [or not].
> Check to see if (OR: whether) the address is correct.
> He asked if the telegram had been sent.

After "Doubt". "Whether" or "that", instead of "if", is usually
used after the word "doubt".

> I **doubt whether** the meeting could have been held.
> We **doubt whether** they really appear in business.
> We do not **doubt that** they can do it.

-ic alphabetic ⎫
-ical parenthetic ⎪ Although these and similar adjectives may end in
    periodic ⎬ either -ic or -ical, the tendency is to use the shorter
    analytic ⎭ form.

Yet the two forms of some such words have grown to have distinct meanings:

> **economic**   pertaining to man's living, as "economic future".
> **economical**   pertaining to thrift or economy, as "an economical budget".
> **historic**   pertaining to things that have made history, as "a historic spot".
> **historical**   pertaining to history, as "a historical tale".
> **periodic**   pertaining to a period of time.
> **periodical**   pertaining to a publication issued at intervals.

kindly   primarily means "in a kind manner"; but it can also mean "obligingly", "helpfully", "graciously", and "with good will". It is in these senses that it is so often used in business letters.

> **Kindly** send us a receipt for this.
>   (MEANING: "Please", which in turn means "to have the kindness".)
> Would you be so **kind** as to do this for us.   (obliging, or helpful)

kind of ⎫ These expressions are used colloquially to mean "somewhat" or
sort of ⎬ "rather". "Kind a" and "sort a" are corruptions.

> It sounds kind of strange.   It seems sort of true.

kind of *a*   The "*a*" is superfluous.

>   that kind of thing (NOT: that kind of *a* thing)
>   that sort of person (NOT: that sort of *a* person)
>   in this kind of country
>   the same kind of transaction
> COLLOQUIAL: ⎰ ...written in kind of *a* dictionary style. ⎱ (omit "kind of")
>   ⎱ ...written in a kind of dictionary style. ⎰
>   COMMON: What kind of *an* administration is coming?
>   FOR: What kind of administration is coming?

kind of   **style of** ⎫
sort of   **form of** ⎪ These words, and the words combined with them,
brand of   **type of** ⎬ may be singular or plural, according to the sense
make of   **class of** ⎭ of the sentence, as

>   make of engine (one make of one engine)
>   makes of engine (several makes of a similar engine)
>   make of engines (one make of similar engines)
>   makes of engines (several makes of different engines)
> the kind of man   the kinds of man   the kind of men   the kinds of men
> type of letter   types of letter   type of letters   types of letters
>   That sort of question is hard to answer.
>   ...in the sort of questions that occur in print.
>   ...used in all three sorts of question.
>   ...and were asked all sorts of questions.
> Note: When "these" and "those" are used, plurals such as "kinds" and "sorts" must be used. To say "*those* kind of people", or "*these* sort of things", is like saying "those style of paper", or "these make of engines".

USE: those kinds of people   OR: that kind of people
these sorts of things   this sort of thing
these kinds of paper   this kind of paper
those sorts of lights   that sort of lights
NOT: We like these better than those *kind.*
(USE: those kinds   OR: that kind)

like takes an object. It should not introduce a subject and verb.

as
as if } may introduce a subject and verb.

Note: The above distinction is not always adhered to by good writers. A possible reason for their deviation from the rule is given below—but first a few examples of the correct forms.

"Like" takes an object, and means "similar to" or "similarly to". Test it by substitution.

It looks **like rain.** (similar to rain or the condition of rain)
It looks **as if** it might rain. ("as if" introduces a subject and verb)
... **like a child** with a new toy.
... **like the man** who sees blindly.
It sounded **like a Spaniard** singing.
It was **like coming** in out of a storm.
...a distinction **like being** a survivor of...
He behaved **like a prisoner** sentenced to die.
This works **like that.**
He fought **like a tiger.**
We mean, **like the natives,** to live in peace.

"Similar to" or "similarly to" can be substituted in all these constructions.

"As" or "as if" introduces a clause, with a subject and verb.

It looks **as if** it were worn out.
   (NOT: *like* it was worn out)
It is not **as if** we hadn't played fair.
   (NOT: *like* we hadn't)
Do **as** we do. (NOT: *like* we do)

These sentences will not take the substitution.

BUT: Do **like** us. ("similarly to us" may be substituted)

If a "like" phrase occurs between a subject and its verb, it is usually, but not always, set off by commas.

Natural talk, **like ploughing,** should turn up a surface...
They plead that better men **like Johnson and Scott** have set the precedent.
(Do not attempt to construe that "like" here introduces a subject and verb. "Like Johnson and Scott" modifies "men".)

Reason for Deviation From the Rule. The flaw in the above scheme is that understood words are not taken into account when they seemingly should be. For instance:

Send us some like you sent before.
(Perfectly in order if "those" is understood after "like". Substituting: Send us some similar to those you sent before.)
It is better than a homemade one like they usually use. (UNDERSTOOD: like that which they usually use)
...fogs like they have in London. (like the ones they have)

14

Because some writers do not, and because some readers will not, supply the understood words, a misunderstanding exists.

But it would seem that wherever the small word "like" can take the place of the longer phrase "like those", or "like that which", etc., its use is to be preferred.

like in
like at
Under the general rule for "like", these constructions are disapproved, because "like" should introduce a noun or pronoun; but here again usage is more lenient in supplying understood words than grammar is, and so the prepositional phrases are often used.

> USAGE: ...certain blues like in deep seas.
> RULE: ...certain blues like those in deep seas.   (OR: blues as in deep seas)
> USAGE: And now, like in 1918, we have to face another situation... (like the situation we had to face in 1918)
> RULE: And now, as in 1918, we have to face another... (as we had to face in 1918)
> USAGE: Here, like at Washington, we have the facilities... (like the facilities they have at Washington)
> RULE: Here, as at Washington, we have the facilities... (as they have at Washington)

like if   is an expression of the uneducated.

> CRUDE: Some unforeseen condition *like if* they failed to...
> IMPROVED: Some unforeseen condition like their failure to...

like me
like him   (See Pronouns, p. 53.)
like them

majority   more than one-half of the total votes cast.   Also the number by which a majority exceeds one-half.

relative majority   the excess of the majority number over the total of the remaining numbers.

plurality   the largest number of votes cast for one person.   Or the excess of the largest number over the next largest number. (A plurality may exist without a majority.)

quorum   an agreed-upon number of members necessary to transact legal business for a group or body.   (Usually a majority, but not necessarily so.)

Example of votes received:

Candidate A	Candidate B	Candidate C	Total Votes
25	10	5	40

Candidate A has a majority of 5 votes.   (5 more than ½ the total)
He has a relative majority of 10 votes.   (10 more than the sum of the other two)
He has a plurality of 15 votes.   (15 more than the nearest candidate)
A quorum of 35 persons was necessary in order to vote.
Forty were present and voted.

15

mutual implies reciprocal feeling or action.
common means shared by two or more.

mutual regard	common sorrow
mutual promises	common claims

"Mutual friend" is derived from "mutual friendship", and is an expression largely used in preference to "common friend", which has an inferior implication.

never refers to a period of time.
not refers to one time.

> NOT: I *never* got the message.
> BUT: I did not get the message.
> It will never come again. (not ever)
> It will not come again. (at no one time)

of Never use "of" for "have", as "should *of*", etc. (See p. 85.)

nice a handy little word with many meanings, which has led to its being noticeably overworked. It should be restricted in use; but there is no other reason to avoid it. Primarily, it conveys the idea of discrimination, which may be either tasteful, delicate, or exact.

a nice distinction	a nice choice of words
a nice treatment of a subject	nice judgment
a nice page	a nice gesture

not only is completed by "but" or "but also". The parts of the sentence introduced by "not only" and "but" should be of like construction—should balance.

> NOT: Their prices not only change with the seasons, but with each new customer.
> BUT: Their prices change not only with the seasons, but with each new customer.
> ("Change" is a part of both phrases and should therefore be before the "not only".)
> NOT: They are not only unreliable, but they are dishonest.
> BUT: Not only are they unreliable, but they are dishonest.
> NOT: He does not succeed only in interesting them, but he gains their confidence.
> BUT: He not only succeeds in interesting them, but gains their confidence.
> NOT: To add not only to the equipment but to provide...
> BUT: Not only to add to the equipment but to provide...

The complementary "but" is sometimes omitted.

> Not only must there be banks; it is essential that there be businesses.

(See also Subjects, p. 75.)

no use in {These are the correct phrases; but they are sometimes
of no use to idiomatically reduced to "no use".

16

There's no use insinuating... (FOR: no use in insinuating)
It is no use arguing... (FOR: is of no use to argue)
It's no use to continue. (FOR: It's of no use to continue.
   OR: It's useless to continue.)

only The placement of this word has much to do with the meaning of a sentence. It should, if possible, be placed immediately before the word or phrase it modifies.

Only he could work the puzzle. (no one else)
He could only work the puzzle. (not explain it)
He could work only the puzzle. (nothing else)

Avoid the use of "only" before a verb, unless it is expressly meant to modify the verb.

I only heard about the accident. (I didn't see it)
I heard only about the accident. (nothing else)
They only guarantee bank loans. (they do not make them)
They guarantee only bank loans. (nothing else)
...which only added to the confusion. (merely)
We can only consider that unfair treatment. (no less than)

Misplaced "only":

The campaign only commenced with the upturn.
   (USE: commenced only with the upturn)
People will only buy the paper they like. (USE: will buy only the paper)

Colloquial uses—so common that no misunderstanding of the meaning can exist:

It only costs a dollar.	FOR:	It costs only a dollar.
I only have a quarter.		I have only a quarter.
They only sell for cash.		They sell only for cash.
He only waited a minute.		He waited only a minute.
We only expect what is right.		We expect only what is right.

If "only" is out of its logical position, commas may be placed around it for clarity or emphasis.

The president, only, was authorized to sign.
Papers could be signed by the president only. (no comma necessary)

Similar words that require care in their placement are:

alone	at least	hardly	merely
almost	even	just	scarcely

only may be used as a conjunction in the sense of "except that". Yet if "but" is more applicable than "except that", "but" instead of "only" should be used.

They sounded convincing, only they seemed hesitant.
It sounds plausible only it won't work.
   (Here "but" would be better.)

"Only" should not be used with the prepositional force of "but" or "except" in such sentences as

> Nobody could decipher it only the inventor. (USE: but)

(See also Double Negatives, p. 111.)

others is the plural of "other". "*Other*" as a plural is obsolete.

> There are others than these to be sent. (NOT: *other* than)
> NOT: No *other* than those are known. (USE: No others)

over may be used to mean "because of", "about", or "more than".

> If feelings are injured over that... (because of that)
> Over six percent of the judges voted for... (More than)

per properly belongs in Latin phrases, as "per annum", "per diem", etc. However, it is widely used in commercial phrases to mean "by the", as

> per yard   per day rate   miles per hour   dollars per hundred

But wherever the meaning of "by the" is not foremost, the use of the simpler "a" or "an" is to be preferred.

> 50¢ an hour   RATHER THAN: 50¢ per hour
> $5 a day $5 per day

persons used when the individuality of each person is considered, as "alike to all persons", "the persons in that company".

people used when the individuality of each person is not considered.

> The room was full of people.
> Three people spoke.

party a person or a group participating in a contract or action. (A legal and commercial term, useful because it can represent either a person or a company, as "the party to the contract", "the party receiving the goods".) Colloquial, when used to refer to an ordinary person.

individual a person. (This word has been discountenanced because of overuse; nevertheless it may properly be used to represent one person as contrasted with a body or class of people, as in referring to "the conduct of some individual", etc.)

reason is because This combination has been condemned, first, because of incorrect grammatical construction, and, secondly, because of overlapping meanings—"because" means "for the reason that", and one would not say "the reason is for the reason that". However, "the reason why" is approved, and it may be similarly analyzed in such sentences as "He didn't know the reason why."

Modern usage has decided that "the reason is because" is "good everyday English". (The National Council of Teachers of English.)

But do not use "the reason why...is *because*", as there are here three words implying cause.

18

NOT: The reason why that location is unsuitable is *because* it is...
BUT: The **reason why** that location is unsuitable **is that** it is...

Now that "the reason is because" may be used, it is in order to say that it is preferable to "the reason is due to" or "the reason is on account of", which were poor attempts to circumvent "the reason is because".

But of course the correct form, "the reason is that", may always be used in preference to any of the other combinations.

said meaning "afore-mentioned" is commonly used as an adjective in legal and commercial phrases, as "comply with said terms".

same meaning "the aforesaid thing" is commonly used as a pronoun in legal and commercial phrases, as "terms covering same".

the same as is often used as a commercial shortening for "in the same manner as".

> They draw interest the same as the other bonds. (FOR: in the same manner as the other bonds do)

But "the same" should not be used if it is superfluous.

NOT: ...if they will work *the same* as he does.
BUT: ...if they will work as he does.

In many phrases "the same" represents a noun.

> This is the same as that.
> It is considered the same as money.
> The increase is the same as shown here.

seldom if ever means in few if any instances.
seldom or never means in few or no instances.
seldom or *ever* has no meaning.

"Seldom ever" and "rarely ever" are colloquial contractions of "seldom if ever" and "rarely if ever". In these phrases "ever" can usually be dropped as superfluous.

"Scarcely ever" and "hardly ever" are modifications of "never".

> "What, never?" "Well! hardly ever..."—Pinafore.

so is widely used for "therefore"—often beginning sentences.

> There was yet a judicial principle to be established. So there was ordained a Supreme Court...—The Saturday Evening Post.

some say **they say** ⎫ These phrases may be used to refer indefinitely to
people say **by many** ⎭ people.

> Some approve of that method.   It is felt by many to be undesirable.
> They have seasons in the tropics.   People say it is valuable.
> (The objection to such phrases is that they are often carelessly used.)

somehow or other ⎫
sometime or other ⎬ These are idiomatic forms in good use. "Or
somewhere or other ⎭ other" emphasizes the first word.

19

such is often used as a pronoun in legal and commercial phrasings.

> The law provides a redress; but **such** cannot be had.

such a is used to indicate a singular, particularized thing (the "a" being used when it would be used if "such" were not there). "Such" alone is used before plural words, and words that express abstract or general ideas.

GENERAL	PARTICULARIZED
Use such paper as this.	Use such a paper as this.
(Use paper such as this.)	(Use a paper such as this.)
Buy such food as is recommended.	Buy such a food as wheat.
(Buy food such as is...)	(Buy a food such as wheat.)
if they accept such payment	accept such a payment
(a general method of payment)	(one payment)
put it to such use	put it to such a use
(a general use)	(a particular use)
enjoy such liberty	enjoy such a liberty
(general freedom)	(one privilege)
receive such honor	receive such an honor
until such time as	until such a time as
in such manner	in such a manner
to such degree	to such a degree
to such length	to such a length

"Such" alone may be used to indicate a thing previously mentioned, as in legal phraseology.

> A notice should be sent to each nonresident officer, if **such officer** has not...

Also "such" alone is used if a modifier such as "any", "one", "no", or "another" occurs before it.

> in **one such** place   **any such** thing
> **no such** excuse   **another such** situation

such...as is the correct combination, not "such...*who*", "such...*where*", "such...*which*", nor "such...*when*".

> NOT: ...for such men *who* contemplate that.
> BUT: ...for **such** men **as** contemplate that.
> NOT: ...from such conditions *which* exist in the cities.
> BUT: ...from **such** conditions **as** exist in the cities.

Understood words can often be supplied to make the sentence clear.

> FAULTY: ...to such territories in which irrigation is impossible.
> BETTER: ...to **such** territories **as** those in which irrigation...
> FAULTY: ...covering such acreage where crops are not grown.
> BETTER: ...covering **such** acreage **as** that where crops are not grown.

Do not use "such as" for "as" before a prepositional phrase.

> NOT: ...*such* as in magazines.   (USE: **as** in magazines)
> NOT: ...*such* as for traveling.   (USE: **as** for traveling)
> NOT: ...*such* as by methods of distillation.   (USE: **as** by methods)

Conversely, do not use "as" for "such as".

> NOT: Under conditions as we have been accustomed to...   (USE: conditions **such as** we have)

And lastly, do not overwork "such as". Substitute "that", "those", "which", or "like".

such that   is used in two ways:

> CORRECTLY: Conditions are such that it is impossible...
> ("That" is a connective here.)
> LESS CORRECTLY: ...from such that can afford it.   (USE: such as can afford)

that   may be omitted in certain sentences and smoothness gained thereby. But it should not be omitted if it is needed to retain the meaning of the sentence.

> OMITTED: Supposethey question the terms.
> We will sign providedthey agree to that.
> We grantit is a common occurrence.
> NECESSARY: We understand **that** the man might be wrong.
> The President emphasized **that** the Government will exercise its power...
> They should know **that** inflated credit could not in itself bring prosperity.
> NOT: The message pointed outno one country can handle the situation.   (INSERT: that)

that that   is a correct combination. "Which" may sometimes be used with "that" to avoid repetition, but it is not always appropriate.

> ...for those who here gave their lives **that that** nation might live.
> ...and enjoy **that which** is the gauge of life.

that...that   The repetition of "that" in introducing a clause is a very common and noticeable error.

> **"It often happens to a writer to embark upon a...'that-clause', to find that it is carrying him further than he reckoned, and to feel that the reader and he will be lost in a chartless sea unless they can get back to port and make a fresh start. His way of effecting this is to repeat his initial 'that'. This relieves his own feeling of being lost; whether it helps the inattentive reader is doubtful; but it is not doubtful that it exasperates the attentive reader, who from the moment he saw 'that' has been on the watch for the verb that it tells him to expect, and realizes suddenly, when another 'that' appears, that his chart is incorrect."**
> -Fowler, **"A Dictionary of Modern English Usage", p. 633.**

One "that" unnecessary:

> They now say **that** if we will agree to their terms *that* they will consent to the reduction.
> We hope **that** when you look over the papers *that* you will find everything in order.

21

(Test the sentences by arranging the clauses in their natural order, as "We hope that you will find everything in order when you look over the papers.")

The use of more than one "that" in a sentence to introduce separate clauses is, of course, correct. No "that" should be omitted unless it can be legitimately spared. Both "thats" necessary:

> There is no doubt of the fact **that** it is true **that** only because he did not begin his campaign...
> ...but if they realize **that** at the same moment **that** payment is stopped they are jeopardizing...

too for "too much" } are accepted in commercial English without
very for "very much" } question.

> He was too interested to give up.
> (FOR THE CORRECT: too much interested)
> We were very disappointed in the outcome.
> (FOR: very much disappointed)

Expressions like "very tired" and "too tired" are accepted as idiomatic.

unless introduces a subject and verb.
without takes an object.
Do not use "without" where "unless" could be substituted.
"Without" in the sense of "unless" is dialectal.

> They cannot sell unless (NOT: *without*) they consult the authorities.
> They cannot sell without consulting the authorities.
> ("Consulting" here stands as a noun—the object of "without".)

Note that "without", not "unless", is the common word before an -ing word.

> NOT: No one can get a seat *unless* making reservations. (USE: without making a reservation)

If "unless" is used before an -ing word, it signifies that some words are missing.

> They never use that form unless quoting prices. (UNDERSTOOD: unless they are quoting prices)

Other constructions are often used after "unless", with words understood.

> That is not ordinarily done unless in connection with educational work. (UNDERSTOOD: unless it is in connection)
> There is no occasion to use it unless as a sample. (UNDERSTOOD: unless it is used as a sample)

unlike follows the same general rules as "like": it should not introduce a subject and verb, nor should it be followed by a prepositional phrase. A noun or pronoun should follow it.

NOT: And now, unlike *it was* in 1918, we are forced...
NOR: And now, unlike *in* 1918, we are forced to...

To remedy such a situation, a few words may be moved up—

THUS: And now we are forced, as we were not in 1918, to...

Usage often overrides the above rules, depending on understood words to give the proper meaning.

USAGE: ...but here, unlike *at* Washington, we have not the facilities for... (unlike conditions at Washington)
RULE: ...but here we have not, as at Washington, the facilities for... (as they have at Washington)
OR: ...but here, in contrast with Washington, we have not the facilities for...

un-
in-
il- } The selection of these prefixes for the formation of negative words
im- has departed so often from any definite rule that usage has
ir- arbitrarily established many of the forms.

> **"The choice of the fitting negative prefix...is largely governed by established usage..."**
> **—Vizetelly, "How to Use English", p. 436.**

Note some of the varieties:

unable	but	inability
unadvised	but	inadvisable
unexpressive	and	inexpressive (both used)
unlawful	but	illegal
unlimited	but	illimitable
unmoved	but	immovable
unpractised	but	impractical (unpractical is also used)
unresponsive	and	irresponsive (both used)
inartistic	and	unartistic (both used)
incomplete	but	uncompleted
inexperienced	and	unexperienced (both used)
insanitary	and	unsanitary (both used)
irremovable	and	unremovable (rare)
irreparable	and	unrepairable (rare)

is where
is when } Avoid these expressions when giving definitions.

NOT: A "pool" *is where* several groups agree to...
BUT: A "pool" is an agreement between several groups...
NOT: A "low ceiling" *is when* the atmospheric conditions...
BUT: A "low ceiling" means that the atmospheric...

A different and permissible use, with words understood:

Two o'clock is (the time) when the meeting is to be held.
Mexico is (the place) where they have pyramids older...

-ward

afterward	inward	skyward	All written without the final -s,
backward	landward	southward	which is the preferred form in
downward	northward	toward	American usage. This not
eastward	onward	upward	only shortens the words, but
forward	outward	westward	in many instances makes them
homeward	sideward		more euphonious.

-ways
-wise

anywise	lengthwise	The generally preferred ending for these words
crosswise	nowise	is -wise, rather than -ways, with the excep-
edgewise	sidewise, or	tion of "sideways", which is considered
endwise	sideways	established.

-where

anywhere	All written without the final -s. To add -s is termed
everywhere	"illiterate". To substitute "any place", "every
nowhere	place", "no place", and "some place" is termed
somewhere	"careless".

> NOT: We couldn't find them ∧ *any place.* ("in" omitted)
> (One would not say or write "We couldn't find them *any town.*"
> THEREFORE USE: anywhere, which means "in any place".)

---

who   refers to persons (rarely to animals).
which   refers to animals and things (and to persons, in questions).
that   refers to persons, animals, and things.
whose   is the possessive for all the above words. It may refer to either animate or inanimate things.

The choice between "who" and "that" when referring to persons:
who   signifies the individual, or the individuality of each member of a group.
that   signifies type, class, or an impersonal number of people.

> The man **who** is in charge... (a certain individual)
> Anyone **that** believes in the future... (a type or class of men)
> The man that stands by himself... (the type of man)
> Is he the person that he appears to be? (the type)
> People who do such things... (the individuals)
> The people that live in northern climates... (the species)

The choice between "which" and "that" when referring to animals and things: These words are interchangeable (except in "nonrestrictive clauses", which see below). Their use is a matter of personal preference. A writer usually selects the word that for him gives the better effect or has the more euphonious or forceful sound.

"Which" is the more noticeable word, and writers are no doubt often influenced toward its use as a means of emphasis.

24

Emerson used "which" and "that" interchangeably:

The power **which** resides in him is new in nature...
The other terror **that** scares us from self-trust is our consistency...

Ruskin used them interchangeably:

The best image **which** the world can give of Paradise...
...the only supreme flowers **that** the lowlands can show...

Some writers believe that "that" has enough work to do in the language without being substituted for "which"; and so on occasions that call for a choice between these two words, they use "which". Huxley might have followed this method in his writings:

We live in a world **which** is full of misery and ignorance...

Some writers follow a certain distinction between "that" and "which" and assign each word a special job to do. They use

which to introduce a clause that is **"nonrestrictive"** (that is, a clause that does not restrict the meaning and which could be lifted out of the sentence—therefore it is set off with commas).

that to introduce a **"restrictive"** clause (that is, a clause that restricts the meaning and which could not be dispensed with without impairing the sentence—therefore no commas are around it).

The protests, **which always follow,** are again with us.
Should we forgo all **that is valuable in our lot?**
Note that the "which" nonrestrictive (parenthetic) clause may be removed; but the "that" restrictive clause must stay if its sentence is to have its real meaning.

"Which" is often used to avoid a repetition of "that".

...and enjoy **that** friendly association **which** is the life of business.

If the reference is to both persons and things, use "that", as it is applicable to both.

Men and machines **that** turn out that work... (NOT: *which*)
The forty men and eight horses **that** could be transported in one car... (NOT: *which* NOR: *who*)

Special uses of "who": "Who" may refer to personified things.

A tree...**who** intimately lives with rain...—Kilmer.

"Who" is sometimes used to refer to an animal, if later in the sentence the animal is designated by a pronoun such as "he" or "she".

Fleeting, **who** was the most brilliant horse of **his** time, won...

But wherever "that" can be used in such sentences, it is to be preferred.

The dog **that** led **his** team-mates in the hazardous trek...

The choice between "who", "which", and "that", when referring to collective nouns:

25

who should be used when referring to a noun that signifies a collection of persons, wherein personalities exist (especially if "they" or "their" is used later in the sentence).

> That firm, **who have** (NOT: *which has*) given us **their** business for years, **are** worthy of special consideration.
> That part of the audience **who** (NOT: *which*) demanded **their** money back...
> ...of the number of passengers **who** (NOT: *which*) **were** saved.

which or⎫ should be used when the collective noun exists as a single thing
that ⎭ (especially if "it" or "its" is used later in the sentence).

> That firm, **which has** given us **its** business for years, **is** worthy of special consideration.
> That group, **which is** of course in Wall Street, **has** had to retrench in **its** buying.
> Any company **that deals** fairly with us **is** entitled to **its** profits.

Do not mix "who" and "which" in the same sentence when referring to a collective noun.

> NOT: That company, **which is** composed of ten men, **is** one company in *whom* (USE: which) we have the greatest confidence.

which⎫ Either word may refer to a particular thing or to several things.
what ⎭

> Which team won?
> What crews will row this year?
> Decide which you want.   (the individual things)
> Decide what you want.   (the quantity, or kind of thing)
> They are brokers or bankers, but we are not sure which.
>   (they are one or the other)
> They may be brokers or bankers, but we are not sure what.
>   (they may be any one of a number of things)

what may mean "that which" or "those which".

> ...it fairly teems with **what** are in one sense or another false issues.   (MEANING: those which)

which usually refers to the word that immediately precedes it; but it may refer to the entire clause that precedes it.

> It soon becomes a badge of gentility **which** is adopted generally.   ("Which" here refers to "badge".)
> It soon becomes a badge of gentility, after **which** it is adopted generally. ("Which" here refers to the becoming a badge.)

"Which" is sometimes used before a word to fix definitely the reference.   The phrase **"in which case"** is also used by authorities.

> They suggested an alternative, **which** suggestion was not welcome.

whichever indicates one or another of a number and may refer to persons as well as things.

> ...to be sent to the buyer or the seller, **whichever** is to pay the insurance.

FASHIONS
IN WORDS

❖

There are styles in words as in
other things

❖

"EVERY fall-season Dame Fashion builds beautiful linguistic houses of cards which last until spring; then the showers wash them away, and new ones are erected only to be burned down by summer heat, to be followed by others that blow away with the falling of the leaves, ultimately to be buried from sight by winter snows. The performance is continuous and the terminology of the dress-goods trade of a quarter of a century ago is to-day as dead as Cæsar. New terms are being introduced constantly, and every season brings a fresh crop which it is not advisable to place on record because the lives of such terms are short—the lexicographer can not be charmed by the vagaries and varieties of fashion as represented by words of but ephemeral character."

—Vizetelly, "How to Use English".

FASHIONS IN WORDS

Passing Fancies

aunt
depot
envelope
gladiolus
humble
humor 〉The pronunciation of these words has returned to normal.
interesting
kilometer
pianist
programme
vase

all right—has withstood the onslaught of "alright" and "allright".

authoress—is losing out to "author".

aviatrix〉
poetess〉 are having a hard time to stay.

concern—although condemned by some when used to mean "a business organiza-tion", is so given in the dictionaries, and so used by business authoritier

depot—has been largely replaced by "station", when meaning a passenger station. But it is used to mean a storehouse or supply base.

kiddies—has been displaced by "children".

Pleased to meet you—has been investigated and found to be correct English, if somewhat old-fashioned.

I am very glad to have met you—is quite all right.

render a bill—has been returned to favor.

someone's else—has given way to the more common "someone else's".

Discountenanced Words

	FOR:	
ain't		isn't, or aren't
complected		complexioned
consumption, or *T.B.*		tuberculosis
consumptive		tuberculous
Frisco		San Francisco
Hindu (for any but a real Hindu)		East Indian
nigger		Negro
Portugee		Portuguese
saleslady		saleswoman
Xmas		Christmas

Words and Phrases Being Countenanced

ad—is widely used in commercial phrases for "advertisement". Note that it is written without a period.

anxious—used for "eager".

awfully—used for "very", as "awfully bad".

29

Britisher—formerly classed with "Irisher", but it is now very generally used instead of "Briton".

burglarize—used for "commit burglary upon".

don't think so—very generally used for "think not".

drive slow
drive slowly } both used.

enthuse—used for "become enthusiastic".

have got
have gotten } both used.

healthy climate
healthful climate } both used.

If it was not for that—used for "If it were not for that".

I wish I was rich—used for "I wish I were rich."

individual—used for "person" when contrasted with a group or class of people.

It's me—used for "It is I."

peruse—used for "look over". (The supposedly correct meaning is "to read carefully".)

phone—for "telephone". It needs no apostrophe now.

quite—used for "rather". ("Quite" really means "wholly".)

reason is because—used for "reason is that".

shall and will—used interchangeably now in many instances.

that—used for "so", as "They're not that busy", for "They're not so busy as that."

this—used for "thus" or "so", as "They're never this late", for "They're never so late as this"; or "about this high" for "about so high"; or "after working this far" for "after working thus far".

Who do you mean?—used in conversation for "Whom do you mean?"

Many shortcuts are favored in commercial phrases, as

write him	FOR:	write to him
phone us		telephone to us
sent us		sent to us
work nights		work at night
if they want out		if they want to get out

The announcement will be Wednesday. (FOR: will be made on)

He was in town the first three days of last week. (FOR: in town during the first three days)

I will write it when I am home. (FOR: when I am at home)

But a word or phrase should not be omitted if an ambiguous sentence is liable to result.

NOT: . . . when he was home sick. (FOR: was at home, sick)

COLLOQUIALISMS

A "colloquial" expression does not necessarily mean a condemned expression —although some of them are—but rather an expression heard chiefly in conversation. Discountenanced colloquialisms are italicized below.

a—for "of". Do not say "what time *a* day" or "that sort *a* thing".

ahold—for "hold", as "take *ahold* of the proposition". (FOR: take hold) But "take a hold on the ladder" is right.

all kinds of—for "many" or "much", as "all kinds of money", "all kinds of mistakes".

all the further—for "as far as".

COLLOQUIAL: {"Is that all the further you got?"
{"Is that all the faster it can go?"

FOR: {Is that as far as you got?
{Is that as fast as it can go?

There is an approved use of "all the farther", "all the faster", etc., when "all" means "so much".

It will go all the faster with the new tires.
We can see all the better from here.

around—for "about" or "near", as "around the holidays", "around ten o'clock". "Around" in this sense is a much-used colloquialism.

as—for "that". NOT: "I don't know *as* I do." (FOR: that I do)
NOT: "We can't see *as* it will." (FOR: that it will)

as like as not—for "likely". "As like as not it will break."

balance—for "rest" or "remainder", as "the balance of the week", "the balance of the supplies". When actually referring to a financial balance, it is correct, as "the balance of the account".

bank on—for "rely on". "You can bank on that."

blame it on—"We can't blame it on anything in particular."
FOR: We can't blame anything in particular for it.

cable—meaning a cabled message, is listed as correct by some authorities, and as "a colloquialism" by others. It is a widely used "commercialism".

cablegram—is noted as correct by one authority, as "a colloquialism" by another, and as "a barbarism" (a hybrid derivative) by a third. It, also, is widely used in commercial work, but the shorter word "cable" threatens to supersede it.

can't seem—for "seem unable". "They can't seem to see it."

Chinaman—for a Chinese.

considerable—as a noun, as "nothing to lose, but considerable to gain".

don't ever—for "never". "Don't ever do that." (FOR: Never do that.)
"If we don't ever see it again..." (FOR: If we never see)

expect—for "suppose". "I expect so." (a British colloquialism)

fine—for "well" or "finely". "It grew fine."

folks—for "relatives".

funny—for "strange", "puzzling", "odd", "queer", etc.

going on—for "approaching" or "about". "He is going on fifty."

guess—for "think", without uncertainty. "I guess I'll go to work."

hear—for "have heard". "We hear they are doing well."

in our midst—for "among us". The latter is preferable.

inside of—for "within", as "inside of a month".

Jap—for a Japanese.

learn—for "have learned". "I learn from them that..."

leave go—for "let go". This is not sanctioned, but

leave off—for "quit" or "stop" is approved, as "Where did we leave off?"

locate—for "settle". "They located in Kansas."

lose out—for "fail to succeed" or "be left out". "We might lose out."

mighty—for "very", as "It was mighty kind of them."

31

most—for "almost", as "most any day", "most always", "on most every page". While "most all the time" (meaning "almost all of") is colloquial, "most of the time" (meaning "the largest part of") is naturally correct.

mostly all—for "almost all", or "nearly all". "It has mostly all evaporated."

on the side—for "besides". "A dividend and a bonus on the side..."

operate—for "operate on"—used in medical parlance, as "The patient was operated at six o'clock." This usage is not, however, considered correct.

outside of that—for "other than that", "besides that", or "except that".

overly—for "too much", as "not overly pleased".

photo—for "photograph".

plenty good enough—for "sufficient" or "good enough".

posted—for "informed".

price—for "ask the price of", as to "price articles".

proposition—for "business venture".

put in—for "spent" or "worked". "The men each put in ten hours."

real—for "very". "That's real nice." "It works real well." "Really" may be substituted, but it carries the meaning of "actually" rather than "very". "That's really nice." "It works really well", or "It works very well."

read where—for "read that". "I read where they are selling..."

right—for "very". "It is progressing right well."

run—for "manage", as to "run a business".

see where—for "see that". "I see where the market went up..."

see—for "have seen". "I see by the papers..." (FOR: I have seen in the papers)

shape—for "condition". "It is in good shape."

show—for "chance". "It doesn't stand a show."

some—for "somewhat" or "a little". "That helped some." "They talked some of doing that."

sure—for "yes". "Will it work? Sure, it will." This use may be derived from the older phrase, "to be sure".

"Sure" may properly be used for the adverb "surely".

> They are going forward today, sure.
> And sure enough it stopped.
> It will return as sure as we live.

But "sure" should not be used in a typically slang manner to mean "certainly" or "indeed", as

> "We were *sure* glad to get it."
> "It *sure* works well."

take in—for "see". "We took in the exhibition."

take sick—for "become sick". "He took sick last week."

through—for "finished", as "When will it be through?"

wait on—for "wait for". "We can't wait on them."

way—for "away", "considerably", or "far". "They are way off." "They went way around the subject."

ways—for "way", as "a long ways off".

win out—for "succeed". "Who will win out?"

32

wire—meaning a telegram, is listed by some British authorities as correct, and by American authorities as "a colloquialism". It is a very practical, concise, and widely used "commercialism".

woods—for "wood", as "in a large woods nearby". "Woods" is plural.

⚬═══════════⚬

SUPERFLUOUS WORDS

Do not burden a sentence with unnecessary words. Superfluous words are italicized in the following expressions.

again **regain**—could be used only if once before something had been regained—but not the first time it is regained.

ago **since**—NOT: "It is ten years *ago* since we have seen..."

alone...*only*—One word or the other is superfluous in such sentences as "That alone is the *only* reason."

also...*too*—NOT: "They also want that *too.*" Use one or the other.

and **etc.**—would mean "*and* and so forth".

at **about**—NOT: "It happened *at* about three o'clock."

bars *out*—NOT: "This bars *out* the possibility that..."

both alike—"Both" is unnecessary if it is obvious that two are meant; otherwise "both" may be used.

The terms are both alike. (the two terms)

The terms are alike. (many terms)

NOT: "There is no question but that *both* employer and worker alike will profit." ("both" unnecessary)

both...*also*—One word is unnecessary in such expressions as "for the purpose both of improving the product and *also* of reducing the cost".

both equally—If it is obvious that two are meant, the "both" is superfluous; otherwise "both equally" may be used, as "The propositions submitted were both equally good", or "The two propositions were equally good."

both together—"Both" is often superfluous in this combination, as "Were the two messengers *both* together?" But "both together" is necessary at times, as "Use one word or the other, but not both together." (meaning one following the other)

continue *on*—NOT: "Let them continue *on* with the work."

continue to **remain**—NOT: "If they *continue to* remain as they are..."

converted *over*—NOT: "...to be converted *over* into a new loan."

cooperate *together*—NOT: "Can they not cooperate *together?*"

customary **practice**—"Practice" means a customary action.

each in its respective way—used for emphasis instead of "each in its way".

either...*or else*—NOT: "They either start a new business or *else* are taken over by..."

else **but**—NOT: "No one *else* but him..."

enclosed herewith—is a common commercial phrase, although the second word is superfluous.

attached *herewith*—"Herewith" in this combination is not only superfluous, but wrong. "Attached hereto" would be more nearly right, but the "hereto" is also unnecessary.

encore *again*—could be used only if once before something or someone had been encored.

endorse on the back—"Endorse" usually means to "inscribe on the back of", but not always. Certain papers may be endorsed "on the face"; hence "on the back" may be added to "endorse" for definiteness.

equally as good as—used for emphasis for "as good as", or "equally good".

finish off—"Off" is unnecessary but in good usage, as in "something to finish off the design".

first before—used for emphasis, as "Investigate first before buying."

first begin—used for emphasis, as "When they first begin to see..."

follows after—"Follows" implies "after", yet this is a usual phrase.

free **gratis**—"Gratis" means free. (Observe that "gratis" is pronounced grā′tis, not *grăt′is*.)

in **among**
in **around**
in **back of** ⎬ These are usually simply careless constructions. Sometimes, but rarely, they are justifiable, as
in **between** ...like dancers weaving in around the Maypole.
in **under** ...it was slipped in among the papers.

inside of—"Inside the city limits", rather than "inside of". "Within an hour", or colloquially "inside of an hour".

joint partnership—"Partnership" often implies "joint ownership", but not always. There are several kinds of partnership; hence "joint partnership" may be used to designate a certain kind.

like *for*—for "like", as "We should like *for* them to see it."

near *to*—NOT: "near *to* a school" or "near *to* town".

new **beginner**—One person alone could not be a "*new* beginner"; but if there were several beginners and a new one arrived, he then might be the "new beginner".

not *a* **one**—Use "not one".

off *of*, or **off** *from*—NOT: "...fell off *of* the pedestal."

often **accustomed to** ⎱ NOT: "He was *often* in the habit of going..."
often **in the habit of** ⎰ NOR: "He was *often* accustomed to going..."
 BUT: People are often accustomed to hardships.

outside of—"Outside the jurisdiction", rather than "outside of". "Other than that", "besides that", "beyond that", or "except that", is better than the colloquial "outside of that".

over *with*—NOT: "We're glad that's over *with*."

pair of twins—This phrase is explained by the fact that "a twin" may be used to designate one of two persons known as "twins". Thus in a group there may be "three twins", none of whom are related. Therefore, two that are related may be referred to as "a pair of twins", which seems as defensible as to say, correctly, "a pair of glasses".

pretend *like*—NOT: "They pretend *like* they haven't heard it."
 BUT: They pretend they haven't heard it.

remember *of*—NOT: "We don't remember *of* it." "Not that I remember *of*." But "know of" is used to mean "know about".

repeat *again*—Only if a thing has been repeated before, can it be repeated again.

same **identical**—"Identical" means "the very same".

such as (**as** or **like**)...**etc.**—A widely used combination, even in dictionaries.

think *for*—for "think", as "more than you think *for*".

those *ones*—NOT: "It refers to those *ones* that are crossed out."
 BUT: ...to those...OR: ...to the ones...

34

up **above**—for "above". "It is *up* above the headwaters."
up **until**—"Until" itself means "up to the time of".

...**up**

burn up	open up	
buy up	pay up	
call up	polish up	
climb up	rest up	
connect up	run up	
count up	scar up	
cripple up	scratch up	
divide up	settle up	The "up's". Some "commercial", some "col-
double up	shape up	loquial", some "correct". All used.
end up	show up	
even up	size up	
finish up	start up	
fix up	strike up	
follow up	talk up	
hurry up	turn up	
mar up	wake up	
mix up	write up	

"Legal" Duplication. For particular emphasis, a duplication of words is often indulged in by commercial writers. (In some of the following well-known phrases, the words are not duplications but of different meaning, which adds to definiteness.)

if and when	save and except
due and payable	each and every
unless and until	one and the same thing
over and above	good and sufficient reasons

FAMILIAR PHRASES

Familiar phrases often vary slightly in wording, spelling, or meaning from preconceived ideas of them. (Familiar phrases are usually to be found in the dictionary under the principal word in each phrase.) The following are examples of phrases that are sometimes misconstrued.

anchors aweigh—not "anchors *away*". (Compare "under way", below.)
All is not gold that glisters—is the old proverb. "All that glisters is not gold" is the way Shakespeare and many authors have written it; and it is now commonly seen as "All that glitters is not gold", and "All is not gold that glitters."
at first blush—means "at first glance". Also written "at the first blush".
at swords' points—not "at *sword* points".
balled up—spelled differently from "bawled out".
beyond the pale—also "outside the pale", or "without the pale" ("pale" meaning an enclosed territory, or a protective realm).
brand-new—not "*bran*-new".
by the bye—has been written "by the by" and "bye the by"; but the first is considered correct.

35

by and by—not "by and *bye*".

chock-full—or "choke-full", or "chuck-full"; but the first is preferred.

edge on—or "egg on".

derring-do—not "*daring*-do", although the meaning is literally "daring to do" (daring courage).

gave way—is the phrase in the following uses, not "gave *away*": "The bridge gave way." "The mob gave way." "They gave way to their grief."

gentlemen's agreement—or "gentleman's"—an agreement of honor.

if worse comes to worst—more logical than "if worst comes to worst".

hail-fellow-well-met—not "*hale*". Used chiefly as an adjective, hence hyphened.

had as lief
would as lief⎰not "*leave*".

hand in glove—or "hand and glove". The latter is older.

make assurance double sure—is the Shakespearian quotation, which is now often written "doubly sure".

new lease of life—is the older phrase from which "new lease on life" sprang.

not by any manner of means—rather than "not by any manner or means".

on the wrong tack—is the seafarer's expression that the landsman has changed into "on the wrong track".

hem'd and haw'd
hum'd and ha'd ⎰in fact any combination desired may be used.
hum'd and haw'd

hotchpotch ⎰Although "hotchpot", which exists in legal use, is nearest to the
hodgepodge ⎰ original French "hochepot".

Nothing venture, nothing have—from the old English proverb "Nought venter, nought have." It has been variously interpreted as "Nothing venture, nothing win", "Nothing ventured, nothing gained", etc.

plane sailing—is the nautical term, from which "plain sailing" has been derived. Both are used.

rack and ruin—now common instead of "wrack and ruin".

read the riot act—not "*right*" nor "*Wright*" act. (An act in England for the suppression of mobs.)

round robin—(not capitalized). Signatures written in a circle to avoid making any name stand first.

rule of thumb—means measurement by the thumb; hence a practical rather than a scientific method.

run the gamut—to run the whole scale of anything.

run the gantlet—to experience hazards. (Formerly a punishment between rows of men with clubs.)

stormy petrel ⎰One fond of storm and strife. (A bird said to portend storms.)
storm petrel ⎰ (pron. pĕt'rĕl)

the three R's—"reading, 'riting, and 'rithmetic".

three sheets in the wind—not "*from* the wind". A sailors' term.

To err is human; to forgive, divine—Pope. (pron. ĕr or ûr)

NOT: "To err is human; *forgiveness is divine*."

to the manner born—is sometimes written "to the manor born", but the former is regarded as correct.

swan song—is a writer's or composer's last work before death. (From the fabled song of a dying swan.)

under way—rather than "under weigh". Originally from a ship's gaining motion or starting on its way. The deduction "under weigh" is presumably from a ship's weighing anchor before it starts.

Vanity of vanities; all is vanity—a Biblical quotation (implying futility).

NOT: "*Vanity, vanity, all is for vanity.*"

walk the plank—to be expelled or forced out. (A pirates' method of putting prisoners to death at sea.)

walk Spanish—to be forced along on tiptoe through being seized by the collar and the seat of the trousers; to walk gingerly; to be thrown out.

weighed in the balances, and found wanting—is from a Biblical quotation.

NOT: "*. . . weighed and the balance found wanting.*"

COLLECTIVE WORDS

A collective word is a word that represents the grouping of two or more things. It may be treated as a singular or as a plural, according to the sense of the sentence.

Plural, when the persons or parts are considered separately:

The **company have** agreed upon a course of action.

Singular, when considered as one unit:

The **company is** financially strong.

BUT: After establishing a collective word as a singular in a sentence, **keep it singular;** or after establishing it as a plural, **keep it plural.**

NOT: That **firm** never *employs* (sing.) a man unless he has been recommended by someone **they** (pl.) know. (USE: employ)

NOT: The **company announces** *their* new policy of... (USE: its new policy OR: announce)

NOT: The **Board** of Directors *has* prepared a code for **their** own use. (USE: have)

NOT: The **family** *is* all grown now and **have** scattered. (USE: are)

NOT: The **jury** *was* out but twenty minutes, when **they** returned a verdict. (USE: were out OR: when it)

Note that "who" when used to refer to a collective word represents the individuals that comprise the group, and therefore makes the collective plural.

NOT: There **was** an **element** in that district *who were*... (USE: district that was)

NOT: It is not the small-town **audience who** still *believes*... (USE: who still believe OR: that still believes)

NOT: In that little province there *exists* a **people who are** unknown. (USE: exist OR: that is unknown)

The following long sentence establishes "humanity" as a singular, and then changes it to a plural:

Has not **humanity** always ignored the advice of philosophers, and gone on leaning farther and farther to one side, until even the **majority** could not help seeing that in another instant all would be lost, and then with a feeling of panic, righted **themselves** and **begun** to lean as much too far the other way?

(At first reading we might suppose that "themselves" refers to "majority", and puzzle about "begun". But upon second consideration we see that "begun" goes back to "humanity" and takes "themselves" with it. The simplified construction is: **Has** not humanity always ignored...and gone on leaning...and...righted **themselves** and begun... "Have" should have been used instead of "Has" if the rest of the sentence is to stand.)

Company Names. May be either singular or plural. Those with a distinctly plural ending or makeup are usually considered plural; and those distinctly singular are considered singular.

> Blaine Brothers **are** our sole **distributors**...(or agents, importers, etc.)
> Scott & Lee Publications, Inc., **have** announced **their**...
> Jerome Lane, Hatter, **offers his** new fall...
> Arlington, Inc., **is** the **distributor** for...(or agent, importer, etc.)

A name ending in "Corporation" or "Company" may be either singular or plural, according to the sense of the sentence.

Common Collectives. The number of collective words is unlimited, and has grown to include almost any word that represents the grouping of two or more things.

The following is a list of the common collectives:

army	company	flock	pair
assembly	congregation	generation	party
association	corporation	government	people (meaning a
audience	council	group	populace)
band	counsel	herd	population
board	couple	jury	press
bulk	crew	majority	public
cabinet	crowd	mankind	race
class	department	mass	royalty
clergy	element	minority	society
clientele	enemy	mob	troop
club	family	nation	union
committee	firm	number	United States
community	fleet	pack	youth

For example:

committee The **committee are** debating the question. (among themselves)
The **committee is** considering the proposition. (acting as one unit)

counsel While the **counsel are** attempting to agree...
Counsel for the company closed **their** arguments...
His **counsel objects** to that.

couple A* **couple have** been issued since then.
...to help the **couple insure their** home.
Records reveal that the **couple was** last seen...

majority The **majority come** from the lowlands.
The **majority was** strong in its position.
A* **majority** of people **are** against it.

number A* **number** of improvements **are** to be made.
The **number** of alterations **is** small. (the actual number)

pair This* **pair match** well.
That **pair looks** new.

* Notice that "a" or "this" may stand before a plural collective word.

COLLECTIVE WORDS

press   Never **has** the **Press** been so royally received.   (newspapermen)
The **Press were** accorded places of honor.   (newspapermen)
The **press has** sufficient power to. . .   (publications)
The **press are** in accord on the issue.   (publications)

Small Collectives.   The following small words may be singular or plural, according to their reference.

all	more	none	that	who
any	most	some	what	which

For example:

all   **All has** been used.   (a quantity)
All have been used.   (separate things)
any   **Any** of the motors **responds** instantly.   (any one)
Are there **any** left?   (any separate things)
Is there **any** left?   (any portion)
none   **None** of these things **find their** way into print.   (not any)
Of all the predictions, **none is** to be fulfilled.   (not one)
("None" in the plural is the commoner construction.)
that   The crowd **that was** cheering was in the bleachers.
The group **that were** objecting were questioned.
which   **Which are** to be insured?   (which ones)
Which is to be registered?   (which one)
who   **Who is** to sign it?   (what person)
Who are to sign it?   (what persons)

Fractions or Parts.   Fractions or parts may be singular or plural, according to the sense of the sentences.

first	part	portion	rest
half	percent	proportion	three-quarters
last	percentage	remainder	whole

For example:

first   The **first** of the shipments **have** arrived.   (the first ones)
The **first** of the shipments **was** damaged.   (the first one)
half   **Half** of the pages **are** proofread.
Half is proofread.   (half of the book)
part   **Part** of the crowd **was** held back.   (a portion)
A **part** of the crowd **were** unable to see.   (the individuals)
percent   Eighty **percent** of us **despise** the conditions. . .
Explain why this thirteen **percent was** released.
NOT: This ten percent *was* chosen, but who sponsored **them?**   (USE: were chosen)
percentage   A large **percentage are** sold by subscription.   (separate things)
A large **percentage has** been sold.   (quantity)
proportion   A considerable **proportion** of the extracts **are** from newspapers.
A larger **proportion** of the trade **is** expected to subscribe within a few weeks.
three-quarters   **Three-quarters** of the year **has** passed.
Three-quarters of the committee **were** against it.
rest   The **rest were** little more than mediocre.   (separate things)
The **rest is** in good condition.   (quantity)

39

Singulars and Plurals

Some seemingly plural words may be used as singulars, and some seemingly singular words may be used as plurals.

-ics Words. Almost all the -ics words may be construed as either singular or plural, although the -s is the old plural form (compare "music", "logic", and "arithmetic", which have retained the singular form).

They are regarded as singular if they refer to one thing, as to a science, a course of study, etc.; plural if they refer to several things that make up a whole, as qualities, activities, etc.

> **Acoustics is** the science of sound. (one thing)
> The **acoustics are** good in that building. (the several qualities of sound)
> **Athletics is** a required subject. (one study)
> **Athletics are** too important to dismiss. (the several sports included)

civics[1]	gymnastics[2]	mechanics[1]
dramatics[2]	heroics[4]	physics[1]
dynamics[3]	hysterics[4]	politics[3]
economics[1]	italics[4] (italic, sing.)	statistics[2]
ethics[3]	mathematics[1]	tactics[2]

[1] Usually singular.   [2] Usually plural.   [3] Either singular or plural.   [4] Always plural.

Often a modifier, like "the", "such", "his", etc., will induce the choice of a plural verb.

> **The** mathematics of it **are** complicated.
> **Such** ethics **are** not practised.
> **His** politics **are** interfering with his judgment.

Or a singular complement (representing the subject under discussion) will induce the choice of a singular verb.

> Dramatics **is a diversion** with some...
> Economics **is** also the **study** of wealth.

-s Words. Some words end in -s and yet are singular.

> **apparatus** plural may be "apparatus" or "apparatuses", but is rarely used.
> **gallows** plural is "gallowses".
> **lens** plural is "lenses".
> **news** always singular. In such sentences as "Last week the following were news:", the word "following" is plural, with "items" understood, and "news" is still singular. ("News" was formerly used as a plural.)
> **summons** plural is "summonses".
> **taps** as "Taps was sounded."
> **whereabouts** as "His whereabouts has been ascertained."

Some words ending in -s may be either singular or plural.

alms	gross	series
amends	means (way to an end)	species
chassis	measles	sweepstakes
corps	mumps	works (a factory)
goods		

"Chassis" and "corps", although spelled the same in the singular and plural, are differentiated by pronunciation:

singular $\begin{cases} \text{shăs'e} \\ \text{kōr} \end{cases}$ plural $\begin{cases} \text{shăs'ez} \\ \text{kōrz} \end{cases}$

The **goods were** marked.   (any sort of goods)
The **goods was** faded.   (dress goods)
No other **means was** in sight.   (one thing)
What other **means are** offered.   (several things)

Some -s words, plural in form and used with plural verbs, are singular, or collective, in meaning.

archives	lodgings	proceeds	tidings
earnings	means (income)	quarters	trumps
falls	nuptials	riches	wages
headquarters	oats	savings	winnings
leavings	odds	sweepings	woods
links (golf)	pains	thanks	works (mechanism)

The names of two-part tools and appliances, ending in -s, are considered as plurals although designating but single things.

bellows	pincers	scissors
forceps	pliers	shears
glasses	scales	tongs

When the word "pair" is used before certain of these words, it may induce the choice of a singular verb.

Unchanging Words.   Some words singular in form are unchanged in the plural.

aircraft	elk	quail
Chinese	grouse	salmon
cod	Japanese	sheep
deer	Portuguese	trout

Plurals in -s may be conceived for some of these; for instance, if several kinds of trout are meant, "trouts" may be used, as "Trouts flourish in northern waters", etc.

Some collectives with no plural are used as plurals—

cattle   gentry   police

and some are used as singulars (or occasionally as plurals):

livestock   mankind

Idiomatic Plurals.   Some words idiomatically take their singulars as plurals in certain constructions.

cannon   After the cannon die down...
brick   a ton of brick
dozen   several dozen of them
duck   When the duck fly south they foretell winter.
fish   All the fish in the stream were trout.   (as a whole)
        All the fishes in the stream were silver.   (each fish separately)
head   Some six million head of cattle were...
heathen   ...take advantage of what the heathen make possible.

41

pair	two pair of gloves or	two pairs of gloves
	several pairs of gloves	many pairs of gloves

score three score and ten

shot Four shot were embedded in the wood. ⎫
Shot was falling fast. ⎬ (lead pellets)
Ten shots were fired. (firearm discharges)

ton ten ton of lead

yoke six yoke of oxen

Abstract Collectives. There is another kind of word ("abstract" or general noun) whose singular often has a plural application, that is, when the word represents a common feeling, emotion, or action, etc.; but if a common or general idea is not foremost, the regular plural should be used.

Where the singular alone is applicable:

attention People will buy if we can attract **their attention.** (NOT: *attentions*)
consent Several gave **their consent** to the proposition. (NOT: *consents*)
sense ...according to the **sense of the different phrases.**
force These and others have shown **their force.**
interest **Their interest** was not in buying.
　　　　BUT: **Their interests** were elsewhere.
leaving We cannot prevent **their leaving** once in a while.
　　　　BUT: We cannot govern **their comings** and **goings.**
work It will not interfere with **their work.**
　　　　BUT: It will not interfere with **their careers.**
failure The **contractors' failure** to fulfill their contracts will be sufficient reason for...
　　　　BUT: What accounts for **their failures?**

Where singular or plural is applicable:

meaning ...according to **their meaning.** (OR: meanings)
measure If we can take **their measure** first... (OR: measures)
opinion Others expressed **their opinion** on the subject. (OR: opinions)
business We know men better if we know **their business.** (OR: businesses)
use What **use** can be made of such devices? (OR: uses)
tendency People have a **tendency** to do things that... (OR: tendencies)
time The only **time** those rules are in order is when persons fail to make payments...
　　　　OR: The only **times** those rules are in order **are** when persons fail to make payments...
payment ...if they fail to make **payment** on their notes. (would indicate final payment)
　　　　OR: ...if they fail to make **payments** on their notes. (would indicate installments)

COMPARISON

-er indicates comparison between two, as "the better of two things".
-est indicates comparison between three or more, as "the best of all".

Which way is farther? (of two)
Which way is the farthest? (of three or more)

COMPARISON

The following comparisons stand as opposites:

much, more, most   little, less or lesser, least
  (referring to quantities or degrees)
many, more, most   few, fewer, fewest
  (referring to numbers)
good
well } better, best   bad
ill } worse, worst
great, greater, greatest   little, less or lesser, least
large, larger, largest   small, smaller, smallest
big, bigger, biggest   little, smaller, smallest (littler, littlest [colloq.])
high, higher, highest   low, lower, lowest

fewer   refers to number of—by count. Wherever "a smaller number of" could be mentally supplied, "fewer" should be used. (Consequently, before plurals.)

less   refers to amount, degree, or quantity of. (Chiefly used before singulars.)

They have fewer (NOT: *less*) delays than before.   (a smaller number of)
They have less delay than before.   (a smaller amount of)

fewer men	less time
fewer animals	less work
fewer advantages	less opportunity
fewer troubles	less trouble

less than ten minutes   (means less time)
fewer than ten minutes (means a smaller number of minutes)

less   of two.
least   of three or more.

Which is the less commercial?   (of the two)
Which is the least commercial?   (of all)

lesser   means "smaller" or "in a less degree".

...no lesser fate than India.
Fog prevailed to a lesser extent.

"Less" is commonly used instead of "lesser".

This lamp gives the lesser light.
USUAL: This lamp gives less light.
...papers of lesser importance.
USUAL: ...papers of less importance.
...to a greater or lesser degree.
USUAL: ...to a greater or less degree.
USUAL: ...makes the difference less and not greater.

had best
had better
is best
is better } These are idiomatic combinations, used apparently without regard for comparison, but according to the degree of forcefulness desired.

Such literature **had best** be destroyed.
Such literature **had better have been** destroyed.
It **is best** to be consistent and use this method rather than that.
That **is better** avoided.
OR: That **is best** avoided.

to get the worst of it   compares with "to get the best of it".
to get the *worse* **of it**   is not used.
to get the better of⎫
to get the best of⎬ are both used.

best of all⎫ rather than "best of any", "most of any", etc.
most of all⎭

> We like that the best of any.
> FOR: We like that the best of all.
> (See "any" and "all", p. 5.)

Words Representing the Highest Degrees. Some words are supposed not to admit of comparison, representing in themselves the ultimate degrees, as

accurate	flawless	inseparable	sufficient
complete	fundamental	perfect	supreme
correct	genuine	perpendicular	unanswerable
dead	ideal	preferable	unique
decisive	impossible	real	universal
eternal	incessant	round	unprecedented
exact	incurable	square	vertical
faultless	indelible	stationary	wrong

However, since perfection in anything is rare, there must be degrees of approaching perfection or of appearing perfect, accurate, round, ideal, universal, etc.   It is in this sense of "more nearly" or "most nearly" that comparisons are often made.

> ...in order to form a **more perfect** Union....—The Constitution.
> If we know the meaning of a word, how much **more accurately** we can use it.
> For **more complete** information, write to...
> ...a **very complete** and interesting work.
> They seem **more dead** than alive.
> What could be **more eternal?**
> ...**more or less exact.**
> ...something that is **less indelible.**
> Which is **more correct?**
> ...a delusion that was **extremely real.**
> ...under the **most ideal** conditions possible.
> This is **far preferable** to that.
> The ground plan looks **too square.**
> The **rounder** the circle, the better.
> The idea is **most unique.**   (most unusual)
> ...a **rather unique** arrangement.
> Make it **so unique** that it can't be copied.
> If it is **unique enough** to be considered new...
> ...one of the **most universally** known facts.
> Is this **as unanswerable as** that?

The dictionaries give:

blind	blinder	blindest
choice	choicer	choicest
extreme	extremer	extremest
full	fuller	fullest

44

divine	diviner	divinest
pure	purer	purest
straight	straighter	straightest
true	truer	truest
excellent	more excellent	most excellent

From all of the above, it is to be assumed that practically any adjective or adverb may be compared, if the comparison makes sense.

ADVERBS AND ADJECTIVES

When adverbs and adjectives overlap, these guides may be applied.

Use an adjective when describing the subject:
(TEST: Substitute "is", "are", "was", or "were" for the verb.)

The **movement** grew **rapid**.   (TEST: The movement was rapid.)
He arrived **safe**.   (He was safe.)
Stocks closed **irregular** today.   (Stocks were irregular.)
They desire that their **records** be kept **secret**.   (are secret)
She acts **natural** always.   (She is natural [true to her nature] always.)
He feels **different** now.   (He is different [changed] now.)

Use an adverb when describing the verb:
(TEST: Substitute "in a...manner" for the -ly word.)

The movement **grew rapidly**.   (TEST: The movement grew in a rapid manner.)
Stocks **sold irregularly**.   (Stocks sold in an irregular manner.)
Their records were **kept secretly**.   (kept in a secret manner)
She **acts naturally**.   (acts in a natural manner)
He feels **differently** about it now.   (considers it in a different manner)

– – – –

"In some cases either the adjectival or adverbial form would be correct, and the choice between them is a matter of force, emphasis, or individual taste."
—Vizetelly, "How to Use English", p. 40.

Many Words Have Two Adverbial Forms.   When a word has two adverbial forms, the choice between them is a matter of usage. (The two forms give rise to two comparison forms, as "walk slower" and "more slowly", "think quicker or quickest" and "more or most quickly", etc.)

cheap	cheaply	sell cheap	travel cheaply
clean	cleanly	sweep clean	cut cleanly
close	closely	knit close	bind closely
deep	deeply	drink deep	think deeply
direct	directly	ship direct	talk directly to
fair	fairly	play fair	treat fairly
full	fully	full-grown	fully known
heavy	heavily	rests heavy	suffer heavily
high	highly	price high	praise highly
light	lightly	weigh light	step lightly
loud	loudly	speak loud	call loudly
quick	quickly	think quick	act quickly
right	rightly	guess right	understand rightly
sharp	sharply	turn sharp	watch sharply

45

short	shortly	stop short	answer shortly
slow	slowly	drive slow	move slowly
soft	softly	speak soft	touch softly
straight	straightly (rare)	think straight	remember straightly
wide	widely	open wide	space widely
wrong	wrongly	figure wrong	accuse wrongly

Often the two forms convey different meanings, as

| rest heavy | ship direct | stop short | play fair |
| lose heavily | directly opposed | go shortly | fairly well |

Adverbs Before Prepositions. When a preposition immediately
follows an adverb, the adverbial (-ly) form is usually used; but occasionally the adjectival form is idiomatically preferred.   The following are
examples of common phrases:

> **according to** ...done according to directions.   (NEVER: *accordingly* to)
> **agreeably to** }
> **agreeably with** } ...performed agreeably to the terms thereof.
> **agreeable to** }
> **agreeable with** } are also used adverbially.
> **conformably to** }
> **conformably with** } ...prepared conformably to their wishes.
> **conformable to** is also used.   ...done in accordance with or conformable
> to the law.
> **consistently with** It works consistently with our plan.
> **contrary to** ...signed contrary to their orders.
> **differently from** ...operates differently from that.
> **exclusively of** ...judged exclusively of the testimony.
> **independently of** ...financed independently of the bank.
> **irrespective of** ...bought irrespective of conditions.
> **previous to** ...was granted previous to that.
> **preparatory to** ...was arranged preparatory to leaving.
> **pursuant to** ...was made pursuant to their request.
> **regardless of** ...was spent regardless of the consequences.
> **separately from** ...was sold separately from the others.
> **similarly to** ...handled similarly to the other order.
> **subsequently to** ...dated subsequently to the contract.

The summary of this might be: Theoretically, the adverbial form (-ly)
in the above and similar uses is always grammatically correct.   But
usage has sometimes rejected the adverbial and preferred the adjectival
form.   Therefore, if in doubt about the proper word to use in any of these
adverbial constructions, choose the adverb, unless the adjectival form
is so common as to sound correct.

according as is an idiomatic expression which means "just as" or
"precisely as".   "Accordingly" is not used in this
combination.

> ..done one way or the other, **according as** the thought is in the performer's
> mind.

as near as } Adverbs between "as...as" often take the shorter adverbial
as late as } form.

46

...as **near** as I can remember them. (RATHER THAN: as nearly as)
...occurred as **late** as 1930. (RATHER THAN: as lately as)
We can buy as **cheap** as anyone.

bad The adjective "bad" is used where "offensive", "defective", "disagreeable", "wicked", "sorry", or "ill" is meant.

He looks bad. (ill)	It tastes bad. (offensive)
He feels bad. (ill)	It sounds bad. (disagreeable)
We feel bad about it. (sorry)	That looks bad. (defective)

    (TEST: Substitute a similar adjective: "sad", "glad", or "mad".
        One would not say or write "I feel *sadly*", etc.)

badly The adverb "badly" is used where "in a bad manner" is meant.

He behaved badly.	He was injured badly.
He acts badly on all occasions...	It stains badly.
They look badly upon it. (disagreeably)	

"Badly" is colloquial when used for "very much".

    COLLOQUIAL: They wanted to close the deal badly. (very much)
    COLLOQUIAL: He needed the money badly. (very much)

clean
clear
These words, when used as adverbs, may mean "wholly", or "quite". However, in some such constructions they have a colloquial sound.

    Such methods are **clean** against established practice.
    ...swept the audience **clear** off its feet.
    Shut it **clear** off.
    ...threw it **clear** across the room.

electric
electrical
Both are adjectives, but the shorter "electric" is widely used in preference to "electrical", except in a few phrases such as "electrical work", "electrical engineer", etc.
electrically is the adverb.

    There is to be electric lighting. (adjective)
    The plant is to be electrically lighted. (adverb)
      (NOT: *electric* lighted)
    There is to be electric welding throughout. (adjective)
    The tower is to be electrically welded throughout. (adverb)
      (NOT: *electric* welded)

fast is the adverbial form. "Fastly" is archaic.

    It was fast locked. ...seeping fast toward the bridge.

first, second, third and **first, secondly, thirdly** (See p. 402.)

hard
hardly
are both adverbs; but "hardly" is usually reserved for use when "scarcely" is meant; and "hard" is used in all other instances.

47

hard-hit	RATHER THAN:	hardly hit
hard-put		hardly put
hard-fought		hardly fought
our hard-won liberties		our hardly won liberties
took it hard		took it hardly

ill
illy are both adverbs, but "ill" is usually preferred. "Illy" has not yet become "established" by usage.

He was ill advised.
...an ill-balanced sentence.
The man was ill clad.
The decision was ill made.
The speech was neither well nor ill received.
They took the news illy. (OR: ill)

low
lowly are both adverbs; but "lowly" is usually reserved for use when "meekly" is meant; and "low" is used at other times.

swing low   threw low   talked low
They lowly submitted to the laws.

most   as an adverb, means "in or to the greatest degree".
mostly   means "chiefly", or "for the most part".

They were most concerned over the strike. (worried, or concerned in the greatest degree)
They were mostly concerned about wages. (chiefly concerned)

muchly   no longer exists. "Much" is the adverb.

It was much overdone. (NOT: *muchly*)

rather a...
quite a... These combinations are perhaps as much used as "a rather ..." and "a quite..."

It is rather a difficult process.
...in rather a quiet manner.
It was quite a satisfactory reward.
...at quite a late hour.

-sized
-faced
etc. are the usual adjective forms, but "-size", "-face", etc., are coming into use. The -ed words convey the idea of actual action. For instance, "a low-priced car" conveys the idea of the actual pricing of the car; whereas "the low-price field" conveys the idea of a field where the prices are low. "Letter-sized paper" might convey the idea of the actual sizing of the paper; while "letter-size paper" would represent a size usually used for letters.

Some other examples are:

medium-sized loans	AND:	medium-size loans
a large-sized space		a large-size space
bold-faced type		boldface type
a black-faced comedian		a blackface show
gilt-edged bonds		gilt-edge securities
an old-fashioned house		an old-style building

a life-size portrait
medium-weight manuscripts
ordinary-type goods
ten-letter words

"Of" is often understood after "size" in commercial phrases—

what size unit   any size machine   that size paper

which compare with the common terms:

what type (of) unit   what make (of) machine   what color (of) paper

thusly is colloquial. "Thus" is the usual adverb.

It is significant when considered thus. (RATHER THAN: thusly)

PRONOUNS

A pronoun's form depends always upon the grammatical construction of the sentence, and not upon the pronoun's position in the sentence. For instance, a pronoun used as a subject may be found far after its verb, or a pronoun used as an object may and often does stand somewhere before its verb.

One of the chief confusions concerns the forms to be used when pronouns occur in combinations.

for him and me } The simple test to determine the form of these pronouns
to her and them } is to make each pronoun stand alone.
by us and him   }

NOT: This is for you and *I* to learn.
       ("I" could not stand alone in this construction.   NOT: This is for *I* to learn.   Therefore "me" must be used.)
THUS: This is **for you** and me to learn.
NOT: To you and *he* belongs the credit.
       ("He" could not stand alone; therefore, "him".)
THUS: **To you** and him belongs the credit.
       It is now ready **for him** and his **committee** to sign.   (NOT: *he* and his committee)

Let's you and me

NOT: Let's you and *I* subscribe.
       (The simple sentence is: Let us subscribe.   "You and I" then is only an explanation of "us" and must be in the same form as "us"; therefore "me" must be used because "I" could not stand alone, as "Let *I* subscribe.")
THUS: Let's **you** and me subscribe.
       (Let us—you and me—subscribe.)
       Let **him** and **them** figure it out.   (NOT: *he* and *they*)

called him and me
told him and me

NOT: They called him and *I* to report for work.
       (Again "I" cannot stand alone; therefore, "me".)

THUS: They **called him** and **me** to report for work.
NOT: They told both *he* and *I* that the deal was closed.
(They told him, and they told me...)
THUS: They **told** both **him** and **me** that the deal was closed.

for us workers
We workers

NOT: It is a good rule for *we* **workers** to follow.
(The simple construction is: It is a good rule for us to follow.
"Workers" merely explains "us".)
THUS: It is a good rule **for us workers** to follow.
BUT: **We workers** should follow that rule.
(The simple sentence is: We should follow...)
NOT: Strange ways *us* **travelers** have to take.
(The simple sentence is: Strange ways we have to take.
"Travelers" explains "we".)
THUS: Strange ways **we travelers** have to take.

between you and me
between him and them } "Between" is a preposition. To test the pro-
between us three nouns, substitute another preposition.

NOT: This is just between you and *I*.
(Substitute "for" as a test preposition, and the sentence would
incorrectly read: This is just for you and *I*. Since "I" could
not stand alone in this construction, the word is therefore
"me".)
THUS: This is just **between you** and **me**.
NOT: Between *he* and *they*, we see no peace.
(Substitute "for" for "between", and "*he* and *they*" must
become "him and them". AS: For him and them, we see no
peace.)
THUS: **Between him** and **them**, we see no peace.
NOT: ...an agreement between *we* three.
(Simplified it is: an agreement between us. "Three" simply
explains "us".)
THUS: ...an agreement **between us** three.
NOT: The difference between the man who reads and *he* who only listens
is...
(The simple construction should be: The difference between the
man and him is... "Who reads" modifies "man", and "who
only listens" modifies "him".)
THUS: The difference **between** the **man** who reads and **him** who only
listens...

After Forms of the Verb "Be"

It is I	I am he	It should be they	It could be I
It is we	He is I	It will be I	It may be I, he, we, they
It is he	We are they	It was we	It might have been I, he, we, they
It is they	They are we	They were we	It has always been I, he, we, they

The simple rule is that these pronouns should be capable of replacing
the words to which they refer. Test them by substitution.

It is me is favored by the British in conversation, and is generally used in America. (It has been sanctioned as a "good coiloquialism".)

BUT: If **I were he**... (NOT: *him*)
(SUBSTITUTING: If he were I...)
It **was I** who wrote. (I was it [the person] who wrote.)
No matter what comes, **he will** always **be he.** (NOT: *him*)
Still **I am I,** and you are you.
Among those named **were he and we.** (NOT: *him* and *us*)
(An inverted sentence: He and we were among...)
If any man is right, it should **be he.** (NOT: *him*)
They imagined **it was we,** and we thought **it was they.** (NOT: *us* NOR: *them*)
How can **they be we?** (NOT: *us*)
The **defendants are he, they, and we.** (NOT: *him, them,* and *us*)
Is **it he** that they refer to? (NOT: *him*)
They thought that the **applicant was I.** (NOT: *me*)
If **it had been I,** I should have done differently.
("If it had been me" is colloquial.)
These are they. (NOT: *them*)

If these uses sound unnatural or pedantic, repeat them often enough to become accustomed to them, and the stilted sound will disappear.

being he
ae being

They were concerned over **its being we.** (NOT: *us*)
(over our being it)
No one thought of **its being he.** (NOT: *him*)
The **person** in charge **being he,** there can be no change in policy. (NOT: *him*)
(He being the person in charge...)
There being a definite place for him, and **he** (NOT: *him*)
being the logical man, we decided...

let it be him } Here also the pronoun must be capable of changing
let us be them } places with the word to which it refers.

If anyone profits, **let it be him.** (NOT: *he*) (SUBSTITUTING: ...let him be it.)
Let us be them that give. (OR: Let us be **those who** give.)

to be he
to be him } Again the rule holds: A pronoun after "to be" should be
to be I } capable of replacing the word to which it refers.
to be me

The **fugitive** was thought **to be he.**
REPLACING: **He** was thought **to be** the **fugitive.**
They thought the **fugitive to be him.**
REPLACING: They thought **him to be** the **fugitive.**
They knew **it to be him.**
It seems **to be he.**
I am often taken **to be he.**
(**He** is often taken **to be I.**)
Some take **him to be me.**
(Some take **me to be him.**)

51

We are sure it was **to have been they.**
Whom did they suppose **him** to be? (NOT: *who*)
(Straightening the sentence we have: Did they suppose
him to be whom?)
There was a man standing by the door **whom** the officers
unfortunately took **to be him** (NOT: *he*) whom they
intended to arrest.
("Him" refers to "whom" rather than to "man". The
clause is: the officers unfortunately took **whom to be him.**)

as being
as (when it means "to be") } When "as being" or "as" (meaning "to
be") is used, the pronoun that follows
should be capable of replacing the word
to which it refers.

You were disguised **as he.** (to be he)
They disguised **you as him.** (to be him)
That **man** was remembered **as being he** who blocked...
(**He** was remembered **as being that man**...)
They remembered the **man as him** who blocked...
(They remembered the **man to be him**...)

him me Sometimes "to be" is understood, as "They thought him me."
Similarly used pronouns should be capable of replacing the
words to which they refer.

They thought the **slacker him.** (NOT: *he*)
(They thought the **slacker to be him.**)
They adjudged the **winner me.** (NOT: *I*)
(They adjudged **me to be the winner.**)
We thought the **signers her and him.** (NOT: *she* and *he*)
He seemed to think **us them** whom he was supposed to meet. (OR: **those**)
(He seemed to think **them to be us**—he was supposed to meet whom.)

become we
become they } "Become" in its meaning of "come to be" falls under
the general rule: All pronouns following forms of the
verb "to be" should be capable of replacing the words
to which they refer.

...until **you become they,** and they become you.
(...until **you come to be they**)
He lived in the character so long that it finally **became he.**
(...that **he** finally **became it**)
It is not possible for **us to become them.**
(It is not possible for **them to come to be us.**)

as good as I
as much as he } Pronouns following "as" take the forms they would
as well as they take if the sentences were complete.

They are as good **as we.** (NOT: *us*)
(They are as good as we are.)
We like him as much **as them.**
(We like him as much as we like them.)
We like him as much **as they.** (as they like him)
We can fight as well **as they.** (as they can)
He will have to fight us **as well as them.** (as well as fight them)

You will be notified as soon **as I.**   (as I am)
They will notify you as soon **as me.**   (as soon as they notify me)
It should be up to them as well **as us** to get results.   (as well as to us   **NOT:**
as well as *we*)
We were informed as well **as they.**   (**NOT:** *them*)   (as well as they were)

so...as he } "As" here still takes the form of pronoun necessary
such...as he } to complete the phrase.

> They are not **so** dependable **as he.**   (**NOT:** *him*)   (as he is)
> They are not **so** much interested **as you and I.**   (**NOT:** *me*)
> There are always **such as they.**   (**NOT:** *them*)
> **NOT:** ...if such **as** *him* should win.   (**USE:** such as he [is])
> A DEVIATION: It is for **him** and **such** offenders **as him** that these laws are
> made.
> (This "him" is given license to match the preceding
> "him".)

like him } Since "like" means "similar to" or "similarly to" and
like them } takes an object, "as" should be used wherever a subject
like me } and verb are introduced. (See also Words Misused,
p. 14.)

> He is **like me.**   (similar to me)
> (**NOT:** He is like *I am.*   It could not read: He is similar to *I am.*)
> He writes **as I do.**   (in the manner that I do)
> (Note that "as" introduces a subject and verb.)
> He writes **like me.**   (similarly to me)
> Men **like him and you** should not be involved.   (**NOT:** *he*)
> ("Like him and you" means "similar to him and you" and does not intro-
> duce a verb, but explains "men".   The simple sentence is: Men should not
> be involved.)
> Artists **like her and him** are interested in...   (**NOT:** like *she* and *he*)
> Those who, **like them,** have spent a fortune...   (**NOT:** like *they*)
> People **like them** can't tell the difference.   (**NOT:** like *they are*)

but me } When these introductory words have the meaning of "except"
but him } or "besides", they may logically be considered prepositions
save me } and followed by "me", "us", "him", "her", and "them".

> Everyone signed **but him.**   (except him)
> Everyone **but him** was notified.
> (The simple sentence is: Everyone was notified.   "But him", meaning
> "except him", modifies "everyone".)
> No one **but you and me** is to receive a check.   (**NOT:** No one but you and I
> *are* to...)
> All **save him** were drowned.   (except him)

When "but" stands as a conjunction and does not have the meaning
of "except", it takes the pronoun necessary to complete its clause.

> We, **but not he,** expect to join.
> (We expect to join—but he does not.)
> They are interested, **but not I.**   (**NOT:** *me*)
> (They are interested—but I am not.)
> It is not they who are right, **but he.**   (but it is he)
> It benefited not them, **but him.**   (but it benefited him)

53

than I
than he ⎫ Pronouns following "than" take the forms they would take
than me ⎬ if the sentences were complete.
than him ⎭

It is a test of you more **than me.**   (than it is of me)
You are being tested more **than I.**   (than I am)
They like you more **than he.**   (than he likes you)
They like you more **than him.**   (than they like him)
None have worked for it more **than we.**   (NOT: *us*)
Financially you rate higher **than he.**   (than he rates)
The Credit Bureau rates you higher **than him.**   (than it
   rates him)
He is no better **than you or I.**   (NOT: *me*)
   (He is no better than you are or I am.)
If any nation that is stronger **than we**...   (NOT: *us*)
The man who plans is more valuable **than he** (NOT: *him*)
   who only plods.   (than he is who only plods)
Praise is given more often to the man who asks for it **than
   him** who deserves it.   (than to him who deserves it)
The peasants are voiceless and no more **than we** (NOT: *us*)
   to be censured.   (no more to be censured than we are)
We disliked both of them—but **him more than her.**   (but
   we disliked him more than we disliked her)
Both were dishonest—but **he more than she.**   (but he was
   more dishonest than she was)
A DEVIATION: It defeated not only **him,** but men much stronger **than him.**
   (This "him" is given license to match the preceding
   "him".)

other than*

It was none **other than he** who sent the message.   (than he is)
It is someone **other than I** that they mean.   (than I am)
They spoke to someone **other than me.**   (than to me)
No one, **other than they,** knows about it.   (NOT: No one, other than *them know*
   about it.)

rather than*

They should be responsible, **rather than we.**   (than that we should)
The firm is involved **rather than he.**
...look to the firm **rather than him.**   (than to him)
We, **rather than they,** are entitled to consideration.

*"Than" phrases such as this are, by some writers, regarded as having the prepositional force of "except", "besides", "instead of", etc., and are therefore followed by the pronouns "me", "us", "him", "her", and "them".

than whom is an idiomatic combination, with "than" having the
   prepositional meaning of "in comparison with".

Midas **than whom** no man was richer...
The working people, **than whom** no more trusting souls exist, voted for...

who and whom can be either singular or plural, or first person, second
   person, or third person, according to the words to
   which they refer.

54

...for **you who have** worked.   (for you, you have **worked**)
...for **him who has** worked.   (for him, he has **worked**)
...for **those who have** worked.   (usage for "for **them who**")
...for **us who have** worked.   (for us, we have worked)
...for **me who have** worked.   (for me, I have worked)
It is **I who am** interested.   (NOT: who *is*)
  (It is I, I am interested.)
He **who** never **wastes** anything...
You **who** never **waste** anything...(NOT: *wastes*)
  (You, you never waste anything...)

The fundamental guides in choosing "who" or "whom":

Use "who" wherever "he" or a similar pronoun could be substituted. Use "whom" wherever "him" or a similar pronoun could be substituted.

They couldn't tell **whom** the cable was **from.**   (NOT: *who*)
  (They couldn't tell—the cable was from whom [him].)
Guess **whom** we saw today!   (NOT: *who*)
  (Guess—we saw whom [him] today!)
Who does he think he is?   (NOT: *whom*)
  (Does he think—he is who?)
Whom does he think he's hurting?   (NOT: *who*)
  (Does he think—he's hurting whom?)
Who could it have been?   (NOT: *whom*)
  (Could it **have been who** [he]?)
Don't you know **who** it was?   (NOT: *whom*)
  (Don't you know—it was who [he]?)
Here is a man **whom** no one can accuse of being selfish.
  (Here is a man—no one can accuse whom [him] of being...)

Remember that entire clauses or phrases may be subjects or objects and "who" may be just a part of such a clause or phrase.

Now you know **who should be given preference.**   (NOT: *whom*)
  (Now you know—who should be given preference.   The entire clause "who should be given preference" is the object of "know".)
You have observed **who is always first.**   (NOT: *whom*)
  (You have observed—who is always first.)
The matter of **who should pay** was not determined.   (NOT: *whom*)
  (The matter of—who should pay—was not determined.)
But there are people **whom to admire** is difficult.
  (There are people—to admire whom [them] is difficult.   The entire phrase "to admire whom" is the subject of "is difficult".)
There was no question about **who the winner would be.**
  (There was no question about—who would be the winner.)
It depends on **who is meant.**   (NOT: *whom*)
  (It depends on—who is meant.)
It depends on **whom they mean.**   (NOT: *who*)
  (It depends on—they mean whom.   Here "whom" is the object of "mean", and the entire clause "they mean whom" is the object of "on".)

In speech, "who" is sometimes used for "whom".

Established colloquialisms:

Who are you looking for?   (whom)
Who do you mean?   (whom)
I don't remember who with.   (with whom)

55

The verb form "to be" often affects the construction of "who" or "whom". (See also "to be he", "to be him", etc., p. 51.)

> **Whom** did they take **it** to be?
> (Did they take **it** to be **whom** [him]?)
> Is he **who** he pretends to be?
> (Is he—**who** pretends to be **he?**)

he who	OR: him who	
they who*	them who	To test these pronouns break the sentences
we who	us who	into their separate clauses.
I who	me who	

> Everything comes to **him who** waits. (NOT: *he*)
> (Everything comes to him—who waits. "Him" is the object of "to", and "who" is the subject of "waits". "Who waits" modifies "him" To use "*he* who" would give two subjects to "waits".)
> **He who** waits will find that everything comes.
> (He—who waits—will find that everything comes.)
> **Him who** is loyal, repay. (Repay him—who is loyal.)
> It was **he whom** they summoned. (NOT: *him who*)
> (It was he—they summoned whom [him].)
> Give **him who** runs a chance to read. (Give him—who runs—a chance...)
> **He who** runs has no time to read. (He—who runs—has no time to read.)
> It was **they who** told. (NOT: *them*) (It was they—who told.)
> It was **they whom** you told. (It was they—you told whom [them].)
> ...but **they who*** cannot yet read English, can read this.—Emerson.
> ...traders might ask whether **they, who** have the excuse of having to contend with a merciless competition, are alone to be blamed.—Spencer.
> ...returned with his prisoner to **them that** sent him...—Emerson.
> (Usually "to those that" or "to those who")
> They wonder why security is not for **them, who** have always worked.
> He told **them who** was to be the next chairman. ⎱ different meaning
> He told **them whom** we had decided to make chairman. ⎰
> The results of this will be important only to **those whom** it concerns.
> **We who** have had that experience do not doubt it.
> What is in line for **us who** have that training?
> It was **I who** was called upon. OR: It was **I whom** they called upon.
> They called upon **me whom** no one knew.
> (They called upon me—no one knew whom [me].)
> It was like willing a ranch in Texas to **me who** live in Wales. (NOT: *lives*)
> (...to me—who [I] live in Wales.)

* "They who" and "them who" have been almost entirely displaced by "those who".

whoever means "anybody who".
whomever means "anybody whom".

The "anybody" belongs to what goes before the word, and the "who" or "whom" to what follows.

> A political trap was set for **whoever** would fall into it.
> (...was set for anybody—who would fall...)
> They set a political trap for **whomever** they could catch.
> (...for anybody—whom they could catch.)
> This applies to him or **whoever** is given the job. (NOT: *whomever*)
> (...to him or anybody—who is given...)
> **Whoever** is successful they dislike. (NOT: *whomever*)
> (They dislike anybody—who is successful.)

56

Whomever he envies he dislikes. (NOT: *whoever*)
(He dislikes anybody—whom he envies.)
Whomever they want, will be the next chairman. (NOT: *whoever*)
(Anybody—whom they want—will be the next chairman.)
To **whoever** writes in, we will send a sample. (NOT: *whomever*)
(To anybody—who writes in...)
To **whomever** they designate, we will send samples. (NOT: *whoever*)
(To anybody—whom they designate...)
Appoint **whoever** is suited for the position. (NOT: *whomever*)
(Appoint anybody—who is suited...)
Appoint **whomever** you wish. (NOT: *whoever*)
(Appoint anybody—whom you wish.)

whosever is the possessive, rather than "whoever's".

whosoever ⎫
whomsoever ⎬ are the more formal and precise forms.
whosesoever ⎭

as to who means "regarding who [is]".
as to whom means "regarding whom".

> A debate **as to who** should be appointed took up most of the afternoon.   (NOT: *whom*)
> (A debate regarding—who should be appointed—took up...   The entire clause "who should be appointed" is the object of "as to" [regarding].)
> A question might arise **as to who** is responsible. (NOT: *whom*)
> (A question might arise regarding—who is responsible.)
> ...an investigation **as to whom** the Court is shielding. (NOT: *who*)
> (...an investigation regarding—the Court is shielding whom [him].)

If another "to" is necessary after "as to" to complete the "whom", it is better to rewrite the sentence.

> INCOMPLETE: No decision was made as to whom the contract should be awarded.
> (Another "to" is necessary if the sentence is to be complete: **as to whom** the contract should be awarded **to**.)
> BETTER: No decision was made **as to who** should be awarded the contract.

Intervening Statements After "Who" and "Whom". Explanations, suppositions, asides, etc., are often inserted immediately after "who" and "whom", and tend to cloud the construction. If such intervening statements can be temporarily removed without destroying the basic meaning of the sentences, they are not considered in determining upon "who" or "whom".

> Who **did they say** is leaving tomorrow?
> ("Did they say" is the intervening statement. "Who is leaving tomorrow?" is the simple question.)
> Whom **did they say** the speaker meant?
> (The speaker meant whom?)
> ...a man who **we thought** needed the work. (NOT: *whom*)
> (...a man who needed the work.)
> ...a man whom **you would think** they could interest.
> (...a man whom they could interest.)

57

...someone who **they specified** could live at home.
Send it to anyone who **you think** will be interested.
Send it to anyone whom **you think** they would care to interest.
...a representative who **the interpreter said** could act for us.
...a mechanic who **they well knew** could not do the work.
...an investor whom **the company stated** they did not want.
...who **we believe** are the proper persons.
Who **do you suppose** is the donor?
Whom **do you suppose** this is from?
They paid those who **they felt** might bring suit.
...an agent who **I think they imagine** was not playing fair.
NOT: He is the banker *whom*, rumor makers say, is investing...
    ("Rumor makers say" is parenthetic.)
NOT: The playwright *whom*, the critics say, is recounting his life...
    ("The critics say" is parenthetic.)

When similar statements cannot be even temporarily removed without destroying the sense of the sentences, they govern the form of "who" or "whom".

The man **whom I knew**, was made president. (irremovable)
(The man—whom I knew—was made president.)
He was the man **whom I believed** to be our pilot.
(To remove "I believed" would destroy the sentence. so: He was the man—I believed whom [him] to be our pilot.)
The man **whom we thought** to be our client deserted us.
(The man—we thought whom [him] to be our client—deserted us.)
We do not visit even those **whom we think** our friends.
("We think" here means "we consider". so: ...we consider whom [them] our friends.)

If such statements could be temporarily removed, but if their removal would destroy the true sense of the sentences, they must be considered in determining upon "who" or "whom".

There were but a few natives left, **whom we found** engaged in gambling.
(...we found whom [them] engaged in gambling.)
BUT: There were but a few natives left who, **we found**, engaged in gambling.
(Here "we found" may be removed, giving the sentence a different meaning.)

one   The indefinite "one" refers to "anyone" or "everyone".
one's is the possessive, written with the apostrophe.
oneself is now written solid. It was formerly "one's self".

If the indefinite "one" is introduced into a sentence, the impersonal form should be maintained throughout.

One must work out **one's** own salvation. (NOT: *his* NOR: *their*)
One should not take **oneself** too seriously. (NOT: *himself* NOR: *themselves*)

one   Definite. This "one" refers to one person, and is followed by "he", "his", "her", or a corresponding pronoun.

One [man] improves **his** mind to grow rich; another to grow wise.
No one [person] likes to think that **his** fortune is founded on sand. (NOT: *their*)

As **one** [person] who knows a bargain when **he** sees it, I believe... (NOT: when *I see* it)

you   Indefinite. This "you" means "anyone". Do not mix it with "one" in the same sentence. Keep one point of view.

If **you** are responsible for a debt, **you** (NOT: *one*) should pay it.

we   Indefinite. This "we" may mean the writer and the reader, or people in general. It should not be mixed indiscriminately with other indefinite pronouns.

We now come to a theory which **we** (NOT: *one* NOR: *you*) cannot readily prove.

— — — —

A jumbled viewpoint:

If **one** is inclined to doubt the truth of this **you** should investigate it, because **we** cannot always tell from the surface just what the situation is.

From one viewpoint:

If **you** are inclined to doubt the truth of this, **you** should investigate it, because **you** cannot always tell from the surface just what the situation is.

— — — —

Editorial "we"   The "editorial we" should be used only when "we" actually implies the opinion of the editors, or of a corresponding group; it should not be used to state the opinion of one writer, one speaker, or one thinker.

National "we"   The "national we" may be used by anyone, to mean a nation; but it should not be mixed with the "editorial we" in the same sentence.

NOT: We [editorial] are not attempting to dictate to Washington, but **we** [editorial] believe that **we** [national] should now take **our** [national] first fearless or fearful step.

BUT: ...we believe that **the nation** should now take **its** first fearless or fearful step.

Sovereign "we"   The "sovereign we" or "royal we" is used instead of "I" by royalty and governing officials, who consider themselves a part of, and spokesmen for, their people. **"Ourself"** instead of "ourselves" is used with this "we".

Personification Pronouns. Do not break off into personification after establishing a word as a neuter thing.

NOT: If the **world** should somehow find peace within **itself**, so that all **her** people would stop fighting everlastingly...
("Itself" establishes "world" as a neuter, but "her" personifies it.)
USE: ...world...itself...its people...
OR: ...world...herself...her people...

59

myself
ourselves
yourself
yourselves
himself
herself
itself
themselves

} These pronouns should be used to reflect or intensify nouns or pronouns that have been expressed. In the absence of such introductory words, regular pronouns should be used.

Reflecting:

He laughed at **himself**. ("Himself" reflects "he".)
The man saw **himself** in that situation.
People appoint **themselves** to such positions.

Intensifying:

I **myself** will attend to it. ("Myself" intensifies "I".)
...for the **doctor, himself,** to take.
Note that commas may or may not be used around "myself", "himself", etc., according to the emphasis desired.

The -self pronouns may be used in combination with other pronouns.

He saved a place for **himself** and **me**. (NOT: *myself*)
I saved a place for **him** and **myself**. (NOT: *himself*)
They saved places for **him** and **me**. (NOT: *himself* and *myself*)

Occasionally these pronouns stand alone in sentences, when the words they reflect or intensify are implied but not expressed.

There is no one to blame but **himself**. (He has no one...)
Keep it for **yourself**, alone. (You keep it...)
But as for **themselves**—nothing is too good. (But they think...)
So many people, including **myself**, have started on that course. (including me myself)

The following constructions are commonly seen; but most of them could be improved if the shorter pronouns were used as indicated.

My associates and **myself** are interested in... (USE: I)
Yourself and directors are requested to consider... (USE: You and your directors)
There must be other persons like **myself**... (USE: me)
Nobody knows how to operate it but **myself**. (USE: me)
They insinuated that it was Barton and **ourselves** who...
   ("We" [it was Barton and we] might sound a bit strained in this everyday sentence, but should be used on all formal occasions.)
Send it to **myself** at the above address. (USE: me)
Both Mr. Hale and **myself** are writing him direct. (USE: I)
We do not think that any American manufacturer other than **ourselves** is quoting.
   ("We", while correct here, would not appear to bridge the gap so well as "ourselves". Some writers would treat "other than" as a preposition meaning "besides", and use "us". Others would avoid the pronoun and use "our Company".)

60

"Yourself" is commonly used in the following phrases:

Regards to **yourself** (OR: you) and Mrs. Hale.
Regards to **yourself** (OR: you) and your associates...
Note that "yourself" or "you" is placed first in these combinations, as a courtesy to the reader.

"Yourselves" is often used in such sentences as the following, because it expresses the plural; whereas "you", in itself, does not.

I was pleased to find letters from both **yourselves** and the Fulton Company.
Patents have been issued to **yourselves**.
("You" might be ambiguous here, in that it might seemingly refer to but one person—the reader of the letter.)

Possessive Pronouns in Combinations.

your and our
yours and ours
her and their
hers and theirs } When using two or more possessive pronouns, check each one separately to make sure that its form is correct for its position in the sentence.

NOT: This is **his**, *yours,* and **my** problem. (USE: your)
    (his problem—your problem—my problem)
BUT: This problem is **his, yours,** and **mine.** (NOT: *your*)
    (is his—is yours—is mine)
NOT: *Theirs* instead of **his** instructions will be followed.
    (their instructions—his instructions)
BETTER: **Their** instructions instead of **his** will be followed.
NOT: *Theirs* and **our** offices adjoin. (USE: Their)
    (their offices—our offices)
NOT: It is for *hers* as well as **his** benefit. (for her benefit—as well as
    his benefit)
BETTER: It is for **her** benefit, as well as **his.**
NOT: It must have been *mine* and not **their** car. (my car—their car)
BETTER: It must have been **my** car and not **theirs.**
OR: The car must have been **mine** and not **theirs.**

Possessive Pronouns Before -ing Words and Phrases.

your going
my being
his asking
their writing { An -ing word may serve as a noun; and a phrase containing a word ending in -ing may express one thought (as if it were one word). The possessive form of pronoun should be used before an -ing word or phrase standing as a noun.

Their having finished the work proves that it can be done.
    (The entire -ing phrase, "Their having finished the work", is the subject of "proves".)
They, having finished the work, **now desire compensation.**
    (Here the -ing phrase simply modifies "They".)
His having read the speech caused much comment. (NOT: *He*)
    (Again the entire -ing phrase is the subject.)
He having read the speech, **the committee adjourned.**
    (Here the -ing phrase is again a modifying phrase.)
It is hard to conceive of **their not doing good work.** (NOT: *them*)
    (The entire -ing phrase is the object of "of".)

If the one-thought -ing phrase is broken into by another phrase or clause, the possessive cannot of course be used.

> It isn't pleasant to contemplate him **who really wants to work** being forced to accept charity.
> (The simple sentence is: It isn't pleasant to contemplate **his being forced to accept charity.** But "who really wants to work" breaks in, and "his" cannot be used. Therefore, the next best pronoun is "him".)

Guard against the splitting of these one-thought -ing phrases. Not only does it make a phrase very difficult to follow, but a sentence can be made wholly meaningless thereby. The best rule is to rearrange the sentence.

> The debate had been personal, and the question arose regarding it, **which should not have been a part of the minutes anyway,** being stricken from the record.
> (The simple clause is: . . . the question arose regarding **its being stricken from the record.** But another long clause intrudes, ruining the grammatical construction of "its" and making the whole sentence a puzzle.)

(See also Possessives, p. 124.)

Pronouns Used Parenthetically or in Apposition. Pronouns used parenthetically, or in apposition, should be of the same form as the nouns or pronouns which they explain, or which they could replace.

> They sent **us, him and me,** on the mission.   (NOT: *he* and *I*)
> ("Him and me" explains "us". SUBSTITUTING: They sent him and me, us, on the mission.)
> **We** should be cautious, **we** Americans, that we do not. . .
> ("We Americans" explains "we" and could be substituted for it.)
> Let **us** be cautious, **us** Americans, that we do not. . .
> ("Us Americans" here explains "us".)
> **We** can take a lesson from them, **we** Americans, and begin again.   (NOT: *us* Americans) (Again "we Americans" is of the same construction as "we" and should not be influenced by "them".)
> **Who** won—**you** or **I?**   (NOT: *me*)
> (Who—you or I—won?)
> Let's start the wheels turning—**you and me**—and before. . .
> ("You and me" explains the "us" of "Let us" or "Let's". Let you and let me, us, start the wheels turning. . .)
> They wanted **us** both, **me** as well as **him.**   (NOT: *I* as well as *he*)
> ("Me as well as him" simply explains "us both". They wanted me as well as they wanted him—us both.)
> All were interested—**he, they,** and **we.**   (NOT: *him, them,* and *us*)
> It was interesting to all—**him, them,** and **us.**
> To treat a **man** so despicably, **him** (NOT: *he*) who is bigger than they.
> ("Him" explains "a man". To treat him so despicably, a man who is. . .)
> The **man** was treated despicably, **he** (NOT: *him*) to whom they owed everything.
> (He was treated despicably, the man to whom. . .)
> It encourages the **planter,** even **him** who is skeptical.   (NOT: *he*)
> ("Him" may replace "the planter". It encourages him, even the planter who is skeptical.)
> The **planter** is encouraged, even **he** who is skeptical.   (NOT: *him*)
> (He is encouraged, even the planter who is skeptical.)

Misleading Pronouns. If a pronoun is liable to be misleading in its reference, it should not be used. Either the word in question should be repeated, or the sentence should be rearranged.

> The solution to this problem is still a matter of guesswork, but it looks as if it could be brought about by analyzing its four fundamental causes.
> (The first "it" is general; the second "it" refers to the solution; and the third "its" refers to the problem. Better to discard the last "its" and use "the": ...but it looks as if it could be brought about by analyzing the four fundamental causes.)
> The secretary admitted that it was **his** own fault that the president had been asked to resign. (Whose fault?)
> ("His" presumably refers to "president", but the reader does not know that until late. Better to rearrange: It was the president's own fault that he had been asked to resign, the secretary admitted. Or if a different meaning applies, and a rearrangement is not desirable, parentheses may be used: The secretary admitted that it was his (the secretary's) fault that the president had been asked to resign.)
> Without explanation **he** informed **him** that **he** must leave.
> (Who must leave—the speaker or the listener? BETTER: Without explanation he informed him that he found it necessary to leave. Or if another meaning applies: Without explanation he asked him to leave.)
> Men giving charity to men less fortunate than they, **who** desire that their names be kept secret, seek such obscurity because...
> (Which men desire that their names be kept secret?—the reader does not immediately know. BETTER: Men who desire that their names be kept secret when giving charity to men less fortunate than they, seek such obscurity... OR: Men who, in giving charity..., desire...)

Clear Reference. Pronouns should agree in person and number with the words to which they refer.

After establishing a word as a singular, keep it singular.

> NOT: This nation should be able to protect its (sing.) resources if we (pl.) are called upon to do so.
> (Use "it is", instead of "we are", to agree with the first "its".)
> If a worker is justified in tendering his (NOT: their) resignation, he (NOT: they) should receive...

The masculine pronouns ("he", "his", "him") are used to refer to nouns of indefinite gender, as "everyone", "a person", etc., and also to antecedents of mixed gender, as "every man and woman". (See also Subjects, pp. 71 and 72.)

> Everybody told **his** side of the story. (NOT: *their* side)
> Everyone wants **his** outlook to be bright. (NOT: *their*)
> Each desires a place for **himself** in the sun. (NOT: *themselves*)
> Which of us is to have **his** way? (NOT: *our* way)
> If a man or a woman meets **his** equal... (NOT: *their* equal)
> Every girl and boy looks to **his** future. (NOT: *their* future)

"His or her" is sometimes used for exactness.

> If a man or a woman changes his or her mode of dress... (NOT: *their*)
> If a man or a woman wants to obscure himself or herself... (NOT: *him or herself*)

The feminine pronoun "she" or "her" may of course be used if the reference is clearly to women.

> **Everyone** should include this in **her** wardrobe. (NOT: *their*)
> **Each** of the teachers subscribed **her** share. (NOT: *their* share)

"He or it" or "his or its" is not usually used in an attempt to avoid "they" or "their". Either "they" or "their" is used (in the absence of a fitting singular pronoun), or the sentence is rearranged.

> UNUSUAL: If **a person** or **an event** is mentioned in the text, **he or it** should be clearly identified.   (OR: they)
> REARRANGED: If mentioned in the text, a person or an event should...
> OR: If persons or events are mentioned in the text, they should be clearly identified.

PREPOSITIONS

Prepositions overlap each other in meaning; but an attempt should always be made to select the best word for the sentence in hand.

after } used interchangeably in such phrases as "30 days after date",
from } "ten days from today".

among used when three or more things are referred to.
between used when two things are referred to.   If used with more than two things, it brings each into individual relationship with the others.

> An agreement between France, England, Germany, and Italy.

It sometimes groups them in twos, as

> ...between the pages of a book.

at implies geographical location, and can mean either **in** or **near** a city, as "the airport **at** New York", "the races **at** Palm Beach", "a plant **at** Toledo".
in usually means actually **within** the boundaries of a city, as "The Olympic Games were held **in** Los Angeles."
on implies geographical location **on** a wide or long area, as "**on** the Coast", "**on** an Indian reservation", "**on** a street".

> He is **on** the Coast, **in** San Francisco, **at** the Lakeside Hotel.
> A person lives **on** a street **in** a city.

"In the street" is a commercial phrase meaning in the financial district of a city, as "in Wall Street".
"In...street" is common in British usage, instead of "on...street", as "living in Waverley Street".

in implies within.
into implies entrance; or change of form.
in to two separate words.

He walked **in** the office.   (within the office)
He walked **into** the office.   (he entered)
...divided **into** three parts.
Send the telegrams **in to** them immediately.

next   may be used as a preposition meaning "nearest to".

Place this one **next** the other.
("To" is unnecessary after "next" in this construction.)

on   indicates position.
onto   indicates movement toward.
on to   two separate words.

The cadets marched **on** the field.
The cadets marched **onto** the field.
They marched **on to** the next encampment.

on } are interchangeable.   Their use is a matter of choice.
upon }

up on   two separate words.

On further consideration...
That depends **upon** the man...
He has climbed **up on** the ladder since then.

within...**of**   is often used to mean "within...from", "within... after", "within...before", "within...above", or "within ...below".

...**within** two hours **of** its receipt.   (after)
...**within** ten degrees **of** the boiling point.   (below)
...**within** ten days **from** the date hereof.   (NOT: *of*)
...**within** an hour's ride **from** here.   (OR: *of*)

"Within" can be confusing if not carefully used, as

All bids must be deposited **within** ten days **of** the meeting of the Board.   (ten days before or after?)
DEFINITE: All bids must be deposited within the ten days immediately preceding the meeting of the Board.

PREPOSITIONS COMBINED WITH OTHER WORDS

There is no definite rule for the combining of prepositions with other words. Some combinations are established idioms, and are therefore used because they "sound right".   Other combinations are deduced by analogy; that is, meanings are applied as tests.   The following is a list of the ordinary combinations:

accompanied by—is usual, rather than "accompanied with".
acquiesce in—is usual.   "Acquiesce to" and "acquiesce with" are older forms.
admit of—is used in the sense of "permit" or "allow", as "too numerous to admit of any classification".   In ordinary uses, the "of" does not apply, as "He will not admit defeat."
agreeable to—is usual; although "agreeable with" is also used.
all of—(See p. 4.)
allow of—is similar to "admit of".

analogous to—means "correspondent to". "Analogous with" is seldom used.

angry at—a thing.

angry with—a person.

appposition with } are used interchangeably. Grammarians favor "in apposition
apposition to } with".

approve of—is a common combination; although just "approve" is better in most instances.

apropos of—is the usual combination, not "apropos *to*".

at hand
to hand } are all used. The first two refer to something "within reach"; and
in hand } the last to something "in preparation", or "being dealt with".

aversion to—is usual. "Aversion toward", "for", or "from" is rare.

beneficial to—not *"for"*— meaning "useful, helpful, or advantageous to".

bill of } are both used in referring to amounts, as "a bill of $85" (in the amount
bill for } of), or "a bill for $85" (a statement for).

both of—(See p. 9.)

buy from—rather than "buy of". By analogy: "to purchase from" rather than "to purchase of".

cause of—means that which produces the result of, as "the cause of action".

cause for—means the reason for, as "a cause for action".

compare to—is used when things are only likened, as "an electric light compared to the sun".

compare with—is used when things are, or may be, compared in detail, as "one man compared with another".

compatible with—is the usual combination; although "compatible to" is used, probably by deduction from "agreeable to".

compliance with—is usual, not "compliance *to*".

conceive of—is a common combination.

concur in—an opinion, an action, a belief, a decree.

concur with—a person, or a thing.

conducive to—is usual, not "conducive *of*".

conform to
conform with } both used. "Conform to" is usual.

consequent to—is usual, rather than "consequent upon".

consist of—means "is made up of".

consist in—means "lies in", or "dwells in".

> Life **consists of** little things.   (is made up of)
> Enjoyment **consists in** work as well as pleasure.   (dwells in)
> The error **consists in** writing only what we hear.   (lies in)

contrast with
contrast to } interchangeable when "contrast" is a noun.

> What is that in contrast with?
> ...a candle in contrast to the sun.

When "contrast" is a verb form, "with" follows it.

> ...the eye contrasted with a camera.
> That is like contrasting night with day.

correspond to—means "to be analogous to"; also "to match".

correspond with—means "agree with"; also "to communicate with".

credit for—is usual, not "credit of", as to "get the credit for".

cure of—is usual, rather than "cure from".

danger in—means the danger that lies in.

danger of—means the full danger of, or the possibility of. "The **danger in** introducing this is the **danger of** establishing that."

die by—to die by the process of, as by violence, by suffocation, by drowning.
NOT: "He died *from* drowning." (drowning is dying)
BUT: "...narrowly escaped death by drowning."

die from—to die from the effects of some outward agent, as from exposure, from suffocation, from wounds, from want.

die of—to die from the effects of some inward agent, as of a disease, of fever, of old age, of grief.

die with—to die with (or by) the sword, or with (or of) humiliation.

different from—is the preferred combination.

different than—is used, although mildly condemned by some.

different to—is used colloquially in England.

It was **different from** that.   is no doubt better than
It was **different than** that.   but
It was **different than** I thought.   because of its smoothness is no doubt better than
It was **different from what** I thought.

"Than" permits many shortcuts:

They have **different** methods today **than** in 1910.
(Is surely more practical than: They have **different** methods today **from those which they had** in 1910.)
We are considering it from a **different** angle **than** they.
(Is surely better than: ...from a **different** angle **from that from which** they are.)

disappointed in—is the usual combination. "Disappointed with" is also used.
"Disappointed of" things not obtained is sometimes used.

discrepancy in—a thing.

discrepancy between—two things.

discretion—"At the discretion of" and "in the discretion of" are both used.

dispense with—not "dispense *of*".

dissent from—is usual, not "dissent *with*", nor "dissent *of*".

enamored of—is usual, rather than "enamored by", or "enamored with".

foreign to—is usual. "Foreign from" is also used.

free from—is the common combination; although "free of" is also used, as "free of (OR: from) foreign entanglements".

half of—The "of" is used before pronouns, as "half of these"; and before nouns when the fractional part is thought of, as "half of the boxes". But it may be dropped when a quantity rather than an actual part is meant, as "Half the sales were not consummated."

identical with—is usual, meaning "uniform with"; rather than "identical to", meaning "equal to".

incompatible with—is usual.

in distinction from—is usual. "In distinction to" is rare.

ill with—a disease, rather than "ill of".

67

indifferent to—not "indifferent *of*".

in regard to ⎱ are both used. Note that "regard" and not *"regards"* is used in
in respect to ⎰ the first phrase.

insensible to—means "indifferent to", as "insensible to pain" or "fear", etc.

insensible of—means "not aware of", as "insensible of danger".

instill into—is the idiomatic combination, not "instill *in*".

monopoly of—means "control of"; yet "monopoly on" is widely used.

motive for—is usual, as "the motive for being honest"; rather than "motive in".

necessity of—means the unavoidable obligation of.

necessity for—means the urgent occasion for.

need of—means the lack or want of something, as "the need of money".

need for—means the urgent occasion for, as "the need for financing".

oblivious of—means "unaware of", "unmindful of", "forgetful of". "Oblivious
to" is not a correct deduction from the meaning.

occasion of—means "cause of", as "Such things are the occasion of much
suffering."

occasion for—means "call or reason for", as "There was no occasion for that."

omit in—is usual, although "omit from" is also used.

on behalf of—means "on the part of".

in behalf of—means "in the interest of".

opposite to—"To" is often dropped after "opposite", as "Place this opposite
that." But either "to" or "from" may be used if necessary, as
"This is opposite to that", "done opposite to (OR: from) their
way", "took the opposite side from him".

opposite of—is used when "opposite" is a noun, as "This is the opposite of that."

parallel to—is usual.

parallel with—is used when comparison with is meant.

payment of—as "in payment of the invoice".

payment for—as "in payment for the goods ordered".

permission of—as "with the permission of the author" (with the consent of).

permission from—as "by permission from the publishers" (by authorization
from).

permit of—The "of" is sometimes used, but it is often superfluous. (See
"admit of", above.)

prevent from—is a usual combination. (See also Possessives, p. 125.)

prohibit from—is usual.

purpose of—means the object or idea of, as "the purpose of doing that".

purpose in—means the intention in, as "his purpose in doing that".

recommend to—A person or thing is recommended to someone for consideration.

recommend above ⎫ should be used if one thing is recommended more
recommend more than ⎬ than or rather than another thing, as "We recom-
recommend rather than ⎭ mend this rather than that." (NOT: *to* that)

reconcile to—means to bring to quiet submission to, as "I have reconciled
myself to poverty."

reconcile with—means to make consistent with, or to harmonize with, as to
"reconcile one thing with another", or "reconcile one person
with another".

recover from—rather than "of" a disease, as "recovered from fever".

rests on—means "is based on", as "The essential difficulty rests on the charge
of the salesmen that..."

rests in—means "lies in", as "The significance of the term rests in the idea of
obligation."

68

retroactive to—means "active backward to". "A wage increase, retroactive to June 10", not "retroactive *from*".

right of—takes a noun, as "the right of organization, of veto, of search, of protest, of trading, of self-determination".

right to—takes a verb, as "the right to organize, to protest, to trade".

sick with—a disease, rather than "sick from".

speak to or talk to
speak with or talk with } largely interchangeable. The former may be particularly applied to the addressing of words to a person whether he replies or not. The latter may be particularly applied to conversation.

subscribe for
subscribe to } Strictly speaking, one subscribes one's name to a document for a periodical, or stock, etc. The New York Times uses "subscribe for", "a subscription for", etc.; but some other publishers use "subscribe to", "a subscriber to", etc.

under the circumstances—indicates action under given conditions.

in the circumstances—indicates situation in given conditions.

upward of—means "more than". (Dialectal) "about".

vary from—means "differ from", as "one thing varies from another".

with regard to
with respect to } are both used. Note that "regard" and not "*regards*" is used in the first phrase.

with the view of—means "with the purpose of".

with a view to—means "with an outlook toward".

> Note that "the" is used with "of", and "a" is used with "to"; not "with a view *of*", nor "with the view *to*".
>
> Note also that an -ing word usually follows "with a view to", as "with a view to **curtailing** production", rather than "with a view to **curtail** production".

SUBJECTS

The **true subject** of a verb is often obscured by an intervening phrase, or an inverted construction.

> "Some writers are as easily drawn off the scent as young hounds. They start with a singular subject; before they reach the verb, a plural noun attached to an 'of' or the like happens to cross, and off they go in the plural; or vice versa."
> —Fowler, "A Dictionary of Modern English Usage", p. 389.

To determine the true subject:

Break down the sentence structure and test it.

Intervening Phrases.

> NOT: The total of the bills which were charged to "campaign expenses" *were* high. (USE: was high)
> (The simple sentence is: The total was high.)
> NOT: The shape of the heads *show* that... (USE: shows)
> (The shape shows...)
> NOT: A large amount of information and news *are* to be found there. (USE: is)
> (A large amount is to be found there.)

69

ENGLISH

NOT: The only times the gentlemen are photographed *is* when...
   (The only times are when...)
NOT: **Reports** that the long **battle** between the two shipping interests
   over intercoastal service *were* settled in New York **were** denied.
   (Reports were denied that the long battle was settled.)
NOT: A new set of rules and regulations *have* been adopted.
   (A new set has been adopted.)
NOT: His association with big industries and foreign governments *make*
   him the most sought-after... (USE: makes)

Inverted Constructions. Many writers have a tendency, when a subject follows its verb, to allow what precedes to govern the verb. But a plural verb should be used wherever necessary to prepare the reader for a plural subject; and a singular verb, for a singular subject.

NOT: ...in which *was* stored the books.
   (in which the books were stored)
NOT: If out of this depression *comes* the results that...
   (If the results come out of...)
NOT: But from these extracts *are* gleaned one single thought...
   (One thought is gleaned from...)
NOT: Clearly visible against the sky *was* the *peak* of Mount Rainier and
   Mount Adams. (USE: were the peaks)
NOT: ...a forecast in which *is* seen two bright spots. (USE: are)
NOT: To him *falls* the duties of... (USE: fall)
NOT: From that source *has* frequently come to us many enlightening
   facts. (USE: have come)
   Awaiting the outcome was a new government and an old.
   (To use "was" might mean that the new government and the old
   were one. Use "were" if two distinct governments are meant.)
   On the success of this conference hang the future happiness and
   prosperity of the world.
   (If "hangs" had been used, "happiness and prosperity" would
   have been considered a single thought. See One-Thought
   Subjects, p. 79.)

"One of". When "one of" occurs in a sentence, it is often misleading. To test it, determine upon the simple sentence first, and then decide whether a singular or plural verb should follow the object of "of".

It is one of the things that are worth doing. (NOT: *is* worth)
(It is one—of the things—that are worth doing. "It is one" is the simple sentence; "of the things" modifies "one"; and "that are worth doing" modifies "things".)

The following sentences will bear the same analysis. The simple sentences are set off by dashes.

He is one—of those people who are (NOT: *is*) cautious.
Now we come to one—of the very few men who have (NOT: *has*) ever served their (NOT: *his*) country in such a capacity.
That is just one—of the exclusive features that make (NOT: *makes*) our product the finest.
A planet is one—of the opaque bodies of the solar system that revolve (NOT: *revolves*) around the sun.
One—of the things which have (NOT: *has*) interested us most—is the perfection of a new accelerator.
(The simple sentence is: One is the perfection.)

70

On that date one—of the most spectacular sky disturbances that have (NOT: has) taken place in our generation—will occur about midnight.
He is one—of those hosts who entertain by giving lectures.   (NOT: *entertains*)
It was one—of those interesting days that carry us back...   (NOT: *carries*)

Note the difference in meaning in the following sentences:

He is one—of our customers who do not pay promptly.
(There are a number who do not pay promptly.)
Here is one of our customers—who doesn't pay promptly.
(Here is perhaps the only one who doesn't pay promptly.)
It was considered one—of the finest of its kind that have (NOT: *has*) ever been grown.
(It was one—of the finest that have been grown.)
It was considered the finest of its kind that has (NOT: *have*) ever been grown.
(It was the finest—that has ever been grown.)

Singular Subjects.   The following words are singular and should be followed by singular verbs and singular pronouns.

anybody
anyone   (meaning anybody)
any one   (meaning any one thing, or any one of a group)
anything
each
either   (singular when used alone.   See also "either...or", p. 73.)
every
everybody
everyone   (meaning everybody)
every one   (meaning every one of a number of things, or every one of a group)
everything
neither   (singular when used alone.   See also "neither...nor", p. 73.)
nobody
no one
nothing
one
a person
somebody
someone   (meaning somebody)
some one   (meaning some one thing, or some one of a group)
something

Does anyone ever **consider** that **his** (NOT: *their*) lot is fair?
Has any one of them **stopped** to consider **his** (NOT: *their*) own interests?
Each resident is allowed $100 of **his** (NOT: *their*) purchases...
Each of us **is** what circumstances make **him.**   (NOT: *us*)
Each of them **has** to answer that question for **himself.**   (NOT: *themselves*)
But **each has** chosen to go **his** separate **way.**   (NOT: *their...ways*)
Has each of you decided upon **his** course?   (NOT: *Have* each of you decided upon *your courses?*)
The tricks that **each is** in the habit of playing...   (NOT: *are*)
Everybody wants enough money to satisfy **his** needs.   (NOT: *their*)

71

Every one of them **was** asked to prepare **his** story. (NOT: *their* story NOR: *their stories*)

Every American will have to pay **his** part. (NOT: *their*)

Nobody knows what is in store for **himself.** (NOT: *themselves*)

Not one of them **has** (NOT: *have*) given **his** (NOT: *their*) consent.

No one thinks it is **himself** (NOT: *themselves*) who **is** (NOT: *are*) meant.

If **either** of these terms **is** (NOT: *are*) accepted... (SIMPLIFIED: If either [one] is accepted...)

Either of the men **is** (NOT: *are*) influential enough to control the situation. (Either one is...)

Does **either** of you care to join? (NOT: *Do*)

Is **either** of you going to investigate it? (NOT: *Are*)

There are two reasons, **neither** of which **is** (NOT: *are*) important. (SIMPLIFIED: ...neither [one] is important.)

Neither of them **knows.** (SIMPLIFIED: Neither knows.)

Neither of the two solutions **is** (NOT: *are*) right.

A person presumes that **his** (NOT: *their*) luck will not desert **him** (NOT: *them*).

Someone who **is** not always trying to prove **his** (NOT: *their*) theories...

Some one of the group will be rewarded for **his** (NOT: *their*) perseverance.

Even when two of the above subjects are joined by "and" they take a singular verb.

Anything and **everything is** to be sold.

Anybody and **everybody was** invited.

Something and **somebody is** to be considered in each case.

There **is something** to be criticized and **something** to be praised in that.

Grouped subjects, preceded by "each", "every", "no one", etc., also remain singular.

Every man and **woman** in America **is** interested in **his** tax **bill.** (NOT: *are* interested in *their* tax *bills*)

As an experiment, **each city, county,** and **state is** to elect **its** own **representative.** (NOT: *are* to elect *their* own *representatives*)

No one country and **no one ruler has** a right to be so honored.

Some one man and **some one organization is** sure to profit.

no This word, like "none", can mean "not one" or "not any". Hence, it can modify either singular or plural nouns.

No man and **no woman was** exempt. (no one)

No time and **money was** spared. (not any)

No group of people **are** so secure that **they** can afford to ignore the future. (not any of the individuals of the group)

No data are to be submitted.

everybody⎫ These words are sometimes regarded as collectives, and
everyone ⎬ followed by "they", "their", or "themselves"—if not
etc.   ⎭ restricted by singular verbs.

Everybody could have more profit if **they** would work together toward a common end.

Everyone voted but **they** could not **agree.**

Should **every nation** go off the gold standard **they** would find no difficulty in adjusting **themselves.**

Every one of them would fight for what **they** believe **is their** just due.

SUBJECTS

each (when in apposition with a plural subject)

In ordinary sentences, a parenthetic or explanatory "each" may be inserted before a plural verb (or its complement); the plural form is undisturbed and should be continued throughout.

> The stockholders each expect to receive their dividends. (NOT: *dividend*)
> Washington, London, and Paris, each hope to succeed in turning their trade concessions into gold.
> The directors each want their own way.
> (For the use of the singular "way", see p. 42.)
> The directors, each for his own sake, want their candidates elected.
> The president, the vice president, and the secretary, each wrote their own speeches. (NOT: *speech*)
> There are three directors who, each in turn, plan to carry on their private campaigns. (NOT: *campaign*)
> They each have fortunes in their own right.
> (For the use of the singular "right", see p. 42.)

In formal writings, the parenthetic or explanatory "each" should be set after the plural verb (or its complement). In this position, the words that follow "each" are governed by it and are singular.

> The stockholders expect each to receive his dividend.
> The president, the vice president, and the secretary wrote each his own speech.
> There are several kinds of bills, each of which serves (NOT: *serve*) a special purpose.
> They have fortunes, each in his own right.

more than one This phrase, although plural in implication, is used as a singular, undoubtedly because of the necessity of joining a singular noun to "one".

> More than one tear was shed.
> BUT: More tears than one were shed. (NOT: *was*)
> More than one person in the employ of the Commissioners was needed to keep the peace. (NOT: *were*)

many a This phrase also conveys a singular idea, and the verb should be singular.

> Many an hour and day was spent in contemplation.
> Although there has (NOT: *have*) been many a trying day...

"many's the time" is the shortening of the colloquial phrase, "many is the time". Do not write "many's a time".

When Alternative Subjects are Introduced by "Or", or by

either...or } "Or" and "nor" do not blend words into one subject; **neither...nor** } they simply join alternative subjects.

If the subjects are singular, the verb must be singular:

> A feast or a famine is (NOT: *are*) always to be expected.
> If this, that, or the other thing is (NOT: *are*) to be used...
> One or the other of those men is (NOT: *are*) responsible.
> Either one method or the other is (NOT: *are*) to be tested.
> Neither imagination nor industry is (NOT: *are*) to be found in...
> Neither page nor paragraph is given.

73

If one subject is singular and the other plural:

There is a difference of opinion regarding this. The rule most commonly followed is that the verb should agree with the subject nearer it—if no later complications arise. Another rule is that a plural verb should be used regardless of the position of the subjects. A third rule is to evade the problem by reconstructing the sentence.

1. Using a verb to agree with the subject nearer it:

One or more **men are** needed.
Neither the men nor the **machine accomplishes** the work.
Neither the machine nor the **men accomplish** the work.
Do real **hazards** or only a slight risk **present themselves?**

But this method can lead into difficulties, as

Neither the men nor the **machine accomplishes** its? (their?) allotted work.
Does only a slight **risk** or real hazards **present** itself? (themselves?)

2. Using plural verb regardless of position of subjects:

Neither the men nor the machine **accomplish their** work.
Do only a slight risk or real hazards **present themselves?**

3. Reconstructing:

Neither do the men accomplish their allotted work, nor does the machine.
Does only a slight risk present itself, or real hazards?

If the subjects are of different person:

Either you or he is (are?) to be the judge of that.
Neither he nor I am (is?) the one to decide.
Is he or I to be responsible?

This awkwardness should be overcome by reconstruction.

Either you are to be the judge of that, or he is.
Neither is he the one to decide, nor am I.
Is he to be responsible, or am I? or
Is he, or am I, to be responsible?

Words or Phrases That do not Affect Subjects. An explanatory, modifying, or parenthetic phrase, introduced by or containing a word similar to those listed below, and inserted immediately after a subject, does not combine with the subject nor influence the verb.

The verb agrees with the true subject. Commas or dashes may be used to set off the intervening phrase, if a definite separation is deemed necessary. However, if the intervening phrase causes the construction to be awkward, the sentence should be rearranged; or a verb to agree with the phrase should be used.

after   Snow **after the rains** delays the coming crops.
along with   This document, **along with the other papers,** completes the exhibit.
also   But certainly the first, **and the second also,** is to be considered.
as well as   A day, **as well as years,** changes a life.
before   In that instance the merchant, **before the customers,** was to be considered.
besides   Who **besides them** is to sign the contract?
but   No one **but you and him** is aware of it. (See "but him", p. 53.)

certainly This dealer—and **certainly** those that you mentioned—is fair.
else It gives the distinction that he **and everybody else** wants.
He **and who else** is to report?
especially South America, **especially** Venezuela and Brazil, has products that we cannot produce.
etc. Lumber, **etc.**, was to be shipped by rail.
even America, **and even England**, has become interested.
every other He **and every other buyer** knows the difference.
except The book, **except** two certain parts, is finished.
for that matter This new account, **and for that matter** several old ones, is questionable.
in addition to That fact, **in addition to the other testimony**, is enough...
including The mortgage, **including the notes**, is to be signed...
in fact That company—and **in fact** all its subsidiaries—is to be investigated.
instead of The product, **instead of the prices**, is to be changed.
like Our workmanship, **like our prices**, is right.
much less No European country, **much less any of the Asiatic countries**, has reason to...
much more England, **and much more France**, is looking toward...
no less than The depositor, **no less than the directors**, is interested in...
no more than The banker, **no more than the depositors**, is to be...
not Great wealth, and **not meager savings**, is what causes...
Not great wealth, but meager savings are what build...
not even Nobody, **not even presidents**, is immune.
often A grownup, **and often a child**, is inclined to...
other That job **and other work** is to be done.
AWKWARD: France, **and other European countries**, is...
BETTER: France and other European countries are...
other than No equitable offer, **other than those**, has been made.
particularly Reckless driving, **particularly cutting-in**, tends to...
perhaps One, **and perhaps two**, seems to be necessary.
plus That amount, **plus interest**, gives a net...
together with This, **together with those**, is to be transmitted...
too It appears that this, **and that too**, is incorrect.
AWKWARD: It appears that he, **and they too**, is to benefit.
BETTER: It appears that he and they too are to...
usually The first copy, **and usually the second**, is clear.
with This **with that** is sufficient.
The sight draft **with documents attached** is to be...
without One **without the others** is incomplete.

not only...but ⎰ When these introductory words are used, the subject nearer the verb governs it.

Not only **are those** to be sent, but this also.
Not only those but **this** also is to be sent.
It is true that not only the health, growth, and prosperity, but also the mental **development** of a nation **depends** (NOT: *depend*) on...
Behind the remarkable progress *is* (USE: **are**) seen not only persistent **ideals** but a vast knowledge...

Participles Modifying a Subject, such as

accompanied by...
followed...
following...   These and similar verb forms do not join words
considered...   into plural subjects. The phrase introduced by
considering...   the particle simply modifies the true subject.

75

The gray plane **pursued by the red bomber** was (NOT: *were*) plainly seen.
("Pursued by the red bomber" modifies "plane".)
The gray plane **pursuing the red bomber** was next seen.
That letter, **followed by these,** is (NOT: *are*) quite enough proof.
That, **considered in the light of these,** is not surprising.
The code message, **accompanied by a translation,** was delivered.

There is...
There are...
Here is...
Here are...
Where is...
Where are...
"There", "here", or "where" may stand in the place of either a singular or a plural subject. To determine the correct verb form, substitute the true subject.

There **are** (NOT: *is*) to be two **discounts.**
(Two discounts are to be...)
There **are** (NOT: *is*) approximately **twenty** in the company.
There **were** (NOT: *was*) the **six** of them—sitting in silence.
There **appear** (NOT: *appears*) to be **conditions** which govern...
There **stand** (NOT: *stands*) the **monuments** to our prosperity.
Where **go** (NOT: *goes*) the American **dollars**...
Here **begin** (NOT: *begins*) the **histories** of two nations.

When a compound subject follows and clearly indicates two or more distinct things, a plural verb is used.

There **were** an **industry and** several **arts** to be considered. (several distinct things)
There **were** a **postmaster and** two **consuls** to be appointed. (three people)
Here **are quality and quantity** at last. (two distinct things)
Where **are man and woman** so equal?
There **have been** a large **number** of plays that have been censored.
(The collective "number" is here regarded as a plural.)

But when the compound subject indicates one thought or idea, a singular verb may be used.

There **is distinction and truth** in that slogan. (a combination of qualities)
There **was neatness and dispatch** in that order. (a combination of qualities)
There **was** a **beach and palm trees** in the foreground. (one scene—a beach with palm trees)
Here, before us, **is the problem and its solution.** (one thing—the problem with its solution)
Where **is the power and the glory** that was ours? (one greatness)

Or when the parts of the compound subject are separated by several words, or are listed, the verb may be considered to be understood before each subject after the first.

There **is** a lake **camp** in that vicinity and several **resorts.**
(There is a camp...and [there are] resorts.)
There **was** a report **charge,** a filing **charge,** a time **fee,** and a copying **charge.**

What is...
What are...
"What" may be singular or plural. It may mean "that which" or "the thing which" and be considered a singular; or it may represent "those which" or "the things which" and be considered a plural.

76

What they require **is** five or six good salesmen.
  (The thing which they require is...)
Material advantages **are what** make people **strive**...
  (...are the things which)
Here **are what** appear to be the reasons.
  (...are the things which)

What is...is ⎰ After establishing "what" as a singular, keep it
What are...are ⎱ singular. Or after establishing it as a plural, keep it
  plural.

Singular:

What is needed **is** (NOT: *are*) laws to govern...
  (The thing which is needed is laws...)
What seems to be the cause of the trouble **is** (NOT: *are*) the promises on the part of the sellers...
  (The thing which seems to be the cause is...)
What delays the deliveries **is** (NOT: *are*) the transfers...
  (The thing which delays...is...)

Plural:

But **what were** fairly good points **were** overlooked.
  (The things which were good points were...)
What appear to be nuisances sometimes **turn** out to be advantages.
  (The things which appear...turn...)

all some ⎫
any that ⎪ These words may stand as singular or plural subjects,
more who ⎬ according to the sense of their sentences. (See Collec-
most which ⎪ tives, p. 39.)
none   ⎭

NOT: He is among the few authors **who** *does* not experience difficulty
    with... (USE: do)
    (He is among—the few authors **who do** not...)
NOT: **Who** can outwit *their* own shadow? (USE: his own shadow)

"Is" or "Are". The true subject of a sentence is the subject that is being discussed. It may occur after the verb or before it.
In questions, the true subject follows the verb.

What guarantee **are** these promises of your ability to pay?
  ("These promises" becomes the true subject by the rearrangement of the question.)

But in straight sentences—

  "...when...subject and complement can change places without alteration of sense, so that it may be doubted which is which, the verb must agree with what precedes, and not with what follows...."
  —**Fowler, "A Dictionary of Modern English Usage", p. 29.**

An ever-present **threat was** price **reductions.**
Price **reductions were** an ever-present **threat.**
Possibly **taxes are** a tender **spot** in that issue.
Possibly a tender **spot** in that issue **is taxes.**
Dr. Jekyll and Mr. Hyde are the same **person.**
The same **person is** at different times **Dr. Jekyll and Mr. Hyde.**
His **wages are** his only **income.**
His only **income is** his **wages.**
("Wages" was formerly regarded as singular, as in the Biblical phrase, "The wages of sin is death.")

"Is" After Numbers. When a number and a plural noun represent a singular idea, they are followed by a singular verb.

Twenty years is long enough.
(The period of twenty years is long enough.)
Fifty dollars is not too much.
(The sum of $50 is not too much.)
Seventy inches is usually figured for that pipe.
(The length of **70** inches is...)
A million dollars is a lot of money.
One hundred men is the quota for each division.
There **is just $100** involved.

But when the individual parts are thought of, a plural verb is used.

Twenty **years have** now passed since...
One hundred **men are** needed to fill that quota.
There **are hundreds** of dollars wasted.
There **are ten** in the organization.

"Is" or "equals" is now generally used in arithmetical calculations.

Two times three is six.
One hundred plus fifty is one hundred and fifty.

However, when "and" is used, "are" usually follows.

Five thousand and **four hundred are** five thousand, four hundred.

"And" Joining Two Subjects. When "and" joins two true subjects, whether they are both singular, one singular and one plural, or both plural, they form a compound subject and take a plural verb. (Unless but one thought is conveyed by the two subjects—see One-Thought Subjects, below.)

NOT: We shall assume no new obligation until times and our own future *looks* (USE: look) more promising.
("Times" and "future" are the subject of "look".)
NOT: The services rendered by these people and their share in making the work a success *is* (USE: are) to be commended.
("Services" and "share" are the subject.)
NOT: Trees and lakes and even a mountain *was* (USE: were) on the place.
("Trees" and "lakes" are the subject.)

"And" Introducing Explanatory Phrases After a Subject.

and also

and certainly

and even

and especially

and every other

and often

and other

and particularly

and perhaps

and usually

"And" often introduces an explanatory or parenthetic phrase which does not compound the subject. (See p. 74.)

Commas or dashes may be used to set off such explanatory or parenthetic phrases, if a definite separation is deemed necessary.

> Every idle telephone in this city—and millions of other telephones—stands ready to obey.

One-Thought Subjects. When the parts of a compound subject blend into one idea, they may be treated as a singular subject.

> **"If two or more nouns can fairly be considered as together expressing a single idea, a singular verb may be used with them."**
>
> **—Ives, "Text, Type, and Style: A Compendium of Atlantic Usage", p. 244.**

> **"Two nouns of closely allied meaning are often felt to make no more than a single notion..."**
>
> **—Fowler, "A Dictionary of Modern English Usage", p. 641.**

The **tumult and the shouting dies**...—Kipling. (the excitement dies)

The **beginning and end lies** somewhere in that. (the entirety)

The **wear and tear is** to be considered. (the depreciation)

The **rise and fall** of the tide **has been** measured... (the movement)

The **organization and commencement** of business **is** announced. (the beginning)

To see clearly and to act wisely is sometimes difficult. (to pursue a course)

Prosperity on the one hand **and poverty** on the other **is** not a pretty picture. (one vision)

Mexico and the far Southwest is the fairest and finest of lands. (one land)

Singular Subject Made Plural by Modifiers. If a singular subject is so modified as to suggest two different things, a plural verb may be used.

> ...but American and East Indian **culture** in many respects **are** not alike. (two different kinds of culture)
>
> Modern and ancient **architecture present** many similarities. (two styles)

When a Second Verb is Understood, in Inverted Constructions. "And" does not compound two subjects if a second verb can be reasonably understood from the first.

> ...wallowing in the channel was (NOT: *were*) a freighter, and farther along a whaler. (and farther along was a whaler)

VERBS

Many verbs are misused because the meanings are not thoroughly understood. The definitions of troublesome verbs should be applied as tests when doubt arises regarding correctness.

affect   to act upon; to alter; to assume; to adopt.

effect   to bring about. (As a noun it means: that which is brought about, as a result or an impression.)

Remember that "affect", which begins with "a", means four things that begin with "a"—act upon—alter—assume—adopt.

The one test meaning of "effect"—bring about—can be applied wherever "effect" is a verb.

Testing by substitution:

> Would that **affect** their decision?   (act upon or alter)
> That might **affect** our school system.   (alter or act upon)
> He just **affects** that manner.   (assumes)
> They always **affect** the trend in styles.   (adopt)
> Can they **effect** the compromise?   (bring about)
> ...if unable to **effect** delivery.   (bring about)
> They **effected** a solution.   (brought about)
> What was the **effect** of it?   (the result of, or impression made by)

Sometimes either word might suit; in that event the exact meaning must decide the matter.

> One act may **effect** both things.   (bring about)
> One act may **affect** both things.   (act upon or alter)
> ...to **effect** a law.   (bring it about)
> ...to **affect** a law.   (act upon or alter)

A few further aids toward determining the difference:

"Affect" is not used as a noun, except in rare medical phrases. Therefore, if a noun is necessary, "effect" is the word, meaning a result or an impression.

> ...a far-reaching **effect**.   (NOT: *affect*)
> ...as soon as it takes **effect**.   (NOT: *affect*)

"Affect" in its meaning of "to assume" may be remembered by association with "affectation".

> English grandees **affect** to be farmers.—Emerson.

Study the following simple sentences which illustrate the different uses:

> That law cannot **affect** us, although it may **effect** great changes as soon as it goes into **effect**.
> It **affected** some but had no **effect** on others.

Wrong choices:

> Its advance is apparently having an *affect* on the price of gold.
> ("Effect" was meant—having a result or making an impression.)
> A drop in the price would not *effect* it seriously.
> ("Affect" was meant—act upon or alter it.)
> ...if we are able to *affect* the transfers.
> ("Effect" should have been used—to bring about.)
> ...unless it *affects* radical reform.
> (Again, "effects"—brings about.)
> It may have a telling *affect* on such cases.
> ("Effect" is the noun—a result or impression.)

as follows } "As follow" might seem correct for the introduction of
as follow } plurals, as

> The items are as follow:

But "as follows" has come to be generally used for both singular and plural, as

> The items are as follows:

From this it should not be deduced that "follows" should always be used for the plural.

> NOT: ...in the examples of the forms of advertising that *follows*. (USE: follow)

bring to carry toward.
take to convey away from.
Never carelessly use "bring" when "take" is intended.

> NOT: May I *bring* that book home tonight? (USE: take)
> You may **take** it home if you will **bring** it back tomorrow.

can signifies ability to do: is able, is competent, has a right, or is empowered to do.

may signifies permission. Also it may signify a possibility. Wherever **permission** is involved, use "may".

> Can he read the chart? (Has he the ability?)
> May he read the chart? (asks permission)
> Can he draw up the agreement? (Is he able to?)
> May he draw up the agreement? (asks permission)
> We can expect no more. (have no right to)
> He cannot sign checks. (is not empowered to)
> I think we can count on that. (are able or have a right to)
> I think we may count on that. (a possibility)

come } These words are often confused by letter writers when writing
go } to persons about proposed trips. The writer should take into consideration the reader's geographical position. For instance, when writing to a person in New York, do not say:

> I expect to go to New York this fall.
> (Use "come", which will sound correct from the reader's viewpoint.)

But when writing to a person at any point other than the destination, use "go".

do have FOR: **have** } As a general rule (which has exceptions) when pos-
does have **has** } session is implied, "have" alone is used; "do",
did have **had** } "does", or "did" being considered unnecessary before it.

IDIOMATIC USAGE	GRAMMATICAL USAGE
Does he **have** time to do it?	**Has** he time to do it?
Do they **have** a cable address?	**Have** they a cable address?
Did he **have** recommendations?	**Had** he recommendations?
Does he **have** the papers?	**Has** he the papers?

They **have** quite a collection.
Have they?   (RATHER THAN: **Do** they?)
He **has** an appointment to Germany.
Has he?   (RATHER THAN: **Does** he?)

But when possession is not implied, "do", "does", and "did" are used with "have" to avoid very great formality or awkwardness.

Did you **have** a pleasant vacation?   (NOT: Had you a...)
   (Did you experience a pleasant vacation?)
We **don't have** to do it their way.
   (We are not compelled to do it their way.)
Does he **have** to go back next year?
   (Will he be obliged to go?)
Did they **have** an X-ray made?
   (Did they obtain an X-ray?)
Did they **have** an accident?
   (Did they experience or suffer an accident?)
Do they **have** benefit performances every year?
   (Do they hold benefit performances every year?)

At times, even though possession is implied, "do", "does", or "did" is used before "have" as a mark of special emphasis—particularly in negative sentences.

He **did** not **have** the courage to say so.   (did not possess)
He **did have** the courage to say so.
When the letters **do** not **have** that significance...
ORDINARY: They **don't** all **have** incomes.
FOR: They all haven't incomes.

did ⎫
have ⎬ "Have" should be used instead of "did" in questions where it is
has ⎭ desired to cover all points of time up to the moment of asking
        the question, as

Have they come yet?   NOT: *Did* they come yet?

"Did" represents past or closed action; whereas "have" continues the action up to the present moment.

Did you hear from them yesterday?   (past action)
Have you heard from them this morning?   (OR: Did you hear...)
Did they agree to that?   (OR: Have they agreed to that?)
Have they agreed yet?   (NOT: *Did* they agree yet?)
Have they finished it already?   (NOT: *Did* they...)

don't   is a contraction of **"do not"**.
doesn't   is a contraction of **"does not"**.

To say "he *don't*", "she *don't*", "it *don't*", etc., is like saying "he *do* not", "she *do* not", "it *do* not", etc.

"Doesn't" should always be used with "he", "she", and "it", and with any other word that requires "does not".

To use "don't" with these words is as conspicuous an error as to say illiterately, "I *seen*", and "I *done*".

A headline from a paper published in 1876 reads:

What General Kidder Knows and *Don't* Know.

graduate Strictly speaking, a school graduates a student. The student is graduated from the school.

He was graduated (OR: is to be graduated) from the University in June.

But common usage also favors:

He graduated (OR: will graduate) in June.

had better have been
had rather have been
would rather have been } In these idiomatic phrases the word "have" must always be used before "been".

He had better be careful. (He should be careful.)
BUT NOT: He had better been careful. (He should been careful?)
CORRECT: He had better have been careful. (He should have been...)
NOT: He would rather said nothing at all. (He would said...?)
BUT: He would rather have said nothing at all.

had I *have* known it
had we *have* done that
if I had *have* seen it } "Have" is totally unnecessary in these phrases, and is termed "illiterate".

Had I known it, I could have called.
Had we done that, we should have profited.
If I had seen it, I should have told you.
OR: Had I seen it, I should have told you.

had *of* Never use "had *of*" for the almost equally bad "had *have*".

CRUDE: Had we *of* heard it... (FOR: Had we heard it...)
If we had *of* known it sooner... (FOR: If we had known it...
OR: Had we known it...)

has got
have got } "Has got" or "have got" is colloquial when used where "has" or "have" alone will suffice.

That's all we have to say. (COLLOQUIAL: have got to say)
COLLOQUIAL: Has he got the money? (FOR: Has he the money?)
COLLOQUIAL: We have got to go. (FOR: We have to go.)
BUT: He did not seek recognition, but he **has**, indeed, **got** it.
(meaning "has obtained" or "has been awarded")

learn to acquire knowledge.
teach to impart knowledge.
It would seem to be unnecessary to mention the distinction between these two words, except to say that once they were interchangeable To use one for the other now is, by the dictionaries, termed "a vulgarism"

lend is the usual verb, meaning the opposite of borrow.
loan is also used as a verb, especially in financial writings, as to "loan money on goods of value".
Possibly the tendency to use "loaned" for all purposes is caused by a desire to avoid "lent", which is a perfectly good word.

They lent us their drawings.

lay to put.
lie to rest or stay; or to take a position of rest.

⎱ "Lay" represents the actual putting down of something; and "lie" represents the resting or reposing there.

lay, laid, laid, laying take an object.
Something must always be laid (put) down by someone.
lie, lay, lain, lying do not take an object.
Something lies (rests or stays) somewhere.

> Now I **lay** me down to sleep. (put myself down)
> He maketh me to **lie** down in green pastures. (to take a position of rest)
> **Lie** down and rest. (take a position of rest)
> Had you **lain** down before? (rested)
> **Lay** it over there. (put it)
> Let it **lie** there. (stay there)
> The soldiers **lay** in the mud. (stayed or rested)
> They **laid** their guns in a row. (put)
> The papers **lay** on the desk unsigned. (stayed)
> The papers were **laid** on the desk. (put)
> The fields **lie** unploughed. (stay)
> The fields **lay** unploughed for years. (stayed)
> It has **lain** there all these years. (stayed)
> It seems to have **lain** dormant for many years. (stayed)
> The years have **laid** wisdom at his feet. (put)
> Time is **lying** heavy upon his hands. (resting)
> Time is **laying** heavy hand upon him. (putting)
> The blame **lies** with them. (rests)
> **Lay** the blame on them. (put)
> The ship is **lying** in the harbor. (staying)
> Land **lying** to the north... (staying)
> The story is **laid** in England. (set)

Common uses, in which it will be noted that "lay" takes its object; but in the nautical phrases the object is unexpressed:

> to **lay** stress on...to **lay** out a plan...to **lay** in supplies
> to **lay** [cars] over (stop over)...to **lie** over (be deferred)
> to **lay** goods down (deliver), as "goods laid down in Chicago"
> NAUTICAL: ⎰ to **lay** forward (to **lay** oneself forward) ⎱ to **lay** to the oars (to **lay** hand to the oar)
> **lie** in wait, as "He lay in wait." (NOT: *laid*)
> **lie** low (NOT: *lay* low)
> a ship **lies** to the wind (stays toward the wind)
> land **lies** (stays or rests)
> The one phrase, "the lie of the land", is more frequently written "the lay of the land"; but "lie" would seem preferable, to conform to other uses, as "see how the land lies", etc.

may expresses a **strong** possibility.
might expresses a **weak** or **remote** possibility.
These words are practically interchangeable. Still there remain distinctions that are observed.

> It **may** be true. (present—a strong possibility)
> It **might** be true. (present or future—a remote possibility)

It **may** (OR: **might**) have been true.   (a past possibility, which may be strong or weak)

We **may** (OR: **might**) donate something.   (a present possibility, which may be strong or weak)

The same question **may** (OR: **might**) arise years hence.   (a future possibility, which may be strong or weak)

This **may** prove to have been an aid.   (a present, strong possibility)

They **might** have seen him.   (a past, weak possibility)

That **may** have encouraged him.   (a past, strong possibility)

It **may** have turned out all right.   (a past, strong possibility)

Wherever a possibility is contrary to fact or is a mere supposition, **might** should be used.

Had they telephoned, they **might** have got the order.   (contrary to fact—they didn't get the order)

They **might** have subscribed, but they were not asked.   (contrary to fact—they didn't subscribe)

Even some Roman pagan **might** have realized the plight of ancient Rome. (a supposition)

I think of it as it **might** have been...   (a supposition)

The reader may have observed how the story **might** have been written.   (The first is a strong possibility; the second, a supposition.)

It was something that he himself **might** have said.   (a supposition—he did not say it)

It looks as if it **might** work out.   (a supposition)

May should be used when **present permission** is implied.   **Might** may be used when **past permission** is implied.

May I do that?   (RATHER THAN: Might I do that?   [subjunctive])

May I have the honor...   (RATHER THAN: Might I have the honor...)

They do not know whether they **may** venture to print that.   (whether they would be permitted to)

Might he stay? he inquired with mild politeness.   (a past asking)

They asked if they **might** be permitted to use our name.   (a past request)

The sequence of tenses should be preserved if there is no other indication for a choice between the words.

They **think** that it **may** be to our advantage.

They **thought** that it **might** be to our advantage.

may *of*		
might *of*	**should** *of*	To use "*of*" for "have" in these verb forms is
must *of*	**would** *of*	termed "illiterate". Use "may have", "might
could *of*	**ought to** *of*	have", "should have", etc.

need } "To" may be omitted after these forms in an idiomatic use, usually in questions and in negative sentences.   But if the "to" is used, the regular verb forms should be used.
dare

NEED

IDIOMATIC: No one **need** hesitate about doing that.

REGULAR: No one **needs** to hesitate about doing that.

BUT NOT: No one need *to* hesitate...
    NOR: No one *needs* hesitate...
IDIOMATIC: No journalist **need** be told that...   (NOT: *needs* be NOR:
    need *to* be)
    ...unless it is assumed that the layman **need** be warned.
    ...though no notion of time **need** be introduced.
    Need it be mentioned that...?   (Does it need to be...?)
    One **need** only glance through the pages...
    It was done sooner than it **need** have been.
    OR: It was done sooner than it **needed** to be.   (BUT NOT: than it
    need *to* have been)

DARE

IDIOMATIC:	He **dare** not sign it. AND:	**Dare** he sign it?
SOMETIMES:	He **dares** not sign it.	**Does** he **dare** sign it?
REGULAR:	He **does** not **dare** to sign it.	**Does** he **dare** to sign it?
BUT NOT:	He dare not *to* sign it.	Dare he *to* sign it?
IDIOMATIC:	No one **dare** criticize the plan.	...if one **dare** do it.
SOMETIMES:	No one **dares** criticize the plan.	...if one **dares** do it.
REGULAR:	No one **dares** to criticize the plan.	...if one **dares** to do it.
BUT NOT:	No one dare *to* criticize the plan.	...if one dare *to* do it.

needs   meaning "of necessity", is an adverb, and its form is invariable

    We must needs inform him...
    They needs must have...

ought to   should never be preceded by "had" or "hadn't".
    "Ought to" in itself can represent present, past, or future time—it needs no introductory word.

    It **ought to** be finished now.   (present)
    (NOT: It *had* ought to be finished now.)
    It **ought to** have been finished yesterday.   (past)
    (NOT: It *had* ought to have been...
    NOR: It ought to`been finished...)
    It **ought to** be finished next week.   (future)
    (NOT: It *had* ought to be...)
    It **ought** not to be told.   (OR: ought not be)
    (NOT: It *hadn't* ought to be told.)
    Nothing **ought to** be said about that, ought it?   (OR: should it?)
    (NOT: *had* it?—which would mean "*had* it ought?")

    "To" should always be used after "ought"—unless "to" is supplied in another verb form; or unless it is understood, as in negative sentences

    NOT: Many people ought`and do give generously.
    BUT: Many people **ought to** and do give generously.
    They ought and are to have the privilege.   (Here "to" is supplied in another verb form.)
    They seem disinclined to do that, but we think they **ought**.   ("To" has already been supplied.)

Negative sentences without "to":

Perhaps they ought not be sent.
This use ought not, however, be confused with that.

ought not   is formal.
oughtn't   is colloquial.

> He ought to pay for that, ought he not?   (formal)
> He ought to pay for that, oughtn't he?   (colloquial or ordinary)
> BUT NOT: He ought to pay for that, *hadn't* he?
> ("Hadn't" should not be used before an implied "ought to", which would make "*hadn't* he ought to?")

prefer...to   is a correct combination.
prefer...rather than   is a correct combination.
prefer...than   is a colloquial shortening of "prefer...rather than".

REGULAR: { We should **prefer** standing pat **to** trying to win.
   { We should **prefer** to stand pat **rather than** to try to win.
COLLOQUIAL: { We should **prefer** standing pat **than** trying to win.
   { We should **prefer** to stand pat **than** try to win.
REGULAR: We should **prefer** dealing with them **rather than** (dealing) with anyone else.
COLLOQUIAL: We should **prefer** dealing with them **than** anyone else.

The expressions after "prefer" and "to" or "rather than" should balance as nearly as possible; that is, if an -ing word has been used after "prefer", an -ing word should follow "to", etc.

NOT: We prefer **to sell** than **buying.**
BUT: We prefer **selling** to **buying.**
OR: We prefer **to sell** rather than (**to**) **buy.**

raise   to lift something.
rise   to move upward by itself.
raise, raised, raised, raising   take an object.
   Something must be raised (lifted) by someone or something.
rise, rose, risen, rising   do not take an object.
   Something rises (moves upward) of its own accord.

USES OF "RAISE" (NOTE THE OBJECT)	USES OF "RISE" (NO OBJECT)
to raise money	funds rise
to raise a question	a question arises
to raise a voice	a voice rises
to raise a price	a price rises

They **raised** the price.   (they lifted or boosted it)
Prices are **raised.**   (by someone)
Prices are **rising.**   (moving upward themselves)
Prices seem to **raise** themselves.   (to lift themselves)
They are going to **raise** wages.   (to lift wages)
Wages will soon **rise.**   (move upward themselves)
The sun **rises.**   (moves upward itself)
The river **rose** several feet.   (moved upward itself)
The temperature **rose** ten degrees.   (moved upward itself)

87

The sun **raised** the temperature. (lifted the temperature)
The temperature was **raised** ten degrees. (lifted by outside force)
Raised bread is baked from dough made to **rise** by a leavening agent.
The mist is **rising** rapidly. (moving upward itself)

Rise is the noun meaning a self-increase.

a rise in salary	a rise in temperature
a rise of two points in the market	a rise in price

Raise may be used as a noun if it represents that which has been **raised** by some outside force and which did not rise by itself.

price raises (liftings or boostings)	a salary raise
the raise of wages	a raise of an inch (a lifting)

We expected a rise in salary. (a self-increase)
The Government effected a salary raise. (a lifting or boosting)

Rising and **raising** are both used as nouns.

"Raising" is used to denote the act of something's being raised by some outside force.
"Rising" is used to denote the act of something's moving upward by itself.
We watched the **raising** of the tower.
(The tower was raised by someone.)
We watched the **rising** of the sun.
(The sun rose by itself.)
We witnessed the **rising** of the floods.
(The floods moved upward themselves.)
the raising of wages ⎫
the price-raising campaign ⎬ raised by people
the raising of the question ⎭

rise ⎱ These verbs are interchangeable; but "arise", probably because of
arise ⎰ its poetic flavor, has given way to "rise" in most instances.

men rise to the occasion (RATHER THAN: arise)
farmers rise early (RATHER THAN: arise)

Arise is used when "comes up" or "springs up" can be substituted.

a question arises	debates arise	occasions arise

Arisen is the past participle, not "arose".

It is declared to have suddenly arisen. (NOT: *arose*)

raised ⎱ practically interchangeable as applied to persons. "Reared" is
reared ⎰ favored in some sections of the United States; "raised" in others. "Brought up" may be used to avoid either.

set to place. ⎱ "Set" represents the actual placing down of something;
sit to rest. ⎰ and "sit" represents the resting or reposing there.
set, set, set, setting usually take an object.
Someone must set something.
sit, sat, sat, sitting do not take an object.
Someone or something sits.

88

To remember the forms of the two verbs, associate them with these ideas:
People themselves sit—sat—have sat—are sitting. (rest or repose)
People set things—set things—have set things—are setting things.
    (place things)
When inanimate objects are said to "sit" or be "sitting", they are
really personified.

> The President **sat** there once. (rested)
> The President **set** the statue there. (placed)
> Responsibilities **sit** heavy upon him. (rest)
> He **sets** his responsibilities before his opportunities. (places)
> ...having a **sitting** for a portrait. (resting or posing)
> ...the court **sits** tomorrow. (sits down or convenes)
> ...in a **sitting** room. (resting room)
> The cowboy **sits** his horse well. (sits on)
> ...inclined to **sit** (NOT: *set*) out a dance. (rest)
> The committee expects to finish the business at one **sitting**. (a session)
> The suggestion did not **sit** well with them. (rest well)
> **Sit** down and tell me about it. (rest)
> When I had **sat** (NOT: *set*) down to think... (rested)
> **Set** a price on it. (place)
> The sun **sets**. (places itself below the horizon)
> ...in a rural stage **setting**. (placement)
> ...goods **set** down in Chicago. (placed down)
> The men **set** to work on it. (placed themselves at work)
> ...**setting-up** exercises...cement **sets** (hardens)...gelatin **sets** (congeals)

Overlapping uses:

> **Sit** the guest there. (cause to sit) ⎫
> **Set** the guest there. (place) ⎬ (OR BETTER: **Seat** the guest there.)
>   ⎭
> "A **sitting** hen" was supposed to be the proper term, but
> "A **setting** hen" has been heard so often as now to be recognized as correct.

When inanimate objects are referred to, often some other word than
"sit" is appropriate.

> The building **sits** (USE: stands) on government land.
> BUT: The house **sits** back from the road.
>   (A house may appear to "sit" in its surroundings.)
> That landmark has **sat** (OR: has been) there for years.
> The machinery was **sitting** (OR: resting) on the ground.
> Let the mixture **sit** for an hour. (BETTER: stand)
> The table is **set**, but the dishes **sit** (OR: remain) untouched.
> The coat **sits** (OR: fits) well across the shoulders.
>   (The "set" of a coat is colloquial.)

Likewise, another word is sometimes more appropriate than "set".

> The building will be **set** (USE: placed, built, or erected) on government land.

shall ⎫
will ⎬ The simple rule:

Use **shall** in the first person, **will** in the second and third, to
denote simple futurity.

⎧ I shall
⎪ we shall
⎨ you will
⎪ he will
⎩ they will

89

Use **will** in the first person, **shall** in the second and third, to denote determination or command—or willingness, promise, consent, or choice.

$$\left.\begin{array}{l} \text{I will} \\ \text{we will} \\ \text{you shall} \\ \text{he shall} \\ \text{they shall} \end{array}\right.$$

In commands, "will" is often used instead of "shall" to soften the tone, or by way of courtesy, as

> You will then report to the New York Office.
> You will then proceed with the work.

The above general distinctions between "shall" and "will" are still followed. But the finer shades of usage have led to so much confusion that even these broad differences are disappearing.

> "Unfortunately the distinction in meaning of 'shall' and 'will' is being effaced..."
> —Vizetelly, "How to Use English", p. 539.

British usage is more definite in its differentiation between "shall" and "will". For a discussion see Fowler, "A Dictionary of Modern English Usage", pp. 526 and 729.

should ⎱ These words follow mainly the simple rule that applies to "shall"
would ⎰ and "will".

Some verbs, such as the following, already signify willingness, promise, or choice; therefore only simple futurity need be expressed before them.

> I should like to see them. (RATHER THAN: I would)
> I should not care to read it.
> We should be glad to do it.
> I should be pleased to comply.
> I should be content to work alone.
> I should not find it difficult, I'm sure.
> We should be willing to sign it.
> I should prefer not to talk.

"Would" is accordingly used with the second and third persons:

> You would like it, I'm sure.
> They would like to go too.
> You would not find it difficult.
> They would be willing to sign it.

"Should" is of course used wherever "ought to" is meant.

stay means to remain for a time. ⎱ "Stop" for "stay" is colloquial.
stop means to pause or halt. ⎰
One "stays" at a hotel, rather than "stops".
One may "stop" in a town on a journey.

> We **stopped** in St. Louis and **stayed** at the Parkland Hotel.
> At what hotel are you **staying?** (COLLOQUIAL: stopping)

90

suffice it to say ⎱ is a form of the subjunctive, meaning "let it suffice to
OR: say". Often the "it" is dropped, as
suffice to say ⎰

> Suffice to say that the matter has been settled.
> FOR: Suffice it to say that the matter has been settled.

than comply	INSTEAD OF:	**than to comply**	In such sentences as the following, "to" is often
but ask		**but to ask**	not used with verbs
except listen		**except to listen**	after "than", "but",
besides tell		**besides to tell**	"except", and "besides"
than complying			—usually when these
than complied			words are introduced by
			"do", "did", or "done".

After "than":

> USUAL: ⎧ They **do** little more than **comply** with the rules.
> ⎨ They **did** little more than **comply** with the rules.
> ⎩ They **have done** little more than **comply** with the rules.

> UNUSUAL: ⎧ They **do** little more than **to comply** with the rules.
> ⎨ They **did** little more than **to comply** with the rules.
> ⎩ They **have done** little more than **to comply** with the rules.

> NOT: ⎰ They **did** little more than *complied* with the rules.
> ⎱ They **have done** little more than *complied* with the rules.

> BUT: They **have** more than **complied** with the rules.
> (Here "have complied" is a single verb form.)

> USUAL: They **will do** more than **comply** with the rules.

> USUAL: They are **doing** more than **complying** with the rules.
> (Here, they are actually "complying", but below they are not.)

> IDIOMATIC: . . . **doing** that rather than **comply** with the rules.
> (Here, they are not "complying"; hence "[to] comply" is used.)

> USUAL: It **has done** more than **demonstrate** the value of study and **prove** the value of work.

> UNUSUAL: It **has done** more than **to demonstrate** the value of study and **to prove** the value of work.

> NOT: It **has done** more than *demonstrated*. . .and *proved*. . .

> BUT: It **has** more than **demonstrated**. . .and **proved**. . .
> (Here "has demonstrated and proved" is the full verb form.)

> USUAL: Most persons **know** better than **to try** to stop progress.
> (NOT: *than try*)

> USUAL: . . .like one who **perishes** sooner than **submit**. (UNUSUAL: to submit NOT: *submits*)

After "but", "except", and "besides":

> USUAL: They **have done** everything but **ask** advice. (INSTEAD OF: to ask NOT: *asked*)

> USUAL: He **has done** little except **listen** attentively. (INSTEAD OF: to listen NOT: *listened*)

> USUAL: It **does** nothing besides **tell** the direction of the current. (INSTEAD OF: to tell NOT: *tells*)

91

to do   OR: to doing
to use   to using
to work   to working
to call   of calling

Whether to use an -ing verb form or a plain verb, is often a question. Idiomatic usage influences some combinations; therefore, if in doubt about the proper form, test both to see which "sounds right". The idiomatic use should be distinguishable by its familiar sound; if it is not, and one phrase seems to fit as well as the other, choose the -ing form— it is almost always right.

Some idiomatic combinations are:

They had no hope **of succeeding.** (NOT: *to succeed*)
BUT: They had no desire **to succeed.**
They are not equal **to meeting** the demands. (NOT: *to meet*)
BUT: They are not able **to meet** the demands.
They set themselves **to performing** the task. (NOT: *to perform*)
BUT: They set **to work** on it.
They had every opportunity **of becoming** acquainted with it.
BUT: They had every chance **to become** acquainted with it.
...with an aim **to help** rather than (to) **hinder** progress.
OR: ...with an aim **at helping** rather than **hindering** progress.
...**intention to appeal,** to wed, to build, to resign, etc.
...no **intention of going,** allowing, retiring (OR: *to retire*)
...interested **in knowing.** (OR: *to know*)
...take the liberty **of calling** their attention. (OR: *to call*)
They should reserve the right **of deciding** in each case. (OR: to decide)
They should be credited with the ability **to make** their way. (RATHER THAN: for making NOT: *of making*)
Things that we remember long ago **to have** taken delight in. (OR: having BUT NOT: *of having*)
...terms that they have been **accustomed to use** (OR: to using)
We have become so **accustomed to seeing** that in print...
They have not been **accustomed to doing** it in that manner.
are **used to doing** (RATHER THAN: are used to do)

see your way clear {to handle this / to help us / to assist us / to do this}   RATHER THAN: {to handling / to helping / to assisting / to doing}

try and come
come and see
look and see
be sure and tell

The use of "and" instead of "to" with these verbs is termed "colloquial". Yet some of the combinations are widely used; the word "and" appearing to strengthen the verbs by implying result.

Try and come to some conclusion.
(Means more than "try to come". It means first to try and then actually to come to some conclusion.)
Look and see for yourself if it is...
(Means more than "look to see". It means first to look and then to see or be convinced.)

But phrases which really imply but one thought had better be written with "to".

Come to see us.   Be sure to tell them.

92

used to is the form that means "was accustomed to" (pron. ūzd to; Br. ūst to).

use to is obsolete.

> That firm **used to** pay promptly.   (NOT: *use* to)
> CLUMSY: Didn't they use to pay promptly?
> FOR: They used to pay promptly, didn't they?
> CLUMSY: We didn't use to do it that way.
> FOR: We used not to do it that way.

would have Never use this combination for "had", after "if".

> NOT: If they *would have* done that they might have succeeded.
> BUT: If they had done that...
> OR: Had they done that...
> NOT: If they *would have* asked, we could have told them.
> BUT: If they had asked...
> OR: Had they asked...

TIME EXPRESSED

To bring out the meanings of sentences, select the verb forms that best express the time elements involved.

is represents an existing fact or condition.

was represents a past or closed fact or condition.

> The message said that thousands **are** starving.
> (The condition still exists.)
> The message said that thousands **were** starving.
> (The condition may have been remedied.)
> The lecturer said that Fuji **is** an extinct volcano.
> ("Is" represents an existing fact—Fuji is still an extinct volcano.)
> It was demonstrated that air **is** composed chiefly of oxygen and nitrogen.
> (An existing fact—air is always composed of these elements.)
> In the argument they maintained that America **was** less democratic than Europe.
> (In the argument they probably said "America is...", but since they did not prove it, it is now a past statement.)

Some writers prefer to maintain the sequence of tenses, and use verbs in the past tense to express existing facts.

> How did you guess that I **was** an American?
> (RATHER THAN: that I **am** an American)
> He said his name **was** Stanfield.   (RATHER THAN: is)
> ...but for that ancient sailor who knew that the earth **was** round.

will be represents a future fact or condition.

is may also represent a future fact or condition.

> The train **is** to be sent on a trial run.   (OR: will be)
> The Olympic Games **are** to be held next year.   (OR: will be)
> The Olympic Games **are** next year.   (FOR: are to be held)
> Tomorrow **is** Wednesday.   (FOR: will be)
> Next year **is** presidential election year.   (FOR: will be)
> Christmas **is** on a Sunday this year.   (FOR: will be)

93

Although expressions such as the last four and the following are by some considered "colloquial English", they are widely used.

This year he is in Japan, and next year he **goes** to Spain. (FOR: will go)

has } represent an action which still exists, or the result of which still
have } exists.
had represents a past or closed action.

> He **said** that he **had** taken it up with them. (a past action)
> He **says** that he **has** taken it up with them. (an existing action)
> They **returned** last week from Florida where they **had been** spending the winter.
> ("Returned" closes the fact that they were in Florida; therefore "had been" is used rather than "have been". Their vacation should not continue past their returning.)
> They **have been** spending the winter in Florida.
> (The vacation still exists.)
> At least he **had** the courage to say what he **thought.** (past action)
> At least he **has** the courage to say what he **thinks.** (existing action)
> ...but one who **has** a real claim to fame **would have done** otherwise.
> ("Has" indicates an existing claim to fame.)
> At the trial they **swore** that they **had** always given away the tickets.
> (They swore to what had happened previously.)
> NOT: At the trial they **swore** that they *have* always given away the tickets.
> (They could swear only to what had gone before, not to what is still their practice.)

has been represents an action which still exists, or the result of which still exists.
was represents a past or closed action.

> The manager **was** forced to resign. (past action)
> The manager **has been** forced to resign. (existing action)

to be }
to do } imply the same time as the main verbs, or future time.
to have }
to have been }
to have done } imply time before the main verbs.
to have had }

> The flyers **were thought to be** near Berlin at six o'clock.
> ("To be" indicates the same time as "were thought".)
> The flyers **were thought to have been** near London at noon.
> ("To have been" indicates time prior to "were thought".)
> It **would have been** simple **to do** that.
> NOT: It **would have been** simple *to have done* that.
> ("To have done" places the action further into the past than "would have been".)
> NOR: It *would be simple to have done* that.
> ("To have done" places the action before the being simple, which is not the meaning.)

94

FOUR WAYS OF EXPRESSING TIME:

> These changes **seem** to us **to be** for the better. (all present)
>
> These changes **seemed** to us **to be** for the better. (all past)
>
> These changes **seem** to us **to have been** for the better. (The changes that were made in the past now seem or still seem to be for the better.)
>
> These changes **seemed** to us **to have been** for the better. ("To have been" places the time into the distant past, before "seemed" which is itself in the past.)

NOT: It **has been** pleasant *to have met* you. (USE: to meet you)

> ("To have met" places the meeting before the being pleasant.)

NOT: We **hoped** *to have completed* the job before the new year. (USE: to complete)

> ("To have completed" places the action before the hoping.)

NOT: They **would have been** the last *to have admitted* defeat. (USE: to admit)

NOT: It **would have been** enough *to have told* them that. (USE: to tell)

NOT: We **intended** *to have shipped* the goods sooner. (USE: to ship)

NOT: He **said** that he **had hoped** *to have seen* them before that.

> ("To have seen" places the seeing into the distant past, beyond "had hoped", which is still beyond "said", which is itself in the past.)

USE: He **said** that he **had hoped to see** them before that.

should have liked
would have liked

> These expressions should be followed by the present instead of the past of verbs with "to". (See "to be" and "to have been", above.)

NOT: I **should have liked** *to have seen* it.

BUT: I **should have liked** to see it.

> ("To have seen" in the first sentence places the seeing in the far past, before the liking, which is itself in the past.)
>
> I **should like to have seen** it. (has a different meaning)
> (This means that the desire or the liking exists now, after the sight or the seeing is past.)
>
> I **should like** very much **to have gone**.

BETTER: I **should have liked** very much **to go**.

NOT: I know I **would have liked** very much **to have had** a similar guide.

BUT: I know I **should have liked** very much **to have** a similar guide.

NOT: We **should have disliked** *to have been forced* to do that.

BUT: We **should have disliked being forced** to do that.

JUMBLED: I **would have liked to see** you and *talked* about this.

CORRECTED: I **should have liked to see** you and (to) **talk** about this.

being
doing } imply the same time as the main verbs, or future time.

having been
having done } imply time before the main verbs.

Even when used as nouns or adjectives, -ing verbs can be governed by time.

> There **was** no question of his not **doing** his work.
> ("Doing" implies that the work was going on at the time the question might have arisen.)

95

There **was** no question of his not **having done** his work.
("Having done" implies that the work was finished at the time the question might have arisen.)
The writer **was quoted** as **saying** in his article...
("Saying" implies the same time as the quoting.)
The writer **was quoted** as **having said** in his article...
("Having said" implies time prior to the quoting.)
He, **being told** to report, **refused** to go.   (OR: having been—if the refusing occurred after the being told)
NOT: It is true, *being* announced yesterday.   (USE: having been)

after having   is an idiomatic expression that is commonly used—even by authorities.   Some writers condemn it on the ground that "after" definitely places the action before the main verb, and the word "having" is superfluous.

After having talked we decided the issue.   (OR: After talking)
He was instructed to see the President, **after having had** his company's views made clear to him.   (OR: after having his company's views)
He wandered to safety out of the deep woods here today **after having been** lost for two days.   (OR: after being lost)

would be
should be } imply the same time as the main verbs, or time after the main
could be   verbs.

would have been
should have been } imply time before the main verbs.
could have been

It **was** not **thought** that funds **could** so easily **have been obtained.**   (OR: could be)
("Could have been" places the obtaining before the thinking; whereas "could be obtained" would imply the same time as the thinking, or time after the thinking.)
They **decided** that it **would have been** unwise to do that.
("Would have been" indicates a possible action before the deciding. "Would be" would indicate a possible action after the deciding.)
We should not have sent the statement if we **had known** that it *would have embarrassed* them.   (USE: would embarrass)
("Would have embarrassed" puts the embarrassing before the knowing, which is not what is meant.)

shall have been
will have been { indicate action performed before some future time. They may also indicate action performed before the present time.   But should not be used to indicate action performed before some past time.

We **shall have received** instructions before then.   (future time)
The news **will have been dispatched** by now.   (before the present time)
It **will have occurred** to the reader that...   (before this time)
The check **would have been paid** before they **received** our letter.   (NOT: *will* have been)
The check **will have been paid** before they **receive** our letter.   (before a present or future time)

Proper Relation of Tenses

Although there are no definite rules to govern the selection of tenses, the verbs in one sentence should be in agreement; that is, they should present a smooth and logical continuity of time and thought.

> NOT: Four days after his release from the Navy, he enlisted in the Army, joining comrades with whom he *went* to war.
> ("Went" places the time of going to war with the time of enlisting. USE: had gone to war)
> NOT: We saw the wing of the plane break and later *dropped* (USE: drop) into the sea. (MEANING: and later we saw it drop)

When nothing is to be gained by shifting from one tense to another, keep the tenses the same.

> NOT: The Mayor **said** that as soon as he *learns* the provisions of the bill he **would cooperate** with...
> BUT: The Mayor **said** that as soon as he **learned**...he **would**...
> OR: The Mayor **says** that as soon as he **learns**...he **will**...
> NOT: As one thing **becomes** necessary, another thing *has become* useless. (USE: becomes...becomes)
> NOT: He **thought** he *can* meet his payments tomorrow.
> BUT: He **thinks** he **can**...
> OR: He **thought** he **could**...

can expresses present or future ability.
could expresses past or future ability.

These verbs should agree with the other verbs in a sentence.

> NOT: He **could** do the work if he *will*.
> BUT: He **can** do the work if he **will**.
> OR: He **could** do it if he **would**.
> NOT: He **said** he *can* do it.
> BUT: He **says** he **can** do it.
> OR: He **said** he **could** do it.
> NOT: If I **thought** that he *can* do the work...
> BUT: If I **thought** that he **could** do the work...

can have } The proper one of these verbs should be selected to preserve
could have }   the logical relationship of time in a sentence.

> It **can** not **have been received** if they **say** it **has** not. (all present)
> It **could** not **have been received** if they **said** it **had** not. (all past)
> No one who **has observed** them **can have failed** to note...
> No one who **had observed** them **could have failed** to note...
> That **is** an instance in which the display **can have been prompted** only by pride.
> That **was** an instance in which the display **could have been prompted** only by pride.

should...would { A past-tense clause usually follows a "should",
should...will { "would", or "could" clause, to maintain the
                   { sequence of tenses.

But the present tense is sometimes employed in the second clause to give force or reality to the second verb (called "vivid sequence").

97

We **should** appreciate it if he **would** do that. ⎫ (regular sequence of tenses)
We **shall** appreciate it if he **will** do that. ⎬
We **should** appreciate it if he **will** do that. (vivid sequence)
("Will" brings out the last verb—makes it real or positive of accomplishment.)
I **should** not be surprised if he **succeeded.** (regular sequence)
I **should** not be surprised if he **succeeds.** (vivid sequence)
If we **could** guess what they **would** do... (regular sequence)
If we **could** guess what they **will** do... (vivid sequence)
I **should** be glad to do it provided I **returned** from the trip in time. ⎫ (regular
I **shall** be glad to do it provided I **return** from the trip in time. ⎬ sequence)
I **should** be glad to do it provided I **return** from the trip in time. (vivid sequence)
If there are any further questions you **would** like to take up with me, I **shall** be glad to answer them.

Principal Parts

Verbs seem constantly to undergo change. Usage makes one form popular and discards another. Some quaint old forms show how far we have progressed, or digressed—

snown	*catched*	*awoken*	*washen*	*teached*
ruinate	*foughten*	*growed*	*sitten*	*stang*

The following forms are set down to point out the fluctuations or idiosyncrasies of verbs and to point up the advice:
When in doubt, consult the dictionary.

bankrupt—bankrupted—bankrupted
They have bankrupted the county. (NOT: have *bankrupt*)
He was bankrupt. (Here "bankrupt" is an adjective.)
He was bankrupted by the crash. (Here "was bankrupted" is the verb.)

bear—bore—born or **borne**
"Born" is used when "given birth to" is the meaning.
"Borne" is used when "carried" or "endured" is meant.

beat—beat—beaten or (colloquial) **beat**
COLLOQUIAL: It can't be beat.   FOR: It can't be beaten.

begin—began—begun
It began to look promising. (NOT: *begun*, which is archaic)
It has begun... (NOT: has *began*)

bet—bet or **betted—bet** or **betted**
They bet on the race and lost.
...even time can be betted away.

bid—bade—bidden or **bid** (to command; to address)
They were bidden to come.
We try to do as we are bid.
"Bade" is pronounced băd, not *bāde*.

bid—bid—bid (to make an offer)
But they bid above us last week.
Twenty dollars was bid.
We might as well have bid twelve spades.

bite—bit—bitten or (colloquial) **bit**
                It was bitten by the frost.
      COLLOQUIAL: He has bit the dust.

bless—blessed or **blest—blessed** or **blest**
    "Blessed" (the verb) is pronounced blĕst.
    "Blessed" (the adjective) is pronounced blĕs'ĕd, as "the blessed day".

blow—blew—blown
    "Blowed" is considered "dialectal".
    The storm has blown several buildings down.   (RATHER THAN: has blowed)

break—broke—broken
    "It was broke" is obsolete or archaic.
      USE: It was broken...   It got broken..., etc.

broadcast—broadcast (or -ed)—broadcast (or -ed)
    "Broadcast" is more commonly used for the past than "broadcasted"—although
either is correct—as
    The news was broadcast yesterday.

build—built—built
    "Builded" is archaic or poetic.

burst—burst—burst
    "Bursted" is dialectal, as "The keg had bursted."
    "*Bust*" or "*busted*" is considered "inelegant".

buy—bought—bought
    "Boughten" is archaic as the past participle of "buy", as "I have boughten a
suit." But it is still used colloquially as an adjective, as "boughten cake",
"boughten goods", etc.

climb—climbed—climbed
    Never, of course, say "*clum*", as "had *clum*".

copyright—copyrighted—copyrighted
    In the copyright notices, as "Copyright, 1937, by...", the owner is simply
declaring his claim of copyright—the right to produce copies, etc.—which claim
he may subsequently have registered in the Copyright Office. "Copyrighted"
is the commonly used term for "registered for copyright".

dig—dug—dug
    "*Digged*" is archaic.

dive—dived—dived
    "*Dove*" is colloquial in the United States.
    Use "dived into the water" rather than "*dove* in".

drag—dragged—dragged
    Never use "*drug*" for the past of "drag", as "The play *drug*."
    "Drug" is a verb in its own right, meaning to stupefy with drugs.

drink—drank—drunk
    Do not attempt to avoid "had drunk"; it is the only correct form. "Had *drank*"
does not exist.
      NOT: He had not *drank* any of it.
      BUT: He had not drunk any of it.
    "Drunken" is sometimes used as an adjective, as "a drunken stupor".

fit—fitted—fitted
        It fitted well. (NOT: *fit*)

99

flow—flowed—flowed
> NOT: The mud had *flown* down and covered the fields.
> BUT: The mud had flowed down...
"Flown" is the past participle of "fly".

forbid—forbade—forbidden
"Have forbid" is archaic; use "have forbidden".
"Forbade" is pronounced fôr-băd′, not -bāde.

forecast—forecast—forecast
"*Forecasted*" is considered awkward.

forget—forgot—forgotten or forgot
"Have forgot" may be used, but there is much to favor the better sounding "have forgotten".

get—got—got or gotten
"Gotten" is still used to a slight degree in the United States, though scarcely now in England, except in such phrases as "ill-gotten", or "the rate per ton gotten".
> A British sentence: That invention should be got rid of.
"Gotten" is sometimes used as a modifier, as
> The amount of money gotten back was small.
> Performances gotten up by amateurs are usually...
"Gotten" is often superfluous, as
> The oil (gotten) from that field tests high.
> The leases (gotten) on that timberland are not...

hang—hung or hanged—hung or hanged
"Hanged" is used in referring to death by hanging, as
> The prisoner is to be hanged.
"Hung" is used in all other instances.

hide—hid—hidden or hid
"Have hid" is commonly used.

hyphen, hyphenate, or hyphenize may be used as the verb.
hyphen—hyphened—hyphened—is to be preferred because it is shorter.

lead—led—led
Note that the past forms are spelled "led" and not "*lead*", as is sometimes seen, the writers evidently thinking of "read".

light—lighted or lit—lighted or lit
"Lighted" is usually preferred to "lit".

mow—mowed—mowed or mown
> They were mowed (OR: mòwn) down.
"Mown" is used as the adjective, not "*mowed*", as "mown weeds".

plead—pleaded—pleaded
"Plead" and "pled" as the past forms are colloquial, as
> "They have all pled guilty."

prove—proved—proved or proven
"Proven" is rapidly coming into use again, especially in legal phrases, as "not proven".
It is also used as an adjective, as "proven land", "proven facts".
> CORRECT: It has sometimes proven true that... (OR: proved true)

ring—rang or **rung—rung**

While "rung" may be used instead of "rang" for the past tense, it is not generally so employed.

He rang the bell. (RATHER THAN: rung)

He has rung the bell. (NEVER: has *rang*)

run—ran or (dialectal) **run—run**

We ran into a thick fog. (DIALECTAL: run into)

"Had run" is correct, though some find it hard to say and waver along with "had *ran*".

saw—sawed—sawed or **sawn**

The board has been sawed in two. (RATHER THAN: has been sawn)

Both "sawn" and "sawed" are used as adjectives, as "the sawn strip", "sawed lumber".

shape—shaped—shaped

"*Shapen*" is archaic.

shine—shone—shone

"Shined" is archaic in any sense but "to shine shoes".

show—showed—shown or (less commonly) **showed**

They had shown that they understood it. (RATHER THAN: had showed)

shrink—shrank—shrunk

"It shrank" and "It has shrunk" are used.

NOT: It shrunk. NOR: It has *shrunken*.

"Shrunken" is used as an adjective, as "shrunken goods".

sing—sang or **sung—sung**

"Sang" is preferable to "sung" for the past tense.

They sang his praises. (RATHER THAN: sung)

They have sung their swan song.

sink—sank or **sunk—sunk**

"Sank" is preferable to "sunk" for the past tense.

It sank into the sand. (RATHER THAN: sunk)

It has sunk down. (NOT: has *sunken*)

"Sunken" is used as an adjective, as "a sunken grave".

slay—slew—slain

NOT: They could have *slayed* him.

BUT: They could have slain him.

NOT: He *slayed* the thought.

BUT: He slew the thought.

slide—slid—slid or **slidden**

It had slid past. (RATHER THAN: had slidden)

sneak—sneaked—sneaked

"Snuck" is dialectal.

sow—sowed—sown or **sowed**

They have sown the crops. (RATHER THAN: have sowed)

speak—spoke—spoken

He has spoken about that. (NOT: has *spoke*, which is archaic)

spin—spun—spun

"*Span*" is an older form.

"Spinned" is not a recognized form.

101

spring—sprang or **sprung—sprung**
"Sprang" is preferable to "sprung" for the past tense.
They sprang a surprise. (RATHER THAN: sprung)

sting—stung—stung
"*Stang*" is archaic.
It stung.   It has stung.

stride—strode—stridden
"*Strid*" is, of course, obsolete.
After they, like soldiers, had stridden past.

strike—struck—struck or **stricken**
"Stricken" is used in court phrases, and when meaning "struck by misfortune".
"Struck" is used elsewhere.
LEGAL: It shall be stricken from the record.
SPECIAL: They were stricken with calamity.
COMMON: That has been struck out.

string—strung—strung
"Stringed" is rare but is sometimes used as an adjective, as "stringed instruments".

swell—swelled—swollen or **swelled**
The funds have swollen. (OR: have swelled)

swim—swam or (dialectal) **swum—swum**
Things swam by us. (RATHER THAN: swum)
Never use "had *swam*" for "had swum" as in the following line from a newspaper story:
He had *swam* out to save his ten-year-old brother.

swing—swung—swung
"*Swang*" is archaic.
It swung past them. (NOT: *swang*)
It has swung into a new cycle.

thrive—thrived or **throve—thrived** or **thriven**
They thrived on it. (OR: throve)
They have thrived on it. (OR: have thriven)

wake—waked or **woke—waked** or (dialectal) **woke** or (rarely) **woken**
awake—awoke or **awaked—awaked** or (rarely) **awoke**
awaken—awakened—awakened
waken—wakened—wakened
wake }
waken } usually apply to physical rousing from slumber.
awake }
awaken } usually apply to mental awakening.
awake is the adjective, as
They are awake to the possibilities.

wring—wrung—wrung
"Wringed" is very rare; and "*wrang*" is obsolete.
Things wrung dry.

Wrong Forms Used as Modifiers.   A common mistake in the use of verbs is the selection of the wrong form as the modifier of a noun.
As a test, substitute a full clause as a modifier.

...like a race run (NOT: *ran*) against time.
(like a race **that is run** against time)
...followed by a song sung (NOT: *sang*) by the audience.
(a song **that was sung** by the audience)

102

They were poisoned by water drunk from a well.   (NOT: *drank*)
(by water **that was drunk** from a well)
The new study, begun last year, is to be continued.   (NOT: *began*)
(study, **which was begun** last year)

··◄◊▬▬▬▬▬▬▬▬▬◊►··

SUBJUNCTIVES

It is admitted that the subjunctive mood is dying.   Its last stand
is in the use of the two verbs "be" and "were".

"Subjunctives are nearly dead..."
—Fowler, "A Dictionary of Modern English Usage", p. 67.

The reason for the survival of a few forms of the subjunctive is that
they allow the writer or speaker to imply that what he is saying is not a
fact, or that he does not believe it is a fact.   Ordinary verb forms refer
to facts or assumed facts.

be   indicates uncertainty.
were   indicates unreality.

$\left.\begin{array}{l}\textbf{is}\\\textbf{was}\end{array}\right\}$indicate reality.

The subjunctive **"be"** is properly used to express uncertainty or
doubt; although many writers find it more natural to use "may be",
"might be", "should be", etc.   (See also Subjunctives of Other Verbs,
p. 105.)

UNCERTAINTY:
$\left\{\begin{array}{l}\text{If this \textbf{be} treason, make the most of it.}\\\text{(If this might be considered treason..., but the speaker}\\\text{does not believe that it is.)}\\\text{Though its meaning \textbf{be} beyond us, we can still... (the}\\\text{meaning may be beyond us)}\\\text{...unless they \textbf{be} known to live. (they may be known to}\\\text{live)}\end{array}\right.$

Modern usage is rapidly discarding the subjunctive "be" where it
does not imply doubt or uncertainty, but means no more than "is" or
"are".

If that **be** the case, most of our efforts are useless.   (BETTER: If that is the
case...)
...whether the methods used **be** direct or indirect.   (BETTER: ...are direct or
indirect.)
Though there **be** no reason, still it is done.   (BETTER: Though there is no
reason...)

"...there is no question that the 'prim and pompous be' is
rapidly passing out of use, together with all similar forms."
—Ives, "Text, Type, and Style: A Compendium of Atlantic
Usage", p. 268.

The subjunctive **"were"** is properly used to express an imaginary
state (present or future) that is contrary to fact, as in a supposition or
wish.   It is the most used of surviving subjunctives.

103

UNREALITY:

If that **were** true, we might..
  (The "were" indicates plainly that it is not true.)
If I **were** rich, nothing could...
  ("Were" indicates that I am not rich.)
If I **were** he, I should...
  (Purely imaginary, I cannot be he.)
If it **were** not for the fact that it is overdue, we should...
  (an imaginary condition outside the fact)
If that **were** the end of the matter, it would...
  (Imaginary—it is not the end.)
Were it not for that, we should be glad to comply.
I wish it **were** possible.
It would be impossible, even **were** it desirable, to...
...just suppose this city **were** to be destroyed.
Though that **were** so, it would not help.
No person would use those methods unless he **were** dealing with experts.

The subjunctive "were" is not often used in referring to **past time** (it usually refers to present or future time); **"was"** or **"had been"** is used to express unreality in the past.

It seemed as if it **was** winter. (RATHER THAN: were)
If it **had been** (NOT: *were*) raining when they took off, they would have had a hard time of it.
(The writer presents an imaginary condition in the past.)
If it **was** raining when they took off, they must have had a hard time of it.
(The writer assumes a past fact.)
If it **were** raining today, they could not go up. (a present imaginary condition)

Assumed Facts. When a writer assumes a fact, "is" or "was" should be used to express it. In such suppositions "if" is sometimes almost equal to "when". (Note that a writer may treat a supposition as a fact and base his conclusions thereon without knowing the actual truth or untruth of the situation.)

REALITY:

If that **is** true, why do we ponder it? (NOT: *be*)
  (The writer assumes or has been told it is true.)
If he **is** rich, why did he not contribute? (NOT: *were*)
  (The writer assumes or knows that he is rich.)
If it **was** as you say, he should have been told.
  (Assuming it was true, he ought to have been told.)
If it **was** not for the reason you mention, what was the reason?
  (assumed fact)
If the company **was** solvent, why did it fail?
They were still necessary if the business **was** to maintain its standing.
So they compromised, believing if that **was** done the thing would die of itself.
The occasion on which it was done (if it really **was** done) was the meeting at...
He did not know of any cause, unless it **was** human folly.
He threatened to leave if his request **was** not granted.
They asked him if he **was** aware of the offense.
The mistake looks almost as if it **was** due to avoidance of an imagined danger.

104

Subjunctives of Other Verbs. When verbs are used to express indefinite time, without an introductory "should", "shall", "might", "may", etc., they are "subjunctive".

> REGULAR: It is important that he should go.
> SUBJUNCTIVE: It is important that he go.

This kind of subjunctive occurs usually in "that" clauses, introduced by such expressions as

ask that	is necessary that
require that	is essential that

These uses may be tested by simply inserting "shall", "should", "may", "might", etc.

> It is necessary that **one of us remain.** (should remain)
> We must ask that **he attend** to business. (should attend)
> To be accurate requires that **one make** use of... (should make)
> ...on the condition that **someone** with experience **draft** the bill. (should draft)
> They demand that **industry increase** the number of... (shall increase)
> It is essential that **he do** this. (should do)
> We move that **he be** nominated. (shall be)
> The Court rules that **he be** awarded... (shall be)
> It is necessary that exact **figures be** used. (should be)
> We have repeatedly urged that **this be** done. (should be)
> They were afraid to announce it, lest **it fail.** (lest it should fail)
> Note that "remains", "attends", "makes", etc., would not be appropriate in these sentences.

as if
as though ⎰ Since these interchangeable introductory words always imply condition, past conditional verb forms are used after them rather than verbs in the present tense.

> It looks **as if** it **would** rain. (NOT: *will* rain)
> It looks **as if** it **might** rain. (NOT: *may* rain)
> It seems **as if** a new courage **had been born** (NOT: *has* been) which **would** (NOT: *will*) save the race.
> It looks **as if** they **were** going to win. (NOT: *are*)
> It looked **as if** he **was** going to lose.
> ("Was" rather than "were" is usually used to express past time.)
> It appears **as if** he **knew** it. (NOT: *knows*)
> They feel **as though** the barrier **were** (OR: was NOT: *is*) about to lift.
> **As though** they **didn't** care. (NOT: *don't*)

Mixed Constructions. Do not mix a subjunctive and a regular verb in a combined construction. Two verbs with the same subject must both be subjunctive or both regular.

> MIXED: If that **be done** and *turns* out badly, we shall see...
> ALL SUBJUNCTIVE: If that **be done** and **turn** out badly...
> ALL REGULAR: If that **is done** and **turns** out badly...

General Guide for Subjunctives. As a closing remark on subjunctives: Whenever a sentence offers a puzzle regarding the use of the subjunctive "were" or "be", or the regular verb "was" or "is", choose the regular verb and dismiss the subjunctive.

> They swore that they would not deviate from their policy in the event that any agreement reached at Geneva **were** thereafter broken. (OR: was OR: should be)
> There were implied threats that their delegates would walk out unless action **were** (OR: was) taken at once.
> Assuming one of us **were** (OR: was) to tackle the job and it proved too much... (OR: Assuming one of us tackled the job...)
> No trader would defy the law if he knew he **were** (OR: was) liable to arrest.
> I wish I **were** (OR: was) experienced in that work.
> ("Was" after "I wish" is considered "established usage".)
> If this **be** (USE: is) done, the balancing of the books will be facilitated.
> Unless that **were** (OR: is OR: was OR: has been) done on all jobs, they should not expect it here.
> _ (Here, four different meanings can be expressed; and the exact meaning must decide the choice of the verb.)

SPLIT INFINITIVES

"Splitting an infinitive" is simply placing a word, or several words, between "to" and its verb.

SPLIT INFINITIVES	SIMPLE INFINITIVES
to harshly criticize	to criticize
to steadily maintain	to maintain
to slyly hint	to hint
to further hope	to hope
to quickly comprehend	to comprehend
to painstakingly prepare	to prepare
to never tell	to tell
to sometimes hear	to hear
to often see	to see
to never even think	to think
to thus permit	to permit
to so desire	to desire

Although there is much prejudice against the split infinitive, it has been used by good writers of all times.

> "The 'split' infinitive has taken such hold upon the consciences of journalists that, instead of warning the novice against splitting his infinitives, we must warn him against the curious superstition that the splitting or not splitting makes the difference between a good and a bad writer."
> —Fowler, "The King's English", 3d Ed., p. 329.

The commonly suggested remedy is to remove the intervening word and place it before "to" or after the verb, as

> so to arrange the work   TO AVOID: to so arrange
> to prepare carefully   to carefully prepare
> It is impossible **fully to satisfy** everyone.
> OR: It is impossible **to satisfy** everyone **fully.**

However, some split infinitives are to be preferred to any rearrangements that suggest stiffness, or permit vagueness or ambiguity.

> They intend **to partially do away** with ceremonies.
> BETTER THAN: They intend partially to do away with ceremonies.
> OR: They intend to do away with ceremonies partially.
> He agreed **to personally supervise** the group employed.
> BETTER THAN: He agreed personally to supervise the group employed.
> OR: He agreed to supervise the group employed personally.
> ...if they want **to so regulate** activities.
> BETTER THAN: ...if they want so to regulate activities.
> Even now measures **to severely restrict** racing are...
> BETTER THAN: Even now measures severely to restrict racing are...
> They are planning **to vigorously protest** hasty action.
> BETTER THAN: They are planning vigorously to protest hasty action.
> OR: They are planning to protest hasty action vigorously.

Note this distinction:

> " 'To really understand' is a split infinitive;
> 'to really be understood' is a split infinitive;
> 'to be really understood' is not one;
> the havoc that is played with much well-intentioned writing by
> failure to grasp that distinction is incredible."
> —Fowler, "A Dictionary of Modern English Usage", p. 558.

to readily observe
to readily be observed
to readily have observed
to readily have been observed }are split infinitives.

to be readily observed
to have readily observed
to have readily been observed
to have been readily observed }are not split infinitives.

The simple infinitives above are:

to observe   to be   to have

The completed infinitives are:

to be observed   to have observed   to have been observed

But the splitting takes place in the simple infinitive, not in any combination of the verbs that complete the simple infinitive.

Two sentences used by authorities:

It is still **to be so classed** as to...
They are liable **to be carelessly combined.**

Observe, too, that an -ing word following "to" is a noun form; and no splitting of an infinitive is involved in such constructions as

They came nearest **to really solving** the problem by admitting that it did not matter.

107

DOUBLE NEGATIVES

Double negatives are often incurred when the negative implication of certain words is overlooked. When one negative cancels another, an affirmative is the result.

but that   means "that...not" in some questions and negative sentences. (Ordinarily it means "except that".)

but what   is colloquial when used for "but that". (Ordinarily it means "but that which".)

Common uses:

There is no question **but that** he will sign. (MEANING: There is no question that he will **not** sign.)

We have no fear **but that** they will pay. (that they will not pay)

There is no thought **but that** he will accept.

We don't know **but that** that's right.

We have had no word **but that** they are coming. (MEANING: except that OR: that they are **not** coming.)

We don't know **but what** we can arrange it. (colloquial) (MEANING: We don't know that we **cannot** arrange it.)

They do nothing **but what** they care to. (but that which)

Double negative:

Who can tell **but that** this might *not* prove a boomerang?
(MEANING: that this might **not** *not* prove)

RIGHT: Who can tell **but that** this might prove a boomerang? (MEANING: that this might **not** prove)

not but what   is colloquial and should be avoided in favor of "not but that". A double negative is often formed with this construction.

DOUBLE NEGATIVE: Not but what we could *not* do it if we tried.
RIGHT: Not **but that** we could do it if we tried. (MEANING: Not that we could **not** do it...)

but   doubles the negative in some sentences, because of its meaning of "only" (in the sense of "no more than").

NOT: There *weren't* but four left.
FOR: There were but four left.
NOT: They *hadn't* but two orders last week.
FOR: They had but two orders last week.
NOT: It *won't* take but a second.
FOR: It will take but a second.
OR: It won't take a second.
NOT: We *couldn't* see but a few feet ahead of us.
FOR: We could see but a few feet ahead of us.
NOT: One *doesn't* have to take but half a glance at it to see...
FOR: One has to take but half a glance at it to see...

"But", with its meaning of "except", may of course be used after negatives, as

Nobody but him went. (except him)
We have none but that. (except that)

108

but only In some sentences, "but" is a duplication of "only".

> NOT: We have *but* only two left.
> FOR: We have only two left.
> OR: We have but two left.

"But only" is sometimes necessary: when "but" is a connective, as

> They will sometimes applaud, **but only** when extremely pleased.

can but ask means "can only..."
cannot but ask means "can do nothing except..."
cannot help asking means "cannot avoid..."
cannot help but ask is colloquial or idiomatic, but appears to be giving
way to the shorter "cannot help asking".

Ordinary uses:

> We **can but** ask them. (MEANS: We can only ask them.)
> We **cannot but** ask them. (MEANS: We can do nothing except ask...)
> We **cannot help** asking them. (MEANS: We cannot avoid asking...)

Colloquial or idiomatic (and practically a double negative):

> We cannot help but ask them. (MEANS: We cannot avoid not
> asking them.)
> BETTER: We **cannot help asking** them.

Mixed:

> No one can help *believe* the next two years will... (FOR: No one **can help**
> believing...)
> We cannot help *make* the suggestion that... (FOR: We **cannot help making**...)

doubt that is usually used with negative statements, or questions.
doubt whether is usually used with affirmative statements.
doubt but ⎱ is idiomatic, meaning "doubt that...not"—wherein
doubt but that ⎰ "doubt" has the meaning of "question".
doubt but what is colloquial for "doubt but that".

> I **doubt whether** it is true. (affirmative statement)
> Who can **doubt that** it is true? (question)
> I do **not doubt that** it is true. (negative statement)
> There is **no doubt that** it is true. (negative statement)
> There is little **doubt but that** it is true. (established idiom)
> There is little **doubt that** it is true. (approved usage)

Some writers always avoid the use of "but that" after "doubt",
preferring simply "that". But since "doubt" may sometimes mean
"question" with the further implication of "misgiving" or "suspicion",
it would seem that "but that" is required in certain sentences to keep
the meaning clear.

> OBSCURE: We don't think there's a doubt in the world that you'll like it.
> ("But that you'll like it" would have seemed clearer—
> MEANING: We don't think there is a suspicion that you will
> not like it.)

109

hardly } These words contrive to form double negatives because of
scarcely } their negative implication of "not quite".

The simple double negatives are:

> We *haven't* hardly enough time.   (WOULD MEAN: We haven't not
>   quite enough...)
> RIGHT: We have hardly enough time.
>   I *can't* hardly believe it.   (MEANS: I can't not quite...)
> RIGHT: I can hardly believe it.
>   That *doesn't* seem scarcely enough.
> RIGHT: That seems scarcely enough.

The more concealed forms are:

> *Nothing* in the world scarcely is ever found without search.
> FOR: Scarcely anything in the world is ever found...
>   *No one* in our organization hardly would agree to that.
> FOR: Hardly anyone in our organization...
>   After twenty years scarcely *nothing* remains.
> FOR: After twenty years scarcely anything remains.
>   They seem to succeed without *hardly* trying.
> FOR: They seem to succeed almost without trying.
>   It was unnecessary to say *scarcely* anything about it.
> FOR: It was unnecessary to say anything much about it.   (OR: much at
>   all)
> OR: It was necessary to say scarcely anything about it.

not is used in simple questions, with the suggestion of a positive rather
than a negative answer.

> That is right, is it not?
> May we not hear from you?
> **Is it not true** that they have failed?
> ("Is it not true?" is the simple question.)

But if "not" appears in a clause attached to the simple question,
it regains its negative force.

> Is it true **that they have not failed?**

Disregard of this distinction causes many double negatives.

> Is it **untrue** that they have *not* failed?   (MEANS: Is it untrue
>   that they have succeeded?)
> RIGHT: **Is it not untrue** that they have failed?
>   Who can **deny** that they have *not* tried?   (MEANS: Who can deny
>   that they have shirked?)
> RIGHT: Who can deny that they have tried?
>   How can they **refuse to admit** that aviation has *not* succeeded?
>   (that aviation has failed?)
> RIGHT: How can they refuse to admit that aviation has succeeded?

Superfluous "nots":

> We wouldn't be surprised if they *didn't* bring it along.   (MEANS:
>   We shouldn't be surprised if they left it.)
> RIGHT: We shouldn't be surprised if they brought it along.
>   It wouldn't surprise us if they *hadn't* made a fortune.
> RIGHT: It wouldn't surprise us if they had made a fortune.
>   It depends upon whether *or not* they can or cannot see it.

RIGHT: It depends upon whether they can or cannot see it.
 OR: It depends upon whether or not they can see it.
  At present we are trying to figure how much may *not* be charged
  to overhead.
RIGHT: ...how much may be charged to overhead. (which is the
  intended meaning, not how much is not chargeable)
  We must look to our future, lest we be *not* enslaved.
RIGHT: We must look to our future, lest we be enslaved.
  Nothing is too trivial *not* to be included.
RIGHT: Nothing is too trivial to be included.
  Let us *not* end this unpleasant controversy. (perhaps intended
  as a question)
RIGHT: Let us end this unpleasant controversy.
 OR: Should we not end this unpleasant controversy?

only conflicts with the negative in some sentences.

  They will *not* work only when they are forced to.
RIGHT: They will work only when they are forced to.
  They do *not* want to sell, only a part of it.
RIGHT: They want to sell only a part of it.
  That can*not* be understood only by scientists.
RIGHT: That can be understood only by scientists.

In some sentences "only" may be used in a second clause, after a
negative, if certain words carry over to give it support.

  They cannot realize that they have grown old, only that time has passed.
  (they can realize only that time has passed)

Miscellaneous:

  No American city is less *un*blurred by hurry. (USE: is more unblurred OR: is
  less blurred)
  The Army *nor* any other Government agency should **never** be called upon
  to... (USE: The Army or any other Government agency... OR BETTER:
  Neither the Army nor any other Government agency should ever be called
  upon to...)
  Irregardless of that, let us proceed. (USE: Regardless)
  Such a course would give nothing to *no one*. (USE: would give nothing to
  anyone)
  ...for which we make—*nor* need to make—no apology. (USE: or)

Several "nots" may appear in close formation, if the writer knows
his way about when using them:

  The distinction is not only not useless, but not even arbitrary.—From a Fowler
  sentence.

And seeming double negatives appear in literature:

  If this be error and upon me proved,
  I never writ, **nor no** man ever loved.—Shakespeare.

FOREIGN PLURALS

Many words adopted from foreign languages have both original and
English plurals. Some have only their original foreign plurals.

111

If the plural of a foreign word is not given in the dictionary at hand, form a simple English plural.

Regarding the use of Latin or English plurals:

> "All that can safely be said is that there is a tendency to abandon the Latin plurals, and that when one is really in doubt which to use the English form should be given the preference."
> —Fowler, "A Dictionary of Modern English Usage", p. 316.

Observe the pronunciation of vowel sounds in foreign words, especially the long vowels in Latin. They are marked in some words below.

SINGULAR	ENGLISH PLURAL	FOREIGN PLURAL
addendum		addenda
alumna (fem.)		alumnae (fem.)
alumnus (mas.)		alumnī (mas., or mas. and fem.)
analysis		analysēs
antenna	antennas (radio)	antennae
āpex	apexes	ăpicēs
apparātus	apparātuses	apparātus (NOT: apparati)
appendix	appendixes	appendicēs
aquarium	aquariums	aquaria
automaton	automatons	autŏmátá
axis		axēs
bacterium		bactēria
bandit (It. bandito)	bandits	banditti (Italian)
basis		basēs
bureau	bureaus	bureaux (French)
cactus	cactuses	cactī
candelābrum	candelābrums	candelābra

("candelābra" is sometimes used as a singular, with "candelābras" as plural)

château		châteaux (French)
cherub	cherubs	cherūbim (Hebrew)
crisis		crisēs
criterion	criterions	critēria
curriculum	curriculums	curricula
datum		dāta
dēsiderātum (a thing desired)		dēsiderāta
diagnōsis		diagnōsēs
dilettante	dilettantes	dilettanti (Italian)
discus	discuses	disci (dĭs'ī)
dogma	dogmas	dogmáta
emphasis		emphasēs
errātum		errāta
eucalyptus	eucalyptuses	eucalyptī (New Latin)
Fascista		Fascisti (Italian)
focus	focuses	foci (fō'sī)
formula	formulas	formulae
fungus	funguses	fungi (-jī)
genius (a spirit)		genīī
genius	geniuses	
gladiolus	gladioluses (common)	gladĭolī (scientific)

("gladiolas" is a corruption of "gladioluses")

112

gymnasium	gymnasiums	gymnāsia
hīātus	hiatuses	hīātūs
hippopotamus	hippopotamuses	hippopotamī
hypothesis		hypothesēs
ignorāmus	ignorāmuses	(NOT: *ignorami*)
impediment (-um)	impediments	impedimenta
index	indexes (common)	indicēs (scientific)
insignē		insignia
libretto	librettos	libretti (Italian)
literātus (a scholar)		literātī (men of letters)
loggia	loggias	loggie (Italian)
Magus		Magi (mā′jī) ("wise men")
mātrix	matrixes	mătricēs
maximum	maximums	maxima
medium	mediums	mēdia
memorandum	memorandums	memoranda
metropolis	metropolises	metropoleīs (Greek)
minimum	minimums	minima
minutia		minutiaē (small details)
narcissus	narcissuses	narcissī
nemesis		nemēsēs
nucleus	nucleuses	nucleī
oasis		oasēs
octopus	octopuses	octopī, or octopodes
opera (It.)	operas (musical compositions)	
opus (a literary or musical composition)		opera (Latin)
paralysis		paralysēs
(no singular)		paraphernalia
parenthesis(may mean one or both curves, or the expression enclosed, as "a parenthesis")		parenthesēs
phenomenon	phenomenons	phenomena
planetārium	planetariums	planetāria
radius	radiuses	radiī
residuum	residuums	residua
rostrum	rostrums	rostrā
sanatōrium	sanatoriums	sanatōria
sanitārium	sanitariums	sanitāria
sērum	serums	sērā
solo	solos	soli (-lē) (Italian)
spectrum	spectrums	spectra
sphinx	sphinxes	sphinges (sfĭn′jēz)
stadium	stadiums	stādia
status	statuses	(NOT: *stati*)
stigma	stigmas	stigmăta
stimulus		stimulī
strātum	stratums	strāta
streptococcus		streptococci (-kŏk′sī)
synopsis		synopsēs
tableau	tableaus	tableaux (French)

113

tempo	tempos	tempi (Italian)
terminus	terminuses	terminī
thesis		thēsēs
trousseau	trousseaus	trousseaux (French)
ultimātum	ultimatums	ultimāta
vacuum	vacuums	vacūa
vertebra	vertebras	vertebraē
vortex	vortexes	vorticēs

Note that the familiar form of some words is the foreign plural; therefore, a plural verb is required.

Data are (NOT: *is*)... Bacteria are... Insignia are... Addenda are...
Advertising media are... Paraphernalia are... Phenomena are...
One of the vertebrae... (NOT: one of the *vertebra* NOR: *vertebraes*)

Remember, too, that the foreign **singular** is required wherever a similar English word would be singular.

NOT: *gladioli* bulbs, *cacti* plants BUT: gladiolus bulbs, cactus plants
(One would not write "*tulips* bulbs" or "*roses* bushes".)

Also note that the foreign plural forms require plural modifiers and plural pronouns.

this memorandum	BUT:	these memoranda
this medium		these media
that phenomenon		those phenomena
that datum		those data
that analysis		those analyses
this insigne		these insignia

PLURALS

If the plural form of an unusual noun is not given in the dictionary at hand, form a plural as simply as possible, by adding -s; or if the word ends in -s, add -es. (See Spelling, p. 141.)

Names Ending in -s. To form the plural of names ending in -s, -x, -z, or a sibilant sound, add -es.

The Simses	The Essexes	The Kurzes
Harrises	Rexes	Lentzes
Evanses	The Blanches	
Lewises	Frenches	

Names Ending in -y. Simply add -s to proper nouns ending in -y. Do not change any letters, or strange-looking words will result.

The Montgomerys	The Marys
Macys	Henrys
Gregorys	Cicelys

Names Followed by Jr., 2d, or III. The plurals of names followed by "Jr.", "3d" or "III", etc., may be formed in two ways:

FORMAL: The John B. Blaines, Jr.
The Jason Lloyds, III (or 3d)
INFORMAL: The John B. Blaine, Jrs.
The Jason Lloyd, 3ds (or IIIs)

A Common Title Before a Common Name. If two persons of the same name bear the same title, they may be referred to in the following manners:

FORMAL	INFORMAL
The Doctors Nevins	The Doctor Nevinses
The Attorneys McLeod	The Attorney McLeods
The Captains Linden	The Captain Lindens
The Superintendents Lewis	The Superintendent Lewises
The Presidents Markham	The President Markhams
The Messrs. Lee	The Mr. Lees
The Mesdames Harland	The Mrs. Harlands
The Misses Stewart	The Miss Stewarts

If an indefinite number of people is meant, the informal form is used.

They would defy all the Governor Harrises in the states.
There were several Major Hills on our list.
All the Mrs. Browns were to be honor guests.

Nouns Ending in -s or -ss. To form the plurals of common nouns ending in -s or -ss, add -es.

businesses	processes	buses
actresses	classes	lenses
witnesses	masses	apparatuses

Words ending in silent -s do not change form in the plural. In pronunciation the plural may be indicated by sounding the -s.

two corps	several faux pas
ten chassis	many Mardi Gras
two early Degas	all the King Louis

Words as Words. When words are referred to as words, the plurals may be indicated by the simple addition of -s—if the words are common, and such plurals are clear.

pros and cons   ifs and ands   ins and outs   ups and downs

If the words are uncommon, or may be misread, the plurals should be indicated by an 's.

or's and nor's   which's and that's

Further, if the words are liable to be read into the text incorrectly, or if special emphasis is desired, they may be quoted.

All of their "whereas's" are indefinite.
There are numerous "ifs" and "buts" in their language.
(See also Quotation Marks, p. 241.)

If the word to be pluralized already contains an apostrophe, the -s alone is added.

don'ts and doesn'ts RATHER THAN: don't's and doesn't's
        BUT NOT: *dont's* and *doesnt's*
do's and don'ts   'tis's (both apostrophes necessary)

115

The following words have established plurals which are used rather than the 's.

| ayes (or yeses) and noes | RATHER THAN: | yes's and no's |
| yeas and nays | | yea's and nay's |

· If the plural and the possessive both become necessary, the sentence had better be rearranged.

We do not understand his ifs' implication. (NOT: *if's*)
BETTER: We do not understand the implication of his "ifs".

Compound Words. The plural of compound words is formed on the main word, that is, on the word telling what the principal is.

attorneys general	(they are attorneys, not *generals*)
governors general	(they are governors, not *generals*)
major generals	(they are generals, not *majors*)
adjutants general	(they are adjutants [assistants], not necessarily generals)
judge advocates	(they are military prosecutors, not *judges*)
courts-martial	(they are military courts)
heirs apparent	(they are heirs)
notaries public	(they are notaries, not *publics*)
trade-unions	(they are unions)
sums total	(they are sums—"total" is a modifier)

Prepositional phrases, as "of war", "in law", "in chief", "de [of] camp", are descriptive of the main words.   Hence plurals are ordinarily formed on the main words.

commanders in chief	men-of-war	attorneys at law
ambassadors at large	sisters-in-law	rights of way*
chargés d'affaires	mothers-in-law	bills of lading
aides-de-camp	maids of honor	letters of credit

* United States Government usage is "rights-of-way".   Webster's New International Dictionary prefers "rights of way".   It gives, as an Australian usage, the plural form "right of ways".

A few such plurals are idiomatically formed on the last word.

| jack-in-the-boxes | jack-in-the-pulpits | will-o'-the-wisps |

When a preposition is hyphened to a noun, the noun is pluralized.

lookers-on	passers-by	listeners-in
fillers-in	runners-up	goings-on
hangers-on	tryers-out	callers-up
backers-up	times-out*	helpers-out

* The plural "time-outs" is used in official football guides.

Where neither word is a noun, the plural is formed on the last word.

also-rans	hand-me-downs	lay-offs
come-ons	pick-me-ups	take-offs
go-betweens	strike-overs	run-ins
higher-ups	sell-outs	tie-ins

Both parts are pluralized in some compounds—where the words are of almost equal importance.

116

men cooks   Heads of Departments OR: Department Heads
men drivers   Directors of Research Divisions
women pilots   Courts of Appeals (sing., Court of Appeals)
    (For plurals in such phrases as "types of radios", see p. 13.)

Solid Compounds. The plural is formed at the end of a solid compound.

armfuls	cupfuls	pocketfuls	teaspoonfuls
basketfuls	handfuls	spoonfuls	tumblerfuls

If the word is broken into and the plural formed on the first part, the meaning is changed.

two arms full of wood	(MEANS: two arms filled at one time)
two armfuls of wood	(MEANS: two armloads)
four bucketfuls of earth	(one bucket filled four times)
four buckets full of earth	(four separate buckets)
about two shelffuls of paper	(enough to fill two shelves)
two shelves full of paper	(two shelves filled)

A word denoting a class of people may be pluralized in the regular way, or by adding -ers.

tenderfeet or tenderfooters   webfeet or webfooters   greenhorns or greenhorners

Plurals.—Collective Words, p. 37.   (Company Names, p. 38.)
Plurals as in "Ohio and Hudson Rivers".   (See pp. 8, 9, and 133.)
Plurals of Abbreviations.   (See Abbreviations, p. 538.)
Plurals of Figures, Weights and Measures.   (See pp. 268 ff.)
Plurals of Letters.   (See Abbreviations, p. 538.)
Plurals of Quoted Words.   (See Quotation Marks, p. 241.)
Plurals of Unusual Words.   (See Spelling, p. 141.)

POSSESSIVES

Possessives of Singular Words Ending in -s, -x, and -z.   In modern usage an 's is commonly added to form the possessive of singular words ending in -s, -x, and -z.   Formerly only the apostrophe was used.

Adams's election	Essex's victory
Paris's fame	Knox's products
Dumas's works	Cortez's journey
The Times's circulation	Diaz's life
The Mardi Gras's legend	Louis's reign

The apostrophe alone may, of course, be used in all such possessives, if it is preferred.   Or it may be used in special instances, for the sake of euphony, if several s's occur together.

      Confucius' sayings   Essex' sailing
Caution: Do not go back into a word and place the apostrophe before
      the final -s.
    NOT: *Keat's*   The *Time's*
    BUT: Keats's or Keats'   The Times's or The Times'

Descriptive Words. Some words are considered to be more descriptive than possessive; hence the possessive is not used.

United States laws	state rights*
Massachusetts roads	the Hastings ranch
Federal Waterways Bill	a merchants exchange
the Bureau of Standards circular	the company name
	the shipping and mails section

* Possessive not used in singular, but used in plural—states' rights.

Possessives of Plurals. It is easy to misplace the apostrophe when forming plural possessives.

Form the plural of the word first; then add the possessive. If the plural ends in -s, all that is needed is an apostrophe. If the plural does not end in -s, an 's is needed.

NOT: *childrens'* protection	*womens'* votes	*boy's* and *mens'* interests	
BUT: children's protection	women's votes	boys' and men's interests	

SINGULAR	SINGULAR POSSESSIVE	PLURAL	PLURAL POSSESSIVE
boy	boy's	boys	boys'
man	man's	men	men's
woman	woman's	women	women's
workman	workman's	workmen	workmen's
child	child's	children	children's
lady	lady's	ladies	ladies'
witness	witness's, or -ness'	witnesses	witnesses'
mass	mass's, or mass'	masses	masses'
deer	deer's	deer	deer's
Mr. Hayes	Mr. Hayes's	The Hayeses	The Hayeses'
Mr. Essex	Mr. Essex's	The Essexes	The Essexes'
Mr. Burns	Mr. Burns's	The Burnses	The Burnses'
Mr. Montgomery	Mr. Montgomery's	The Montgomerys	The Montgomerys'

Note that the word following a plural possessive is plural, unless a combined possession is intended.

> those authors' **styles** (NOT: those authors' *style*) (not one style, but several)
> the rich men's **fortunes** (not one fortune, but many)
> BUT: those men's consent (their combined consent)
> those buyers' business (a common or combined business)
> those speakers' use of the word (a common use)
> those speakers' uses of the word (means that they used it differently)
> (See also Collective Words, p. 42.)

Possessive When a Common Title Precedes a Common Name. If the possessive is to be used when a common title precedes a common name, it may be added in the following manners:

FORMAL	INFORMAL
The Messrs. Blake's theory	The Mr Blakes' office
The Mesdames Hill's reception	The Mrs. Hills' tearoom
The Misses Davis's School	The Miss Davises' shop
(OR: The Misses Davis' School)	
The Attorneys McLeod's suit	The Attorney McLeods' case

118

Possessives in Phrases.   Phrases like the following are sometimes called "double possessives", because of the "of phrase" (which, as well as an 's, signifies possession).   But good usage has so long sanctioned such phrases that they are regarded as idiomatic.

> a friend of Mr. Gale's (INSTEAD OF: Mr. Gale's friend OR: a friend of Mr. Gale)
> a friend of mine (INSTEAD OF: my friend OR: one of my friends)
> a friend of Whittier's and mine (NOT: of Whittier and mine)
> a book of theirs
> a habit of his
> a rule of Ralph's
> a painting of Whistler's

An instance where the possessive is not used:

> ...although the voice cannot be that of Wagner.   (NOT: that of *Wagner's*)

Do not tack a possessive on a pronoun that is already possessive.

> NOT: a client of *ours'* building
> BUT: the building of a client of ours
> NOT: a friend of *mine's* car
> BUT: the car of a friend of mine
> NOT: at a *neighbor's* of *his* house (NOR: at a *neighbor*)
> BUT: at the house of a neighbor of his

Phrases such as the following should be avoided in writing.   But they occur in conversation, and if started should be finished correctly.

> in one of the men's desks (NOT: men's *desk*)
>   (The simple phrase is "in one of the desks".)
> from one of our relatives' vineyards (NOT: *vineyard*)
> at one of the girls' homes (NOT: *girl's home*)
> BETTER: { in the desk of one of the men
>   { from the vineyard of one of our relatives
>   { at the home of one of the girls

With Names Consisting of Several Words.   The possessive may be placed at the end of a name composed of several words, if the construction remains clear.

> the Standard Oil Company of California's offer
> the American Relief Association's report
> the Attorney General's office
> Columbus, Ohio's most famous citizen
> Bard Winton, Jr.'s account   The Bard Winton, Jrs.' cards
> Philipp Whitney, III's plane   The Philipp Whitney, IIIs' home
> Stanfield, Inc.'s order
>   (See also Possessives of Abbreviations, p. 538.)

If the construction is awkward, an "of phrase" should be used.

> AWKWARD: the delegates from Way Down East's vote
> BETTER: the vote of the delegates from Way Down East
> AWKWARD: the Manager of Construction and Repair's report
> BETTER: the report of the Manager of Construction and Repair
> AWKWARD: the Society for the Prevention of Cruelty to Animals' action
> BETTER: the action of the Society for the Prevention...

119

With Explanatory Words. Explanatory words or phrases usually carry the possessive. But if they are distinctly set off by commas, the possessive may be formed on the main words as well.

> Dumas the elder's writings
> That was John the handy man's idea.
> That idea was John the handy man's.
> NOT: He wants to have a role in his *friend*, James Hopewell's, play.
> BUT: He wants to have a role in his friend's, James Hopewell's, play.
> (OR: [without commas] in his friend James Hopewell's)
> NOT: It is the same at his local *broker*, George Lane's.
> BUT: It is the same at his local broker's, George Lane's.

Compound Possessives. The possessive of compound words is formed by adding an 's to the last word.

> sister-in-law's   commander in chief's   listener-in's
> brother-in-law's   ambassador at large's   passer-by's

With names that already contain a possessive, an "of phrase" should be used.

> NOT: after Villon's-at-the-Beach's style
> BUT: after the style of Villon's-at-the-Beach
> NOT: Benson's-by-the-Sea's orchestra
> BUT: the orchestra of Benson's-by-the-Sea

When a plural and a possessive are both involved, use an "of phrase" to show possession.

> the governors general's decisions
> BETTER: the decisions of the governors general
> his brothers-in-law's estate
> BETTER: the estate of his brothers-in-law
> the listeners-in's viewpoint
> BETTER: the viewpoint of the listeners-in

Joint Possession. When joint possession is intended, the possessive may be formed on the last of two or more nouns—if there is no possibility of a misreading.

> James, Robert, and Charles's business venture
> the Soldiers and Sailors' Club
> Randall & Ives's "Chronicles"
> Coolidge and Dawes's administration
> Blake and Hayward's note
> Davis and Clayton's truck

But if the possibility of an error in reading exists, each noun should be made possessive.

> NOT: They held John *Blake* and Don Hayward's note.
> BUT: They held John Blake's and Don Hayward's note.
> ("Note" indicates that it was one note.)
> OR: They held the note of John Blake and Don Hayward.
> NOT: George *Davis* and Ralph Clayton's truck was damaged.
> BUT: George Davis's and Ralph Clayton's truck was damaged.
> NOT: Is this a *farmer* and a merchants' bank?
> BUT: Is this a farmers' and a merchants' bank?

120

Or if a pronoun is involved, each word is possessive.

> James's, Robert's, and his business venture
> Bankwell's and my refusal
> Rand's and our agreement

Separate Possession. If separate possession is intended, each noun should be possessive.

Note that the thing possessed is plural, unless it is something that can be commonly possessed, as "attention", "consent", "use", etc.

> Those are the owner's, lessee's, and mortgagee's rights.
> ...given to soldiers' and sailors' clubs.
> Lincoln's and Roosevelt's administrations can be compared.
> James Bryson's and Daniel Mack's fathers were childhood friends. (NOT: James *Bryson* and Daniel Mack's fathers...)
> The lot between Harmon's and Hazelton's beach homes was sold. (NOT: beach *home*)
> It is desirable that the sender's and addressee's names and addresses appear on both portions...—U.S. Official Postal Guide.
> That is apparently Gray's (and other authors') use of the word. ("Use" here represents a common use.)
> Note: For clarity, the noun is often moved forward, as "from both the reader's standpoint and the writer's".
> Or the noun is repeated, as "the Artists' **Club** and the Florists' **Club**".

Alternative Possession. If alternative possession is indicated, each noun should be possessive.

Note that the thing possessed may be either singular or plural, to conform to the rest of the sentence.

> a boy's or a girl's effort   an author's or an editor's opinion
> men's or women's interests   the authors' or editors' opinions
> a man's or a period's style   in a senator's or a member's language

Parallel Possession. Do not forget the possessive when a word stands parallel with another possessive.

> NOT: A child's food requirements differ from the *adult* in that...
> BUT: A child's food requirements differ from an adult's in that...
> NOT: ...a navy to equal *Britain* or the *United States*.
> BUT: ...a navy to equal Britain's or the United States'.
> NOT: ...whose faults were no worse than their *neighbors*.
> BUT: ...whose faults were no worse than their neighbors'.
> NOT: Like a *watchmaker*, his work is exacting.
> BUT: Like a watchmaker's, his work is exacting.

Words Understood After Possessives. Often the thing possessed is understood.

> Send it to Blackmore's [shop] for repair. (NOT: *Blackmores*)
> It can be bought at Clarendon's. (NOT: *Clarendons*)
> NOT: At your *druggist*.   At your *dealer*.   At your *grocer*.
> BUT: At your druggist's.   At your dealer's.   At your grocer's.   [store]
> OR: From your druggist.   At your drugstore.   At your grocery.

121

Piled-up Possessives. Avoid the piling of one possessive on another.

> It was sent at *his partner's brother's* request.
> BETTER: It was sent at the request of his partner's brother.
> It was caused by that company's representative's being absent.
> BETTER: It was caused by the absence of that company's representative.
> The Authors' League's report...
> BETTER: The report of the Authors' League...
> The firm's New York manager's signature was necessary.
> BETTER: The signature of the firm's New York manager was...
> That corporation's attorney's decision...
> BETTER: The decision of that corporation's attorney...
> ALLOWABLE: ...depend on one's hearers' readiness to... (which is comparable to "his hearers'")

Titles Containing Possessives. In some titles the apostrophe is omitted.

> Citizens National Bank
> Farmers Valley
> Governors Island
> Harpers
> Teachers College
> Funk & Wagnalls Practical Standard Dictionary

In other titles it is retained.

> Scribner's
> McCall's
> Veterans' Administration
> The Ladies' Home Journal
> State Teachers' College
> Webster's Collegiate Dictionary

Abbreviated Possessives. (See Abbreviations, p. 538.)

Quoted Possessives. (See Quotation Marks, p. 241.)

Idiomatic Possessives. Some grammarians state that possession should not be given to inanimate things (it personifies them); but this has been done throughout good literature for hundreds of years, and has grown in present usage to such an extent that it can hardly be put aside now.

Some idiomatic possessives are:

> a moment's notice
> an hour's time
> a day's work
> a month's* interest
> 6 months'* subscription
> in one year's* time
> a twenty-one years'* struggle
> five dollars'* worth
> a dollar's* worth
> ten cents' worth
> New Year's Day
> at arm's length
> a stone's throw

* Note the use of the singular and plural possessives.

> ...that 1930's cost of living was but a percentage of 1914's.
> ...and April's level showed a similar gain over March's.

The final -s is omitted in the following idiomatic possessives (that is, with words that end in an s sound).

> for acquaintance' sake
> for appearance' sake
> for conscience' sake
> for goodness' sake
> for justice' sake
> for peace' sake

But the 's is used with other words.

for charity's sake	for mercy's sake	for pity's sake
for art's sake	for heaven's sake	for honor's sake

General Possessives. Certain general possessives may be written as singulars or as plurals. The idiomatic use is singular; but logic favors the plural.

	OR:	
writer's cramp		writers' cramp
fuller's earth		fullers' earth
printer's ink		printers' ink
artist's oil		artists' oil
mariner's needle		mariners' measure
surveyor's level		surveyors' measure
printer's ream		printers' ream
a child's disease		a children's disease
a man's club		a men's club

Anybody Else's. The vogue for saying "anybody's else" seems to have passed, and the "else's" have been restored.

anybody else's	nobody else's
anyone else's	no one else's
everybody else's	somebody else's
everyone else's	someone else's

"Whose else", however, remains; but "who else's" will undoubtedly supplant it, to conform to the rest.

whosever is usually preferred to "whoever's", but the latter may yet become the accepted form to agree with similar possessives.

whosesoever is the possessive of "whosoever"—used in formal writings.

anybody's
everybody's Since these words are singular, the possessives are singular.
another's Do not write: *anybodys'*, each *others'*, etc.
each other's

WRITE:

anybody's	nobody's	one's
anyone's	no one's	another's
everybody's	somebody's	one another's
everyone's	someone's	each other's

each other's and **one another's** are usually followed by plural nouns.

We saw each other's **faces.**—Merriam-Webster dictionaries.
...cutting one another's **throats** without hatred.—Macaulay.

But if the plural noun would convey an **unintended meaning,** the singular is used.

Artists are not inclined to admire each other's talent.
    ("Talents" would give a different meaning.)
They did not ask each other's opinion.
Men take each other's measure.
    ("Measures" would give a different meaning.)
...an appraisal of each other's power.

123

others' is plural.

. . . others' troubles.   (NOT: other's, unless referring to only one)

its is the possessive of "it". "It's" was formerly used, but the apostrophe has long since been dropped to avoid confusion with "it's" meaning "it is".

Possessives Before -ing Words and Phrases. The possessive form should be used before an -ing word or phrase when the -ing word or phrase stands as a noun.

> NOT: We did not object to *them* selling.
> (It is the selling that is under discussion, not the people themselves.)
> THEREFORE: We did not object to **their selling.**

Some writers disregard this form of possessive, believing that a sentence is clear without it; but a perusal of the sentences below should be sufficient to convince the reader that the possessive makes the -ing word clearer and more meaningful in most instances. (To test a sentence, substitute a possessive pronoun, such as "his" or "their", before the -ing word.)

> NOT: Can we depend on *you* doing that?
> BUT: Can we depend on **your** doing that?
> NOT: They insisted upon *me* writing the letter.
> BUT: They insisted upon **my** writing the letter.
> NOT: It would result in *him* losing his job.
> BUT: It would result in **his** losing his job.
> NOT: . . . if it comes to *us* being called.
> BUT: . . . if it comes to **our** being called.
> NOT: It depends on the *President* accepting the compromise.
> BUT: It depends on the **President's** accepting the compromise.
> NOT: . . . that leads to *it* being misinterpreted.
> BUT: . . . that leads to **its** being misinterpreted.
> NOT: There is no reason for the *people* waiting there.
> BUT: . . . for the **people's** waiting there.
> NOT: The *president,* the *secretary,* and the *manager* having to resign caused a sensation.
> BUT: The **president's,** the **secretary's,** and the **manager's** having to resign . . .
> NOT: The First National Bank of the *North* closing made . . .
> BUT: **The First National Bank of the North's** closing made . . .
> COMMON: They had not considered the possibility of anything destroying the crops.
> FOR: . . . of **anything's** destroying the crops.
> COMMON: We can't imagine anybody caring to do that.
> FOR: . . . **anybody's** caring . . .
> COMMON: It resulted in the hotel operating at a loss.
> FOR: . . . in the **hotel's** operating . . .
> COMMON: They are responsible for New York being so street-conscious.
> FOR: . . . for **New York's** being so street-conscious.
> COMMON: . . . the possibility of the event never happening.
> FOR: . . . of the **event's** never happening.
> COMMON: That should be left to those who can rely on their words not being misunderstood.

124

FOR: ...on their **words'** not being misunderstood.
COMMON: If you don't like that prophecy coming true...
    FOR: If you don't like that **prophecy's** coming true...
COMMON: No danger of the rule being broken...
    FOR: ...of the **rule's** being broken...
COMMON: It was caused by a night watchman falling asleep.
    FOR: ...by a night **watchman's** falling asleep.
COMMON: We must insist on all employees being punctual.
    FOR: ...on all **employees'** being punctual.
COMMON: ...instead of the proceeds being collected through an agent.
    FOR: ...instead of the **proceeds'** being...
COMMON: You can rely on our goods arriving on time.
    FOR: ...on our **goods'** arriving on time.
COMMON: It was caused by the printer or the editor mistaking...
    FOR: ...by the **printer's or the editor's** mistaking...
COMMON: ...with neither buyer nor seller being advised of it.
    FOR: ...with neither **buyer's nor seller's** being advised of it.
COMMON: Instead of labor and capital working together...
    FOR: Instead of **labor and capital's** working together...
COMMON: That is like an hors d'oeuvre being served after dinner.
    FOR: That is like an **hors d'oeuvre's** being served after dinner.

If a singular verb follows an -ing phrase, check to see whether or not a possessive is needed before the -ing phrase to make it a singular thought.

NOT: The small banks extending credit **violates** the law.
BUT: The **small banks'** extending credit violates the law.
OR: The small **banks** extending credit **violate** the law.

"This" and "that", and naturally "these" and "those", do not take the possessive.

We had not heard of **that** being done. (NOT: *that's*)
There is no likelihood of **those** being sold.
There is a chance of **this** going on indefinitely.

After **"prevent"**—the possessive is used if an -ing word immediately follows; but it is not used if "from" is employed.

NOT: A guard was called to prevent *them* carrying away souvenirs.
BUT: ...to prevent **their** carrying away souvenirs.
OR: ...to **prevent them from** carrying away souvenirs.
NOT: There was nothing to prevent the *broker* selling.
BUT: ...to prevent the **broker's** selling.
OR: ...to **prevent the broker from** selling.
NOT: We could not prevent the *men* going ahead with it.
BUT: ...prevent the **men's** going ahead with it.
OR: ...**prevent the men from** going ahead with it.

When Possessives are not Used Before -ing Words and Phrases.
Not all -ing words and phrases require the possessive. The sense of the sentence must be considered first. Test it by inserting "who is" or "that is" before the -ing word.

It depends upon the man reporting the proceedings whether or not we get the whole story.
(This means that it depends on the man who is reporting.)

It depends upon the man's reporting the proceedings whether or not we get the whole story.
(This means that it depends on the reporting.)
The convention being held in Chicago will bring many on to New York.
(This means that the convention itself will bring.)
The convention's being held in Chicago will bring many on to New York.
(This means that the being held in Chicago will be the cause of bringing.)
A man spending everything he earns is like an improvident beaver tossing away everything it gathers.
(This means that the man is like the beaver.)
A man's spending everything he earns is like an improvident beaver's tossing away everything it gathers.
(This means that the spending is like the tossing.)
We watch the newcomer struggling for a foothold...
(We watch the newcomer himself.)
We watch the newcomer's struggling for a foothold...
(We watch the struggling.)

If the one-thought -ing phrase is broken into by another phrase or clause, the possessive, to avoid awkwardness, is not used.

We appreciated the difficulty of a man with so slight an education accomplishing the task.
(The simple sentence is: We appreciated the difficulty of a man's accomplishing the task. But "with so slight an education" intervenes.)

Also, in other sentences where the possessive would be awkward, it is not used.

The possibility of his **absence** being considered as evidence...
We object to its **truth** being assumed without...
They insist on **none** being left out.
There was no necessity for **all the rest** declining.

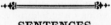

SENTENCES

Logical ideas are the first step toward clear writing.
Simple words are the next.
Clean sentence construction is the next.

Singulars and Plurals Mixed. Singulars and plurals may be logically used in the same sentence; but often there is an indiscriminate mixing of singulars and plurals that leads to ambiguity.

Therefore, the best practice is to make all singulars conform to singulars and all plurals to plurals, where nothing is to be gained by writing them otherwise.

ILLOGICAL: Write the names (pl.) on the backs (pl.) of each receipt (sing.).
("Each receipt" could not have "backs".)
BETTER: Write the **name** on the **back** of **each receipt**. (specific)
OR: Write the **names** on the **backs** of **all receipts**. (general)
ILLOGICAL: When meeting **a person**, shake hands if **they** extend **their hand.**
BETTER: When meeting **a person**, shake hands if **he extends his hand.**
OR: When meeting **people**, shake hands if **they extend their hands.**

126

ILLOGICAL: I was pleased to find **a letter** from both you and the National Company.

BETTER: I was pleased to find letters...

ILLOGICAL: Above the skyline rose the **top of** the Flagler and Southern buildings.

(Until the reader reaches "buildings" he believes it one building.)

BETTER: Above the skyline rose the tops...

ILLOGICAL: All of them had their heads buried in **a book.**

BETTER: All of them had their heads buried in books.

ILLOGICAL: Both men and women must be 21 years of age before they can become a registered **voter.**

BETTER: ...before they can become registered voters.

ILLOGICAL: Both of them will receive **a silver dollar.**

BETTER: Both of them will receive silver dollars.

OR: Each of them will receive a silver dollar.

ILLOGICAL: Those **officers** wear **a rating badge** on **their arm.**

BETTER: Those officers wear rating badges on their arms.

OR: Those officers wear a rating badge on their arms. (if it is the same kind of badge)

ILLOGICAL: Today **men** send their **boy** to college that **he** may become "**a gentleman".**

BETTER: Today men send their boys to college that they may become "gentlemen".

OR: Today a man sends his boy to college that he may become "a gentleman".

Singulars and plurals are sometimes idiomatically mixed, when the singular represents a class of things.

IDIOMATIC: If they are treated as if they were **beginners,** it is only because their writings are available and those of the **beginner** are not.

REGULAR: ...and those of the beginners are not.

Omitted Words. Omitted words and supposedly understood words are the cause of much controversy regarding grammatical construction.

Commercial usage countenances certain omissions, for the sake of brevity, if the omitted words can be readily understood. But in formal writings most missing words should be supplied.

NOT: They are as good, if not better, than these.

BUT: They are as good as, if not better than, these.

OR: They are as good as these, if not better.

NOT: They had no knowledge or faith in the proposition.

BUT: They had no knowledge of, or faith in, the proposition.

NOT: The conference is being watched by shipping men with as much interest, possibly more, than that of any other group.

BUT: ...with as much interest as, possibly more than, that of...

NOT: They arrange prices for the benefit of the industry and the detriment of the consumer.

BUT: ...for the benefit of the industry and to the detriment of...

Small words, such as "the", "a", "an", "our", "some", etc., should be repeated wherever necessary for definiteness.

The vice president and secretary signed for the firm.

(This could mean one officer.)

The vice president and the secretary signed for the firm.   (two officers)
...a blue and black car.   (one car)
...a blue and a black car.   (two cars)

Carry-Over Constructions.   When a construction carries over in a sentence and depends on a later word for completion, it should agree with the form of the word expressed.   A word should be mentioned before any reconstruction of it is assumed.

> FAULTY: It was in one of the late, if not the latest, **editions.**
> (Testing each phrase to see if it carries over: ...one of the late editions...if not the latest editions?)
> REARRANGEMENT: It was in one of the late editions, if not the latest.
> (Here "edition" can be understood after "latest", because "editions" has been mentioned before.)
> FAULTY: They always have and still **pay** all their own expenses.
> (Testing each verb to see if it carries over: ... always have pay?...and still pay)
> BETTER: They always have paid and still pay all their...
> FAULTY: No one has or ever will **paint** such a living thing.   (No one has paint...?)
> BETTER: No one has painted, or ever will paint, such a...

The following are examples of sentences in which the constructions carry over.

> He was one of the best, if not the best, **of scholars.**
> (Testing each phrase: ...one of the best of scholars...if not the best of scholars)
> They can and will **pay** all their own expenses.   (...can pay...will pay)

Often a clause appears before the word on which it depends; but if the sentence were in its natural order, the clause would follow the word, as

> They, just as we would, **took** no notice of it.
> (Straightening the sentence: They took no notice of it, just as we would [take].)

But more often such a clause should stand after the word on which it depends.

> FAULTY: ...at the old hotel where Washington, as did Lafayette, **lived** during...
> BETTER: ...at the old hotel where Washington lived, as did Lafayette, during...

Balanced Construction.   To acquire clean sentence construction, make similar parts of a sentence balance as nearly as possible.

> DEFECTIVE: They neither spare man nor beast.
> BALANCED: They spare **neither man nor beast.**
> ("Spare" applies to both words, hence should stand before "neither".)
> DEFECTIVE: We are not only interested in that but also in this.
> BALANCED: We are interested **not only in that but also in this.**
> ("Interested" applies to both parts, hence should stand before the "not only".)

128

DEFECTIVE: They have started buying and to look for new bargains.
BALANCED: They have started **buying** and **looking** for new bargains.
OR: They have started **to buy** and **to look** for new bargains.
DEFECTIVE: They expect to go to Chicago, as well as going to St. Louis.
BALANCED: They expect to go to **Chicago, as well as St. Louis.**
DEFECTIVE: They are now more interested in buying than was the case prior to 1929.
BALANCED: **They are** now more interested in buying **than they were** prior to 1929.
DEFECTIVE: The best way to do that is by doing this.
BALANCED: The best way **to do that** is **to do this.**
DEFECTIVE: It foretells a good future as well as giving warning.
BALANCED: It **foretells** a good future **as well as gives** warning.
DEFECTIVE: It checked buying rather than causing sales.
BALANCED: It **checked** buying **rather than caused** sales.

Clear Reference. Definite word reference is necessary to good construction.

The reference of the words "which" and "that" is often vague. They will pick up and reflect whatever is immediately before them. (See also "which", p. 26.)

CONFUSING: They have a pamphlet covering the idea, which is to be sold by the separate copy.
(The reader first believes that "which" refers to "idea", but later finds that it refers to "pamphlet".)
BETTER: They have a pamphlet which covers the idea and which is to be sold by the separate copy.
CONFUSING: This is the list showing the names of the dealers that we spoke to you about yesterday.
PUNCTUATED: This is the list, showing the names of the dealers, that we spoke to you about yesterday.
OR BETTER: This is the list that we spoke to you about yesterday, which shows the names of the dealers.

Pronouns are also often confusing in their reference. (See p. 63.)

"Dangling" or "Hanging" Words. There has been much talk about the status of the -ing word (adjective) that is suspended in a sentence with no definite word upon which to lean. The -ing words that are nouns can of course stand alone—unsupported. But an -ing word that is an adjective should supposedly have a definite word to modify.

Seeing is believing. (both nouns)
Seeing it there, we could hardly believe...
(Here "seeing" modifies "we", as "We, seeing it there, could...")
Seeing it there, it appeared much larger...
(Here "seeing" cannot modify "it", so must call upon understood words for support, as "Upon our seeing it there...", which makes "seeing" a noun.)

Thus, because a pronoun, or a pronoun with a preposition, can so easily be understood before an -ing word, the objection to the simple unsupported -ing word may be overcome.

Sentences such as the following are in general commercial usage:

> Being a retired officer, his pension was assured.
> ("He being a retired officer" is understood.)
> Investigating the situation, several new angles were uncovered.
> ("By our" is understood before "investigating".)

The real objection to the "dangling participle" is aimed at downright awkward constructions, and at constructions that can readily be changed for a marked improvement.

> MEANINGLESS: Being in the bank, we were not concerned over our certificates being stolen.
> ("Being" immediately attaches itself to "we"; but it was not "we" who were in the bank, but the certificates.)
> IMPROVED: Being in the bank, our certificates were in no danger of being stolen.

Arrangement. The ill arrangement of words in a sentence may cause a reader to reread in order to puzzle out the meaning.

> INVOLVED: The notice was sent to all those whose payments for the quarter our treasurer had not received.
> CLEARER: The notice was sent to all those whose payments for the quarter had not been received by our treasurer.
> INVOLVED: The marks indicate that all coupons were with the original bonds and must have been detached if not there now.
> CLEARER: The marks indicate that all coupons were with the original bonds and, if they are not there now, they must have been detached.
> INVERTED: And so the changes have gone on until only very recently has been felt the influence of the papers.
> CLEARER: And so the changes have gone on until only very recently the influence of the papers has been felt.
> JUMBLED: His actions revived the insinuations before he was elected by many newspapers.
> CLEARER: His actions revived the insinuations made by many newspapers before he was elected.
> MISLEADING: To be meaningful, the writer should rewrite the sentence.
> CLEAR: To be meaningful, the sentence should be rewritten.

Every inverted or introductory phrase should have a definite connection with the rest of the sentence. Test an inverted phrase by placing it later in the sentence.

> NOT: In reply to your inquiry relative to the issuance of licenses, such licenses are issued by the district offices.
> (Rearrangement shows improper connection: Such licenses are issued by the district offices, in reply to your inquiry relative to the issuance of licenses.)
> BETTER OPENING: The licenses that you asked about in your letter of April 6 are issued by the district offices.
> (By beginning with the subject, the writer avoids the use of the unnecessary and old-fashioned "we wish to say that", which is required if the original phrasing is to be properly connected.)

Long Sentences. A sentence may be long if it is perfectly clear. Long sentences create a slow tempo; short sentences, a fast tempo.

Short sentences can become as monotonous as long ones. Do not overwork either style.

Forceful Beginnings and Endings. The attention-catching part of a sentence is at the beginning; the climax is at the end.

Notice the difference in emphasis in the following sentences:

> WEAK: The decision should be final to be fair.
> FORCEFUL: To be fair, the decision should be final.

Sentences Beginning With "And", "But", "For", etc. A sentence may correctly begin with "and", "but", "for", "or", etc. It is usually started thus for emphasis, or as a continuation or a summing up. The only restriction is that the device should not be overused.

> **And** information is to be found in the 24 volumes of the Britannica of such unquestionable authority...
> **And** now at last the highest truth on this subject remains unsaid... —Emerson.
> **And** it is perhaps already time to mark what advantage and mischief... —Ruskin.
> **But** it is only by deliberate effort that I recall the long morning hours of toil, as regular as sunrise...—Ruskin.
> **But** the sense of joint discovery is none the less giddy and inspiriting. **And** in the life of the talker...—Stevenson.
> **But** call it worship, call it what you will...—Carlyle.
> **For,** in fact, I say the degree of vision that dwells in a man is a correct measure of the man.—Carlyle.
> **And** the evening and the morning were the first day.—The Bible.

Various sentence beginnings are shown in these successive sentences:

> **Nor** is this all. If digestion were a thing to be trifled with... **And** were I to return to my own place... **Or,** if nothing better were to be had... **Hence** it appears to be a matter of no great moment...—Huxley.

Prepositions at the End of Sentences. A sentence may end with a preposition. Often the final preposition is superfluous, which has undoubtedly led to the prejudice against its use. Sometimes it is rather awkward; but more often it is a very effective ending.

Effective endings:

> The world we live in.
> But dost thou love life? Then do not squander time, for that's the stuff life is made of.—Franklin.

Common endings:

It is difficult to account for.	Those are things to get rid of.
Not that I know of.	See that the matter is attended to.
Where are they from?	Give us money to buy things with.
What is it for?	That's what I'm talking about.

131

Superfluous endings:

It means more than we think *for*.   Where am I *at?*

Awkward endings:

What are they going there for?
BETTER: Why are they going there?
A preposition is not a good word to end a sentence with.
(awkward but effective)

Rearrangement:

Send the machines our men are accustomed to work with.
Send the machines with which our men are accustomed to work.
(Some writers prefer the first method, others the second.)

Sentences Without Subjects or Verbs.   A phrase may stand as a sentence—and often does.

Now to get down to business.
Hence the grief over wars.
So much for that.

❖

132

CAPITALIZATION

Capitalize sparingly. Overindulgence detracts from the value of the capitalized word. The dictionary denotes words to be always capitalized.

Proper Names. The purpose of the capital letter is to designate the name or title of a specific person or thing.

CAPITALS (SPECIFIC NAMES)	SMALL LETTERS (GENERAL DESIGNATIONS)
the Army	an army of men
the Navy	build a navy
New York City	from the city
State of Wyoming	in any state in the Union
Congress convenes	appoint a congress
the Government requires	a form of government
General Land Office	the different offices
the Republican Party	a republican form of government
President Lincoln	when Lincoln was president
the Governor spoke on	the governor of a state
our Company has	a company was formed
our Accounting Department	in any accounting department
the Club voted	that club was not represented
the Old World, the New World	in a new world
New Year's Day	that day is a holiday
Canary Islands	the island of Cuba

Business Titles. Are usually capitalized in business papers when they refer to specific persons. They are not usually capitalized in printing.

R. C. Blake, President of the Park Association
Len Barr, Vice President of Rochester & Co.
He is Secretary and Treasurer of Hammond Bros.

... when he was Chairman of the Board.
OR: ... when he was chairman of the Board.

Geographic Names. Some publications do not capitalize the words "river", "ocean", "county", etc., after geographic names. But other publications regard these words as part of the titles, and therefore capitalize them. Such capitalization is usual in typewritten work.

	OR:	
Pacific Ocean		Pacific ocean
Mississippi River		Mississippi river
Westward County		Westward county
Atlantic and Pacific Oceans		Atlantic and Pacific oceans
Colorado and Columbia Rivers		Colorado and Columbia rivers
Tenth and Main Streets		Tenth and Main streets

133

After long use in certain constructions, some geographic words are written without capital letters.

| transatlantic | **BUT:** | mid-Atlantic |
| transpacific | | trans-Siberian |

Directions. "North", "South", "East", and "West" are capitalized when used as the names of certain sections of the country.

out West	living down East
in the West	Middle West
back East	Southern California
in the East	Northern Ireland
going West	Western Australia
coming East	Eastern Shore (Md.)
from the South	in the Far East
from the North	the Western World

When used as nouns or adjectives to designate natives or residents of certain sections, they are capitalized.

| a Westerner | an Easterner | Southerners |
| Western buyers | an Eastern visitor | a Southern drawl |

They are not capitalized when used as simple directions or to refer to parts of the country.

east of Chicago	in the north of Ireland
traveling west	in the south of France
toward the south	in northern Italy
looking north	in western Canada

When used as adjectives to describe things in general, they are not capitalized.

| a northern winter | eastern mountains | a western settlement |
| a southern spring | the eastern part | middle western towns |

Seasons. The names of the seasons are not capitalized unless they are personified.

| spring | summer | autumn or fall | winter | midwinter |

The. The word "The" should be capitalized when part of a title.

The Hague   BUT: the Netherlands
The New York Times OR: The Times
The Guaranty Bank
The Associated Press   BUT: "the Associated Press story", because here "the" refers to "story", and Associated Press as a modifier can stand without its "The".

Nations and Nationalities. The names of nations, languages, and nationalities should always be capitalized. There are, however, certain instances where such names have, after long use, lost association with their countries and are no longer capitalized.

134

Japanese	BUT:	japan (varnish)
the Orient		oriental customs
Chinatown		china (chinaware)
India		indiarubber
Negro (the race)		negro dialect, negro songs
Moroccan		morocco (leather)
Roman architecture		roman type
from Manila		manila paper

Hyphened Words. Both parts of a hyphened word are capitalized if each part is ordinarily capitalized.

Spanish-American War   the East-West game   a President-Congress debate

In a heading or title, both parts may be capitalized to conform to the general style. (That is, capitalize the words that would be capitalized if the hyphens were not there.)

Out-of-Town Exchanges	A Down-and-Outer's View
Strong Mid-April Buying	Air-Cooled Theaters
The Up-State Vote	The Ever-Present Threat
Forty-Second-Street Signs	Our Listeners-In
The Wage-Earning Masses	Make-Believe Pacts

Note: Some publications, following rules of style, capitalize only nouns used as the second parts of hyphened words; others capitalize no second parts unless they are proper names; however, the above method is the newspaper style, and is largely used by good authorities.

In the text, the first part only, or the last part only, may be capitalized, according to the manner in which the single words are ordinarily written.

...up-State...Forty-second Street...ex-Governor Hayward...(but, an ex-governor)...non-Christian...pro-British...the President-elect...(but, a president-elect)...mid-April...un-American...English-speaking people

Biblical References. All words denoting the Deity should be capitalized.

our Saviour	God
All-Wise	Godforsaken land
Father	God-given right
the Almighty mercy	an act of God
in the year of our Lord	

BUT: a savior of men, a heathen god, godless, a godsend, godlike

Pronouns referring to the Deity should be capitalized if they stand for His name.

His   Him   He   Thee   Thou

But if such pronouns immediately follow the name of the Deity, they need not be capitalized.

And on the seventh day God ended his work which he had made...—Bible.

Likewise, pronouns that refer to other designations of the Deity are not capitalized, as

who   whom   whose   thy   thine

Biblical references and terms should be capitalized.

The Ten Commandments	Heaven (meaning God), but not
Bible, also Biblical	as in "a heaven on earth"
Scriptures, but scriptural	Hades, but not hell

Principal Words in Headings or Titles. The important words in headings or titles are capitalized, such as nouns, pronouns, verbs, adverbs, and adjectives.

Small or unimportant words are not capitalized, such as prepositions ("of", "in", "to", "by", etc.), conjunctions ("and", "but", "or", etc.), articles ("a", "an", and "the"), the abbreviation "etc.", and often the small verbs "is", "are", and "be".

The Battle of the Marne
Markets or Exchanges, etc.
How to Write a Short Story
Whence are We So Lately Come?

However, prepositions and other small words may be capitalized in headings if they are stressed, or if of more than three letters, as

Decide Before not After Doing
Standards In Business and Out

The main words in the titles of schools, colleges, associations, and business enterprises should be capitalized.

University of Washington
Emerson School of Applied Science
The Association for the Benefit of the Unemployed

Sun, Moon, Stars. The common names of heavenly bodies are not capitalized unless used in connection with the names of other planets or stars that are always capitalized.

sun   earth   moon   stars   polestar   lodestar
...studying Mercury, Arcturus, the Sun, Mars, the Earth, etc.

Imaginative names are capitalized, as

the Milky Way   the Great Bear   Southern Cross   Dog Star

Sentences Within Sentences. If a complete sentence is introduced within another sentence, it may or may not begin with a capital letter, according to the emphasis desired. (If the complete sentence is quoted, it always begins with a capital.)

The debated question was, Is there work for all?
The point is this: There is no alternative.
There are two stands: one is questionable, the other commendable.
Their reply was, "Conditions will not warrant it."

If only a part of a sentence is quoted, it should not begin with a capital letter.

They talked about "price cutting and price fixing".

136

If several sentences are introduced into one sentence, but are joined by "and", or "or", etc., they are not usually capitalized.

> There are three reasons: we are experienced in the work; we are equipped to do it; and our prices are undoubtedly right.
> (For further examples, see the Punctuation section pp. 237 and 246.)

Words Before Figures. (For the capitalization of words in combination with figures, such as "Chapter 10", "Fig. 7", "No. 2", etc., see Numbers, p. 275.)

Personified Things. The name of a personified thing may be either capitalized or written with a small letter, according to the distinction or emphasis to be accorded it. (Note that if capitalization is used, only the thing personified is capitalized, not what it is, nor what it does, nor what it possesses.)

the wheel of Fortune	OR:	the wheel of fortune

> ...when Necessity is the mother of invention.
> ...as Time spins a thread.
> After life's fitful fever, he sleeps well.—Shakespeare.

Poetry. The first word of every line of poetry is usually capitalized.

> There are gains for all our losses,
> There are balms for all our pain;
> But when youth, the dream, departs,
> It takes something from our hearts,
> And it never comes again.—Richard Henry Stoddard.[1]

There is no definite rule for the indention of lines of poetry. Each poem is a law unto itself; and the lines may be indented or not, in any style that best suits the meaning.

Modern poetry often dispenses with capitalization, to achieve a certain effect.

> if I had the lake
> in my own front yard
> I never would work at all
> just smoke my pipe
> and dream
>   by the waves
>   from April
>   to frosty fall
>   and in winter
> I'd skate
>   from early to late
>   wrapped up
>   in a Paisley
>   shawl
> —Riq.—As quoted in "A Manual of Style",
>   The University of Chicago Press.

[1] Reprinted by permission from Charles Scribner's Sons, New York.

Familiar Forms of Address. The words "father", "mother", "aunt", etc., are capitalized when used as titles or names.

> Ask Father and Aunt Sarah to sign.
> Tell Brother Jack to send the papers.

They are not capitalized when mere reference is made to the persons.

> My father and aunt will sign.
> Our brother Jack will send the papers.

Foreign Names. "Van", "von", "du", "de", etc. (meaning "from", "of", etc.) in foreign names are not capitalized, unless such foreign names begin sentences, or stand alone within sentences (that is, are not preceded by forenames or titles).

> The writer Guy de Maupassant...   (with forename)
> De Maupassant, the writer...   (beginning sentence)
> The writer De Maupassant...   (standing alone)

Many foreign names have become Americanized and are written with capital letters. The preference of the owners of the names usually governs in this.

> De Laval OR: de Laval   Van Dyke OR: van Dyke
> Du Pont BUT: the firm name is still carried as E. I. du Pont de
>   Nemours & Co.
> Van Rensselaer (still written "van Rensselaer" also)

Prefixed Names in Caps. When prefixed names are being set in caps, the prefixes, if disjoined, are set in caps.

> DES MOINES   LA SALLE   VON GRISWOLD

But if the prefixes are joined, they are made clearer if only the first letter is capitalized.

> McDONALD   RATHER THAN: MCDONALD
> MacDOWELL   MACDOWELL

Attempt to be uniform in capitalization. Do not capitalize a word at one time and not at another, when using it in the same construction.

❖

SPELLING

The business rule:

Constantly consult the dictionary.

It is the exceptions that prove this rule.
Question the spelling of every unusual or infrequent word.

Words Frequently Misspelled

(Notice how "right" most of the "wrong" words appear at first glance.)

absorption	NOT:	*absorbtion*	gnawing	NOT:	*knawing*
accommodate		*accomodate*	government		*goverment*
acquiesce		*aquiese*	grammar		*grammer*
analyze		*analize*	heart-rending		*heartrendering*
antarctic		*antartic*	hemorrhage		*hemorrage*
asinine		*assinine*	hindrance		*hinderence*
auxiliary		*auxillary*	hygiene		*hygeine*
banana		*bananna*	idiosyncrasy		*idiocyncracy*
bankruptcy		*bankrupcy*	inflammable		*inflameable*
brethren		*bretheren*	intercede		*intersede*
Britain		*Britian*	interfered		*interferred*
Britannia		*Britainia*	khaki		*kahki*
		Brittania	kimono		*kimona*
buoyancy		*bouyancy*	liquefy		*liquify*
Carnegie		*Carneige*	liquefaction		*liquefication*
chauffeur		*chauffuer*	maintenance		*maintainance*
chimneys		*chimnies*	management		*managment*
		chimleys	maneuver		*manuveur*
colossal		*collosal*	navy		*navey*
commitment		*committment*	nickel		*nickle*
committee		*commitee*	nineteenth		*ninteenth*
concede		*consede*	ninth		*nineth*
conscientious		*conscientous*	nowadays		*nowdays*
consensus		*concensus*	occasionally		*ocassionaly*
controversy		*controvercy*	occurrence		*occurence*
corrugated		*corrigated*	pamphlet		*phamplet*
cynical		*synical*	persuade		*pursuade*
deuce		*duece*	Philippines		*Phillipines*
diphtheria		*diptheria*	Pittsburgh, Pa.		*Pittsburg*
ecstasy		*ecstacy*	plagiarism		*plaigarism*
embarrass		*embarass*	playwright		*playwrite*
existence		*existance*	prairie		*prarie*
February		*Febuary*	preceding		*preceeding*
fiery		*firey*	precipice		*presipice*
Filipino		*Philipino*	presumptuous		*presumptous*
forthright		*fortright*	privilege		*privelege*
forty		*fourty*	psychological		*psycological*
George Eliot		*George Elliot*	propeller		*propellor*

publicly	NOT:	*publically*	safety	NOT:	*safty*
questionnaire		*questionaire*	scissors		*sissers*
recipient		*resipient*	seize		*sieze*
relevant		*revelent*	separate		*seperate*
renown		*renoun*	shepherd		*sheperd*
rhapsody		*raphsody*	similar		*similiar*
rhododendron		*rhododrendon*	souvenir		*souviner*
rhubarb		*ruhbarb*	suing		*sueing*
rhythm		*rythm*	vegetable		*vegatable*
Rio de Janeiro		*Rio de Janerio*	Wednesday		*Wedensday*
sacrilegious		*sacreligious*	weird		*wierd*

Simplified or Modern Spelling. Simplified or modern spelling should be used only in **informal work,** such as interoffice communications, intercompany letters, etc.

Regular Spelling. Regular academic spelling should be used in all **formal** letters, documents, and legal papers, and in all copy for publication.

Adding -ed or -ing. When -ed or -ing is to be added, and it is permissible to use either a single or a doubled consonant, American and especially business usage prefers the simpler form.

labeled, signaling, etc. PREFERRED TO: labelled, signalling, etc.

The "rule of accent" may be used as a guide. The rule is: When the accent falls on the **last syllable** of a word ending in a **single** consonant (except h or x) preceded by a **single** vowel, the final letter is doubled in adding -ed or -ing (or another suffix beginning with a vowel):

committed controlling occurred referring equipped (u equals w)

This of course includes all such words of one syllable, as without the doubled letter there would be danger of confusion with similar words:

barring fatted pinning planned ragged stripped tubbing

The continuation of this rule is that if such a word is not accented on the last syllable, the final letter is not doubled:

ben'efited can'celing e'qualed fo'cusing to'taling trav'eled

(Some writers carry the rule out even in such words as "kidnaped" and "worshiped"; but they except "handicapped", "humbugged", "outfitted", "wigwagged", "zigzagged", and "chagrined".)

Do not drop or change a final letter when forming an unusual -ed or -ing ending. If the form is not given in the dictionary at hand, leave the word intact. It is more easily recognized.

tabooed ballyhooed taxied taxiing relayed NOT: *relaid*

The 'd instead of -ed may be used to preserve the appearance of unusual words.

ski'd shanghai'd subpoena'd visé'd (or visaed)

Endings -cede, -ceed, and -sede. It will repay a writer to take a few minutes to memorize the following:

"Only one word ends in *sede* (supersede); only three end in *ceed* (exceed, proceed, succeed); all other words of this class end in *cede* (precede, secede, etc.)."

—Style Manual of the United States Government
Printing Office (1935), p. 47.

140

In this connection, it should be noted that the three words ending in -ceed ("exceed", "proceed", and "succeed") change form when taking different endings—as "procedure", "procession", "excess", and "successive".

Endings -ize and -ise. American preference is for the -ize ending, and British preference is largely becoming so.

characterize	humanize	economize	criticize

Consequently, when forming new words use the -ize form, as

publicize	notarize	BUT: televise (stemming from television)

Many established American words, however, retain the -ise form.

advertise	merchandise	enterprise	surprise

Endings -able and -ible. The more usual suffix, and the living form, is -able. It is generally employed in forming new words.

incorporable	connectable	tryable	publishable

The -ible form is retained on many established words.

forcible	convertible	susceptible

Words Ending in -c. If -ed, -er, -ing, or -y is added to a word ending in -c, the letter k is inserted for clarity, to prevent the c from being sounded as s.

frolicking	shellacked	panicky	picnicker (NOT: *picknicker*)

But the k is not used in forming the plurals of such words, because here the c's sound of k is undisturbed.

panics	picnics	frolics	almanacs	critics

Plural Forms of Unusual Words. When the plurals of words ending in -y, -o, -i, -f, -a, or -e, are not given in the dictionary at hand, form the plurals in the simplest possible way: by adding -s only.

taxis	hoofs	visés	mesas	Filipinos	Januarys
Hopis	scarfs	coupés	lavas	avocados	Alleghenys

Or if the word ends in -s, add -es.

buses	citruses	censuses	compasses

æ and œ. The ligatures æ and œ are not commonly used in business spellings. Not only is it difficult to write them on the typewriter, but the dictionaries now very generally drop the silent letter.

maneuver	RATHER THAN:	manœuvre
medieval		mediæval
encyclopedia		encyclopædia

In some words, especially in trade names, both letters are retained but the ligature is dismissed.

Aetna	Aeolian	subpoena	aesthetic	aeon

141

British and American Variations. British and American spelling often differs in minor particulars. The following are examples:

AMERICAN	BRITISH
acknowledgment	acknowledgement
judgment	judgement
analyze	analyse
ax	axe
check	cheque
connection	connexion
counselor	counsellor
enroll	enrol (but enrolling)
kilogram	kilogramme
program	programme
honor	honour
humor	humour (yet humorous)
offense	offence
totaling	totalling
traveling	travelling
theater	theatre
caliber	calibre
center	centre (makes centring)

Foreign Spellings. Foreign and American spellings sometimes differ in the names of cities.

AMERICAN	FOREIGN	
Antwerp	Anvers	(French)
Brussels	Bruxelles	(French)
Cologne	Köln	(German)
Copenhagen	Köbenhavn	(Danish)
Cordova	Córdoba	(Spanish)
Florence	Firenze	(Italian)
Geneva	Genève	(French)
	Genf	(German)
Gothenburg	Göteborg	(Swedish)
The Hague	's Gravenhage	(Dutch)
Havana	La Habana	(Spanish)
Moscow	Moskva	(Russian)
Munich	München	(German)
Prague	Praha	(Czech)
	Prag	(German)
Rumania ⎱ Roumania ⎰	România	(Rumanian)
Venice	Venezia	(Italian)
Vienna	Wien	(German)
Warsaw	Warszawa	(Polish)

The names of several foreign cities have been permanently changed.

FORMERLY	Now	
Christiania, Norway	Oslo	(ōs'lō)
Constantinople, Turkey	Istanbul	(ē'stän-bōōl')
St. Petersburg ⎱ Petrograd ⎰ Russia	Leningrad, U.S.S.R.	(lĕn'ĭn-grăd)
Peking, China	Peiping	(bā'pĭng')
Pernambuco, Brazil	Recife	(rā-sē'fĕ)
Porto Rico	Puerto Rico	(pwĕr'tō)
Queenstown, Irish Free State	Cóbh, Ireland (Eire)	(kōv)

Russian words are seen spelled in different ways.

Czar OR: Tsar   Romanof OR: -off, -ov, -ow   Grozny OR: -sny
Dostoyevsky   Dostoyefsky   Dostoïeffsky   Dostoevski   Dostoevskii
Dostoevsky   and   Dostoievsky

Standardize on Spellings. If two or more forms for spelling a word exist, adopt the preferable form and use it consistently.

For instance, "employee" is usually preferred to the French form "employé" so that it will be uniform with "payee", "lessee", etc.

Remember spellings by association of ideas, or by photographing words on the mind, with the troublesome parts magnified, as

aCCoMModate   ecStaSy   coMMiTTee   sepArate   oCCuRRence

Also, learn to **spell by syllables,** carefully pronouncing each one so that certain letters may be remembered by sound, as

absorption arctic authoritative government prescription tempestuous

An understanding of the construction of a word will often be of assistance. For instance, the prefixes **dis-** and **mis-** have but one s; and two s's occur only when the joining word begins with s.

disappear	dissatisfied	misapply	missent
disapprove	dissimilar	misguided	misspell
disprove	dissolve	mismanage	misstate

In the ending **-ful,** the l is single unless an -ly is added.

careful	restful	tearful	wishful
cheerful	skillful	thoughtful	wistful
cupful	spoonful	useful	woeful
hopeful	successful	willful	youthful
carefulness	hopefulness	skillfulness	willfulness (older, willfullness)
carefully	hopefully	restfully	skillfully thoughtfully willfully

Technical and unusual words often present a spelling problem unless they can be quickly verified. Such words should be entered—when first encountered or first looked up—in a small indexed notebook, or compiled into a list and kept in the front of a small dictionary. In a large office, new words to be added to the list should be posted on a bulletin board.

This notebook or list can be made to act as a "stylebook" or "style sheet", such as is used by printers and publishers, to keep the spelling, capitalization, division, hyphenation, and abbreviation of words uniform throughout a writer's or a company's work.

❖

PRONUNCIATION

❖

WORDS

❖

"**E**MERSON says that reading lists of words may inflame the imagination."

* * *

"**C**ONRAD once wrote:...'Give me the right word and the right accent, and I will move the world.'"

—Ellsworth, "Creative Writing",
Funk & Wagnalls Company, New York.

❖ ❖ ❖

Pronunciation undergoes change. Know first, however, that which is correct, then gradually adopt the change . . . .

Abbreviations Used in This Section

✤

abbr.	abbreviation	**L.**	Latin
adj.	adjective	**mas.**	masculine
adv.	adverb	**n.**	noun
Am.	American	**naut.**	nautical
Ar.	Arabic	**Nor.**	Norwegian
Aus.	Austrian	**Pg.**	Portuguese
Boh.	Bohemian	**pl.**	plural
Br.	British	**Pol.**	Polish
colloq.	colloquial	**prep.**	preposition
Du.	Dutch	**pron.**	pronounced, or pronunciation
Eng.	English	**Prus.**	Prussian
fem.	feminine	**Rus.**	Russian
Fr.	French	**sing.**	singular
Ger.	German	**Sp.**	Spanish
Gk.	Greek	**Sw.**	Swedish
Hung.	Hungarian	**syl.**	syllables
It.	Italian	**U.S.**	United States
Jap.	Japanese	**v.**	verb

PRONUNCIATION

PRONUNCIATION SYMBOLS

Marking	Sound	As in
ā	long a	āle
ă	short a	ădd
â	the ăr sound	câre
ä	the Italian a	ärt
ȧ	between ä and ă	fȧst
a̤	the aw sound	a̤ll
a	(unmarked) a soft sound	about
ch	soft ch	chin
ē	long e	ēve
ĕ	short e	lĕt
ē̤	the uh sound	fē̤rn
e	(unmarked) a soft sound	moment
g	hard g	go
ī	long i	īce
ĭ	short i	ĭll
i	(unmarked) a soft sound	habit
j	soft	jet
k	hard	park
K	German ch sound	ich, ach
ṅ	French nasal tone	embonpoint (äṅ'bôṅ'pwăṅ˝)
ō	long o	ōld
ŏ	short o	ŏdd
ô	the or sound	nôrth
o	(unmarked) a soft uh sound	won
o͞o	long double o	mo͞on
o͝o	short double o	fo͝ot
ou	the ow sound	out
oi	the oy sound	oil
ū	long u	ūse
ŭ	short u	ŭp
û	the ur sound	bûrn
ṳ	same as short double o — o͝o	fṳll
u	(unmarked) a soft sound	submit
ü	a muted e sound, as in a German umlaut (as if one started to say o͞o and said ē)	München (mün'Kĕn)
′	primary accent	
′	secondary accent	

Foreign Pronunciations. In the lists of foreign words, the pronunciations given are those commonly used in English, whether they are the foreign pronunciations or English versions thereof. If the foreign and English pronunciations differ widely, both are given.

147

PRONUNCIATION

To speak correctly signifies accuracy.

COMMON WORDS DAILY MISPRONOUNCED

A

abdomen ăb-dō'men
ablution ăb-lū'shŭn
abnormality ăb'nôr-măl'i-ty
abstemious ăb-stē'mi-us
accent (n.) ăk'sent
accent (v.) ăk-sĕnt'
accidentally ăk-si-dĕn'tal-ly, not
-dent-ly
acclimate ă-klī'mat
accompaniment ă-kŭm'pà-nĭ-ment, not
-kump'nē-
accompanist ă-kŭm'pà-nĭst, not
-pa-nē-ist
accurate ăk'ū-rat, not _ak-rit_
acrimony ăk'rĭ-mō-ny
acumen a-kū'men, not _ăk'_
addict (n.) ăd'ikt
addict (v.) ă-dĭkt'
address ă-drĕs' (note accent)
adept (adj.) ă-dĕpt'
adept (n.) ăd'ĕpt
admirable ăd'mĭ-ra-bl, not _ad-mīr'_
adult à-dŭlt' (note accent)
advertisement ăd-vĕr'tĭz-ment, or
ăd'vĕr-tīz'ment
aeon ē'ŏn, not _ā'on_
aerial ā-ē'ri-al, or âr'
aesthetic ĕs-thĕt'ik (Br. ēs-)
affluent ăf'lū-ent, not _a-flu'_
agape à-gāp', or à-găp'
aged ā'jed, as "an aged person"
ājd, as "aged 47"
aggrandizement ă-grăn'dĭz-ment, or
ăg'grăn-dīz'ment
albeit ạl'bē'it, not _ăl-_
albino ăl-bī'nō (Br. ăl-bē'nō)
albumen ăl-bū'mĕn
alchemist ăl'ke-mĭst
alias ā'lĭ-as

alienate āl'yĕn-āt
align a-līn'
alleged a-lĕjd', not _a-lej'ed_, but
allegedly ă-lĕj'ed-ly
alloy ă-loi', or ăl'oi
almanac ạl'ma-năk, not _ăl-_, nor _ăl-_
altercation ạl'ter-kā'shun, or ăl'
alternate (n. & adj.) ạl'tĕr-nat, or ăl'
alternate (v.) ạl'tĕr-nāt, or ăl'
altruism ăl'trōō-izm, not _awl-_
aluminum a-lū'mĭ-num, not _-mē-um_
ambergris ăm'ber-grēs
ambiguity ăm'bĭ-gū'i-ty
amen ā'men', or
ä'men', in singing
amenable a-mē'na-bl, but
amenity a-mĕn'i-ty
analogous a-năl'ō-gŭs, not _-ajus_
analytical ăn'a-lĭt'i-kal, not _-lĕtt_
anathema a-năth'e-ma (a curse)
ăn'a-thē'ma (a consecrated
thing)
antarctic ănt-ärk'tĭk
antipathy ăn-tĭp'a-thy
antipodes ăn-tĭp'ō-dēz
apparatus ăp'a-rā'tus
appellate ă-pĕl'āt (note accent)
applicable ăp'li-ka-bl (note accent)
appreciate a-prē'shĭ-āt, not _-see-ate_
aquamarine ăk'wà-mà-rēn', or ā'kwà-
aquaplane ăk'wà-plān', or ā'kwà-
aqueduct ăk'we-dŭkt
arbiter är'bĭ-ter, not _-bīte'_
archangel ärk'ān'jĕl
archipelago är'ki-pĕl'a-gō, not _arch-_
archives är'kīvz
aristocrat a-rĭs'tō-krăt, or ăr'ĭs-
artistically är-tĭs'ti-kal-ly, not _-tick-ly_
artistry är'tis-try
asinine ăs'i-nīn, or _-nĭn_

āle, ădd, câre, ärt, fàst, ạll, about | ēve, lĕt, fērn, moment | īce, ĭll, habit | ōld, ŏdd, nôrth, won | mōōn, fŏŏt |

148

asphalt ăs′fălt, or -fălt
aspirant ăs-pīr′ant
associate ă-sō′shĭ-āt, not -see-ate
asterisk ăs′ter-ĭsk, not -rich
athlete ăth′lēt, not atha-
atrophy ăt′rō-fĭ, not -fĭ
attacked a-tăkt′, not a-tak-ted
attar ăt′ar
attorney ă-tûr′ny, not atawr-
audacious a-dā′shus, not -dăsh
aunt ȧnt, or änt
aura a′rȧ, not ō-ra
austere as-tēr′, not -tĕr
authoritatively a-thŏr′i-tā′tiv-ly, not
        a-thor′a-tively
autocracy a-tŏk′ra-sy
automaton a-tŏm′a-tŏn
autopsy a′tŏp-sy, not autop′sy
auxiliary ag-zĭl′ya-ry
aviation ā′vĭ-ā′shun
avoirdupois ăv′or-du-poiz′, not adver-
avuncular à-vŭn′kū-lar
awry a-rī′, not aw′ry

B

baccalaureate băk′a-la′rē-āt
bacchanalian băk′a-nā′li-ăn, not -năl
bagatelle băg′a-tĕl′, not -teel
bailiwick bāl′i-wĭk, not băl-
bakelite bā′kĕ-līt
balderdash bal′der-dăsh, not băl-
balsam bal′sam
baptize băp-tīz′, not bab-
barbecue bär′be-kū, not barber-
beleaguer bē-lē′ger, not -lĕgūar
benignant bē-nĭg′nănt
bequeath bē-kwēthe′ (like "breathe")
bestial bĕs′chal
betrothed bē-trōthe′d, or -trôtht′
bibber bĭb′er, not bĭber
Biblical bĭb′lĭ-kal, not bib-i-kal
binocular bĭn-ŏk′ū-lar, or bī-nŏk′
biography bĭ-ŏg′ra-fy, not bee-
bituminous bĭ-tū′mĭ-nus, not bĭ-
blackguard blăg′ärd
blaspheme blăs-fēm′, not -fĕm
blatant blā′tant, not blăt-
brethren brĕthe′rĕn, not -ern
brigand brĭg′and (note accent)
brogan brō′gan, or brō-găn′
buncombe bŭn′kum

bureaucracy bū-rŏk′rȧ-sy, or -rō′
burglar bûr′glar, not berg-u-ler

C

cachinnation kăk′ĭ-nā′shun
calumny kăl′ŭm-ny, not calum′
cantonment kăn-tŏn′ment, or -tōn′
        (Br. kăn-tōōn′)
caramel kăr′a-mĕl, not karm-el
carburetor kär′bū-rĕt′ĕr
cartridge kär′trĭj, not cat-
cater-cornered kăt′er-, or kā′ter-
cavil kăv′il
Cayenne pepper kī-ĕn′, or kā-ĕn′
centaur sĕn′tôr
centrifugal sĕn-trĭf′ū-gal, not -trifical
chaos kā′ŏs, not ka-ŏss′
chasm kăz′m
chastisement chăs′tĭz-ment
        (note accent)
cherubic che-rōō′bĭk (note accent)
chimera kī-mē′ra, or kĭ-
chimney chĭm′ny, not chim-ley
circuitous sĕr-kū′i-tus, not serkit-
clandestine klăn-dĕs′tin (note accent)
claret klăr′ĕt, not klary-et
cleanly (adj.) klĕn′ly
cleanly (adv.) klēn′ly
cognomen kŏg-nō′men (note accent)
coleslaw kōl′slaw, not cold-
collegiate kŏ-lē′ji-at, or -āt
columnist kŏl′ŭm-ist, or kŏl′ŭm-nist
comatose kō′ma-tōs, or kŏm′a-tōs
combatant kŏm′ba-tănt (note accent)
commandant kŏm′an-dänt′, or -dănt′
communal kŏm′ū-nal, or kŏ-mū′nal
comparable kŏm′pa-ra-bl
        (note accent)
condolence kŏn-dō′lens, or kŏn′dō-
conduit kŏn′dwit, or kŏn′dōō-it
confiscate kŏn′fis-kāt, not -fisti-
conical kŏn′i-kal, not kōn-
conjugal kŏn′ju-gal (note accent)
connubial kŏ-nū′bi-al, not -nŭb
constable kŭn′sta-bl, or kŏn′
construe kŏn-strōō′, or kŏn′strōō
contemplate kŏn′tem-plāt, or -tĕm′
contiguous kŏn-tĭg′ū-us
contour kŏn′tōōr, or kŏn-tōōr′
contrast (n.) kŏn′trăst
contrast (v.) kŏn-trăst′

oil, out | ūse, ŭp, bûrn, full, submit; ü—a muted e | chin; go; jet; park; K—Ger. ch; Fr. ṅ—a nasal tone

149

controversial kŏn′trō-vēr′shal
conversant kŏn′ver-sant, or -vērs′
Cordovan kôr′dō-van
corroborate kŏ-rŏb′ō-rāt, not *cor-rōb′*
costermonger kŏs′ter-mŭn̄′ger, not
    -mŏng
counterfeit koun′ter-fĭt, not *-feet*
covert kŭv′ert, not *kō-vert*
crayon krā′on, not *krĕn*
credence krē′dĕns, not *krĕd-*
crematory krē′ma-tō′ry, or krĕm′
cretonne krē-tŏn′ (Br. krĕt′ŏn)
crucial krōō′shal
culinary kū′lĭ-nĕr′y, not *kŭl-*
curator kū-rā′tor (note accent)

D

daguerreotype da-gĕr′ō-tīp
dais dā′is, not *dī-*
damask dăm′ask, not *da-mask′*
daub dạb, not *dŏb*
dawdle dạ′dl, not *dwă-*
deaf dĕf
decadence dē-kā′dĕns, or dĕk′ȧ-
decathlon dē-kăth′lŏn, not *-a-lon*
decorous dē-kō′rus, or dĕk′o-
decoy dē-koi′, not *dee′koy*
decrepit dē-krĕp′it, not *-id*
defalcation dē′făl-kā′shun, or dĕf′
degradation dĕg′ra-dā′shun
delete dē-lēt′, not *dā-*
demesne dē-mān′, or -mēn′
demoniacal dē′mō-nī′a-kal
depot dē′pō (Br. dĕp′ō)
deprivation dĕp′rĭ-vā′shun
derelict dĕr′ĕ-lĭkt, not *deer-*
derisive dē-rī′sĭv, not *-rĭs*
despicable dĕs′pĭ-ka-bl, not *dē-spik′*
desultory dĕs′ŭl-tō-ry
detail dē-tāl′, or dē′tāl
detestation dē′tĕs-tā′shun
detonation dĕt′ō-nā′shun, or dē′tō-
diagnosis dī′ăg-nō′sis, not *-nŏs*
diffident dĭf′i-dĕnt, not *div-*
digest (n.) dī′jĕst
digest (v.) dĭ-jĕst′, or dī-jĕst′
diminution dĭm′i-nū′shun, not
    de-min-u-a-shun
dirigible dĭr′i-jĭ-bl
discharge dĭs-chärj′ (note accent)
disconcerting dĭs′kŏn-sĕrt′ing

discretion dĭs-krĕsh′un, not *-krā*, nor
    -krē
dishevel dĭ-shĕv′el, not *dis-hevel*
dissoluble dĭ-sŏl′ū-bl, or dĭs′ō-lū-
distillate dĭs′tĭ-lāt, or dis-tĭl′āt
docile dŏs′ĭl (Br. dō′sīl)
dolor dō′lor, but
dolorous dŏl′ĕr-us, not *do-lōr′*
domicile dŏm′i-sĭl (Br. -sĭl)
donor dō′nor, not *dŏnner*
dotage dōt′ĭj, not *dŏt-*
drama drä′ma, or drăm′ȧ
dramatize drăm′a-tīz, not *drăm-*
dross drôs, not *drōss*
drowned dround, not *drown-ded*
duchy dŭch′y, not *duke-y*
dynamite dī′na-mīt, not *dăn-*
dynamo dī′na-mō, not *dăn-*
dynasty dī′nas-ty (Br. dĭn′)

E

eclipse ē-klĭps′ (note accent)
economical ē′kō-nŏm′i-kal, or ĕk′ō-
edict ē′dĭkt
eerie } ē′ry, not *ĕrr′y*
eery }
egg ĕg, not *āg*
ego ē′gō, or ĕg′ō
electrolysis ē-lĕk′trŏl′i-sis, not *-trōl*
embroider ĕm-broi′der, not *-ry*
embryo ĕm′brĭ-ō
emeritus ē-mĕr′i-tus, not *-ī′tus*
emolument ē-mŏl′ū-ment
empiric ĕm-pĭr′ik, not *-pĭr*
ensign ĕn′sīn (Navy ĕn′sĭn)
envelope ĕn′vĕ-lōp (Fr. än̄′vē-lōp′)
environment ĕn-vī′run-ment, not
    envir-ment
epaulet ĕp′ō-lĕt
ephemeral ĕ-fĕm′er-al
episodic ĕp′i-sŏd′ik, not *-sŏd′*
epitome ē-pĭt′ō-mē
equanimity ē′kwa-nĭn′i-ty, or ĕk′
equinox ē′kwĭ-nŏks, or ĕk′
era ē′ra, not *ĕrr′a*
escalator ĕs′ka-lā′tor, not *escū-*
exigency ĕk′sĭ-jĕn-sy, not *eggs-*
exit ĕk′sit, or ĕg′zit
experiment ĕks-pĕr′i-ment, not
    -pēr-ment
exquisite ĕks′kwi-zit (note accent)

āle, ădd, cȧre, ärt· fȧst, ạll, about | ēve, lĕt, fērn, moment | īce, ĭll, habit | ōld, ŏdd, nôrth, won | mōōn, fŏŏt|

extol ĕks-tōl′, or -tŏl′
extraneous ĕks-trā′nē-us
extraordinary ĕks-trôr′di-ner′y

F

February fĕb′rŭ-er′y, not *febū-*
finagle fĭ-nā′gl
finance fĭ-năns′, or fī′
flaccid flăk′sĭd, not *flăss-*
flagrant flā′grant, not *flăg-*
forehead fŏr′ĕd, not *four-head*
formidable fôr′mĭ-da-bl, not *for-mid′*
forum fō′rum, not *four-um*
fossil fŏs′il, not *faws-*
fracas frā′kas (Br. fră′kä)
   (Fr. frà′kä′)
fragile frăj′il (Br. -īl)
fraternize frăt′er-nīz, not *fratra-*
funereal fū-nē′rē-al

G

gainsaid gān′sĕd′, not *-sād*
gala gā′la, not *găl′a*
genealogy jĕn′ē- or jē′nē-ăl′ō-jy, not
   -ŏlogy
genuine jĕn′ū-in, not *-u-wine*
giblet jĭb′lĕt
gigantic jī-găn′tik, not *jĭ-*
government gŭv′ērn-ment, not *guvver-*
granary grăn′a-ry, or grān′a-ry
grievous grēv′us, not *-i-ous*
grimace grĭ-mās′, not *grĭm-us*
grimy grīm′y, not *grĭmy*
groceteria grō′se-tē′rĭ-a, not *-tĕrr*
grovel grŏv′l
gubernatorial gū′bēr-na-tō′rĭ-al, not
   gŭb-
guillotine gĭl′ō-tēn
gums gŭmz, not *gōōmz*
gyroscope jī′rō-skōp, not *guy-*

H

halo hā′lō, not *hăl-o*
harass hăr′as, or hà-răs′
hearth härth, or hĕrth
heathen hē′then, not *-ern*
hegira hĕj′ĭ-ra, or hē-jī′ra
height hīt, not *hīthe*
heinous hā′nŭs
heraldic hĕ-răl′dĭk

Herculean hĕr-kū′lē-an, not *hurk-ya-lān*
hiatus hī-ā′tŭs
hierarchy hī′er-är′ky
holocaust hŏl′ō-kôst, not *hōl-*
homage hŏm′ĭj, not *hōm-*
homicide hŏm′ĭ-sīd, not *hōme-*
honorary ŏn′ĕr-ĕr′y, not *oner-ry*
hoof hōōf, not *huf*
horizon hō-rī′zun
hospitable hŏs′pi-ta-bl (Br. hŏs-pĭt′)
hostage hŏs′tĭj, not *hōst-*
hostile hŏs′tĭl (Br. -tĭl)
hovel hŏv′el, or hŭv′l
hover hŭv′er, not *hō-*
humble hŭm′bl, rarely ŭm′bl
humor hū′mor, rarely ū′mor
hundred hŭn′drĕd, not *-derd*
hurricane hûr′i-kān, not *hĕr-*
hysteria hĭs-tēr′ĭ-a, not *-tĕrr*

I

identify ĭ-dĕn′ti-fī, not *ĭden-*
ignominy ĭg′nō-mĭn-y
ignoramus ĭg′nō-rā′mus, not *-răm*
illustrate ĭl′us-trāt, or illŭs′
imbecile ĭm′be-sĭl (Br. -sēl, or -sĭl)
impious ĭm′pĭ-us
implacable im-plā′ka-bl, or -plăk′
impotent ĭm′pō-tent, not *impōt′nt*
improvisation im′prŏv-i-zā′shun, or
   -prō-vī-zā′
inaugurate in-a′gū-rāt, not *-auger*
incidentally in′sĭ-dĕn′tal-ly, not *-dent-ly*
incognito in-kŏg′nĭ-tō, not *-nee′to*
incongruous in-kŏng′grŭ-us
indefatigable in′dē-făt′ĭ-ga-bl
indigenous in-dĭj′e-nus
indomitable in-dŏm′ĭ-ta-bl, not
   -dom-nit-
inebriety in′ē-brī′e-ty
inexplicable in-ĕks′plĭ-ka-bl, not *-plĭk′*
infamous ĭn′fà-mus
infantile ĭn′făn-tĭl, or -tĭl
inflammable in-flăm′a-bl
inherent in-hĕr′ent, not *-hĕrr*
inquiry in-kwīr′y, or ĭn′kwĭ-ry
interesting ĭn′tĕr-est-ing (Br.-trĭs-ting)
inveigle in-vē′gl, or -vā′
irate ī′rāt′, not *ĭr-*
ironical ī-rŏn′i-kal, not *ĭr-*
irradiate ĭ-rā′di-āt

irrelevant ĭr-rĕl′e-vant, not *irrev-*
irremediable ĭr′rē-mē′di-a-bl
irreparable ĭ-rĕp′a-ra-bl
irrevocable ĭ-rĕv′ō-ka-bl
isolate ī′sō-lāt, or ĭs′ō-
itinerary ĭ-tĭn′ēr-er′y, not *-tin-e-ry*

J

jejune jē-jōōn′
jocose jō-kōs′
jocund jŏk′und
juvenile jōō′ve-nĭl (Br. -nĭl)

K

kerosene kĕr′ō-sēn′, not *kăr-a-*
kilometer kĭl′ō-mē′ter, not *kilŏm′*
Ku Klux Klan kū′klŭks′klăn, not *klōō-*

L

lamentable lăm′en-ta-bl, not *lament′*
lasso lăs′ō, not *lă-sōō′*
latent lā′tĕnt, not *lăt-*
Latter-day Saint lăt′er, not *lāte-*
laundered lạn′dĕrd
laundried (colloq.) lạn′drēd
learned (adj.) lûr′ned, not *lernd*
legerdemain lĕj′er-dē-mān′
leisure lē′zhur, or lĕzh′, not *lā-*
lethal lē′thal
lever lĕv′er, or lē′ver
limn lĭm
limner lĭm′ner
limning lĭm′ing, or lĭm′ning
lissome lĭs′um, not *lī-*
literary lĭt′ĕr-er′y, not *lit-re-ry*
literature lĭt′er-a-tūr, or -chụr
longevity lŏn-jĕv′i-ty
long-lived -līvd (Br. -lĭvd)
lowering lou′er-ing, not *lō′er-*
    (glowering)
lugubrious lū-gū′bri-us, not *-gŭb′*

M

macadamized măk-ăd′am-īzd
machinal mȧ-shēn′ăl, or măk′i-năl
machination măk′i-nā′shun, not *mash-*
magneto măg-nē′tō
maintenance mān′te-nans, not
    mān-tān′
malefactor măl′ē-făk′tor, not *māl-*

malevolent ma-lĕv′ō-lent
marcasite măr′ka-sīt, not *-zĭt*
marshmallow mȧrsh′măl′ō, not *—mĕllo*
mausoleum mạ′sō-lē′um, not *mō-*
medieval mē′dĭ-ē′val (Br. mĕd′)
melancholia mel′ăn-kō′lĭ-a, not *-kŏĭ*
melodic mē-lŏd′ik, not *-lōd*
menace mĕn′as, not *men-ance*
mercantile mēr′kăn-tĭl, or -tĭl
mercury mēr′kū-ry, not *murk-ry*
metallurgy mĕt′a-lûr′jy
metamorphosis mĕt′a-môr′fō-sis
    (note accent)
microscopic mī′krō-skŏp′ik, not *-skōp*
mineralogy min′er-ăl′ō-jy, not *-ŏl′*
miniature mĭn′ĭ-a-tūr, or -chụr
minority mĭ-nŏr′i-ty, or mī-
minute mĭ-nūt′, or mī-nūt′ (tiny)
mischievous mĭs′chĭ-vŭs
misnomer mis-nō′mer, not *-nŏm*
modicum mŏd′ĭ-kŭm, not *mōd-*
momentous mō-mĕn′tus, not *-tu-ous*
monetary mŏn′e-ter′y, or mŭn′
mongrel mŭng′grĕl, or mŏng′
monologist mō-nŏl′ō-jĭst, or
    mŏn′ō-lôg′ist
morganatic môr′ga-năt′ik (4 syl.)
moron mō′rŏn (note accent)
mountebank moun′tē-bank (3 syl.)
municipal mū-nĭs′i-pal, not *muni-sip′ul*

N

napery nā′pēr-y, not *năp-*
naphtha năf′tha, or năp′
nomad nō′măd (Br. nŏm′ăd)
nomenclature nō′men-klā′tūr, not *nŏm′*
nuptial nŭp′shal, not *-tĭ-al*

O

oaf ōf, not *ōōf*
obdurate ŏb′dū-rāt
obese ō-bēs′
obesity ō-bēs′i-ty, or ō-bĕs′
obituary ō-bĭt′ū-er′y
obsequies ŏb′sē-kwĭz
occult ŏ-kŭlt′, or ŏk′ult
octogenarian ŏk′tō-je-nâr′i-an
often ôf′n, or ôft′n
ogle ō′gl, not *ŏg′l*
ogre ō′ger, not *ôrg*

oleomargarine ō'lē-ō-mär'jȧ-rēn, or -mär'gȧ-

olfactory ŏl-făk'tō-ry, not ōle-

omen ō'men, not ah-men, but

ominous ŏm'i-nus

omnipotent ŏm-nĭp'ō-tent, not omni-potent, but

omnipresent ŏm'nĭ-prĕz'ent

onerous ŏn'er-us, not ōn-, but

onus ō'nus

onyx ŏn'iks, or ō'niks

orgy ôr'jy, not org'y

overalls ō'ver-ȧlz, not -halls

P

pageant păj'ent, rarely pā'jent

pandemonium păn'dē-mō'ni-um, not -mōm'

panorama păn'ō-rä'ma, or -răm', not -rām'

pantomime păn'tō-mīm, not -mine

papal pā'pal, not păp-l

paradisiacal păr'a-dĭ-sī'a-kăl, not -dizzy-kl

paraffin păr'a-fĭn

paraphernalia păr'a-fēr-nā'li-a

parasitic păr'a-sĭt'ik, not -sīt

parboil pär'boil', not păre-

parliament pär'lĭ-ment, not -li-a-

parochial pa-rō'kĭ-al

pastoral pàs'tōr-al, not pastōr'al

pecuniary pe-kū'ni-er'y

pedagogy pĕd'a-gō'jy

pedantry pĕd'ănt-ry

penalize pē'nal-īz, not pĕnnal-

peninsula pĕn-ĭn'sū-la, not păn-in-sa-la

penury pĕn'ū-ry (note accent)

percolate pēr'kō-lāt, not percū-

perfume (n.) pēr'fūm, rarely pēr-fūm'

peroration pĕr'ō-rā'shun, not prē-

perspiration pēr'spĭ-rā'shun, not prĕs

pessimistic pĕs'ĭ-mĭs'tik, not pesta-

philanthropy fĭ-lăn'thrō-py, not -fy

phosphorus fŏs'fō-rus, not fŏss-for'

pianist pĭ-ăn'ist (Br. pē'a-nĭst)

piteous pĭt'ē-us, not pit-yus

placard plăk'ard

placate plā'kāt, or plăk'āt

placer plăs'er, not plā- (mining)

poem pō'ĕm, not pŏm

poignant poin'yănt, or -ănt

portrait pōr'trāt, or -trit

posthumous pŏs'tū-mus, not pōst-

precedence prē-sēd'ens, but

precedent prĕs'e-dent

predecessor prĕd'ē-sĕs'er (Br. prē')

predicament prē-dĭk'ȧ-ment, not pûr-

prediction prē-dĭk'shun, not pûr-

preferable prĕf'er-a-bl

premature prē'ma-tūr' (Br. prĕm'a-)

premonition prē'mō-nĭsh'un, not prĕm-

prerogative prē-rŏg'a-tiv, not per-og-

presage (v.) prē-sāj'

presage (n.) prĕs'ĭj

prescience prē'shĭ-ĕns, or prĕsh'

prescription prē-skrĭp'shun, not per-

presentation prĕz'en-tā'shun, or prē'

pretty prĭt'y, not pŭrty, nor prĕty

preventive prē-vĕn'tiv, not -ta-tiv

process prŏs'ĕs (Br. prō'sĕs)

prodigal prŏd'i-găl, not proj-i-găl

produce (n.) prŏd'ūs, or prō'dūs

profile prō'fĭl (Br. prō'fēl)

program prō'grăm, not -grŭm

progress (n.) prŏg'rĕs (Br. prō'grĕs)

promulgate prō-mŭl'gāt (Br. prŏm'ŭl-)

pronunciation prō-nŭn'sĭ-ā'shun, not pro-nown-

propaganda prŏp'a-găn'da, not prōp-

puerile pū'er-ĭl (note accent)

pulpit pu̇l'pit, not pŭlp'it

pyramidal pĭ-răm'i-dăl

Q

qualitative kwŏl'i-tā'tĭv, not kwol-i-tive

quantitative kwŏn'ti-tā'tiv, not kwon-ti-tive

R

raillery rāl'er-y, or răl'

rancor răng'kĕr, not ran-ser

rapier rā'pĭ-er, not ră-peer

ration rā'shun, or răsh'un

recluse (n.) rē-klōōs', or rĕk'lōōs

reconnoiter rĕk'ō-noi'ter, or rē'kŏ-

recuperate rē-kū'per-āt, not re-cōōp-

regatta rē-găt'a

renege rē-nēg', not -năg

repast rē-pàst', not ree'past

reputable rĕp'ū-ta-bl (note accent)

research rē-sērch', or rē'

reservoir rĕz'er-vwôr, not -voi

---

oil, out | ūse, ŭp, bûrn, fu̇ll, submit; ü—a muted e | chin; go; jet; park; K—Ger. ch; Fr. n̄—a nasal tone

respite rĕs′pĭt, not *ree′spūte*
revocable rĕv′ō-ka-bl, not *re-vōk′*
rhapsodical răp-sŏd′i-kal, not *raf-sō′*
ribald rĭb′ald, not *rī-bawld*
rigmarole rĭg′ma-rōl, not *riga-*
rinse rĭns, not *rench*
risible rĭz′ĭ-bl, not *rīse-*
robot rō′bŏt, or rŏb′ŏt, not *rō-bōt*
robust rō-bŭst′ (note accent)
roily roil′y, not *rīle-y* ("Rile"
   is colloquial for "roil".)
romance rō-măns′, or rō′măns
rotund rō-tŭnd′ (note accent)

S

saccharine săk′a-rĭn, or -rĭn, or -rēn
sacrifice (n.) săk′ri-fīs, not *-fĭs*
sacrilegious săk′ri-lē′jus, or -lĭj′
salve săv, or säv
sapient sā′pĭ-ent, not *săp-*
satiety sá-tī′ĕ-ty
satirical sá-tĭr′ĭ-kal, not *-tīr*
scenic sē′nik, or sĕn′ik
schism sĭzm, not *skism*
scintillate sĭn′ti-lāt, not *sink-*
scion sī′un
scourge skûrj, not *skōrj*
secondhand -hand, not *-handed*
secretive sē-krē′tiv, or sē′krĭ-tiv
seismograph sīz′mō-graf, not *sīs-a-mo-*
senile sē′nīl, or -nĭl
sepulchral sē-pŭl′krăl
sergeant sär′jent
servile sûr′vĭl (Br. sûr′vīl)
short-lived -līvd (Br. -lĭvd)
significant sĭg-nĭf′i-kănt, not *-gant*
simultaneous sī′mŭl-tā′nē-us, or
   sĭm′ul-
skillet skĭl′et, not *skĕl′*
sobriety sō-brī′e-ty
solace sŏl′as, not *sōl-*
solder sŏd′er (Br. sô′der)
solemnize sŏl′em-nīz (note accent)
solstice sŏl′stis
somersault sŭm′er-sôlt ⎱ (inter-
somerset sŭm′er-sĕt ⎰ changeable)
sonorous sō-nō′rus (Br. sŏn′ō-rus)
soot sŏŏt, or sōōt
sophomore sŏf′o-mōr (3 syl.)
spa spä
spontaneity spŏn′ta-nē′i-ty, not *-nā′*

spurious spū′rĭ-us
squalor skwŏl′or, rarely skwā′lor
stabilize stā′bi-līz, or stăb′
stereotype stĕr′ē-ō-tīp′, or stēr′ē-
stipend stī′pĕnd, not *stĭp-*
strategic stră-tē′jik, or -tĕj′ik
stupendous stū-pĕn′dus, not *-jus*
subsidiary sub-sĭd′ĭ-er′y (5 syl.)
succinct sŭk-sĭnkt′
superb sū-pērb′, not *su-berb*
superfluous sū-pēr′flu̯-us
surprise sûr-prīz′, not *săp-*
surreptitious sûr′ĕp-tĭsh′us, not *sū-*
sword sōrd, not *s′ward*
sycophant sĭk′ō-fant, not *sin-ko-*

T

tapestry tăp′ĕs-try, not *tāpe-*
tassel tăs′el, not *tôss-*
tedious tē′dĭ-us, or tē′jŭs
telegrapher te-lĕg′ra-fer, or tĕl′e-graf′er
telescopic tĕl′e-skŏp′ik, not *-skōpik*
temperament tĕm′pēr-à-ment (4 syl.)
temporal tĕm′pō-ral, not *tempō′ral*
tensile tĕn′sĭl, or -sīl
tepid tĕp′id, not *tee-pid*
terrestrial tĕ-rĕs′trĭ-al, not *te-reschal*
textile tĕks′tĭl, or -tīl
the thû, before a consonant sound, as
   "the temple", "the proceeds"
   thĭ, before a vowel sound, as "the
   end", "the act"
   thē, for emphasis, before either a
   vowel or a consonant sound, as
   "The End", "He is just the man."
theater thē′à-ter, not *the-ā′ter*
thermometer thēr-mŏm′e-ter, not *thŭh-*
tiara tī-âr′à, or tē-ä′rà
toupee tōō-pē′ ⎱ (both used)
toupet (Fr.) tōō-pā′ ⎰
tournament tŏŏr′nà-ment, or tûr′
toward tōrd, or tō′ard
translate trăns-lāt′, not *tran-si-*
trek trĕk, not *treek*
tremendous trē-mĕn′dŭs, not *-jus*
trenchant trĕnch′ănt
trespass trĕs′pàs (note accent)
tribunal trī-bū′nal, or trĭ-
truculent trŭk′ū-lent, or trōō′kū-
tryst trĭst, or trīst
tumultuous tū-mŭl′tū-us, not *-mul-tus*

āle, ădd, câre, ärt, fȧst, ạll, about | ēve, lĕt, fẽrn, moment | īce, ĭll, habit | ōld, ŏdd, nôrth, won | mōōn, fŏŏt |

tune   tūn
turgid   tûr′jid
tyro   tī′rō

U

ultimatum   ŭl′tĭ-mā′tum, not -*măt*
umbrella   ŭm-brĕl′a, not *umber-ella*
usurp   ū-zûrp′
utensil   ū-tĕn′sil, not -*tĭn*

V

vagary   vȧ-gā′ry, or -gȧr′ (Br. vā′gȧ-ry)
vagrant   vā′grant, not *văg′*
vague   vāg, not *văg*
valiant   văl′yant
vapid   văp′id, not *vāp-*
vase   vās (Br. väz)
vehement   vē′e-ment, not *ve-heem′*
vehicle   vē′ĭ-kl, not *ve-hĭk′l*, but
vehicular   vē-hĭk′ū-lar
veldt   vĕlt, not *vĕld*
verbose   vẽr-bōs′, but
verbosity   vẽr-bŏs′i-ty
versatile   vẽr′sȧ-tĭl, or -tīl
veteran   vĕt′ẽr-an, not *vet-run*
viand   vī′ănd, not *vee-*
vicarious   vī-kâr′ĭ-us, or vī-kā′
viceroy   vīs′roy, not *vĭs-e-roy*
victual   vĭt′l

viscid   vĭs′ĭd, not *vis-kid*
viscount   vī′kount′, not *vĭs-*
visor ⎱ vī′zer, or vĭz′er
vizor ⎰
vivacious   vī-vā′shus, or vĭ-

W

waistcoat   wĕs′kŭt, or wāst′kōt′
⎰ wharves   (U.S.) hwôrvz
⎱ wharfs   (Br.) hwôrfs
width   wĭdth, not *with*
wrestle   rĕs′l, not *răssel*

X

Note that x at the beginning of a word has a z sound.
xenial   zē′nĭ-al
xylography   zī-lŏg′ra-fy

Y

⎰ yolk   yōk, or yōlk
⎱ yelk   yĕlk

Z

zealot   zĕl′ut, not *zeel-*
zenith   zē′nith (Br. zĕn′ith)
zodiacal   zō-dī′a-kal
zoological   zō′ō-lŏj′i-kal, not *zōō-*
zoology   zō-ŏl′ō-jy, not *zōō-*

ANIMALS—BIRDS, FISH, ETC.

abalone   ăb′a-lō′nē
aigrette   ā-grĕt′, or ā′grĕt
anchovy   ăn-chō′vy, not -*kōv*
bovine   bō′vīn
canine   kā′nīn (Br. kăn′īn)
capon   kā′pŏn
caterpillar   kăt′er-pĭl′ar, not *catta-*
chameleon   kȧ-mē′lē-on, not *sha-*
chimpanzee   chĭm′păn′zē′, not *shim-*
cicada   sĭ-kā′da, or sĭ-kä′da
cobra   kō′bra, not *kor-*
dinosaur   dī′nō-sôr
elephantine   ĕl′e-făn′tĭn, or -tīn
equine   ē′kwīn

falcon   fą′kn, or fąl′kun
feline   fē′līn
Gila monster   hē′la, not *gee-la*
jaguar   jăg′wär, not *jag-u-ar*
leonine   lē′ō-nīn, or -nĭn
muskrat   mŭsk′răt′, not *mush-*
⎰ orangutan   ō-răng′ōō-tăn′
⎱ orangoutang   ō-răng′ōō-tăng′
plover   plŭv′er
reptile   rĕp′tĭl, not -*tīle*
salmon   săm′un, not *săm-*
serpentine   sẽr′pĕn-tēn, or -tīn
tarantula   ta-răn′tū-la, not -*ulȧr*

ARCHITECTURE

acoustics   a-kōōs′tĭks, or a-kous′
architect   är′kĭ-tĕkt
balcony   băl′kō-ny, not *bawl-*

bas-relief   bä′rē-lēf′
Byzantine   bĭ-zăn′tĭn, or bĭz′ăn-tĭn
clapboard   klăp′bōrd, or klăb′erd

oil, out | ūse, ŭp, bûrn, fųll, submit; ü—a muted e | chin; go; jet; park; K—Ger. ch; Fr. ṅ—a nasal tone

coping kōp'ing, not kŏp'
cupola kū'pō-la, not -lō
Della Robbia dĕl'lä rōb'byä (It.)
façade fà-säd', or fà-
figurine fĭg'ū-rēn'
foyer fwä'yā', or foi'er
gargoyle gär'goil
Gothic gŏth'ik, not gō-
Ionic ī-ŏn'ik, not -ōn
loge lōzh
loggia lŏj'à (It. lôd'jä)
metope mĕt'ō-pē
mezzanine mĕz'a-nēn, or -nĭn

Moorish mŏŏr'ish, or mōr'
pediment pĕd'ĭ-ment
pergola pĕr'gō-la, not pergōh'la
piazza pĭ-ăz'a, not pĭ- (It. pyät'sä)
porte-cochere pôrt'kō'shâr'
promenade prŏm'e-näd', or -näd'
proscenium prō-sē'nĭ-um, not -sĕn
roof rōōf, not ruf
rotunda rō-tŭn'da
terrazzo tĕr-rät'sō (flooring)
Tuscan tŭs'kăn
veranda ve-răn'da, not -rähn
wainscot wăn'skŭt, not -kōt

ARTISTS

Bellini (It.) bĕl-lē'nē
Bonheur, Rosa (Fr.) bō'nûr'
Botticelli (It.) bŏt'tē-chĕl'lē
Cellini, Benvenuto (It.) chĕl-lē'nē, bĕn'vä-nōō'tō
Corot (Fr.) kō'rō'
Correggio (It.) kōr-rĕd'jō
da Vinci, Leonardo (It.) dä vēn'chē, lā'ō-när'dō
Degas (Fr.) dĕ-gä'
Dürer, Albrecht (Ger.) dü'rēr, äl'brĕKt
El Greco (Gk.) ĕl grā'kō (Sp., The Greek)
Gainsborough (Eng.) gānz'bŭ-rŭ, or -brō
Goya (Sp.) gō'yä
Hals, Frans (Du.) häls, fräns

Holbein, Hans (Ger.) hōl'bĭn, häns
Michelangelo (It.) mĭ'kĕl-än'jĕ-lō (It. mē'kĕl-än'jä-lō)
Millais (Eng.) mĭ-lā'
Millet (Fr.) mē'lĕ', or mĭ-lā'
Monet (Fr.) mō'nĕ'
Murillo (Sp.) mū-rĭl'ō (Sp. mōō-rēl'yō)
{ Raphael răf'ā-ĕl, or rä'fā-ĕl
{ Raffaello (It.) räf'fä-ĕl'lō
Rembrandt (Du.) rĕm'bränt
Renoir (Fr.) rē-nwár'
Rodin (Fr.) rō'dăn'
Titian (It.) tĭsh'an
Velásquez (Sp.) vā-läs'kāth
Watteau (Fr.) và'tō', or wä'tō'
Zuloaga (Sp.) thōō'lō-ä'gä

BRITISH

again a-gān'
ate ĕt (in England, and especially Ireland)
Asquith ăs'kwĭth
Avon (Stratford on) ā'von
Axminster ăks'mĭn-ster, not -minister
been bēn
Berkeley bärk'ly
Berkshire bärk'shĭr
bomb bŭm
Buckingham bŭk'ing-am, not -ham
Bulwer-Lytton bul'wēr-lĭt'un, not -līt
Cheltenham chĕlt'nam
Chisholm chĭz'ŭm
Cholmondeley chŭm'ly
cinema sĭn'e-ma, not kĭn-

clerk klärk
Covent Garden kŏv'ent, or kŭv', not kō'
Derby där'by
Edinburgh ĕd'in-bŭ-rŭ
either, and neither ī-ther, and nī-ther
epoch ē'pŏk
Eton ē'tn, not e-tän'
evolution ē'vō-lū'shun
Gladstone glăd'stŭn
Glasgow glás'gō, or -kō
Gloucestershire glŏs'tēr-shĭr, or glôs'
Leicester lĕs'tēr
lieutenant lĕf-tĕn'ănt (naut. lĕ-tĕ'nánt)
Michaelmas mĭk'ĕl-más, not mīke-
Midwick mĭd'ik, not -wick

āle, ădd, câre, ärt, fàst, ạll, about | ēve, lĕt, fērn, moment | īce, ĭll, habit | ōld, ŏdd, nôrth, won | mōōn, fŏŏt |

Pall Mall pĕl'mĕl', or păl'măl'
patent pā'tĕnt
petrol pĕt'rŏl (gasoline)
plaid plād (Scotch)
quieten dialectal English
Reading rĕd'ing
Salisbury sạlz'bur-y
schedule shĕd'ūl
scone skōn (Scotch), or skŏn
Sealyham sē'lĭ-ăm, or -hăm
Shrewsbury shrōz'bûr-y

Shropshire shrŏp'shĭr
Southampton south-ămp'tŭn
St. George sĕnt jôrj', or sĭn'jôrj'
St. John sĭn'jen
Taliaferro tŏl'i-ver
Thames tĕmz
Trafalgar trȧ-făl'gẽr
Warwick wŏr'ik, not -wick
Westminster Abbey wĕst'mĭn'ster, not -minister
Yorkshire yôrk'shĭr

When speaking of England, Great Britain, etc., note the following distinctions:
England is the southern division of the island of Great Britain.
Great Britain is the island of England, Scotland, and Wales.
United Kingdom is Great Britain and Northern Ireland.
British Empire is the United Kingdom and its colonies and dependencies.
Commonwealth of Nations is now an association of eight nations: United Kingdom, Canada, Australia, New Zealand, South Africa, India, Pakistan, and Ceylon.

CHRISTIAN NAMES—MEN

Abraham ā'bra-hăm (note accent)
Adolph ȧ-dŏlf', or ăd'ŏlf
Anthony ăn'tō-ny, or ăn'thō-
Aubrey ạ'brĭ (fem. Audrey)
Basil băz'ĭl, or bā'zĭl
Bernard bẽrn'ard (note accent)
Cecil sĕs'ĭl, or sē'sil
Clive klīv
Cyril sĭr'ĭl
Eli ē'lī
Elihu ē-lī'hū, or ĕl'ĭ-hū
{Emil ē'mĭl, or ā'mĭl
{Émile (Fr.) ā'mēl'
Eric ĕr'ik
Ernst ĕrnst, not ûrnst
Evan ĕv'ăn
Evelyn ēv'lĭn (fem. ĕv'ĕ-lĭn)
Francis frăn'sĭs (fem. Frances)
Giles jīlz, rarely gĭlz
Gouverneur gōō'vẽr-nẽr' (Fr.)
Grosvenor grōv'nẽr (Br.)
Gustavus gŭs-tā'vŭs, or -tä'

Hans häns, not hăns (Ger., John)
Henri än'rē' (Fr.)
Hilary hĭl'ȧ-ry
Isaac ī'zák (ē'zäk', foreign)
Ivan ī'van (ē-vän'; Rus., John)
Jacques zhák (Fr., James or Jacob)
Juan hwän (Sp., John)
Laurence } lạ'rĕns
Lawrence }
Leslie lĕz'lĭ, or lĕs'lĭ
Louis lōō'ĭs (Fr. lōō'ē')
Maurice mạ'rĭs (Fr. mō'rēs')
Miguel mē-gĕl' (Sp., Michael)
Nigel nī'jĕl
Pedro pā'drō (Sp., Peter)
Philippe fē'lēp' (Fr.)
Pierre pyâr (Fr., Peter)
Ralph rălf (Br. rāf)
Simon sī'mon (Fr. sē'môn')
Ulysses ū-lĭs'ēz
Wilhelm vĭl'hĕlm (Ger., William)

CHRISTIAN NAMES—WOMEN

Adela ăd'e-la (note accent)
Agatha ăg'a-tha (note accent)
{Alicia (It.) ä-lē'chä
{Alícia (Sp.) ä-lē'thē-ä
Antoinette ăn'tŏ-nĕt' (Fr. än'twȧ'nĕt')
Athalie ăt'ȧ-lē (Fr. ȧ'tȧ'lē')

Audrey ạ'drĭ (mas. Aubrey)
Beatrice bē'a-trĭs (note accent)
Bernice bûr'nis, or bûr-nēs'
Caroline kăr'ō-lĭn, or -lĭn
{Cécile (Fr.) sä'sēl'
{Cecily sĕs'i-ly

oil, out | ūse, ụ̄p, bûrn, fụll, submit; ü—a muted e | chin; go; jet; park; K—Ger ch; Fr ṅ—a nasal tone

157

Charlotte shär′lŏt (Fr. shår′lôt′)
{ Clarice klăr′ĭs
{ Clarisse (Fr.) klá′rēs′
Corinne kō′rĭn′, or -rēn′
Deborah dĕb′ō-ra
{ Diana dĭ-ăn′a
{ Diane (Fr.) dē′än′
Dolores dō-lō′rĕs
Enid ē′nĭd
Evangeline ē-văn′je-lēn, -lĭn, or -lĭn
Evelyn ĕv′ĕ-lĭn (mas. ēv′lĭn)
Frances frán′sĕz (mas. Francis)
Greta grĕt′a, or grē′ta (Ger. grä′tä)
Helena hĕl′e-ná
Honora hō-nō′ra
Janet jăn′ĕt, or ja-nĕt′
Jeanne zhán (Fr.)
Joan jōn
Margot mär′gō, or mär′gŏt

Maria mä-rē′a, or má-rī′a
Olivia ō-lĭv′ĭ-a
Pamela păm′ĕ-la, or pá-mē′la
Paulina pạ-lĭ′na (Sp. pou-lē′nä)
Penelope pe-nĕl′ō-pē (note syl.)
Philippa fĭ-lĭp′a (note accent)
Rosalie rŏz′á-lē, or rōz′
Rosalind rŏz′á-lĭnd
Rosamond rŏz′á-mŭnd
Rowena rō-ē′na
Sarah sâr′a, or sā′ (Fr. sá′rä′)
Sheila shē′la
Stéphanie stā′fá′nē′ (Fr.)
{ Theresa tĕ-rē′sa
{ Teresa (Sp.) tā-rä′sä
Ursula ûr′sū-la
Vivienne vē′vē-ĕn′ (Fr.)
Wilhelmina vĭl′hĕl-mē′nä
Zoe zō′ē

COMPOSERS

Bach (Ger.) bäK
Beethoven (Prus.) bā′tō-vĕn (note accent)
Berlioz (Fr.) bĕr′lē-ōs′
Brahms (Ger.) bräms
Chopin (Pol-Fr.) shō′păn′
Dvořák (Boh.) dvôr′zhäk
Gabrilowitsch (Rus.) gá′brĭ-lŭv′ĭch (note accent)
Handel (Ger.) hăn′dl (Ger. hĕn′dĕl)
Lehár (Hung.) lĕ′här
Liszt (Hung.) lĭst
Mendelssohn (Ger.) mĕn′dĕl-sōn, not -sŭn

Mozart (Aus.) mō′tsärt
Offenbach (Jewish-French) ŏf′ĕn-bäK (Fr. ô′fáṅ′bák′)
Paderewski (Pol.) pá′dĕ-rĕf′skē
Rachmaninov } (Rus.) räK-mä′nē-nôf
Rachmaninof } (note accent)
Respighi (It.) rĕs-pē′gē
Schubert (Aus.) shoo′bĕrt
Schumann (Ger.) shoo′män
Tchaikovsky }
Tschaikovsky }
Tschaikowsky } (Rus.) chī-kôf′skē
Chaykovski }
Weber (Ger.) vā′bĕr

(For other composers, see Operas, below.)

EAST INDIAN

amah ä′ma (a servant)
Benares bĕ-nä′rĕz
Brahma brä′ma
Buddha bụd′a, not boo-da
copra kŏp′ra, not kōp-
Delhi dĕl′ē, not -hĭ
gymkhana jĭm-kä′na (athletic meet)
Himalaya hĭ-mä′lá-yá (note accent)
{ ketchup kĕch′up
{ catchup kăch′up
{ catsup kăt′sup

khaki kä′kĭ, not kăk-
maharaja má-hä′rä′já (a ruler)
maharani má-hä′rä′nē (a queen)
mahatma má-hät′má (Eng. -hăt′) (a great soul)
sahib sä′ĭb (Sir or Mr.)
Taj Mahal täj má-häl′
yogi yō′gē, not yo-jē

āle, ădd, câre, ärt, fást, ạll, about | ēve, lĕt, fērn, moment | īce, ĭll, habit | ōld, ŏdd, nôrth, won | moon, foot |

158

EGYPTIAN AND ARABIC

Aladdin ȧ-lăd'ĭn
Ali Baba ä'lē bä'bä, not *ȧ-lī*
Allah ăl'a (Ar. ȧl-lä')
Arab ăr'ab, not *ȧ'rab*
Bedouin bĕd'u̯-ĭn, or -ēn
burnoose bûr-nōōs'
Cairo kī'rō, not *kā*
caliph kā'lĭf, or kăl'ĭf
{caravansary kăr'ȧ-ⁿĭn'sȧ-ry
{caravanserai kăr' văn'sĕ-rī
Cheops kē'ŏps
dromedary drŏm'e-der'y (Br.
        drŭm'e-dûr-y)
Fatima făt'ĭ-ma, or fä'tē-mä (note
        accent)

harem hä'rĕm, or hâr'ĕm
houri hōō'rĭ, or hou'rĭ
khedive kĕ-dēv'
minaret mĭn'a-rĕt'
{Mohammed mō-hăm'ĕd
{Mahomet mȧ-hŏm'ĕt (Br. mä'ŏm-ĕt)
muezzin mū-ĕz'ĭn
Port Said sä-ēd', or säd, not *sĕd*
{Rameses răm'ē-sēz
{Ramses răm'sēz
Sahara sȧ-hä'rȧ, or -hâr'
salaam sȧ-läm', not *-lăm*
Scheherazade shĕ-hä'rȧ-zä'dĕ
sheik shēk, or shāk

FRENCH

Note that in French pronunciation the main accent is usually at the end of the word. Some speakers, however, stress the syllables evenly.

(See note on Foreign Pronunciations, p. 147.)

aide-de-camp ād'dĕ-kȧṅ'
à la mode ȧ'lȧ-mōd'
amateur ăm'ȧ-tûr' (Eng. ăm'ȧ-tūr)
apéritif ȧ'pä'rē'tēf' (Eng. ȧ-pĕ'rĭ-tēf)
aplomb ȧ'plŏṅ'
artiste ȧr'tēst' (mas. or fem.)
atelier ȧ'tē-lyā'
attaché ȧ'tȧ'shä'
au gratin ō' grȧ-tăṅ'
au naturel ō' nȧ'tü'rĕl'
au revoir ō' rĕ-vwär', not *rĕ-voi*
Autre temps,   ō'tr täṅ',
    autres mœurs. ō'tr mûrs' (Other
                times, other manners.)
ballet bă-lā' (sometimes in Eng. băl'ĕt)
baton bȧ'tŏṅ' (Eng. băt'un)
beau monde bō' mŏṅd'
belles-lettres bĕl'lĕt'r
bête noire bât' nwȧr' (Eng. bāt' nwär')
bon ami bŏṅ'nȧ'mē' (good friend)
bon mot bŏṅ' mō' (pl. bons mots—
        bŏṅ' mōz')
bon vivant bŏṅ' vē'väṅ'
bon voyage bŏṅ' vwȧ'yȧzh'
bouquet bōō-kā'
bourgeois bōŏr-zhwȧ'
boutonnière bōō'tŏ-nyȧr'

Braille brä'l̇ (Eng. brāl) (printing
        system for the blind)
buffet bu̯-fā' (Br. bŭf'ĭt)
cabaret kăb'ȧ-rā'
camaraderie kȧ'mȧ-rä'dĕ-rē
Camembert kȧ'mäṅ'bâr'
canaille kȧ'nä'ĭ (Eng. kȧ-nāl')
carte blanche kȧrt' bläṅsh'
cause célèbre kōz' sä'lĕb'r (celebrated
            case, not *cause* [law])
chaise longue shȧz' lŏṅg' (Eng. shāz)
chargé d'affaires shȧr'zhä' dȧ'fâr'
charivari shä'rē-vä'rē (Am. shĭv'ȧ-rē)
cherchez la femme shĕr'shä' lȧ fȧm'
                (Find the woman.)
chic shēk
clientele klē'äṅ-tĕl' (Eng. klī'ĕn-tĕl')
cloisonné klwȧ'zŏ'nä' (Eng. kloi'zŏ-nā')
Coeur de Lion kûr' dĕ lē'ŏṅ'
communiqué kŏ-mū'nĭ-kā'
compagnie kŏṅ'pȧn-yē' (abbr. Cie)
comte kŏṅt (a count)
comtesse kŏṅ'tĕs' (a countess)
concierge kŏṅ'syĕrzh' (mas. or fem.)
confrère kŏṅ'frâr'
congé kŏṅ'zhä'
connoisseur kŏn'ĭ-sûr'

oil, out | ūse, ŭp, bûrn, fu̯ll, submit; ü—a muted e | chin; go; jet; park; K—Ger. ch; Fr. ṅ—a nasal tone

contretemps kôṅ′tr-täṅ′
cortège kôr′tĕzh′
coterie kō′t-rē′
coup d'état kōō′ dä′tá′
coup de grâce kōō′ dē gräs′
coupon kōō′pŏn, not *kū*
crème de la crème krâm′ dlȧ krâm′
Croix de guerre krwȧ′ dē gâr′, not
　　　　　　　kroy
cuisine kwē-zēn′
danseuse däṅ′sûz′
debacle dā′bä′klē (Eng. dē-bä′kl, or
　　　　-bǎk′)
debris dā′brē′
debut dā-bü′ (Eng. dĕ-bū′)
débutante dā′bü′täṅt′ (Eng.
　　　　　dĕb′ū-tänt′)
déclassé (mas.) ⎱ dā′klȧ′sā′
déclassée (fem.) ⎰
de luxe dē lüks′ (Eng. dē lŭks′)
dénouement dā-nōō′mäṅ
dernier ressort dĕr′nyä′ rē-sôr′
dernier cri dĕr′nyä′ krē′ (last word)
de trop dē trō′
diablerie dē′ä′blē-rē′
distingué dĭs′täṅ′gā′
⎰divorcé (mas.) ⎱ dĭ′vōr′sā′
⎱divorcée (fem.) ⎰
⎰divorcee (Eng.) dĭ-vōr′sē′ (any
　　　　　　divorced person)
⎰double entente dōō′bl äṅ′täṅt′
⎱double-entendre dōō′bl-äṅ′täṅ′dr
éclaircissement ā′klâr′sēs′mäṅ′
éclat ā-klä′
élan ā′läṅ′
elite ā-lēt′, not *ē-lēt*
en banc äṅ bäṅ′ (in full authority)
encore äṅ-kōr′, not *ĕn-*
enfant terrible äṅ′fäṅ′ tĕ′rē′bl
en masse äṅ mȧs′, not *ĕn masee*
ennui äṅ′nwē′ (weariness)
en passant äṅ pä′säṅ′
en route äṅ rōō′, not *ĕn rout*
ensemble äṅ′säṅ′bl
entente cordiale äṅ′täṅt′ kôr′dyȧl′
entourage äṅ′tōō′räzh′
entr'acte äṅ′träkt′
entrée äṅ′trä′
entre nous äṅ′tr nōō′ (between us)
esprit de corps ĕs-prē′ dē kôr′

etiquette ĕt′ǐ-kĕt, not *-kwĕt*
exposé ĕks′pō-zā′
fait accompli fĕ′tȧ′kôṅ′plē′
　　　　　(accomplished deed)
fiancé (mas.) ⎱ fē′äṅ′sā′
fiancée (fem.) ⎰
filet mignon fē′lĕ′ mē′nyôṅ′
fleur-de-lis flûr′dĕ-lēs′, or -lē′, not *flūr*
force majeure fôrs′ mȧ′zhûr′ (major
　　　　　　force, or act of God)
frère frâr (brother)
garage gȧ-räzh′ (Br. gắr′ǐj)
genre zhäṅ′r
grand prix gräṅ′ prē′
Gruyère grü′yâr′
habitué ȧ′bē′tü-ā′ (Eng. hȧ-bǐt′ū-ā)
hauteur hō-tûr′, not *haw-tūr*
hors de combat ôr′ dē kôṅ′bȧ′ (out of
　　　　　　　the combat)
hors d'oeuvre ôr′ dû′vr (an extra)
impasse äṅ′päs′ (Eng. ǐm-pȧs′)
ingénue äṅ′zhā′nü′
insouciance äṅ′sōō′syäṅs′
je ne sais quoi zhē-nē-sä-kwä′ (I know
　　　　　　　not what.)
julienne zhül-yĕn′
laissez faire lĕ′sā′ fâr′ (let do, that is,
　　　　　　noninterference)
légionnaire lä′zhon′nâr′ (Eng.
　　　　　　lē′jŭn-âr′)
l'envoi läṅ′vwȧ′
Le roi est mort, lē rwȧ′ ĕ môr′,
vive le roi! 　vēv′ lē rwȧ′ (The
　　　　　　king is dead, long
　　　　　　live the king!)
⎰lèse-majesté lĕz′mȧ′zhĕs′tā′ (treason)
⎱lese majesty (Eng.) lēz mȧj′ĕs-ty
liaison lē′ä′zôṅ′ (Br. lǐ-ā′zn)
lingerie läṅ′zhĕ-rē′, or läṅ′
lorgnette lôr′nyĕt′, not *lorg-*
madame mȧ′dȧm′ (Eng. mǎd′ǎm)
mademoiselle mȧd′mwȧ′zĕl′ (colloq.
　　　　　　mȧm′zĕl′)
maître d'hôtel mȧ′tr dō′tĕl′
Mardi Gras mär′dē grä′
⎰marquis (mas.) mȧr-kē′ (Eng.
⎱　　　　　　mär′kwǐs)
⎰marquise (fem.) mȧr-kēz′
Marseillaise mȧr′sĕ′yȧz′ (Eng.
　　　　　　mär′sĕ-läz′)
mauve mōv, not *mawv*

ȧle, ȧdd, cȧre, ärt, fȧst, ạll, about | ēve, lĕt, fẽrn, moment | īce, ĭll, habit | ōld, ŏdd, nôrth, won | mōōn, fŏŏt |

mayonnaise mà'yô'nâz' (Eng.
  mā'ŏ-nāz')
mélange mā'länzh'
mêlée mâ'lā' (Eng. mā'lā)
memoir mĕm'wär, rarely mēm'wär
ménage mā'nàzh'
menu mĕ-nü' (Eng. mĕn'ū)
mésalliance mā'zà'lē'äńs'
mesdames mā'dàm'
messieurs mā'syų' (Eng. mĕs'ērs)
milieu mē'lyû'
mirage mē-räzh'
mise en scène mē'zäń sân' (stage
  setting)
monsieur mĕ-syų'
moyen âge mwà'yĕ'näzh' (Middle
  Ages)
naïveté nä-ēv'tā'
née nā, not nee
n'est-ce pas? nĕs-pä' (Isn't it true?)
noblesse oblige nō'blĕs' ō'blēzh'
  (nobility is obliged to
  be noble)
nom de plume nôń' dē plüm' (Eng.
  nŏm'dē plōōm')
nonpareil nŏn'pà-rĕl'
nouveau riche nōō'vō' rēsh' (newly
  rich)
nuance nü'äńs'
objet d'art ôb'zhĕ' dàr'
outré ōō'trā'
papier-mâché pà'pyā'mä'shā' (Eng.
  pā'per-ma-shā')
pari-mutuel pà'rē'mü'twĕl' (Eng.
  păr'ĭ-mü'tū-ĕl, not Paris
  mu-chel) (mutual wager; a
  betting machine)
patois pà'twà'
penchant päń'shäń' (Eng. pĕn'chant)
pièce de résistance pyĕs' dē rā'zēs'täńs'
pierrot pyĕ'rō'
pierrette pyĕ'rĕt'
pince-nez păńs'nā'
piquant pē'kănt, not peek-went
plaque plàk, not plāke
poilu pwà'lü' (French soldier)
portière pôr'tyâr', not -teer
poseur pō-zûr'
potpourri pō'pōō'rē'
praline prä'lēn

première prē-myâr'
prestige prĕs-tēzh' (Eng. prĕs'tĭj)
qui vive kē vēv', not kwee
raison d'être rā'zôń' dâ'tr (reason for
  existence)
régime rā-zhēm'
rendezvous räń'dä-vōō' (Eng. rän'dĕ-)
{ repartee (Eng.) rĕp'ēr-tē', not -tā
{ repartie (Fr.) rē-pàr-tē'
répertoire rā'pĕr'twàr' (Eng.
  rĕp'ēr-twär)
restaurant rĕs-tō-räń' (Am.
  rĕs'tō-rant, not rest-urnt)
résumé rā'zü'mā'
reveille rā-vĕ'ĭ (Am. rĕv'ĕ-lē')
  (Br. rĭ-vĕ'lĭ)
risqué rēs'kā'
Roquefort rōk'fôr' (Eng. rōk'fērt)
rôtisserie rō'tēs'se-rē'
rouge et noir rōōzh' ā nwâr' (red and
  black)
sabotage sà'bō'täzh' (Eng. sà'bō-tĭj)
sang-froid säń'frwà' (coolheadedness)
sans gêne säń' zhân' (without
  embarrassment)
sans souci säń' sōō'sē' (without care)
savant sà'väń'
savoir-faire sà'vwàr-fâr' (tact; poise)
séance sā'äńs'
s'il vous plaît sēl' vōō plĕ' (if you please)
soirée swà'rā'
solitaire sŏl'ĭ-târ', not -tar-ee
sobriquet sō'brē'kā' (a nickname)
soupçon sōōp'sôń'
suave swäv (Br. swāv)
surveillance sür'vĕ-yäńs' (Eng.
  sûr-vāl'yăns)
table d'hôte tà'bl dōt'
thé dansant tā' däń'säń'
timbale tăń'bàl' (Eng. tĭm'băl)
tout ensemble tōō'täń'säń'bl
valet văl'ā (Br. vă'lĭt)
vaudeville vōd'vēl' (Eng. vōd'vĭl)
vers libre vâr' lē'br (free verse)
vignette vēn-yĕt' (Eng. vĭn-yĕt')
vis-à-vis vē'zà-vē'
{ vive vēv
{ viva (It.) vē'vä
voilà vwà'là' (look, or there it is)
wagon-lit và'gôń'lē'

oil, out | ūse, ŭp, bûrn, fųll, submit; ü—a muted e | chin; go; jet; park; K—Ger. ch; Fr. ń—a nasal tone

161

FRENCH CITIES, PLACES OF INTEREST, ETC.

Arc de Triomphe àrk' dĕ trē'ônf'
Bastille bȧs-tēl' (Fr. bȧs'tē'y)
Biarritz bē-ȧ'rēts'
⎰Bretagne brĕ-tȧn'yĕ
⎱Brittany (Eng.) brĭt'ȧ-ny
Cannes kȧn
Champs Élysées shäṅ'zä'lē'zä'
     (Elysian Fields)
Château-Thierry shä'tô' tyĕ'rē'
Cherbourg shĕr'bŏŏr'
Eiffel Tower ĕ'fĕl' (Eng. ī'fl)
Fontainebleau fôṅ'tän'blō'
Île de France ēl' dĕ fräṅs'
⎰Le Havre lĕ ȧ'vr
⎱Havre (Eng.) hä'vĕr, not harv
Lille lēl
Limoges lē'mōzh'
Lourdes, Our Lady of lŏŏrd

Louvre lŏŏ'vr, not louve
⎰Lyon lē'ôṅ'
⎱Lyons (Eng.) lī'unz
⎰Marseille mȧr'sĕ'ĭ
⎱Marseilles (Eng.) mär-sālz'
⎰Menton mäṅ'tôṅ'
⎱Mentone (It.) mĕn-tō'nä
Neufchâtel nû'shä'tĕl'
Notre Dame nô'tr dȧm'
Pyrenees pē'rä'nä' (Eng. pĭr'e-nēz)
Reims rȧṅs (Eng. rēmz)
Rue de la Paix rü' dĕ lȧ pĕ' (Street of
     Peace)
Saint-Cyr săṅ'sēr'
Saint-Mihiel săṅ'mē'yĕl'
Versailles vĕr'sä'ĭ (Eng. vĕr-sālz')
Vosges vōzh
Ypres ē'pr (in Belgium)

GEOGRAPHIC NAMES—FOREIGN

Adriatic ā'drĭ-ăt'ĭk, or ăd'
Azores ȧ-zōrz' (note accent)
⎰Bagdad băg'dăd
⎱Baghdad bȧg-däd'
Bahamas bȧ-hä'maz (Br. -häm')
Banff bămf
Barbados bär-bā'dōz, not -băd'us
Barranquilla bär'än-kēl'yä, not -kwilla
Bering Strait bēr'ing, or bâr'
Bethlehem bĕth'lē-ĕm, not -hăm
Borneo bôr'nē-ō, not barn-
Bosporus bŏs'pō-rŭs (note accent)
Capri kä'prē
Caribbean kăr'ĭ-bē'an, or kȧ-rĭb'
⎰Carlsbad kärlz'băd
⎱Karlsbad kärls'bät
Caspian kăs'pĭ-ăn, not kăsa-
Colón kō-lōn', not -lŏn
Costa Rica kŏs'ta rē'ka
Crimea krī-mē'a, or krĭ-
Edam ē'dăm, or ā'däm'
Etna (L. Aetna) ĕt'nȧ, not eet-
European ū'rō-pē'an, not -peen
Gatun gä-tŏŏn'
Gobi gō'bē
⎰Gotham (England) gŏt'am
⎱Gotham (N.Y.C.) gō'thăm, or gŏth'am
Haiti hä'tĭ, not -tī

Iraq⎫
Irak⎬ ē'räk
Java jä'va, not jăv-a
Levant lē-vănt' (note accent)
Lima lē'mä
Mediterranean mĕd'ĭ-tĕ-rā'nē-an, not
     -trăn-yan
Newfoundland nū'fŭnd-lănd', or
     nū'found-lănd'
Nicaragua nĭk'ȧ-rä'gwȧ (Br. -răg'ū-ȧ)
Pago Pago ⎱ päng'ō päng'ō
Pangopango⎰
Palestine păl'ĕs-tīn, not -teen
⎰Papeete pä'pä-ā'tä (4 syl.)
⎱Papéiti pä'pä-ē'tē
Peiping bā'pĭng' (formerly Peking)
⎰Prague (Eng.) präg
⎱Praha (Czech) prä'hȧ
⎰Prag (Ger.) präK
Puerto Rico pwĕr'tō rē'kō
Rhodesia rō-dē'zhĭ-a, not -dĕss
Rio de Janeiro rē'ō dä zhȧ-nä'rō
     (Pg., River of January)
Saint Helena sänt hĕ-lē'na, not hĕl'ena
     (Napoleon's last exile)
Santiago sän'tē-ä'gō, not sănte-ā'
Santo Domingo sän'tō dō-mĭng'gō, or
     sän'tō, not -tȧ
Stromboli strōm'bō-lē (note accent)

āle, ădd, câre, ärt, fȧst, ạll, about | ēve, lĕt, fērn, moment | ice, ĭll, habit | ōld, ŏdd, nôrth, won | mŏŏn, fŏŏt |

GERMAN AND HUNGARIAN

Tahiti tä-hē′tē, not *ta-hāy′te*
Tibet tĭ-bĕt′, or tĭb′ĕt
Transvaal trăns-väl′, not *-văl*, nor *-vāl*

Valparaiso văl′på-rī′sō (Sp.
        văl′pä-rä-ē′sō)
Venezuela vĕn′e-zwē′la

GEOGRAPHIC NAMES—UNITED STATES

Abilene, Tex. ăb′i-lēn
Adirondacks ăd′ĭ-rŏn′dăks, not
    adrē-on-
Albuquerque, N. Mex. ăl′bū-kúr′kē
Arkansas är′kăn-saw (official)
Baton Rouge băt′ŭn rōōzh′
Boise, Idaho boi′zē
Cincinnati sĭn′sĭ-nă′tĭ
Colorado kŏl′ō-rä′dō, or -răd′ō
Concord, Mass. kŏng′kērd
Des Moines dē moin′, not *moins*
{Greenwich, Conn. grēn′wich, or
      grĭn′ich, or grēn′
{Greenwich Village, N.Y.C. grĕn′ich
{Greenwich, England grĭn′ĭj
Haverhill, Mass. hā′vēr-ĭl
Helena, Mont. hĕl′e-na, not *he-lēn′a*
Hoboken, N.J. hō′bō-kĕn (note accent)
Illinois ĭl′ĭ-noi′, or -noiz′
Laredo, Tex. lå-rā′dō
Los Angeles lôs ăn′jĕl-ĕs (Sp.
    lōs äng′hä-lās)
Louisiana lōō-ē′zē-ăn′a, not *looz-*
Miami mī-ăm′ĭ, not *mē-äm′ē*
Missouri mĭ-sōō′rĭ, not *mi-zur-ree*
Mobile mō-bēl′, not *mō′bĭl*
Mojave Desert mō-hä′vä

Nevada nĕ-văd′a, or nĕ-vä′då
New Orleans ôr′lē-ănz (note accent)
Niagara nī-ăg′å-rá, not *-ag-ra*
Palo Alto, Calif. păl′ō ăl′tō, or
    pä′lō ăl′tō
Passaic, N.J. pă-sā′ĭk
Peekskill, N.Y. pēks′kĭl, not *pigs-*
Pierre, S.Dak. pēr
Poughkeepsie, N.Y. pō-kĭp′sĭ
Puget Sound pū′jĕt, not *pug-*
Quincy, Mass. kwĭn′zĭ, not *kwins′ē*
Reading, Pa. rĕd′ĭng, not *read-*
Rio Grande rē′ō grän′dä
San Diego săn dē-ā′gō
San Jose, Calif. săn hō-sā′
Santa Fe săn′ta fā, not *-fee*
Sault Sainte Marie sōō′ sänt må-rē′
    (Fr. sō′săṅt′må′rē′)
Shreveport shrĕv′pōrt, not *shrĕv′*
Spokane spō-kăn′, not *-kain*
St. Louis lōō′ĭs, or lōō′i
Terre Haute tĕr′ē hōt′
Tucson, Ariz. tōō-sŏn′
Waco, Tex. wā′kō
Willamette wĭ-lăm′ĕt
Worcester, Mass. wųs′ter
Yosemite, Calif. yō-sĕm′ĭ-tē

GERMAN AND HUNGARIAN

Note that in the pronunciation of the German combinations ie and ei, a long sound is given to whichever letter stands last:

ie is pronounced ē
ei is I

auf Wiedersehen ouf′ vē′dēr-zā′ĕn
Baden-Baden bä′dĕn-bä′dĕn, not
    bäden-
Bremen brä′mĕn (Eng. brĕm′en)
Budapest bų′då-pĕst′, or bōō′
dachshund däKs′hųnt′, not *dash-hound*
Deutschland doich′länt′
edelweiss ā′dĕl-vīs, not *ĕd-*
frankfurter frănk′fŭr-ter not *-fritter*
Frau frou
Fräulein froi′līn, not *frou-*

{Hungary hŭng′gå-ry (note accent)
{Ungarn (Ger.) ųn′gärn
Ich dien ĭK dēn′ ("I serve"—motto of
    the Prince of Wales)
kindergarten kĭn′dēr-gär′ten, not *-garden*
meerschaum mēr′shŭm, not *mŭr-*
{Munich mū′nĭk
{München (Ger.) mün′Kĕn
Nazi nä′tzĭ (Nationalsozialistische
    Deutsche Arbeiterpartei—German
    National Socialist Labor Party)

---

oil, out | ūse, ŭp, bŭrn, fųll, submit; ü—a muted e | chin; go; jet; park; K—Ger. ch; Fr. ṅ—a nasal tone

163

PRONUNCIATION

Oberammergau ō'bĕr-äm'ĕr-gou' (scene of the Passion Play)

rathskeller räts'kĕl'er

Reichstag rīKs'täK (Assembly, or Diet)

Rhenish (Eng.) rĕn'ish, not *rain-* (the German is "rheinisch")

Roentgen
Röntgen } rûnt'gĕn (note hard g)

Tirol
Tyrol } tē-rōl' (Eng. tĭr'ŏl)

Viennese vē'ŏ-nēz', not *-nāz*

von fōn (of, or from)

wanderlust vän'dĕr-lụst'

Weltschmerz vĕlt'shmĕrts' (world sorrow)

Wien vēn (Vienna)

wienerwurst vē'nĕr-vụrst' (Eng. wē'nĕr-wûrst) (Vienna sausage)

Zeitgeist tsīt'gīst' (spirit of the time)

zwieback tsvē'bäk (Am. swī'băk)

GREEK

Note the long vowel sounds that predominate in Greek words.

Adonis á-dō'nĭs

Aeolian
Eolian } ē-ō'lĭ-ăn, not *ā-o-liun*

Aesop ē'sŏp

Aeschylus ĕs'kĭ-lŭs (Br. ēs')

alpha and omega ăl'fá and ō-mē'gá, or ō-mĕg'á

Androcles ăn'drō-klēz

Aphrodite ăf'rō-dī'tē

Archimedes är'kĭ-mē'dēz

Aristophanes ăr'ĭs-tŏf'á-nēz

epicurean ĕp'ĭ-kū-rē'ăn

Eros ē'rŏs, or ĕr'ŏs

Euripides ū-rĭp'ĭ-dēz

Hippocrates hĭ-pŏk'rá-tēz

hoi polloi hoi'pŏ-loi', not *oi-poloi*

Mephistopheles mĕf'ĭ-stŏf'e-lēz

naiad nā'yăd, or nī'ăd

Nemesis nĕm'ē-sĭs

Olympiad ō-lĭm'pĭ-ăd

paean
pean } pē'an

Pegasus pĕg'á-sŭs (note accent)

Pericles pĕr'ĭ-klēz

Pierian pī-ē'rĭ-ăn

Pleiades plē'yá-dēz, or plī'

pseudo sū'dō

Pygmalion and pĭg-mā'lĭ-ŏn and
Galatea găl'á-tē'á

Socrates and sŏk'rá-tēz and
Xantippe zăn-tĭp'ē

Sophocles sŏf'ō-klēz

Stygian stĭj'ĭ-an (note accent)

Terpsichore tĕrp-sĭk'ō-rē, not tûrp'sē-kōr

{ Venus of Milo vē'nŭs of mī'lō, or mē'lō
{ Vénus de Milo (Fr.) vā'nüs dĕ mē'lō

HAWAIIAN

aloha á-lō'hä

Hawaii hä-wī'ē, not *-wī-á*

Hilo hē'lō

Honolulu hō'nō-lōō'lōō (Eng. hŏn'ō-)

Kamehameha kä-mā'hä-mā'hä (first king of Hawaii)

Kanaka ká-năk'á (a native)

lanai lä-nä'ē (a veranda)

lehua lä-hōō'ä (a Hawaiian flower)

lei lä'ē (a wreath)

Liliuokalani lē'lē-ụ-ō-kä-lä'nē (last queen of Hawaiian Islands)

luau lōō'ou (a feast)

Mauna Loa mou'nä lō'ä (active volcano)

Molokai mō'lō-kä'ē (leper island)

Oahu ō-ä'hōō

Pele pä'lä (a goddess)

poi pō'ē, or poi, not *pwäh* (a native dish)

ukulele ū'ke-lä'lē, or ōō'kụ-lä'la

Waikiki wä'ē-kē'kē

The Hawaiian Islands were formerly called the "Sandwich Islands", but are no longer so designated. There are other Sandwich Islands in the South Atlantic.

HISTORICAL NAMES

Alden, John ạl'dĕn, not ăl-

Antony, Mark ăn'tō-ny, not anth'

Appian Way ăp'ĭ-ăn (ancient paved
road from Rome to
Brindisi)

Babel bā'bĕl, not băb'el (the Tower of
Babel)

Carnegie kär-nĕg'ĭ

Cleopatra klē'ō-pā'tra, or -pät'

Croesus krē'sŭs

Curie, Madame kü'rē', not ku-rā

Disraeli dĭz-rā'lĭ, not -răl, nor -rĕl

Du Barry dü bá'rē' (note accent)

Elizabethan ē-lĭz'à-bē'thăn, or -bĕth'ăn

Faneuil Hall făn'l (in Boston)

Jeanne d'Arc zhȧn'dȧrk' (Eng.
Joan of Arc)

Lusitania lū'sĭ-tā'nĭ-à

Magna Charta măg'na kär'ta, not
char- (a guarantee of
liberty)

Marconi mär-kō'nē, not -kŏni

Rockefeller rŏk'e-fĕl'er, not rocka-fella

Roosevelt rō'zĕ-vĕlt, not rōōs-

INDIAN (AMERICAN)

{Algonquian ăl-gŏng'kĭ-ăn, not -kwin
{Algonquin ăl-gŏng'kĭn

Arapaho à-răp'à-hō

bayou bĭ'ōō, not bā-ō (Choctaw)

Chinook chĭ-nōōk'

Choctaw chŏk'tạ, not chōk-

Hiawatha hĭ'à-wä'tha (a Mohawk
chief)

Hopi hō'pē

Maya mä'yä, not mā-

Navaho }
Navajo } năv'à-hō, not năv-

Nez Percé nä'pĕr'sā', commonly nĕz
pērs (French for "pierced
nose")

Osage ō'sāj'

Powhatan pow'há-tăn', not powee-tan
(a chief, father of Pocahon-
tas)

Pueblo pwĕb'lō, not pū-eb-lo

sachem sā'chĕm, not săch-em

Shoshone shō-shō'nē

Ute ūt, or ū'tē

Yakima yăk'ĭ-mạ, not ya-kĭ'ma

Yaqui yä'kē, not yăk-e

IRISH

colleen kŏl'ēn, or kŏ-lēn', not kōl-

Dail Eireann dôl âr'ĭn (lower house of
Legislature of Ireland)

Eire âr'ĕ (Gaelic name for Ireland)

Erin go brath! }
Erin go bragh! } âr'ĭn gŭ brạ', or
ē'rĭn gō bräK' ("Ire-
land forever!", an
ancient war cry)

shillelagh } shĭ-lā'là, or
shillalah } shĭ-lā'lē

Sinn Fein shĭn fān (a political party)

ITALIAN

(See note on Foreign Pronunciations, p. 147.)

al fresco ăl frĕs'kō, or äl (in the open
air)

ballerina bäl'lā-rē'nä (Eng. băl'ĕ-rē'nȧ)

Bologna bō-lōn'yä

bravo brä'vō

Brindisi brēn'dē-zē (note accent)

campanile käm'pä-nē'lä (Eng.
kăm'pȧ-nē'lē) (bell tower)

Chianti kē-än'tē, not shĭ-

cognoscente } kō'nyō-shĕn'tä
conoscente } (a connoisseur)

con amore kōn ä-mō'rä (with love)

{dilettante dē'lĕt-tän'tä (Eng.
dĭl'ĕ-tăn'tĭ)
{dilettanti (pl.) dē'lĕt-tän'tē

dolce far niente dōl'chä fär nyĕn'tä
("sweet do-nothing-
ness")

Duce, Il ēl dōō'chä (The Leader)

oil, out | ūse, ŭp, bûrn, fụll, submit; ü—a muted e | chin; go; jet; park; K—Ger. ch; Fr. ṅ—a nasal tone

Fascisti fä-shē'stē (pl.)

Fata Morgana fä'tä môr-gä'nä

Firenze fē-rĕnt'sä (Florence, Italy)

{ Genoa jĕn'ō-á, not je-noh'a
{ Genova (It.) jĕn'ō-vä

ghetto gĕt'ō

gondola gŏn'dō-lá (note accent)

imbroglio ĭm-brōl'yō

intaglio ēn-täl'yō (Eng. ĭn-tăl'yō)

Italian ĭ-tăl'yăn, not ī-tăl'

italics ĭ-tăl'ĭks, not ī-tăl'

Lido lē'dō

maestro mä-ĕs'trō

maraschino măr'á-skē'nō, not -shee

Medici mĕd'ē-chē (note accent)

{ Milan mĭ-lăn'
{ Milano (It.) mē-lä'nō

Pisa pē'sä (Eng. pē'zá)

Riviera rē-vyâ'rä, not rivi-era

scenario shä-nä'rĭ-ō (Eng. sē-nâr'ĭ-ō)

sotto voce sōt'tō vō'chä, or sŏt'ō

Trieste trē-ĕs'tä (Eng. trē-ĕst')

{ Venice vĕn'ĭs, not vi-nees'
{ Venezia (It.) vä-nĕt'syä

villa vēl'lä (Eng. vĭl'á)

JAPANESE

geisha gā'sha

hara-kiri hä'rä-kēr'ĭ (a method of suicide)

jinrikisha }
jinricksha } jĭn-rĭk'sha̤

jujitsu jōō-jĭt'sōō, not jew-jitski

kimono kĭm'ō-nō (Eng. kĭ-mō'nō)

Nagasaki nä'gá-sä'kē, not năg-a-săk-e

Nippon nĭp'pŏn' ("Land of the Rising Sun")

LATIN WORDS AND PHRASES

There are two methods of pronouncing Latin—the **Roman** (taught in schools), and the **English**, with long vowels (used in law, etc.), as shown below. See Webster's New International Dictionary, p. liv.

absente reo ăb-sĕn'tē rē'ō (in the absence of the defendant)

a datu ā dā'tū (from the date)

ad finem ăd fī'nĕm (to the end)

ad litem ăd lī'tĕm (for the suit or action)

alma mater ăl'má mā'ter, or äl'ma mä'ter (fostering mother)

alter ego ăl'ter ē'gō (a second self)

anno Domini ăn'ō dŏm'ĭ-nī (in the year of our Lord)

ante bellum ăn'tē bĕl'ŭm (before the war)

a priori ā' prĭ-ō'rī (deductive; from cause to effect)

aqua pura ā'kwá pū'rá, or ăk'wá (pure water)

aurora borealis a̤-rō'rá bō'rē-ā'lĭs (the northern lights)

ave ā've (It. ä'vä) (hail)

bona fide bō'ná fī'dē, not bŏnna fĭd (in good faith)

casus belli kā'sŭs bĕl'ī, not kăshus (a cause for war)

caveat emptor kā'vē-ăt ĕmp'tôr (let the buyer beware)

Corpus Christi kôr'pŭs krĭs'tĭ, or -tī (the body of Christ)

corpus delicti kôr'pŭs dē-lĭk'tī (the body of the crime, that is, the facts of a crime)

corpus juris kôr'pŭs jōō'rĭs (the body of the law)

cui bono? kī' bō'nō (Who benefits?)

cum laude kŭm la̤'dē, or kŭm lou'dĕ (with praise or honor)

data dā'tá, or dä'tá, not dătta (plural of "datum")

de facto dē făk'tō (actually; in fact)

de jure dē jōō'rē (by lawful right)

dramatis personae drăm'á-tĭs pēr-sō'nē (the characters in a play)

Ecce Homo ĕk'sē hō'mō (Behold the Man!)

E Pluribus Unum ē plōō'rĭ-bŭs ū'nŭm (one out of many)

ergo ĕr'gō (therefore)

erratum ĕ-rä'tŭm (an error)

āle, ădd, câre, ärt, fást, a̤ll, about | ēve, lĕt, fērn, moment | ïce, ĭll, habit | ōld, ŏdd, nôrth, won | mōōn, fŏŏt |

et tu, Brute! ĕt tū brōō'tē (Even thou, Brutus!)
ex cathedra ĕks kȧ-thē'drȧ (from the chair; with authority)
ex libris ĕks lī'brĭs (from the books [of])
ex officio ĕks ŏ-fĭsh'ĭ-ō (from office; by virtue of position)
ex parte ĕks pär'tē (pertaining to only one side)
facile princeps făs'ĭ-lē prĭn'sĕps (easily first)
fiat fī'ăt (let it be done; hence, a sanction)
homo sapiens hō'mō sā'pĭ-ĕnz (the species—mankind)
in re ĭn rē (in regard to)
in situ ĭn sī'tū (in [the original] place)
in statu quo ĭn stā'tū kwō (in the same state)
lapis lazuli lā'pĭs lăz'ū-lī, or lăp'ĭs lăz'ū-lī (a stone)
lares et penates lā'rēz ĕt pē-nā'tēz (household gods)
lex loci lĕks lō'sī (the law of the place)
lis pendens lĭs pĕn'dĕnz (a pending lawsuit)
literati lĭt'ĕ-rā'tī (men of letters)
Magi mā'jī (the "wise men")
magna cum laude măg'nȧ kŭm lạ'dē, or kụm lou'dĕ (with great praise or honor)
magnum opus măg'nŭm ō'pŭs (a great work)
mala fide mā'lȧ fī'dē, not *mălla fīd* (in bad faith)
nolle prosequi nŏl'ē prŏs'ē-kwī (to be unwilling to prosecute)
modus operandi mō'dŭs ŏp'ĕ-răn'dī (mode of operating)
modus vivendi mō'dŭs vĭ-vĕn'dī (mode of living)
ne plus ultra nē plŭs ŭl'trȧ (the highest point of achievement)
non sequitur nŏn sĕk'wĭ-tûr (it does not follow)
O tempora! O mores! ō tĕm'pō-rȧ ō mō'rēz (O the times! O the manners!)
paterfamilias pā'tēr-fȧ-mĭl'ĭ-ăs (head of a household)
per diem pĕr dī'ĕm, not *deem* (by the day)
per se pĕr sē (by itself)
persona non grata pĕr-sō'nȧ nŏn grā'tȧ (an unacceptable person)
prima facie prī'mȧ fā'shĭ-ē (on the face of it)
pro rata prō rā'tȧ (in proportion)
prosit prō'sĭt (may it benefit you)
quasi kwā'sī (seeming, or in a way)
quo vadis? kwō vā'dĭs, or vä' (Whither goest thou?)
rara avis rā'rȧ ā'vĭs (a rare bird)
re rē (in regard to)
requiem rē'kwĭ-ĕm, or rĕk' (rest—a Mass for the dead)
requiescat in pace rĕk'wĭ-ĕs'kăt ĭn pā'sē (R.I.P.—rest in peace)
res judicata ⎱ rēz jōō'dĭ-kā'tȧ (a thing adjudicated; a matter previously and
res adjudicata ⎰ finally decided by law, on which suit cannot be brought again)
salve săl'vē (a greeting)
sanctum sanctorum sănk'tŭm sănk-tō'rŭm, not *-torium* (the holy of holies)
semper fidelis sĕm'pĕr fĭ-dē'lĭs (always faithful)
sic semper tyrannis sĭk sĕm'pĕr tī-răn'ĭs (Thus ever to tyrants—motto of Virginia)
sic transit gloria mundi sĭk trăn'sĭt glō'rĭ-ȧ mŭn'dī (So passes away the glory of the
    world.)
sine die sī'nē dī'ē (without [fixing a] day [on which to reconvene])
sine qua non sī'nē kwā nŏn' (an indispensable thing)
status quo stā'tŭs kwō (the existing state) (See "in statu quo", above)
sui generis sū'ī jĕn'ēr-ĭs (of its own kind; in a class by itself)

oil, out | ūse, ŭp, bûrn, fụll, submit; ü—a muted e | chin; go; jet; park; K—Ger. ch; Fr. ṅ—a nasal tone

summa cum laude sŭm'à kŭm là'dē, or sụm'mä kụm lou'dĕ (with highest praise or honor)
ultima Thule ŭl'tĭ-mà thū'lē (distant or mystical region)
ultra vires ŭl'trà vī'rēz (beyond the powers [of a corporation])
vale vā'lē (farewell)
veni, vidi, vici vē'nī vī'dī vī'sī (I came, I saw, I conquered. Caesar's announcement of a victory)
verbatim et literatim vĕr-bā'tĭm ĕt lĭt'ĕr-ā'tĭm (word for word and letter for letter)
via vī'à (by way of)
vice versa vī'sē vĕr'sà, not *vīs vĕrsa* (conversely)
vox populi vŏks' pŏp'ū-lī (the voice of the people)

LITERATURE

Admirable Crichton, The ăd'mĭ-ra-bl krī'ton
Alcott, Louisa May ạl'kŭt, not *ăl-*
Americana à-mĕr'ĭ-kā'nà, or -kä', or -kăn'
ana ā'nà (scraps of literature)
Ananias ăn'à-nī'ăs
Anna Karenina än'ä kä-rĕn'yĭ-nà
Apocalypse à-pŏk'a-lĭps
Balzac (Fr.) bàl'zàk' (Eng. băl'zăk)
Baudelaire (Fr.) bōd'lâr'
Blasco Ibáñez (Sp.) bläs'kō ē-bän'yäth
Boccaccio (It.) bōk-kä'chō
Candide kän'dēd'
Cather, Willa kăth'er (th as in breathe)
Cervantes (Sp.) thĕr-vän'täs (Eng. sĕr-văn'tēz)
Chekhov (Rus.) chĕ'Kōf
Coleridge (Eng.) kōl'rĭj, not *cōōl-*
Cowper kōō'per, or kou'
Cyrano de Bergerac sē'rà'nō' dē bĕr'zhē-ràk'
Dante (It.) dän'tā (Eng. dăn'tē)
D'Artagnan dàr'tà'nyäṅ' (a Dumas hero)
Daudet (Fr.) dō'dĕ'
Diderot (Fr.) dēd'rō'
Don Juan dōn hwän' (Sp.) (Eng. dŏn jōō'ăn)
Don Quixote dōn kē-hō'tā (Sp.) (Eng. dŏn kwĭk'sot)
Dostoevski (Rus.) dôs'tŏ-yĕf'skē
Dumas (Fr.) dü'mä'
Endymion ĕn-dĭm'ĭ-ŏn
Flaubert (Fr.) flō'bâr'
Forsyte Saga fôr-sīt' sä'gà
Galsworthy, John (Eng.) gạlz'wûr'thĭ
Gautier (Fr.) gō'tyā'

Goethe (Ger.) gû'tĕ
Heine (Ger.) hī'nĕ
Hugo (Fr.) ü'gō' (Eng. hū'gō)
Jekyll jē'kĭl (Dr. Jekyll and Mr. Hyde)
Lagerlöf, Selma (Sw.) lä'gēr-lûf
La Rochefoucauld (Fr.) là rôsh'fōō'kō'
Les Misérables lā mē'zä'rá'bl
Machiavelli (It.) mä'kyä-vĕl'lē (Eng. măk')
Maeterlinck (Belgian) (Du. mä'tĕr-lĭngk) (Eng. mä')
Maupassant, Guy de (Fr.) mō'pà'säṅ', gē dē
Molière (Fr.) mōl'yâr'
Montaigne (Fr.) môṅ'tàn'yē (Eng. mŏn-tān')
My Ántonia än'tōn-ē-äh (note accent)
Nietzsche (Ger.) nē'chĕ
Omar Khayyám (Persian) ō'màr kī-yäm' (note last accent)
Ouida (Eng.) wē'dà (a pen name)
Pepys (Eng.) pēps, or pĕps
Perrault (Fr.) pĕ'rō'
Prévost (Fr.) prā'vō'
Pulitzer Prizes pū'lĭt-sēr, or pōōl'
Rabelais (Fr.) rà'bē-lĕ'
Renan (Fr.) rĕ-näṅ'
Rousseau (Fr.) rōō'sō'
Rubáiyát rōō-bī'yät'
Shavian shā'vĭ-an (pertaining to George Bernard Shaw)
Southey (Eng.) south'y, or sŭth'y (th as in breathe)
Stendahl (Fr.) stäṅ'dàl'
Sue (Fr.) sü, not *sōō-ā*
Tolstoy (Rus.) tŏl-stoi' (Eng. tŏl'stoi)

Turgenev (Rus.) tŭr-gĕn'yĕf
Villon, François (Fr.) vē'yôn',
       frän'swä'
Volpone vŏl-pō'nē (It., old fox)

Voltaire (Fr.) vôl'târ'
Wassermann (Ger.) väs'ēr-män
Zola (Fr.) zō'lá' (Eng. zō'là)

MEDICAL TERMS

acidophilus milk ăs'ĭ-dŏf'ĭ-lŭs
ague ā'gū, not ăg-
allopathy ă-lŏp'á-thy, not *allō-pathy*
asafetida ăs'á-fĕt'ĭ-dà, not *-fĭt-ity*
astigmatism á-stĭg'má-tĭzm
basal metabolism bās'ăl mĕ-tăb'ō-lĭzm,
       not *basic*
caffeine kăf'ēn, or -ē-ĭn
cerebral se-rē'brăl, or sĕr'ē-brăl
chiropodist kī-rŏp'ō-dist, not *shi-*
chloroform klō'rō-fôrm, not *klera-*
cholera kŏl'ēr-à, not *kŏl-ry*
cocaine kō-kān', or kō'ká-ĭn
delirium tremens trē'mĕnz, not *-mers*
diabetes dī'á-bē'tēz (colloq. -tĭs)
digitalis dĭj'ĭ-tăl'ĭs, or -tā'lĭs
diphtheria dĭf-thē'rĭ-à, not *dĭp-*
eczema ĕk'zē-má (note accent)
erysipelas ĕr'ĭ-sĭp'ĕ-lăs, or ĭr'
Eustachian tube ū-stā'kĭ-ăn, not *-shŭn*
febrile fē'brĭl, or fĕb'rĭl
formaldehyde fôr-măl'de-hĭd, not *-mala'*
glycerin glĭs'er-ĭn
heroin hĕr'ō-ĭn, or he-rō'ĭn

hiccup } hĭk'ŭp
hiccough }
homeopathy hō'mē-ŏp'a-thy (5 syl.)
iodine ī'ō-dīn, or -dĭn
ipecac ĭp'e-kăk, not *ĕpp-*
jugular jŭg'ū-lēr, or jōō'gū-lar
larynx lăr'ĭnks, not *lär'nicks*
leprosy lĕp'rō-sy, not *leper-sy*
meningitis mĕn'ĭn-jī'tĭs
neuralgia nū-răl'já, or -jĭ-á not *-roul*
orthodontist ôr'thō-dŏn'tist, not *-den'*
pharmaceutical fär'má-sū'tĭ-kăl
pharmacist fär'má-sĭst, not *-tist*
pleuropneumonia plōō'rō-nū-mō'nĭ-à
psychiatry sī-kī'á-try
psychopathy sī-kŏp'á-thy (note accent)
pulmonary pŭl'mō-nĕr'y, not *pŭll-*
quinine kwī'nīn (Br. kwĭ-nēn')
rabies rā'bĭ-ēz, or rā'bēz, not *răb'*
sarsaparilla sär'sá-pá-rĭl'à, not *sáss-*
sclerosis sklē-rō'sĭs, not *slĭ-*
veterinary vĕt'ēr-ĭ-nĕr'y, not *veta-*
virus vī'rŭs

MUSIC

adagio á-dä'jō
allegro äl-lā'grō
andante än-dän'tä
Ave Maria ä'vä mä-rē'ä
basso profundo bäs'sō prō-fŭn'dō, not
       -found
berceuse bĕr'sûz', not *bŭr-sūs'*
calliope ká-lī'ō-pē, not *calē-ōpe*
cantabile kän-tä'bē-lä
cantata kán-tä'ta
cello chĕl'ō
coloratura kŭl'ēr-á-tū'rá (It.
       kō'lō-rä-tōō'rä)
concerto kōn-chĕr'tō
diva dē'vá
finale fē-nä'lä
fugue fūg (note hard g)
hautboy hō'boi (an oboe)
impresario ĭm'prä-sä'rĭ-ō

intermezzo ĭn'ter-mĕd'zō, not *-met-so*
madrigal mădri-găl
mezzo mĕd'zō, not *met-so*
Miserere mĭz'e-rē'rē, or -rä'rē
oboe ō'bō (a hautboy)
oboist ō'bō-ĭst
orchestral ôr-kĕs'trăl, or ôr'
Peer Gynt Suite pēr' gĭnt' swēt (Nor.
       pâr' günt')
prelude prĕl'ūd, or prē'
prima donna prē'má dŏn'á
roundelay roun'dē-lä
scherzo skĕr'tsō, not *shertso*
soprano sō-prä'nō, or -prăn'
Stradivarius străd'ĭ-vâr'ĭ-ŭs
Träumerei troi'mĕ-rī'
trio trē'ō, or trī'ō
violoncello vē'ō-lŏn-chĕl'ō, not *violin-*
xylophone zī'lō-fōn, or zĭl'

oil, out | ūse, ŭp, bûrn, fųll, submit; ü—a muted e | chin; go; jet; park; K—Ger. ch; Fr. n̈—a nasal tone

PRONUNCIATION

NATIONALITIES AND RACES

Anglo-Saxon ăng'glō-săk'sn (English)
Breton brĕt'un (of Bretagne [Brittany])
Briton brĭt'un (of Great Britain)
Celtic sĕl'tik ⎱ (usually refers to Irish)
Keltic kĕl'tik ⎰
Creole krē'ōl (does not necessarily signify race mixture. The American Creole in Louisiana is a French or Spanish descendant of the Louisiana Settlers, speaking a French or Spanish dialect.)
Czech (n. & adj.) chĕK (a native, or the language, of Bohemia, a western province in the Slavic countries.)
Danish dān'ish, not *dăn-*
Deutscher doich'er (a German)
Dutchman a Hollander
Gaelic gāl'ik (Irish, Scottish, etc.)
Gallic găl'ik (French)
Iraqi ē-rä'kē (rather than "Iraqian")
Javanese jăv'a-nēz' (of Java)

Latin races French, Italian, Spanish, etc., whose languages come from the Latin
Nipponese nĭp'ŏ-nēz' (Japanese)
⎰**Panamanian** păn'à-mā'nĭ-an (usual)
⎱**Panaman** păn'á-män' (rare)
⎰**Panameño** (Sp.) pä-nä-mā'nyō
Portuguese pōr'tū-gēz (colloq. -gē)
Romany rŏm'á-ny, not *rōme-* (pertaining to the gypsies)
Semitic sē-mĭt'ĭk (pertaining to the Hebrews and Arabs)
Senegalese sĕn'ē-gạl-ēz' (of Senegal)
Singhalese sĭng'gà-lēz' (of Ceylon)
Sino- sī'nō, or sĭn'ō (Chinese, as Sino-Russian, Sino-Japanese)
Slavic släv'ĭk, or släv' (pertaining to the Slavs: Russians, Bohemians, Bulgarians, Serbians, Slovaks, etc.)
Teuton tū'tŏn (German)
Yugoslav⎱ yōō'gō-släv', or -släv'
Jugoslav⎰

NAUTICAL TERMS

boatswain bō'sn, rather than bōt'swān
bow bou, not *bō*
bowsprit bō'sprĭt, or bou'
conning tower kŏn'ing, not *kōn-*
coxswain kŏk'sn, rather than kŏk'swān
flotsam flŏt'sam, not *float-sum*
forecastle fōk'sl, rather than fōr'kás-l
gunwale gŭn'l

larboard lär'bĕrd ("port side", or a ship's left side)
leeward lū'erd, rather than lē'ward (opposite of windward side)
mainsail măn'sl, rather than măn'sāl
maritime măr'ĭ-tīm, or -tĭm
sou'wester sou'wĕs'ter
starboard stär'bĕrd (a ship's right side)

NORWEGIAN AND NORSE

fiord⎱ fyôrd
fjord⎰
maelstrom māl'strŏm, not *măl-*

ski shē (Eng. skē)
Valhalla văl-hăl'a
Valkyrie văl-kĭr'ĭ, or văl'kĭ-rĭ

OPERAS

Opera	Composer
Aïda ä-ē'dà	**Verdi** (It.) vâr'dē
Cavalleria Rusticana kä'văl-lä-rē'à rōō-stē-kä'nà (rustic chivalry)	**Mascagni** (It.) mäs-kän'yē
Die Meistersinger dē mīs'ter-sĭng'er	
Die Walküre dē văl-kü'rĕ (The Valkyrie)	**Wagner** (Ger.) väK'nēr (Eng. văg'ner)
	Wagner
Faust foust (Fr. fōst)	**Gounod** (Fr.) gōō'nō'

āle, ădd, câre, ärt, fást, ạll, about | ēve, lĕt, fērn, moment | īce, ĭll, habĭt | ōld, ŏdd, nôrth, won | mōōn, fŏŏt |

Götterdämmerung gŭt′ĕr-dĕm′er-ŭng	Wagner
Hänsel und Gretel hĕn′sĕl ŭnt grä′tĕl	Humperdinck (Ger.) hŭm′pĕr-dĭngk
Il Trovatore ēl trō′vä-tō′rä (The Trou- badour)	Verdi
Iolanthe ī′ō-lăn′thē	Gilbert and Sullivan (Eng.)
Iris ē′rĭs	Mascagni
La Bohème lä bô′ĕm′	Puccini (It.) pōōt-chē′nē
L'Africaine lä-frē-kān′, or -kĕn′	Meyerbeer (German-Jewish) mī′ĕr-bär
La Gioconda lä jō-kōn′dä	Ponchielli (It.) pōn-kyĕl′lē
Lakmé läk′mä′	Delibes (Fr.) dē-lēb′
La Traviata lä trä-vyä′tä	Verdi
Lohengrin lō′ĕn-grĭn (note accent)	Wagner
Lucia di Lammermoor lōō-chē′ä dē läm′mĕr-mōōr′	Donizetti (It.) dō′nē-dzĕt′tē
Lucrezia Borgia lōō-krät′sē-ä bôr′jä	Donizetti
Manon Lescaut mä′nôn′ lĕs′kō′	Puccini
Mignon mē′nyôn′	Thomas (Fr.) tō′mä′
Pagliacci päl-yä′chē	Leoncavallo (It.) lä′ōn-kä-väl′lō
Parsifal pär′sĭ-fäl	Wagner
Pelléas et Mélisande pĕ′lä′às′ ā mä′lē′zänd′	Debussy (Fr.) dē-bü′sē′
{ Salome (Eng.) sà-lō′mē { Salomé (Fr.) sà′lō′mä′	R. Strauss (Ger.) shtrous
{ Samson and Delilah (Eng.) săm′sn and dē-lī′là { Samson et Dalila (Fr.) sän-sôn′ nä dà′lē-lä′	Saint-Saëns (Fr.) săn′säns′
Siegfried sēg′frēd (Ger. zēK′frēt)	Wagner
Tannhäuser tän′hoi-zēr	Wagner
Thaïs tá′ēs′	Massenet (Fr.) mà′s-nĕ′
{ The Barber of Seville (Eng.) sē-vĭl′, or sĕv′ĭl { Il Barbiere di Siviglia (It.) ēl bär-byä′- rä dē sē-vēl′yä { Le Barbier de Séville (Fr.) lē bàr-byä′ dē sä-vēl′	Rossini (It.) rôs-sē′nē
The Pirates of Penzance pĕn-zăns′	Gilbert and Sullivan
Tosca tōs′kä	Puccini
{ Tristan and Isolde (Eng.) trĭs′tăn and ĭ-sōld′ { Tristan und Isolde (Ger.) trēs-tän′ ŭnt ē-zōl′dĕ	Wagner
Turandot { tōōr′än-dō (It.) { tŭ′rän-dŏt (Ger.)	Puccini

RUSSIAN

Baku bà-kōō′	borzoi bôr′zoi (a wolfhound)
balalaika băl′a-lī′ka (a guitarlike instrument)	caviar kăv′ĭ-är′ (from Turkish)
	Cossack kŏs′ăk, not kōs-
{ Bolshevik (sing.) bŏl′shĕ-vĭk, or bōl′ { Bolsheviki (pl.) bŏl′shĕ-vē′kē, or bōl′	droshky drŏsh′ky (a carriage)
	icon ī′kŏn (from Greek)

oil, out | ūse, ŭp, bûrn, fŭll, submit; ü—a muted e | chin; go; jet; park; K—Ger. ch; Fr. n̄—a nasal tone

intelligentsia ĭn-tĕl'ĭ-gĕnt'sĭ-à, or
-jĕnt'
Lenin lyĕ'nēn (Eng. lĕn'ĭn)
Leningrad lĕn'ĭn-grăd, not -grād
{ Moscow mŏs'kō, or -kou
{ Moskva (Rus.) mŏs-kvà'
Pavlova }
Pavlowa } pàv'lō-và (note accent)

Rasputin ràs-pụ'tēn
Russian rŭsh'an, not rōōsh'
soviet sō'vĭ-ĕt', or sō'
steppes stĕps, not steeps
Ufa ụ'fà (a river)
ukase ū-kās' (an official decree)
Vladivostok vlà'dĭ-vŏs-tôk' (note accent)

SPANISH, MEXICAN, AND SPANISH AMERICAN

Standard Spanish or pure Spanish is Castilian (kăs-tĭl'yăn) spoken by the citizens of Castile, the old ruling kingdom of castles.

Mexican language is a combination of Castilian and Andalusian Spanish, and some of the best elements of several of the native Indian tongues. It is a very rich and flexible language.

Spanish American is the language spoken in the Spanish American countries. It is largely Castilian, but may be, as the Mexican language is, a combination of Spanish and native tongues.

(See note on Foreign Pronunciations, p. 147.)

adios ä'dē-ōs'
adobe ä-dō'bä, not do-be
Agua Caliente ä'gwä kä'lē-ĕn'tä
alameda ä'lä-mä'dä (Eng. ăl'à-mē'dà)
amigo ä-mē'gō (a friend)
apartado ä'pär-tä'dō (post office box)
Armada är-mä'dà (Eng. -mä')
arroyo är-rō'yō (Eng. ă-roi'ō)
bolero bō-lä'rō, not -lĕra
{ bravado brä-vä'dō (Br. -vä'dō)
{ bravada (Sp.) brä-vä'dä
Buenos Aires bwä'nōs ī'räs (Eng. bō'nŏs âr'ēz)
caballero kä'bäl-yä'rō
cabaña kä-bä'nyä (a cabin)
cafeteria kä-fä-tä-rē'ä (Eng. kăf'e-tēr'ĭ-a)
cañon kä-nyōn' (Eng. canyon—kăn'yun)
centavo cĕn-tä'vō
chaparajos chä'pä-rä'hōs (Short Am. form, chaps—shăps)
chaqueta chä-kᴀ'tä (a jacket)
Chihuahua chē wä'wä, not shē-
{ desperado dĕs'pĕr-ä'dō, or -ä'dō
{ desesperado (Sp.) dĕs-ĕs-pä-rä'dō
Don dōn (Sir) (Eng. dŏn)
Doña dō'nyä (Lady)
{ dueña dwä'nyä
{ duenna (Eng.) dū-ĕn'a

El Camino Real ĕl kä-mē'nō rä-äl' (the King's Highway)
embarcadero ĕm-bär'kä-dä'rō (wharf)
enchilada ĕn'chē-lä'dä
fiesta fē-ĕs'tä
frijoles frē-hō'läs (beans)
hacienda ä-thē-ĕn'dä (Eng. hä'sĭ-ĕn'dä)
hidalgo ē-däl'gō (Eng. hĭ-dăl'gō)
Hispano-Suiza ĭs-pä'nō sụ-ē'thä (means Spanish-Swiss)
hombre ōm'brä
{ incomunicado in-kō-mụ-nē-kä'dō
{ incommunicado (Eng.) in'kŏ-mū'nĭ-kä'dō
Joaquin wä-kēn'
licenciado lē-thĕn-thē-ä'dō (attorney)
Llano Estacado lä'nō ĕs'tä-kä'dō
{ Majorca (Eng.) mà-jôr'kà
{ Mallorca (Sp.) mäl-yôr'kä
mañana mä-nyä'nä (tomorrow)
mantilla män-tē'yä (Eng. măn-tĭl'a)
mesa mä'sä
Montevideo mōn'tä-vē-thä'ō (Eng. mŏn'tē-vĭd'ē-ō)
olla-podrida ōl'yä-pō-drē'dä (Eng. ŏl'à)
padre pä'drä
{ palmetto păl-mĕt'ō
{ palmito (Sp.) päl-mē'tō
patio pä'tyō

āle, ădd, câre, ärt, fàst, ạll, about | ēve, lĕt, fērn, moment | īce, ĭll, habit | ōld, ŏdd, nôrth, won | mōōn, fŏŏt)

{ peccadillo pĕk'a-dĭl'ō
{ pecadillo (Sp.) pā-kä-dēl'yō
peón pā-ōn'
peseta pā-sā'tä
peso pā'sō
plaza plä'thä (Eng. plä'za)
poncho pŏn'chō (a cloaklike blanket)
presidio prā-sē'dyō (Eng. prē-sĭd'ĭ-ō)
{ pronunciamento prō-nŭn'sĭ-à-mĕn'tō
{ pronunciamiento (Sp.) prō-nụn'thyä-
     myĕn'tō
quién sabe? kyĕn sä'bä (Who knows?)
{ riata rē-ä'ta
{ reata (Sp.) rā-ä'tä
rodeo rō-dā'ō (Am. rō'dē-ō)

señor sä-nyôr'
señora sä-nyō'rä
señorita sä'nyō-rē'tä
sierra sē-ĕr'rä
siesta sē-ĕs'tä
sombrero sŏm-brä'rō
Tampico täm-pē'kō
tapadera tä-pä-dā'rä (Eng. tăp'à-)
{ tomato tō-mä'tō, or tō-mä'tō
{ tomate (Sp.) tō-mä'tä
tornado tŏr-nä'dō (Eng. tôr-nä'dō)
tortilla tōr-tē'yä
vaquero vä-kä'rō (Am. buckaroo)
vigilante vē-hē-län'tä (Eng.
     vĭj'ĭ-lăn'tē)

SWISS

There is no Swiss language. The languages of the surrounding countries are
spoken.

Alpine ăl'pĭn, or -pĭn
chalet shă-lä' (Fr. shá'lĕ')
hospice hŏs'pĭs (Fr. ôs'pēs')
Jungfrau yụng'frou'
Lausanne lō'zàn'
Matterhorn mät'ĕr-hôrn, not măt-

Saint Bernard săn bĕr'när' (Eng.
     sänt bĕr-närd')
{ Saint Moritz sänt mō'rĭts (Fr.
{   săn mō-rēts')
{ Sankt Moritz (Ger.) zängkt mō'rĭts

UNIVERSITIES, COLLEGES, AND SCHOOLS

Amherst College—Mass. ăm'ĕrst
Antioch College—Ohio ăn'tĭ-ŏk, not
     -oak
Bowdoin College—Maine bō'dn
Brigham Young University—Utah
     brĭg'am, not
     bring'ham
Bryn Mawr College—Pa. brĭn'mär', not
     more
Canisius College—N.Y. kà-nĭsh'ŭs
Colgate University—N.Y. kōl'gāte, not
     kŏl-
Dartmouth College—N.H. därt'mŭth
DePauw University—Ind. dē-pạ'
Duquesne University—Pa. dụ-kān'
Fordham University—N.Y. fôrd'ăm

Gonzaga University—Wash. gŏn-ză'gà
Groton School—Mass. grŏ'ton, not
     grŏt-
Juniata College—Pa. jōō'nĭ-ăt'à
Loyola University—Ill. loi-ō'là
Mount Holyoke College—Mass.
     hōl'yōk, not
     holy-oak
Notre Dame, University of—Ind.
     nō'ter däm'
Rutgers University—N.J. rŭt'gĕrz
Wellesley College—Mass. wĕlz'ly, not
     wel-es-ly
Wesleyan University—Conn. wĕs'lĭ-ăn
Xavier University—Ohio zāv'ĭ-er

college—a small or restricted institution of higher learning, granting degrees in
     specialized subjects.
university—a large institution of higher learning, comprised of several colleges—as
     colleges of arts, literature, and science—and professional schools or colleges of
     law, medicine, etc.

oil, out | ūse, ŭp, bûrn, fụll, submit; ü—a muted e | chin; go; jet; park; K—Ger. ch; Fr. ñ—a nasal tone

VEGETATION

acacia à-kā′sha, not -kǎsh-ia
almond ä′mŭnd
amaryllis ăm′á-rĭl′ĭs
anemone à-nĕm′ō-nē
apricot ā′prĭ-kŏt, or ăp′rĭ-
arbutus är-bū′tŭs
asparagus ăs-păr′a-gŭs, not a-spar-grass
avocado ăv′ō-kä′dō
banana bà-năn′á (Br. bà-nä′nà)
bougainvillea bōō′gĭn-vē′lē-a
broccoli brŏk′ō-lĭ
camellia kà-mĕl′ĭ-a, or -mēl′ya
camomile kăm′ō-mīl
catalpa cà-tăl′pa, not -tawl
cauliflower kô′lĭ-flou′er, not cŭl-
cereus sē′rē-ŭs
chive chīv
chrysanthemum krĭs-ăn′thē-mŭm, not -thium
cinchona sĭn-kō′na
cineraria sĭn′ĕ-rā′rĭ-a
clematis klĕm′a-tĭs (Br. klē-mā′tĭs)
cranberry krăn′bĕr-y, not cram-
cyclamen sĭk′la-mĕn, or sīk′
dahlia dăl′ya, or däl′ (Br. dāl′ya)
elm ĕlm, not el-um
endive ĕn′dīv, or -dĭv (Fr. äṅ′dēv′)
eucalyptus ū′kà-lĭp′tŭs
{ gladiolus (plant) glăd′ĭ-ō′lus
{ Gladiolus (genus) glà-dĭ′ō-lus
heliotrope hē′lĭ-ō-trōp
herb ûrb (Br. hûrb)
hibiscus hī-bĭs′kŭs

hydrangea hī-drăn′jē-a, not -drain
lichen lī′kĕn
licorice lĭk′ō-rĭs, not lick-rish
lignum-vitae lĭg′nŭm-vī′tē
mesquite mĕz-kēt′
mushroom mŭsh′rōōm, not musha-roon
muskmelon mŭsk′mĕl′un, not mush-
nasturtium năs-tûr′shŭm
papyrus pà-pī′rŭs
passionflower so named because parts of the flower suggest the instruments, or story, of Christ's Crucifixion
pecan pē-kän′, or -kăn′
peony pē′ō-ny (note accent)
pistachio pĭs-tä′shĭ-ō, or -tä′
poinsettia poin-sĕt′ĭ-a, not -setta
pollen pŏl′ĕn, not pōle-
pomegranate pŏm′grăn′at, or pŭm′
pumpkin pŭmp′kĭn (colloq. pŭng′kĭn)
radish răd′ĭsh, not red-
raspberry răz′bĕr-y, or răz′
{ resin rĕz′ĭn
{ rosin rŏz′ĭn
rind rīnd, not rine
saguaro sà-gwä′rō, or sà-wä′rō
sumac shōō′măk, or sū′măk
turmeric tûr′mĕr-ik, not tōōm-
vanilla và-nĭl′a, not -nĕll
{ Wistaria (genus) wĭs-tā′rĭ-a
{ wisteria (plant) wĭs-tēr′ĭ-a
woodbine wŏŏd′bĭn′, not -bĭn
yucca yŭk′á, not yū-

AFTERWORD ON PRONUNCIATION

Many mispronunciations are the result of a hazy idea of the spelling of, or syllables in, a word.

To mispronounce an unfamiliar word is not so noticeable an error as to mispronounce a familiar one. Familiar words are bungled because they are taken for granted.

Do not use a word and then wonder about the pronunciation. Question the pronunciation of every infrequent or unusual word and defer its use until it has been checked with the dictionary.

Memorize the pronunciation by repeating it at least five times when looking up a word. If the pronunciation of a word stays in the memory a day, it is usually indelibly imprinted there.

When two or more pronunciations are given for the same word, choose the one that is the most generally used, whether this pronunciation is given first or last in the dictionary.

When speaking of dictionaries or reference books, note these pronunciations:

Merriam-Webster dictionaries—mĕr′ĭ-ăm, not *mē-*, nor *mĭr-*
Funk & Wagnalls dictionaries—wăg′nalz, not *wäg-*, nor *väg-*
The Roget Dictionary—rō′zhā′, not *rō′jet*
                     (from Roget's Thesaurus)—thē-sô′rŭs
Encyclopædia Britannica—ĕn-sī′klō-pē′dĭ-a, not *-săk-la;*
                  brĭ-tăn′ik-a, not *-tān′*

"The best kind of education is unquestionably that acquired through individual effort—by experience, practise, and research."
—Frank H. Vizetelly in Funk & Wagnalls
Practical Standard Dictionary Introductory, p. iii.

❖

SIMILAR WORDS

Many words are so similar in sound or spelling that they are liable to be interchanged if a writer glances too quickly in the dictionary, or does not stop to comprehend the meanings.

Note: Words that have two spellings, such as "catalogue" or "catalog", "disk" or "disc", "dispatch" or "despatch", "gauge" or "gage", "skeptical" or "sceptical", etc., are not included in the list. Choice of spelling is a matter of usage.

A

abbess	the superior in a convent
abyss	a bottomless depth
abjure	to renounce or reject solemnly (ăb-jŏor′) (noun, abjuration)
adjure	to command or entreat solemnly (ă-jŏor′) (noun, adjuration)
absorption	a taking up or drinking in; engrossment
adsorption	adhesion of gas or liquid to the surface of a solid
accept	to receive with approval
except	to leave out
ad	abbreviation of advertisement (no period)
add	to make an addition
adept	skilled
adapt	to adjust ("adapted"—adjusted; "adaptable"—can be adjusted)
adopt	to choose or take as one's own
admittance	actual entrance; permission or right to enter, as "No admittance", "gain admittance"
admission	entrance for a certain purpose, or with certain rights and privileges, as "admission to a theater", "admission to a club", "admission to a country"
adverse	opposing; unfavorable
averse to	disinclined toward
advice	(noun) information; recommendation (ăd-vīs′)
advise	(verb) to inform; to counsel (ăd-vīz′). (These words, though useful, are overworked in letter writing. They should be limited to instances in which the idea of "recommendation" is involved. "Inform", "tell", "information", etc., should be used at other times.)
affect } effect }	(See Verbs, p. 80)
ail	to affect painfully
ale	a beverage
air	the atmosphere
heir	one legally entitled to inherit an estate (âr)
alinement} alignment}	interchangeable, but the English form "alinement" seems preferable to the French form "alignment"

176

all	the whole of
awl	a tool
allocate	to set apart or assign
locate	to fix or find the place of

allusion	reference by suggestion		allude	allusive
elusion	avoidance or evasion (rare)	Similarly	elude	elusive
illusion	a visual deception; a romantic idea		illude (rare)	illusive
delusion	a false idea		delude	delusive

ally	an associate (ă-lī′, or ăl′ĭ)
alley	a narrow way
aloud	audibly
allowed	permitted
Alpine	pertaining to the Alps (ăl′pīn, or ăl′pĭn)
alpine	of or like the Alps, as "alpine flowers", "alpine heights"
alpen-	(used in compounds) "alpenglow", "alpenhorn", "alpenstock"
already	previously, as "They have already been sent."
all ready	all in readiness, as "The packages were all ready to mail." (not "already")
altar	a place of worship
alter	to change
alternate	a substitute (a person). Occurring by turns (ạl′tĕr-nat, or ăl′)
alternative	a choice (or offering a choice) between two or more courses or things (ạl-tûr′na-tiv)
although } though	interchangeable in most instances; but "although" being slightly more emphatic is often preferred to introduce facts, and "though", suppositions
altogether	entirely, as "They are altogether too light."
all together	in one group, as "Were they all together?" (not "altogether")
amnesia	loss of memory
aphasia	loss of speech
astasia	inability to stand or walk
asphyxia	suffocation; suspended animation
anachorism	something foreign to a place or condition
anachronism	a chronological error
analyst	one who analyzes
annalist	a writer of annals (records)
anecdote	an interesting incident or brief story
antidote	a remedy
angel	a spiritual being
angle	a corner
ant	an insect
aunt	a relative
ante-	a prefix meaning "before". (As a noun) a cardplayer's stake (ăn′tē)
anti-	a prefix meaning "against" (ăn′tĭ, not ăn′tī). (Colloq. as a noun) a dissenting person (ăn′tĭ)
antedate	to date back to some past date (before the present date)
postdate	to date forward to some future date (after the present date)

antiseptic	an agent that destroys bacteria
anesthetic	an agent that produces insensibility
aseptic	free from germs

anyhow } **anyway**	interchangeable. Sometimes used as connectives, as "He says he doesn't need it; anyway, he will buy it."

anyone } **anybody**	interchangeable (See Subjects, p. 71)

anyway	in any event, as "Anyway, we are not interested."
any way	in any one way, as "not interested in any way"

appertain	to belong—more formal than "pertain"
pertain	to belong—denotes a closer relationship than "appertain" } Note
appurtenance	that which belongs; accessory } spellings
pertinent	related; applicable

appraisal } **appraisement**	interchangeable. The shorter form is preferred.

appraise	to estimate the value of
apprise	to inform
apprize	to appraise or apprise (not commonly used)

Arabian	pertaining to the country of Arabia
Arabic	pertaining to the language or numerals of the Arabs (ăr′a-bĭk)

area	surface; extent or range (ā′rē-a)
aria	a melody (ä′rĭ-à)

Argentina	(noun) a republic in South America (är′jĕn-tē′na)
Argentine	(adj.) pertaining to the republic of Argentina (är′jĕn-tēn)

ark	a place of refuge
arc	a curved line

around } **round**	interchangeable in such phrases as "turn round", "all round", etc. (See also p. 6)

arrange	to put in order
arraign	to call into court (ă-rān′, not a-rānj′)

ascetic	austere and self-denying (ă-sĕt′ik)
acetic	sour, as the acid in vinegar (à-sē′tik)

assay	to test, as an ore
essay	to attempt

assent	consent
ascent	a rise
accent	a stress

assurance } **insurance**	interchangeable. "Assurance" is the older form. (See also Insurance, p. 532)

aster	a flower
Astor	a proper name

astray	straying, as "gone astray", not "estray"
estray	a stray (formal, legal). Gone astray, as "estray freight"
stray	a wanderer. To wander

astrology	the study of the influences of the stars on human destinies
astronomy	the science of the heavenly bodies

ate	did eat
eight	a numeral

178

auger	a tool
augur	to foretoken, as "It augurs well..."
aught	anything (for a cipher, see "naught", below)
ought	should
aviary	a place for birds (ā′vĭ-ĕr′y)
apiary	a place for bees (ā′pĭ-ĕr′y)
away	as "away from", or "gone away"
aweigh	(naut.) lifted, as an anchor
way	in the phrase "give way", not "*away*", as "the bridge gave way", "the people gave way", "gave way to grief"
awhile	(adv.) for a while
a while	(noun). Note that "awhile" means "for a while"; therefore, if "for" is used "a while" should be used. "After they experiment for a while..." (not "*awhile*") OR: "After they experiment awhile..."

B

bad	defective
bade	told or commanded (băd, not *bāde*)
bail	to dip up; to parachute from. Release security; pail handle
bale	a large, compact bundle, as "a bale of hay"
bait	a lure. To torment, as "bear baiting"
bate	to moderate, as "with bated breath"
bald	bare
balled	wound into a ball, as "balled up"
bawled	shouted, as "bawled out"
ball	a round object; a dance
bawl	to cry out
barbaric	gaudy; wild
barbarous	cruel; brutal
barbarian	uncivilized
bard	a poet
barred	fastened; excluded
bark	the outer part of a tree; the call of a dog or animal
barque⎱ **bark** ⎰	a three-masted sailing ship
baron	a nobleman
barren	unfruitful
base	a foundation. Small or mean
bass	a deep tone or voice (bās); a kind of fish (băs)
bathos	a descent from the sublime to the ridiculous; absurd pathos (bā′thŏs)
pathos	sadness (pā′thŏs, not *păth-ōs*)
Bayreuth⎱ **Baireuth** ⎰	a Bavarian city, scene of the Wagner festivals (bī′roit′, not *-ruth*)
Beyrouth⎱ **Beirut** ⎰	a city in Syria (bā′rōōt)
bazaar	an exchange place
bizarre	fantastic

be	a verb
bee	an insect
beach	the shore
beech	a tree
bear	to wear, carry, or endure. An animal
bare	unadorned; naked; destitute of ordinary things
beat	to strike; to vanquish
beet	a vegetable
beer	a liquor
bier	a funeral litter
Belgium	a country
Belgian	of or pertaining to Belgium. A native of Belgium
benzine	a product of petroleum
benzene	a product of coal tar (also called "benzol")
berry	a fruit
bury	to cover deeply
berth	a place to sleep; an allotted place for a ship
birth	a coming into life
beside	by the side of, as "beside the roadway"; disjoined from, as "That is beside the issue."
besides	moreover; other than; in addition to, as "Besides stocks, there were bonds."
billed	charged; listed; advertised
build	to construct
blew	moved rapidly
blue	a color
bloc	a combination for political strength, as the "liberal bloc"
block	a piece of wood; a quantity or unit, as a "block of stock"; a pulley; a mold; a city square. To obstruct; to outline
boar	a swine
bore	to drill; did bear. A wearisome thing or person; a high, rushing tide
boor	a peasant; a rude or clownish person (bŏŏr)
Boer	a South African colonist (Boer War) (bōr)
board	a piece of wood; meals; an organized group
bored	pierced; penetrated; wearied
boarder	one who pays for meals
border	edge
bolder	more bold
boulder	a large rock (old spelling "bowlder")
bomb	an explosive device (bŏm, or bŭm)
balm	something that soothes
born	brought into life
borne	carried; supported; endured
bourn	a stream; a boundary; a goal (bōrn)
bow	(bō) a tie; a weapon; a violin bow. To bend
bow	(bou) the forward part of a ship; an inclination of the head. To make a bow
bough	a branch of a tree
beau	a dandy

180

boy	a youth
buoy	a floating signal (bōo′y, or boi)
braze	to solder, join, or cover with metal
braise	to brown and then cook slowly in an oven or braising kettle
breach	a break
breech	the rear or lower part
bread	a food
bred	produced; brought up
break	an opening or fracture
òrake	a device for retarding motion; a thicket
breath	a slight stirring of air
breathe	to respire
breadth	width
bridal	pertaining to a wedding
bridle	a horse's headgear; anything that restrains
Britain	Great Britain—England, Wales, and Scotland
Briton	a native British subject, particularly an Englishman
Breton	a native of Bretagne (Brittany) (brĕt′un)
Britisher	applies to any person of British nationality. Although the word "Britisher" is objected to by some—on the ground that it is no better than "Irisher"—it is noted by American authorities as correct, and is very generally used.
Englishman	pertains only to England. An Irishman or a Scotsman should not be called an "Englishman".
broach	to open; to introduce
brooch	an ornamental pin (brōch, rather than brōoch)
bullion	gold or silver metal
bouillon	a broth (bōo′yòn′)
burrow	a hole for shelter. To dig under
burro	a little donkey
borough	a division of New York City; a village
by	a preposition ("by and by")
buy	to purchase
bye	secondary; in passing, as "by the bye"

C

cagey	
cagy	sly; shrewd (kāj′y)
cadgy	cheerful; wanton (kăj′y)
calendar	a schedule of time; a list
calender	a press for cloth, paper, etc. To glaze
colander	a sieve or strainer
callous	(adj.) hardened
callus	(noun) a hardened surface (pl. calluses)
Calvary	where Christ was crucified
cavalry	mounted military forces
cannon	a gun
canon	a law or rule; "canon law", religious or moral law; a list; a church dignitary

181

canyon cañon (Sp.)	a ravine or narrow valley
cannot can not	the common form of "can not" slightly more emphatic than "cannot"
canvas canvass	strong tent cloth to solicit. An inspection or survey
capital Capitol	chief; vital; first-rate. The head; a capital city; money or assets (capitalized) the official building of Congress in Washington, D.C.; (not capitalized) a statehouse
carat karat caret carrot	a measure for precious stones a measure for gold a correction mark a vegetable
carousal carrousel	a boisterous revel of drinking a military tournament on horseback; a merry-go-round (kăr′ụ-zĕl′)
carton cartoon	a pasteboard box; a target a large sketch or caricature
cash cache cachet	money a hiding place (kăsh) a seal or stamp; hence a distinctive mark, trait, or character (kă-shā′)
cast caste	a group of actors; a mold or pattern; a tinge. To throw off a class of society (kȧst)
caster castor	a small wheel or roller; a cruet a beaver or its fur; a drab color (castor oil)
casual causal	incidental; unimportant pertaining to a cause
casualty casuality causality	a contingency or accident casualness the relation of cause and effect
censor censure censer	an examiner or critic (sĕn′sēr) condemnation; blame (sĕn′shụr) a vessel for burning incense
ceremonious ceremonial	formal; done with ceremony pertaining to a ceremony
chafe chaff	to anger; fret; irritate (chāf) that which is light or worthless. To banter (chȧf)
champaign champagne	level expanse or open country a sparkling white wine
chased chaste	pursued; ornamented, as "chased gold" pure
chassé chasse châsse chassis	a dance step (Fr. shȧ′sā′) the chase; a small glass of liqueur (Fr. shȧs) a coffer for the relics of a saint (Fr. shäs) the framework of an automobile or airplane (Fr. shä′sē; Am. shȧs′e; pl. shȧs′ez)
cheap cheep	not expensive to chirp or peep

182

childish	pettish; small; weak
childlike	innocent; trustful
choose	to select
chews	masticates; meditates
chose	did choose (chōz). (Law) a piece of personal property (shōz)
clamor	noise; outcry
clamber	to climb or scramble up
clause	a group of words
claws	an animal's nails
click	a light, sharp sound
cliché	a stereotyped or trite phrase (klē'shā')
clique	a small social set (klēk)
claque	paid applauders (klǎk)
climatic	pertaining to climate
climactic	pertaining to a climax
climacteric	indicating a crisis
clinch	to grapple; to clamp, as a nail; to conclude, as a deal
clench	to grip tensely, as the fist; to close tightly, as the teeth
clothes	dress
close	to shut; to end (klōz). Near (klōs)
cloths	fabrics (tablecloths)
coal	a mineral
cole	a vegetable ("coleslaw"—a cabbage salad)
kohl	a beauty powder used by Arabian women to darken the eyelids
coarse	unrefined
course	a passage; a way
cocoa	a beverage
cacao	the seeds of the cacao tree, used in making chocolate (kȧ-kā'ō; Sp. kä-kä'ō)
coconut	the fruit of the coconut palm (has no connection with cocoa)
coin	money
quoin	a wedge; a corner block of stone or brick (koin, or kwoin)
collie	a Scotch shepherd dog (kŏl'ĭ)
coolie	an Oriental laborer (kōō'lĭ)
collision	a clash
collusion	a secret scheme to defraud
coma	a state of unconsciousness; a blur of light (kō'mȧ)
comma	a punctuation mark
complacent	self-satisfied (kŏm-plā'sent)
complaisant	obliging; affable (kŏm-plā'zȧnt)
complement	that which completes
compliment	praise
comprehensible	intelligible; understandable
comprehensive	extensive; of wide range
compute	to calculate
commute	to substitute something less severe or burdensome; to travel daily on a commutation ticket
condemn	to pronounce opinion or sentence against
contemn	to despise or view with contempt

183

confidant	(mas.)⎱ one to whom secrets are entrusted (kŏn'fĭ-dănt')
confidante	(fem.)⎰
confident	possessed of firm belief
conjurer	a magician or juggler (kŭn'jûr-er)
conjuror	a confederate; an entreater (kŏn-jōōr'er)
contagious	spreading by contact with diseased persons
infectious	spreading by germs or parasites which attack the body and which may be carried in the air or water (not necessarily by contact with diseased persons)
contemptible	deserving of contempt; despicable
contemptuous	expressing contempt; disdainful
continual	endless; of broken occurrence, but frequently or constantly repeated
continuous	ending, but of uninterrupted progress while it continues
continuation	pertains to length—the prolongation of, extension of, or carrying on of something
continuance	pertains to time—the duration of, lasting of, or succession of things
controller	a private officer who controls accounts or moneys
comptroller	a public officer or accountant who controls public moneys
coral	a small sea animal, or its skeleton (kŏr'al)
corral	an enclosure (kō-răl')
choral	pertaining to a chorus (kō'ral)
chorale	a sacred song, sung in chorus (kō-räl')
cord	a string; tendon; wood measure
chord	musical tones in harmony; a straight line; part of a bridge truss
core	the central part
corps	a body of persons, especially a military division (kōr; pl. kōrz)
corporal	bodily, as "corporal punishment"
corporeal	material or physical, not spiritual
correspondent	one who communicates by letter
corespondent	a joint respondent in a divorce suit (kō'rē-spŏn'dent)
corrosion	an eating away, as by chemical action
erosion	a wearing away, as of land by the action of water
costume	a garment
custom	practice
council	an assembly for legislative or administrative purposes (councilor)
counsel	advice; one who is consulted for advice; an attorney or group of attorneys conducting a case, as "legal counsel" (a camp counselor)
consul	a commercial representative of a foreign country (kŏn'sŭl)
courtesy	a favor; politeness
curtsy	a genuflection
creak	a squeaking sound
creek	a stream (krēk; colloq. krĭk)
crick	a muscular cramp
credible	believable
credulous	prone to believe on slight evidence
creditable	deserving esteem
credit	to give credit for or to
accredit	to attribute; to furnish with credentials as an "accredited repre

sentative"; to certify as maintaining prescribed standards, as "accredited schools"

crevasse	a large fissure or deep crevice (krĕ-văs′)
crevice	a narrow split or crack
cue	a catchword; a signal; a billiard rod
queue	a pigtail; a line of persons waiting
curaçao	a liqueur (kū′rȧ-sō′)
Curaçao	an island in the Dutch West Indies (kōō′rä-sä′ō)
currant	a fruit
current	a flowing or passing; the general course. Of the present time, as "current literature"

D

dam	a barrier
damn	a curse
Dane	a native of Denmark
deign	to condescend
days	plural of "day"
daze	to stun. A stupefied condition
dear	valued highly
deer	an animal
decant	to pour gently
descant	to discourse; to sing or play (dĕs-kănt′)
decease	death
disease	illness
demise	death, as of royalty (dē-mīz′) (See also "device", below)
decent	respectable; proper; fitting
descent	downward progress
dissent	disagreement
decree	a decision or order in the nature of a law
degree	a step or point in a series; an academic title conferred
decry	to censure or discredit
descry	to espy something distant or obscure (dē-skrī′)
definite	clear; fixed; well-defined
definitive	final; conclusive
demean	to behave or conduct [oneself]
demesne	domain; lands; estate (dē-mān′, or -mēn′)
depository	the place where something is deposited
depositary	the person or trustee with whom something is deposited
deprecate	to express disapproval of
depreciate	to decrease in value; underestimate
desecrate	to profane
descendant	(noun) an offspring; a part of the heavens; "in the descendant", on the decline
descendent	(adj.) descending
desert	to abandon. Merit; reward, as "just deserts" (dē-zĕrt′)
desert	barren land (dĕz′ert)
dessert	the last course of a repast (dĕ-zĕrt′)

deserve	to be worthy of
disserve	to treat or serve badly
desirable	worth desiring
desirous	entertaining desire. ("Desirous" for "desirable" is obsolete.)
detract	to take from
distract	to divert the attention of; harass
device	(noun) a contrivance (dē-vīs')
devise	(verb) to contrive; to convey real estate by will (dē-vīz')
demise	to lease; to convey a life estate (dē-mīz') (See "decease")
remise	to surrender title to, as to "remise, release, and forever quitclaim" (rē-mīz')
diary	a daily record
dairy	a place where milk products are made
dictograph	a detective device; an interoffice telephone
dictaphone	a dictation device
die	a tool; a machine; a metal block bearing a design or letters for reproduction. To cease living (dying)
dye	material for staining or coloring. To color (dyeing)
disassemble	to take apart
dissemble	to disguise, or feign
disassociate } **dissociate**	interchangeable, but there is a tendency to use the shorter form
disburse	to pay out
disperse	to scatter
discomfit	to baffle; to overwhelm or defeat (noun, discomfiture)
discomfort	to make uneasy (noun, discomfort)
discreet	prudent (dĭs-krēt')
discrete	distinct or separate (an opposite of "concrete") (dĭs'krēt)
disinterested	impartial; acting without self-interest
uninterested	not interested; indifferent; unconcerned
dispense	to distribute; administer
dispense with	to forgo or do without
disseminate	to spread widely or broadcast
dissimulate	to conceal by pretending
dissoluble } **dissolvable**	interchangeable
distinct	clear; individual; separate
distinctive	distinguishing; characteristic
distrait	absent-minded (dĭs'trā'; Fr. dēs'trĕ')
distraught	distracted (dĭs-trôt')
divers	various or sundry (dī'verz)
diverse	different (dī-vērs')
do	to perform
due	owing; proper, as "in due course"; directly, as "due west" (dū)
dew	condensed moisture, as "the dew point" (dū, not dō͞o)
doe	a deer
dough	a paste

186

dolphin	a fish
dauphin	the eldest son of the king of France (1349 to 1830)
done	performed
dun	a demand for payment; a tannish color
dose	a measured quantity
doze	a light sleep
draft draught	interchangeable; but the shorter "draft", for all uses, is generally preferred
drought drouth	(drout) (drouth) } a parching dryness from want of rain
dual	twofold
duel	a combat between two persons
dungeon	a dark prison
dudgeon	sullen anger; resentment (dŭj′on)
Dutch	pertaining to the Netherlands ("Pennsylvania Dutch"—German)
Deutsch	the German language (doich)
dying	being overcome by death
dyeing	coloring
dieing	cutting or stamping with a die

E

earn	to acquire by effort
urn	a vessel or vase
earnest	serious; sincere; binding, as "earnest money"
Ernest	a man's name
earthy	like earth or soil
earthly	worldly or material (opposed to "heavenly")
East, the	the oriental countries east of the Mediterranean. The East in the United States is regarded as the states east of the Mississippi River; or particularly, the states east of the Allegheny Mountains.
West, the	the Americas (the Western Hemisphere or the New World) and Europe. The West in the United States is regarded as the states west of the Mississippi River; or particularly, the states west of the Rocky Mountains.
East, Far	China, Japan, and neighboring countries—so called because they are the countries farthest east of Europe
East, Near	the Balkan States (Yugoslavia, Rumania, Albania, Bulgaria, Greece, and Turkey in Europe)
East, Middle	the Levant (the countries washed by the eastern Mediterranean: Egypt, Turkey in Asia, Syria, Palestine, and Trans-Jordan), and also Arabia, Iraq [Mesopotamia], and Iran [Persia]
economic economical	(See -ic, p. 13)
effete	worn out; barren (ĕ-fēt′)
au fait	skilled; expert (Fr. ō′fĕ′)
egoism	excessive thought of self
egotism	excessive talk of self; self-conceit
eldest	pertains to the age of persons in one family
oldest	pertains to the age of other persons and things

187

electric ⎰ electrical ⎱	(See p. 47)
emerge ⎰ immerge ⎱	(See "immerge", below)
emigrate	to go from one country (or part of a country) to another to live
immigrate	to come into a country, from another country, to live. (People emigrate out of one country, but they immigrate into another.)
eminent ⎰ emanate ⎱	(See "imminent", below)
emollient	a soothing application
emolument	remuneration; salary
empire	an imperial organization
umpire	a judge or arbiter
referee	one to whom things, or points of a game, are referred for decision
ended	used in phrases that express past time, as "for the week ended May 1"
ending	used in present or future phrases, as "for the week ending Saturday" (this coming Saturday), or "for the week ending June 1" (a future date)
endorse	is the form generally used in business papers
indorse	is used in legal papers
enervate	to weaken
innervate	to stimulate [through the nerves]
energize	to give energy to
enormousness	vastness of size
enormity	greatness of horror or depravity
entomology	insect zoology
etymology	the history of words
envelop	(verb) to wrap around (ĕn-vĕl′up)
envelope	(noun) a cover or wrapper (ĕn′vĕ-lōp; Fr. än′vĕ-lōp′)
epic	a poem of action in heroic style
epoch	a period of time introduced by a memorable event which acts as a turning point in history
epitaph	an inscription for the dead
epithet	an appropriate descriptive word or phrase
epigram	a clever, compact saying
equable	even; uniform
equitable	fair; just
erasable	capable of being erased (ē-rās′a-bl)
irascible	quick-tempered (ĭ-răs′ĭ-bl, or I-răs′)
err	to commit an error (ĕr or ûr)
ere	before (no apostrophe before this word)
e'er	a contraction of "ever"
errant	wandering
arrant	notoriously bad; downright
euphemism	a softened statement; substitution of an agreeable expression for a disagreeable one
euphuism	high-flown speech

188

everyone everybody	interchangeable (See Subjects, p. 71)
exalt	to elevate
exult	to rejoice
exercise	to put into action
exorcise	to drive out, as an evil spirit
exit	a going out; a leaving
exodus	a going forth, as a migration
expatiate	to enlarge upon
expiate	to atone for
extant	still existing
extent	measure
extract	a selected literary passage (usually large)
excerpt	a carefully selected literary passage (usually small)
eye	the organ of sight
I	personal pronoun; a shape, as "I-beam", "I-rail"
aye	yes (ī)
aye	always (ā)

F

facet	one of several small flat surfaces (făs'et)
faucet	a tap
facetious	witty
factitious	artificial
fictitious	not real; like fiction
factious	promoting discontent or a faction
fain	gladly, or reluctantly willing
feign	to pretend
faint	weak
feint	a deceptive movement; a trick
fair	favorable; moderately satisfactory; just. An exhibit
fare	food; cost of transportation. To go [forth]; to live
fairy	an imaginary being
faery faerie	pertaining to fairyland
faker	one who fakes; a peddler
fakir	a wandering religious wonder worker (East India) (fȧ-kēr', or fā'ker)
farther	pertaining to actual distance
further	additional; more advanced
fate	destiny
fete	a festival. To honor (fāt; Fr. fât)
faun	a deity of the woods—half-human, with pointed ears and goat's feet
fawn	a young deer; a yellowish brown color. To court favor
faze	to disturb (also spelled feaze, fease, feese, feeze, phase)
phase	an appearance or angle of a subject; a stage in development
feaze	(dialectal) to unravel (fēz)

189

feet	plural of "foot"
feat	an act of skill or strength
fellow	an associate; one holding a fellowship; an equal
fellah	a laborer in Egypt
felloe	a part of the rim of a wheel
ferment	to change, as with yeast; to be agitated from within
foment	to stir up; instigate
file	a smoothing instrument; a place for filing papers
phial	a small bottle (fī'al) (See "vial", below)
flare	a spreading or blazing out; a torch
flair	instinctive discernment; aptitude; scent
flaunt	to brandish, display, parade, or show off
flout	to insult, taunt, mock
flea	an insect
flee	to speed away from (fled)
flew	did fly
flue	a chimney
flu	(colloq.) influenza
flow	to move smoothly, as in a stream
floe	a flat mass of floating ice
flower	a blossom; a plant that blooms
flour	ground meal
foggy	beclouded; misty
fogy	one behind the times (fō'gy)
follow	to come after
fallow	to plow and harrow land but leave it unseeded for a season, as to "summer-fallow". A pale yellowish color
for	a preposition
fore	first; preceding. The front; a shouted signal in golf
four	a numeral
forbear	to refrain from; to do without
forebear	an ancestor
forceful	full of force; effective
forcible	powerful; accomplished by force, as a "forcible entry"
forgo	to relinquish; to let pass
forego	to go before, as "foregone conclusions"
formerly	heretofore
formally	in a dignified manner
fort	a fortified place
forte	a special talent
forth	forward; outward
fourth	next after the third
forward	eager; bold; advanced
froward	obstinately willful
foul	unfavorable; unfair; unclean. Entangled, as a "foul anchor"
fowl	a bird or chicken
franchise } enfranchise }	(See Legal Terms, p. 473)

190

frank	candid. To dispatch free of charge, as Government letters, etc.
franc	a French coin
frays	skirmishes. Wears out
phrase	a group of words
freeze	to chill, congeal, or become ice
frieze	an ornamental strip; a coarse cloth
funeral	burial
funereal	sad or solemn
fur	the hairy coat of an animal
fir	a tree

G

Gaelic	pertaining to certain branches of the Celts, such as the Irish, Scottish Highlanders, etc. (gāl'ik)
Gallic	pertaining to ancient Gaul or modern France (găl'ik)
gamble	to hazard
gambol	to frolic
gantlet	a punishment, as to "run the gantlet"
gauntlet	a glove
gamut	the scale or range, as to "run the gamut" (găm'ŭt)
gap	an opening
gape	to yawn; to stare stupidly (gāp, găp, or gäp)
gate	the closure for a passageway; an opening
gait	manner of walking or moving
genius	inspired talent; extraordinary creative power; a guardian spirit
genus	a classification of species (jē'nŭs)
gentle	mild; of or pertaining to good birth
gentile	one of a different religious belief; one not a Jew (jĕn'tīl)
genteel	well-bred
gild	to embellish with gold
guild	a group of persons, or plants
gilt	gold-surfacing material. Gilded
guilt	liability for blame or wrongdoing
glazier	a glassworker
glacier	an ice formation
goal	an end or aim
ghoul	a demon (gōol, or goul)
gorilla	an African ape
guerrilla	one who wages irregular or predatory warfare (gĕ-rĭl'a)
grease	fat
Greece	a country
great	large
grate	a frame of bars. To scrape; to irritate
grill	a gridiron
grille	a wrought-iron framework, fence, or barrier
grisly	ghastly (grĭz'ly)
grizzly	somewhat gray (grizzly bear)

191

grove	a group of trees
groove	a hollowed-out space; a rut
guarantee	to warrant the performance of; to secure. A warrant of soundness, reliability, or genuineness
guaranty	a financial security; a surety. (Some writers do not differentiate between these words as nouns, and use "guarantee" in all instances. "Guarantee" is the verb always.)
guest	a visitor
guessed	did guess
Guinea	a gulf and region on the west coast of Africa (gĭn'ĭ) (French Guinea, Spanish Guinea, guinea hen, guinea pig). New Guinea—a large island north of Australia (New Guinea, British; New Guinea, Dutch, or commonly "Dutch New Guinea" or "Netherland New Guinea")
guinea	a coin first made of Guinea gold; now a British monetary term for one pound one shilling (about $5)
Guiana	a region in South America (gē-ä'nȧ) (British Guiana, French Guiana; "Dutch Guiana" is the common name for Surinam [Du. Suriname])

H

hail	frozen rain. To come [from]; to call to. A greeting, as in the phrase "hail-fellow-well-met"
hale	robust. To pull or drag, as "haled into court"
hair	a filament that grows from the skin
hare	a rabbitlike animal
hall	a room
haul	to pull or drag
hay	dried grass
hey	an exclamation (heyday)
heal	to restore or cure
heel	a part of the foot
healthful	producing good health, as "a healthful climate"
healthy	enjoying good health, as "a healthy person". ("Healthful" and "healthy" are interchangeable to a certain extent, and such phrases as "a healthy climate" and "a healthy recreation" are used and sanctioned. But in other than these few phrases, the distinction between the words is rather well observed.)
hear	to perceive by the ear
here	in this place
heard	did hear
herd	a drove
hearsay	rumor
heresy	an opinion opposed to the commonly accepted doctrine (hĕr'ĕ-sy)
heart	a part of the body
hart	a stag
hew	to cut or chop
hue	color; tint. A shout of alarm, as in "hue and cry"
high	lofty
hie	to hasten

192

him	a pronoun
hymn	a sacred song
historic	history-making; famous in history
historical	pertaining to history
histrionic	pertaining to theatricals
hoard	a supply stored away
horde	a roaming tribe or pack
hoes	garden tools
hose	stockings; rubber tubing
hole	an opening
whole	entire
holy	sacred
holey	full of holes
wholly	entirely
holly	a tree or shrub
horse	an animal
hoarse	rough or harsh of sound
huge	immense
Hugh	a man's name
human	pertaining to man
humane	compassionate
hypercritical	overcritical (hī'per-)
hypocritical	deceitful; smug with pretense (hĭp'ō-)
hyphen ⎫ hyphenize ⎬ hyphenate ⎭	All verbs, and interchangeable; but "hyphen", because it is shorter, is preferable.

I

idle	inactive; groundless, as "an idle rumor"
ideal	perfect
idol	an object of worship
idyl	a scene of rustic life
illicit	unlawful
elicit	to draw out
imaginary	nonexistent, that is, existing only in the imagination, as "imaginary fears", "imaginary people" (not real)
imaginative	existing, but created from or characterized by imagination, as "an imaginative drawing", "an imaginative person"
imbue	to saturate; to impress deeply; to tinge deeply or dye
imbrue	to stain or drench [with blood]
endue	to clothe; to invest with some quality
endow	to enrich; to benefit with a gift
immerge	to plunge under; to sink in; to immerse
emerge	to rise out of; to come into view
immersed	sunk in (especially in a liquid)
emersed	standing out of
immersion	a going under; a sinking in
emersion	a rising out of; a coming into view

193

imminent	threatening to happen at once
immanent	inherent
eminent	distinguished; outstanding; evident
emanate	to originate, or start [from]
impassable	not passable; intolerable
impassible	not capable of suffering or feeling pain
imperial	sovereign; pertaining to an empire, or an emperor
empirical	based on practical experience rather than on theory, as rule-of-thumb methods
empyreal	celestial, as "empyreal blue"
impostor	a pretender
imposture	act or conduct of a pretender; fraud
in	a preposition
inn	a tavern
incarnation	embodiment in a living form
incarceration	imprisonment
incidents	occurrences
incidence	a falling upon; an angle; occurrence, as "the incidence of a disease"
inclose } **enclose** }	interchangeable. "Enclose" is preferred in British usage.
incredible	unbelievable
incredulous	unbelieving; skeptical
indention	the setting in of a line in typewriting or printing
indentation	a dent or depression; a notch in a border
indiscreet	imprudent
indiscrete	compact; made up of similar elements
indite	to put into words or writing (in-dīt′)
indict	to accuse (in-dīt′)
ingenious	clever; inventive; resourceful (in-jēn′yŭs) (noun, ingenuity)
ingenuous	candid; artlessly frank (in-jĕn′ū-ŭs) (noun, ingenuousness)
insensate	incapable of sensation; senseless; brutal
insentient	inanimate
insensible	unable to feel; unconscious
insensitive	not sensitive; unimpressionable
insight	mental vision
incite	to instigate
insoluble	incapable of being dissolved (indissoluble)
insolvable	not solvable or explainable
insolvent	pertaining to a debtor who is unable to pay his debts
instance	occasion; example; request
instants	brief moments
insulate	to prevent the transfer of heat, electricity, etc.
insolate	to expose to the rays of the sun
intelligent	possessed of intelligence or understanding
intelligible	understandable
interpolate	to insert
interpellate	to question formally
extrapolate	(note spelling) opposite of "interpolate" (mathematical)

194

interpretative } interpretive }	interchangeable; but the first is usually preferred, except in the phrase "interpretive dancing"
interstate intrastate	between two or more states within one state
irruption eruption	a bursting in a bursting out
isle aisle	a small island a passageway
its it's	possessive of "it" (no apostrophe) contraction of "it is"

J

jam	to crowd; to cause to become wedged, as to "jam a lock"; to thrust with force, as to "jam on the brakes"
jamb	a part of a door
jest	to banter. A joke
geste	(Fr.) a gesture; "beau geste", a gallant gesture; an epic poem (zhĕst)
gest	(Eng.) an exploit or romantic adventure (jĕst)
gist	the main idea involved, as "the gist of the matter" (jĭst)
just	fair. Nearly; exactly
joust	to tilt with lances on horseback (jŭst)

K

Keltic Celtic	(kĕl'tik) } interchangeable; usually refers to Irish, but really includes (sĕl'tik) } several languages
kernel colonel	a seed; the central part a military officer
key quay	that which controls or unlocks a landing place or wharf (kē, not kwā)
kill kiln	to put an end to a furnace (kĭl, or kĭln)

L

laboratory lavatory	a workshop for conducting scientific experiments a place for washing
lain lane	rested; reposed a narrow way; an ocean route
last latest	final last up to the present time } largely interchangeable
later latter	at a subsequent time the second-mentioned; the last, as "the latter part of the year"
lath lathe	a strip of wood (làth) a machine for shaping material (lāthe)
lea lee	a grassland; a textile measure a sheltered place
leaf lief leave	a part of a plant. To bear leaves willingly to go from; to let be; to bear leaves. Permission

195

lean	to incline. Thin
lien	a legal claim (lē'ĕn, or lēn)
led	did lead
lead	a heavy metallic element. To fit with lead
legend	a tradition; an explanation or inscription (lĕj'ĕnd, rather than lē'jĕnd)
legion	a multitude
lesson	a teaching
lessen	to diminish
levy	to assess or collect
levee	an embankment; a wharf; a court reception
liable	responsible; having an unfavorable tendency toward (lī'a-bl) (See "apt", p. 6)
libel	written defamatory statements (lī'bĕl); (adm. law) a complaint
liar	a falsifier
lyre	a musical instrument (līr)
lie	to rest or recline; to deceive (lying)
lye	a caustic alkaline solution or powder
lie ⎱ lay ⎰	(See Verbs, p. 84)
lifelong	lasting throughout life
livelong	seemingly long in passing
lightening	making lighter
lightning	a sudden flash of light
limb	a branch
limn	to draw (lĭm)
linear	pertains to measurement, as "linear feet"
lineal	pertains to ancestral lines or lineage
liniment	an ointment
lineament	a feature (lĭn'ē-à-ment)
links	connections
lynx	an animal
liquor	a liquid, usually alcoholic
liqueur	an alcoholic cordial (lē-kûr')
literal	according to the letter or exact facts
littoral	pertaining to a shore
livid	discolored, as black and blue; lead-colored; ashy pale. "Livid" appears in the names of certain reddish colors, as "livid violet".
lurid	sallow; of red-yellow hue; ghastly (lū'rid, not lûr-)
load	a burden or cargo
lode	an ore deposit
loan	a lending
lone	solitary
loan ⎱ lend ⎰	(See Verbs, p. 83)
loath	averse; unwilling
loathe	to detest

196

lose	to part with unintentionally
loose	not restrained; unfastened
luxuriant	abundant; rich in growth, design, or display
luxurious	promoting luxury or ease

M

madding	raging
maddening	enraging
made	did make
maid	a young girl; a servant
magnet	that which has magnetic attraction
magnate	an influential, rich, or powerful person (măg′nāt)
magnificent	having splendor
munificent	unusually generous or lavish
mail	that which is posted
male	masculine
main	chief
mane	hair on the neck of certain animals
malfeasance **nonfeasance** **misfeasance**	(See Legal Terms, p. 474)
manner	a mode; a way; "to the manner born"
manor	a mansion or estate
mantel	the structure around a fireplace
mantle	a cloak
marshal	an officer. To arrange in order
martial	military
marital	pertaining to marriage
martin	a bird
marten	a fur; an animal
mast	a pole or spar
massed	formed into a mass
masterful	exhibiting dominance or mastery
masterly	exhibiting superior knowledge or skill
material	substance, or parts, of which anything is made
matériel	equipment (opposite of "personnel") (Fr. mȧ′tā′rē-ĕl′)
mean	to intend. Ignoble; average, as a "mean distance"
mien	appearance; demeanor
mesne	(law) middle, as a "mesne encumbrance" (mēn)
meantime **meanwhile**	used interchangeably; but "meanwhile" usually stands alone, and "meantime" is used in the phrase "in the meantime"
meat	a food
meet	to join. Suitable
mete	to measure. Measurement, as in the legal phrase "metes and bounds"
medal	a decoration of reward; a medallion
meddle	to interfere

197

meritorious	deserving of praise
meretricious	tawdry, as "meretricious dress"
meticulous	careful, as "meticulous dress"
metal	a hard, heavy substance
mettle	spirit; courage
meter	a measure
métier	a calling or profession (Fr. mä-tyä′)
millinery	hats
millenary	a 1000th anniversary
miner	one who mines
minor	smaller. A person under age
missive	a letter; a message
missile	an object that is thrown or hurled
mist	vapor; haze
missed	failed to do; noted the absence of
mite	a tiny particle; a small sum of money
might	force. Past of "may"
modal	pertaining to a mode (mōd′ăl)
model	a pattern; design; fashion
mood	disposition; feeling; a grammatical term (mōod)
mode	fashion; method; grammatical mood (mōd)
moral	pertaining to right conduct. A lesson
morale	state of mind; spirit or feeling, as of a body of people (mō-răl′)
morality	virtue; ethics
mortality	occurrence of death; death rate
mores	customs or laws (L. mō′rēz)
Moors	natives of Morocco (mŏŏrz)
moors	heaths (mŏŏrz; Br. mōrz)
morning	early day
mourning	sorrowing; "mourning dove", not "*morning* dove"
motive	the moving power or idea; the theme
motif	(Fr.) the theme; the recurring unit of a pattern (mō-tēf′)
leitmotiv ⎰	
leitmotif ⎱	(Ger.) an identifying phrase in a musical composition (līt′mō-tēf′)
muscle	a part of the body
mussel	a shellfish

N

nap	a doze; a rough surface on fabrics
nape	the back of the neck (nāp)
knap	a mound. To snap off (knapsack)
naught	zero; a cipher
nought	nothing
naval	pertaining to the navy
navel	the central part; a part of the body; a descriptive term, as "navel orange"
nave	the center part of a church (nāv)
knave	a rogue

198

nay	no
née	born (used to designate a married woman's maiden name) (Fr. nā)
neigh	the call of a horse
necessities	things that are urgently needed, as "the necessities of life"
necessaries	things that are usually needed, as "necessaries supplied to a minor"
need	to require
knead	to work into a mass
needed	wanted
needful	necessary
needy	in need
neglect	the act of neglecting
negligence	the habit of neglecting
new	recent; fresh
knew	did know
gnu	an African antelope
night	darkness
knight	one who has been knighted
no	a negative
know	to have knowledge of
nobody } no one }	interchangeable (See Subjects, p. 71)
none	not one
nun	a woman member of a religious order
not	in no way
knot	a tie

O

O } Oh }	(See Exclamation Point, p. 247)
oar	a rowing implement
ore	a natural deposit
o'er	over
obelisk	a tapering column, as "Cleopatra's Needle" (ŏb'ĕ-lisk)
odalisk } odalisque }	a slave in a harem (ō'dȧ-lisk)
observance	act of attending to, complying with, or commemorating, as the "observance of a rule", "observance of a holiday"
observation	act of seeing, watching, noticing, fixing the gaze or mind upon, as "clear observation", "learning by observation"
oculist	one who treats the eyes
occultist	a believer in supernatural powers (ŏ-kŭlt'ist)
optician	one who makes optical glasses
optometrist	one who measures the range or powers of vision
of } off }	These small words are often mixed, simply because of hasty spelling.
one	a single thing
won	did win

199

oral   spoken. ("Oral" suggests the act of speaking.)

verbal   by word of mouth; word for word. ("Verbal", when applied to spoken words, suggests words that are lasting or binding, as a "verbal agreement". "Verbal", when applied to written words, calls attention to the words themselves and means literal, as a "verbal translation".)

ordinance   a law

ordnance   military ammunition and supplies

ordonnance   an arrangement in order

Orient   the Far East

Occident   Europe and the Western Hemisphere

orient   to cause to face the east, hence to get the bearings of; to adjust

orientate   interchangeable with "orient" (as a transitive verb); to face the east (an intransitive verb)

osculate   to kiss

oscillate   to swing back and forth

vacillate   to waver or stagger

our   a pronoun

hour   a measure of time

overdo   to do to excess

overdue   past due

P

pact   an agreement

packed   did pack

pail   a bucket

pale   faint. A stake; an enclosure, or protective realm, as "outside the pale"

pain   a hurt; suffering; care, as to "take pains"

pane   a window glass; a panel; a division

pair   a couple

pare   to cut or peel

pear   a fruit

palate   a part of the mouth

palette   an artist's color board

pallet   a shabby bed, as of straw; a wooden implement; a board; a tool

pall   gloom; a dark covering. To become insipid, as "pleasures pall"

Paul   a man's name

partly   in part, as "wholly or partly destroyed"

partially   to some degree, as "completely or partially established"

past   pertaining to time gone by

passed   gone beyond; transferred; passed an examination, as a "passed master". (A "past master" is one who has been master.)

patience   endurance

patients   persons being treated medically

peace   calm; content; harmony

piece   to put together. A portion; a short composition

peak	a point; the top. To become thin, as to "peak and pine"
peek	to peep
pique	to provoke; to pride [oneself]. Resentment
piqué	a cotton fabric
pedal	a foot lever. Pertaining to the feet
peddle	to sell from house to house
peel	to remove the rind or skin of
peal	to resound, as a bell
peer	to look intently. An equal; a nobleman
pier	a pillar for support; a landing place
pendant	(noun) that which hangs
pendent	(adj.) suspended; overhanging; pending
percent	number of parts to 100. ("Percent" is usually used after a number, but may stand alone as a noun if referring to a definite number, as "What percent were turned back?" Note that "percent" is now written as one word, and without a period—Government Printing Office usage.)
percentage	relationship of a part to the whole of 100 parts. ("Percentage" is often used when the word does not refer to a definite number, as "A small percentage had to be replaced." "Percentage" is used in commerce to mean a rate per hundred, as in commissions, allowances, duties, discounts, etc.)
peremptory	positive; decisive; dictatorial
pre-emptory	having the right of preference; shutting out (usually "pre-emptive")
perfect	faultless; complete. To make perfect
prefect	an official
perpetrate	to carry through; to be guilty of
perpetuate	to make lasting or perpetual
perquisite	an extra profit or privilege
prerequisite	something required as a preliminary
persecute	to torment; oppress
prosecute	to pursue in order to accomplish; (law) to sue
personnel	the persons engaged in a certain service; staff
personal	individual; private
persons } people }	(See Words Misused, p. 18)
perspective	mental or physical view in correct proportion
prospective	expected; anticipated
perspicacious	mentally sharp
perspicuous	clear; understandable
physic	a medicine
psychic	pertaining to the soul or spirit
physique	the structure of the body
physical	material
psychical	mental
picaresque	pertaining to rogues or vagabonds
picturesque	having the rugged, quaint, or charming qualities of a picture
pigeon	a dove
pidgin	a Chinese corruption of the word "business", as "pidgin English" (pĭj'ĭn)

pipe	a tube
piping	a system of pipes
plain	flat; simple; clear. Level prairie land
plane	a flat surface; a level or grade; a tool. To make level. ("Plain sailing" and "plane sailing" are both used.)
plaintiff	(law) the one who brings suit; the accuser
plaintive	mournful
plate	a flat piece. To overlay with metal
plait	to braid (plāt, or plăt)
pleat	to fold cloth (plēt) (sometimes spelled plait)
plat	(not generally used) to braid; to plot [a piece of land]
plum	a fruit
plumb	a weight. To sound or test, as to "plumb the depths"
pole	a long wooden rod; end of a magnet; polar region, as "North Pole"
poll	a voting; the head or top ("poll tax"—a tax per head)
politicly	discreetly; with tact on the surface and shrewdness underneath
politically	with regard to politics
poor	meager; unfortunate; not good
pour	to stream
pore	to ponder. A small opening
poplar	a tree
popular	pertaining to people
populace	the common people
populous	thickly populated
portion	a part. To divide into portions ("apportion"—to allot)
proportion	relationship or ratio of parts. To adjust in relationship
post card ⎫ postal card ⎭	generally interchangeable; but the Post Office Department makes the distinction that a "post card" is a "private mailing card", while a "postal card" is one printed by the Government with the stamp impressed thereon
power	strength; force
prowess	strength and courage
practical	useful; experienced; actual
practicable	usable; workable; possible. (A "practical" thing may not be "practicable" under certain circumstances.)
practice	(noun) performance
practise	(verb) to perform
pray	to beseech
prey	a victim of capture. To plunder; trouble, as "prey on the mind"
precede	to go before
proceed	to advance (noun, procedure)
precedence	priority (prē-sēd'ens)
precedents	established rules (prĕs'e-dents)
predicate	to assert; affirm; (U.S.) to base [on] or establish
predict	to foretell
premier	first; chief. A prime minister (prē'mĭ-er, or prĕm'yĕr)
première	the opening performance of a play; a leading lady (Fr. prē-my&r')

202

SIMILAR WORDS

prescribe	to designate; dictate
proscribe	to outlaw; prohibit
presentiment	a foreboding
presentment	a presentation [of commercial papers for payment]; a report by a grand jury
presentation	a presenting; a showing
presents	gifts; (law) present writings, as "to whom these presents shall come"
presence	the state of being present; bearing; alertness, as "presence of mind"
pretend	to make believe; to lay claim [to]
portend	to foreshow; to indicate by an advance sign
principal	(adj.) chief; main. (Noun) a capital sum; the most important
principle	(noun) a rule of conduct; a general truth; inherent character; a fundamental part or element, as "Oxygen is a principle of air."
proceeding	moving forward. A course of action, as "legal proceedings"
preceding	going before, as "the preceding page"
prodigy	a marvel
protégé	(mas.) one cared for by another (prō'tā'zhā')
protégée	(fem.)
progeny	offspring
profit	gain
prophet	one who foretells
program	a plan; a list
pogrom	devastation; massacre (pō-grŏm')
prophecy	(noun) an inspired prediction (prŏf'e-sĭ)
prophesy	(verb) to foretell (prŏf'e-sī)
proportional / **proportionate**	interchangeable (See also "portion", above)
protagonist	the chief actor or advocate; the leader
antagonist	an opponent; foe
provided	on condition that (used when a stipulation is involved)
providing	furnishing (should be used when "furnishing" or "supplying" is meant)
provisional	based on temporary conditions
provincial	pertaining to a province or small region; narrow
Provençal	pertaining to Provence in France, especially to the language of the troubadours (Fr. prō'vän'sȧl')
purpose	(verb) to intend. (Noun) intention; object
propose	to offer for consideration; to intend

Q

quarts	measures
quartz	a mineral
questionnaire / **questionary**	interchangeable; meaning a set of questions
quiet	still; calm
quite	wholly; considerably
quit	to stop; leave

203

| quire | a paper measure |
| choir | a company of singers |

R

| rabbit | an animal; "Welsh rabbit", rather than "rarebit" |
| rabbet | a groove; a joint |

| rack | a framework; thin clouds; a gait; a gearing. To harass |
| wrack | debris cast ashore by the sea; wreck (now rare, except as "rack" in "rack and ruin") |

| rail | a bar. To scold |
| railing | a continuous bar, composed of several rails |

| railroad ⎰ railway ⎱ | interchangeable. in American usage. "Railway" is preferred in British usage. |

rain	falling waterdrops
rein	a part of a bridle; a curb; restraint
reign	to rule. Time or term of power, as "a king's reign"

raise	to lift something; to produce something. A lifting
raze	to destroy; demolish
rays	beams
rise	to lift itself or oneself. A self-increase (See also Verbs, p. 87)

| rap | to strike a quick blow |
| wrap | to enfold |

rapt	engrossed
rapped	struck with quick blows
wrapped	enfolded

| read | to interpret by reading |
| reed | a bamboolike plant |

| real | true; existing; actual |
| reel | a winding device; a spool; a dance. To whirl |

| realty | real estate |
| reality | that which is real |

| receipt | an acknowledgment of things received |
| recipe | a formula for ingredients, as for cooking or medicine |

| recognizance | (law) a recorded promise (rē-kŏn′ĭ-zăns, or rē-kŏg′nĭ-zăns) |
| reconnaissance | a survey tour; act of reconnoitering (rē-kŏn′ĭ-săns) |

| recourse | a resorting to for assistance; resort |
| resource | that supply to which one turns for support |

| redound | to return or flow back; to accrue, as to "redound to one's credit" |
| rebound | to bounce back from impact with another object |

| reek | to fume or smell |
| wreak | to inflict, as vengeance |

| re-enforce | to enforce again |
| reinforce | to strengthen |

| regimen | a regulated course of procedure, or diet, etc. (rĕj′ĭ-mĕn) |
| régime | a term or form of government, as "during a régime" (Fr. rā-zhēm′) |

register	a record; a list; the one who records
registrar	an official keeper of records
registry	the place where a register is kept

204

remediable	capable of being remedied (rē-mē′dĭ-a-bl)
remedial	providing a remedy (rē-mē′dĭ-al)
Renaissance	the revival of art and literature from the 14th to the 16th centuries; hence (not capitalized) any similar period of revived and active interest, especially in things old (rĕn′ĕ-säns′, or rē-nā′sáns)
renascence	a general revival; awakening or being reborn (rē-năs′ĕns)
repulsive	driving back or repelling; causing dislike or disgust
revulsive	causing or caused by a desire to draw back or turn away from
residence	a dwelling
residents	those who reside in a place
respectfully	with respect
respectively	each to each in the order designated
rest	to repose
wrest	to twist or pull away
reverend	worthy of reverence. "The Reverend" is a title of respect.
reverent	expressing reverence
reverence	profound respect. To revere
riffraff	rubbish. The rabble
riprap	a broken-stone foundation. retaining wall, or wearing bed, in water
rifle	a firearm. To rob
riffle	a ripple. To shuffle; to ruffle [through], as a book (rĭf′l)
raffle	a lottery. To give or sell by lottery, as to "raffle off"
right	correct
rite	a ceremony
write	to set down in writing
wright	a workman, as a shipwright, playwright, etc.
rime	hoarfrost
rhyme	a verse (sometimes spelled rime)
ring	to sound; to encircle
wring	to twist
road	a highway
rode	did ride
rowed	did row
roll	that which is rolled; a list, as "roll call"
role	a part in a play
roomer	a lodger
rumor	an unverified report
root	the underground part of a plant (rōot, not rŏŏt); a mathematical quantity. To dig up; (slang) to cheer for
route	a way (rōot). To send over a certain course (usually pronounced "rout" in military and shipping parlance)
rout	to put to flight; to drag forth. An uproar
roster	a list of names (rŏs′ter; Br. rō′ster)
roaster	for roasting
rooster	a chanticleer
rote	repetition, as "by rote"
wrote	did write
row	(rō) a line of things; (rou) (colloq.) a quarrel. To propel a boat
roe	fish eggs; a kind of deer

205

royalty	descendants of kings; the house of kings
nobility	titled persons
rung	sounded. A crossbar
wrung	twisted
rye	a grain
wry	distorted

S

safe deposit ⎱ safety deposit ⎰	both used, but the first is preferable because it is shorter, as "safe deposit box"
sail	to move or glide rapidly, as a ship. A ship's sail
sale	the process of selling
salon	a drawing room; a fashionable reception held periodically; (capitalized) an exhibition of art in Paris (Fr. sȧ'lôṅ')
saloon	a spacious room for a certain purpose, as a "dining saloon"; a barroom (U.S.)
sanatorium	a health resort, primarily where natural remedies, such as altitude. etc., are employed as curatives—usually for tuberculosis
sanitarium	a place where conditions are sanitary and therefore conducive to health, and where medical treatment is given
sane	having a sound mind
seine	a fishing net
Seine	a river in France, running through Paris. On the "left bank" is the educational center or "Latin Quarter" of the city. On the "right bank" is the more modernized section.
sanguine	hopeful
sanguinary	attended with bloodshed
Sargasso Sea	a part of the North Atlantic, where the waters are covered with floating sargasso seaweeds (sär-găs'ō)
Saragossa	a province and cathedral town in northern Spain (sär'ȧ-gŏs'ȧ; Sp. Zaragoza, thä'rä-gō'thä)
scrip	a written document as evidence that the holder is entitled to receive something therefor; a pilgrim's wallet
script	style of handwriting; the working scenario of a motion picture; (law) an original document
sculptor	one who carves
sculpture	the art of sculpturing; carved work
sealing	fastening, as with a seal or glue
ceiling	overhead covering
see	to perceive. A Catholic province
sea	a body of water
C	a shape, as "C-spring" (preferred to "cee spring")
seed	a part of a plant
cede	to give over
seem	to appear
seam	a meeting line; a thin layer of rock
seen	past participle of "see"
scene	a view; a setting; a division of a play

206

seer	a prophet
sear	dry. To burn
cere	to cover with wax
seize	to lay hold of
cease	to stop
sell	to transfer for a price
cell	a small place of confinement
seller	one who sells
cellar	an underground storeroom (saltcellar)
senses	faculties
census	statistics of population
sensible	intelligent; impressible through the senses, as "sensible to pain"
sensitive	quickly affected
sensuous	of the senses as distinguished from the intellect; appealing to the imagination through the senses, as "sensuous poetry."
sensual	of the senses, implying gross or worldly pleasure; carnal
sent	dispatched
scent	an odor. To smell
cent	a coin
sense	intelligence; meaning
serial	in series
cereal	grain used for food
session	assembly; a sitting; the time of being convened
cession	a giving over; a concession
secession	a withdrawal or separation from
cessation	a stopping
sewage	refuse or matter carried in sewers
sewerage	a system of sewers
shear	to cut, clip, or trim
sheer	fine or thin; unadulterated; downright; vertical. To swerve
shone	emitted light
shown	displayed; indicated
shoot	to fire; to hit or kill with a shot; to sprout; to pass over rapidly, as to "shoot the chutes"
chute	a waterfall; a slide; a narrow passage
sight	vision
site	location
cite	to quote; to name or summon
sinecure	a position with few duties (sī'nē-kūr, or sĭn')
cynosure	the North Star, hence the center of attraction (sī'nō-shụr; Br. sĭn'ō-sūr)
Singhalese	the chief race, or one of the race, of people in Ceylon (sĭng'gȧ-lēz')
Senegalese	natives, or one of the natives, of Senegal (sĕn'ē-gạl-ēz')
single	one. To select one from others, as to "single out"
signal	to inform by sign. Outstanding, as a "signal triumph"
Sinicism	that which is peculiar to the Chinese
cynicism	cynical quality
sit } set }	(See Verbs, p. 88)

slack	relaxed; inactive
slake	to allay; to mix lime with water (slāk, not *slăk*)
slay	to kill
sleigh	a winter vehicle
sley	a weaver's reed
slew	killed
slue	to twist; to slide or turn, as "The car slued round."
slough	(slou) a mudhole; a quagmire
slough	(sloō) a marshy place (also spelled slew, sloo, slue)
slough	(slŭf) to cast off
slick	slippery
sleek	glossy
slight	small. To neglect
sleight	skill; a trick; a quick, deceptive movement, as "sleight of hand"
slow	not rapid
sloe	a plumlike fruit (sloe-eyed)
sluff	(See "slough", above)
so	in such a manner, or to such a degree; thus; therefore; in order that
sew	to stitch
sow	to scatter, as seed (sō). A swine (sou)
sough	the sighing or murmuring of the wind (sou, or sŭf)
soared	did soar
sword	a weapon (sōrd)
sward	turf; greensward (swảrd)
soluble	capable of being dissolved
solvable	capable of being solved
some	a portion
sum	an amount; the total
someone ⎱ somebody ⎰	interchangeable (See Subjects, p. 71)
sometime	at an indefinite time, as "It may happen sometime." Former, as "sometime Judge of the Court"
some time	a period of time, as "some time ago", "some time elapsed"
sometimes	now and then
son	a descendant
sun	a heavenly body
sore	painful
soar	to rise aloft
soul	spiritual nature
sole	the under part of the foot; a fish. Single, as "for the sole purpose"
special	not general; specific; pertaining to a single thing, as "a special job", "a special occasion", "a special friend", "special delivery", "for their special benefit" "A special performance has been arranged." "This requires special training."
especial	extraordinary; particular "Take especial care to..." "There is no especial need to hurry."
spatial ⎱ spacial ⎰	pertaining to space (spā'shal)

specially	in a special manner
	"These books were bound specially for me." (a special job)
	"He was specially trained for the work." (special training)
especially	particularly
	"These books were sent especially for me." (particularly)
	"He was especially fitted for the work." (particularly)
specialty	a distinctive thing; a particular line (common in American usage). (Law) a sealed contract
speciality	a distinctive quality; a special characteristic (common in British usage)
specie	coin; "in specie", in U.S. currency (spē′shē)
species	a sort; kind; variety; class (both singular and plural) (spē′shēz)
specter	a ghost; phantom
scepter	a staff carried by a sovereign as a symbol of power
spiritual	pertaining to the spirit. A religious song
spirituel (mas.)	
spirituelle (fem.)	spirited; witty; intelligent (Fr. spē′rē′tü′ĕl′)
spy	to discover by careful or secret examination
espy	to catch sight of
stable	steady; firm. A barn
staple	chief; regular. A principal commercial article; a fastener
stair	a step or a series of steps
stare	a fixed gaze
stamp	to tramp about heavily (stamp out) (stamping ground)
stomp	to bring the foot down forcibly, as in applause or anger
stationary	in a fixed condition
stationery	writing materials
statue	a modeled likeness
statute	an enacted law
stayed	remained; kept back; reinforced; (law) postponed, as "stayed judgment"
staid	sedate
steak	a piece of meat
stake	a pointed stick; a hazard; a prize; a property; grubstake
steel	a metal alloy
steal	to take wrongfully; to go secretly
stimulant	an excitant
stimulus	an incentive
stop	to cease
estop	(law) to bar
estoppel	(law) a bar because of a previous action
strait	narrow; strict. Distress; a water passageway
straight	not curved or broken
stray	(See "astray", above)
style	mode; fashion
stile	a set of steps; turnstile; piece of a door
subtile	delicate; ethereal (sŭb′tĭl)
subtle	sly; clever; deep; fine, as a "subtle distinction" (sŭt′l)

209

subtitle	a secondary title, as in the title of a book or play
subhead	a subdivision heading placed in the center of the page; also a secondary newspaper heading
sidehead	a subdivision heading placed at the side of the page
sucker	a fish; a part of a plant; a valve
succor	relief. To give aid
sue	to prosecute (suing)
sou	an old coin
Sioux	an Indian tribe
suit	a set of things; a court action. To fit
suite	a retinue; a connected series, as a "suite of rooms" or a "music suite" (swēt)
sweet	saccharine; pleasing
summon	(verb) to call or command to appear
summons	(noun) a call or command to appear
surge	a rising and falling roll; a swelling wave
serge	a fabric
suspect	to imagine; surmise; mistrust
expect	to count upon; look forward to
suppose	to think; believe; conclude
sustenance	that which sustains life; nourishment
subsistence	maintenance; livelihood; living expenses (in contracts)
swathe	to wrap or bandage (swāthe)
swath	the sweep of the blade in mowing (swôth)
symbol	an emblem; a sign
cymbal	a platelike musical instrument

T

tail	the end. (Law) restricted [inheritance], as an "estate tail" or "fee tail"
tale	a story; a total, as "the tale of years"; count, as "payment by tale"
talisman	a charm
talesman	(law) one of the persons added to a jury (tă′lēz-man, or tālz′)
tantamount	equivalent
paramount	the highest; chief
taper	to diminish. A candle
tapir	an animal
tare	allowance for the weight of a container
tear	to rend. Depreciation, as "wear and tear"
taught	instructed
taut	tense; tight
tax	an assessment
tacks	small nails
tea	a beverage
tee	a mark in games; a small support for the ball in golf
T	a shape, as "T-iron", "T-square", etc. (preferred to "tee iron", etc.)

210

team	two or more that work together
teem	to abound
tear	a teardrop
tier	a layer; a row in a series, one above another
telegraph blank telegram blank	interchangeable; but the first is preferable since it is general in meaning; whereas the second may refer to but one type of message
temblor	an earthquake (from Sp., to tremble)
trembler	(elec.) a vibrating hammer
tremor	a vibration; a trembling; a slight earth disturbance
temerity	rashness
timidity	shyness
tenor	course; intent; nature; a part in music; (law) an exact copy [of an instrument]
tenure	a holding; a holding term
terminal	the end; especially the end of a railroad line
terminus	the boundary or goal; especially a city at the end of a railroad line
their	a pronoun ⎱ As common as these words are, it is not uncommon to
there	in that place ⎰ see them confused.
they're	they are
therefore	consequently
therefor	for that thing
thrash	to flog; to toss about; (naut.) to sail toward the wind in a choppy sea
thresh	to beat out grain; to argue to a conclusion, as to "thresh the matter out"
through thru	from beginning to end; by means of; because of. ("Thru" is less formal than "through".)
threw	did throw
throw	to fling or hurl
throe	agony, as "in the throes of creation"
thrown	hurled
throne	a royal chair; sovereign power
tide	the rise and fall of the ocean. To carry through, as to "tide over"
tied	fastened
timber	wood
timbre	a quality of tone (tĭm′ber; Fr. tăṅ′br)
time	duration, or a measure of duration
thyme	a plant used as a food seasoning (tīm)
to	a preposition indicating direction, attachment, or connection
too	also; to an excessive degree
two	a couple ("cut in two")
toe	a part of the foot ("toe the mark"); a part of a machine, or rod
tow	to pull along, as to "take in tow"
tortuous	twisting or winding, as "a tortuous path"; not forthright
torturous	inflicting pain or torture; cruelly distorting
track	a footprint or trace; a path or way; a racecourse; a railway
tract	a piece of land; a system ("digestive tract"); a treatise; sacred verses

211

transcribing	copying, as "transcribing notes"
transcription	a copy or reproduction

transmission — the transmitting of something without substance, as news, messages by telegraph, light, heat, and radio waves, etc.

transmittal — the transmitting of something with substance, as papers, goods, etc. A "letter of transmittal" often accompanies transmitted papers.

transmittance — (physics) transmission of radiant energy

travel	journeying
travail	painful toil; anguish suffered for achievement (trăv'āl)
triumphant	victorious
triumphal	pertaining to the celebration of a victory, as a "triumphal return"
troop	a body of soldiers. To march
troupe	a theatrical company. To travel as a troupe; to play any part well
trustee	one who holds property in trust
trusty	reliable. A prisoner with special privileges
tuberculous	pertaining to tuberculosis
tubercular	pertaining to tubercles
turban	a headdress
turbine	a rotary motor
typography	the arrangement of type; art of printing
topography	the geographical or surface features of a region

U

unabridged	entire
abridged	shortened
expurgated	cleared of objectionable things
undoubtedly	without a doubt
indubitably	with too much evidence to doubt
until ⎫	interchangeable. Note that "till" is a word, not a contraction,
till ⎭	and written without an apostrophe.
urban	pertaining to cities or towns (opposite of "rural")
urbane	courteous; suave (ûr-bān')
usable	workable
useful	full of use

V

vain	futile; conceited
vane	a weather indicator; a compass sight
vein	a blood vessel; a strain or streak
vale	a valley
veil	a thin covering that conceals or protects
venal	mercenary
venial	forgivable (vē'nĭ-al)
vender	one who vends
vendor	(law) the seller (opposite of "vendee")
veneer	gloss. To coat or overlay, as with fine wood
venire	a writ to summon jurors (vē-nī'rē)

212

venerable	worthy of respect (because of age)
vulnerable	capable of being hurt or wounded
veracious	truthful
voracious	greedy
verses	divisions of poetry
versus	against
vice	depravity; a defect; a bad habit
vise	a clamp for holding materials securely
visé	an endorsement on a passport (Fr. vē-zā')
visa	(also a French word) a visé (Fr. vē'zà)
vicegerent	an officer appointed to act for another (vīs-jē'rĕnt)
viceregent	a person who acts for a regent. (A regent is a type of vicegerent.)
vile	despicable; loathsome; worthless
vial }	
phial }	a small bottle
viol	a stringed instrument
vindictive	revengeful
vindicative	tending to justify or clear of suspicion (vĭn'dĭ-kā'tĭv)
viscous	(adj.) sticky or adhesive (vĭs'kŭs)
viscose	(noun) a viscous solution (vĭs'kōs)
viscosity	stickiness or resistance to flowing (vĭs-kŏs'ĭ-ty)
vocation	a regular occupation
avocation	an occupation for diversion

W

waist	a narrow central part; a garment
waste	worthless; barren [land]; debris; loss. To expend idly; to lose size gradually
wait	to stay
weight	a measure of heaviness
want	desire; lack
wont	habit (wŭnt; Br. wōnt)
won't	will not
wave	to motion with the hand, as to "wave aside", not "*waive* aside"
waive	to relinquish [a right to], as to "waive preliminary examination"
waver	to fluctuate, or hesitate
waiver	a relinquishment
way	a distance, as "a long way", not "*ways*"; course; manner; (naut.) progress, as "under way"
weigh	to find the weight of; to be a burden; (naut.) to lift [anchor]
ways	the plural of "way". A structure for shipbuilding
weak	not strong
week	a period of seven days
wear	to have on; to bear; to last; to waste; to consume by use or friction. Depreciation, as "wear and tear"
weir	a dam; a water-measuring plate (wēr)
ware	a class of merchandise; pottery

213

weighing	measuring the heaviness of; considering the worth of, as "weighing a proposition"
weighting	loading, or adding weight to
weighted	made heavy; calculated or evaluated from statistics, as a "weighted average", a "weighted wholesale price index", a "weighted opinion" (but "weighed down" rather than "weighted down")
whose	a possessive pronoun
who's	who is
winch	a windlass for hoisting or pulling
wench	a servant
wood	the substance of a tree; a grove
would	the past of "will"

Y

yoke	a working frame for oxen
yolk	the yellow of an egg
you	a pronoun
ewe	a sheep
U	a shape, as "U-bolt", "U-tube', etc.
yew	a tree
your	belonging to you
you're	you are
yore	time gone by, as "of yore"

PUNCTUATION

"PUNCTUATION should be as uniform as possible. Unfortunately not only is there often a difference of opinion in regard to what is the best or the correct punctuation, but also it is difficult for even the same writer to be always consistent in this matter."

—From Webster's Collegiate Dictionary,
Fourth Edition, Copyright 1916, 1925, 1931,
by G. & C. Merriam Co., Springfield, Mass.

❖ ❖ ❖

"I have never yet come across a book on the subject which did not leave me more puzzled than it found me."

—The late Barrett Wendell of Harvard University.

Marks of Punctuation

PUNCTUATION

Authorities are agreed that:

Punctuation is a matter of judgment, and not of definite rule.

It adds expression and meaning to written words.

Open or Close Punctuation. "Open punctuation", or rather the absence of punctuation, is not recommended for use in other than routine work, form letters, etc., where the saving of time is an important factor. Many persons are confused by the absence of punctuation. Others think it eccentric.

The regular or "close" style of punctuation should be used in all dignified correspondence, formal documents, and legal papers. It is always clear and businesslike.

Regarding open punctuation:

> "This style of punctuation is best suited to the more simple, direct forms of writing, such as plain narrative; but if carried to extremes it results in ambiguity and an appearance of slovenliness. The primary aim of punctuation is to convey to the reader the exact meaning intended, and any text should be punctuated more or less 'closely,' according as clearness demands."
>
> —From Webster's Collegiate Dictionary, Fourth Edition, p. 1213, Copyright 1916, 1925, 1931, by G. & C. Merriam Co., Springfield, Mass.

The law recognizes the importance of punctuation:

> "Punctuation may be considered in determining the meaning of a contract, when it is doubtful. 138 U.S. 1."
>
> —Bouvier's Law Dictionary (Baldwin's Revision), p. 1004.

COMMA

Commas give pause and clarity to sentences. Do not attempt to omit them altogether, nor to use them indiscriminately. A wide difference in meaning may be indicated by commas.

Ambiguous:
The seller says the buyer is profiteering.
Unfortunately neglected opportunities cannot be recaptured.
In daylight streets in the Eighties are deserted.
Shortly before this testimony was given by a student who had witnessed the strike.

217

Clear:

The seller, says the buyer, is profiteering.
Unfortunately, neglected opportunities cannot...
In daylight, streets in the Eighties are deserted.
Shortly before this, testimony was given by a...

Commas have six chief uses:
1. Around parenthetic words
2. Around explanatory expressions
3. Between listed words or phrases
4. In place of omitted words
5. After inverted constructions
6. Between clauses.

Parenthetic Words. If pauses are clearly indicated by any of the following words, they may be set off with commas.

But if no real interruptions are caused by such words, they need not be set off with commas.

---

accordingly	furthermore	oftener than not
actually	hence	on the contrary
after all	however	on the other hand
afterward	I believe	originally
again	I think	otherwise
also	if any	perhaps
apparently	in addition	personally
as a matter of fact	in any case	respectively
as a rule	in any event	say
as I see it	in brief	second, or secondly
as it happens	inclusive	so
as it were	indeed	still
as you know	in fact	strictly speaking
at any rate	in other words	that is (i.e.)
at last	in reality	that is to say
at least	in short	then
besides	in the first place	theoretically
better yet	in the meantime	therefore
by chance	in turn	third, or thirdly
by the bye	meanwhile	thus
by the way	moreover	to begin with
consequently	namely (viz)	to be sure
conversely	naturally	too (meaning "moreover or "also")
finally	next	to say the least
first	nevertheless	to tell the truth
for example (e.g.)	no	unfortunately
for instance (e.g.)	notwithstanding	well
for the most part	now	whereas
for the time being	obviously	without doubt
fortunately	of course	yes
further	of necessity	yet

Do not use the abbreviations "e.g.", "viz", and "i.e.", unless in abbreviated work, or in texts where such abbreviations will be perfectly understood

218

Indicated pauses:

That is, **in short,** the story.

In other words, it has got into a snarl.

Send us samples of, **say,** three varieties.

The truth, **of course,** is that it does not, **as a rule,** go anywhere and, **therefore,** nobody has it.

It is true, **yes,** but can they prove it?

It was illegible, **that is,** it was blurred.

Substantially, **indeed,** the depositor is...

A rule, **by the way,** is not necessarily a practice.

Here, **meanwhile,** are some of the characteristics.

Many things, **however,** are neither emphatic nor...

By eliminating, **for the time being at least,** certain...

It may be true, or, **again,** it may be only a rumor.

(The commas around "again" give it the meaning of "on the other hand". Without the commas it could mean "once again".)

Uninterrupted sentences:

It is very necessary **indeed.**

...which **of course** is nonsense.

...but **at any rate** we have tried.

...on Friday and Saturday **respectively.**

...owing **perhaps** to the increased costs.

We **theoretically** sold for that amount.

Commercial activity will **of necessity find...**

It **therefore** involves no prejudices.

Short examples, or namings:

...native birds, **for example,** the ptarmigan and partridge.

...for two apparent reasons, **namely,** that it was due and that it represented an honest debt.

...to get what is worth getting, **namely,** an education.

(For long enumerations, see Semicolon and Colon.)

One comma: Only one comma (or a semicolon) may be used if the parenthetic expression acts as a connective, or blends more naturally with one part of the sentence than with another.

He was going to Europe, **in fact** he was sailing...

They have asked for immediate shipment; **therefore** we must comply.

Two elements, **for instance** mercury and gold, cannot be...

Intervening Phrases or Clauses. If an explanatory phrase or clause breaks into a sentence at any point, it may be set off by commas to give it distinction or to preserve the clear continuity of the sentence.

Note that **two commas** are necessary to segregate completely an explanatory phrase or clause within a sentence.

Men, **like animals,** live in herds. (BUT: Men **like him** live long.)

They often said, **and I believe they were right,** that...

It seems strange, **the circumstances being as you say,** that...

That, **so far as we are concerned,** is the situation.

Remember that, **from the buyer's point of view,** the discount...

Some customers are, **as is sometimes apparent,** not willing...

More snow, **along with rain and a warmer temperature,** is...

These men, **together with Colonel James,** make up the Cabinet.

There is nothing smaller, **in the laboratory or out,** than...

In the mountains, **where rain fell heavily,** fear was...

And we say to you, **advisedly and unqualifiedly,** that...

A ship, **sunk during the war,** has been located...

When we offer them this, **the best of opportunities,** they refuse.

If two phrases have the same continuation, the intervening phrase may be set off by commas to give it definiteness.

> It is as good as, if not better than, the rest.
> The difficulty is due to, and arises with, a lack of...
> ...could be bought as reasonably as, if not more reasonably than, land in other developments.
> ...shall not be used for, nor in connection with, advertising.

Always enclose within commas the full intervening expression, not just a part of it. Test a sentence to determine what constitutes a full phrase or clause and what does not.

> NOT: It is as large as, if not larger, than their holdings.
> BUT: It is as large as, if not larger than, their holdings.
>   (The complete intervening phrase is "if not larger than". The simple sentence is "It is as large as their holdings.")
> NOT: On, but not exactly of the waterfront...
> BUT: On, but not exactly of, the waterfront...
> NOT: No one can equal or even approximate, their work.
> BUT: No one can equal, or even approximate, their work.
> OR: No one can equal or even approximate their work.

As shown in the last example, if it is considered that the intervening phrase or clause does not noticeably break the continuity of a sentence, no commas are used around it.

> If and when reductions are made...
> ...owner of a large and at present none too profitable realty company.
> ...on or near the seaboard.
> ...characteristic of or peculiar to the native.
> Sounder policies must and will emerge.
> ...first to come into and first to go out of the land.

Closing Explanatory Expressions. An explanatory remark at the end of a sentence may be set off with a comma to give it emphasis.

> Some asked for more than they wanted, to make sure of getting enough.
> It is a medium of trade, ever changing.

Contrasts. Emphatic contrasting phrases or clauses may be set off by commas.

> It is work we want, not charity.
> A situation that no one likes, not even the politician.
> We pay for being protected, not for being saved.
> Machines, not men, should do the work.
> We ordered the goods, not because we liked them, but because our customers called for them.
> Unexpected, not unforeseen, is this ruling.

Unemphatic contrasting phrases are not set off by commas.

> They are poor but honest.
> He is satisfied though skeptical.
> It comes not from skill but from patience.
> They are bound not from but to the Orient.

220

Emphatic Words. Single words may be set off by commas if emphasis is desired.

> They must remain invisible, **forever.**
> . . .for the time specified, **only.**
> Some, **foolishly,** imagine that it is good business.

-ing Phrases. A common mistake in punctuation is the cutting into an -ing phrase with a comma and setting some words adrift.

> NOT: The Governor, having finished his investigation, steps are now
>   being taken toward legal action.
>   (To set off "having finished his investigation" with commas
>   leaves "The Governor" to bump into "steps" without reason.
>   The full first phrase is "The Governor having finished his
>   investigation".)
> THUS: **The Governor having finished his investigation,** steps are now
>   being taken toward legal action.

If, of course, the -ing phrase acts as a simple modifier of a word which has another construction, the phrase may be set off with commas; that is, if it could be temporarily removed without impairing the meaning of the sentence.

> The Governor, **having finished his investigation,** now proposes to institute
>   legal action.
>   (In this sentence "Governor" is the subject of "proposes", and "having
>   finished his investigation" is a modifying phrase which could be removed.)
> Such decisions, **wavering as they do,** offer no solution.
> The stock, **having now earned its dividend,** is worth. . .
> We can suggest, **knowing they will understand.**
> They are again together, **continuing a long association.**

But commas should not be used around an -ing phrase if it could not be removed without impairing the meaning of the sentence.

> A statement **modifying his previous views** may be expected.
> The men **working on that project** are to be paid by the day.
> **Running such a risk** is not good business.

"That" and Commas. Keep the word "that" outside the commas which often enclose an inserted explanatory clause or phrase. Guard against repeating "that" in such constructions.

> (TEST: Place the intervening clause or phrase at the end of the sentence.)
> NOT: He maintained, that if prices are lowered, costs must be cut.
> NOR: He maintained, that if prices are lowered, *that* costs must be. . .
> BUT: He maintained that, **if prices are lowered,** costs. . .   (emphatic)
> OR: He maintained that **if prices are lowered,** costs. . .   (usual)
>   The act states that, **before securities can be sold,** they must. . .
>   It proves that, **while we cannot win alone,** we can join. . .
>   He said that, **so long as they believe in freedom,** they will. . .
>   . . .recognize that, **although the ways are many,** there is one. . .
>   . . .declared that, **because of his contributions,** it is fitting. . .
>   . . .suggested that, **where needed,** channels should be opened.

Between Two or More Adjectives. A comma is used between listed adjectives when the word "and" has seemingly been omitted.

221

...a quiet, emicient man.   (a quiet and efficient man)
...a good, reliable old American firm.   (a good and reliable old American...)
...for specific, detailed instructions.
His words were simple, direct, and forceful.

No commas should be used when the adjectives contribute to one complete thought.

...tell the plain honest truth.   ...of a few remaining good
...a tall brown church spire.   tried-and-true methods.

Specific designations may be made by using "and" with the commas.

...red, and white, and blue flags.   (flags of three different colors)
...red, white, and blue flags.   (three-colored flags)

Address.   Words used in direct address should be set off with commas.

Father, forgive them; for they know not what they do.
Et tu, **Brute!**   (Even thou, Brutus!)
At last, **Paul,** you are right.
Don't think, **my son,** that you can't do it.
Is that, **Mr. Ellson,** what you think of the proposition?
I appreciate the honor, **gentlemen,** but I shall be detained.

Identification.   Identifying words or phrases are usually set off with commas.

Our representative, **Mr. Scott,** will call upon you.
The Superintendent, **Mr. Hayes,** should report...
...as J. R. Darton, **one of the drafters of the bill,** testified.
... to be held on Wednesday, **the 24th,** at 10 a.m.
President James, **of Garfield University,** was...
They were sent to Denver, **the state capital,** for...
...an agreement with one nation, **Cuba.**
...to reach the summit of Mount Everest, **the world's loftiest peak.**
Lee, **my brother,** is here.
My brother, **Will,** is in the East.   (indicates that there is but one brother)
My brother Will is in the East.   (indicates that there may be other brothers)

An identifying clause should be set off with commas if it could be removed from the sentence without impairing the meaning.

That plan, **which was to stop all other plans,** is, for the time being, stopped itself.
...and now that company, **which was started in 1841,** leads the field.
The new president, **who is soon to take office,** will be...

But if an identifying clause could not be removed without impairing the meaning of the sentence, it should not be set off with commas.

All members of the committee **who are also members of the Exchange** are requested to meet...
The nation **that looks to its industries** will be the...
The form of barrier **which it represents** cannot be abolished.

Himself, Itself, Myself, etc.   These words may or may not be set off with commas.   They are usually segregated if a definite pause is desired; unsegregated if no pause is desired.

222

He, **himself,** will attend to it.
I **myself** will see to it.
...none other than the Señor, **himself.**
...it was the man **himself.**
Life **itself** has been changed.

Inc., Jr., State Names, etc. "Inc.", "Jr.", etc., after names, and the names of states after the names of cities, are considered explanatory and are set off with commas.

Vernon-Wood, **Inc.,** has announced its autumn prices.
Thomas H. Maynard, **Jr.,** is now associated with...
Washington, **D.C.,** is the center of...
Seattle, **Washington,** had an earthquake on October 27, 1940, at 2:33 p.m.

Inverted Constructions. If a word, phrase, or clause is out of its natural order in a sentence, it may be set off with a comma.

Simultaneously, an extensive program was started.
Elsewhere, bitter cold was endured.
After his speech in the Senate, he returned to his home.
In view of that situation, the Secretary said...
Like them, we are not interested.
Thanks to your insistence, they have been taken care of.
Admitting that an estimate is impossible, he declared that...
If that had been done in the first place, they would not now...
That it is not always easy, we are well aware.
According to that report, 500 stock tickers will...
For us, it amounts to a considerable profit.
If by any chance you agree, you might write...
These, they at any rate know how to sell.

But no comma is necessary after a simple inverted phrase that runs without pause into the rest of the sentence.

In just a few minutes they were dispatched.
Throughout the night they worked on it.

However, do not omit a comma if the end of the inverted construction is not immediately clear.

NOT: And to meet this new taxes are introduced.
BUT: **And to meet this,** new taxes are introduced.
NOT: When the reviewers say that we object.
BUT: **When the reviewers say that,** we object.

Omitted Words. A comma is used to signify the omission of a word or phrase.

This method is easy; that, difficult.
So it seems—the more of the one, the less of the other.
Analogy always wins, is forever successful.
They are interested in no future, no religion, but in...
That law is rigid, ironclad, but now obsolete.
Must we give up, leave the job undone?
They had to do it, could do nothing else.
Something went wrong. What, was not exactly known.

223

Between Listed Words. A comma is placed before the concluding "and", "or", or "nor", in listed words, so that the last two items will not be erroneously grouped. (Publications often omit this final comma.)

> ...assign delivery dates for cotton, tobacco, corn, and wheat.
> (The comma before "and" implies definitely that corn and wheat are not to be grouped in one shipment.)
> ...invested in banks, insurance companies, mortgages and home-building loans. (The last two items are here grouped.)
> Is it for display, distinction, or advertising?
> Ocean, clouds, and hills will still be there.
> ...deliverable when, as, and if issued.
> That will not bring down freight rates, interest, or rents.
> ...sealed, insured, loaded on trucks, and shipped away.
> ...questions of what, who, how, when, and where.
> ...an outgrowth of social, scientific, and cultural life.
> ...someone whose judgment will be practical, firm, and fair.

After Listed Words. No comma is necessary after the concluding word in a list if a verb or phrase **unmistakably applicable to the entire group** follows.

> Ten, twenty, forty, and sixty are the percentages.
> Large shipments of wheat and grains, butter and cheese, wool and flax, sugar and foodstuffs will come out of that country.

But if there is danger of connecting only the last listed item with what follows, a comma should be used after the concluding item.

> The revenue collected by the State from tobacco, candy, and theaters, alone amounts to a large sum.
> Several subjects were discussed—taxes, deterioration, and overhead, in particular.
> They were more balanced, more reserved, than we expected.

If an explanatory or parenthetic phrase or clause applying to the entire group immediately follows listed words, it is set off with commas.

> The promising of notes, certificates, or bonds, **which cannot possibly be delivered,** violates...

But if a phrase or clause follows the list and applies only to the last item, it should be bound to the item it modifies and separated from the following part of the sentence by a comma.

> Bankers, professional men, **and farmers as well as laborers,** are expected to...
> (Here "as well as laborers" is joined to "farmers".)
> Bankers, professional men, and farmers, **as well as laborers,** are expected to...
> (Here "as well as laborers" applies to the entire group.)

Before and After "Etc." Commas are usually placed before and after "etc.", or "et cetera", in a sentence; "etc." being regarded as a parenthetic statement.

> Logs, timber, lumber, **etc.,** are to be shipped...
> Lumber, **etc.,** is to be shipped by water.

224

When Connecting Words are Repeated in Lists. No commas are necessary between listed words if the connecting "and", "or", or "nor" is repeated.

> He had faith in the future and in business and in men.

If emphasis is desired, a comma may be used with the connecting word.

> If we can but have faith in the future, and in business, and in men.

"Such as" Introducing Enumerations. When "such as" introduces an enumeration, it should not be followed by a comma; although it is preceded by one if the writer is pausing to give examples. But if no pause is indicated, and the "such as" enumeration is a vital part of the sentence, which could not be removed without impairing the meaning, no comma should break its connection with the other words.

> Mention is made of many famous men, such as Edison, Burbank, and Bell.
> Men such as Edison, Burbank, and Bell have...

Phrases or Clauses in Series. Commas may be used to separate simple phrases or clauses in series.

> The first is established, the second under way, the third being planned, and the fourth not yet formulated.
> It may be a message from across the street, across the continent, across the sea.

Longer and more complicated phrases or clauses are separated by semicolons.

Between Clauses. A comma is usually placed before a common connective, such as "and", "as", "but", or "since", when it introduces a separate subject and verb conveying an additional idea. The comma prepares the reader for the second clause.

> That is exactly what it is, **and** it can be nothing more.
> The process is slow, **but** it protects the rights of...
> We shall never see them, **for** they are infinitely small.
> The situation is more serious now, **since** it finds workers...
> The shortage is less acute here, **though** of course all parts...
> Certain things cannot be done, **while** certain others can be.

If the clauses are short and the relationship is close, the comma may be omitted before the connective.

> Not only was the time ripe **but** it proved golden.
> We will agree **if** they accept our terms.
> They wrote to us **because** they knew us.
> Responsibility will increase **and** few measures will survive.

Connectives less common than the above-named, such as "otherwise", "nevertheless", "hence", etc., are usually preceded by semicolons, and may or may not be followed by commas. (See Semicolon.)

Around a Connective. If a parenthetic or explanatory expression immediately follows a connective, any one of four methods of punctuation

225

may be used, according to the pause and emphasis desired. The comma may be

Omitted before connective:
It was nicknamed **and,** as usual, the name made it distinctive.
It is highly recommended **and,** if it is as good as they say it is, we shall certainly be interested.
It is perishable **and,** therefore, nobody can afford it.

Used before connective and omitted after it:
This course was followed, **and as a result,** we found...
Has it been canceled, **and if so,** has the record been...
They made a holiday of it, **and by noon,** supplies were...
They belittled that account, **and therefore,** they lost it.

Used both before and after connective:
That is unlikely, **or,** as they put it, the prospects are...
Things will eventually change, **for,** very rapidly, we are...
That had not occurred to him, **but,** on being called to his attention, was received...

Omitted around the parenthetic expression:
They may put up a fight, but **on the other hand** they may not.
We had no recent data, and **therefore** no prices were quoted.

Between Parts of a Subject. If a subject is long or involved, or if the second part is to be emphasized, it may be punctuated with commas. Ordinarily no commas are used.

> The **spelling, and usage** in regard to separating the two parts, are variable.
> FOR EMPHASIS: Its fine **detail, and rich quality** of reproduction, give many striking effects.
> ORDINARY: **That cost and the present market price** do not spell profit.

Between Parts of a Verb. If a compound verb is long or involved, or if the second part is to be emphasized, it may be punctuated with commas. Ordinarily no commas are used.

> Here we find the word **traced** back to its earliest appearance, **and analyzed** into its elements.
> FOR EMPHASIS: We **secured** the volume, **and presented** it to the library.
> This average **is based** on estimates, **and does not include...**
> ORDINARY: They **changed** their tactics **and voted** for the bill.
> He **will investigate** the charges **and report** at once.

Between Subject and Verb. Ordinarily a single comma should not be placed between a subject and its verb. But there are times when a single comma is so used, to hold the subject together, as it were, and to prevent its running into the verb.

> Whatever is, is right.—Pope.
> And what they decide, shall be the law.
> What may seem valueless and unimportant to one class of society, may be the lifeblood of another.
> The record of that company's climb to the name that it now enjoys, is a story in itself.

226

To saddle them and their organizations with the burden
of paying for the folly of others, would be a crime.
To have something to say and to want to say it, are the
main things.
FOR EMPHASIS: The best way to learn to write, is simply to write.
Comma not used:
What happened to them is as yet unknown.
Some of the men who began with us in 1908 are still here.
The subject matter with which that article deals has no bearing on the case.
All of the rules we had then are still in effect.
The best thing to do would be to agree.

Between Verb and Object. Ordinarily a single comma should not
appear between a verb and its object. However, there are times when
a single comma seems as necessary and logical between a verb and its
object, as between a subject and its verb.

NECESSARY: Congress **will submit** to the several states for ratification
by conventions chosen by the people, **a resolution**
providing for...
UNNECESSARY: Congress will submit to the states a resolution...

SEMICOLON

Semicolons are used to separate phrases, clauses, or enumerations.
of almost equal importance, especially when such phrases or clauses
contain commas within themselves.

When Connective is Omitted. If the connecting word between
clauses is omitted, a semicolon is used.

That is old-fashioned; it suggests senility.
Don't let them get the better of you; change your viewpoint.
We are not telling you anything new; we are merely repeating something old.
Not only are they not interested; they feel a resentment toward...
We thought greatness was infallible; we know better now.

When Connective is Used. Even though a connecting word is used,
if the break between clauses or phrases is noticeable, or if the thought
makes an abrupt turn, a semicolon instead of a comma is employed.
Connectives often preceded by semicolons are:

accordingly	hence	moreover	still
also	however	nevertheless	that is
at least	if	notwithstanding	then
besides	indeed	on the contrary	therefore
consequently	in fact	otherwise	thus
for	in short	similarly	whereas
furthermore	likewise	so	yet

This will probably be mentioned again; **for** it is a bit of hard-earned information.
We live in an interesting age; **at least** we know that.
The manual shall be our guide; **if** there is room for doubt we...
All numbers should be indicated; **likewise** all queries should...
It is true that the method is difficult; **but** it is believed to be the better way.
It can be done; **and** we venture to say that it will be done; **but** there are right
and wrong ways of doing it.

227

If the connecting word itself is to be emphasized, a comma is placed after it.

> They argued the question at length; **however,** we were right.
> This reduces the difficulty; **nevertheless,** care must be...
> It is important that we find a substitute; **moreover,** we should not consider...

Before Words Introducing Enumerations. A semicolon is used before a word that introduces a long enumeration or list in a sentence. A comma is placed after the word.

Words and abbreviations usually thus set off are:

e.g.	for example	to wit
i.e.	namely	viz

> ...a large number of exceptions; **namely,** furs, hides, hemp, jute, and copra.

Note that if "namely" had been omitted, a colon would have been used. Or if the enumeration had been spaced, a comma would have preceded "namely" and a colon followed it.

In a Series. Semicolons are used between phrases or clauses in a series, usually when such phrases or clauses themselves contain commas.

> Stocks had reached the following levels: steel, 21; coal, 15; tin, 30; radio, 3; nickel, 4.
> Those affected by the orders are: Lieutenant John Lee, transferred from the Mission to the Presidio; Corporal Joseph Moore, from the Southern to the Potrero; and Patrolman Nelson Brown, from Richmond to Park.
> Miscellaneous freight loaded, 198,000 cars; forest products, 20,024; ore, 6,724; coal, 81,046; livestock, 17,441.
> They were stranded with no income; no outgo; no exchange; no contribution; no distribution.
> Time and space are not considered; where it is, is day; where it was, is night; and history is being made.
> He is forever working; rigging up apparatus; measuring distances; studying curves; pursuing the dozens of other things that tempt the curiosity.
> If a company has made every effort to lower its debt; if it has reduced its overhead to a minimum; if it has undertaken no new obligations; then it is in a position to seek assistance from the Government.

Before Phrases. A semicolon may be used to set off an -ing phrase, or any other phrase, if it is of sufficient importance to warrant such distinction. (But usually a comma is preferable. See also p. 221.)

-ing phrases:
> They have now entered into a definite agreement; it being understood that all profits are to be shared.
> We shall have to charge for them; they falling under the head of "extras".
> It is the wind that blows toward the equator; its main direction being from the northeast.
> The aim has been to improve the product; no effort having been made to increase the output.

Other phrases:
> We often received communications from them; sometimes of a critical nature; sometimes merely seeking information.
> There's nothing more we can do; that is, not just now.

Between Parts of a Subject, and Between Subject and Verb. Semicolons should not ordinarily be used to divide the parts of a compound subject; nor should they otherwise appear between a subject and verb. However, if a strong separation is desired, they are sometimes so used.

UNUSUAL: Valuable papers of which only one copy exists; or original, signed documents; or papers that could not be replaced, should be registered.

USUAL: Valuable papers of which only one copy exists, or original, signed documents, or papers that could not be replaced, should be registered.

UNUSUAL: This information; namely, that we are reducing prices, is not to be released.

USUAL: This information, namely, that we are reducing prices, is not to be released.

In some sentences, semicolons seem the only logical punctuation to use in dividing the parts of a subject.

All financiers; probably 95 percent of the business men, including publishers; a very large part of the women voters; and even a fair number of school children, know that bank credit was practically unobtainable...

COLON

The colon may introduce a summing up, an illustration, quotation, or enumeration, for which the previous words in the sentence have prepared the reader.

A dash is unnecessary after a colon. The colon itself indicates a definite break in the sentence.

As a Mark of Introduction. A colon is usually used when the word "namely" is missing but could be mentally supplied.

The purpose of the organization is told in its name: to further better business relations.
Another thing: they are colorful.
He could offer but one excuse: they were delayed.
...a man once the center of attention: Bryan.
...two things you seldom find together: democracy and capital.
The current thought is: Let down the tariff bars.
...for two reasons: first,...; and second,...
It has two uses: it can be..., and it is...

Introducing Quotations. Long quotations are usually introduced by colons. And short quotations may be introduced by colons if emphasis is desired.

Their motto was: "First come, first served."
We might say to them: "Now it's your move."

Introducing Enumerations. Spaced enumerations are usually introduced by colons.

The witnesses called are:

....
....
....

It will be shipped as follows:

....
....

The orders are, namely:

....
....

If a parenthesis occurs just before the enumeration, it should be placed before the colon, not after it.

NOT: The following are recommended: (because of price)
BUT: The following are recommended (because of price):

If an enumeration is indirectly introduced, a colon is not usually used.

The goods will be shipped in the following order, and an invoice will be mailed for each shipment.

....
....
....

After an Introductory Phrase in a Letter. A colon is often used after an introductory phrase in a letter, to enable the writer to begin his main statement with a paragraph.

Re (or Regarding, Answering, or Referring to) your letter of the 18th:
(Note: Such an opening is not recommended, but it is often dictated.)

Between Subject and Verb. A colon should not ordinarily break into a sentence between a subject and its verb. The matter introduced by the colon usually concludes the sentence.

UNUSUAL: The old familiar saying: All's well that ends well, is proved
    again.
USUAL: The old familiar saying, All's well that ends well, is proved
    again.
UNUSUAL: To say: "It can't be done", is just an evasion.
USUAL: To say "It can't be done" is just an evasion.

Capital Letters After Colons. If a complete sentence follows a colon, it may or may not begin with a capital letter, according as emphasis is desired.

The question naturally arises: Why should it cost so much?
First of all: what is business?
There is but one thing wrong: it costs too much.
The final decision rests with the writer: what looks right usually is right.

DASH

A pair of dashes are necessary to segregate material completely. If but one dash is used. it is in effect to the end of the sentence, or to the end of a parenthesis. A comma, semicolon, or colon does not conclude the authority of a dash.

> "All that follows a dash is to be taken as under its influence until either a second dash terminates it, or a full stop is reached."
> —Fowler, "The King's English", 3d Ed., p. 281.

Punctuation With Dashes. The dash is a definite mark of punctuation and needs no other punctuation to support it. To use commas to set off dashes is double punctuation.

Sentence Commas With Dashes. Commas are used with dashes only when they, the commas, are punctuating the entire sentence. Two methods are employed in the placement of these sentence commas.

— —, First method, one comma after last dash.

> It is not because we have played our last card—we have not done that—, but because we...

,— ,— Second method, a comma before each dash.

> It all seemed so fit, no doubt,—everything as it should be,—we forgot the material it was shaped from.

Sentence Semicolon or Colon With Dashes. A colon or semicolon, if punctuating the entire sentence, may be used after the last dash.

> — —; It sometimes implies encouragement—the effort will succeed—; it sometimes implies assurance—the effort shall succeed.
>
> — —: The following terms are correct—and acceptable—:

Some writers omit the second dash when a colon or semicolon intervenes, preferring to let the reader decide whether the colon or semicolon ends the influence of the dash or whether the dash continues in effect to the end of the sentence.

Sentences in which the dash carries through to the period:

> Today that organization is fifty years old—an age at which it should attain a balance; at which it should lean upon but not be discouraged by experience.
> They seem gentle enough—quite human; in fact, can almost talk.

Sentences in which the dash ends at the semicolon:

> That trouble is easily overcome—by shifting from one hand to another; but when a new difficulty arises, they cannot cope with it.
> The treatment is not even thorough—it is exceedingly sketchy and vague; but somehow he has painted a picture—a scene that is real enough.

Punctuation Within Dashes. Punctuation within dashes pertains to the segregated matter only, and is the same as punctuation in ordinary sentences or phrases. The words within the dashes may or may not be grammatically independent of the rest of the sentence.

> They are always—not unnaturally, considering their position—the first to rebel.
> He handles the material—or should we say the lack of it?—very well indeed.

231

Dashes Following Dashes. Dashes may follow other dashes without extra punctuation.

> People everywhere—doctors, merchants, students, workmen—farmers and city dwellers—all are...
>
> Taking this as a basis—in any case, it is not exaggerated—and taking into consideration that we have far surpassed expectations—by about 200 percent—and this cannot be disputed—, it is quite easy to conclude...

Explanations or Repetitions. Dashes may set off a repetition, explanation, variation, or summary of what has been said.

Repetition:
> Buy now—today—if you can.
> June 19—next Monday—is the date set for...

Explanation:
> That firm—an old customer of ours—has never failed to...
> We feel that we—that is, the average person—could not...
> Do we really want to be governed—told what to do and when to do it?

Variation:
> They feel badly treated—betrayed—and the feeling is...
> It had been known for days—for weeks, in fact—that...
> Business is convalescing—or, to put it another way, its outlook is improving.
> They have given notice of acceptance—in other words, the installation is satisfactory.
> Their future is certain if they elect the right kind of leader—or better yet, the right kind of man.

Summary:
> ...from laborer to merchant prince—they are all included.
> So it goes—trials within trials, all to the same end.
> To believe that what is true for you is true for all—that is genius.

Side Thoughts and Comments. Dashes are used to segregate a quick change of thought or of sentence construction; or to set off an afterthought, comment, or contemplation, provoked by the text but not necessarily a part of it.

> If it is good reading—and it is—the style of the book...
> It, too—with its many sidelights—impressed me.
> By a stroke of good fortune—or so it seemed to me—I was sent...
> ...and—what is worse—they cannot live up to their promises.
> He hardly deserved credit, but he has—anonymously, indeed—got it.

For Emphasis. A dash may be used to set off a single word or expression for emphasis.

> It seems that they lack only—starch.
> They pretended to want the contract very much, and then—they refused it.
> ...a strange situation—and yet, harmonious.
> ...and, then, solemnly vowing they would never give in—gave in.
> Turn from this—to what?
> If you don't know the meaning of a word—look it up.

Instead of Parentheses. Dashes may be used instead of parentheses. They are a slightly less noticeable mark of punctuation than parentheses, and do not so definitely segregate the parenthetic material.

232

The conditions are ripe—with the exception of money circulation—to fulfill the promises...

...ruled that a 6% return—the rate fixed by the Commission—could not be considered.

...an early winter—for this was in October, 1917—added to the gravity of the situation.

Instead of a Colon. A dash is sometimes used instead of a colon, where the word "namely" has seemingly been omitted.

...added these names to the list—Jasper, Lynn, and Martin.

It ended with a query—Will this territory remain undeveloped, forever?

Two things are needed—to get started again, and to keep business...

...turned to the only alternative—the ballot box.

Instead of a Semicolon. A dash is sometimes used instead of a semicolon before the word "namely", or a like word.

There were several questions to be discussed—namely, the deeding of lands to the homesteaders, the placing of...

...three reductions—namely, a lowering of wholesale prices, a lowering of...

A dash may be used instead of a semicolon when a connective has been omitted.

The expense is ours—the saving is theirs.

Broken Sentences. A dash may be used to indicate that a sentence is broken by spacing.

He suggested—
1. That we buy...
2. That we install...
3. That we sell...

Yet spaced sentences are often written without punctuation.

It should be carried in
1. All newspaper advertising, and
2. The annual catalogue.

Let us now consider
The Summary

Regarding the Use of Dashes. Do not employ dashes for any and every purpose. They are an outstanding mark of punctuation; and their value is increased by a restriction of their use.

Still, do not overrestrict the use of dashes and omit them where they seem necessary.

CONFUSING: It is singular that Edison, Burroughs, and Coolidge, man of science, naturalist, and president, all belonged...

CLEARER: It is singular that Edison, Burroughs, and Coolidge—man of science, naturalist, and president—all belonged...

Do not omit the last dash when it is necessary to complete an earlier dash.

NOT: Such leadership sends confidence—even restores courage, to our people.

BUT: Such leadership sends confidence—even restores courage—to our people.

233

Typewriting Dash. In typewritten work, a single mark, with a space on each side, is usually used for a dash. Two marks, with or without a space on each side, may be used if special emphasis is intended.

USUAL: ... – ... – ...　　　　　　EMPHATIC: ... – – ... – – ...

PARENTHESES

Parentheses are a noticeable, and therefore very strong, mark of punctuation, holding the matter enclosed within them entirely to itself. They are used when it is desired to segregate material very definitely.

Punctuation With Parentheses. Parentheses are a punctuation in themselves, and need no additional commas or dashes to set them off.

Use　(　)　　　not　,(　),　　　nor　—(　)—

Another mark of punctuation is used with parentheses only when such other mark is punctuating the entire sentence.

Sentence Marks With Parentheses.

(　),　Comma, semicolon, colon, and dash are always outside the paren-
(　);　theses (unless, in rare instances, they are part of quoted parenthetic
(　):　material).
(　)—

> Thus the matter, so far as we know it (and we have no right to speculate), breaks up into...
> It is in many of our contracts (but not in all); nevertheless, we will agree to...

(　).　A period, exclamation point, or question mark, when punctuating
(　)!　the entire sentence, is outside the parentheses.
(　)?

(　.)　These marks are inside the parentheses when punctuating only the
(　!)　parenthetic material.
(　?)

> It was held in Washington (D.C.).
> (It was held in Washington, D.C.)
> But was the year as late as that (1926)?
> ...to make such a deal (and call it honest!).

Continuous parenthetic paragraphs have an opening parenthesis mark before each paragraph, but a closing one only after the last paragraph.

Punctuation Within Parentheses. This is the same as in ordinary sentences, except that no periods are used, unless after abbreviations, or after parenthetic sentences standing alone, or parenthetic quotations.

> ...on the south lay the valley of the Oro (doubtless shortened from Copa de Oro, meaning the "Cup of Gold" lake; recently, I regret to say, bridged over for the convenience of Mr. Laidlaw, engineer, and others); while on the north...
> Our purpose in using the "reinforced filling" (or "reinforced covering"; the terms seem to be practically interchangeable) was to secure...
> Years ago someone (I haven't forgotten his name, my friend) said that...
> An eminent physician (his name does not matter—any one of a dozen men might have done as well) was called upon...

234

Parentheses may be placed within parentheses, if the two sets are not confusing. However, dashes or brackets are usually used as inner parentheses, or around parentheses.

(( ))   ...according to the locality (see Dutch (Netherland) West Indies).

([ ])   The word is numero (Latin, [by] number).

[( )]   "It was penned by the French philosopher [Voltaire (see below)] and succinctly disposes..."

(— —)   We are not sure of the date (we thought it was 1916—some said 1915—and that it was in the spring).

— ( ) —   It was late for them to be starting on a venture—really gambling on a scheme (a "plan" they called it) of doubtful character—that might yield them nothing.

Capitalization Within Parentheses. The first word of parenthetic material within a sentence is not usually capitalized, unless it is a proper name or used as part of a proper name.

ORDINARY: The prevalent method is there indicated (the newspaper excerpts are exact).

PROPER NAME: They advertised as "The Western Company (Makers of Fine Woolens)".

Occasionally, if the parenthesis is a strong inner sentence, the first word is capitalized.

EMPHATIC: The argument on which their objection is based (We do not do that; therefore we should not do this) is not sound.

ORDINARY: It is only to certain persons that that would occur (or would the reformers prefer another word?)

Grammatical Construction Within Parentheses. The construction of words within parentheses may or may not be grammatically independent of the rest of the sentence.

He does not know a bad bargain when he sees (or even when he makes) one.

But always, the sentence should be grammatically independent of the parenthesis. Enclose within the parentheses only what could be removed without impairing the sentence. If the parenthetic matter could not be removed, parentheses should not be used.

NOT: They operate (like the savages of old upon the western movement), and man fights...

BUT: They operate like the savages of old upon the western movement, and man fights...

NOT: It is (not the first) but the last straw that counts.

BUT: It is not the first but the last straw that counts.

NOT: This is an exception (that instead of destroying) proves the rule.

BUT: This is an exception that (instead of destroying) proves the rule.

Explanations and Identifications. Parentheses are used around explanatory phrases or comments, or phrases of identification or reference, which are not a part of the continuous thought, and which it is desired to set off completely or noticeably from the rest of the sentence.

235

The difference between the old rate (which was legalized) and the new. .
As the gentlemen (Mr. Hanna and Mr. Mills) observed. . .
In the example given (No. 3) the total is correct.
A sinking fund was authorized (see Minutes of Meeting of June 14) for. . .

To Clarify Sentences. If the meaning of a sentence is obscure with ordinary punctuation, parentheses may help to clarify it.

OBSCURE: Our Company will furnish all specified items, with the exception of foundations, all brickwork, and insulating material.

CLEAR: Our Company will furnish all specified items (with the exception of foundations), all brickwork, and insulating material.

QUOTATION MARKS

There are **two methods** of using **periods and commas** with "quotes":

1. The "inside" method—established and preferred in printing—places the **period and comma** always inside the final quotation mark, no matter what the sentence construction. This facilitates typesetting.

" ." Each small country has "rights," and each wants "justice."
" ," "Progress," he reminded us, "means scientific work."

2. The "outside" method*—adopted for exactness by such authorities as those listed on the following page—places the **comma** always outside the quotes, because it punctuates the entire sentence. Likewise, the **period** is placed outside the quotes when it punctuates the entire sentence; and inside the quotes when it punctuates the quoted matter.

" ". Each small country has "rights", and each wants "justice".
" ", "Progress", he reminded us, "means scientific work."
" ." They drove home this truth: "We are not independent."

There is **only one method** (employed by all) for the use of **all other marks of punctuation** with quotation marks.

Semicolon, colon, and dash are always outside the quotes (unless, in a rare instance, one such mark is an actual part of the quotation).

" "; We are told that "Might does not make right"; however, . . .
" ": They came upon a "collector's item": a four-pointed star.
" "— It is "standard equipment"—in fact, indispensable.

Question mark and exclamation point are outside the quotes when punctuating the entire sentence; and inside the quotes when punctuating only the quoted matter. (If in a quotation that ends the sentence, these marks may suffice for punctuation for the entire sentence.)

" "? Why talk about "photoelectric cells"?
" "! . . .forged ahead as if nothing were "impossible"!
" ?" The natural question arose, "Is it legal?"
" !" . . .until they cry "Enough!"

Extra punctuation may be added outside the quotes, if deemed necessary.
" !"? But did anybody say, "Good work!"?
" !"— Someone cried, "Throw him out!"—and there was a . . .

---

* NOTE: If preparing material for a publication, use the "inside" method for all commas and periods. It is suggested that students be taught the "inside" method first; later, with a knowledge of both methods, they can adopt the "outside" method when working in offices that prefer it.

NEWER "OUTSIDE" METHOD OF USING PERIODS AND COMMAS WITH QUOTES

(See footnote on preceding page.)

Among the users of the newer method of placing periods and commas outside the final quotation marks are:

H. W. Fowler (foremost authority on English) in his "Dictionary of Modern English Usage", 1927.

Homer C. House and Susan E. Harman (Professors of English at the University of Maryland) in their "Handbook of Correct English", 1926.

Arthur G. Kennedy (Professor of English Philology at Stanford University) in his "Current English", 1935.

Arnold Smith (a British grammarian) in his "Grammar and the Use of Words", London, 1923.

The United States Department of State in its Style Manual, 1935.

The United States Government Printing Office in all legislative work, such as bills and acts of Congress.

The Oxford University Press in its publications (including the great Oxford English Dictionary).

* * *

Examples showing the United States Government Printing Office style in all legislative work (where it is necessary to be exact):

From the "Civil Aeronautics Act of 1938":

"Interstate air commerce", "overseas air commerce", and "foreign air commerce", respectively, mean the carriage by aircraft...
...by adding "and all air routes", after the words "or parts of railroads".
...the following: "two members from the Civil Aeronautics Authority;", by...
"...appointed only for the unexpired term of the member whom he succeeds:".
...reads ", and may by regulation...or intrastate air commerce.", and...
(Note the semicolon, colon, comma, and period are parts of the quotations.)

From the "Unlisted Securities Act", 1936:

...is amended by striking out "every broker or...of interstate commerce", and inserting in lieu thereof "every broker or dealer registered pursuant to section 15 of this title".

From the "Banking Act of 1935":

...is amended by striking out "upon the date this section takes effect", and inserting..."on and after June 19, 1934"; and by striking out "the par value of...stock", and inserting..."the amount paid by each Federal Reserve bank for stock of the Federal Deposit Insurance Corporation".
...and by inserting after the words "or the Comptroller of the Currency", the words "or the Federal Deposit Insurance Corporation,".
(Note that the last comma is an actual part of the insertion.)
"After the date of...representing stock of a national banking association."
"...the use of the words 'Federal', 'United States', or 'reserve', or..."
...after "the words 'United States' ", the following: "the words 'Deposit Insurance' ";...the following: "nor to any new bank...as amended,"; and...
"...Provided, That...the term 'time deposits' shall include 'savings deposits'."

EXAMPLES OF THE NEWER "OUTSIDE" METHOD BEING USED
IN ADVERTISEMENTS AND COMMERCIAL BOOKLETS

A folder, "The Cost of Four Years at College", published by the New York Life...
Educational Endowment policies, with a "Settlement Agreement", can be made...
...for the full twenty years plus $10,000 paid at the end of the "20-year period".
—**New York Life Insurance Company.**

It is literally a "made job", created by...　—**Aluminum Company of America.**

"Gone With The Wind", produced by...　...it is called "Edison The Man".
...the overworked word "cavalcade".　—**Metro-Goldwyn-Mayer Pictures.**

...of an American Airlines "Flagship".　—**Sinclair Pennsylvania Motor Oil.**

...other factors that contribute to "Traffic Nerves".　—**Union Oil Company.**

It goes "Straight to the Gate".　..."Spirit of St. Louis", New York...
If you go "Coach", enjoy restful...　—**Pennsylvania Railroad.**

...never just a... number—"the passenger in seat six".　—**United Air Lines.**

...becomes their "new favorite", too.　..."almost a meal in itself", you know.
...that says "party" or "special occasion".　...a "find".　—**Campbell's Soups.**

You say "when", "where", and "how fast"...　...powered and "sized", from...
...deep Dodge "luxury cushions", spacious...　—**Chrysler Corporation.**

...cushioned in chair-high seats "amidships", where riding is best...
...in this "only-car-of-its-kind".　—**Lincoln-Zephyr Cars.**

It's the new Nash "Weather Eye", watching...　...roads, "tough going".
A new Nash development called "Hurricane Power".　—**Nash Motors.**

...made to "stay brighter longer".　...on "less price".　—**General Electric.**

...in the fine art of "knowing how".　—**United States Lines.**

...called, aptly enough, "A New Slant on Beauty".　—**Richard Hudnut.**

"Hollywood hands", girls call them...　—**Jergens Lotion.**

...a handlaid Fostoria "Master-Etching", a gem to set...　—**Fostoria.**

"...sang Foster's 'My Old Kentucky Home', and 'Oh! Susanna'."
　—**Veedol Motor Oil.**
...booklet, "Styling with Paint the Dutch Boy Way", which...
...interested in "something different".　—**Dutch Boy Paint.**

"Swift's Premium", "Swift's Select", or "Swift's Arrow" stamped right on...
...flavor millions say is "just-right".　—**Swift & Company.**

...driving of the "golden spike".　...newest is "Roller Freight".　—**Timken.**

..."...essentials of a liberal education". The famous little book, "Fifteen
Minutes a Day", furnishes you with full information about The Harvard Classics.
　—**P. F. Collier & Son Corporation.**

"...fourth dimension of 'Lost Horizon'."　...N.Y. Herald Tribune "Books".
...of the making of "Disraeli",...　—**Little, Brown & Company.**

In the "process", many foods...　...sealed or "closed", it is...
...into "sheet bars".　...in "base boxes".　—**American Can Company** booklet.

...by the "gross profit test", comparing...　...under "accrued liabilities".
...as "surplus arising from revaluation", or...　...the heading "other income".
　—**American Institute of Accountants** booklet.

Two periods, question marks, or exclamation points are usually considered unnecessary, although they may be used.

> Who wrote "Is It Treason?" (rather than   ?"?)
> The boxes were marked "M.C." (rather than   ."?.)

Parentheses With Quotes.

"   (   )."   Parentheses should be inside the quotes if more than the parenthetic matter is quoted.

("   .")   Parentheses should be around the quotes if the entire quotation is parenthetic.

"   "(   )"   ."   Quotes should be broken and renewed when parentheses are inserted containing unquoted matter.

("   .")?   Sentence punctuation marks are added after parenthetic quota-
("   .").   tions.

> When did he make that statement ("I do not intend to pay.")?
> They all bore the same label ("N.Y.").

Inner Quotes.

"   '   '   ."   Single quotes are used for inner quotations.   (British practice favors the use of single quotes for regular quotations, and double quotes for inner quotations.   Some American publishers have adopted this form.   '   "   "   .')

"   '   '".   Punctuation marks are used with inner quotes in the same
"   '   '."   manner as with regular quotes.   (See footnote p. 236.)
"   '   ',"

"   '   ?'?"   Extra sentence punctuation may be used after a punctuated
"   '   ?'"   final inner quotation; but ordinarily the inner quotation's punctuation is sufficient.

> He asked quietly, "What do you suppose they meant by saying, 'Haven't you heard?'" (rather than ?'?")
> He testified: "I heard them say 'It's hopeless!'"

"   '   "   "   ',   ."   A second inner quotation takes the double quotes again.   Quotations should not go beyond this.

"   :'   .';'   ';'   .'"   Example of punctuation with inner quotes:

> He reported, "Their excuses were something like this: 'We don't have the time'; 'We don't have the money'; and an implied 'We don't have the courage.'"

Other Marks.

"   – – –"   Three dashes inside quotes indicate broken-off speech.

"   "– – –   Three dashes outside quotes indicate that the sentence breaks off after the quotation is finished.

"   ..."   Three dots inside quotes indicate that part of the quotation has been deleted.

"   ***   "   Three stars indicate an omission or unprintable words.

—"   "—   Plain dashes may be used around a quoted passage to set it
—"   !"—   off from the rest of the sentence.

"Etc." not Quoted.   "Etc." should not be within the quotes, unless it is actually a part of the quoted matter.

> On the order was marked "Inserts", etc.   (See footnote p. 236.)
> (This indicates that something besides "Inserts" was marked on the order.)
> On the order was marked "Inserts, etc."
> (Here "etc." is a part of what was actually marked on the order.)

Segregating Direct Quotations. A long quotation (of more than three lines) is usually segregated, indented, and introduced by a colon.

> That statement was made by the Secretary, but he added:
> "We are going ahead with the order as if the debt had been canceled, and will put the billings on the books for next year. Our Company can see no improvement in the situation until the small merchants are helped back...."

A short quotation may be segregated if it closes the sentence, and is important enough to be so emphasized. Ordinarily it is not segregated.

> He strode from the room saying:
> "That's ridiculous!"

Conversation. When a conversation is being recorded, the speeches of each speaker are given separate paragraphs, unless the conversation is very short. (See footnote p. 236.)

> "There is no mystery about what they will do", replied the visitor, knowingly.
> "Ah, but they may make a false move!" cried Holman.
> "If they do, they will lose", said the other.
> "No", Holman replied; and with a careless gesture, "whatever they do, they will win. It is their nature."

It is unnecessary to use quotation marks when recording a dialogue if each speech is prefaced by the name of the person speaking, as in court testimony or a play.

Punctuation of Broken Quotations. When quotations are broken by "he said", etc., they are punctuated as they would be if the "he said", with its preceding comma, were omitted. (See footnote p. 236.)

> "The planes did not reach St. Louis", the dispatch said; "they were snowbound in Denver."
> (Without "the dispatch said" the quotation would read: "The planes did not reach St. Louis; they were snowbound in Denver.")
> "We were forced down in Ohio", he testified, "because our craft could not weather the storm."
> "You've set a new record", he smiled—"a record that will be hard to beat."
> "They came through with flying colors", he reported. "Their gasoline supply was sufficient for 1000 miles more, and their engines were faultless."
> "Is everything all right?" he asked—"then let's be off!"

Capitalization in Quotations. The first word in a quotation is capitalized only when it is a proper name, or when it begins a sentence.

A **comma** may be used or omitted before a quotation, according to the pause desired. Fowler favors omission. (Modern English Usage, p. 571.)

> ...with the legend, "We shall see", scrawled upon it. (See footnote p. 236.)
> ...in the passage beginning "Canst thou not minister..."
> ...the old aphorism which says "People who live in glass houses..." is not always remembered.
> He replied, "Money in itself is not a promise."
> He asked, "What does that indicate?"
> He asked them to help, and they said "No."
> He called back, "Who can say?"—and then left.
> "If you make a bad bargain", he said, "stick to it." } (See footnote p. 236.)
> The Vice President emerged with "nothing to say". {

238

Fragmentary Quotations. Pick up a fragmentary quotation with the exact words uttered. Do not include any introductory remarks, or any reconstruction of the spoken words.

> He admitted the goods were "not up to standard".
> (What was probably said was, "I'll admit that the goods **are** not up to standard", which gives the privilege of quoting only "not up to standard"; and which would not permit quoting something like this: He admitted "that the goods *were* not up to standard".) (See footnote p. 236.)
> NOT: They said he "*had* the most analytic mind..."
> BUT: They said he had "the most analytic mind..."
> (What they probably said was, "He **has** the most analytic mind...")

The same caution applies when quoting the exact words from another text: Quote the actual words, and not any rearrangement of them.

> The clipping said that prices were being "forced down because of the general unrest". (See footnote p. 236.)
> NOT: The clipping said "that prices were..."

Also, when quoting a familiar saying or phrase, do not quote words that are not an actual part of the saying or phrase.

> NOT: There is a saying "that if you make a better mousetrap..."
> BUT: There is a saying that if you "make a better mousetrap..."
> NOT: And "your gentle reader" will not long tolerate...
> BUT: And your "gentle reader" will not long tolerate...

Quoted Words Listed. When quoted words or phrases are listed, each has its separate set of quotation marks. (See footnote p. 236.)

> They would refer to each other as "my honorable opponent", "my rival", and "the gentleman of the opposition".
> ...the three compositions, "Serenade", "Prelude", and "Venetienne".

Indirect Quotations. Do not use quotation marks around indirect quotations.

> He said that the order had been checked.
> NOT: He said "that the order had been checked".

Common Expressions not Quoted. Common expressions, not necessarily slang, borrowed from certain vernaculars, or familiar quotations and figures of speech, need not be quoted.

> That ought to take the wind out of their sails.
> The scheme was nipped in the bud.
> Another job is in the bag.
> That would make him the underdog.
> It simply means passing the buck.
> There should be no killing of two birds with one stone.
> That's where he met his Waterloo.
> ...if they should go to the wall.
> There was method in our madness.
> They are more sinned against than sinning.
> We cannot make head nor tail of it.
> The habit of calling a spade a spade...

239

If it seems necessary to quote any such phrases, because of the tone of the writing, quote **all** of the usual phrase, not just a part of it.

NOT: That rather rubs the "fur the wrong way".
BUT: That rather "rubs the fur the wrong way". (See footnote p. 236.)
NOT: They are doubling "in brass".
BUT: They are "doubling in brass".

Colloquial Words. In most writings, words accepted as "colloquial" are not usually quoted.

We make no bones about that.
...in that half-baked manner.
They seem to be getting hard-boiled about it.
...if you think that will get by.
And as for that, they can go hang!

Slang or Coined Words. In most writings, quote slang or coined words, or any phrases which might cheapen the text if it is not known that the writer is aware of them.

That is their own "funeral". (See footnote p. 236.)
He had a "run-in" with their manager.

Humorous Words or Misnomers. If a word or phrase is intended to be awkward, whimsical, or humorous, it may be quoted.

Then, indeed, there might be "trouble in paradise". (See footnote p. 236.)

It is supposed not to be good form to label one's own humor, but it is worse form, in a serious text, to expose one's writing or mentality to criticism by having a light or slang remark taken seriously.

"Most of us would rather be taken for knaves than for fools; and so the quotation marks are usually there."
—Fowler, "The King's English", 3d Ed., p. 58.

Foreign Words. Foreign words need not be quoted if they are common enough to have been embraced by the English language. But if they are likely to be unfamiliar to the reader, they should be quoted.

In printing, foreign words are usually italicized; but that does not necessarily mean that they should be quoted when typewritten.

résumé   visé   incommunicado   communiqué
BUT: "autre temps, autres moeurs"   "mañana"

Technical or Trade Words. If technical or trade words are likely to be unfamiliar to the reader, quote them. If they are familiar, do not quote them.

If a technical or trade word occurs repeatedly throughout a text, it may be quoted on first appearance, and written without quotes thereafter. (Trade names and trade-marks are often written in caps instead of being quoted.)

We shall make a "cut" of the photograph for reproduction.
...and send the cut direct to the printer.

240

They will "spud in" the well on your property next week.
They are spudding in Well 660 on adjoining property today.
A "melon" of $5,000,000 was available.
If they had divided the melon equally...
...and in selling SUNGLOW we are offering...   (trade name)

Nicknames.   Do not quote nicknames if they are familiar enough to be recognized as names.   (See p. 297.)

Words Referred to as Words.   Words referred to as words need not be quoted if they are unusual enough to be distinct from the sentence.

the word quinquennium   the word eternal

But if the words referred to as words are not distinct from the text, they should be quoted.   Commas are unnecessary before them.

The word "that" is interchangeable with "which".   (See footnote p. 236.)

Letters as Letters.   Letters referred to as letters need not be quoted, unless they are liable to be misread.

the letter M   a small y   a capital U
It begins with "a".
The road makes a Y.   V-shaped   I-beam
If A rents to B, and B subleases to C...

Letters representing a common appellation may be quoted, as

...to encourage passengers to ride on the "L".
...a "Y" hut in France.

Possessives or Plurals of Quoted Words.   If the possessive or plural of a quoted word becomes necessary, it is less awkward to include the -s or 's within the quotes than to add it after the quotes.

Possessive:
The "Hudson's" record   RATHER THAN: The "Hudson"'s
The "Y's" advantages   The "Y"'s
The "L's" rates   The "L"'s
Plural:
All the "Leviathans"   RATHER THAN: "Leviathan"s
Several "Last Laughs"   "Last Laugh"s
to refurbish the "L's"   the "L"'s

"So-Called" Expressions.   A word or phrase is usually quoted if the expression "so-called" or "what is termed" can be mentally supplied before it.   (See footnote p. 236.)

The partners meet "in conference" every two weeks.
We do not know their line of "business".
"Panhandling" is conniving or begging...
It is just a "horseback guess".
Public opinion "freezes", and we do not know...
In Peiping, the "Forbidden City" is enclosed in...
Universes that lie "fifty million light years" away...

If any of the defining expressions—"so-called", "entitled", "termed", "signed", "supposed", etc.—are actually used, the words that follow them may or may not be quoted, according to the writer's preference.

241

a so-called "Liberal"	OR:	a so-called Liberal
a supposed "trust"		a supposed trust
what is termed "generosity"		what is termed generosity
the much-talked-of "life"		the much-talked-of life

Titles of Books, Stories, Plays, Paintings, Music, etc. In ordinary writings, titles of compositions should be set in small letters and quoted (with only the main words capitalized).

...the book was "The Virginian" by Owen Wister.
...the short story, "The Apple-Tree", by Galsworthy. (See footnote p. 236.)
Doctor Thomas's article was entitled "Does Tomorrow Come?"

In the publishing trade, titles of books and compositions are often set in caps, and not quoted; or sometimes underlined to indicate that they would be set in italics if in print.

...an order for THE VIRGINIAN by Owen Wister.
...the style of the Oxford English Dictionary.

Credit Lines. In credit lines, the name of the work or book is quoted, unless it is an everyday name. (In printing, it is often italicized.)

—Irving, "Life of Washington", Vol. II, p. 210. (See footnote p. 236.)
BUT: —Webster's Collegiate Dictionary, p. 1217.
(See also Copy for the Press, pp. 423 and 424.)

Ships' Names. In ordinary writings, the names of ships should be set in small letters and quoted (with only the main words capitalized).

the SS. "Transatlantic"   the SS. "Empress of the Seas"
(See Abbreviations, p. 540, for the use of "SS." rather than "S.S.")

In the shipping trade, the names of ships are often set in caps and not quoted. (And no periods are used after the abbreviations SS, MS [motorship], and MV [motor vessel].)

the SS ATLANTICLAND   the MS MONARCH OF THE SEAS

Magazines, Newspapers, Periodicals, and Reference Books. Titles that are being constantly used or seen are not quoted. Do not neglect to capitalize "The" in all such titles when it is a part of the name.

in The Saturday Evening Post   in the New York Herald Tribune
in The New York Times   in The World Almanac

Words Set in Caps. When words are set in caps for distinction, it is not necessary also to quote them.

...hereinafter called the SELLER. (or Seller)

QUOTED MATTER

Paragraphs Quoted. Quotation marks are placed at the beginning of each paragraph of continuous quoted material, but not at the end of each paragraph—at the end of the entire quotation only. This indicates that the quotation is still in effect at the beginning of each new paragraph, and that it does not end until the final quotation mark is reached.

     "..
....
....
     "..
....?
     "..
....
...."

If the material quoted is not continuous, but is extracted from various parts of a text, each extract should be closed with a quotation mark, and stars run between the quotations to indicate intervening space.

     "..
...."
                        *   *   *
     "..
...."

Sentences Quoted. Single sentences are often quoted in block style, with the first quotation mark set one space to the left of the block margin.

       "..
...."

Indenting Quoted Excerpts. Quotations of three or more lines should, as a rule, be set apart and indented from the body of the text. They are usually introduced by colons.

Quotation marks should be used as well as indention. Mere indention in typewritten work does not signify that the material is also quoted.

Elimination of Quotation Marks When Credit Line is Given. If the quoted excerpt is indented and followed by the author's name, or a credit line:

    In printing, quotation marks are often omitted. But they may be retained for a certain definiteness.

    In typewriting, quotation marks are sometimes omitted, but more often retained for exactness.

    In legal papers, they are always used.

Quoting Poetry. An excerpt of poetry should be set in the original form, and quoted, unless the author's name is given before or after the excerpt.

Punctuation Copied in Quoted Matter. When quoting material, copy the punctuation exactly, unless it is obviously or strikingly incorrect. For instance, if the copy has "to-day", retain the hyphen instead of writing "today".

In legal papers, copy the punctuation exactly, right or wrong (underlining any mark that is obviously incorrect). Changing the punctuation may change the meaning.

Remember, however, to change the double quotation marks in the text to single marks in the copy (if quotation marks are being used around the material being copied), as any matter quoted in the original becomes an inner quotation in the copy.

Italicized Words in Quoted Matter. If a word has been italicized for emphasis in the original text, it should be underlined in the quoted typewritten copy. In the following excerpt from Frederic Harrison, the word "must" was originally italicized:

> "For in the wilderness of books most men, certainly all busy men, must strictly choose."

If a word has been italicized instead of quoted in the original text, it should be single-quoted in the typewritten copy. In the following excerpt from Charles Lamb, the words "for" and "against" were originally italicized:

> "When we coveted a cheap luxury...we were used to have a debate..., and to weigh the 'for' and 'against'..."

Quoting Letters or Telegrams. When quoting letters or telegrams, always include the date, with a quotation mark before it; so there can be no possible question about that most important part of the instrument.

The address need not be copied unless some later question might arise regarding the actual addressee. In legal papers the address should always be copied, with a quotation mark before the first word, but not after the last word in the address.

If a letter or telegram is short enough to be copied on one page, only three quotation marks are necessary: one before the date, one before the address or salutation, and one after the last word in the signature.

"April 14, 1950

"Gentlemen:

....

....

....

....

Very truly yours,

(Sgd.) Thomas V. Law
President"

TVL:MB

If the letter or telegram to be copied is long and will carry over to another page, a quotation mark should be placed before each paragraph to indicate the continuation of the quotation.

QUESTION MARK

The peculiarity of the question mark is that it may occur within a sentence without ending the sentence.

Direct Questions. If an answer to a direct question is expected, a question mark should be used.

244

What time is it?
He asked, "Who is responsible for this?"

If an answer is not expected, and the question is intended as a suggestion or request, no question mark is necessary.

> May we ask for a prompt payment.
> Would it not be well to do it that way.
> Will you please send it to this address.
> May we hear from you promptly.
> (A question mark would make this sentence more emphatic: May we hear from you promptly?)

If no answer is expected, but if the question is a supposition or forceful statement, intended to make the reader think, a question mark is used.

> Why cannot nations come to terms?
> But who indulges in the belief that such a thing may yet be realized?
> Why not help others to help themselves?

Indirect Questions. If a question is not directly put, that is, if it is changed from its original form, it does not take a question mark.

> They asked how we would make shipment.
> He wanted to know who won the game.
> It was a question of where and when to talk.
> ...but they wondered what difference it made.

Questions not in Question Form. The question mark alone may make a question of an ordinary expression.

> They said that?
> And so they were going to abandon it?
> They intend to do no more advertising?

Unpunctuated Questions. Some questions ending within sentences are left "open", that is, without question marks, because the question mark would unduly emphasize them.

> Relief has been promised, yet what of it, they ask.
> How can we exist, is the question in every mind.

Quoted Questions. Quoted questions occurring within sentences may be begun with a capital or small letter, according to the importance of the question.

> Someone inquired: "Did you ever hear from them again?"—and no one answered.
> One question is, "from whom did they buy it?"—the other is, "to whom can they sell it?"

Doubt or Irony. If the accuracy or truth of a statement is questionable, a question mark in parentheses may follow it.

> They were discovered in 1886 (?) and were...

Irony, doubt, or humor is sometimes expressed by the question mark in parentheses. Some authorities do not sanction this; but still it is

245

used, and is often a quick and effective means of giving the writer's conclusions regarding his subject when otherwise his statements might be misunderstood.

> They also conducted a business (?) in Boston.

Of course, if the text clearly indicates the irony or doubt of the expression, the question mark is superfluous.

Court Testimony Questions. (For questions and answers in court testimony style, see Court Papers, p. 470.)

Placement of Question Mark. A question mark should immediately follow a question, whether the question ends within a sentence or not. A question mark placed within a sentence does not conclude the thought nor break the continuity of the sentence. No capital letter is necessary after it, and no punctuation other than sometimes a dash.

Commas, semicolons, and colons are not usually used after interior question marks, although of course they may be.

> Will they accept? and if they do, how long will it be before we are notified?
> How can they be superior?—unprincipled and unethical as they are!
> Can such things happen?—well, we all know they do.
> They were fined (but could you call it "fined"?) sixty cents.
> What is that they say?—"Ars longa, vita brevis."
> It's always the same old question, "What's new?", and the same old answer, "Nothing."

Do not insert a question mark before the end of the question.

> NOT: Did you see the press notice? that we wrote about.
> BUT: Did you see the press notice that we wrote about?

Beginning a Question Within a Sentence. A question may originate at any point in a sentence. It may be introduced by a comma, a semicolon, a colon, or a dash.

It may begin with a capital or small letter, according to the emphasis desired; and it is not quoted, unless it is an actual quotation.

> One naturally asks: Why hunt up all those things?
> They debated it from several angles—Was it businesslike? Was it ethical? or, even further, Was it honest?
> In all doubtful cases our first questions will be, what was the author's purpose in choosing such a theme? is it his own, or a borrowed idea? if the latter, did he use it consciously or unconsciously?
> The distinction is far from clear; who can say what would be fair to both?
> This is Thursday, isn't it?

EXCLAMATION POINT

An exclamation point should be used to point up or enliven words used forcefully, but which in themselves might convey only a mild impression.

It may be inserted at any point in a sentence; and it is followed by no mark of punctuation other than sometimes a dash.

Expressing Emotion. An exclamation point is used to punctuate expressions of intense feeling or great emotion.

The king is dead, long live the king!   In other words, war!

Ejaculations or Commands. An exclamation point is used to set off impulsive or emphatic remarks, such as ejaculations or commands.

Impossible!   Splendid!   Very good!
That's absolutely untrue!
I can't believe it!
That sounds strange, indeed!
Something must be done about it, now!
Make the most of it!
For emphasis:
Of all things!
...but, after all, we did it!
...and that goes for them, too!

Exclamation in Question Form. An exclamation point, instead of a question mark, is used after an exclamation in question form.

It might end well, who knows!
How could it be misunderstood!
What difference does it make!

Polite or Satirical Emphasis. An exclamation point may be used to express contempt, irony, doubt, or amusement.

Quite!   Just so!   Not really!   How clever!
They referred the scholar to a tabloid! for information.

Sarcasm, disbelief, or surprise is sometimes expressed by an exclamation point enclosed in parentheses immediately after a word in the text.

The favored position (!) was the first in line.

Mild Exclamations. A comma or period, instead of an exclamation point, is often used after an expression of mild force or pleasant surprise.

Well, well, so that is what you thought.
Truly, we can't believe it.
As if it mattered.

"O" and "Oh". "O" is used when persons or personified things are directly addressed.

O my friends!   O Travelers!

"O" is also used in expressions of plaintive hope or despair.

O the times!   O the manners!   O for a house by the sea!

"Oh" is the more common word and is used in practically all instances except the two above.

Oh, what a life!   Oh! Let it pass!

247

In mild expressions containing "oh", the exclamation point is not used.

> Oh, we do not question their statement...
> You think you can't afford a vacation; but, oh, why not?
> Oh, what's the use?

Note that "O" has no apostrophe after it; is always capitalized; is never used alone; and is not separated from the following words by any mark of punctuation.

Note that "oh" is not capitalized unless it begins a sentence; and that it is usually followed by a comma.

Placement of Exclamation Point. An exclamation point is placed immediately after the words that it describes or dramatizes—in the body of a sentence or at the end.

If in the body of a sentence, it needs no other punctuation mark to support it, except sometimes a dash; nor does it break the sentence sufficiently to require a capital letter after it.

Commas, semicolons, or colons are not usually used after inner exclamation points.

> Imagine that! the only times they have been civil have been the occasions...
> Absolutely incredible!—but what can we do?

If the entire sentence is an exclamation, or if a series of words are exclamatory, the exclamation point is usually reserved for the final word.

> My, how they laughed!
> Why, so it was, to be sure!
> Why, it may cost thousands!
> It was the old, old story of "Going; going; gone!"

If the first words alone are exclamatory, the exclamation point is used immediately after them, and a period or question mark at the end of the sentence.

> Too bad! too bad! we thought, but we could not remedy it.
> Ah! then they haven't told?
> Ho, ho, ho! That's funny, indeed.

Several exclamation points may appear in the same sentence.

> If they cry "Wolf! Wolf!" once more, we'll annihilate them, so help us!

APOSTROPHE

The apostrophe has four uses. It is used in forming
Contractions of words and figures,
Possessives,
Plurals of letters, figures, and words used as words, and
Verb forms of letters and unusual words.

APOSTROPHE

Contractions. The omission of letters in words is indicated by apostrophes.

Note that **a contraction is not an abbreviation.** It does not require a period. To use both an apostrophe and a period is double punctuation.

NOT: *cont'd.*	*Int'l.*	*Dep't.*	*Corp'n.*	*Sec'y.*
BUT: cont'd	Int'l	Dep't	Corp'n	Sec'y
OR PREFERABLY: contd.	Intl.	Dept.	Corp.	Secy.

(Abbreviations are generally preferred to contractions, especially in typewritten work. See Abbreviations, p. 535.)

Common Contractions.

I'll, we'll, you'll, he'll, they'll, it'll, who'll } Colloquial shortenings of "will" and "shall", but "I'll" and "we'll" are so common as no longer to be considered colloquial.

I'd, we'd, you'd, it'd, they'd, he'd, who'd } Colloquial shortenings of "had", "would", and "should".

I've, we've, you've, it's, that's, he's, who's, they've, who've } Shortenings of "have" and "has".

would've, could've, should've—are distinctly colloquial.

I'm, we're, you're, he's, it's, they're, who's, that's, there's, here's, where's } Shortenings of "am", "is", and "are".

haven't, hasn't, needn't, can't, wouldn't, shouldn't, won't, shan't, isn't, aren't, wasn't, weren't, don't, doesn't } Shortenings of "not".

Ain't is condemned as "illiterate".

Make sure that the apostrophe is in the exact place of the omitted letters

isn't not *is'nt*   doesn't not *does'nt*

"Can't", "won't", and "shan't" present the problem of having two places to put the apostrophe. The preferable form for these words is the apostrophe between the n and the t, as in similar contractions. However, "shan't" is also sometimes written "sha'n't".

o'clock	is a contraction of "of the clock"
'tween decks	between decks
sou'wester	southwester
O'Neil	originally meant "of Neil"
M'Donald	used sometimes for "MacDonald"
M'Call	used for "McCall", etc.

The words "till", "O", and "round" are not contractions. They are words in themselves. No apostrophe should be used with them.

"Change", as in "on Change", is a British word and is not considered a contraction of "Exchange". Therefore no apostrophe is used before it.

cello, teens, phone, possum, ricksha, varsity, Halloween } are written now without an apostrophe. They have become known as words and have been forgotten as contractions.

249

Other Uses of Apostrophe. Other uses of the apostrophe are to indicate

Omission of figures:	'49er	'90s	(See Numbers, p. 268)
Plurals of figures:	10's	20's	(See Numbers, p. 273)
Plurals of letters:	ABC's	t's	(See Abbreviations, p. 538)
Plurals of words:	if's and and's		(See Plurals, p. 115)
Addition of -ed or -ing:	comma'd off		(See Spelling, p. 140)
	X'd out, OK'ing		(See Abbreviations, p. 539).
Possessives:	Keats's	men's	(See Possessives, p. 117)

HYPHEN

No two authorities agree on the use of hyphens. Therefore, a writer must be guided by rules of usage in the matter of hyphening or eliminating hyphens and writing solid or separate words.

One-Thought Expressions. When two or more words have the force of one word, that is, convey a single thought, they are hyphened.

ne'er-do-well	Mr. So-and-So
make-believe	on the four-o'clock
a passer-by	a man-of-war
will-o'-the-wisp	a lawyer-banker
a step-saver	a bit of the up-to-date
stick-to-itiveness	cut-and-dried-ness

One-Thought Modifiers Before Nouns. When two or more words have the force of a single modifier before a noun, they are hyphened.

a straight-from-the-shoulder talk	a frivolous-sensible manner
a run-of-the-mine American	a gray-blue uniform
the up-to-the-minute developments	the free-and-easy, first-come-first-
catch-as-catch-can methods	served type
at such-and-such a time	a would-be statesman
a three-minute conversation	an economy-without-injustice
	measure

Modifiers Before and After Nouns. Often when a one-thought modifier is transposed and placed **after a noun,** the construction is changed, giving the words their separate force, and no hyphen is needed.

BEFORE A NOUN	AFTER A NOUN
a well-known name*	a name well known
a worth-while venture	a venture worth while
a so-called law·	a law, so called because
the above-mentioned item	the item above mentioned
an ill-designed plan	a plan, ill designed but worthy
a long, up-hill climb	a long climb up hill

* In "a very well known name", "very" qualifies "well", thus destroying the unity between "well" and "known".

Also, when such an expression follows the noun and other words are added to connect the parts, no hyphen is needed.

BEFORE A NOUN	AFTER A NOUN
an up-to-date record	a record brought up to date
a first-class proposition	a proposition of the first class
a rule-of-thumb calculation	a calculation by rule of thumb
the 800-meter race	a race of 800 meters
a coast-to-coast broadcast	a broadcast from coast to coast
a hand-to-mouth living	a living from hand to mouth

But when such an expression follows the noun and still retains its force as a one-thought modifier, the hyphen is used.

BEFORE A NOUN	AFTER A NOUN
a hand-to-mouth existence	an existence that became hand-to-mouth
a first-class proposition	the proposition is not first-class
the dust-covered street	the street was dust-covered
a breath-taking adventure	an adventure breath-taking and hazardous
an error-proof machine	the machine is not error-proof
poison-tipped arrows	arrows that are poison-tipped
a rust-gold color	a color practically rust-gold

Compound Names as Modifiers. Proper compound names and, in business usage, many ordinary compound names retain their original forms when used as modifiers: if hyphened they retain the hyphen; if not hyphened no hyphen is added—they being naturally joined in the reader's mind.

Civil Service Commission	The Anglo-French pact
Post Office Department	Supreme Court decisions
Far Eastern customs	Postal Union mails

Compound ordinary names as modifiers:

income tax statements	foreign exchange values
civil service examinations	night letter rates
motion picture screens	rural route deliveries
real estate values	safe deposit boxes
daylight saving time	air mail stamps
direct mail advertising	long distance calls

(Many printing establishments hyphen these compound names when used as modifiers, following definite rules of style; but business usage very generally omits such hyphens so as to avoid getting too deep in the matter of hyphening.)

Names of three or more words are usually hyphened when used as modifiers.

bill-of-lading forms	collect-on-delivery service
right-of-way grants	change-of-address cards

Occasionally a proper name is hyphened, if joined in a three- or four-word modifier before a noun, as

the White-House-ruled Cabinet
RATHER THAN: the White House-ruled Cabinet

Although more often the hyphens are unnecessary, as

the Federal Reserve banking methods

251

Adverb Ending in -ly not Hyphened. An adverb ending in -ly is not hyphened to the word that follows, even though the two form a single idea. The -ly itself shows the relationship between the words, by indicating that the first modifies the second; therefore the hyphen seems superfluous.

THUS: a publicly owned corporation   NOT: a *publicly-owned* corporation
        a privately managed business   a *privately-managed* business
        highly valued packages   *highly-valued* packages

Verbs and Verb Forms Hyphened. Verbs composed of two or more words forming a single thought should be hyphened.

blue-pencil the drawing   double-spacing the copy
question-mark the points   if it is cross-referenced

But verbs are not hyphened to prepositions that follow them as adverbs, unless such combinations stand as nouns or adjectives.

As verbs:
   set off such words (NOT: *set-off*)   is marking up the price
   turn down the page   has crossed off the names
As nouns:
   a send-off   a step-down   a cross-out   a tie-in
   But not when only the first part is a noun (unless the combination has a special
      meaning—different from the ordinary sense).
   the writing down of names   the crossing off of figures
   the writing-down of assets   reckless cutting-in (driving)
   the opening up of new fields   the holding over of a play
   the bringing-up of children   the rounding out of the year
As adjectives:
   built-in fixtures   a crossed-out figure
   take-off signals   a marked-up price

When a noun is followed by an -ing word (a verbal noun), no hyphen is necessary unless the combination is used as an adjective.

As nouns: a profit taking   **As adjectives:** a profit-taking period
           a price cutting   a price-cutting war
           in map making   a map-making company
           in letter writing   a letter-writing contest

When an -ed word occurs in a modifier, the preceding word is often hyphened to it; but if the preceding word ends in a comparative -er or -est, which in itself indicates the connection between the words, no hyphen is necessary (unless two meanings could apply).

a high-priced article   { a higher priced article
                                 { the highest priced article
a small-sized book   a smaller sized book
a deep-toned instrument   a deeper toned instrument
a well-established firm   { a better established firm
                                 { the best established firms
a well-informed man   the best informed people

A hyphen to distinguish two meanings:

the lighter shaded portion	(the shaded portion that is lighter)
the lighter-shaded portion	(the portion that is more lightly shaded)
a finer lined ornament	(a lined ornament that is finer)
a finer-lined ornament	(an ornament that is more finely lined)
the best accepted usage	(the accepted usage that is best)
NOT: the *best-accepted* usage	(which would mean the usage that is accepted best)
larger stamped envelopes	(stamped envelopes that are larger)
NOT: *larger-stamped* envelopes	(which would mean envelopes that are stamped with larger stamps)

Words Grow Together or Apart. After long use the hyphen is often discarded. Words grow together or they grow apart.

> "...the conversion of a hyphened word into an unhyphened single one is desirable as soon as the novelty of the combination has worn off, if there are no obstacles in the way of awkward spelling, obscurity, or the like."
> —Fowler, "A Dictionary of Modern English Usage", p. 244.

GROWN TOGETHER	GROWING TOGETHER	GROWN OR REMAINING APART
airplane	airline	air mail
airport	bylaws	all right
counterclockwise	checkbook	common sense
crosscut	deadline	cross reference
fireproof	downtown	day labor
headquarters	highlights	dead letter
inasmuch as	layout	ill will
insofar as	lineup	more or less
letterhead	makeup	motion picture
nevertheless	newsreel	post card
notebook	nonetheless	post office
notwithstanding	payroll	price list
nowadays	setup	question mark
proofreading	shortcut	real estate
scrapbook	sidelights	red tape
showdown	sidestep	right of way
timesaver	standby	sea level
today	trademark*	so far as
tomorrow	transship	title page
tonight	turnover	trade name
viewpoint	waterfront	vice president

* "Trade-mark" is still hyphened in all Government publications.

Some words have difficulty in settling down to a permanent form. The word "cooperate" is still seen in its three stages of evolution:

co-operate	coöperate	cooperate

but the form "cooperate" is now very generally used in business papers.

Three Stages of Transition. Similar words (or the same word) may be seen in any one of three forms: as two words; hyphened; or as a single word.

ONE WORD	HYPHENED	TWO WORDS
blueprint	blue-print	blue print
horsepower	horse-power	horse power
steppingstone	stepping-stone	stepping stone
windshield	wind-shield	wind shield
tintype	tin-plate	tin foil
handwork	metal-work	book work
midwinter	mid-August	mid air
crossroad	cross-examination	cross reference
schoolhouse	road-house	bond house
courthouse	counting-house	clearing house
postmark	post-box	post office

"Suspending" Hyphens. "Suspending hyphens" should be used in a series of hyphened words having a common ending.

> long- and short-term notes
> a chart- or map-maker
> slated for a two- or possibly three-year stay
> a grooved ring in circular-, pear-, or heart-shaped form
> on a 120- or 121-inch wheelbase
> French- and Spanish-speaking provinces
> between a well- and an ill-sounding verse
> twenty-six or -seven

Although some writers prefer to drop the suspending hyphens in common expressions, such as "five and ten-dollar bills", it is perhaps a better plan to use them consistently in all such constructions to avoid the possible danger of an occasional misreading.

Words should be repeated if a part does not naturally carry over.

> NOT: Do they mean a wood-wind or -note instrument?
> BUT: Do they mean a wood-wind or a wood-note instrument?

Solid words are not often separated, although they may be.

> eastbound or westbound   OR: east- or westbound
> handwritten or typewritten matter   hand- or typewritten matter

Hyphening Prefixes and Suffixes. A different meaning may be conveyed by setting a prefix or suffix off with a hyphen.

> recover the loss   re-cover the furniture
> recollect the incident   re-collect the debt
> recount a tale   re-count the votes
> reform a youth   re-form the bylaws
> recreate the mind   re-create a masterpiece
> a fruitless search   a fruit-less diet
> prayers   pray-ers

To avoid the doubling or tripling of letters, prefixes and suffixes may be set off with hyphens.

> re-employ   re-emphasize   shell-like   shell-less

Unusual Words Formed With Prefixes.   Prefixes in coined or unusual words are joined with a hyphen.

co-user	ex-diplomat	post-prosperity period
non-civilian	pre-1929	semi-authentic
pro-inflationist	anti-hopefuls	pseudo-scoffer

Familiar words with these prefixes (except ex-) are written solid.

anticlimax	proslavery	postgraduate	semiannual
coauthor	prehistoric	noncommissioned	pseudofamous

But **self-** is still hyphened: self-explanatory   self-evident   self-made   self-conscious   self-starter   (EXCEPTIONS: selfsame and selfless)

If the prefix is added to a two-or-more-word expression, the entire combination may be hyphened.

anti-British-Rule
  (RATHER THAN: anti-British Rule)
pre-Flag-Day ceremonies
pre-World-War commerce
a pro-National-Republic man
a pseudo-East-Indian art

a semi-American-citizen
(NOT: a *semi-American* citizen)
a semi-well-wisher
the mid-Twentieth-Century exposi-
tion
non-civil-service examinations

Or if such a combination would be misleading, the prefix may stand one space away from the first word.

a pro- ex-Mayor candidate   an ex- G.O.P.
Note the difference between: anti- war demonstrations, anti-war demonstrations, and anti-war-demonstrations (the last form being ambiguous).

Hyphening Long Double Names.   Two familiar long names, each of two words or more, are often joined with a single hyphen.

the San Francisco-New York air mail
a Great Britain-South Africa affair
a Benjamin Franklin-Daniel Webster phrase
the public works-industries control bill
the G. K. T.-Union Corporation securities

Two unfamiliar long names should not be hyphened.   Rather, the construction should be changed.

OBSCURE: A Republic of Cuba-Isle of Pines agreement...
IMPROVED: An agreement between the Republic of Cuba and the Isle of
        Pines...

Capitalization in Hyphened Words.   (See p. 135.)
Numbers Hyphened.   (See pp. 266–74.)
Abbreviations Hyphened.   (See p. 539.)

Titles.
    "Civil and military titles denoting a single office are not hyphened."   —United States Government Printing Office
                        Style Manual (1945), p. 59.

255

CIVIL TITLES	MILITARY AND NAVAL TITLES
Ambassador at Large	Adjutant General
Assistant Secretary	Brigadier General
Attorney at Law	Commander in Chief
Attorney General	Inspector General
Chief Clerk	Lieutenant Colonel
Chief Engineer	Lieutenant Commander
Chief Justice	Lieutenant General
Chief of Police	Major General
Congressman at Large	Quartermaster General
Consul General	Rear Admiral
Deputy Commissioner	Surgeon General
Director in Charge	Vice Admiral
Editor in Chief	
General Manager	
Governor General	
Lieutenant Governor	
Managing Editor	
Postmaster General	
Purchasing Agent	
Secretary of State	
Sergeant at Arms	
Under Secretary	
Vice Chairman	
Vice Consul	
Vice President	

If a title represents two offices, it is hyphened.

Secretary-Treasurer   Auditor-Treasurer

Ex- and -elect are hyphened to titles; and titles of two or more words are hyphened in these combinations.

ex-President   President-elect
ex-Editor-in-Chief   Vice-President-elect
ex-Governor-General   Lieutenant-Governor-elect

Designations of offices are hyphened.

the vice-presidency   the chief-clerkship

Foreign Phrases. It is unnecessary to hyphen a foreign or Latin phrase, even when it is used as a modifier before a noun. Such a phrase is distinct in itself and will be interpreted as one expression without hyphening.

prima facie evidence   per diem employees
bona fide agreements   ex officio member
a bon voyage gift   an ex parte hearing

Letters. Letters used as descriptive words are usually, for definiteness, hyphened to words to form nouns; and are always hyphened to form adjectives.

NOUNS		ADJECTIVES
I-beam	A-frame	S-curved
T-square	C-spring	T-shaped
T-rail	U-boat	V-shaped
X-ray	S-curve	

It is not necessary to quote the letters, as "I" beam; nor is it necessary to spell them out, as "eye beam".

Regarding the Use of Hyphens. Misplacement of a hyphen can completely change a meaning.

NOT:	BUT:
lighter than *air-craft*	lighter-than-air craft
tenement *house-act*	tenement-house act
a hand *tool-box*	a hand-tool box
a forest *fire-lighter*	a forest-fire lighter
check-and-double check service	check-and-double-check service
slow *motion-pictures*	slow-motion pictures

Do not drop a necessary hyphen at the end of a line. Such omitted hyphens often make the reader read twice to get the meaning.

NOT:	BUT:
...they will score good sized gains.	...they will score good-sized gains.
It means a long drawn out process.	It means a long-drawn-out process.
...seek higher interest bearing loans.	...seek higher interest-bearing loans.
...will buy 30 or 60 day paper.	...will buy 30- or 60-day paper.
...several of the out of town exchanges were...	...several of the out-of-town exchanges were...
...if they will buy up to date equipment.	...if they will buy up-to-date equipment.
...such things as a well appointed room.	...such things as a well-appointed room.

DIVISION OF WORDS

Pronunciation governs the division of words. Sound the word and divide between the syllables. If in doubt, consult the dictionary.

Division According to Pronunciation. The following words illustrate the method of division between syllables:

	NOT:	
anx- ious		*an- xious*
bu- gle		*bug- le*
di- shevel		*dis- hevel*
eight- een		*eigh- teen*
fur- nished		*furn- ished*
han- dled		*hand- led*
hin- drance		*hind- rance*
mon- eyed		*money- ed*
prob- ably		*pro- bably*
sci- ence		*scien- ce*
tri- fled		*trif- led*
wrin- kle		*wrink- le*

Dictionaries sometimes differ.

ONE GIVES:	ANOTHER:
assist- ance	assis- tance
attend- ance	atten- dance
preced- ence	prece- dence

257

British and American usage differs.

AMERICAN: bystand- er   BRITISH: bystan- der
distrib- utive   distri- butive
prep- osition   pre- position
prev- alent   pre- valent
prefer- ence   prefe- rence
partic- ular   parti- cular
knowl- edge   know- ledge

Between Doubled Letters. Words are usually divided between doubled consonants.

mas- sive   neces- sary   puz- zled
clas- sic   pas- sage   pos- sible, not *poss- ible*

When the final letter is doubled because of an added -ing, -ed, -er, -est, etc., the division is between the doubled letters, to preserve the original word.

stop- ping   NOT: *stopp- ing*   pit- ted   NOT: *pitt- ed*
run- ning   *runn- ing*   outfit- ted   *outfitt- ed*
begin- ning   *beginn- ing*   hid- den   *hidd- en*
refer- ring   *referr- ing*   thin- nest   *thinn- est*
rob- bing   *robb- ing*   bid- der   *bidd- er*

But if the word itself ends in a doubled letter, the original form is preserved.

pass- ing   NOT: *pas- sing*
pull- ing   *pul- ling*
full- er   *ful- ler*

One-Syllable Words. One-syllable words cannot, of course, be divided.

freight   thought   strength   though
height   width   length   friend
fought   breadth   through   scheme

Note that many words remain but one syllable after taking -ed.

billed   scarred   shipped   flagged
marred   grabbed   stopped   trumped

Contractions. Do not divide contractions, such as

haven't   doesn't   wasn't   shouldn't

Hyphened Words. Divide hyphened words only at the hyphens.

...in the above-   NOT: ...in the *above-men-*
mentioned book.   *tioned* book.

Dividing One or Two Letters. Do not divide on a single letter; and in most instances, do not divide on two letters. Two-letter prefixes are sometimes divided, but usually not two-letter endings.

ex-   -ly
im-   -ty
re-, etc.   -ed, etc.

Proper Names.   Although proper names are divided in printing, they should not be divided in typewriting.

WRITE:	NOT:
. . . . .Theodore Wilson.	. . . . .Theodore Wilson. . . . .
. . . . .Billings, Montana.	. . . . .Billings, Montana. . . . . . .
. . . . .to St. Louis.	. . . . .to St. Louis. . . . .
. . . . .on Wednesday morning.	. . . . .on Wednesday morning.
. . . . .R. B. Hill, President.	. . . . .R. B. Hill, President. . . . .

Initials should not be separated from each other, and preferably not from the surname.

Degree or other letters after a name should not be separated from each other, and preferably not from the surname; yet if they are long, there is often no other choice than to separate them from the name.

"Mr.", "Sr.", "Jr.", and "Esq." should preferably not be separated from surnames.

WRITE:	NOT:
. . . . .Superintendent J. B. Martin.	. . . . .Superintendent J. B. Martin.
. . . . .Baldwin M. Blaine, Ph.D., LL.D., ...	. . . . . . .Baldwin M. Blaine, Ph. D., LL.D., ...
. . . . . .Wm. Mansford, Jr.	. . . . .Wm. Mansford, Jr. . . . .
. . . . .for Mr. Leland.	. . . . .for Mr. Leland.

Figures and Dates.   Never divide figures or abbreviations, nor separate signs, letters, or short abbreviations from that to which they apply.   (Publications sometimes make such divisions to obtain balanced lines.)

WRITE:	NOT:
. . . .$500,126	. . . .$500, 126. . . . .
. . . .	
. . . . .4:20 p.m.	. . . . .4:20 p.m. . . . .
. . . .	
. . . . .36 deg. F.	. . . . .36 deg. F. . . . .
. . . .	
(a).	. . . .(a). . . . .(b)
(b). . . . .(c).	. . . .(c)
. . . . .500 bbls.	. . . . .500 bbls.. . . . .
. . . .	

Divide dates between the day and the year, not between the month and the day.

WRITE:	NOT:
. . . . .February 14, 1937.	. . . . .February 14, 1937. . . . . .

Foreign Words. Do not divide foreign words unless they are familiar enough to have become a part of the English language. Then divide according to pronunciation.

Last Word in a Paragraph, and Last Word on a Page. Do not divide the last word in a paragraph. To do so leaves but a portion of a word for the last line, which is not an effective ending.

Do not divide the last word on a page and carry a portion over to the next page. This is sometimes done in printing to fill out lines; but in typewriting it is unnecessary and should not be practised.

Consecutive Divided Endings. Do not allow more than two consecutive lines to end in word divisions. Divided words are hard to follow; and too many divided words on a page produce a choppy effect.

··◆◀▒══════════▒▶··

DIACRITICAL MARKS

Diacritical marks are carried on some foreign words. But before using any unfamiliar mark, consult the dictionary.

Put all accent marks in by hand, with a pencil rather than with ink. A pencil mark blends more naturally with the typewritten letter than ink does.

Accents and Markings.

French:

		As in:
Acute	é	Champs Élysées, résumé, visé
Grave	à è ù	mise en scène, vis-à-vis
Circumflex	â ê î ô û	tête-à-tête, maître d'hôtel
Dieresis	ë ï ü	naïveté, Noël
Cedilla	ç	garçon
Apostrophe	(denotes omission of letters)	chargé d'affaires, entr'acte

Spanish:

Acute   á é í ó ú   Sí, compañía
(indicates a stress of the syllable, not a change in vowel sound)
Crema   ü
(indicates that u is to be pronounced)
Tilde   ñ   Señor, cañon, doña
(indicates a special pronunciation of n, similar to ny in English)

Italian:

Grave   à è ì ò ù   capacità, abilità
(indicates a stress of the syllable, not a change in vowel sound)

German:

Umlaut   ä ö ü   Götterdämmerung, Walküre
                             (ö is often expressed by oe, as in Goethe, Roentgen, etc.)

English:

Dieresis ·· over a second vowel indicates that the vowels are to be pronounced separately.
coördination   reënter   preëmpt   zoölogical
In printing, it often replaces a hyphen. In typewriting, the hyphen is usually used; or if the word is familiar, it is written solid, without markings.
Grave   indicates that the syllable is to be pronounced separately.
belovèd   learnèd   agèd   blessèd

··◆◀▒══════════▒▶··

ASTERISK

Footnote Indicators. A footnote indicator in a text is placed **after a word,** rather than before it, and in typewritten work may be set before or after any immediate mark of punctuation, according to the part of the sentence to which the indicator refers. If it refers to an entire clause, it may be set after a punctuation mark; if it refers to a single word, it may be set before the punctuation mark.

> They cited a quotation from the "Official Bulletin",* and it was evident...
> It is a sort of office daily—house organ*—which all are expected to read.
> It was adopted by France, England, and Germany (the "key countries"*).

Note: In printing, footnote indicators are, for symmetry, usually placed after any and all immediate marks of punctuation, except the dash.

Not more than three asterisks should be used to indicate footnotes (*, **, ***); some other mark should be used after the number reaches three. Several other footnote reference marks may be made on the typewriter. A raised x is a good substitute for an asterisk. A capital A with a small v struck over it is a good imitation asterisk; as is a capital T with an x struck over it; or a capital O with an x in it. Do not use as indicators, signs that have other meanings, as #, %, and @.

In printing, these signs are used: dagger (†), double dagger (‡), star (*), parallels (‖), section (§), radical (√), degree (°), and paragraph (¶).

Superior (raised) figures or letters may be used if they are not likely to be confused with the text. The Government writes them: 1/ or a/, etc.

> France[1],...England[2],...   Or letters with figures: 1342[a],...2978[b],...
> **Government usage:**   Gold 1/   Fund 2/   or   1940 a/   1950 b/
> In the footnotes: 1/ Gold certificates.   or   a/ Revised list.

In tabulations the indicator may be placed immediately before or after that to which it refers.

> April*   Silver[1]   Gold 2/
> *Finland   1945[a]   a/ 1945

Footnotes. In the footnote itself, the indicator may, for distinction, be set one space before the first word.

> * Formerly the capital

A footnote should be on the same page as its indicator, not one or two pages later (except in tables). (See also Copy for the Press, p. 424.)

Heading Indicators. A "heading indicator" may be an asterisk or other mark which refers the reader to a heading instead of a footnote.

NATIONALITIES

(Nations not using a Latin alphabet are marked *)
Chilean   *Korean
*Chinese   Colombian

DIAGONAL OR SLANT LINE (VIRGULE)

In tabulation headings and in abbreviations, a diagonal line, often called a **"slant"** or a **"shilling mark",** may indicate an omission of words.

barrels/day   for   barrels per day   B/L   for   bill of lading

Two words to be used interchangeably may be connected by a slant, as

and/or   was/were   his/their

OMISSIONS

Omission of Words or Sentences (Ellipsis).   Three dots are used to denote the omission of words in a quoted sentence.   A fourth period may be added to indicate the end of a sentence, if this is deemed necessary.

The agreement specifically stated: " . . . and we will refrain from any action. . .
that might prove damaging to their interests. . . ".
The spice of life is battle. . .   —Stevenson.

Three spaced dots may be used to indicate the omission of entire sentences.

"There is a time when no thing seems worth while.
.   .   .   And that is the key to the situation."

Dots Instead of Other Punctuation.   Three dots are sometimes used—especially in advertising copy—to replace other marks of punctuation. They tend to retard the sentence and hold the reader's attention on the context.

This is a particular series. . .particular in that it is directed toward a special
market. . .a market that is on the march.
The machines are used for proofing. . .for imprinting. . .for duplicating. . .for
addressing. . .for filling in. . .for listing.

Unfinished Sentences.   Three dashes are used to denote an unfinished sentence, or one in which the thought or speech falters and breaks off, or turns sharply.

That cannot happen unless- - -but of course it might.

Unprintable Words.   Three asterisks are used to indicate unprintable words in a quotation or a text.

He said ***—what he thought.

Omission of Paragraphs.   Three spaced asterisks may be used to indicate the omission of paragraphs in copied work.

* * *

Change of Subject Matter.   A row of four dashes may be used to indicate a break between two subjects.

- - - -

End of Manuscript. The end of a manuscript may be indicated by

– – –oOo– – –   or   * * *   or   # # # (printers' mark)
                            * *
                             *

UNDERSCORE

Underline headings with an unbroken line.

Underline parts of the text with an unbroken line, unless each under-lined word or part is to be emphasized separately, in which case break the line at the spaces.

> Delivery is to be made not later than Monday, June 20.
> Deliveries are to be made in June, in September, and in November.

TYPEWRITER SPACINGS

The following typewriter spacings are used in connection with the various marks of punctuation:

period	two spaces (three, with elite type) after each.
question mark } exclamation point }	two spaces (three, with elite type) after each; one space after each within a sentence.
comma } abbreviation period } semicolon }	one space after each.
colon	two spaces after each.
dash	one space on each side.
parentheses	one space before the first parenthesis and one after the last, but no spaces between parentheses and the words enclosed.
quotation marks	spacings are governed by the accompanying marks of punctuation. No spaces between quotation marks and the words they enclose, nor between final quotation marks and other marks of punctuation—except dashes.

BRACKETS

Brackets are used around remarks inserted by a writer when quoting another writer or text, or reporting a procedure.   The words so enclosed are entirely separate from the rest of the sentence in the matter of punctuation and construction.

The first word in the insertion is not capitalized unless it begins a separate sentence or is a proper name.   No break in the quotes is neces-sary for the insertion of a bracketed statement.

Typewritten brackets are made with "slants" and underscores: [ ]

> "Since that time [1859] the right of agents to use..."
> ...said that it was "characterized [by solemn "critics"] in the press as 'stupendous'".

Q. You said the document was a poem?   [Laughter.]
  A. Yes, it seems to be.   [Reads:]
Q. You call that poetry [laughter]; then explain it.

If the year or name of a city has been omitted in a date line and is inserted by the one copying the manuscript, brackets should be used around the insertion.

[New Orleans] May 5 [1936]

BRACE

Braces are used before or after material that is grouped.

The point of the brace should be turned toward the smaller number of lines, or the smaller group.

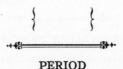

PERIOD

After Sentences.   No sentence should be left "open", that is, with no punctuation, unless it is segregated as a title, heading, or part of a tabulation.

An expression does not necessarily need a subject or verb in order to be followed by a period, question mark, or exclamation point.

Important, if true.
Not to mention other things.
Bare facts, nothing more.
Some good; some bad.
After that—what?
Not in the past, not in the future, and not now!

NUMBERS

When to Use Figures, and When to Use Words. In modern business practice very few numbers are written out. Almost every number that is used is inserted for quick reference or calculation; hence it is in a form to catch the eye.

All definite numbers above ten should be in figures (and below ten, if given for quick reference).

> It is in 24 volumes.
> We will ship 7 cases.
> ...in 20 to 30 days.
> ...27¢ each...at 6%...weighing 8 lbs.
> ...interest for 2 years 5 months and 19 days.
> ...charged $1 for 5 months.

Indefinite numbers are often written out; but if a ready calculation of them is necessary, they may be in figures.

about sixteen hundred tons	OR:	about 1600 tons
sold about sixty percent		about 60%
some twenty-odd years ago		250-odd pages
a fifty-fifty proposition		will split 50–50
ten or twenty years ago		10 or 20 pieces
lost nearly a thousand dollars		almost $1000

At the beginning of a sentence, numbers are usually spelled out if they are short; but if long, they may be written in numerals to avoid a cumbersome lot of words. (Many examples in expensive advertising.)

> Seventy crates, 12 bundles, and 42 cartons were...
> Twenty-five to thirty barrels will be sent.
> 1926 saw the...—Prof. W. E. Atkins, "Gold and Your Money", p. 126.
> 33,612 miles in 5 months is...—Ford Motor Company advertisement.

If two sets of figures occur in a sentence, one set may be spelled out to differentiate it from the other.

> Only three wells were producing 2000 barrels each; twenty-five were producing 1000 each; and thirty-eight were pumping about 100 barrels each.

When two numbers occur together, a comma or dash is used to separate them. Or one of the numbers may be spelled out.

> In 1928, 25 million barrels were shipped.
> Instead of 5, 25 were necessary.
> We ordered 350—50 of which were to be bound.

Note that "million" or "billion" may be spelled out after a number to avoid the use of many ciphers and to afford a quick interpretation of the number.

> 10½ million dollars or $10½ million   3⅗ billions

265

Numbers in legal papers are now commonly written only in figures. (See Legal Papers, p. 460.)

If two numbers form one item, one number, usually the first, is spelled out.

four 6-inch frames	eight 5-gallon cans
six ⅜-inch boards	seven 3¢ stamps
five 3-point recorders	two $1 bills

But if the second number is the shorter, it may be spelled out instead of the first.

85 three-cent stamps   269 five-gallon tins

In tabulations a dash is used to separate such numbers.

12 – 5″ pipes   6 – ⅜″ boards

Commas Separating Thousands From Hundreds. Do not run figures together in a long number without the necessary dividing commas. Long undivided numbers are very hard to read.

Write all numbers above 10,000 with commas, as 1,324,576 instead of 1324576—even in tabulations, unless spaces are left to indicate commas.

Patent numbers, insurance numbers, and other serial numbers are often printed without commas; but good authorities use commas when rewriting these numbers.

The even hundred numbers below 10,000 may be written with or without commas, as 9500, 4200; but when used with other numbers below 10,000, all usually have commas, as 9,500,   9,568,   4,200,   4,234— unless in tabulations.   If written in succession as the foregoing are, two spaces instead of one should be left between the numbers.

Year numbers, page numbers, room numbers, house numbers, and most telephone numbers have no commas.

A comma is not necessary (but it adds to clearness) between the thousands and hundreds when a number is written out.

...nine hundred eighty-five thousand, seven hundred and thirty-two.
(The "and" may be used or omitted.   It is used by many authorities.)

Dollars. When an even amount of money is written in the text, the decimal point and ciphers are usually omitted.

$7 $35 $750 $95,345

The dollar sign is used before definite numbers, rather than the word "dollar" or "dollars" after the numbers.

a $20 note   RATHER THAN: a 20-dollar note, or a twenty-dollar note
a $15-a-week worker
a $100,000 project
a million-dollar outlay (indefinite)
about ten thousand dollars' worth (indefinite)

The dollar sign should be repeated before numbers in succession.

at $75, $154, $196, and $200   NOT: *at $75, 154, 196, and 200*
$10–$20   NOT: *10–$20*   NOR: *$10–20*
between $15 and $20
$10 to $20   OR: ten to twenty dollars (indefinite)
a $10 or $20 fine   OR: a ten- or twenty-dollar fine (indefinite)

(For $ and ¢ in columns of tabulations, see Typewritten Work, p. 405.)

Cents. In ordinary work, the cent sign is used after amounts less than one dollar. "Cts." is seldom used because it is almost as long as "cents". In printing, just "c" is often used.

| ORDINARY: | 35¢ | 2¢ | 87¢ |
| FORMAL: | 35 cents | two cents | 87 cents |

The dollar sign is not ordinarily used with cents alone, as $0.65, unless it is in statistical work or tabulations, or unless the cents are in three or four figures, as $0.4567.

Never write ".75 cents" or ".75¢" unless it is intended. This would mean $75/100$ of a cent. Write "75¢" or "75 cents".

Some ways of writing cents are:

at 75¢ a pound   @ 75¢/lb   a price of 95¢
$0.7535 an ounce
50¢ to 60¢   50 to 60 cents   50 to 60¢
a 5¢-a-pound increase
a 5¢ piece   a 5-cent piece   a five-cent piece
a 6¢ tax   a 6-cent tax   a six-cent tax

Prices Written Out. Prices are usually written in words as well as figures in legal documents; also in some quotations in which the prices are firm. A series or list of prices is written in figures only.

Approximate prices are written in figures only.

The parenthesis containing the figures should be written after the word "Dollars", because the parenthesis can sum up only what has been written before it begins.

The price is Fourteen Hundred Dollars ($1400.00).
The price is Four Thousand, Five Hundred and One Dollars ($4,501.00).

The word "and" is usually written before the numbers below one hundred in prices; but on checks, notes, etc., it is generally omitted. Therefore, if a writer desires not to use this "and", he may omit it.

The price is Five Hundred Fifty-six and $75/100$ Dollars ($556.75), f.o.b. Chicago, Illinois.

Prices in texts are often segregated and indented in order to be quickly seen.

Double-check every written-out price to make sure that the words and figures agree. Many discrepancies occur between these two sets of numbers.

No erasures should be made in the figures of a price; and not more than one letter should be erased in the written-out form.

Terms of Payment. Terms of payment are now usually written in figures only. And for definiteness, the percent sign is repeated down the column.

```
10% – 10 days after date of order
20% – 30 days  "    "    "    "
20% – 2 months "    "    "    "
25% – 4 months "    "    "    "
25% – upon completion of contract.
```

Dates. It is unnecessary to use -st, -d, or -th in dates, unless the day is written before, or is separated from, the month.

> January 2, 1937...January 1...May 28...
> BUT: ...the 1st of January, 1937...the 28th of May...from November 1st to 15th...

Note the distinction between:

> the first of the month (corresponding to the last of the month)
> the 1st of the month (meaning the first day of the month)

Do not abbreviate a date in a text, as 1/7/37, unless it is in tabulated or statistical work.

Foreign Dates. (See Letters, p. 279.)

Dates Written Out. Dates are written out only in the most formal legal documents, such as wills.

> ...this twentieth day of December, A.D. nineteen hundred and thirty-five.

Note that A.D. (meaning "in the year of our Lord") is placed before the year, not after it, and is not followed by a comma. And the numbers in the year are not capitalized.

Years may be abbreviated, as

in the winter of '17	in the '80s
Spirit of '76	in the 1920s and '30s
Class of '98	Government '31s
a '49er	

> Note that -er or -s may be joined without a second apostrophe.

When written in words, these contractions do not take an apostrophe, but may be capitalized for distinction.

in the Eighties	a Forty-niner	back in Eighteen
RATHER THAN:	in the 'Eighties	back in 'Eighteen

It is also unnecessary to use the apostrophe when a diagonal line or a hyphen is used before an abbreviated year.

1/15/36	NOT:	*1/15/'36*
1915-25		*1915-'25*

(For consecutive years indicated by a hyphen, see Omission of Intermediate Figures, p. 274.)

"Of" may be omitted in year phrases, as "the year 1936". Note that the word "year" is not capitalized.

When a month and year are written together, they may be separated by a comma, to indicate the omission of words. Some authorities omit the comma; but others use it, to conform to the usual punctuation in dates.

> April, 1945   OR: April 1945
> That was in June, 1918.
> ...in the November 1936 supplement.
> OR: ...in the November, 1936, supplement.

Hyphening Written-out Numbers. Note that numbers below one hundred are hyphened when written out, but that the hundreds and thousands are not hyphened.

twenty-five	forty-three	seventy-six
fifty-five hundred	eight hundred	three thousand
five hundred thousand	one hundred million	sixty-two million

NOT: *four-hundred*   *seven-hundred-thousand*
NOR: ...almost *six-hundred* feet below.
BUT: ...our one-hundred-and-thirty-fourth report.

Terms of Hours, Days, Months, Years. A figure may be hyphened to a **singular word** to express a single term of hours, days, months, or years. Note that when the description is placed **after** the noun the figure is not hyphened to the word, and a plural word is used (unless of course the figure one or a fraction is used before it).

a 20-minute wait	BUT:	a wait of 20 minutes
a 7-hour day		a day of 7 hours
24-hour-a-day driving		driving for 24 hours a day
60-day options		options for 60 days
a 3-day sight draft		at 3 days' sight
a 16-week term		a term of 16 weeks
a 6-month note		a note for 6 months
a 2-month extension		an extension of 2 months
a 5-year guarantee		a guarantee for 5 years

Periods of time may also be expressed by the possessive, if the idea of a single term is not foremost. The hyphen is not then used.

after six weeks' sailing	give them one month's extension
take six months' leave of absence	within five to ten minutes' time

(For use of the "suspending hyphen" in expressions such as the following, see Hyphen, p. 254.

(For use of the "suspending hyphen" in expressions such as the following, see Hyphen, p. 254.

> a small 30- or 60-day loan)

A term of years, months, and days is considered a single unit and needs no commas within it.

> interest for 3 years 5 months and 17 days

Ages. Ages may be written in figures, or spelled out. The general rule applies: Use figures if the ages are definite and given for quick reference or calculation; write out if the ages are indefinite, or if the writing is formal.

He was 31 years old when first elected. (definite)
A boy about ten years old was... (indefinite)

Note that the plurals "months" and "weeks" are idiomatically used before "old" in the following age combinations, while "year" and "day" are singular, after the usual form.

a 2-year-old animal	a two-year-old plan
a 2-year-old	a two-year-old
a 6-months-old child	a six-months-old debt
or sometimes	or
a 6-month-old child	a six-month-old debt
a 6-weeks-old infant	a six-weeks-old paper
the 10-day-old news	the ten-day-old news
2000-year-old engraving	the sixty-odd-year-old actress

In the following combination of years, months, and days, no commas are used because the age is considered one unit.

His age was 21 years 6 months and 15 days.

Write "aged" instead of "age" in such phrases as

In 1918 he died, aged 21, and his work...
A man, aged 35, was chosen...

Time. (See Clock Time, p. 569.)

Dimensions. In technical work, ′ is used for feet, ″ for inches, and x for "by".

18′ x 9″ x 3′6″
18 x 5 x 6″ indicates that all dimensions are inches.
But to avoid possible misinterpretation the designation is usually written after each number:
18″ x 5″ x 6″   5′ x 3′ x 2′

To indicate exact measurement, dimensions are often written with ciphers for inches.

10′0″ x 5′0″   gauge height 15.0 feet
Fractional dimensions are written: 1/16″   5/8′
Fractions are joined: 7-5/16″ x 16-3/8″ x 9-5/8″
Or disjoined: 7 5/16″ x 16 3/8″ x 9 5/8″

The first method seems preferable because the fractional part is more definitely bound to the unit.

If a dimension is written before a noun, the figure is idiomatically hyphened to a singular word. But if the dimension is written after the noun, the figure is not hyphened to the word, and the word is plural (unless of course the figure one or a fraction is used before it).

270

a 50-foot mast	BUT:	a mast 50 feet high
a 10-inch-wide strip ⎱		a strip 10 inches wide
a 10″-wide strip ⎰		
a 24-foot-diameter tower		a tower 24 feet in diameter
a 500-mile race		a race 500 miles long
a 40-acre farm		a farm of 40 acres
a 1-foot hedge		a hedge one foot high
a ⅓-inch pipe ⎱		
a ⅓″ pipe ⎰		a pipe measuring ⅓ inch
a ⅓-in. pipe ⎰		

Dimensions are abbreviated in ordinary work—and not capitalized In formal work they are written out, but not capitalized.

5 ft. 8 in.	10 yds.	6 mi.
231 sq.ft.	27 cu.yds.	16 sq.mi.
FORMAL: 5 feet 8 inches	27 cubic yards	

Note that no comma is used between feet and inches in the first dimension, as it is considered one unit.

Weights and Capacities. In ordinary work, weights and capacities are abbreviated. In formal papers they are written out. They are not capitalized.

| 8 lbs. 2 oz. | 26,625 lbs. of steel | 2000 bbls. |
| FORMAL: 8 pounds 2 ounces | 2000 barrels | |

Note that no comma is used to separate pounds and ounces in the first weight, because the quantity is considered one unit.

If a weight or capacity is written before a noun, the figure is idiomatically hyphened to a singular word. But if the weight or capacity is written after the noun, the figure is not hyphened to the word, and the word is plural (unless of course the figure one or a fraction is used before it).

a 500-barrel capacity ⎱	BUT:	a capacity of 500 barrels
a 500-bbl. capacity ⎰		
a 10-pound weight ⎱		a weight of 10 pounds
a 10-lb. weight ⎰		
a 75-horsepower engine		an engine of 75 horsepower
a 3¼-ton truck		a truck weighing 3¼ tons
an 8-cylinder engine		an engine with 8 cylinders

Some weights and capacities may be expressed by the possessive, if the idea of a single unit is not foremost.

   ...build a plant of about 500 barrels' capacity.
   ... applied about 10 pounds' pressure. (the pressure of 10 separate pounds)
      ("A 10-pound pressure" would mean a single unit of pressure.)

Fractions. When writing fractions in figures, use the diagonal line, as 5/8, not a hyphen, as 5-8, which can be read "5 to 8".

A fraction is usually joined to a unit number with a hyphen to show that the two definitely belong together.

| 3-9/16 acres | 4-3/8 miles |
| RATHER THAN: | 3 9/16 acres | 4 3/8 miles |

Isolated fractions are often written out. Some authorities hyphen written-out fractions; others do not, unless the fractions are used as modifiers. In business usage all fractions are very generally hyphened, which appears to be good practice, inasmuch as it affords a quick interoretation of the fraction.

```
two-thirds      ...the remaining two-thirds.
one-fourth      ...weigh one-fourth as much.
three-fourths   ...saved about three-fourths of it.
one-half        About one-half was lost.
one half        One half was good, the other bad.   (a special use)
cut in half     is colloquial for "cut into halves".
the first half-dozen notations (modifier)
another half dozen
half-a-dozen books (modifier)
half a yard   half an hour   half a hundred
one-half yard   one-half foot
half-and-half (used as one word)
a quarter of a yard
three-quarters of a mile
a three-quarter turn   or   a three-quarters turn
three-quarter length
```

Do not write one part of a fraction as a figure and the other as a word.

```
seven-eighths-inch pipe⎫
⅞-inch pipe            ⎬   NOT:   7-eighths-inch pipe
⅞" pipe                ⎭
three-fourths of a yard    NOT:   3-fourths of a yard
```

When either part of a spelled-out fraction contains a hyphen, omit the usual connecting hyphen. It is often better, however, to use numerals than to write out such ponderous fractions.

```
nine thirty-seconds of an inch (not secondths)      9/32
ninety-nine one-hundred-sixteenths                  99/116
```

A hyphen can change the meaning of a fraction.

```
forty-two hundredths      42/100
forty two-hundredths      40/200
```

When a fraction is joined to the number "one", the following noun is plural, and the verb singular.

```
1³⁄₁₆ inches   NOT:  inch
1¼ yards   1½ miles
One and seven-eighths inches is required...
One and one-fourth feet makes it right.
A yard and a half is sufficient.
```

(For singular or plural verbs with fractions or parts, see Collective Words, p. 39.)

Decimals. If a decimal occurs in the text with no unit before it, a cipher is usually supplied to point up the decimal.

a 0.65-inch difference   specific gravity 0.3857

But if the decimal itself begins with a cipher, no other cipher is necessary.

an .08-inch difference

In technical work, the extra cipher is often used to express exactness.

0.0144 sq.ft.   0.0010 gram

Percentages. "Percent" may be written as one word or as two words, and now without a period. The United States Government Printing Office writes it as one word, "percent"; and that form, being largely used in business papers, is followed in this book.

Definite percentages in commercial work are written in figures with the percent sign.

at 10%   33⅓%   112%
Our price is $62.50; 5% discount for cash; 2% 10 days; net 30 days.

In formal work, the word "percent" is used instead of the sign " % ", but the numeral is retained before it.

a 20-percent profit   a reduction of 20 percent
one-half of 1 percent   commonly ½ of 1%

Indefinite percentages may be spelled out; but it is not unusual to see them in figures.

Nearly twenty percent were forfeited.
OR: Nearly 20 percent were forfeited.
About sixty percent was lost.

Note that percentages may be singular or plural, according to their meaning or reference. (See Collective Words, p. 39.)

Do not use both the decimal point and the word or sign "percent" unless it is intended.

0.5% is one-half of 1 percent, or 5/1000
For instance, if 65% is intended, do not write: *.65%* nor *.65 percent*, which would be 65/10,000

For definiteness, the percent sign is usually used after each of several percentages in succession.

40% to 50%   10% or 20%   5%, 10%, and 15% discount
SOMETIMES: 40 to 50%   10 or 20%

But if the word "percent" is used, it is written only after the last number.

40 to 50 percent   ten or twenty percent

Plurals of Figures and Characters. The plural of figures and characters may be formed by adding 's. Some publications use only an s.

6's and 7's   OR: 6s and 7s
10's and 20's   10s and 20s
2 x 4's   2 x 4s
Government 5½'s   Liberty 4¼s
Treasury 4's   Treasury 3¾s
&'s, %'s, ¢'s, #'s   &s, %s, ¢s, #s

273

A simple s is usually added to the contraction of a year, to avoid the repetition of the apostrophe, as "in the '80s".

Omission of Intermediate Figures. The omission of intermediate numbers or letters may be indicated by a hyphen (that is, when "to" could be supplied).

years	1885-96	1880-1900	1900-1908	1890-1910	1921-31
months	January-June, 1937		April 15, 1928-June 30, 1934		
pages	pages 47-94	pp. 115-20	pp. 203-9	pp. 2244-3249	
letters	A-M	P-W			

A term of two years may be indicated by a hyphen.

in 1915-1916   the 1929-30 report

If "from" is used before the first number or word, "to" should follow it instead of the hyphen.

from 1885 to 1896   NOT: *from 1885-96*
from May to October, 1936   NOT: *from May-October, 1936*

If a continuous numbering is not intended, a comma should be used instead of a hyphen.

the years 1917, 1921, 1925, and 1930
OR: the years 1917, '21, '25, and '30
BUT NOT: *the years 1917-21-25-30*

If symbols are involved, one should be placed after each number, to prevent the numbers from being read as a fraction. If abbreviations or words are used after the last numbers only, the word "to" should be used instead of the hyphen.

5°-16° F.	OR:	5 to 16 deg. F.
$75-$100		
10%-25%		10 to 25 percent
3#-8#		3 to 8 lbs.

When consecutive items are indicated by a hyphen, it is loosely understood that the last item is "inclusive". But if definiteness is desired, "inclusive" should be written in.

January-June, 1934, inclusive,   P-Z, both inclusive,
pp. 5-29, inclusive,   Nos. 66-168, both inclusive,

Page Numbering. (See Typewritten Work, p. 403.)

No. and #. Avoid the use of "No." or "#" before a number, unless the number is standing alone and it is necessary to identify it as a number.

Room 185	IS CLEARER THAN:	Room *No.* 185	OR:	Room #185
Grade 10		Grade *No.* 10		Grade #10
page 286		page *No.* 286		page #286

"No." or "Nos.", capitalized, is used in ordinary work; "#" is used in tabulations or routine work.

No. 450	Nos. 456-598	Nos. 18, 24, 45, and 64
#4507	#456-598	#18, 24, 45, 64

274

Numbered References. In typewritten work, references to numbered parts of compositions are usually capitalized, with the exception of the common words "page", "line", and "verse". In printing, such designations are often all written with small letters.

	ABBREVIATION		ABBREVIATION
Article 245	Art.	Paragraph 16	Par.
Book I	Bk.	Part II	Pt.
Chapter 14	Chap. or Ch.	Plate III	Pl.
Class 5	Cl.	Reference 18	Ref.
Column 7	Col.	Rule 204	R.
Diagram 3	Diag.	Section 3	Sec.
Division III	Div.	Series 10	Ser.
Figure 9	Fig.	Volume I	Vol.
Illustration 10	Ill.	page 230	p. (pl. pp.)
Number 4	No.	line 19	l. (pl. ll.)
Numbers 5 & 8	Nos. or No.	verse 3	v. (pl. vv.)

Whether these references are capitalized or written with small letters, they should be kept uniform. Do not use a capital in one place and a small letter in another, as
... pursuant to Section 4 of the Act and subject to sections 7 and 10, and any other sections which have a bearing... (WRITE: to Sections 7 and 10)
(The last "sections" may stand because no specific sections are being designated.)

Roman Numerals.

ARABIC	ROMAN	ARABIC	ROMAN
1	I	100	C
2	II	150	CL
3	III	200	CC
4	IV	300	CCC
5	V	400	CCCC or CD
6	VI	500	D
7	VII	600	DC
8	VIII	700	DCC
9	IX	800	DCCC
10	X	900	CM or DCCCC
11	XI	1000	M
12	XII	1500	MD
13	XIII	2000	MM
14	XIV	3000	MMM
15	XV	4000	MMMM or M$\bar{V}$
16	XVI	5000	$\bar{V}$
17	XVII	1,000,000	$\bar{M}$
18	XVIII	DATES	
19	XIX	1600	MDC
20	XX	1700	MDCC
30	XXX	1800	MDCCC
40	XL	1900	MCM or MDCCCC
50	L	1910	MCMX
60	LX	1920	MCMXX
70	LXX	1930	MCMXXX
80	LXXX or XXC	1940	MCMXL
90	XC	1950	MCML
		1960	MCMLX

NUMBERS

RULES FOR READING ROMAN NUMERALS

A repeated letter repeats the value.

III 3   XX 20   CCC 300

A letter occurring after one of greater value is added thereto.

VI 6   LX 60   MC 1100

A letter occurring before one of greater value is subtracted therefrom.

IV 4   XL 40   CM 900

A dash over a numeral multiplies it by 1000.

$\overline{V}$ 5,000 $\overline{L}$ 50,000

$\overline{C}$ 100,000 $\overline{DLVI}$ 556,000

The old form for 500 was a disjoined D—IƆ; but it is no longer used. The old form for 1000 was CIƆ.

The old form for 4 (IIII) is still seen on clocks; but otherwise it is not used.

USE OF ROMAN NUMERALS

Roman numerals should be used to designate the most important divisions of a composition, not the subdivisions.

No period is necessary after a Roman numeral (although it was formerly used). The numeral is not an abbreviation.

Henry VIII   Denis J. Polk, III   William III
George V   Chapter XI

But if used in headings, Roman numerals may be followed by periods, in accordance with the general punctuation.

When writing consecutive Roman numerals, leave an extra space after each numeral to facilitate reading.

Chapters IX, XIV, XL, CL

Roman numerals may be written in small letters, if two sets are being used.

viii   xix   xxvi   xl

First, Second, Third. These are called **ordinal numbers** because they show the order. The shortened forms are regarded as contractions rather than abbreviations; therefore, no periods are used after them.

1st   2nd   3rd   4th   5th   6th

Note that the shorter "2d" is, by some authorities, preferred to "2nd", and "3d" to "3rd". (For further uses, see Typewritten Work, p. 402.)

Superior and Inferior Figures. Superior figures are raised figures that indicate a footnote or reference, or show that a number is to be squared or cubed, etc.

reference[1]   footnote[3] 25^2 10^3 5^5

Inferior figures are lowered figures, used in scientific work to indicate chemical formulas, etc., as H_2SO_4, CO_2. (See also Chemical Symbols, p. 535.)

By the Dozen, By the Hundred, etc. Note that in "by" phrases the singular form of the words "dozen", "pair", "hundred", "thousand", "million", etc., is used **if "the" precedes the words.** The analogy is that a unit is meant, as "by the (unit of one) hundred", "by the (unit of one) pair", etc.

276

But if "the" does not precede the word, the plural is used.

by the dozen	AND: by dozens	INSTEAD OF: by the dozens
by the pair	by pairs	by the pairs
by the hundred	by hundreds	by the hundreds
by the thousand	by thousands	by the thousands
by the million	by millions	by the millions
by the ten dozen	by tens of dozens	by the tens of dozens
by the hundred dozen	by hundreds of dozens	by the hundreds of dozens
by the hundred pair	by hundreds of pairs	by the hundreds of pairs
by the hundred thousand	by hundreds of thousands	by the hundreds of thousands

Hundred, Thousand, Million. "Hundred", "thousand", and "million" are idiomatically singular if a figure or the word "several" is used before them. But if "many" is used before them, they are usually plural.

five hundred books		
several hundred books		
many hundreds of books	RATHER THAN:	many hundred books
ten thousand	OR:	tens of thousands
several thousand		
many thousands of	RATHER THAN:	many thousand
four million people		four millions of people
several million people		
many millions of people		many million people
population of about two million	NOT:	two *millions*
ten or twenty billion dollars' worth		

RATHER THAN: ten or twenty billions of dollars' worth

BUT NOT: ten or twenty *billions dollars* worth

❖

LETTERS

Preferred positions in the business letter:

LETTERHEAD

Date

File No.
Order No.

Address

Attention

Salutation:

Subject

Paragraphs indented 5 or 10 spaces...........
....
....

Body single-spaced........................
....
....
....

....
....
....

Complimentary close,

COMPANY NAME

(Writer's signature)

Writer's typed name, and
Title if used

Initials

Enc.
Explanatory phrases
c.c.

..............Postscript................
....

Date. Place the date where it is naturally looked for—and where it is of value in filing—that is, toward the upper right corner, rather than in the center beneath the letterhead. If placed in the center it is apt to blend with the letterhead and be lost to the casual glance.

Write the date so that the end of the date line will be approximately even with the right margin of the letter below it.

The date is preferably not abbreviated on the first page of a letter.

To make the date instantly clear, write it professionally: that is, write it all on one line; spell out the month in full; write the figures for the day of the month without -st, -d, or -th; and write the year in full without a period after it. Any other form for the date detracts from its quick readability.

February 20, 1951

Date letters the day they were dictated, and not the day they were transcribed (unless otherwise instructed); so that words referring to the dictation day, such as "this morning", or "today", may stand and not be changed to "yesterday", etc. The transcription day may be shown after the initials, if this is thought necessary, as SLH:DM–2/21.

Armed Forces Dates. The Army and Navy have adopted the inverted (foreign) method of writing dates—using no commas or periods.

8 June 1951   abbreviated as: 8 Jun 51   (never *8/6/51*)
(Abbreviation of the month is always the first 3 letters.)

Addresses. (On letters, p. 295; on envelopes, p. 324.)

File References. For convenience and quick reference in filing, set numerical references—file numbers, order numbers, etc.—about four spaces below the date. They should be completely segregated from the subject of the letter.

Avoid placing numerical references too near the date, as the two sets of figures tend to run together and lose distinctness. For clearness give each item a separate line. Do not underline or set in caps; file references should not obtrude. The receiver's reference should be placed first for his convenience in locating files when the letter is received.

Your letter 8/14/51   or   Your File C-SW
Order 3458
Our Job 921

The word "References" is unnecessary. From the placement and context it is known immediately that they are references.

As a matter of courtesy—if the sender's file reference has been given in an incoming letter, indicate it in the reply, whether instructed to do so or not. It is a valuable aid in the office of the receiver of the reply.

Attention. The word "of" after "Attention" is superfluous. A colon has been used instead of "of", but now that is being omitted. In ordinary work, even the word "Attention" is unnecessary. The placement of a name below the company's name and address indicates "Attention of".

The "Attention" line should be placed **below** the main address, not above it. It is less important than the company's name and address, especially in filing, and yet it is a part of the address. Do not place it below the salutation, nor in the center of the page as if it were a subject. It should not be written in caps; and now it is not indented or underlined. Always use the word "Mr." or another title in the "Attention" line.

> Attention Mr. F. C. Gordon, Advertising Director

Do not neglect the "Attention" line. It is of very definite meaning. "Attention" signifies that the letter contains company business; that the person addressed is familiar with or handling it; but that in his absence the letter may be opened and attended to by any other member of the organization. If a letter is addressed simply to an individual, it may lie unopened in his absence, or be forwarded and cause delay.

The salutation "Dear Mr. . . . :" is often used after an "Attention" line. Since the "Attention" is a part of the address, this may properly be done. The letter then has a personal as well as an official tone.

Notations Under "Attention". If a copy of a letter is being sent to a second person in the same company as the addressee, and if the letter is of almost as much importance to the second person as it is to the addressee, the "Copy to" notation may be written immediately beneath the "Attention" line.

> Attention Mr. F. C. Gordon
> Copy to Mr. George Talbot

Ordinarily the carbon copy notation is placed at the end of the letter.

Salutations. A dash is unnecessary after the colon in a salutation; to use both is double punctuation.

A comma is not often used after a salutation, except in informal social correspondence. (It is, however, common in British usage.)

Do not use abbreviations in salutations, other than "Mr.", "Mrs.", and "Messrs."; and capitalize, besides the first word, all titles such as "Sir", etc.

Accepted salutations to men:

Gentlemen:	
Dear Sirs:	not generally used in America, possibly because "Gentlemen:" is easier to write. ("Messrs.:" is never used alone, although "Messieurs:" alone is the French salutation.)
Dear Sir:	is the common, impersonal business form.
Sir: or Sirs:	is the formal, diplomatic salutation.
My dear Sir:	not commonly used in business letters.
My dear Mr. . . . :	is considered more formal than
Dear Mr. . . . :	although the distinction is disappearing.
(In British usage these formal and informal forms are reversed.)	
Dear Jim:	to a friend called by his first name.
My dear Thompson:	to a business associate.
My dear Messrs. Scott and Thomas:	
My dear Messrs. Page:	to two men of the same name.

280

Do not use "My dear Mr. ....:" if a company is to sign the letter. Use "Dear Mr. ....:" or "Dear Sir:".

Salutations to Women. Avoid the use of "Dear Madam:" except in impersonal or routine letters; and especially avoid it when addressing an unmarried woman—it is an unpleasant approach. Use instead:

My dear Mrs. ...:⎱
My dear Miss ...:⎰ which are considered more formal than

Dear Mrs. ...:⎱
Dear Miss ...:⎰ although the distinction is disappearing.

   (In British usage these formal and informal forms are reversed.)

Dear Miss: without a surname, is rarely used.

Madam: is the formal, diplomatic salutation.

To an organization of women use:

Mesdames: or

Ladies: which corresponds to "Gentlemen:". This salutation may seem strange at first, but when used several times it appears preferable to the French "Mesdames:".

My dear Mesdames Page and Lee:
My dear Misses Grant and Thorpe:
My dear Mesdames Rogers:⎱
My dear Misses Duncan:⎰ to two women of the same name.

To an organization of men and women:

Gentlemen: or Ladies and Gentlemen:
My dear Mrs. Grant and Mr. Lowe: or Dear Sir and Madam:

Salutations to Charitable Organizations and Churches.

Gentlemen: or Ladies:
Dear Friends: ("Dear Friend:" is rarely used, however.)

Subject. The word "Subject" or "In re" is unnecessary before the subject on a letter. The placement shows that it is a subject. One would not write "Title" before the title of a story or article; and similarly no such introduction is needed before a letter subject.

Center the letter subject **below** the salutation, not above it. The subject is an introduction to the body of the letter and not a part of the address.

It is unnecessary to set a subject in caps. All capitals are hard to read. Capitalize only the most important words and underline the last line only.

Gentlemen:

Venezuela Land Option, and
Texas Leases Expiring in April

Every letter should bear a subject. This practice is becoming more important every day. It facilitates the handling of letters in both the senders' and the receivers' offices. Especially is it valuable in subject filing and for the distribution of letters to the various departments of an organization. The Government insists upon subjects on its letters.

"One subject in one letter" should be the rule, unless the letter is about matters in general. In that event it may carry headings down the side.

If two or more subjects are included in a letter and the subjects change abruptly, a short dividing line of four dashes may be drawn between the paragraphs to indicate the changes, unless sideheadings are used.

If two or more subjects of equal importance are discussed in a letter, make enough copies so that each subject file will receive a copy of the entire letter.

Sideheadings. Are often used in letters. Place these at the left margin and underline. The subject matter may or may not be indented. Or, to save space, **paragraph headings** may be used, as in this book.

Body of Letter. The professional setup of a letter is:

> Single-spaced, unless unusually short
> Double-spaced between paragraphs
> Paragraphs indented five or ten spaces.

Arrange the letter so that the points to be emphasized, calculated, or answered, will stand out. For instance, set out lists, quoted matter, addresses, etc., by indenting them in block style, as

> Please reply to Mr. H. F. Hale, whose address is:
> Room 6081
> 200 Fifth Avenue
> New York City 10

Paragraphing. (See Typewritten Work, p. 402.)

Complimentary Close. This may be written in block alinement with the signature, or begun five or ten spaces to the left of the signature. The latter arrangement seems preferable in that it assists the eye by keeping the complimentary close from entangling with the signature.

Capitalize only the first word in a complimentary close—it is a simple phrase, not a title. A comma always follows it.

The usual complimentary closings are:

Very truly yours,	the most generally used.
Yours very truly,	
Sincerely yours,	
Yours sincerely,	
Faithfully yours, } Yours faithfully, }	in British usage.
Yours very sincerely, } Very sincerely yours, } Most sincerely yours, }	informal.
Respectfully, } Very respectfully, } Respectfully yours, } Respectfully submitted, }	formal—used in diplomatic correspondence.
Cordially yours,	a friendly closing.
Fraternally yours,	used in brotherhoods.
Thanks,	informal close.
Gratefully yours,	used when acknowledging a favor.
Yours truly,	not generally used in America; but very generally used in England because of its brevity.

Often just one word is used, as
Sincerely,
Faithfully,
Cordially,
Fraternally,
Gratefully,

Always write the complimentary close that is dictated. The dictator may have some reason for saying "Sincerely yours", for instance, rather than "Yours sincerely".

If the complimentary close is not dictated, use a closing that corresponds to the tone of the letter. When in doubt use "Very truly yours".

"I am", "we remain", etc., are often dispensed with before complimentary closings, commas taking their place.

With kindest regards,
    Very truly yours,
With the compliments of the Season,
With the Season's greetings,
Wishing you a merry Christmas,
With best wishes to you and Mrs. ...,
  ("You" is first out of courtesy to the
  receiver of the letter.)
	Often such phrases displace the complimentary closings.
	Best wishes,
	Best regards,
	Kindest regards,
	Kindest personal regards,
	Thanks, OR Thank you,
	Thank you very much,

"I am", or "we remain", etc., is rarely used now, but if dictated, a comma should precede but not follow it.

With kindest regards, I am
Sincerely yours,

Note that "I am", "I remain", etc., originally had this distinction:

"I am" or "we are" was used at the close of the first letter to a correspondent. "I remain" or "we remain" was used at the close of all subsequent letters to the correspondent.

But "I am" or "we are" is now used (if the expression is used at all) in preference to the longer "I remain" or "we remain".

Signatures in General. A signature should be in the lower right corner of the letter and not in the center, nor past the halfway mark toward the left. If a signature is thus misplaced it loses its identity as a signature.

A name should be signed in the form that is expected in the reply; or at least the typed signature should indicate that form.

"Doctor", "Professor", "Colonel", etc., while not used in the pen-and-ink signature, may be indicated in the typed signature in the form of a title.

L. M. Lansdowne, M.D. President	Benj. B. Scott Major General, Chief of Engineers
Edwin T. Masters Professor of Economics	David Ward Blythe, D.D. Chairman, Program Committee

It is better to type the name beneath the signature than to write it in the initials' space. Some readers do not reconcile one name with the other, if the signature is poor.

If a name is printed on the letterhead, it is unnecessary to type it beneath the signature, unless the signature is known to be illegible; in that case the reader may not connect the signature with the printed name.

Punctuation at the ends of the lines in the typed signature may be omitted, if such is the style used in the address.

When to Sign Company Name. If "we" has been used throughout the letter, sign the company's name in caps, **exactly as it is printed on the letterhead.** A discrepancy between these names may cause the answerer to debate which is correct.

Four spaces below the company's name, type in small letters the name of the person signing for the company. "By" or "Per" is unnecessary.

THORNWALL & SONS, INC.   SCOTT & GRANT COMPANY

R. K. Laidlaw   V. O. R. Scott, Vice President
Manager, Sales Department

Some titles are used constantly in typed signatures, and others are not. Individual preference governs in this. But if a letter is of a legal nature and the writer is signing in an official capacity, his title should always be typed after or below his typed name.

Always leave enough space for the signature, so that the name will not be signed over the typed name, which makes both names illegible.

When to Sign Personal Name First. If "I" has been used throughout a formal company letter, or "I" and "we" interchangeably, the writer's name should be typed first, with the company's name beneath it.

Kenneth Meade   Thomas Hill, President
Sales Manager   THE HILL & BRAND COMPANY
THE EMPORIUM

When to Sign Personal Name Only. If "I" has been used throughout, and the tone of the business letter is informal, it is not necessary to use the company's name in the signature—the letterhead is sufficient identification.

The writer's name alone may be signed; or the writer's name, title and/or department, if customarily used.

Hugh Langdon   R. M. Lowe
Travel Editor   Sales Department

Value of the Typewritten Signature. Even though the writer is well known to his correspondent, the name typed beneath his signature is of definite value.

It is an indelible record of correct initials and spelling. If the pen-and-ink signature is difficult to decipher, the typewritten signature will aid members of the receiver's staff in transcribing the name.

The typed name also leaves a record on the carbon copies, thus providing a later reference regarding the signer of the letter. Further, it allows the signer the privilege of simply initialing the line above the typewritten signature if he so desires.

Women's Signatures. On an incoming letter—if "Miss" or "Mrs." is not enclosed in parentheses before a woman's signature, or indicated in the typed signature, it is to be assumed that the title is "Miss".

An unmarried woman may use "Miss" in parentheses before her signature, or include it, without parentheses, in the typed signature.

(Miss) Frances Linton   or   *Frances Linton*
Miss Frances Linton

A married woman may use "Mrs." in parentheses before her signature, or include it, without parentheses, in the typed signature.

(Mrs.) Janet Meade   or   *Janet Meade*
Mrs. Janet Meade

If a married woman wishes to be addressed by her husband's Christian name or initials, she may so indicate in her typed signature. (In social usage she is preferably addressed by her husband's full name.)

Eleanor Martin
Mrs. S. J. Martin

A widow may use her own Christian name, or retain her husband's Christian name or initials, as she chooses.

Mrs. Leland T. Fair   or   Mrs. Elizabeth Fair

A divorced woman uses her own Christian name and her divorced husband's last name, unless she has regained her maiden name. Often she combines her maiden name and her divorced name.

Jeanne Brown Benton   or   *Jeanne Benton*
Mrs. Jeanne Brown Benton   Mrs. Jeanne Benton
or just
Mrs. Brown Benton

Signing for Another. When signing another's name, it is not usually necessary to use "Per" or "By". Simply sign the name and initial it with small but clear initials. (See also Legal Papers, p. 461.)

Deputy signers should be careful to sign the right names. They have a tendency to sign their own names; or if they have prepared the letters, they have a greater tendency to forget to sign them altogether.

"By" is sometimes used when one person signs for another in an official capacity.

Ralph V. James, President
By
Howard Gray

"Secretary to" should be used only by actual secretaries.

Harriet Miller
Secretary to Mr. Stewart

If not officially a secretary, the signer may use "For".

Harriet Miller
For Mr. Kent

After signing and sending dictated letters, always put copies of the letters on the dictator's desk, with a note attached marked "Signed and Sent".

Initials. Put initials on all but legal papers. Initials are important, especially on telegrams. They indicate responsibility.

The easiest and most businesslike way to write initials is to set them in caps and join them with a colon. No typewriter shifting is necessary for this form.

WS:M   or
BTG:LP   (The transcriber ordinarily does not use three initials.)

Other forms are usually time-consuming; and some, with a space instead of a dividing mark, are not always clear.

Typing the entire name of the dictator in the initials' space is not recommended. It is better practice to type the dictator's name beneath his signature so that the eye will not have to travel across the page to compare the signature and the typewritten name.

There is an instance in form letters where it is good practice to write the dictator's name in full in the initials' position—that is, when the letter is dictated and signed by one person for another.

H. M. Granville

W. Benson:JM   ***W. B.***

Director of Purchases

If the letter is to be signed by someone other than the dictator, put the signer's initials first, the dictator's second (joined with a dash), and the transcriber's third (joined with a colon).

WH–DKF:IW   or to signify dictator, transcriber, typist: JTL:IJ:R

The transcriber should not put merely his own initials on a letter or telegram, even though the dictator's name is typed elsewhere. This is confusing in that it suggests that the person whose initials appear also composed the message.

If the letter or wire is composed by the one who types it, that fact may be indicated definitely by the use of single initials in parentheses.

(VT)

"Jr." and "Sr." need not be carried with the initials, unless the Junior and Senior are in the same organization. In that event the initials may be written:

JVTJr:HM

Enclosures. Write "Enc." **below** the initials, and not in caps.

The number of enclosures may be indicated, as "Enc. 3", to guard against the omission of one, especially if a third person is to mail the letter, and to aid the receiver in checking the enclosures.

If the papers to be enclosed are of unusual importance, they should be listed and identified.

Enc. 2:
  Deed – Jason to Hill, June 6, 1936
  Contract – Martin and Lane, April 10, 1936

If they are to be returned, or are being sent separately, write:

Enc. 2 (to be returned)   or   Sep. Cov. 2

Mailing Notations. Type mailing notations (in small letters) below the "Enc." notation, on all letters dispatched otherwise than by regular mail. Questions often arise regarding the delivery of these letters, at both the sending and the receiving ends; and such notations as the following are valuable aids in tracing letters or in computing delivery dates.

Air mail
Registered
By messenger
Special delivery

Carbon Copy Notations. The carbon copy notation, "c.c.", should be the last notation. If it is placed before the mailing and enclosure notations, it would appear that these phrases also pertain to the carbon copy.

"Mr." or a similar title is usually used before the name of the person who is to receive the carbon copy. Indicate the city to which the copy is mailed, if not the ordinary address.

c.c. – Mr. G. Turner, Seattle

It is not necessary to write "Copy to". The "c.c." abbreviation is very generally used and understood to mean "Carbon copy to".

Notations in General. Before removing a letter from the machine, make sure that there is not some notation needed, such as "Enc.", "c.c.", "In duplicate", or "Air mail". A moment's pause here will save time and effort wasted in reinserting the letter for notations.

Drop the notations at least three spaces below the initials. The "c.c." notation especially should be spaced so that it will stand out. If written close to the initials or other notations, it will blend with them and is liable to be overlooked.

"Blind Copy" Notation. If a copy of a letter is to be sent to a second person, and the notation is not to show on the original letter, make the notation at the top (upper left corner) of the carbon copies, not at the bottom. The notation's being at the top of the carbon copies shows that it did not appear on the original letter.

Postscripts. A postscript is usually important; therefore it should stand out. Indent its margin about five spaces from the margin of the letter. If it bears a date different from that on the letter, put the date above it. The abbreviation "PS." or "P.S." may be used, or omitted.

PS. – Samples of the different materials have just arrived, and we will proceed at once with the analyses.
J. B. L.

Sign the initials of the dictator on the typewriter, and if he chooses he can initial over them. If he does not care to read and initial the postscript, it needs no further signature than the typewritten initials.

287

Post-Postscripts. If a second postscript is added, it may bear the abbreviation "P-PS." meaning post-postscript. It is set in the same form as the first postscript.

Second Pages. Never carry only the signature over to the second page of a letter. There must always be two or three lines of writing on the second page to connect the signature definitely with the letter.

Attempt to carry the entire last paragraph over if it is very short. This gives good balance and a nice finish to a letter.

Second-Page Notations. In the second-page headings use "Mr." or another title before the addressee's name. In formal correspondence the company's name is carried before the individual's name.

It is unnecessary to write "Page 2". Use just the figure. Put the page number in the center of the page, and not under the name, where it is not easily seen.

Mr. Kingston   –2–   Feb. 20, 1951

Note that the date is now usually written as shown, and not abbreviated to 2/20/51. It is considered of more trouble to code and decode the latter form, with a chance of error, than to write simply the date with only the month abbreviated.

It is unnecessary to draw a line or put dots beneath the second-page notation to separate it from the letter. But leave at least four spaces (preferably six) between the heading and the body of the letter. Particularly, set the second-page notations well down on the page if there is very little writing to follow. Too often a letter is seen jammed to the top of the second page with three-quarters of the page below it blank.

Diplomatic and Personal Letters. In diplomatic correspondence, and in personal letters that are slightly formal, the address may be placed at the bottom of the letter above the initials. The word "To" is not necessary before it.

The date should remain in its regular position at the top of the letter and not be brought down to the bottom.

September 14, 1951

My dear Mr. Harland:

. . . .
. . . .
. . . .
. . . .

Sincerely yours,

Mr. James F. Harland
428 Coronado Terrace
Cleveland 66, Ohio

PJC:TR

The writer's name is not typed beneath his signature if he is well known to his correspondent. If he is not well known to the addressee, his name should be typed beneath his signature. His address—if it

288

does not appear on the letterhead—should be typed above the date, or below his signature.

Initials on Social and Personal Letters. The writer's and transcriber's initials are not used on social letters. They are used on personal business letters, unless a letter is confidential, in which instance they are omitted so that it will not appear that a third person has knowledge of a strictly private matter. (But they can be shown on the carbons.)

"Personal" Business Letters. Business letters that are marked "Personal" are written in regular business letter style on business letterheads, with the word "Personal" above the receiver's name and address, which is at the top of the letter. The sender's name may be typed beneath his signature as usual.

Business Letters on Plain Paper. If a business letter is written on plain paper, the sender's address may be typed either above the date line or below the typewritten name in the signature. The latter arrangement is preferable from the reader's viewpoint, in that it puts the writer's address conveniently close to his name.

> Robert V. Pierce
> 5426 University Ave.
> Omaha 33, Nebraska

Letter Conveying a Message for Another. The writer should never insinuate himself into a letter written to convey a message for another. The other person's name should always appear first and foremost.

> NOT: I am glad to inform you that Mr. Scott...
> This is to inform you that Mr. Scott is unable...
> I should like to know the amount of Mr. Scott's dividend...
> BUT: Mr. Scott has asked me to say that...
> Mr. Scott regrets that...
> In Mr. Scott's absence, I have been asked to obtain...

Letters of Introduction. Letters of introduction are written in the regular form, and are usually begun:

> This will introduce Mr. ..., who is...

A letter of introduction should be left unsealed, as a courtesy to the bearer. He may seal it if he cares to.

The receiver's address should be in the ordinary place on the envelope, and above it to the right may be typed if desired:

> Introducing Mr. ...

Letters of Recommendation. Letters of recommendation should be dated. It is important to a prospective employer to know the date of the applicant's association with another company.

No heading is required if the letter is a general letter of recommendation, addressed to no one in particular; but such letters are often headed "To Whom It May Concern:".

No salutation is necessary on a general letter of recommendation, nor is any complimentary close.

Letters of Transmittal. Always write a letter of transmittal when mailing papers of any value, if no other letter accompanies them.

Describe briefly the papers, enumerating or identifying what is being sent so that a permanent record may be had in the carbon copy of the letter, and further so that the receiver will not be confused by receiving just a bunch of papers. A letter is always looked for with papers; even though the receiver knows they are coming he wants to be told again, if in no other words than simply "Here are the papers we mentioned."

Register letters containing original papers which could not be replaced if lost, or of which there exist no other copies.

Invitations, Announcements, and Programs. Modern and correct forms for invitations, announcements, and programs may be obtained from any reliable printer or stationer.

When replying to an invitation use the form that is employed in the invitation. If it is formal and worded in the third person, use the third person in reply. If it is informal and uses the first person, reply in that person. It is usual to reply in handwriting.

No excuse is necessary when declining a formal invitation.

Letter Writing. Begin a business letter with the **subject,** if possible, and state what **action** is to be taken regarding it.

The...(subject)...that you ordered (or asked about, enclosed, etc.) in your letter of...has been (or is, will be, etc.)...

Write as you would speak. Natural expressions make good openings.

Thank you for... You are right in... Yes, we issue the... Here are the... Please send... Do you publish...? There are... It has been... We are sending... I know that... Of course... Evidently... Since...

Do not waste time reviewing the incoming letter—merely mention it.

It is permissible to begin a letter with "I", "We", or the name of a person or company, if no other opening presents itself. Do not, however, mix "I" and "we" indiscriminately in a letter.

Avoid hackneyed, uninteresting, or old-fashioned phrases at the beginning and end of a letter.

Do not be too enthusiastic or ingratiating in a letter. Be very dignified, definite, and sincere.

Consider the reader's time and make all letters as short and concise as possible. Vary the sentence lengths. Short sentences increase the pace; long sentences retard it. Either form constantly employed can become monotonous.

Avoid the repetition of any certain word in a sentence or throughout a letter. Check the meaning and spelling of all unusual words.

Use "Mr." or a proper title when introducing a name into a letter; do not introduce the name alone. Thereafter the person may be referred to by his last name only, if he is familiarly known to both writer and reader, or if his name occurs repeatedly in an impersonal manner.

If a letter is to contain a disappointment to the reader, state the reason for the disappointment first, as a preliminary to the final unfavorable news.

Never write a letter in anger—wait a day.

Old-Fashioned Phrases. Many old-fashioned phrases are being discarded from letters in favor of the "direct approach" and businesslike end.

Among the phrases classed as stereotyped or cumbersome are:

We hand you herewith...   (FOR: We are enclosing)
Your favor at hand...   ⎰Instead of "favor" use "letter", "order",
...your esteemed favor.   ⎱ "note", "card", "request", or "report".
As per your inquiry...   ⎧FOR: The...(subject)...that you asked about
In reply to yours of...   ⎨ (or requested, etc.) in your letter of...is (or
In re...   ⎩ has been, will be, etc.)
We beg to state...or wish to say...or to **advise**...(better omitted entirely)
at the **present writing**   (FOR: now OR: at present)
even date   ⎫
recent date ⎪   The definite date is now usually used instead of
instant   ⎬   these forms.
ultimo   ⎪
proximo   ⎭
contents noted
valued order
Thanking you **in advance,** we remain
Believe me to be...
Your obedient servant,
and oblige

Some old phrases such as the following are still used in business letters and probably will remain until displaced by better terms.

Enclosed *please find*...   ⎰FOR: We are enclosing...   or
Enclosed *herewith*...   ⎱   A check for $5 is enclosed.
under separate cover   (FOR: by mail, by express, is being mailed, etc.)
as stated above...by return mail...went forward...earliest convenience
Trusting this will be satisfactory, we are   (FOR: This will, we trust, be...)
Thanking you, we are   (FOR: Thank you for...)

All **-ing letter endings** (Hoping, Trusting, Thanking, etc.) are condemned; but some are still dictated by older writers who have become accustomed to participle endings and prefer them to modern phraseology.

Most **-ing beginnings** (Replying, etc.) are avoided by good writers.

The **telegraphic style** is also censured, as "Received check for $100." Do not omit necessary words. Write "We received your check for $100."

"The writer" is an appellation very generally used by letter writers who wish to remain obscure as individuals—especially when a company name is to be signed to a letter and "we" is used throughout.

But "the writer" should not be used if "I" or "me" follows.

NOT: Your letter has been referred to *the writer.* I am pleased to.
(USE: to me)

Negative Expressions. Avoid the making of negative suggestions or the calling up of unpleasant thoughts in letters, business papers, advertisements, etc.

Never suggest failure, inaptitude, or possible trouble. Acknowledge difficulties, but acknowledge them in a positive way, as if something would immediately be done to rectify them.

Words and phrases that create a bad impression are:

complaint	damage	inability	unfortunately
trouble	delay	mistake	failure, etc.

"If this information is not sufficient, kindly call upon us for more."
(Why suggest that it is insufficient? Why not say "If any further information is desired, please call upon us.")

"We regret our inability to comply with your request."
(Do not admit any inability. Better to rest the inability on the request— "We regret that your request cannot be complied with.")

"This industry's soundness can best be gauged by the number of failures recorded within it—only 4 in 60 years."
(Why not say "by the few failures" or "by the almost complete absence of failures" instead of "by the number of failures" which immediately sounds large.)

"Unfortunately, your letter was misplaced, and we cannot..."
(The unfortunate part should be subdued, not emphasized—"Your letter was misplaced, unfortunately, and we...")

"The Purchaser shall withhold payment until guarantees are met or not met."
(Omit the "or not met". It puts the idea in the purchaser's mind that perhaps the guarantees will not be met. Also, how long should the purchaser withhold payment if "guarantees are not met"?)

"All conflicts and controversies shall be settled in accordance with the California State Code."
(This sounds like trouble. Wouldn't it give a better feeling to say "The California State Code shall govern in all questions to be settled between the parties hereto.")

"The Contractor shall be responsible for any and all liens filed during the course of construction."
(This actually predicts the filing of many liens, which would give the owner an uncomfortable feeling. Would not this be easier to contemplate: "If any lien whatsoever is filed during the course of construction, the Contractor shall be responsible therefor.")

Instead of saying "Thanks for all your trouble..." why not say "Thanks for the assistance..." And so on.

Spacing. Setup is of first importance in a business letter. It is the most noticeable feature of a letter and can interest or prejudice a reader at a glance.

Lopsided letters, top-heavy letters, letters running off the bottoms of pages, all bespeak of inefficiency and reflect on the merits of the senders. If an ill-balanced letter is received, it suggests that all other products of the sending company might be as carelessly constructed.

No matter how busy you are, take a moment to contemplate each letter before writing it. Change the setup on the typewriter **for every letter,** if necessary, to get the proper spacing. A uniform style of work will be the reward. Employers are not usually in as much of a hurry for letters as they are concerned over the finished product.

Center every letter, with the left margin always slightly wider than the right margin. And keep the right margin as even as possible. Long letters should have a left margin of about an inch and a quarter, and a right margin of at least an inch. Longer lines in single-spaced letters

LETTERS

Example of a Top-Heavy Letter

Example of a Letter Set Too Low

These unbalanced arrangements are caused by an inability to judge the length of letters.

Examples of Lopsided Letters

These misarrangements result from failure to change the left marginal stop for each letter.

293

are difficult to follow. Short letters may have still wider margins. Very short letters should be double-spaced or even triple-spaced.

If a letter turns out noticeably off balance, **rewrite it.** This is good self-discipline in the matter of space judging.

Critics that a writer is not aware of notice and comment upon the merits of typewritten work: the staff at the receiving end of the line. Their conclusions, good or bad, may influence their employer in doing business with a company. They are harsh judges of what they consider inefficiency, or ignorance, or both.

Efficient Method of Preparing Letters, and of Handing Them In. Proofread each letter as it is finished. If this is done, all typed letters will be ready at any time they might be called for. Do not write several letters and then proofread them.

Proofread slowly so that no typographical errors will be overlooked. No defense can be offered for these. Check carefully all initials, addresses, reference numbers, and the spelling of words not frequently used.

Every page must be immaculately clean: **no struck-over letters,** no half erasures, and no finger marks or smudges.

Clip the pages of each letter together **in the upper left corner,** not in the center, nor on the right.

Clip pencil notations to letters that require special handling. These notations can remind the dictator of things to be done, as "Check to accompany this", "Date necessary", "Enclosures necessary", "To be held", etc.

If there is a question about a certain letter, write it on a note and clip it to the letter; the dictator can then answer when he returns the letters and at his convenience.

In special instances when another than the dictator is to sign the letter, clip a note to that effect over the place for signature. This will prevent the dictator from absent-mindedly signing the letter.

Manila File Folder for Letters to be Signed. When handing in letters, put them in a manila file folder on which is marked "For Signature". The manila folder not only keeps the letters all together so that they can be considered at one time, but keeps them clean, and keeps them private.

Arrange the letters in the folder in the order of their importance; the most important always on top.

It is not necessary to clip the envelopes or enclosures to the letters (unless the dictator prefers that this be done). This extra bulk makes the letters awkward to handle when they are being signed.

When to Address Envelopes. Address the envelopes from the carbon copies, while the letters are being read and signed. **This saves time.**

Assume responsibility for correct addresses, the manner of dispatch of letters, and enclosures. If any change is made in an address on a signed letter, **correct the envelope first,** then the letter.

Carbon Copies to be Mailed Out. (See Carbon Copies, p. 416.)

ADDRESSES

Style of Address. The block style of address is the form most generally used on letters. The indented style should be used on envelopes.

"Open punctuation" (that is, no punctuation at the ends of lines) is now very generally used in addresses—the segregation into lines being sufficient punctuation. "Close punctuation" may also be used; but if a large number of letters and envelopes are being addressed, the punctuating of every line takes a noticeable amount of extra effort and consumes a definite amount of time.

An address may be written in two lines if it is very short: the name on one line, the city and state on the next. Or an address may be written in four or five lines if it is long. It is much better to give all of an address and make it clear than to leave out some part and allow it to be vague.

Street Numbers, Names of Buildings, Hotel Names. (See p. 325.)

Care of. Do not use "In care of" before a company's name if the person addressed is employed by or is a member of the company named. If he is not connected with the company, use "In care of".

Or if a letter is being sent in care of a third person, use "In care of" (usually expressed by "c/o" on the typewriter).

Cities and States. The name of the state may be abbreviated in the address on the letter; but it should be written in full on the envelope, to facilitate the sorting of mail by postal workers.

"New York City" is gradually supplanting "New York, N.Y.", although the latter is considered formally correct.

Never abbreviate the name of a city in a letter, as "N.Y." for New York City, "Phila." for Philadelphia, "L.A." for Los Angeles, "Balto." for Baltimore, etc.

Personal or Confidential. Write "Personal" or "Confidential" (whichever has been dictated) about three spaces above the address on the letter. It is not necessary to set it in caps; but it may be underlined for distinction.

"Confidential" should not be used on the envelope; it applies only to the contents of the letter, and is not considered a part of the address. Use "Personal" on the envelope if "Confidential" is used on the letter.

Messrs. Is used before the names of two or more men associated in business, when their association is more of a personal combination or partnership than a company.

"Messrs." is usually used before the names of firms of attorneys.

Messrs. Logan, Spencer & Raeburn

It is not used before company or corporate names.

Lord & Lyons (a company)
Jackson Bros., Inc. (a corporation)

Two men of the same name may be addressed as

Messrs. R. W. and S. J. Hale (formal)   or   The Mr. Hales (informal)

Never use "Messrs.:" alone as a salutation; use "Gentlemen:". (See also Salutations, p. 280.)

"Messrs." is the English abbreviation of the French "Messieurs", which is pronounced mĕs′ĕrs, or French mā′syu̧′, but not *mĕ-sū′ers*. "MM." is the French abbreviation.

Esquire. Is not generally used in the United States, except after the names of distinguished attorneys. In England, however, it is quite generally used after the names of persons prominent in the social, diplomatic, or business world. It may be combined with titles as follows:

K. V. T. Stuart, Esq., President
J. Leslie Snowden, Jr., Esq.

If "Dr.", "Mr.", or a similar title is used before a name, "Esq." is of course not used after it.

Junior and Senior. As a matter of courtesy to the bearer of the name, capitalize the abbreviation for "Junior" or "Senior" when it is part of a personal name. A comma may or may not be used to separate "Jr." or "Sr." from the name. The separating comma is very commonly used, however, to conform to the general method of making additions after names.

Mr. Lewis Hamilton, Jr.   or   Mr. Lewis Hamilton Jr.

"Jr." or "Sr." may be used in combination with any title.

Mr. Max Hildreth, Jr., President   Paul Thomas, Jr., M.D.

The possessive is formed as follows:

John B. Blaine, Jr.'s office   The John B. Blaine, Jrs.' home

The plural is:

The John B. Blaine, Jrs. (informal)
The John B. Blaines, Jr. (formal)

"Sr." is not usually used unless the two identical names are closely associated. "Jr." and "Sr." are usually dropped after the death of father or son; although in some instances they are retained for identification.

Second and Third. These designations after names are now usually written in the common numerals: "2d" and "3d". Formerly they were written in Roman numerals. Either form is correct; and a comma may or may not be used to separate the numeral from the name. The separating comma is very commonly used, however, to conform to the

296

general method of making additions after names. No period is necessary after either form.

Mr. Jason Lloyd, 3d   or   Mr. Jason Lloyd, III
PLURAL: The Jason Lloyd, 3ds (or IIIs) (informal)
The Jason Lloyds, 3d (or III) (formal)
POSSESSIVE, SINGULAR: 3d's or III's   PLURAL: 3ds' or IIIs'

Personal Names. A personal name should be written exactly as the bearer writes it. If he uses initials, or abbreviates his first name, it is permissible to follow that form. The common abbreviations are:

Benj.	Benjamin	Geo.	George	Sam'l	Samuel
Chas.	Charles	Jas.	James	Thos.	Thomas
Dan'l	Daniel	Jno.	John	Wm.	William
Edw.	Edward	Robt.	Robert		

Check surnames to make sure that they are spelled exactly as the bearers spell them. There is nothing a person is so particular about as his own name. Many common names are spelled in different ways, as

Dickson	Dixon	Stewart	Stuart
Frederick	Fredericks	Stevens	Stephens
Louis	Lewis	Thompson	Thomson

Nicknames. Nicknames or shortened forms of names should not be used in addresses, unless a shortened form is the actual name.

They may be used in salutations and need not be quoted. No periods are required after them; they are not considered abbreviations, but shortened forms, or substitute names.

Dear Tom: Dear Hap: Dear D.B.:   Dear Doc: Dear Syd:

When used in the body of a letter, a nickname need not be quoted if it is as commonly known as a true name.

Bill Gibson   Hap West   J.B.   Tim O'Connor

Company Names. Write a company's name exactly as it appears on that company's letterhead; or in the absence of a letterhead as the company writes its name in an advertisement; or as the name is listed in the telephone book.

Do not abbreviate or hyphen a company name, or use "&" in it, unless the company itself does so. If a company name has "The" before it, use "The" in the address.

If there is a slight discrepancy between the way a company name is signed and the way it appears on the letterhead, take the letterhead as a guide—it should be authentic.

Note whether or not an organization is a "company" or a "corporation". A "corporation" usually dislikes being called a "company", and vice versa. Many large concerns are companies, as

Standard Oil Company

Sometimes there are both a company and a corporation of the same name, as

Bethlehem Steel Company   and   Bethlehem Steel Corporation

Check to make sure that each name is **right,** not almost right. There are various ways to confuse names:

The Johns Hopkins University	NOT:	*John* Hopkins University
	NOR:	*John's* Hopkins Univ.
Hamburg-American Line		Hamburg-*America* Line
Holland-America Line		Holland-*American* Line
American Telephone and		American *Telegraph* and
Telegraph Company		*Telephone* Company
Johns-Manville Corporation		*John Mansville* Corp.

Divisions and Departments. When addressing a division or department of a company or an organization, put the company's or organization's name first, because it is more important than the division's or department's, and because this form will be useful later for reference and filing.

The name of a division or department may also be written in the "Attention" line.

Hanover & Sons, Inc.	OR:	Hanover & Sons, Inc.
Accounting Department		230 Park Ave.
230 Park Avenue		New York City 17
New York 17, N.Y.		
		Attention Accounting Dept.

On the envelope the name of the division or department should be placed in the "Attention" space in the lower left corner.

Personal Names With Company Names. If a letter is intended for the consideration of but one person, the personal name may be placed above the company name. This placement signifies that the letter is of a semi-personal nature.

But if the letter pertains to company business and should be opened and handled in the absence of the person addressed, the personal name should be written below the address, in the "Attention" line.

Do not neglect to write the company name when addressing a person connected with a company. The company's name may seem superfluous in the address, but it is of value for later reference, and it is of definite value on the envelope in assisting the postman to locate the person if the address has been changed or is wrong.

WRITE: Mr. Thornton J. Mills	NOT:	*Thornton J. Mills*
Harrison Wells Company		*160 State*
160 State Street		*Boston, Mass.*
Boston 2, Mass.		

Attention. (For "Attention" line and salutation, see pp. 279–280.)

Personal Names Used as Company Names. It is unnecessary to use "Mr." or "Messrs." before personal names used as company names (unless the concerns are law firms or similar organizations—for which see "Messrs.", p. 295). The salutation should be "Gentlemen:".

Lord & Lyons	John Harper
1401 K St., NW.	50 W. 50th St.
Washington 5, D.C.	New York City 20
Gentlemen:	Gentlemen:

Women's Names.   (See Women's Signatures, p. 284.)

Madam or Madame.   "Madame" is the original French form and is used only in connection with foreign names.   (pron. mȧ'dȧm')   The abbreviation is "Mme" (with no period).

The English form, "Madam", should be used only in salutations on impersonal or routine letters.   (pron. măd'ăm)

(See also Salutations to Women, pp. 281, 309, and 310.)

Mesdames.   Is used before the names of two or more married women (or one married and one unmarried) associated in business. (pron. mā'dȧm')   The abbreviation is "Mmes" (with no period).

Mesdames Meade and Hammond   or   Mrs. Meade and Mrs. Hammond

Two married women of the same name may be addressed as

Mesdames J. V. and T. L. Stevens (formal) or The Mrs. Stevenses (informal)

(See also Salutations to Women, p. 281.)

Misses.   May be used before the names of unmarried women associated in business.

Misses Hazelton and Mills   or   Miss Hazelton and Miss Mills

Two unmarried women of the same name may be addressed as

Misses Joan and Ellen Taylor (formal)   or   The Miss Taylors (informal)

(See also Salutations to Women, p. 281.)

Master.   Is the proper designation for a small boy.   The plural is "Masters".

Masters Weldon and Blaine Cartwright

Two boys of the same name may be addressed as

The Masters Turner (formal)   or   The Master Turners (informal)

Business Titles in Addresses.   The modern tendency is to omit business titles in addresses, unless the title is needed for identification, or unless the letter is of a legal nature and it is desired to address the person in his official capacity.

A business title, if used, may be written on the line with the personal name, or on the line with the company name, or on a line by itself, whichever arrangement gives the best balance.

Mr. J. G. Barnes, President
Merchants Association of Brentwood

Mr. Hamilton W. Pennington, Jr.
Secretary, Maitland Bros., Inc.

Mr. Nathaniel W. Burke
Vice President and General Manager
The Stone and Marshall Company
720 N. Michigan Ave., Chicago 11, Illinois

(The last example is one of the reasons why titles are being discontinued. They can make addresses needlessly heavy and long.)

299

A business title may be used after a name even though a professional title or "Mr." has been used before it.

Prof. Blake Taylor, Treasurer
Dr. Emerson F. Lowell, President
Capt. J. O. Helm, Chairman
The Rev. David Blythe, Secretary

"**Mr.**" is always correct before any man's name if the proper title is not known.

Titles Unhyphened. Titles are no longer hyphened unless they represent two titles. (See Hyphen, p. 255.)

Vice President   Editor in Chief
Lieutenant Governor   Major General
    BUT: Secretary-Treasurer (two titles)

Abbreviating Titles. A title may be abbreviated if it stands before a full name, that is, a name containing a Christian name or initials; but if a title stands immediately before a last name it is not abbreviated.

Prof. John C. Reade   BUT: Professor Reade
Lieut. William Rogers   Lieutenant Rogers

Hence in salutations titles are usually written out.

My dear Professor Reade: My dear Lieutenant Rogers:

Doctor. Other titles may be used in connection with "Dr.", except "M.D." or other degree letters that mean "Doctor".

Dr. J. Mason Blake
Superintendent of Education

Dr. James C. Hartwell
President, Southwestern Institution

Dr. Stephen E. Lee
Professor of Economics

Dr. Joseph B. Blair, Chairman

In the salutation, "Doctor" may be written out, to conform to the rule of writing out titles before surnames; or it may be abbreviated.

My dear Doctor Blake: (formal)   Dr. and Mrs. L. V. Merriville
Dear Dr. Blake: (informal)   Dear Dr. and Mrs. Merriville:

If the addressee is the holder of a doctor's degree, and is referred to in the address by a title other than "Doctor", he may be referred to as "Doctor" in the salutation.

ADDRESS: President Lawrence Merrill
SALUTATION: My dear Doctor Merrill: or   Dear Dr. Merrill:

Do not use "Doctor" without a surname in the salutation, unless it is in personal correspondence.

PERSONAL: My dear Doctor: or   Dear Doctor:

300

If a married woman is a doctor, her title is sometimes—in social correspondence—abandoned in addressing her and her husband.

Mr. and Mrs. James O. Madison

But in professional writings, a woman doctor is accorded her title and separate name. (Many professional women retain their maiden names.)

Dr. Mary C. Hartwell, and
Mr. James O. Madison

My dear Doctor Hartwell and Mr. Madison:

Or if both are doctors, and she uses her married name:

Dr. Mary H. Madison, and
Dr. James O. Madison   or   The Doctors Madison

My dear Doctors Madison:

Many doctors of medicine prefer the degree letters "M.D." after the name to the title of "Dr." before it, because of the large number of persons now using the title "Dr."

Mary C. Hartwell, M.D.   James O. Madison, M.D.

When two doctors are being addressed, the word "Doctors" or the abbreviation "Drs." may be used.

Doctors Blake and Mason (before surnames)
Drs. S. G. Blake and V. M. Mason (before initials or Christian names)

Two doctors of the same name may be addressed as

The Doctors Madison (formal)   or   The Doctor Madisons (informal)

Degree Letters. Letters signifying college degrees or honorary degrees are used chiefly in published works and in formal writings, where it seems desirable to apprise the reader of a person's academic standing. Degree letters (with the exception of "M.D." and "D.D.") are not commonly used in addresses on business letters and envelopes.

If degree letters are used in the address, neither "Mr." nor "Dr." should precede the name.

James Blake, M.D.   Daniel B. Stephens, Litt.D.
President of...   Editor of...
                    Ellen M. Lowden, Ph.D.
                    Dean of the College of Fine Arts

A title (other than "Dr.") is sometimes used before a name when degree letters follow it—in writings other than addresses.

Professor Jason Stanfield, Ph.D.
President Edward L. Masters, LL.D.
The Reverend David A. Merrill, S.T.D.
Rev. John Wayne, D.D.   (Note that "Rev." does not signify "D.D.")
...the Honorable W. Park Wills, Sc.D.
Dean Hugh C. Reade, A.M., Ph.D.
Captain Leland F. Scott, M.A.
Miss Jessica Harland, Litt.D.
Sir Sidney Graystone, LL.D., D.Litt.

Occasionally "Dr." is used before a name with the explanatory degree letters shown in parentheses after the name.

Dr. Paul T. Nelson (Ed.D.)

Degree letters are arranged after a name so that the most important degree is given last, or so that the degree most important to the text is mentioned last.

Keith M. Taylor, B.S., A.M., LL.D.
Leslie A. Ryan, Ph.D., M.D., Medical Director
John F. Franklin, Ph.D., Litt.D., Editor
James E. Russell, M.D., Dr.P.H., Instructor in Hygiene

Professor. The title "Professor" should be used only for instructors of the highest rank, or persons upon whom the title has been conferred by academic authority. It should not be used indiscriminately for all teachers. Since the title "Professor" signifies rank, it is usually preferred to "Doctor" by those who also hold doctors' degrees.

"Professor" should be written in full if used alone with a surname; but it may be abbreviated if used before a Christian name or initial. Accordingly, it is usually abbreviated in an address, but written in full in the salutation.

Prof. Samuel J. Linden   My dear Professor Linden:

"Professor" is not generally used without a surname in the salutation, unless it is in personal correspondence.

PERSONAL: My dear Professor: or   Dear Professor:

In an address to a professor and his wife, "Professor" is commonly written in full, but it may be abbreviated if the name is long.

Professor and Mrs. E. B. Masters
Prof. and Mrs. Alexander B. Hawthorne

If the wife is the professor, her title is abandoned in the combination of names.

Mr. and Mrs. R. B. McGregor

But if the names are used to represent official capacities, they may be separated, as

Dr. E. B. Trainor, President, and
Prof. Caroline V. Trainor, Secretary
The Wilkes School of Fine Arts

My dear Doctor and Professor Trainor:

When addressing two professors, write "Professors" in full, not "*Profs.*"

Professors S. J. Linden and E. B. Trainor

Two professors of the same name may be addressed as

The Professors Linden (formal)   or   The Professor Lindens (informal)

Reverend

In all formal writings, "The" should always precede "Reverend"; but the long "The Reverend" is usually abbreviated to "The Rev." or just "Rev." in addresses on business letters and envelopes, in advertisements, and in church notices.

Rev. John J. Polk

The title of "The Reverend" is used in the following manners:

The Reverend — before the names of most clergymen.
The Very Reverend ⎫ before the names of the higher dignitaries in
The Right Reverend ⎬ various churches. (See Forms of Address,
The Most Reverend ⎭ p. 318.)

"The Reverend" should not be used with a surname only, as "The Reverend Clarkson". "The Reverend" is a title of respect, not one of rank or office. To say "The Reverend Clarkson" is like saying "The Respected Clarkson", which of course immediately suggests a correction to "The Respected Mr. Clarkson" or "The Respected Benjamin C. Clarkson". Hence there must always be an intervening Christian name or initial, or a title such as "Doctor", "Mr.", "Professor", etc., between "The Reverend" and the surname.

The Reverend Mr. Clarkson
The Reverend Doctor Phillips
The Reverend Professor Meredith
The Reverend R. M. Alden, Chaplain
The Very Reverend President Blythe
The Very Reverend Father Wayne

"The Reverend" does not necessarily signify "Doctor of Divinity" (D.D.). "Doctor of Divinity" is an honorary degree conferred upon clergymen. Hence "The Reverend" is often used in connection with "D.D.", or other degree letters signifying "Doctor".

The Reverend Paul Kenworth, D.D.
The Reverend John Lane, S.T.D.
BUT NOT: *The Reverend Doctor Parsons, D.D.*

A clergyman is addressed as "Mr." in conversation unless he has a doctor's degree, then he is addressed as "Doctor".

Not in Salutations. "Reverend" should not be used in a salutation before a surname. Use "Mr.", "Doctor", or another appropriate title.

My dear Mr. Clarkson: My dear Professor Meredith:
My dear Doctor Phillips: My dear President Blythe:

To a Clergyman and His Wife. When a clergyman and his wife are being addressed, "The Reverend" is usually abbreviated to shorten the address, since the full name must be used, not the last name alone.

The Rev. and Mrs. Benjamin C. Clarkson
(NOT: *Rev. and Mrs. Clarkson*)

My dear Mr. and Mrs. Clarkson:
My dear Doctor and Mrs. Clarkson:

If the full name is not known, the address may be:

> The Reverend Mr. Clarkson and Mrs. Clarkson

Plurals. Two clergymen of the same name should not be addressed as "The *Reverends*..." They may be addressed as "The Reverend Messrs..." or "The Reverend Doctors..."; or "The Reverend" or "Rev." may be used before each man's full name.

> The Reverend Messrs. Parke ⎱ or Rev. S. J. Parke, and
> The Reverend Doctors Parke ⎰   Rev. Daniel Parke

In Texts. "The" is not capitalized when the title occurs in the body of a letter or in a text, but "Reverend" is always capitalized.

> ...given by the Reverend Dr. John Phillips.

In Lists. "The *Reverends*" or "*Revs.*" should not be used as a plural title before a list of names. "The Reverend Messrs." or "the Reverend Doctors" may be used; or "the Reverend" or "Rev." may be repeated before each name. Or if the word "clergymen" or "clergy" is mentioned in the introduction to the list, the first "the Reverend" will serve for all the names. ("Revs." is sometimes seen in catalogues and directories, but it should not be used in formal writings.)

> ...present were the Reverend Messrs. Clarkson, Blythe, and Parke.
> ...among the clergy were the Reverend J. Polk, Mr. Clarkson, David Blythe, and Doctor Page.
> ...addresses will be delivered by the Rev. J. Polk, Rev. Mr. Clarkson, Rev. David Blythe, and Rev. Doctor Page.

Honorable

There is a tradition that "Honorable" should not be used without "The" before it; but "The Honorable" is now very generally abbreviated to "Hon." in all addresses to government officials.

> Hon. Stephen Sanderson

Use of "Honorable". Regarding the use of "The Honorable" or "Hon." remember that:

In the United States it is a title of respect accorded to government officials, and that any official of the government, from the highest to the lowest, may be addressed as "Honorable".

"Most Honourable" and "Right Honourable" are used in Great Britain.

Not With Surname Only. "The Honorable" should never be used before a surname only, as "*The Honorable Gray*". "The Honorable" is a title of respect, not one of rank or office. To say "*The Honorable Gray*" is like saying "*The Respected Gray*", which of course immediately suggests a correction to "The Respected Mr. Gray" or "The Respected Frank J. Gray". Hence there must always be an intervening Christian name or initial, or a title such as "Doctor", "Mr.", "Colonel", etc., between "The Honorable" and the surname.

The Honorable Mr. Fulton	The Honorable Colonel Houston
The Honorable George Fulton	The Honorable Doctor Star

Alike for Men and Women. "The Honorable" or "Hon." may be used alike for men and women; and no other title is necessary with the full name.

Hon. Josephine Lande	Hon. Douglas Mills
RATHER THAN: Hon. Mrs. Josephine Lande	Hon. Mr. Douglas Mills

But if the first name or initial is not known, another title must be used with "The Honorable", as

The Honorable Mrs. Lande	The Honorable Professor Bentley
The Honorable Miss Merrick	The Honorable Mr. Mills

Never in Salutations. "Honorable" is never used in a salutation. "Mr." or a similar title may be used; or the title of the office may be employed.

My dear Mr. Fulton:	My dear Governor Clayton:
My dear Mrs. Lande:	My dear Mr. Secretary:

To an Official and His Wife. When an official and his wife are being addressed, the full name should be given, not the last name alone.

The Hon. and Mrs. Benjamin J. Flagg
(NOT: *Hon. and Mrs. Flagg*)

My dear Mr. and Mrs. Flagg:

If the full name is not known, the address may be:

The Honorable Mr. Flagg and Mrs. Flagg

If the wife is "The Honorable", her title may be abandoned in the combination of names.

Mr. and Mrs. J. Evan Downing

In Texts. "The" is not capitalized when the title occurs in the body of a letter or in a text, but "Honorable" is always capitalized.

...given by the Honorable Theodore Adams.

In Lists. "The *Honorables*" or "*Hons.*" should not be used as a plural title before a list of names. "The Honorable Messrs." may be used, or "the Honorable" or "Hon." may be repeated before each name.

...defeating the Honorable Oscar Adams, the Honorable Seth Blackmore, and the Honorable Joseph Anderson.
...was supported by the Honorable Messrs. Clarke, Goodfellow, Thomas, Carlton, and Reade.

Not Permanent Title. "The Honorable" is not a permanent title, but pertains to an office. When an official has returned to private life, the title is no longer applicable (although it is sometimes conferred as a matter of respect). "Mr.", or a like title, is then the proper designation.

Address Book. The most convenient size for an address book is 5 by 7 inches. Larger books are unwieldy and smaller books do not afford space enough for long addresses.

A loose-leaf book is not necessary, since it is more convenient to make entries by hand than on the typewriter.

Make all entries in ink; pencil notations become indistinct with constant handling.

Enter the names according to companies. List the names of the men connected with each company beside the company's name. For instance, under W list:

Telephone
Washington Corporation ⎧H. L. Andrews, Pres.
385 Madison Ave.   ⎨J. J. Higgins, Secy.   Cal. 5-7234
New York City 17   ⎩L. M. Clayton

Make it a rule that every name that is entered in the address book is absolutely correct: written exactly as a company prints its name on its letterhead, or as a man writes his own name (spelling, initials, abbreviations, punctuation, etc.). Make the address book a final authority on names.

Adopt the further rule of entering, when first encountered, every name that will undoubtedly be needed again, even if this necessitates several pauses in the course of a busy day. If this is not done, addresses will be overlooked, and the efficiency of the address book impaired. Time seems much more valuable when wasted in an attempt to look up an address in the files than when used simply to write down a name.

Addresses of Personnel. The correct name, home address, and telephone number of every person in the organization should be written in the address book or kept in a convenient place in the files. These addresses and telephone numbers are often of vital importance when an endeavor is being made to reach someone connected with the organization.

Temporary Addresses. Temporary addresses (traveling addresses, etc.) should be written on slips of paper and clipped into the address book at the proper places. These can be removed when no longer useful, and the address book will not then contain a number of scratched-out names.

Traveling Addresses. (For addresses to Trains, etc., see p. 369.)

Foreign Addresses

English Lettering. All foreign addresses on envelopes should be in English or in English lettering. English is understood in every country in the world. If an address is in a foreign script, an English translation should be interlined.

The foreign titles corresponding to "Mr.", "Mrs.", and "Miss" may be used if desired, even if the rest is in English. But "Mr.", "Mrs.", and "Miss" may always be used and will be changed to the proper titles in translation.

306

Capitalization of Foreign Names. (For the capitalization of "de", "von", etc., in foreign names, see Capitalization, p. 138.)

Name of Country and Postal District. Every foreign address should be complete, with the name of the country as well as the city. A letter addressed, for instance, simply to "London" could be sent to England or to Canada. (Note that Pakistan is a country, not a part of India.)

Canadian addresses should always carry "Canada", even though the name of the province is given, as

> Victoria, B.C.
> Canada

In many foreign addresses, postal districts are written after the names of the cities, as

> London, E.C. 2 (East Central)   Paris 16ᵉ
> Berlin, W. 8   Toronto 2

Mexico City is now a Federal District, similar to the District of Columbia in the United States. Letters are addressed

> Mexico, D.F.—which means "Mexico, Distrito Federal"

Obtaining Foreign Addresses From Telephone Books. Foreign addresses may often be obtained from, or verified in, foreign telephone books in the business offices of the telephone companies. The Long Distance Chief Operator will state whether or not the desired foreign telephone book is available; but no foreign addresses will be given over the telephone.

Translation Bureaus. Translation bureaus are listed in the classified sections of telephone books, under T.

Large public libraries usually have foreign departments that will assist in short translations.

FOREIGN TITLES CORRESPONDING TO "MR.", "MRS.", AND "MISS"

American	French		German		Spanish		Italian	
	Title	Abbr.	Title	Abbr.	Title	Abbr.	Title	Abbr.
Mr.	Monsieur	M.*	Herrn‡	†	Señor	Sr.	Signor	Sig.
Messrs.	Messieurs	MM.*	Herren	†	Señores	Sres.	Signori	Sig.ri
Mrs.	Madame	Mme*	Frau	Fr.*	Señora	Sra.	Signora	Sig.ra*
Miss	Mademoi-selle	Mlle*	Fräulein	Frl.*	Señorita	Srta.	Signorina	Sig.na*
Mesdames	Mesdames	Mmes*			Señoras	Sras.*	Signore	Sig.re*
Misses	Mesdemoi-selles	Mlles*	Fräulein	Frl.*	Señoritas	Srtas.*	Signorine	Sig.ne*

* Abbreviation not often used in addresses. The title is written out.
† Abbreviation not used.
‡ Form used in addresses because it implies "to".

Don—is a Spanish title of respect, corresponding to the English "Esquire". It is used only before Christian names or initials, as

Don Juan   Señor Don Francisco Diaz
Don Alfonso Don L. Diaz   BUT NOT: *Don* Diaz

Doña—is the corresponding feminine Spanish title of respect.

Doña Dolores Montez Doña Dolores   BUT NOT: *Doña* Montez

Sir—The British title "Sir" is never followed by a last name only. It must be followed by a forename, initial, or title.

NEVER: *Sir* Lindon ALWAYS: Sir George Lindon
                               Sir George
                               sir knight

ADDRESSES TO GOVERNMENT OFFICIALS

"No title of nobility shall be granted by the United States."
—The Constitution of the United States, Art. I, Sec. 9.

From the above, it follows logically enough that any official of the government may and should be addressed with simplicity.

Flowery wordings are outmoded—charming when sometimes used by the older generation, but not in keeping with the new.

Use of Personal Name. In ordinary correspondence with government offices, titles of offices rather than personal names should be used, as

The Commissioner of Patents   The Attorney General
The Register of Copyrights   The American Consul

In special correspondence, the personal name may be used in the address.

Names of Government Officials. Names of the United States Government officials may be found in the Congressional Directory in any public library; or in the current World Almanac. (See also Reference Books, p. 590, and Government Departments, p. 486.)

Names of state officials may be found in the state directory or roster in the public libraries in each state. The names of the governors of the different states are given in the current World Almanac. (See also Reference Books, p. 594.)

Names of city officials may be obtained from the city hall, or from the public library, in each city.

Addressing "The Office of". In seeking general information from any office, it is well to address simply "The Office of...", as

The Office of the Secretary of State
The Office of the Attorney General

The salutation to an office is "Gentlemen:".

Women Officials. Women holding official positions are accorded the same titles and forms of address as men. "Madam" is substituted for "Mr." in the diplomatic salutation, as "My dear Madam Secretary:", "My dear Madam Mayor:", etc. (alike for "Miss" and "Mrs.").

"Madam Secretary" (the American form) is preferred, in Government usage, to "Madame Secretary" (the French form). The latter is sometimes seen in texts in publications.

Retired Officials. When an official returns to private life, his title is no longer applicable. Even presidents become "Mr." again.

Retired military and naval officers, however, retain their titles.

Capitol and Capital. Note that "capitol" means a building (a statehouse); while "capital" means a city. "The Capitol" in Washington, D.C., is the building where Congress convenes; whereas Washington, D.C., is the capital of the United States.

Wives of Officials. In American usage, wives do not share their husbands' titles. Their title is always "Mrs."

> The President and Mrs. Hanover
> Governor and Mrs. John Kellogg   or   The Governor and Mrs. Kellogg
> The Honorable and Mrs. Stephen Scott

State Department Forms. The Department of State in Washington, D.C., by reason of its traditional dignity and because of its large diplomatic correspondence, employs certain ceremonious forms that are not used by other Departments of the Government, or by the general public.

For instance, the State Department uses always the full title "The Honorable", formally spaced on a separate line, in addresses; whereas other Departments, in the ordinary course of their voluminous correspondence, have long since omitted the "The" and use just "Honorable" or "Hon." before the names in addresses.

Official Complimentary Closings. The ordinary complimentary closings may be used in all forms of official correspondence. Common official closings are:

Very truly yours,	Respectfully,
Yours very truly,	Very respectfully,
Sincerely yours,	Respectfully yours,
Very sincerely yours,	Faithfully yours,

The diplomatic closing employs the title or name, as

> I am, my dear Mr. President,
> Very sincerely yours,

❖

ADDRESSES

FORMS OF ADDRESS

All forms given herein have been checked by, or furnished by, representative offices.

To make the forms of address applicable to women as well as men, it is to be assumed that feminine titles may be used wherever masculine titles are shown.

Mrs. or Miss	may be substituted for	Mr.
Madam: or Dear Madam:	for	Sir: or Dear Sir:
My dear Madam Secretary:		My dear Mr. Secretary:
My dear Madam Commissioner:		My dear Mr. Commissioner:
My dear Madam Mayor:		My dear Mr. Mayor:

TO FEDERAL GOVERNMENT OFFICIALS

(For postal zone numbers of Government offices, see p. 486.)

If personal name is not used: If personal name is used:

THE PRESIDENT

The President
The White House
Washington 25, D.C.
My dear Mr. President:

The Honorable...(full name)...
The White House
Washington 25, D.C.
My dear President........:

THE VICE PRESIDENT

The Vice President   or
The President of the Senate
United States Senate
Washington 25, D.C.
Sir: or
Dear Mr. Vice President:

The Honorable...(full name)...
The Vice President of the
    United States
Washington 25, D.C.
My dear Mr. Vice President: or
My dear Mr.........:

THE SPEAKER OF THE HOUSE

The Speaker of the House of
    Representatives
Washington 25, D.C.
Sir:

The Honorable...(full name)...
Speaker of the House of
    Representatives
Washington 25, D.C.
My dear Mr. Speaker: or
My dear Mr. ....:

CABINET MEMBER

Formal, diplomatic form:
The Honorable
The Secretary of ....
Washington 25, D.C.
Sir:

     or similarly
The Honorable
The Attorney General
Washington 25, D.C.
Sir:

Business form:
The Secretary of ....
Washington 25, D.C.
Dear Sir:

The Honorable ...(full name)...
Secretary of ....
Washington 25, D.C.
My dear Mr. Secretary: or
My dear Mr. ....:
     or similarly

The Honorable ...(full name) ...
The Postmaster General
Washington 25, D.C.
My dear Mr. Postmaster General: or
My dear Mr. ....:

     or to an Administrator
My dear Mr. Administrator:

FORMS OF ADDRESS

If personal name is not used:

If personal name is used:

COMMISSIONER, DIRECTOR, OR CHIEF OF A GOVERNMENT BUREAU

The Commissioner of the Bureau of ....
Department of ....
Washington 25, D.C.

Dear Sir:

and similarly to

The Director or Chief of a Bureau

Hon. ....
Commissioner of ....
Department of ....
Washington 25, D.C.

My dear Mr. Commissioner: or
My dear Mr. ....: or
Dear Sir:

and similarly to

The Director or Chief of a Bureau*

SENATOR

Hon. ....
United States Senate
Washington 25, D.C.

or to a home address

Hon. ....
United States Senator
(Street Number)
(City, and State)

My dear Senator: (alike for men and women) or
My dear Senator ....: or
My dear Mr. ....:   or
Dear Sir: (rare)

REPRESENTATIVE

Hon. ....
House of Representatives
Washington 25, D.C.

or to a home address

Hon. ....
Representative in Congress
(Street Number)
(City, and State)

My dear Congressman: (alike for men and woment) or
My dear Mr. ....: or
Dear Sir: (rare)

TO DIPLOMATIC REPRESENTATIVES

The diplomatic representatives are ambassadors, ministers, and occasionally chargés d'affaires.

It is customary to address a foreign representative as "His Excellency". This is followed by "Mr." before his name, unless he has a personal title (as used in his own country). The names and titles of diplomatic representatives may be found in the Congressional Directory in any public library, or in the current World Almanac.

Note that where the diplomatic representative is an ambassador, the office is called an "embassy"; and where the representative is a minister, the office is a "legation".

Ordinary communications should be addressed to the Secretary of the Embassy, or Legation, and not to individual members of the staff.

* Although "My dear Mr. Commissioner:" is used as a salutation, "My dear Mr. Director:" is never used, and "My dear Mr. Chief:" is not considered possible.

† "Congresswoman" is a term not generally liked by congresswomen. The term "Congressman" bids fair to become the general term for both men and women, similar to "chairman", "spokesman", "juryman", etc.

311

If personal name is not used:	If personal name is used:

AMBASSADOR

His Excellency The Ambassador of .... Washington, D.C.	His Excellency Mr. (or personal title) .. .... Ambassador of .... Washington, D.C.
The Honorable The American Ambassador (Foreign Capital, and Country)	Excellency: (formal) My dear Mr. Ambassador: (informal)
Sir: or My dear Mr. Ambassador:	The Honorable .... (full name) .... The American Ambassador (Foreign Capital, and Country) Sir: (formal) My dear Mr. Ambassador: (informal) My dear Mr. ....: (personal)

MINISTER

His Excellency The Minister of .... Washington, D.C.	His Excellency Mr. (or personal title) .... Minister of .... Washington, D.C.
The Honorable The American Minister (Foreign Capital, and Country)	The Honorable ....(full name).... The American Minister (Foreign Capital, and Country)
Sir: or My dear Mr. Minister:	Sir: (formal) My dear Mr. Minister: (informal) My dear Mr. .... : (personal)

CHARGÉ D'AFFAIRES

The Chargé d'Affaires The ....Legation (or Embassy) Washington, D.C Sir:	Mr. (or personal title).... Chargé d'Affaires The ....Legation (or Embassy) Washington, D.C. Sir: (formal) My dear Mr. ....: (personal)

DIPLOMATIC OFFICERS

The diplomatic officers are:

Ambassador. A diplomatic representative of the highest rank. The full title is "Ambassador Extraordinary and Plenipotentiary", meaning an ambassador vested with special and full power to transact business.

Minister. A diplomatic representative of high rank. The full title is "Envoy Extraordinary and Minister Plenipotentiary".

Chargé d'Affaires. The officer in charge during the absence of, or instead of, an ambassador or minister.

Counselor of Embassy or Legation. The adviser of the embassy or legation; one versed in matters pertaining to the certain country.

Secretary of Embassy or Legation. One who handles the official papers of the diplomatic office.

Attaché. A subordinate officer attached to a diplomatic corps. There are military, naval, and commercial attachés.

Aide-de-Camp. A special representative of, or assistant to, a sovereign—a naval or military aide.

312

FORMS OF ADDRESS

TO COMMERCIAL REPRESENTATIVES

The commercial representatives are:

Consul General. The officer in charge of all or several of the commercial representatives of a country.
Consul. A commercial representative of a country.
Vice Consul. A substitute or subordinate consul.
Consular Agent. A representative of a principal consular officer.

American consular officers are located in all of the principal commercial cities of the world.

Foreign consular officers are located in all American cities where the certain countries have interests—usually in seaport cities.

The names of the foreign and American consular officers and the cities where consulates are located may be found in the Congressional Directory in any public library; the current World Almanac gives lists of the cities where consulates are located.

If personal name is not used: If personal name is used:

AMERICAN CONSUL

The American Consul   ...., Esq.
(Foreign City, and Country)   American Consul
Sir: (Foreign City, and Country)
                                                  Sir: (formal)
                                                  My dear Mr. ....: (personal)

FOREIGN CONSUL

The French Consul   Hon. ....
(American City, and State)   French Consul
Sir: (American City, and State)
                                                  Sir:

(Because consular officers are transferred frequently, and their duties call them away from their posts, it is better to address the office than the individual. Hence the form in the left column is the preferable form of address, alike for consuls general, consuls, vice consuls, and consular agents.)

TO STATE OFFICIALS

GOVERNOR

The Governor of........   Hon.. ......
    or the diplomatic form: Governor of........
The Honorable   (State Capital, and State)
The Governor of........
(State Capital)   My dear Governor: or
                                                  My dear Governor........: or
Sir: Dear Sir:

LIEUTENANT GOVERNOR

The Lieutenant Governor   Hon. ....
State of ....   Lieutenant Governor
(State Capital, and State)   State of ....
Dear Sir: (State Capital, and State)
                                                  Dear Sir: or
                                                  My dear Governor ....: or
                                                  My dear Mr. ....:

313

ADDRESSES

If personal name is not used:	If personal name is used:

HEADS OF STATE DEPARTMENTS
*(Secretary of State, Treasurer, Auditor, Attorney General, Commissioners, etc.)

The Secretary of State or The State Treasurer or The Attorney General State of . . . . (State Capital, and State) Dear Sir:	Hon. . . . . Secretary of State or Hon. . . . . Attorney General (State Capital, and State) Dear Sir: or My dear Mr. . . . . :

TO MEMBERS OF THE STATE LEGISLATURE
STATE SENATOR

Senator from . . . . (District) . . . . The State Senate (State Capital, and State) Dear Sir:	Hon. . . . . The State Senate (State Capital, and State) Dear Sir: or My dear Senator: or My dear Senator . . . . : or My dear Mr. . . . . :

STATE ASSEMBLYMAN, REPRESENTATIVE, OR DELEGATE

(In some states the lower branch of the legislature is called the "Assembly"; in other states, the "House of Representatives"; and in still others, the "House of Delegates".)

Assemblyman from . . . . (District) . . . . The State Assembly or Representative from . . . . (District) . . . . House of Representatives (State Capital, and State) Dear Sir:	Hon. . . . . The State Assembly (State Capital, and State) Dear Sir: or My dear Mr. . . . . : and similarly to a member of a House of Representatives or House of Delegates

TO COUNTY OFFICIALS
SUPERVISOR OR COMMISSIONER

The Board of Supervisors (or Commissioners) . . . . County (County Seat, and State) Gentlemen:	Hon. (or Mr.) . . . . Supervisor, ... County (County Seat, and State) Dear Sir: or My dear Mr. . . . . : and similarly to a Commissioner of a County

HEADS OF COUNTY OFFICES
(County Clerk, Sheriff, Treasurer, Recorder, Auditor, etc.)

County Clerk (or Clerk of the Superior or Circuit Court) or Sheriff of . . . . County or County Treasurer or County Recorder (County Seat, and State) Dear Sir:	Hon. (or Mr.) . . . . County Clerk (County Seat, and State) Dear Sir: or My dear Mr. . . . . : Hon. (or Mr.) . . . . Sheriff, ... County (County Seat, and State) Dear Sir: or My dear Sheriff . . . . :

* Certain of the older states, such as Massachusetts, Pennsylvania, and Virginia, are known as "commonwealths" rather than "states". Their officers are accordingly addressed as "The Secretary of the Commonwealth", "The Auditor of the Commonwealth", etc.

FORMS OF ADDRESS

If personal name is not used:	If personal name is used:

PROSECUTING ATTORNEY, COUNTY ATTORNEY, STATE'S ATTORNEY, OR DISTRICT ATTORNEY

The Prosecuting Attorney or The State's Attorney .... County (County Seat, and State) Dear Sir:	Hon. .... Prosecuting Attorney or State's Attorney (County Seat, and State) Dear Sir: or My dear Mr. ....:

TO CITY OFFICIALS

MAYOR

The Mayor of the City of .... (City, and State) Dear Sir: or My dear Mr. Mayor:	Hon. .... Mayor of the City of .... (City, and State) Dear Sir: or My dear Mr. Mayor: or My dear Mayor ....:

CITY COUNCILMAN, ALDERMAN, OR SELECTMAN

The City Council City Hall (City, and State) Gentlemen:	Hon. (or Mr.) .... Councilman, City of .... City Hall (City, and State) Dear Sir: or My dear Mr. ....:

HEADS OF CITY OFFICES

(City Clerk, Treasurer, Chief of Police, etc.)

City Clerk or City Treasurer City Hall (City, and State) The Chief of Police (City, and State) Dear Sir:	Hon. (or Mr.) .... City Clerk or City Treasurer or Chief of Police (City, and State) Dear Sir: or My dear Mr. ....:

TO JUDICIAL OFFICERS

CHIEF JUSTICE OF THE UNITED STATES

The Chief Justice of the United States Washington 13, D.C. My dear Mr. Chief Justice:	The Honorable ...(full name) ... Chief Justice of the United States Washington 13, D.C. or Mr. Chief Justice ...(last name)... Supreme Court of the United States Washington 13, D.C. My dear Mr. Chief Justice:

ASSOCIATE JUSTICE OF THE SUPREME COURT OF THE UNITED STATES

	The Honorable ...(full name)... Justice, Supreme Court of the United States Washington 13, D.C. or Mr. Justice ...(last name) Supreme Court of the United States Washington 13, D.C. My dear Mr. Justice:

ADDRESSES

If personal name is not used:	If personal name is used:

CHIEF JUSTICE, CHIEF JUDGE, OR PRESIDING JUDGE
STATE SUPREME COURT OR COURT OF APPEALS

The Chief Justice
Supreme Court of the State of ....
(State Capital, and State)
Dear Sir:
    and similarly to
The Chief Judge or
The Presiding Judge
	Hon. ....
	Chief Justice of the Supreme Court
	(State Capital, and State)
	My dear Chief Justice .... : or
	Dear Sir:
	    and similarly to a
	Chief Judge or Presiding Judge
	My dear Judge .... :

ASSOCIATE JUSTICE OR ASSOCIATE JUDGE
STATE SUPREME COURT OR COURT OF APPEALS

	Hon. .... Associate Justice of the Supreme Court (State Capital, and State) My dear Justice .... : or Dear Sir: and similarly to an Associate Judge My dear Judge .... :

JUDGE

	Hon. .... Judge of the .... Court (City, and State) My dear Judge .... : or Dear Sir:

JUSTICE OF THE PEACE

The Justice of the Peace .... District (City, and State) Dear Sir:	.........., Esq. or Hon. (or Mr.) .... Justice of the Peace (City, and State) Dear Sir: or My dear Mr. .... : or My dear Judge........ :

CONSTABLE

The Constable of ... (District) ... (City, and State) Dear Sir:	Mr. ...., Constable (Street Address) (City, and State) Dear Sir: or My dear Mr. .... :

TO SCHOOL OFFICIALS

(The names and addresses of educational officials may be found in the "Educational Directory" issued by the U.S. Office of Education, or in "Patterson's American Educational Directory", in public libraries. The names of the governing officials of American colleges and universities may be found in the current World Almanac.)

FORMS OF ADDRESS

If personal name is not used:	If personal name is used:

PRESIDENT OF A SCHOOL

The President of ....
(City, and State)
Dear Sir:

*Dr. ....
President of ....
(City, and State) or

President ....
University of ....
(City, and State)

My dear Doctor ....: or
My dear President ....:

CHANCELLOR OF A SCHOOL

The Chancellor of ....
(City, and State)
Dear Sir:

*Dr. ....
Chancellor of ....
(City, and State) or

Chancellor ....
University of ....
(City, and State)

My dear Doctor ....: or
My dear Chancellor ......:

PRESIDENT OF A RELIGIOUS SCHOOL (PROTESTANT)

The President of ....
(City, and State)
Dear Sir:

†The Reverend ....
President of ....
(City, and State)

My dear President ....: or
My dear Doctor ....:

DEAN

Dean of the College of ....
.... University
(City, and State)
Dear Sir:

Prof. (or Dr. or Mr.) ....
Dean of ....
............University
(City, and State) or

Dean........
School of ....
University of ....
(City, and State)

My dear Professor ....: or
My dear Doctor ....:   or
My dear Dean ....:

PROFESSOR

Professor of ....
.... University
(City, and State)
Dear Sir:

Prof. ....
Department of ....
.... University
(City, and State) or

Dr. (or Mr.) ....
Professor of ....
University of ....
(City, and State)

My dear Professor ....: or
My dear Doctor ....:   or
My dear Mr. ....:

* "Dr." is the usual title for the president or chancellor of a school, since most of such officials are the holders of doctors' degrees. "Dr." is used in preference to degree letters in such addresses.

† "The Reverend" is used unless the president of a school is entitled to a higher ecclesiastical title, such as "The Very Reverend". (For Catholic Schools, see p. 320.)

If personal name is not used:	If personal name is used:

STATE SUPERINTENDENT OF PUBLIC INSTRUCTION, OR SCHOOLS, OR STATE COMMISSIONER OF EDUCATION

The Superintendent of Public Instruction or The Commissioner of Education (State Capital, and State) Dear Sir:	Mr. (or Dr.) .... Superintendent of Public Instruction or Commissioner of Education (State Capital, and State)
	My dear Mr. .... : or My dear Doctor .... : or Dear Sir:

SUPERINTENDENT OF SCHOOLS

The Superintendent of .... (City, and State) Dear Sir:	Mr. (or Dr.) .... Superintendent of .... Schools or Supt. .... Schools (City, and State)
	My dear Mr. .... : or My dear Doctor .... : or Dear Sir:

PRINCIPAL OF A SCHOOL

The Principal of .... School (City, and State) Dear Sir:	Mr. .... Principal of .... School (City, and State)
	My dear Mr. .... : or Dear Sir:

TEACHER

	Mr. .... (School) .... (City, and State)
	My dear Mr. .... : or Dear Sir:

MEMBER OF SCHOOL BOARD OR BOARD OF EDUCATION

The .... School Board or The Board of Education (City, and State) Gentlemen:	Mr. .... Member, ... School Board (City, and State)
	My dear Mr. .... : or Dear Sir: and similarly to a Clerk, Chairman, Director, etc., of a School Board or Board of Education

TO CHURCH DIGNITARIES AND OFFICIALS
Roman Catholic Church

(The name and correct title of any official or dignitary of the Catholic Church may be obtained from "The Official Catholic Directory" to be found in any large public library, or in the offices of any large Catholic Church. The names of cardinals, archbishops, and bishops may be found in the current World Almanac.)

THE POPE

His Holiness, the Pope Vatican City Rome, Italy Most Holy Father:	His Holiness Pope .... Vatican City Rome, Italy Most Holy Father:

318

FORMS OF ADDRESS

If personal name is not used:	If personal name is used:

CARDINAL

His Eminence (first name) Cardinal (last name)
(as "His Eminence James T. Cardinal Vincent")
Your Eminence:

CARDINAL ARCHBISHOP

His Eminence (first name) Cardinal (last name)
Archbishop of ....
Your Eminence:

ARCHBISHOP

The Archbishop of	The Most Reverend .... (full name) ....
Your Excellency:	Archbishop of ....
	Your Excellency:

BISHOP

The Bishop of	The Most Reverend ... (full name) ...
Your Excellency:	Bishop of ....
	Your Excellency:

*MONSIGNOR

The Right Reverend Monsignor ... (full name) ...
or abbreviated as
The Rt. Rev. Msgr. ....
My dear Monsignor ....: or
My dear Monsignor:

PRIEST

The Pastor of	The Rev. ... (full name) ...
Dear Father:	Dear Father: or
	Reverend dear Father: or
	Dear Father..........:

MOTHER SUPERIOR

The Reverend Mother Superior	The Reverend Mother ... (full name) ...
Reverend Mother: or	Reverend Mother: or
Dear Reverend Mother:	Dear Reverend Mother: or
	Dear Reverend Mother ....:

SISTER

	Sister ... (full name) ...
	My dear Sister: or
	Dear Sister ....:

SUPERIOR OR DIRECTOR OF A BROTHERHOOD

Brother Superior or	Brother ... (full name) ...
Brother Director	Dear Brother ....:
Dear Brother:	

MEMBER OF A BROTHERHOOD

	Brother ... (full name) ...
	My dear Brother: or
	Dear Brother..........:

* There are two classes of Monsignori: one (Domestic Prelates) are addressed as "The Right Reverend"; the other (Papal Chamberlains) are addressed as "The Very Reverend". The Official Catholic Directory will give the correct designations. In the absence of definite information it is always courteous to address any Monsignor as "The Right Reverend".

319

ADDRESSES

If personal name is not used:	If personal name is used:

ABBOT

The Abbot of .... Abbey Dear Father Abbot:	*The Rt. Rev. ...(full name)... Abbot of .... or The Rt. Rev. Abbot...(last name)... Reverend dear Father .... :

VICAR GENERAL, SUPERIOR, PRIOR, CHANCELLOR, RECTOR, DEAN, CANON, PROVINCIAL, ETC.

(These are titles of offices or appointments, and are used in much the same manner as "President" or "Director" would be. By courtesy, the holders of these offices are accorded the title "The Very Reverend", unless, of course, they are entitled to a higher designation, as "The Right Reverend" or "The Most Reverend".)

The Vicar General or The Chancellor of........ or The Dean of .... Dear Father:	The Very Rev. ...(full name)..., V.G. (for a Vicar General) or The Very Rev. ...(full name)... Chancellor of.......... or The Very Rev. ...(full name)... Dean of .... Very Reverend dear Father:

HEADS OF CATHOLIC COLLEGES, UNIVERSITIES, AND SEMINARIES

(By courtesy are addressed as "The Very Reverend", unless by their ecclesiastical standing they are entitled to a higher designation, as "The Right Reverend" or "The Most Reverend".)

The President of .... or The Chancellor of .... or The Rector of .... Dear Father:	The Very Rev. ...(full name)... President, ... University Very Reverend dear Father: and similarly to a Chancellor or Rector

Protestant Episcopal Church

(The names of the clergy of the Episcopal Church may be found in "The Living Church Annual—The Year Book of the Episcopal Church", in most public libraries. The names and addresses of Episcopal bishops may be found in the current World Almanac.)

BISHOP

The Bishop of .... My dear Bishop: or Dear Sir:	The Right Reverend ...(full name)... Bishop of .... My dear Bishop: or My dear Bishop .... :

ARCHDEACON

The Archdeacon of .... My dear Archdeacon:	The Venerable ...(full name)... Archdeacon of .... My dear Archdeacon: or My dear Archdeacon .... :

DEAN

The Dean of .... My dear Dean:	The Very Reverend ...(full name)... Dean of .... My dear Dean: or My dear Dean .... :

* "The Right Reverend" is used unless the Abbot is of higher ecclesiastical standing and entitled to be addressed as "The Most Reverend".

320

FORMS OF ADDRESS

If personal name is not used:	If personal name is used:

CANON

The Canon of ....
My dear Canon:

The Reverend ...(full name)...
Canon, ...
My dear Canon: or
My dear Canon .... :

RECTOR

The Rector of ....
My dear Sir:

The Reverend ...(full name)...
My dear Mr. .... : or
My dear Doctor .... :

Other Churches

METHODIST BISHOP

(The names and addresses of the bishops of The Methodist Church may be found in the current World Almanac.)

The Bishop of .... Area
The Methodist Church
(City, and State)

My dear Bishop: or
Dear Sir:

Bishop .... (full name)....
My dear Bishop .... : or
My dear Bishop:

JEWISH RABBI

The Rabbi of ....
My dear Rabbi:

Rabbi ....(full name).... or
Dr. ....
My dear Rabbi: or
My dear Rabbi .... : or
My dear Doctor .... :

CLERGYMEN OF VARIOUS DENOMINATIONS

(The names and addresses of prominent clergymen in the United States may be found in the "Yearbook of American Churches", in public libraries.)

The Pastor of ....
My dear Sir:

The Rev. (or Dr.) ....(full name)....
My dear Mr. .... : or
My dear Doctor .... :
If the first name or initial is not known, use
The Rev. Mr. (or Dr.) ....

TO MILITARY AND NAVAL OFFICERS AND ENLISTED MEN

Officers and enlisted men in the Army and Navy should be addressed by their titles rather than by "Mr."

"As a general rule, the delivery of a letter to the addressee will be expedited if it is addressed to him by rank or rating on the envelope, instead of by the term 'Mr.'"

* * *

"...every officer in the Navy shall be designated and addressed by the title of his rank without any discrimination whatever."

—Navy Department.

Titles Abbreviated in Addresses. Titles of rank or rating are usually abbreviated in addresses. Relative rank is:

ARMY	NAVY
General..............	Admiral..............
Lt. Gen.	Vice Adm. ....
Maj. Gen.	Rear Adm. ....
Brig. Gen.	Commo. ....
Col.	Capt. ....
Lt. Col.	Comdr. ....
Maj.	Lt. Comdr. ....
Capt.	Lieut. ....
1st Lieut.	Lieut. (jg) ....
2d Lieut.	Ens. ....
Cadet........... .	Midshipman ....
Sgt.	For petty officers the title is written after the name, as
Cpl.	
Pvt.	.........., Gunner's Mate (1 cl.)

U.S.A., A.U.S., U.S.N., etc. (See footnote, p. 323.) "U.S.A." (United States Army), "U.S.N." (United States Navy), "U.S.M.C." (United States Marine Corps), or "U.S.C.G." (United States Coast Guard), may be added after the branch of the service in the address, or after the personal name.

Lieut. ....
Civil Engineer Corps, U.S.N.

Capt. ...., U.S.A.
Company G, Seventh Infantry

Salutations to Military and Naval Officers. The business salutation for all ranks, rates, and grades is

Dear Sir:

In informal letters, the titles (unabbreviated) may be used in the salutations.

ARMY
My dear General ....:
(Alike for General, Lt. Gen., Maj. Gen., and Brig. Gen.)
My dear Colonel ....:
(Alike for Colonel and Lt. Col.)
My dear Major ....:
My dear Lieutenant ....:
(Alike for First and Second Lieutenants)

NAVY
My dear Admiral ....:
(Alike for Admiral, Vice Adm., and Rear Adm.)
My dear Captain ....:
My dear Commander ....:
(For Commander, but not Lt. Comdr.)

For all ranks, grades, or rates below Commanders in the Navy and Second Lieutenants in the Army, the title **"Mr."** may be used in the salutations on letters (and in oral address). (For **"Dr."** in the Medical Corps, see footnote, p. 323.)

My dear Mr. ....:

To an Officer and His Wife. Since all officers of the Navy, and all officers and noncommissioned officers of the Army, are addressed by the titles of their rank in official written communications, so are they being addressed in social written communications. (Many examples of this "accepted usage" may be found in newspapers and magazines reporting social events.)

Colonel and Mrs. ...(full name)...
Lieut. and Mrs..........
(Alike for 1st and 2d Lieut.)
Sgt. and Mrs. ....

Captain and Mrs. ...(full name)...
Lt. Comdr. and Mrs. ....
Lieut. (jg) and Mrs. ....
Ensign and Mrs. ....

The salutations follow the forms for salutations given above.

322

FORMS OF ADDRESS

If personal name is not used: If personal name is used:

ARMY OR NAVY CHAPLAIN

The Chaplain of ....   Chaplain ... (full name)...
My dear Chaplain: My dear Chaplain: (formal)
                             My dear Chaplain ....:
                             Dear Chaplain ....: (informal)

To a Chaplain and his wife:

Chaplain and Mrs. ... (full name)...
Dear Chaplain and Mrs. ....:

TO MILITARY OFFICIALS

Adjutant General, Inspector General, Judge Advocate General, Quartermaster General, and Surgeon General are titles of office, not of rank.
The heads of these offices are usually addressed by office, as

The Adjutant General
Department of the Army
Washington 25, D.C.
Dear Sir:

Or they may be less formally addressed by their military titles, as

Maj. Gen. ....
The Adjutant General
Department of the Army
Washington 25, D.C.
Dear Sir: or
My dear General..........:

State Adjutant General. An Adjutant General is the military administrative officer in each state. "The Adjutant General" may be addressed as

Official: Informal:
The Adjutant General   *Brig. Gen. ....
State of ....   The Adjutant General
(State Capital, and State)   State of ....
Dear Sir: (State Capital, and State)
                            My dear General ....:

* Adjutants General may be of different military rank. They are not always Brigadier Generals.

The **United States Army (USA)** is the Regular Army—the permanent, professional military force.

The **Army of the United States (AUS)** is the wartime army, composed of the Regular Army, the National Guard, the Organized Reserves, and the Selective Servicemen of the National Army.

The **United States Navy (USN)** is the Regular Navy—the permanent, professional naval force.

The **United States Naval Reserve (USNR)**—the trained, inactive peacetime naval force—is a part of the wartime navy.

- - - -

Doctor. In the Army Medical Corps, officers of the grade of Captain and above are orally addressed by their military titles—"Captain", "Major", "Colonel", and "General". Lieutenants may be orally addressed as "Doctor".

In the Naval Medical Corps, officers below the rank of Commander may be orally addressed as "Doctor".

❖

ENVELOPES

Preferred positions on the business envelope:

Return Address	Stamps, or Delivery Method AIR MAIL, or SPECIAL DELIVERY REGISTERED FIRST CLASS, etc.
PERSONAL Name	
Attention	Room, Apartment, or Box Number
Division or Department	Street Address
Holding or Forwarding	City
Directions	State

Official Form of Address. The United States Post Office Department approves of but one form of address, and asks that the public cooperate in writing all addresses in this form so that mail can be handled with the rapidity and accuracy to which it is entitled:

Although this is the postal pref-
erence in style of address on
envelopes, several other styles
are used by business offices and
are acceptable.

> Mr. Thomas J. Stevens
> Room 1820-B
> 465 California Street
> San Francisco 4
> California

Note that the address is in five lines and indented form, which gives a better segregation for the eye than the block style. The post office reads from the bottom up.

Notice, too, that the name of the state occupies a line by itself, and is spelled in full. The Post Office Department has this to say about abbreviations of state names:

> "When the name of the State is abbreviated, frequently Va. and Pa., Md. and Ind., Colo. and Calif., Miss. and Minn., and others are confused and mail missent, as in many instances post-office names are repeated in several different States."

Do not place addresses high on envelopes, nor far to the left. The post office looks for them in the lower right portion of all letters.

The open style of punctuation, that is, the omission of punctuation at the ends of lines, may be used to advantage on envelopes.

Building Names. On letters not mailed for local distribution, a street address is preferable to a building name, unless the building is

324

very well known. The reason for the preference of the street address is that train mail sorters arrange each city's mail according to street numbers, and if the street number of a building is unknown to them, they must group that building's mail in a separate package for re-sorting when it reaches the city to which it is destined.

If the name of a building is given in an address, the room number should also be given, if it is known. With a building name it is unnecessary to write the word "Room" or "No."—just the number, as

820 Highcourt Bldg.

Hotel Names. What has been said above regarding building names applies also to hotel names: if the hotel is large or well known, the street address is not necessary, but if the hotel is small or not well known, the street address should also be given.

The word "Hotel" is preferably written after the name of a large hotel.

Highland Hotel   RATHER THAN: Hotel Highland

Do not address a person "In care of" a hotel. Omit the "In care of"—it is understood.

"No." or "#" Unnecessary. It is unnecessary to write the abbreviation "No." or "#" before a number in an address.

Street Numbers. In formal correspondence, if the avenue or street name is a number below ten, it is spelled out. But now in informal work —in everyday business addresses—all street names that are numbers are usually in figures, with –st, –nd, –rd, or –th after them.

A dash, not a comma, should be used between a house number and a street number. A dash separates numbers and makes each distinct.

FORMAL: 500 Fifth Avenue   INFORMAL: 500 – 5th Ave.
245 East Second Street   245 E. 2nd St.
5022 – 17th Avenue, NE.   5022 – 17th Ave., NE.

"Avenue", "Street", and "Building" are usually abbreviated "Ave.", "St.", and "Bldg." in addresses on ordinary letters and envelopes. In formal correspondence they are written out.

"City". Never use the word "City" in an address, unless on routine mail such as billing.

Letters for local delivery should bear the name of the state as well as the name of the city—and the postal zone number.

Room, Apartment, or Box Number. A room, apartment, or box number should be written in the address itself, and not in the lower left corner of an envelope.

Postal sorters and carriers look for all numbers that pertain to their handling of the mail in the address proper, not down at the side.

Any notation or instruction that pertains to the mail after it is delivered, such as "Attention Mr. . . . .", or "Hold for Arrival", may be placed in the lower left corner.

325

Full Addresses. Give a complete address on an envelope always; for instance, do not omit the company name when addressing a person connected with a company. Should the street address or room number be incorrect, the post office will make every endeavor to locate the company from the directory. However, local letters with insufficient addresses will not be given "directory service", but will be returned.

Do not omit **street addresses** on mail to towns of any considerable size, even though the persons or companies addressed are well known. There may be several persons or companies of similar or like name in one city. "Letters without street addresses or box numbers are subject to delay."—Post Office Department.

The **postal zone number** must be given in addresses to large cities.

County names are not required in addresses; but if one seems necessary, as "Julian, San Diego County, California", it should be typed on a separate line in the main address, between the city and the state name.

If a letter is returned because of an incorrect address, it should be placed in a new envelope, never remailed in the one showing the error.

Return Addresses. "A return address should be on everything deposited in the mails."—Post Office Department.

The return address should be in the upper left corner of every piece of mail, **not on the back,** nor on the bottom of an address tag or label.

It is unnecessary to specify the number of days that a piece of mail is to be held before it is returned; post office regulations govern this.

"Mr." and **"Miss"** are not used in return addresses. Other titles are.

When using hotel or club envelopes, write a personal return address beneath the hotel or club name. Mail is not returned to hotels, clubs, schools, and other public institutions whose names appear on the envelopes as advertisements.

Dispatch Method. If a letter is to be dispatched by a special postal method, this information should be noted in capital letters below the stamps. Such a notation not only serves as a reminder to the one stamping the mail in an office, but aids postal clerks when sorting the mails.

AIR MAIL	should be marked on every air mail letter, unless the letter is in a regular air mail envelope.
SPECIAL DELIVERY	should appear below all special delivery stamps.
REGISTERED	should be written on letters to be registered.
Return Receipt	should appear if such a receipt is desired.
FIRST CLASS	should be marked on all first-class mail that is not ordinarily sent first class, and on all odd-sized first-class pieces.

If a letter is marked REGISTERED, or AIR MAIL, etc., and it is finally not to be sent by that method, obliterate the words, or confusion in the post office handling will result.

Foreign Routing. (For the method of addressing mail via certain ships, see p. 356. For other foreign mail markings, see pp. 353 ff.)

When addressing a foreign letter on which 5¢ postage will be required, mark "5¢" in pencil in the stamp position, as a reminder to use foreign postage.

Delivery Method. If the delivery method is to be by hand, a notation to that effect should be written in the upper right corner, as

By Messenger, or
Courtesy of Mr. .... or Kindness of Mr. ....

Without one of these notations a question might later arise in the receiving office regarding the method of delivery. Someone will ask, "How did this come?" or "Who left this?"

Personal. PERSONAL, when used, should be written in capital letters above the address.

"Confidential" should not appear on an envelope. It applies only to the contents, not to the delivery, and should be written only on the letter. Use the word PERSONAL on the envelopes of such letters as are marked "Confidential". The word "Private" is not generally used.

Attention. "Attention" should appear in the lower left corner. It is unnecessary to write "of" after "Attention"; and on letters between companies well known to each other, even the word "Attention" may be omitted. The personal name or the name of the division or department in the lower left corner signifies "Attention".

Holding or Forwarding Directions. "Hold for Arrival" should appear in the lower left corner of every piece of mail that is likely to arrive before the arrival of the addressee.

"Please Forward" should be written in the lower left corner of every piece of mail that is likely to arrive after the departure of the addressee.

Hotel addresses especially should carry these notations. Many misunderstandings arise because it is believed that these instructions will be naturally assumed. They are not always.

Addressing a Number of Envelopes. To address a large number of envelopes with the least effort, feed them into the machine in a continuous line, that is, feed a new envelope next the roller and beneath the edge of the envelope that is being addressed. This saves turns of the roller by bringing a new envelope into position as each envelope is removed.

Preparing Letters for Envelopes. Before any letter is placed in an envelope, check it for **signature, corrections,** and **enclosures.** And lastly, check to make sure that the right letter is being placed in the right envelope.

Staple the pages of a letter together with a small wire staple placed neatly in the upper **left corner.** (This is done in the receiving offices, and may as well be done in the sending offices.)

If the enclosures accompanying a letter are to be a permanent part of the letter, staple them to the letter in the manner above.

The use of pins in letters is not approved by postal authorities.

A metal clip, if used, should be placed on the upper left corner, and the letter folded so that the clip will be within the folds and not next the envelope. The letter should be placed in the envelope so that the clip is at the left end of the envelope. If it is at the right end—under the stamp—it will interfere with the stamp-canceling machine and make the postmark blur.

Enclosing Stamps. Stamps are not usually enclosed for reply to any but charitable organizations.

It is a nice courtesy, however, to enclose stamps for reply to an inquiry if the information desired is to benefit only the inquirer.

It is unnecessary to send stamps to the Federal Government offices, unless an air mail reply is desired (then postage must be enclosed). Government ordinary mail is "franked"—sent postage free.

Folding Letters. Letters should be folded carefully, not haphazardly. The fold of a letter adds to or detracts from its appearance when received. Because so many letters are folded into unshapely forms, the following well-known advice is here repeated:

For a legal-sized envelope, fold a letter over equal distances from the top and from the bottom—just two folds.

For a letter-sized envelope, fold it in half from the bottom to the top, and then fold each side in, an equal distance—making three folds in all.

Sealing. Do not seal letters until they are ready to be sent out. If anything is forgotten or to be added, it can be put in without the necessity of making a new envelope and destroying the one that has been sealed.

Use a wet sponge or device for sealing envelopes. Never "lick" them. Not only is it unsanitary, but the sharp edges of the paper may cut the mouth.

Do not moisten the envelopes too much in sealing; too much water may dampen the letters enclosed and cause them to be crinkly; or the glue may run, and if several letters are piled together one may stick to the back of another and go astray. This has happened many times.

Conversely, do not attempt to seal the envelopes with too little moisture. They will dry and crack open before being received.

To seal a number of envelopes, spread them (address side down) so that the gummed edges of the opened flaps will fall one beneath the other in a row. Run a moistener over the gummed edges and seal the letters one at a time.

A clean blotter is an aid in sealing envelopes. It not only absorbs all extra moisture and glue, but keeps the envelopes and hands clean.

Stamping. Use a moistener for stamps. Never "lick" them.

Do not affix stamps carelessly, upside down or out of place, or at a crooked angle. This not only reflects on the merits of the company mailing such letters, but causes postal clerks extra work when canceling the stamps.

If one stamp overlaps another—according to postal rules—the one that is partly covered is not counted.

328

Make sure that every stamp is thoroughly stuck to the envelope. Many important letters have been returned because of lost stamps. Postal clerks are not required to affix stamps to mail.

To stamp a number of envelopes rapidly: pile them in a stack; tear the stamps in rows; moisten a row of five or six stamps, and pull them apart as each is affixed, pushing each envelope down as it is stamped to make room for the next stamp.

Mutilated or defaced stamps cannot be used as postage. Therefore, care should be taken in tearing stamps apart to see that no portions of stamps are torn away.

Weighing. Weigh every piece of mail about which there can exist the slightest doubt regarding postage. It will be weighed in the post office and "postage due" charged the addressee if insufficient postage is affixed. Not only is it annoying to receive postage-due mail, but if it occurs repeatedly from any one correspondent, it is unforgivable.

Keep the postal scales accurate by balancing them through an adjustment of the screw at the top or side. In weighing a piece of mail, if the scales balance on an ounce line, that ounce may be figured; but if they balance on the slightest fraction of an inch above an ounce line, the ounce next above must be figured. The sender is not given the benefit of this shade of weight difference.

Do not estimate weights. Mail too heavy to be weighed on the office scales should be taken to the post office.

An office postal scale of sufficient size to weigh moderately heavy mail is a good investment. It saves frequent trips to the post office, or the much disliked "postage due" on heavy mail.

The postal pound is the standard or avoirdupois pound of 16 ounces.

Mailing. The Post Office Department urges that mail be posted throughout the day:

> "Avoid delay by depositing mail early and continuously throughout the day, thus insuring prompt dispatch. Much mail is deposited just at the close of the business day, and frequently such congestion follows that all of it can not be distributed in time to be given the first dispatch."

Before mailing make three final checks: (1) see that each letter is sealed; (2) that the proper postage is on; and (3) that the address is correct.

Letters have been sent out unsealed, infrequently of course; but more frequently without proper postage; and altogether too frequently with incorrect addresses.

Do not put heavy mail down a chute—it may break open from the long fall.

And also, do not leave mail outside a box on the street. It may be blown away, or if it is of any value it is very liable to be stolen.

Mailing on Trains. Only first-class mail may be posted in train mails. Parcel post is not accepted.

It is not necessary to write the name or time of the train on the envelope. Train mails are given the first possible dispatch.

ENVELOPES

Train mail boxes are located at most railroad stations. If a train mail box is not available, first-class mail may be posted in a slot on the mail car.

It is not possible to send a letter to a train by special delivery.

If it is imperative that a letter or package reach a passenger on a train, such mail may be dispatched by air mail in care of a telegraph company (**preceded by a wire prepaying messenger service**), and the telegraph company will deliver it to the train. It should be addressed in the following manner:

Return Address

AIR MAIL

Please deliver to:
  Mr. H. C. James   The Western Union Telegraph Co.
  Care of Conductor
  Santa Fe Train 20,   Albuquerque
  Eastbound
  Car 78, Compartment 4   New Mexico
  Due Santa Fe Station, May 15,
  10:30 p.m.
  Albuquerque, New Mexico

POSTAL INFORMATION

Compiled from the United States Official Postal Guide, and by consultation
with the Post Office Department.

The general divisions of mail matter are:

First Class	handwritten or typewritten matter, and all matter **sealed against postal inspection.** Post cards and postal cards are included in first-class matter.
Second Class	newspapers, magazines, and periodicals, containing notice of second-class entry.
Third Class	all mailable matter not in the first and second classes, and which **weighs not more than 8 ounces.**
Fourth Class	parcel post—all mailable matter not in the first and second classes, and which **weighs more than 8 ounces.**

The difference between third- and fourth-class mail is a matter of weight.
The **postal pound** is the standard or avoirdupois pound of 16 ounces.

Domestic Mail Matter. This term includes matter deposited in the mails of
the United States or its possessions, for delivery in the United States or its
possessions. Alaska and Hawaii are included in the term "United States".
Puerto Rico, the Virgin Islands of the U.S., Guam, American Samoa, and the
Canal Zone are included in the term "Possessions of the United States".

United States Official Postal Guide contains complete postal information.
It is issued (in two parts) by the United States Post Office Department, and
placed on sale about September 1. It should be ordered direct from the Superintendent of Documents, Government Printing Office, Washington 25, D.C.

> Part I, domestic mails, and foreign money orders. Cloth-bound; biennial . . $2.00
> Part II, foreign mails, except foreign money orders. Paper-bound; annual .   .75
> Supplements [pamphlets] issued quarterly (1½-year subscription) 1.25
> Postal Bulletin: current mail changes; (twice a week); 1-yr. subscription . . .   2.00

The countries of the world are treated separately in the Postal Guide. The
rates, conditions of mailing, air mail and parcel post specifications, etc., to each
country are given in a clear and concise style.

A list of **all post offices in the United States** is included; the **name of the
county** in which each post office is located is also given; and **county seats** are
indicated. Also there is shown the number of boxes served by rural or star
routes from each office having such service, and the number of post office boxholders at other than city letter carrier offices.

The Official Postal Guide may be consulted at any post office.

FIRST-CLASS MAIL

Rate

Letters; handwritten or typewritten matter, and carbons or duplicate } 3¢ an ounce
copies thereof; and all matter sealed against postal inspection.

"Drop letters" may still be mailed for 2¢ an ounce in towns having no letter carrier service, provided
the letters are not intended for rural or star route delivery.

Typewritten manuscripts accompanying proof sheets are an exception to the rule that all typewritten matter must be sent first class. These manuscripts, after being set in type, may accompany the proof sheets as third- or fourth-class mail, according to weight.

For mimeographed or multigraphed copies of letters, etc., see Third-Class Mail.

Weight Limit: Same as for parcel post.

Mark Pieces FIRST CLASS. If sending a large or odd-sized envelope or package first class, mark on it conspicuously in large letters, or stamp it with a rubber stamp, FIRST CLASS. This insures against any oversight that might cause the article to be sent with mail of a lower class.

Government Postal Cards. 2¢ each. By air mail, 4¢ each.

"Postal" cards have the stamp impressed thereon.

Post Cards. 2¢ each. By air mail, 4¢ each.

Included under this term are picture post cards, and in fact any regular-sized post card. Cards unmailable as post cards are those larger than $3\frac{9}{16}''$ × $5\frac{9}{16}''$ or smaller than $2\frac{3}{4}''$ × $4''$, and those that bear particles of glass, metal, mica, sand, tinsel, or similar substances that might rub off in the mails; also those bearing statements of past due accounts, or anything of a dunning or defamatory nature.

Cards larger or smaller than post card sizes, but bearing the words "Post Card" or "Private Mailing Card", are subject to the letter rate of postage, regardless of whether they are printed or otherwise written upon.

Small-Sized Cards and Envelopes. The Post Office Department says that "The use of small 'greetings' cards and envelopes is very objectionable from a postal standpoint" because the sending of small cards and envelopes, usually at Christmas time, "seriously retards and disarranges the work in post offices at a time when the facilities are taxed to the utmost." Frequently the stamps on small-sized cards and letters must be canceled by hand, because such mail will not fit in the canceling machines. Also it does not fit the separating cases, and cannot be tied securely with other mail. Furthermore, there is no space for forwarding directions when it is necessary to forward such matter.

Double or Reply Post Cards. 2¢ each.

The postage on the reply half need not be affixed until it is detached for return mailing; or the reply half may be a "business reply card". Double or reply cards must be folded before mailing, so that the return address is on the inside; but it is not necessary to fasten the two portions together. The two edges may be fastened with a plain sticker or seal, but metal clips cannot be used.

Enclosures are prohibited.

The specified use of double or reply cards is the obtaining of orders or specific information. If used for statements of account, letter rates apply.

Business Reply Cards. 3¢ each. 5¢ each via air mail.

Business Reply Envelopes. A 1¢ **collection fee** on each letter or card makes the rate 1¢ higher than the ordinary rate:

	4¢ for first ounce; 3¢ thereafter.
Local:	(Same as above)
Air mail:	7¢ for first ounce; 6¢ thereafter.

The heavy parallel bars printed down the right end of these cards and envelopes are the flag of "postage due". They guide this mail into the postage-due channels, and indicate to the postman that he is to collect postage when delivering such mail back to the original sender.

Permits for the issuance of business reply cards or envelopes are necessary, and may be obtained by application to the postmaster. There is no charge for these permits.

All printing on the address side of such cards and envelopes must be done at the expense of the sender and must be in strict accordance with forms prescribed by the post office. The Government prints no business reply cards or envelopes.

Reply mail may be distributed in any quantity desired **in the United States or its possessions, except the Canal Zone.** It should not be sent into foreign countries, such as Canada and Mexico, as it cannot be returned from any foreign country without prepayment of postage.

No deposit is required when the cards or envelopes are sent out, in view of the permit holder's guarantee to pay the postage on all that are returned.

SECOND-CLASS MAIL

Rate

Newspapers, magazines, and other periodicals (bearing notice of second-class entry). These rates and conditions apply when such matter is mailed by others than the publishers or registered news agents.
⎱ 2¢ for first 2 ounces, & 1¢ each add. 2 oz., or fourth-class rate, whichever is lower

No Weight or Distance Limit—in the United States.

Stenciled or Mimeographed Publications. Alleged periodical publications produced by the stencil, mimeograph, or hectograph process, or in imitation of typewriting, are not admissible as second-class matter. (See Third-Class Mail.)

Wrapping. Unsealed—and no writing permissible; except on the wrapper may be written, if desired, "Marked Copy" or "Sample Copy", or both, as the case may be.

"On the matter itself the sender may place all that is permitted on the wrapper; correct typographical errors in the text; designate by marks, not by words, a word or passage in the text to which it is desired to call attention. Other writing will subject the package to the first-class rate."

A wrapper for such mail may be made by slitting the ends of an envelope, and rolling the newspaper or magazine into it.

Address. Write SECOND CLASS above the address.

If the addresses are close together on the wrapper, write "From" before the return address, and "To" before the receiver's address. Addresses are often so placed on this type of mail as to be indistinguishable.

Communications. May be attached to second-class matter, in the same manner as described under Parcel Post.

Ordinary Large Mail Boxes. May receive second-class mail. But if a package is large enough to become parcel post, it should be taken to the post office, especially to determine whether the second- or the fourth-class rate applies.

THIRD-CLASS MAIL

Rates

Miscellaneous printed matter, circulars of all kinds, photographs, drawings, proof sheets and accompanying manuscript, and merchandise packages too small for parcel post.
⎱ 2¢ for first 2 ounces & 1¢ each add. oz.

Catalogues and commercial booklets (of 24 pages or more) including the covers, and of which at least 22 are printed), seeds, cuttings, bulbs, roots, scions, and plants.
⎱ 2¢ for first 2 ounces & 1½¢ each add. 2 oz.

333

Weight Limit: 8 ounces. Above that weight it becomes parcel post.

Mimeographed or Multigraphed Copies. These and similar reproductions of handwriting or typewriting may be mailed as third- or fourth-class matter, provided they are mailed at a post office window or other depository designated by the postmaster in a **minimum number of 20 identical, unsealed copies,** either separately addressed or in one package.

Such reproductions, **when bound as pamphlets or books,** may be mailed as third- or fourth-class matter regardless of the number of copies mailed.

When not mailed in accordance with the above conditions, they will be subject to the first-class rate.

No Writing Permitted. Writing is not permitted in or on any third-class mail, except as follows:

On the wrapper, besides the necessary addresses, may be written a designation of the contents, as PRINTED MATTER, PHOTOGRAPH, etc. The inscription "Do not open until Christmas", or words to that effect, may also be written on the wrapper; but no further directions or requests can be inscribed thereon, as "Please send out", or "Post up", etc.

On the matter itself, as on a photograph, there may be written a simple inscription, not in the nature of personal correspondence, as "With best wishes", "Merry Christmas", etc.

Communications. May be attached to third-class matter, in the same manner as described under Parcel Post.

Printed Christmas Cards in Unsealed Envelopes. Printed Christmas cards, or other greeting cards, may be mailed in unsealed envelopes at the third-class rate (2¢ for 2 ounces) if they bear but simple written inscriptions, like "Merry Christmas" or "Best wishes", and the names and addresses of the senders. Greeting cards bearing **written** messages, other than simple inscriptions (and cards smaller than 2¾" × 4" or larger than 9" × 12"), are subject to a 3¢ charge. It is often more desirable to send such cards in sealed envelopes at the first-class rate because of the better service, forwarding, etc., accorded first-class mail.

Birth-Announcement Cards. These cards filled out in **writing** (and cards smaller than 2¾" × 4" or larger than 9" × 12"), cannot be sent in unsealed envelopes at the third-class rate. They are subject to a 3¢ charge.

Breakable Mail. When mailing photographs, drawings, charts, etc., enclose a cardboard protection, and mark on the envelope the nature of the contents, as PHOTOGRAPH—DO NOT BEND.

Wrapping. Third-class mail should be so wrapped that the contents can be easily examined by postal authorities.

THIRD CLASS should be written on the wrapper.

Local Advertising Matter. Advertising matter for delivery to **post office boxholders** at offices not having city letter carrier service, and **on rural or star routes,** may be mailed without individual addresses on the various pieces. Instead, uniform addresses may be used (on each piece), in any one of a number of styles, as

Post Office Boxholder Local	or	Rural (or Star) Route Boxholder Local

Box 75
Rural Route 1
Clear Lake
South Dakota

All pieces for the same post office should be put up by the mailer, so far as practicable, in packages of 50; each package to be labeled, preferably by means of a facing slip, as follows, according to the distribution desired:

334

THIRD-CLASS MAIL

1. For distribution to rural or star route boxholders
   . . . .
   (Post office, and State)
2. For distribution to post office boxholders
   . . . .
   (Post office, and State)

Such advertising matter is accepted at the regular third-class rates, prepaid in money by permit without stamps affixed, or with precanceled stamps; also at bulk third-class rates under permit. Delivery may be restricted to specified rural or star routes, if an advertiser desires to reach only certain localities.

Matter for delivery on **city or village letter carrier routes** must bear individual addresses on the various pieces. Such matter may be addressed by name, including local address, or as follows:

> Occupant (or Householder, or Patron)
> 7895 Foothill Blvd.
> Cincinnati 44 } or Local
> Ohio

Sealing.   Ordinarily, third-class mail is unsealed.

However, third-class merchandising packages (except circulars and other miscellaneous printed matter) may be sealed if they bear **printed** labels which show the nature of the contents and give permission for postal inspection, as described under Parcel Post, Sealing, below.

Ordinary Large Mail Boxes.   May receive third-class mail in small quantities, unless of course it is to be registered or insured.

◆◆❖〓〓〓〓〓〓〓〓〓❖◆◆

BULK MAILINGS (UNDER SECTION 34.66, P.L. & R.)

What May be Mailed in Bulk.   **Identical pieces** of third-class matter may be mailed in bulk lots of not less than either **20 pounds or 200 pieces.**

But EACH PIECE MUST NOT WEIGH MORE THAN 8 OUNCES, and the separately addressed pieces must be uniform in size and weight.*

Permits for Bulk Mailings.   Permits are issued by the postmaster for bulk mailings under Section 34.66 of the Postal Laws and Regulations. A permit costs **$10 for each calendar year,** or portion thereof, for any number of mailings.

Rates per pound (16 ounces):

Circulars and merchandise . . . . 14¢ a pound
Catalogues and commercial booklets (of 24 pages or more, includ- } 10¢ a pound
ing the covers†); Seeds, bulbs, plants, etc.
Minimum charge (max. wt. per piece: 1.143 oz. and 1.6 oz., resp.). . 1½¢ a piece*

* Odd-shaped pieces (round, etc.); big (over 9″ × 12″); small (under 2¾″ × 4″); lumpy (from contents); and tagged (in bags), are subject to a minimum charge of 3¢ each.
"Controlled circulation" advertising publications (not "house organs") may exceed 8 oz. each
Rate: 10¢ a pound; minimum 1¢ a piece weighing not more than 1.6 oz.
† Booklets of less than 24 pages, or with less than 22 printed pages, are not considered "books", and must be sent at the 14¢-a-pound rate.

Methods of Paying Postage.   The postage may be paid under a bulk-mailing permit (which now costs $10 a year) in any one of four ways:

1. **Without postage stamps affixed**—the postage being paid in money, and the permit **printed** on the matter; thus no time or labor is required to affix stamps.
2. **As metered mail.**   A meter is used to imprint the postage on each piece.
3. **With precanceled postage stamps affixed.**   (Uncanceled stamps cannot be used.) Precanceled stamps (sold at post offices) afford such mail fast handling.
4. **In precanceled Government stamped envelopes.**   (Sold at post offices.)

FOURTH-CLASS MAIL

PARCEL POST

Fourth-class mail is parcel post. It includes all mailable matter weighing over 8 ounces and not included in the first and second classes. It is usually unsealed.

Size Limit:* 100 inches in length and girth combined. Parcels weighing less than 10 pounds but measuring over 84 inches in length and girth combined, are subject to the 10–pound rate.

Weight Limit:* 70 pounds for all zones. (A pound is 16 ounces.)

* For parcels (except books and agricultural products) mailed at any first–class post office for delivery at any other first-class post office, the size limit is 72 in. in length and girth combined, and the weight limit 40 lbs. for the 1st and 2nd zones, and 20 lbs. for the 3rd to 8th zones.

Books (parcels weighing over 8 ounces, but not over 70 pounds) as described on the next page.

Rate, for all zones: 8¢ for the first pound, and 4¢ for each additional pound or fraction.

Mark such parcels BOOKS.

Library books (parcels weighing over 8 ounces, but not over 70 pounds), from or to non-profit libraries for delivery anywhere in the 1st, 2nd, or 3rd zone, or within the state in which mailed.

Rate: 4¢ for the first pound, and 1¢ a pound thereafter (or the 3rd– or 4th–class rate, whichever is lower).

Mark such parcels LIBRARY BOOKS.

PARCEL POST RATES

POUNDS	Local	1-2 Up to 150 miles	3 150 to 300 miles	4 300 to 600 miles	5 600 to 1,000 miles	6 1,000 to 1,400 miles	7* 1,400 to 1,800 miles	8† Over 1,800 miles
		Zones (For mileage, see table of distances, p. 566.)						
1		15¢	17¢	17¢	19¢	21¢	23¢	25¢	27¢
2		17	20	21	24	28	33	37	41
3		18	22	24	29	35	42	48	55
4		19	25	28	34	42	51	60	69
5		20	27	31	38	48	60	71	83
6		22	29	35	43	55	70	83	97
7		23	32	38	48	62	79	94	$1.11
8		24	34	42	53	69	88	$1.06	1.25
9		25	37	45	57	75	97	1.17	1.39
10		27	39	49	62	82	$1.07	1.29	1.53
11		28	41	52	67	89	1.16	1.40	1.67
12		29	44	56	72	96	1.25	1.52	1.81
13		30	46	59	76	$1.02	1.34	1.63	1.95
14		32	49	63	81	1.09	1.44	1.75	2.09
15		33	51	66	86	1.16	1.53	1.86	2.23
16		34	53	70	91	1.23	1.62	1.98	2.37
17		35	56	73	95	1.29	1.71	2.09	2.51
18		37	58	77	$1.00	1.36	1.81	2.21	2.65
19		38	61	80	1.05	1.43	1.90	2.32	2.79
20		39	63	84	1.10	1.50	1.99	2.44	2.93
21		40	65	87	1.14	1.56	2.08	2.55	3.07
22		42	68	91	1.19	1.63	2.18	2.67	3.21
23		43	70	94	1.24	1.70	2.27	2.78	3.35
24		44	73	98	1.29	1.77	2.36	2.90	3.49
25		45	75	$1.01	1.33	1.83	2.45	3.01	3.63
26		47	77	1.05	1.38	1.90	2.55	3.13	3.77
27		48	80	1.08	1.43	1.97	2.64	3.24	3.91
28		49	82	1.12	1.48	2.04	2.73	3.36	4.05
29		50	85	1.15	1.52	2.10	2.82	3.47	4.19
30		52	87	1.19	1.57	2.17	2.92	3.59	4.33
31		53	89	1.22	1.62	2.24	3.01	3.70	4.47
32		54	92	1.26	1.67	2.31	3.10	3.82	4.61
33		55	94	1.29	1.71	2.37	3.19	3.93	4.75
34		57	97	1.33	1.76	2.44	3.29	4.05	4.89
35		58	99	1.36	1.81	2.51	3.38	4.16	5.03
36		59	$1.01	1.40	1.86	2.58	3.47	4.28	5.17
37		60	1.04	1.43	1.90	2.64	3.56	4.39	5.31
38		62	1.06	1.47	1.95	2.71	3.66	4.51	5.45
39		63	1.09	1.50	2.00	2.78	3.75	4.62	5.59
40		64	1.11	1.54	2.05	2.85	3.84	4.74	5.73
41		65	1.13	1.57	2.09	2.91	3.93	4.85	5.87
42		67	1.16	1.61	2.14	2.98	4.03	4.97	6.01
43		68	1.18	1.64	2.19	3.05	4.12	5.08	6.15
44		69	1.21	1.68	2.24	3.12	4.21	5.20	6.29
45		70	1.23	1.71	2.28	3.18	4.30	5.31	6.43
50		77	1.35	1.89	2.52	3.52	4.77	5.89	7.13
55		83	1.47	2.06	2.76	3.86	5.23	6.46	7.83
60		89	1.59	2.24	3.00	4.20	5.69	7.04	8.53
65		95	1.71	2.41	3.23	4.53	6.15	7.61	9.23
70		$1.02	1.83	2.59	3.47	4.87	6.62	8.19	9.93

* 7th zone covers Puerto Rico and U.S. Virgin Islands.
† 8th zone covers U.S. Territories and distant possessions.

CATALOGUES. Free catalogues, individually addressed (i.e., single copies of each kind, with order forms, etc., enclosed) and similar printed advertising matter in bound form, consisting of 24 or more pages, weighing over 8 ounces but not in excess of 10 pounds, are mailable at the following rates. No mailing permits required.

Each piece must be stamped "Sec. 34.77 P.L. & R." Add the word CATALOGUE.

Catalogue rates	Local	Zones							
		1	2	3	4	5	6	7	8
First pound	10¢	11¢	11¢	12¢	13¢	15¢	16¢	17¢	18¢
Each additional pound	1½	2½	2½	3	4	5½	7	9	11

Winter mails to Alaska are restricted, effective about October 1 of each year.

Books. A special rate, irrespective of domestic destination, now applies to **permanently bound** books that are wholly reading matter or textbooks (or largely music, pictures, or maps) and contain **no advertisements** except book announcements. Mark such packages BOOK or BOOKS. No special permit is necessary. (For permissible enclosures, consult a postal authority.) This rate does not apply to second-class matter, periodicals, house organs, promotional publications, directories, reports, rate books, sheet music, loose-leaf and handwork books.

No Communications Enclosed. Typewritten or handwritten matter cannot be enclosed in parcel post packages, except as follows:

Invoices and customers' orders may be enclosed with the merchandise to which they relate, provided all references to articles not enclosed are obliterated.

No communications regarding merchandise are permissible (as "Please exchange for size 7", "Please extend credit", etc.) when articles are being sent for replacement or repair, or are being returned for credit, or when films are being sent for development, etc.

Inscriptions, such as "Merry Christmas", "With best wishes", etc., may be written on or enclosed in parcel post packages. Books may bear simple written dedications or inscriptions not in the nature of personal correspondence.

Communications Attached to Parcels. When it is desired to send a letter with a parcel post package, the letter should be placed in a separately addressed envelope and securely glued to the address side of the package, without obscuring the address on the package. Postage must be paid on the letter at the letter rate and on the package at the parcel post rate. They will be dispatched as fourth-class matter.

If special delivery is desired, only one special delivery fee is necessary (on the parcel, at the fourth-class special delivery rate).

Wrapping and Packing. Anything dentable, crushable, or breakable requires extra packing in an extra-heavy cardboard container. If not packed in extra-heavy corrugated cardboard containers, such articles must be crated. Wooden boxes or crates with lids nailed or screwed on may be used.

Heavy manila wrapping paper is standard for the outside wrapping of all parcel post packages. A strong wrapping paper is necessary to withstand the many handlings and the friction of the mail bags.

Do not use dark paper, nor red. The latter color is prohibited by postal authorities because of the difficulty of seeing stamps and reading addresses thereon.

Cord. Tinsel string is prohibited. It rubs off in the mails and causes difficulties.

Heavy cord or twine should be used, wrapped twice around the package in each direction and pulled tight; and all crossings should be securely tied. Packages loosely tied often become unwrapped in the mails, or their wrappers so badly torn that the contents are in danger of being lost. Reported failures to receive articles mailed are often explained by reason of flimsy or insufficient wrapping.

Fragile and Perishable. Mark all parcels containing perishable matter, PERISHABLE. It is recommended that such parcels be sent special delivery.

Mark all parcels containing fragile articles, that is, articles easily broken, FRAGILE, and pack in a strong box with sufficient cushioning material to absorb all shocks.

No extra charge is made for parcels marked FRAGILE or PERISHABLE, but they should **always be insured** to secure careful handling.

337

POSTAL INFORMATION

Mailable liquids* in glass containers cannot be mailed unless specially packed. The bottle must be of strong glass, sealed against leakage, wrapped in sufficient absorbent to insulate it against shocks and to absorb completely the contents of the bottle if broken; and all must be packed in a metal, wooden, or heavy papier-mâché container, marked FRAGILE—LIQUID when in quantities of 16 ounces or less, and FRAGILE—LIQUID—THIS SIDE UP when in quantities of more than 16 ounces.

Mailable liquids* in one-gallon or more, extra-strong metal containers with handles, and with friction tops soldered on in six different places, equally spaced, may be mailed without boxing or crating.

Addresses. All addresses should be written in ink or on the typewriter. Pencil should not be used; pencil addresses rub and become illegible.

The **return address** of the sender **must be on the face of every parcel post package,** or the package may be rejected for mailing.

If the two addresses are close together on a small package, write "From" before the return address, and "To" before the receiver's address, the latter being below and to the right of the former address.

Do not put any addresses on the back of the package.

Tags should not be used unless there is insufficient room on the packages for the addresses. If a tag is used, the addresses of the sender and receiver should also be written on a card and placed inside the package for identification in case the tag is lost.

No Christmas seals or stickers should be placed on the address side of mail.

Sealing. Ordinarily, parcel post packages should not be sealed. If postage stamps, or any other stickers or seals, are so placed that they seal the package against inspection of the contents, the parcel will be subjected to the first-class rate of postage.

Merchandising packages may be sealed if they bear **printed** labels which show the nature of the contents, and give permission for postal inspection, as

```
CONTENTS—MERCHANDISE

Postmaster: This parcel
may be opened for postal
inspection if necessary.
        From
(Name and return address)
_____
Return Postage Guaranteed

              For ...........................
                 ...........................
                 ...........................
```

Note: The sender's name and address may be written or printed, but the indicia as to contents and inspection must be printed.

Mailing. Parcel post packages should be mailed at post offices, and not deposited in mail boxes.

Special Handling. This service accords a parcel the most expeditious handling, transportation, and delivery practicable (but not special delivery).

* Unmailable liquids are poisons, intoxicating liquors, explosives, inflammables, and corrosives.

338

"Special handling" applies to **parcel post only.** It means "fast or first-class dispatch", and **does not insure** a package.

Write or stamp SPECIAL HANDLING immediately below the stamps.

Fees. Are according to weight (in addition to regular postage):

Up to 2 lbs.....15¢   Over 2 and up to 10 lbs.....20¢   Over 10 lbs.....25¢

For "Special Handling with Special Delivery", see Special Delivery.

INSURANCE

Only third-class and parcel post mail may be insured.

Insuring a package provides for careful handling and indemnity against loss, rifling, or damage. No indemnity is payable on ordinary (uninsured) packages in case of loss, rifling, or damage.

(Write on each insurance receipt the name of the person or company to whom the package was sent. Identify the contents in a few words.)

Fees. Are according to valuation (in addition to regular postage):

$ 5 valuation..... 5¢ $25 valuation.....15¢ $100 valuation.....30¢
10   " 10   50   " 20   200   " (limit).35

Return Receipts. May be had on insured mail. As a reminder to ask for a receipt, write RETURN RECEIPT below the space for stamps. The fees are:

7¢ if requested at time of mailing   15¢ if requested after mailing
31¢ if requested at mailing, to show to whom, when, and address where delivered.

Small Valuable Articles. Small articles of value, such as precious stones, jewelry, money, etc., should be sent as sealed, first-class registered mail.

Indemnity up to $1000 is paid on registered mail.

Restrictions in Delivery. (Same as for Registered Mail.)

AIR MAIL

Anything mailable, **sealed or unsealed,** may be sent by air mail, at air mail rates, except articles liable to damage from freezing. (Cut flowers, however, may be sent.)

Rate

6¢ an ounce*
Post cards, 4¢ ea.

* Rate for all air mail weighing up to 8 oz. Above 8 oz. it is "Air Parcel Post". (See p. 340.)

Air mail may be **registered** (if thoroughly sealed); or **insured** (if prepared as third- or fourth-class mail); or sent **C.O.D.,** or **special delivery.**

Size Limit: 100 inches length and girth combined. **Weight Limit:** 70 pounds.

Domestic air mail rates, and weight and size limits, now apply to and from **Alaska, Hawaii, Guam, Canton Island, Canal Zone, Puerto Rico, Virgin Islands of the United States,** and any other place where the United States mail service is in operation, which includes mail to and from the **United States Armed Forces** (and civilian personnel) stationed outside the continental United States.

Foreign Air Mail. (See pp. 355 and 356.)

Preparing Air Mail. Whenever possible, put air mail **letters** in red-white-and-blue-edged envelopes. (Stamped air mail envelopes are sold at post offices.) Ordinary stamps may be used on air mail; but the use of air mail stamps on other than air mail is not permissible. On **ordinary envelopes** and **parcels,** write or stamp—between two blue-pencil lines—AIR MAIL (or paste a sticker) **immediately below the stamps.** An air mail stamp alone is not sufficient.

On **air parcels,** also write or stamp AIR MAIL (or preferably paste a sticker) on each end and side. The sender's **return address** must be on each parcel.

"Postage Due" on Air Mail. A "short-paid" air mail letter will be dispatched by air if at least 6¢ in stamps is attached. If less than 6¢ is prepaid, the letter will be returned for additional postage, or dispatched by ordinary mail.

Short-paid air parcel post will be returned, or dispatched by surface mail.

Air Mail Schedules. Obtain air mail schedules from the post office, and post air mail in sufficient time to arrive at the post office before the closing of the desired air mails. Check to determine whether air mail will reach its destination late Saturday, on Sunday or a holiday, or after the last carrier delivery on other days; if it will, and immediate delivery is desired, send it also **special delivery.**

Air Parcel Post

Parcels of **any class of mail,** sealed or unsealed, may be sent by air mail.

Registered and **C.O.D. first-class packages** must be **securely sealed.**

Insurance indemnity will be paid only on fourth-class packages.

Weight limits: Over 8 ounces and up to 70 pounds. {Less-than-10-pound parcels over 84 inches in length + girth, take 10-pound rate.
Size limit: 100 inches, length and girth combined.

AIR PARCEL POST ZONE RATES

Zone	Miles†	First pound (over 8 oz.)	Each additional pound*	
1 & 2	up to 150	60¢	48¢	* All classes of mail take the same air parcel post rates.
3	150 to 300	60	48	
4	300 to 600	65	50	
5	600 to 1000	70	56	
6	1000 to 1400	75	64	
7§	1400 to 1800§	75	72	
8‡	over 1800‡	80	80	

† For mileage, see table of distances, p. 566. (Same zones as for surface parcel post.)
§ 7th zone covers Puerto Rico and U.S. Virgin Islands.
‡ 8th zone covers U.S. Territories and distant possessions, and Armed Forces overseas.

SPECIAL DELIVERY

Any piece of domestic mail matter may be sent special delivery—sealed or unsealed.

Air mail, registered, insured, or C.O.D. mail, and parcel post may be sent special delivery.

Special delivery does not insure unusual safety, nor a personal delivery to the addressee. When valuables are so sent they should also be r gistered or insured.

Fees. Are according to weight (in addition to regular postage):

First Class

Up to 2 pounds	20¢
Over 2 and up to 10 pounds	35
Over 10 pounds	50

Other than First Class (includes also Special Handling [fast dispatch])
Up to 2 pounds   35¢   Over 10 pounds   60¢
Over 2 and up to 10 pounds   45

Special delivery postage on second-, third-, and fourth-class mail entitles it to the same dispatch and expeditious handling as is accorded first-class mail, and also to special delivery at destination.

Air mail sent special delivery is subject to the special delivery rates that would apply if the same pieces were sent by regular mail.

340

REGISTERED MAIL

Hours of Delivery:

From **7** a.m. to 11 p.m. at city delivery offices.
From **7** a.m. to **7** p.m. at all other offices, or until after the last mail arrives, if not later than 9 p.m.
Sundays and holidays from all post offices.

Service Limits:

In large towns, special delivery mail is delivered within city delivery limits; or within one mile of the main post office or delivery station or branch thereof.
In small towns with no fixed delivery limits, special delivery mail will be delivered within one mile of any post office.
On rural routes, delivery is by rural carriers on their regular trips, and then only to persons residing within one-half mile of the rural routes.

Stamps. Ordinary stamps may be used for special delivery, but when used, the words SPECIAL DELIVERY **must be written** directly below the stamps.

In fact, the words SPECIAL DELIVERY should be written below the stamps on all special delivery mail, even though special delivery stamps are used. The stamps themselves are not sufficiently noticeable in the rapid handling to which mails are subjected. Especially should SPECIAL DELIVERY—AIR MAIL be written on all mail on which special delivery air mail stamps are being used.

If insufficient postage is affixed, mail marked SPECIAL DELIVERY will be returned to the sender for additional postage; or if this course would greatly delay such mail, it will be dispatched and given special delivery service, with the postage due collected from the receiver.

REGISTERED MAIL

First-, second-, and third-class mail may be registered; and fourth-class matter (parcel post) if it is sealed and the first-class rate of postage is paid thereon. **Second- and third-class matter valued in excess of $100, upon which a registry fee in excess of 85¢ is paid, must be sealed and first-class postage paid thereon.** Air mail may be registered.

Special delivery mail may be registered.

Fees. In addition to regular postage and surcharge, if any:

Limit of indemnity	Fee	Limit of indemnity	Fee
No indemnity*	30¢	$ 400	$1.15
$ 5	40	500	1.25
25	55	600	1.35
50	65	700	1.45
75	75	800	1.55
100	85	900	1.65
200	95	1000 (limit)	1.75
300	$1.05		

* On matter having no intrinsic value, such as correspondence and notices.

A small **registry surcharge** must be paid in addition to the registry fee when the value of a registered article exceeds the limit of indemnity prescribed for the registry fee paid. The sender is required to declare the full value (or the known or estimated cost of duplication in the case of nonnegotiable securities), even though the article may be covered by commercial insurance and the sender willing to accept only the $5 limit of indemnity for the fee of 40¢.

Indemnity. Indemnity to be paid in case of loss, rifling, or damage is limited to an amount not exceeding $1000, but private insurance may be carried on registered mail if the sender desires to protect an article fully.

Return Receipts. If proof of delivery is desired, a return receipt should be requested at the time of mailing. Articles for which return receipts are desired should be plainly marked: REGISTERED—Return Receipt, or Return Receipt Showing Address Where Delivered.

Charges for return receipts are:

> 7¢ if requested at time of mailing
> 15¢ if requested after mailing
> 31¢ if requested at mailing, to show to whom, when, and address where delivered.

What Should be Registered. Money should always be registered, if not sent, preferably, by money order.

Valuable papers of which only one copy exists, or original, signed documents, or papers that could not be replaced if lost, should be registered.

Valuable articles, such as jewelry, precious stones, etc., should be sent by registered mail instead of by insured parcel post, because of the additional safeguards provided for registered mail.

Sealing. Mail to be registered (other than second- or third-class mail valued at not more than $100) should be **securely sealed** in every part with glue or mucilage. While the use of sealing wax, paper strips, or paper seals is allowable, it is not encouraged. Wax is unsatisfactory as it is often knocked off or broken in handling. Paper strips or seals, if used, must bear the name and address of the sender, and should not be so affixed as to prevent the registered articles from being properly postmarked.

Restrictions in Delivery. May be made by the sender or the receiver. Letters that the sender desires delivered to the receiver in person should be plainly marked above the address: **Deliver to Addressee Only,** or **Deliver to Addressee or Order.** A 20¢ charge is made for such delivery.

If the delivery is not so restricted, registered mail will be delivered to any responsible person who customarily receives the ordinary mail. The word PERSONAL does not restrict delivery.

Mailing Registered Mail. Breakable articles should be marked FRAGILE.

Write REGISTERED on the envelope or wrapper beneath the place for stamps. This prompts the one who stamps the article to have it registered. If a return receipt is desired, write REGISTERED—Return Receipt.

If for any reason an article is not to be sent registered after it has been so marked, obliterate the word REGISTERED, or confusion in the post office handling will result.

(Note on the back of each registration receipt the name of the addressee and the article sent, for future reference.)

Firm mailing books are available, without cost, to patrons customarily registering three or more articles at a time. These books save time, labor, and expense on the part of the mailer as well as the post office.

Registration Closing Time at Post Offices. Registered mail is closed earlier than ordinary mail at post offices. Air mail and foreign mail to be registered should be sent to the post office in time to meet this earlier closing hour.

MONEY ORDERS

Do not send money in ordinary mail. This is an incitement to theft.

Obtain a money order; or send the mail registered if it is necessary to send currency.

Money orders are issued for sums from 1¢ to $100. More than $100 may be sent by additional money orders.

A small supply of blank applications for money orders should be kept in every office, so that they may be filled out on the typewriter.

Fees. Are according to the amount sent:

From	1¢ to $ 5.00........10¢	From $10.01 to $ 50.00.......25¢
	$5.01 to 10.00.........15	50.01 to 100.00........35¢

Postal notes have been discontinued.

Express money order fees are from 5¢ to 30¢. (See p. 365.)

Bank money orders for amounts up to $100, and **cashier's checks** or bank drafts for any amounts, may be obtained at banks for approximately 15¢ to 25¢ each. (See p. 505.)

Payment. A money order will be paid to the payee named therein, or his endorsee, or to his agent or attorney upon his written order.

Only one endorsement on a postal money order is permissible; but a bank money order may be endorsed any number of times—like a check.

Postal money orders will be cashed at **any** money order office in the United States, within 30 days after issuance; thereafter they must be taken to the office drawn on, or the office of issue.

If cashed at any office other than the one drawn on, or at which issued, a small fee, equal to the fee charged for the original money order, will be collected.

Money orders may be cashed at or deposited in banks.

Identification. Proof of identity is required in cashing a money order at a post office.

Signatures known to the post office officials may be affixed for the purpose of identifying the payee or endorsee, or of guaranteeing his signature.

Also, a remitter may submit a specimen of the payee's signature to the issuing post office, to be mailed to the paying post office for identification of the payee.

COLLECT-ON-DELIVERY SERVICE

Third- and fourth-class mail, and sealed domestic matter of any class bearing postage at the first-class rate, may be sent C.O.D.

C.O.D. mail sealed against postal inspection and bearing postage at the first-class rate may also be registered.

Limit of C.O.D. Collection: $200.

Purpose of C.O.D. Service. C.O.D. first-class-mail service is "intended primarily for the sending of deeds, abstracts of title, insurance policies, bills of lading representing freight shipments, valuable lightweight merchandise, etc."

C.O.D. shipments **must be based on bona fide orders or understandings.** C.O.D. service cannot be used for the collection of debts.

Inspection. No examination of the contents of a C.O.D. article is permitted until the article has been receipted for and all charges paid.

Insurance. C.O.D. fees automatically insure articles against loss, rifling, damage, or nonreceipt of returns.

343

Fees (in addition to regular postage). For collection or insurance of:

$5...........30¢	$25.........60¢	$100.........80¢	$200......$1.00
10.........40	50....... 70	150...... 90	(limit)

Registered C.O.D. collections and indemnity limited to:

$10.........80¢	$50.......$1.10	$100.......$1.20	$200.....$1.40

Registered C.O.D. collections not exceeding $200, but indemnity up to:

$300.......$1.50	$500......$1.70	$700.......$1.90	$1000....$2.10
400....... 1.60	600...... 1.80	800....... 2.00	(limit)

Demurrage.....5¢ a day   Changing terms.....10¢   Notification nondelivery.....5¢

C.O.D. collection fees and postage **must be prepaid by the sender.** But they may be included in the amount of the C.O.D. collection if the sender desires to be reimbursed in this amount.

Restriction in Delivery. (Same as for Registered Mail.)

FORWARDING MAIL

Only first-class mail (including post cards) may be forwarded from one city to another without a new payment of postage. The number of times first-class mail may be forwarded is not limited.

Second- and third-class mail (including permit mail) and parcel post may be forwarded locally (from one street address to another) without a new payment of postage. But such mail must have new postage affixed if forwarded to another city (unless it is of "obvious value", or forwarding postage has been pledged). If the forwarded articles are small and the changed addresses are liable to be confusing, the articles should be rewrapped.

Perishable fourth-class mail of obvious value may be forwarded, and the forwarding postage collected on delivery.

Local letters (2¢ drop letters) may be transferred to local addresses without a new payment of postage; but if forwarded to another city, the deficient postage at the regular letter rate of 3¢ an ounce will be collected on delivery.

Air mail (up to 8 ounces) may be forwarded by air without new postage.

Air parcel post is forwarded by air and charged forwarding postage.

Registered first-class mail may be forwarded without extra charge.

Special delivery mail may be forwarded under the same rules as ordinary mail; but special delivery will not be made at the final address if an attempt was made to deliver the article at the first address, unless another special delivery stamp is affixed when the mail is forwarded.

Several pieces of mail addressed to the same person cannot be assembled in one package and sent at a bulk rate.

But **"Audience"**, **"Advertiser's"**, or **"fan"** mail may, if it has not been opened, be remailed **in bulk** at the third- or fourth-class rate. If the letters are opened and then offered for remailing in bulk, or if remailed singly, they are subject to the first-class postage rate.

A forwarding address **on a window envelope** should be written at the side, not on the window.

Changes of address should be made **in ink,** not in pencil.

Insufficient Postage or Incorrect Address. If mail is returned to the sender because of insufficient postage or for better direction in the address before dispatch to another post office, the postage already placed thereon is still good.

Opened by Mistake. Mail opened by mistake upon misdelivery may be sealed with stickers and endorsed "Opened by Mistake", and signed or initialed by the person who opened it.

344

Such mail may be dropped in a mail box or handed to a postman.

Mail Forwarded to Government Employees. Mail of all classes may be forwarded without a new payment of postage to persons in the Government service (civil, military, or naval) whose change of address is caused by official orders. Such forwarded mail must be endorsed "Address Changed by Official Orders".

Forwarding Foreign Mail

Incoming foreign mail of all classes (except parcel post) may be forwarded to any point in the United States, or to another foreign country, without a new payment of postage.

Incoming foreign parcel post packages should have a new payment of postage when forwarded; or they may be forwarded "postage collect" to any point in the United States. They cannot be forwarded to another foreign country without new wrapping, a new customs declaration, and new postage.

Domestic mail that is to be **forwarded to a foreign address** should have new postage added to that thereon to equal the rate to the country addressed. If such mail is forwarded with postage due, the receivers will, in some foreign countries, be charged double the amount of the deficient postage.

MAIL, GENERAL

Recall of Mail. Mail collectors are not permitted to return mail that has been posted in a mail box. For the recall of mail, the sender must make a written application at the post office; and a similarly addressed envelope or wrapper must be presented for identification.

Mail cannot be recalled by telephone.

Mail may be recalled by telegraph—by the postmaster, at the sender's expense—if it is necessary to stop delivery.

Change of Address. A change of address should immediately be registered with the post office on a regular pink change-of-address card; or the information may be given in a letter addressed to the postmaster.

Neglect to notify the post office of a change of address causes annoyance to persons at the old address. The post office is reliable in the forwarding of mail.

The change-of-address cards may be obtained from any postman or from the post office. When filled out by the addressee (they must bear the addressee's signature) they may be dropped in a mail box for local delivery, without postage, or handed to a postman. If mailed from another city they must be enclosed in an envelope addressed to the postmaster, with full postage paid thereon.

(If a person has failed to register his change of address, a card should be obtained and mailed to him, to be filled out and returned.)

Mail will be forwarded for a period of two years on a change-of-address card. General delivery mail will be forwarded for a period of 30 days only, unless the request is renewed.

Sender May be Notified of Changes of Address. If the sender of ordinary third- and fourth-class mail desires to be notified of addressees' changes of address, he may have printed in the lower left corner of the address side:

Form 3547 Requested

(The sender's return address should appear in the upper left corner of the address side.)

This is a notice to the postmaster that if the addressee has moved and his new address is known, the sender wishes to be so notified on Form 3547, postage for which is guaranteed. In any case, the undeliverable matter will be returned to the sender, rated with return postage due.

Form 3547 applies only to ordinary business third- and fourth-class mail and cannot be used on first-class mail nor in the collection of accounts.

Certificates of Mailing. If proof is desired that certain ordinary mail was mailed, a sender's receipt may be had upon payment of 1¢ for each piece of mail posted. (This applies to both foreign and domestic mail.)

Mailing Lists. Postmasters may correct addresses on any **bona fide mailing lists,** but cannot compile lists.

The charge for correcting lists is 1¢ a name, with a minimum charge of 25¢ for lists bearing less than 25 names. At small post offices with no city delivery service, the charge is now the same.

Postmasters cannot give information regarding the persons on the lists.

Lists used for the purpose of collection cannot be corrected by postmasters.

Stamps for Collections. The current and many discontinued issues of postage stamps may be obtained at face value by applying to: The Philatelic Agent, Division of Stamps, Post Office Department, Washington, D.C.

No old or rare stamps are on sale. A list showing available stock will be sent upon application.

The Post Office Department does not purchase canceled postage stamps; nor can it furnish information regarding the collection value of rare stamps.

Stamps cannot be canceled in any color of ink but black. If a clear cancellation is desired, write PHILATELIC MAIL near the stamps.

Internal Revenue Stamps. May be purchased at any large post office, or at any post office located in a county seat.

Publications not Desired. When a subscription to a newspaper, magazine, or other periodical has expired, and the publication is no longer desired, the receiver should mark all copies REFUSED and return them to the post office.

"The Post Office Department does not determine questions regarding the liability of a subscriber for the subscription price of a publication."

Nonmetered Mail. Permits may be had for the mailing of first-, second-, third-, and fourth-class mail without stamps affixed but with printed indicia thereon, the postage being paid in money; provided the mailings are presented in accordance with certain regulations. Persons or companies who frequently send out large quantities of mail should take advantage of this method of prepaying postage. A charge of $10 is made for a permit to mail, indefinitely, **nonmetered** matter of any class without postage stamps but with **printed** indicia thereon. (**Bulk mailings** now cost an extra $10 a year.)

Precanceled Stamps. Permits may be had for the mailing of first-, second-, third-, and fourth-class mail with precanceled stamps affixed; or in Government stamped envelopes or on postal cards, with the stamps precanceled; provided the mailings are presented in accordance with certain regulations.

There is no charge for these permits (except $10 a year for bulk mailings).

The advantage of precanceled stamps is that they facilitate the handling of "quantity mail" in the post offices, thereby affording such mail a quick dispatch.

Metered Mail. Permits may be had for the privilege of using a meter device on any class of mail.

There is no charge for these permits (except $10 a year for bulk mailings).

Metered mail does not mean that the mail is sent at any reduced rates, the meter simply being used to save time and the work of affixing stamps.

Any color of ink that is a strong contrast to the paper may be used for meter indicia on any class of mail. Frequently the color of the like denomination of stamp is used.

Postage stamps may be affixed in addition to the meter indicia if it is necessary to pay extra postage on a piece of metered mail.

Franked Mail. "Franked" and "penalty" mail is sent without charge to the senders, who are in the service of the Government, or who have been granted the franking privilege by the Government.

Franked mail cannot be sent by air without a payment of the air mail rate.

Stamped Envelopes. Government stamped envelopes may be purchased in different sizes and with different denominations of stamps embossed thereon.

Stamped envelopes may be had in:

Two grades—standard, and extra quality, and

Three colors—white, blue, and amber.

Air mail stamped envelopes may be purchased at post offices.

Window stamped envelopes may also be had.

When stamped envelopes are ordered from the post office in lots of 500 or its multiple, of a single size, quality, and denomination, the Post Office Department will, upon request, print a return address on the envelopes.

Government stamped envelopes with return addresses to be printed thereon should be ordered **20 days in advance** of the date of contemplated use.

Unmailed **misaddressed or damaged** stamped envelopes may be redeemed.

Envelopes of Unusual Size or Shape. The Post Office Department does not sanction the use of envelopes, folders, cards, etc., of unusual size or irregular shape (as triangular or circular).

Mail matter of unusual shape or size cannot be tied into packages with other mail without damage to its edges. Also it does not fit into the stamp-canceling machines, and frequently the stamps on such mail must be canceled by hand.

Dark-Colored Cards or Envelopes. Dark-colored stationery is objectionable because of the difficulty of reading addresses thereon. White, or **very light tints** of yellow, pink, blue, or manila, should be used for all envelopes, cards, folders, and wrappers.

Excessive Printing on Address Side. Not less than 3½ inches of clear space should be left for the address, postage, postmark, etc., on the right end of mail matter that bears printing.

Unmailable Matter. Covers the following things:

Defective address.

Insufficient postage.

Overweight or oversize.

Game, unlawfully killed, or prohibited from mailing.

Meat and meat-food products, without certificate of inspection.

Plants and plant products not accompanied by required certificate. Certain plants are prohibited from shipment into certain states by quarantine order. (Before attempting to mail plants, consult a postal authority.)

Poisons; intoxicating liquors; and explosive, inflammable, or corrosive articles.

Live animals, except day-old chicks, bees, etc.

Foul-smelling articles.

Firearms capable of being concealed on the person. (with exceptions)

Matter tending to incite arson, murder, assassination, insurrection, or treason.

Indecent matter, written or other.

Defamatory, dunning, or threatening matter on post cards, or on the outside of any piece of mail.

Lottery, gift or endless-chain enterprises, or fraud matter.

347

Approximate Mail Time by Train between Principal Cities of the United States

Approximate Number of Days or Hours

d = days
h = hours
1 day = 24 hours
Note: The days or hours herein given are estimated traveling times for mails. Additional hours must be allowed for collection and delivery.

From: \ To:	Atlanta, Ga.	Boston, Mass.	Chicago, Ill.	Cleveland, Ohio	Denver, Colo.	Fort Worth, Tex.	Los Angeles, Calif.	Memphis, Tenn.	Mexico, D.F.	Miami, Fla.	Montreal, Canada	New Orleans, La.	New York City	Omaha, Nebr.	Salt Lake City, Utah	San Francisco, Calif.	Seattle, Wash.	St. Louis, Mo.	St. Paul and Minneapolis, Minn.
Atlanta, Ga.																			
Boston, Mass.	1½d−																		
Chicago, Ill.	1d−	1d																	
Cleveland, Ohio	1d+	15h	8h																
Denver, Colo.	2½d	2½d	1½d	2d															
Fort Worth, Tex.	1d+	2d+	1d+	1½d	1d−														
Los Angeles, Calif.	3d	3½d	2½d	3d	2d−	2d−													
Memphis, Tenn.	12h	2d−	12h	1d	1½d+	14h	2½d												
Mexico, D.F.	3d+	4d+	3d	3½d	3d	2d	2½d−	2½d											
Miami, Fla.	1d−	2d	2d−	2d−	3½d	2d+	4d	1½d	4d+										
Montreal, Canada	1½d	12h	1d	15h	2½d	2½d	4d−	2d	4½d	2d									
New Orleans, La.	14h	2d−	1d−	1½d−	1½d	15h	2½d−	9h	2d−	1½d−	2d								
New York City	1d−	5h	18h	13h	2½d−	2d	3½d	1½d	4d	1½d	8h	1½d							
Omaha, Nebr.	1½d	1½d+	12h	1d	1d	1d	2d	1d	3d	2½d	1½d	1½d+	1½d−						
Salt Lake City, Utah	2½d+	2½d	1½d	2d	1d	2d	1d	2d	4d	4d−	2½d	3d−	2½d	1d					
San Francisco, Calif.	3½d	3½d+	2½d−	3d	2d	2½d−	12h	3d	3d−	4½d	3½d	3d−	3½d	2d	1d				
Seattle, Wash.	3½d	3½d	2½d	3d	2d	3d+	2d	3d	4½d	4½d	3½d	4d−	3½d	2d+	1d+	1½d			
St. Louis, Mo.	1d−	1d+	7h	11h	2d	1d−	2½d−	8h	3d−	1½d	1½d	1d−	1d	1d−	2d	3d	3d		
St. Paul and Minneapolis, Minn.	1½d	1½d	10h	1d	1½d+	1½d	2½d	1d	3d+	2½d−	1½d	1½d−	1½d−	12h	1½d	2½d	2d	1d	
Washington, D.C.	15h	11h	21h	12h	3d−	1½d+	3½d	1d+	3½d+	1d	14h	1d+	5h	1½d	2½d	3½d	3½d	1d	1½d

AIR MAIL TIME

Approximate Air Mail Time between Principal Cities of the United States

Approximate Number of Hours

Note: The hours herein given are estimated flying times for mails. To calculate delivery times:
Add 1 hour for airport-to-post-office transmittal;
For eastbound mail, add the time-zone-difference hours between mailing point and destination.
(For air mail time from New York City to foreign places, see The World Almanac.)

ALASKA

Seattle to { Juneau 5 · Fairbanks 9 · Nome 15 }

HAWAII

San Francisco } to Honolulu 10
Los Angeles }

From: Atlanta, Ga.; Boston, Mass.; Buffalo, N.Y.; Chicago, Ill.; Cincinnati, Ohio; Cleveland, Ohio; Denver, Colo.; Detroit, Mich.; El Paso, Tex.; Fort Worth, Tex.; Indianapolis, Ind.; Jacksonville, Fla.; Kansas City, Mo.; Los Angeles, Calif.; Memphis, Tenn.; Miami, Fla.; Minneapolis, Minn.; Nashville, Tenn.; New Orleans, La.; New York, N.Y.; Omaha, Nebr.; Pittsburgh, Pa.; Portland, Oreg.; Salt Lake City, Utah; San Francisco, Calif.; Seattle, Wash.; St. Louis, Mo.; Washington, D.C.

To: Atlanta, Ga.; Boston, Mass.; Buffalo, N.Y.; Chicago, Ill.; Cincinnati, Ohio; Cleveland, Ohio; Denver, Colo.; Detroit, Mich.; El Paso, Tex.; Fort Worth, Tex.; Indianapolis, Ind.; Jacksonville, Fla.; Kansas City, Mo.; Los Angeles, Calif.; Memphis, Tenn.; Miami, Fla.; Minneapolis, Minn.; Nashville, Tenn.; New Orleans, La.; New York, N.Y.; Omaha, Nebr.; Pittsburgh, Pa.; Portland, Oreg.; Salt Lake City, Utah; San Francisco, Calif.; Seattle, Wash.; St. Louis, Mo.

Destination (To)	Approximate hours (by origin, in table order)
Atlanta, Ga.	7+, 13½, 8½, 10, 6½, 4, 2—, 8—, 15¼, 5—, 5—, 8—, 1¾, 3—, 6½, 10, 6+, 18½, 16, 20, 18, 6+, 4¾
Boston, Mass.	5, 13, 15, 10, 11½, 6½, 8, 20½, 8½, 10½, 3¾, 19½, 16½, 20½, 19, 8½, 3+
Buffalo, N.Y.	1½, 11½, 1½, 16½, 11½, 6, 8½, 7+, 8, 11, 6, 3¼, 15½, 13—, 17, 15+, 5, 2¼
Chicago, Ill.	2, 5½, 2—, 7, 10, 2+, 6+, 4¼, 2½, 3¾, 12½, 8¼, 13, 15+, 12, 4½, 4¾
Cincinnati, Ohio	3¾, 7¼, 5, 4, 4½, 4, 4¼, 4, 15, 15½, 3¼, 2½
Cleveland, Ohio	3+, 7+, 6½, 6½, 6½, 9¾, 5½, 9—, 9+, 2½, 4¼, 14—, 11, 15—, 14¼, 5, 2½
Denver, Colo.	9¾, 15½, 5+, 7¼, 13½, 18½, 11, 11½, 14, 10½, 2¾, 9, 8½, 3, 7¼, 9¾, 9+, 10½
Detroit, Mich.	4½, 8, 6—, 1—, 6½, 10½, 4½, 5¾, 7, 3+, 6, 2—, 14½, 12+, 16, 14, 4, 3¾
El Paso, Tex.	9¼, 13¾, 6½, 4½, 6+, 16½, 14¼, 7½, 9, 12¾, 10, 12, 12, 8, 13½, 8¼, 11+
Fort Worth, Tex.	8, 9, 4¾, 8, 3, 11+, 10+, 16, 13, 12, 7+, 10¾, 16, 13, 12, 17¾, 5, 8—
Indianapolis, Ind.	6+, 3, 13, 4½, 9+, 4+, 7+, 5, 6+, 14—, 12, 15+, 13½, 1½, 3¾
Jacksonville, Fla.	2½, 10¼, 4, 5¾, 6, 13—, 6+, 20½, 19½, 23½, 20, 9—, 4½
Kansas City, Mo.	13, 4, 5½, 6+, 8—, 1+, 14½, 8, 11¾, 15½, 1½, 7
Los Angeles, Calif.	21¼, 13, 6+, 14½, 17+, 10¼, 15½, 4—, 2, 7¼, 11, 15¾
Memphis, Tenn.	10, 7½, 1½, 2¼, 6½, 11+, 7+, 13, 17, 17+, 1¾, 5
Miami, Fla.	7+, 8½, 8½, 13, 15, 8½, 23, 22, 26+, 22½, 11½, 7
Minneapolis, Minn.	6¾, 7+, 2½, 7, 10½, 12, 17, 10, 3¾, 7½
Nashville, Tenn.	4+, 5+, 8, 6, 9, 14, 16+, 15½, 4½, 4—
New Orleans, La.	9—, 14, 10, 20, 19½, 18, 19½, 4½, 7
New York, N.Y.	7½, 2, 17½, 13½, 17+, 17, 7—, 7
Omaha, Nebr.	11, 6½, 7½, 9¾, 6—, 10¼
Pittsburgh, Pa.	15½, 4¾, 1+, 10¼, 16, 12, 15¾
Portland, Oreg.	1, 16½, 1+, 17½, 13½
Salt Lake City, Utah	5½, 12+, 13½, 17+, 4
San Francisco, Calif.	5+, 13½, 17+
Seattle, Wash.	15½, 15+, 17+
St. Louis, Mo.	—

The postal laws provide severe penalties for mailing articles in several of the above classes.

Postal Savings. Is a Government savings system in which the deposits are guaranteed.

Deposits are accepted only from individuals, not from corporations, associations, societies, firms, or partnerships.

Limit of account—$2,500. Interest at the rate of 2% for each full year.

Any person above 10 years of age may make deposits at any post office authorized to accept postal savings deposits.

"The account of a married person is free from any control or interference by the husband or wife."

Full information regarding Postal Savings may be obtained from any post office.

INTERNATIONAL MAIL

Pieces of mail for foreign countries are classified in general as

Letters, and Letter Packages	Samples of Merchandise
Post Cards	Eight-Ounce Merchandise Packages
Commercial Papers	Small Packets
Printed Matter	Parcel Post

Letters and Post Cards to Foreign Countries.

Rates

To all countries of North, Central, and South America (except British Honduras, and the Guianas); and to Cuba, Haiti, Dominican Rep., Philippines, and Spain and its possessions } Letters—3¢ an ounce
Post cards—2¢ each

To all other foreign destinations, including British Honduras and the Guianas } Letters—5¢ for first ounce and 3¢ for each additional ounce
Post cards—3¢ each

Weight limit: 4 pounds 6 ounces (except to Canada, where it is 60 pounds).

Maximum letter dimensions to all foreign destinations:
Length, breadth, and thickness combined—36 inches.
Greatest length—24 inches.
Rolls—length (maximum 32 inches) plus twice diameter is limited to 40 inches.
Indivisible rolls to 3¢-letter countries may be: 40″ long + (2 × diameter) = 48″.
Maximum post card dimensions: 6″ × 4¼″.
Minimum dimensions: It is recommended that any article in the foreign mails measure not less than 4″ × 2¾″.

Letter Packages. Articles liable to customs duty may be forwarded in letters or packages prepaid at the letter rate of postage, provided the importation of such articles in the form of letters is permitted by the country of destination. (Some countries have expressed an unwillingness to accept letter packages.)

An invoice or a customs declaration form must be enclosed in the letter. A green customs label must be affixed to each letter package, showing that the article is to be submitted to customs examination.

Commercial Papers. Unsealed—no customs tag or declaration necessary. Commercial papers are:

"All papers and all documents written or drawn, in whole or in part, which do not have the character of actual personal correspondence, such as old opened letters and old post cards (even though such articles bear the canceled postage stamps used for their original dispatch) which have already reached their original destination, as well as copies thereof:

papers of legal procedure; documents of all kinds drawn up by ministerial officers; waybills or bills of lading; invoices; certain documents of insurance companies; copies of or extracts from documents under private signature on stamped or unstamped paper; scores or sheets of music in manuscript; manuscripts of works or newspapers sent singly; original and corrected exercises of students with the exclusion of all indications not relating directly to the execution of the work."

Rate to all foreign destinations:
$1\frac{1}{2}¢$ for each 2 ounces, with a minimum charge of 5¢.
Weight limit: 4 pounds 6 ounces.
Maximum dimensions: same as for Letters, above.

Wrapping: same as for Printed Matter, below.

Write COMMERCIAL PAPERS on the wrapper.

Printed Matter. Unsealed—no customs tag or declaration necessary. The following are considered as printed matter:

"Newspapers and periodicals, books, pamphlets, sheets of music (except perforated paper rolls for automatic musical instruments), visiting cards, address cards, printing proofs with or without the relative manuscript, engravings, photographs, and albums containing photographs, pictures, drawings, plans, maps, cut-out patterns, catalogues, prospectuses, advertisements, and printed, engraved, lithographed, or autographed notices of various kinds, and, in general, all impressions or copies obtained upon paper, or material assimilable to paper, parchment, or cardboard, by means of printing, engraving, lithography, autography, or any other easily recognized mechanical process, with the exception of the copying press, stamps with movable or immovable type, and the typewriter. Motion-picture films and phonograph records are not acceptable for transmission under the classification of prints."

Reproductions of manuscript or typewritten originals, when obtained by a mechanical process, may be mailed as "Printed Matter" if mailed at a post office window in lots of not less than 20 pieces, containing identical copies.

Rate to all foreign destinations: $1\frac{1}{2}¢$ for each 2 ounces.
Book rate: 5¢ lb., to Mexico; Cuba; P.I.; and most of Central and South America.
Weight limit to most foreign destinations: 6 pounds 9 ounces; to some countries, 22 pounds. For single volumes of books: from 11 to 22 pounds.
Maximum and minimum dimensions: same as for Letters, above.

Wrapping: "Prints must be placed either under wrapper, in rolls, between boards, in a case open at both ends, or in an unsealed envelope, or be wrapped with a string which is easily untied; or simply folded. In those instances when printed matter is enclosed in unsealed envelopes, the latter must, if need be, be provided with easily removable fasteners offering no danger, or be fastened with a string which is easily untied. Care should be exercised in all instances to see that articles of printed matter are not prepared in such a manner as to allow other articles to slip into them."

Write PRINTED MATTER on the wrapper.

Samples of Merchandise. Unsealed—no customs tag or declaration necessary.

Rate to all foreign destinations:
$1\frac{1}{2}¢$ for each 2 ounces, with a minimum charge of 3¢.
Weight limit: 18 ounces.
Maximum dimensions: same as for Letters, above.

Wrapping: Samples must be placed in bags, boxes, or removable envelopes. Packing must be in accordance with certain regulations for various articles.

Write SAMPLE—NO COMMERCIAL VALUE on the wrapper.

Eight-Ounce Merchandise Packages. Unsealed—no customs tag or declaration necessary.

351

Eight-ounce merchandise packages may be sent only to the countries to which the 3¢ letter rate applies.

Rate to the above countries: 2¢ for each 2 ounces.
But when contents are seeds, scions, plants, cuttings, bulbs, or roots, the rate is 1½¢ for each 2 ounces.

Wrapping: These packages are not regarded as parcel post, hence need not have the customs declarations attached, and must not be sealed. (Packages to Canada may be sealed if marked with a printed label: "This package may be opened for postal inspection if necessary." C.O.D. packages to Mexico may be sealed.)

Write 8-OUNCE MERCHANDISE PACKAGE on the wrapper.

Small Packets. Unsealed—green label and paper form of customs declaration necessary.

Mailable only to certain foreign countries. Some countries have expressed an unwillingness to accept small packets.

Small packets may contain articles liable to customs duty, but they **may not contain** coins, bank notes, paper money, or any values payable to the bearer; platinum, gold, or silver; precious stones, jewelry, or other precious articles. Invoices may be enclosed.

Rate: 3¢ for each 2 ounces, with a minimum charge of 15¢.
Weight limit: 2 pounds 3 ounces.
Maximum dimensions: same as for Letters, above.

Wrapping: In general, subject to the provisions applicable to Samples of Merchandise, above, with respect to preparation and packing. A green customs label must be on each packet. A paper form of customs declaration must be enclosed in the package.

Write SMALL PACKET on the wrapper.

Letter Attached to Sample of Merchandise or Printed Matter. A letter, prepaid at the letter rate, may be attached to an unsealed container with samples of merchandise or printed matter therein, prepaid at the appropriate rate, for dispatch to certain countries. Information regarding the countries allowing such "combination packages" may be had at the post office.

Commercial Papers, Samples, and Printed Matter Grouped. Commercial papers, samples of merchandise, and printed matter may be grouped in one package, provided:

1. That each article taken singly does not exceed the limits applicable to it in regard to weight and dimensions;
2. That the total weight does not exceed 4 pounds 6 ounces;
3. That the postage paid is at least the minimum charge for commercial papers, if the article contains commercial papers; or the minimum charge for samples, if it is composed of printed matter and samples.

Grouping of Mail in One Package. Only articles subject to the same rate of postage may be grouped in one package. If articles requiring different rates are detected, the entire package will be charged for at the highest rate of postage represented therein.

Packages of printed matter from or to foreign countries, having articles of merchandise concealed therein, are subject to the letter rate, and postage due is collected thereon.

Letters Within Letters, or Packages Within Packages. Separately addressed letters within letters, or packages within packages, are prohibited, unless such

352

enclosed letters or packages are for members of the original addressee's household, or for persons residing at his address.

Registered Mail—Foreign. Regular mail may be registered to practically all foreign destinations. Parcel post packages may be registered only to certain countries. Foreign air mail may be registered.

> **Fees** for each piece of regular mail:
>   25¢ in addition to postage
>   5¢ for return receipt; 10¢ for return receipt if requested after mailing.
> **Restricted delivery** (by addressee in U.S., to himself or his order): 20¢.

All foreign mail to be registered should be in heavy envelopes or wrappers. Registered letters must not bear any trace of having been opened and resealed before mailing.

Regular mail articles containing the following valuables must be registered: coins, bank notes, paper money, or any values payable to the bearer; platinum; gold or silver (under certain restrictions) manufactured or unmanufactured; precious stones, jewelry, or other precious articles.

Certain countries prohibit the following incoming articles whether registered or not: money in cash, bank notes, or values payable to the bearer.

If the mail is especially valuable, inquiry should be made about indemnity in case of loss. Indemnity varies from $2 to $25 in the different countries.

Special Delivery—Foreign. Special delivery service may be had in a considerable number of the countries of the world. But since some countries, such as Spain, U.S.S.R., etc., have not the service as yet, it is well to inquire at the post office before marking a letter for foreign special delivery.

> **Fee:** 20¢ in addition to the regular postage. (Domestic fees apply to Canada.)

Two United States special delivery stamps may be used, or ordinary stamps in the amount of 20¢. Below the stamps write boldly in red ink (or obtain a label from the post office):

EXPRÈS
SPECIAL DELIVERY

In Canada, only articles prepaid at the letter rate may be sent special delivery. In other countries, practically all pieces of mail **except parcel post packages** may be sent special delivery.

If insufficient postage is affixed, mail marked for foreign special delivery will be sent by ordinary mail; unless, without seriously delaying its dispatch, the article can be returned to the sender for collection of the deficiency.

General Delivery—Foreign. General delivery for foreign post offices should be marked at the left of the address:

POSTE RESTANTE

This French marking is universally accepted for general delivery, although the English words GENERAL DELIVERY may also be used. The number of days that foreign general delivery mail is held in foreign post offices varies according to the regulations of the different countries.

Parcel Post—Foreign.

Parcel post packages may be sent to practically every country in the world. **But before preparing a parcel for foreign delivery, consult a postal authority for regulations of the country of destination.**

Rates: 14¢ a pound to all countries. To many countries there is an additional "transit charge", often amounting to three or four times the parcel post charge.

Weight limits vary with the different countries, from 11 pounds in some countries to 44 pounds in others. To certain cities in China and to Panama, the limit is 50 pounds.

Maximum dimensions: In general, the greatest length is $3\frac{1}{2}$ feet; and greatest length and girth combined, 6 feet. Variations of these dimensions apply to certain countries.

Extra-heavy packing is necessary on foreign parcels to withstand the numerous handlings and risks of concussion to which parcels for foreign destinations are unavoidably subjected. Packages should be packed in canvas or similar material; heavy wrapping paper, or waterproof paper, lined with linen gauze; double-faced corrugated cardboard boxes; solid fiber boxes or cases; or strapped wooden boxes made of material at least a half inch thick. **Ordinary pasteboard containers are wholly inadequate.**

A fragile or easily breakable article, as of china, crockery, or glass, should be packed in a strong (preferably wooden) box and cushioned with a liberal supply of excelsior, crushed paper, wood wool, or cotton, etc., between the article and the top, bottom, and sides of the box.

Liquids and substances which easily liquefy must be packed in **two receptacles.** Between the first (bottle, flask, etc.) and the second (box of metal, strong wood, strong corrugated cardboard, strong fiberboard, or receptacle of equal strength) there must be left a space to be filled with sawdust, bran, or other absorbent material in sufficient quantity to absorb all the liquid in case of breakage.

The **sealing** of parcel post packages (with wax, lead seals, or other material) is compulsory to some countries, while to others it is optional with the sender. There are a few countries which prohibit the sealing of parcel post packages.

Christmas seals or stamps must not be affixed to the address side of a foreign parcel. They may, however, be affixed to the back of the article.

All addresses should be typewritten, or written in ink; pencil addresses are not permitted. (See also Foreign Addresses, p. 306.) The receiver's address and the sender's return address should appear on the face of the package; and they should also be written on a slip of paper enclosed in the package. Nothing should be written on the back of the package.

Alternative disposition must be indicated by the sender; that is, if the parcel is undeliverable as originally addressed, it is to be either (1) tendered for delivery at a second address in the country of destination, (2) treated as abandoned, or (3) returned to the sender.

If a package is returned, it will be at the sender's expense.

Foreign parcel post mail cannot be addressed **via any certain ship.**

All foreign parcel post packages must be **mailed at post offices,** not in mail boxes.

Customs declaration tags, in the required number, and a **yellow parcel post sticker** are necessary on every parcel. In addition, special customs declarations are required to some countries; and also to some countries a dispatch note is required. **Consular invoices** are necessary in some foreign parcels. **Certificates of origin** must accompany parcel post packages addressed to certain foreign countries.

Special Handling on Foreign Parcel Post. If it is desired that foreign parcel post packages receive the same dispatch as letter mails in the United States, special handling may be had thereon to the port of dispatch, where they will be forwarded on ships carrying letter mails, if practicable.

354

Write SPECIAL HANDLING on the wrapper. Fees are the same as domestic special handling fees.

Registered and Insured Packages—Foreign. Parcel post packages may be registered or insured to a number of foreign countries. If the package is valuable, inquiry should be made regarding the indemnity that will be paid in case of loss, rifling, or damage. Indemnity varies greatly with the different countries.

The registration or insurance, as the case may be, of parcels containing coin, bullion, jewelry, or any other precious articles is obligatory.

Insurance fees: from 20¢ to $1. (To Canada, same as domestic insurance fees.)
Registration fees: 25¢ to 40¢. Return receipts: 5¢; after mailing, 10¢.

C.O.D. Parcels—Foreign. Registered C.O.D. parcels (sealed) may be sent to Mexico, which service includes printed matter, eight-ounce merchandise packages, and small packets. Information may be obtained from the post office.

The maximum amount to be collected is $100. Fees range from 30¢ to 60¢.

Money Orders—Foreign. Money orders payable in almost any country in the world are obtainable at all of the larger post offices and at many of the smaller ones. Such orders are payable at foreign post offices in foreign currency.

Fees in general are:
From 10¢ for each $10 or less, up to $1 for $100.
(Fees to some countries are the same as domestic money order fees.)

Certificates of Mailing—Foreign. If proof is desired that certain ordinary mail, air mail, or parcel post, was mailed—or for additional evidence of the mailing of registered or insured articles—a sender's receipt may be had, if requested at the time of mailing. Fee: 1¢ for each piece of mail posted.

Air Mail—Foreign. There are now three different rate classes for foreign air mail: (1) letter class; (2) papers, prints, and samples; (3) air parcel post. Each piece of mail should be prepared exactly as it is for surface transportation.

All foreign air mail postage **must be fully prepaid.**

INTERNATIONAL AIR MAIL RATES
(For Letters, Letter Packages, and Post Cards) *
Weight limit: 4 pounds 6 ounces, to most countries.

North and South America per ½ oz.		Europe, Asia, and Africa per ½ oz.	
To: Cuba	8¢	To: All of Europe and Azores	15¢
West Indies and Bermuda	10	Turkey	15
Central America	10	Australia and Philippines	25
South America	10	Asia	25
		Africa { North Africa	15
		{ South Africa	25

To **Canada and Mexico**, the rate is 6¢ an ounce for letter-class air mail, from any point in the United States or its possessions. Post cards by air: 4¢ each.

World Air Letter (a single, folding sheet, sold at post offices). No enclosures permitted; and it cannot be registered. Rate to all countries...10¢.

*Commercial papers, printed matter, samples of merchandise, small packets, and 8-ounce merchandise packages,** have a special 2-ounce air rate, which is slightly less than ½ the 4-ounce air parcel post rate. (For sample air parcel post rates, see next page.)

Marking Foreign Air Mail. It is desirable that all international letter-class air mail be in distinctive air mail envelopes.

All international air mail should bear a blue PAR AVION sticker below the

stamps. (These stickers are free at post offices.) In the absence of a sticker, the words should be written boldly in ink below the stamps. (pron. pår á′vyôn′)

PAR AVION
By Air Mail

International Air Parcel Post. Air parcel post service is in effect to most countries of the world. The transportation is by air to the countries of destination, and then by surface transportation in the respective countries (with a few exceptions).

Size limitations, packing, customs declarations, and other regulations governing international surface parcel post, apply, in general, to air parcels.

EXAMPLES OF INTERNATIONAL AIR PARCEL POST RATES
Weight limits: In general, 11, 22, or 44 pounds, according to regulations of various countries.

Country	1st 4 oz.	Ea. add. 4 oz.	Country	1st 4 oz.	Ea. add. 4 oz.
EUROPE			**MEXICO & ISLANDS**		
Belgium	.98¢	43¢	Bermuda	.76¢	13¢
France	$1.22	44	Cuba	.80	15
Great Britain	1.00	41	Dom. Republic	.86	22
Italy	1.08	50	Haiti	.72	21
Sweden	.85	49	Mexico	.64	18
AFRICA			**CENTRAL AMERICA**		
Belgian Congo	$1.38	79¢	Costa Rica	.79¢	29¢
Egypt	1.35	64	Guatemala	$1.01	25
Gold Coast	1.18	64	Honduras, Rep.	.78	28
Tunisia	1.11	54	Nicaragua	.80	29
U. So. Africa	1.31	94			
FAR EAST			**SOUTH AMERICA**		
Australia	$1.62	$1.27	Argentina	$1.51	76¢
India	1.70	96	Brazil	1.48	64
Japan	1.27	91	Chile	1.31	56
Philippines	1.81	1.26	Colombia	1.21	40
Thailand (Siam)	2.29	1.50	Uruguay	1.26	76
			Venezuela	1.27	36

Addressing Mail via Special Ships. It is the practice of the Post Office Department to dispatch mails on ships of United States and foreign registry.

Senders desiring to have their mail (letters, post cards, and daily papers) forwarded via certain ships to which mails have not been assigned should plainly indicate the name of the ship diagonally across the face of each piece of mail between the address and the return address, as follows:

Per SS. BRITANNIA   via   New York (or port of departure)

Letters Mailed at Ship's Side. Supplementary mail is that posted after the mails have been closed at the post office of the port from which the vessel sails, and must be handed to a post office representative at the pier or taken to a designated post office. Such mail must be prepaid with double the usual postage.

Closing Time for Foreign Mails. The closing hours for mails to be dispatched on ships are printed each day in seaport newspapers, under the shipping and mails sections.

The hours in the papers are the closing hours at the post office of dispatch. Branch post offices usually close such mails one hour before the post office of dispatch. Therefore, mail for a certain ship should be in a branch post office at least **one hour before the closing hour in the paper.**

If such mail is to be deposited in a mail box in the business district, it should be in the box **at least three hours before the closing hour in the paper.**

356

Registered mail, parcel post, and ordinary printed mail matter is closed from one to two hours earlier than other mail; therefore, such mail must be in branch post offices from **two to four hours** before the closing hour in the paper.

Preparation for Mailing. All regular mail articles for foreign countries should be securely wrapped in heavy paper or enclosed in heavy envelopes, to withstand the many transfers and handlings and the friction of the mail bags in transit to destination.

Do not use sealing wax in sealing letters. Not only does it break off, but letters so sealed often stick together, and addresses are destroyed when the envelopes are pulled apart.

Commercial papers, printed matter, samples of merchandise, eight-ounce merchandise packages, and small packets should be conspicuously marked to indicate the class of mail to which they belong.

Consult a postal authority before preparing any package or questionable piece of mail for foreign delivery.

Foreign Addresses. (See Addresses, p. 306.)

Customs Declarations and Duties. Customs tags, labels, and declaration forms are obtainable at post offices.

Customs duties cannot be prepaid; they must be collected from the addressees when the articles are delivered. (An exception is that customs duties may be prepaid on advertising matter for Australia, Canada, Newfoundland, Labrador, and the Union of South Africa; and on merchandise for the U.S.S.R.)

Although an article may be marked GIFT, with the nature of the article and the valuation written below, it is liable to customs inspection and duty in the country of destination.

Prepayment of Foreign Mail. Mail to all foreign destinations should be fully prepaid. The sender should never guess at the postage applicable to articles for foreign countries.

In certain foreign countries, if there is postage due when mail arrives, the addressee is charged **double the amount of the deficient postage.** Therefore, the importance of fully prepaying foreign mail.

Reply Coupons. As a means of supplying foreign correspondents with reply postage, reply coupons may be purchased (price 11¢ each) and sent to foreign countries. A reply coupon entitles a correspondent abroad to receive return postage for an ordinary letter, without charge, upon presentation of the coupon at his post office. Most countries will accept several coupons for an **air mail reply.**

Reply Cards—Foreign. Each half of a double or reply post card must be fully prepaid if sent into a foreign country. Such post cards must have printed on the first part the French heading: "Carte postale avec réponse payée" (post card with reply paid); and on the second part, "Carte postale réponse" (reply post card). The card must be folded, but not closed in any manner.

Business reply cards or envelopes should not be sent into foreign countries; they cannot be returned without a prepayment of postage.

Return of Unclaimed Foreign Mail. **A return address** should be on every piece of foreign mail, preferably on the address side.

Undeliverable regular mail articles which have been fully prepaid to foreign destinations are returned to the senders without charge, except eight-ounce merchandise packages and periodicals mailed by publishers or registered news agents, on which there is a return charge.

An undeliverable parcel post package returned to the United States, upon which the return postage has not been prepaid, is subject on delivery to the sender to a postage charge equal to the amount originally prepaid thereon; and

357

on undelivered parcels returned from certain countries, the senders must pay, in addition to the above postage charge, storage, customs clearance, and other postal charges.

Samples and mail without value will not be returned; unless a sender, by a notation on an article, requests its return and guarantees payment of return postage.

MAIL DAYS TO FOREIGN COUNTRIES AND U.S. POSSESSIONS

The days listed in the following table are approximated from the Official Postal Guide, with very little time figured for mail connections at various points. Sailings to some distant countries or isolated islands are "four times a month", "every two weeks", or "irregular". Therefore, several days may elapse in some ports while mail is waiting for a ship.

The days given apply to **letter mails only.** Parcel post mails usually take several days longer; and to some distant or isolated countries, several weeks longer.

Christmas foreign mail should be dispatched early; it should be posted in sufficient time to arrive at the Atlantic or Pacific seaports at least one day before the approximate dates given in the table below. Parcel post packages should be mailed at least ten days before the dates given in order to receive the earliest possible dispatch, because of customs formalities that retard delivery.

APPROXIMATE NUMBER OF LETTER MAIL DAYS

To:	Mails dispatched from:				Christmas mail dates (approximate)*
	New York	San Francisco	Seattle	New Orleans	
Abyssinia (See Ethiopia)					
Aden, Arabia..................	18	.....	.....	.....	Nov. 27
Afghanistan..................	26				
Africa (See individual countries)					
Alaska					
Juneau or Skagway.........	.....	.....	4	.....	Oct. 1†
Fairbanks..................	.....	.....	6		
Albania......................	10				
Algeria......................	10				
Anglo-Egyptian Sudan.........	16				
Angola......................	29				
Arabia......................	18				
Argentina....................	18	.....	.....	.....	Nov. 24
Ascension....................	22				
Australia....................	.....	19–24	24	.....	Nov. 18
Austria (now in Germany).....	7–9	.....	.....	.....	Dec. 10
Azores......................	8–15	.....	.....	.....	Nov. 26
Bahamas....................	3 (From Miami, 1 day)		.....	.....	Dec. 15
Balearic Islands..............	10				
Barbados....................	10	.....	.....	.....	Dec. 10
Bechuanaland................	33				
Belgian Congo...............	34				
Belgium.....................	6–9	.....	.....	.....	Dec. 14
Bermuda....................	2	.....	.....	.....	Dec. 17
Bolivia......................	18	20	.....	19	Nov. 28‡
Borneo (See North Borneo, Brunei, and Sarawak)........					
Brazil.......................	13–15	.....	.....	.....	Dec. 2
British Cameroons............	26				

APPROXIMATE NUMBER OF LETTER MAIL DAYS—contd.

To:	Mails dispatched from:				Christmas mail dates (approximate)*
	New York	San Francisco	Seattle	New Orleans	
British Guiana................	12–17	.....	.....	.....	Dec. 2
British Honduras..............	6	.....	.....	3	
British Somaliland.............	20				
British Togoland..............	27				
British West Indies............	6–16				
Brunei.......................	.....	34	34		
Bulgaria......................	11	.....	.....	.....	Dec. 7
Burma........................	24				
Cameroons (See British and French Cameroons)					
Canal Zone...................	5–9	8–9	.....	5–7	Dec. 14‡
Canary Islands................	13–16				
Cape Verde Islands............	15–22	.....	.....	.....	Nov. 12
Caroline Islands...............	.....	30	30		Nov. 18
Celebes.......................	.....	32	32	.....	Nov. 18
Ceylon.......................	24	.....	.....	.....	Nov. 23
Chile.........................	14–20	17–22	.....	16–19	Nov. 28‡
China........................	.....	17–24	15–17	.....	Nov. 28
Chosen (Korea)...............	.....	18	16		
Colombia.....................	7–12	11	.....	.....	Dec. 6
Corsica.......................	9				
Costa Rica....................	9	12	.....	7	Dec. 8‡
Crete.........................	13				
Cuba.........................	3 (From Miami, 12 to 24 hours)			2	Dec. 18‡
Cyprus.......................	15	.....	.....	.....	Nov. 23
Czecho-Slovakia...............	7–9	.....	.....	.....	Dec. 10
Dahomey.....................	25				
Denmark......................	6–9	.....	.....	.....	Dec. 10
Dominican Republic...........	6–8	.....	.....	.....	Dec. 13
Dutch East Indies (Indonesia)..	.....	26–36	24–32	.....	Nov. 18
Dutch Guiana (Surinam).......	12–19	.....	.....	.....	Nov. 28
Dutch West Indies.............	7–13				
Ecuador......................	9–13	12–15	.....	9	Dec. 2‡
Egypt........................	10–16	.....	.....	.....	Dec. 2
El Salvador...................	9	9	.....	5	Dec. 10‡
England......................	5–8	.....	.....	.....	Dec. 14
Eritrea.......................	16–21				
Estonia.......................	10	.....	.....	.....	Dec. 8
Ethiopia (Abyssinia)...........	17				
Falkland Islands...............	22				
Fanning Island	.....	12 (transit time, but service from Honolulu onward twice every 3 months)			
Faroe Islands (Faeroes)........	12				
Fed. Malay States (Malaya)....	.....	26–30	26–30	.....	Nov. 18
Fernando Po..................	30				
Fiji Islands...................	.....	14	16		
Finland.......................	10–12	.....	.....	.....	Dec. 7
Formosa (Taiwan)..............	.....	20	17		
France.......................	5–8	.....	.....	.....	Dec. 14
French Cameroons.............	27				
French Equatorial Africa (French Congo)..............	28–36				
French Guiana................	14–20	.....	.....	.....	Nov. 28
French Guinea................	21				
French India..................	24				
French Indo-China............	.....	22–30	20–26		
French Oceania................	.....	10–12			
French Somaliland.............	18				
French Sudan.................	18				
French Togoland..............	26				
Friendly Islands (See Tonga Islands)					

POSTAL INFORMATION

APPROXIMATE NUMBER OF LETTER MAIL DAYS—contd.

To:	Mails dispatched from:				Christmas mail dates (approximate)*
	New York	San Francisco	Seattle	New Orleans	
Gambia	19				
Germany	6–9	.....	.....	.....	Dec. 14
Gibraltar	6–11	.....	.....	.....	Dec. 9
Gilbert and Ellice Islands	.....	25			
Gold Coast Colony	25				
Great Britain	5–8	.....	.....	.....	Dec. 14
Greece	9–13	.....	.....	.....	Dec. 7
Greenland	25				
Grenada (See Windward Islands)					
Guadeloupe	9	.....	.....	.....	Dec 10
Guam	.....	20	22		
Guatemala	7	8	.....	3	Dec. 12‡
Guiana (See British, French, and Dutch Guiana [Surinam])					
Guinea, Africa (See French, Portuguese, and Spanish Guinea)					
Haiti	4–6	.....	.....	.....	Dec. 15
Hawaiian Islands	.....	6–8	.....	.....	Dec. 12
Hejaz, Nejd, and Dependencies (See Saudi Arabia)					
Holland (See Netherlands)					
Honduras	7	.....	.....	4	Dec. 12‡
Hong Kong Colony	.....	20–28	18–24	.....	Nov. 26
Hungary	7–9	.....	.....	.....	Dec. 10
Iceland	16				
India, and Pakistan	21–24	.....	.....	.....	Nov. 23
Indo-China, French	.....	22–30	20–26		
Iran (Persia)	18–28	.....	.....	.....	Nov 23
Iraq (Mesopotamia)					
Letters and post cards	13–16				
Other mail	30				
Ireland (Eire)	6–9	.....	.....	... .	Dec. 14
Ireland, Northern	6–9	.....	.....	.....	Dec. 14
Italian Somaliland	25				
Italy	7–11	.....	.....	.....	Dec. 14
Ivory Coast	24				
Jamaica	5–6	.....	.....	4	Dec. 15‡
Japan	.....	14–20	11–14	.....	Dec. 3
Java	.....	29	29	.....	Nov. 18
Jugoslavia (See Yugoslavia)					
Kenya	25	.....	.....	.....	Nov. 12
Korea (See Chosen)					
Labrador	8				
Latvia	10	.....	.....	.....	Dec. 10
Lebanon	15–20	.....	.....	.....	Dec. 1
Leeward Islands	6–7	.....	.....	.....	Dec. 10
Liberia	23	.....	.....	.....	Nov. 20
Libya	10–13				
Liechtenstein	6–9				
Lithuania	9	.....	.....	.....	Dec. 10
Luxemburg	6–9	.....	.....	.....	Dec. 14
Macao	.....	24	21		
Madagascar	35				
Madeira Islands	13	.....	.....	.....	Dec. 6
Majorca	10				
Malay States	.....	26–30	26–30	.....	Nov. 18
Malta	11	.....	.....	.....	Dec. 8
Martinique	10	.....	.....	.....	Dec. 10
Mauritania	24				
Mauritius	36				
Mesopotamia (See Iraq)					
Monaco	7				

APPROXIMATE NUMBER OF LETTER MAIL DAYS—contd.

| To: | Mails dispatched from: | | | | Christmas mail dates (approximate)* |
	New York	San Francisco	Seattle	New Orleans	
Morocco......................	8–13				
Mozambique.................	32	.....	.....	.....	Nov. 17
Nauru Island.................	.....	25			
Netherlands..................	6–9	.....	.....	.....	Dec. 14
New Caledonia and Dependencies........................	.....	26			
Newfoundland................	3–5	.....	.....	.....	Dec. 15
New Guinea..................	.....	26–33			
New Hebrides................	.....	36			
New Zealand.................	.....	16–19	19	.....	Nov. 20
Nicaragua...................	8–12	11	.....	5	{ Dec. 4‡, ‖ { Dec. 12‡, ¶
Niger.......................	28				
Nigeria.....................	26				
North Borneo................	.....	34	34		
Northern Ireland............	6–9	.....	.....	.....	Dec. 14
Norway.....................	7–10	.....	.....	.....	Dec. 10
Nova Scotia (Halifax)........	2				
Nyasaland...................	33				
Palestine....................	12–19	.....	.....	.....	Dec. 1
Panama.....................	5–9	8–9	.....	5–7	Dec. 14‡
Papua.......................	.....	26–33			
Paraguay....................	21	.....	.....	.....	Nov. 24
Pemba......................	30				
Persia (See Iran)					
Peru........................	12–14	12–15	.....	11–16	Dec. 1‡
Philippines..................	.....	21–26	21–26	.....	Nov. 23
Poland......................	7–9	.....	.....	.....	Dec. 10
Port Said, Suez Canal........	10–16	.....	.....	.....	Dec. 2
Portugal....................	7–10	.....	.....	.....	Dec. 8
Portuguese East Africa.......	32	.....	.....	.....	Nov. 17
Portuguese Guinea...........	20				
Portuguese India............	26				
Puerto Rico.................	5	.....	.....	.....	Dec. 14
Réunion Island..............	38				
Rhodesia....................	32				
Río de Oro..................	16				
Rumania....................	8–12	.....	.....	.....	Dec. 7
Russia (See U.S.S.R.)					
Saint Helena Island..........	16–23				
Saint Kitts (See Leeward Islands)					
Saint Pierre and Miquelon.....	5				
Salvador (See El Salvador)					
Samoa (Pago Pago)...........	.....	11	19		
Santo Domingo, Distrito de (See Dominican Republic)					
Sarawak....................	.....	32	32		
Sardinia....................	9				
Saudi Arabia................	18				
Scotland....................	6–9	.....	.....	.....	Dec. 14
Senegal.....................	18				
Seychelles..................	34				
Siam (now Thailand)..........	29	31	28	.....	{ Nov. 12‡ { Nov. 18§
Siberia (See U.S.S.R.)					
Sicily......................	9				
Sierra Leone................	21	.....	.....	.....	Nov. 28
Somaliland (See British, French, and Italian Somaliland)					
South Africa, Union of........	19–28	.....	.....	.....	Nov. 21
South-West Africa............	23–32				
Spain......................	6–9	.....	.....	.....	Dec. 8

APPROXIMATE NUMBER OF LETTER MAIL DAYS—contd.

To:	Mails dispatched from:				Christmas mail dates (approximate)*
	New York	San Francisco	Seattle	New Orleans	
Spanish Guinea................	30				
Straits Settlements.............	.....	26–30	26–30	.....	Nov. 18
Suez Canal (Port Said).........	10–16	.....	.....	.....	Dec. 2
Sumatra......................	.....	28	28	.....	Nov. 18
Surinam (Dutch Guiana).......	12–19	.....	.....	.....	Nov. 28
Sweden.......................	7–12	.....	.....	.....	Dec. 10
Switzerland...................	6–9	.....	.....	.....	Dec. 14
Syria.........................	15–20	.....	.....	.....	Dec. 1
Tahiti........................	.....	11			
Tanganyika Territory..........	30				
Tasmania.....................	.....	25			
Timor, Portuguese.............	.....	36	36		
Togoland (See British and French Togoland)					
Tonga (Friendly) Islands.......	.....	16	18		
Trans-Jordan.................	17				
Trinidad and Tobago..........	10–14	.....	.....	.....	Dec. 6
Tunisia (Tunis)...............	8–12				
Turkey.......................	9–13	.....	.....	.....	Dec. 6
Turks Islands.................	5	.....	.....	.....	Dec. 1
Uganda.......................	27	.....	.....	.....	Nov. 12
Union of South Africa..........	19–28	.....	.....	.....	Nov. 21
Uruguay......................	17	.....	.....	.....	Nov. 28
U.S.S.R. (Russia)..............	8–12	.....	.....	.....	Dec. 6
Vladivostok, Siberia..........	23	.....	.....	.....	Nov. 25
Vatican City..................	8	.....	.....	.....	Dec. 14
Venezuela....................	7–13	.....	.....	.....	Dec. 10
Virgin Islands.................	5–7	.....	.....	.....	Dec. 12
Western Samoa................	.....	11	19		
Windward Islands.............	7–16	.....	.....	.....	Dec. 6
Yemen.......................	20				
Yugoslavia...................	7–10	.....	.....	.....	Dec. 7
Zanzibar.....................	30				

* The definite "latest dates of dispatch" for Christmas mails may be obtained from post offices—in November of each year.

† Winter mails to Alaska are greatly restricted, beginning about October 1; however, some mails are sent in later. Definite information may be obtained from post offices.

‡ Dispatched from New York.

§ Dispatched from San Francisco.

‖ To Corinto, Nicaragua.

¶ To Bluefields, Nicaragua.

INCOMING MAIL

Opening Mail. When a person is new in a position, he should ascertain office preferences regarding the opening of mail or telegrams. Do not open any mail until instructions to do so have been received. This is one of the points that cause misunderstandings in an office.

Some one person in an office should open all mail addressed to the company and "route" it, or see that it is attended to in the absence of the addressees. Do not open mail if the person delegated to open the mail is only temporarily absent. Sort out the individually addressed letters and distribute them.

362

Slitting Envelopes Open. Before slitting an envelope open, shake the contents down so that the letter opener will not catch the papers and cut them in two. If a check or a piece of currency is cut in two, it may be pasted together with transparent tape. The bank will accept it in this form.

Incoming Envelopes. Save incoming envelopes if they bear addresses that do not appear on the letters, or if they show forwarding or any other marks of delay. Clip such envelopes to their letters.

Check every envelope to see that it is empty before it is thrown away. Valuable small enclosures are often thrown into the wastebasket.

Attending to Parts of Letters. If some part of a letter or wire is answered or attended to before it is delivered to the addressee, clip a note to that effect to the incoming paper; or write "Noted" and initial it.

If a letter or wire refers to certain correspondence, hand that correspondence to the addressee with the incoming paper.

Check all enclosures carefully; if any are missing, clip a note to that effect to the incoming letter. Note the omission also on the bottom of the letter opposite "Enc."

Distributing Mail. Distribute letters immediately to the persons to whom they are addressed, unless the persons are in conference; in that case do not disturb them with mail, unless it is with special communications they have been waiting to receive.

Incoming mail that has been opened may be distributed in separate folders marked "Incoming Mail", if the quantity is sufficient to make this advisable.

Opening Magazines and Circulars. Open all magazines, circulars, and advertisements; unfold or unroll them; and clip or staple all papers pertaining to each item together before placing them on the addressee's desk.

Absent Addressees. If a person is to be absent from the office for a period of time, ask his preference regarding the opening, forwarding, answering, or acknowledging of his mail.

If the mail is to be opened and important letters forwarded, determine whether the originals or copies thereof are to be sent. If the originals are sent, make copies for the office. Transient mail is sometimes undelivered because of changes in traveling schedules. Anything of unusual importance should be registered.

A letter of transmittal should accompany all mail so forwarded, in order that a record may be had of the letters sent.

Every letter of importance should be acknowledged in the addressee's absence. The correspondent should be informed that his letter has been received, and that it is being forwarded or will be held awaiting the return of the addressee.

❖

EXPRESS SERVICES

Shipments of any value, and any transportable size or weight, may be made by express.

Pickup and Delivery Service. Express companies have free pickup and delivery service in all large cities and in many small towns. The drivers can accept prepayment of charges; or shipments may be made "express collect".

Express companies in one city will accept orders for pickups in other cities, and deliver the articles "express collect".

Charges and Insurance. Shipments may be sent prepaid, collect, or C.O.D.

EXAMPLES OF RAIL EXPRESS RATES
(First class. Rates per pound)

Rail Miles	1 lb.	5 lbs.	10 lbs.	25 lbs.	50 lbs.	100 lbs.
200	$1.50	$1.50	$1.52	$1.96	$2.68	$ 4.12
500	1.50	1.50	1.71	2.41	3.59	5.93
1000	1.50	1.54	1.85	2.71	4.19	7.14
2000	1.50	1.71	2.19	3.62	6.01	10.77
3000	1.50	2.06	2.89	5.36	9.49	17.72

C.O.D. charges range from 38¢ (for amounts not over $2.50) to $6.56 (for $1000). (Note that there is a difference between "C.O.D." and "collect". "C.O.D." means a collection of the invoice value of the article [and the express charges on the package may be prepaid or collect]; while "collect" means a collection of the express charges only.)

Free insurance is given up to $50 on each 100 pounds or less; or 50¢ a pound over 100 pounds. Additional insurance may be carried for 15¢ per $100.

Charges are usually made on actual weight; and two or more pieces from one shipper to one receiver are grouped and charged for on the basis of the combined weight (provided the weight is sufficient to give an average of not less than 10 pounds a package). Or two or more packages from one shipper to one receiver may be tied together and will be charged for as if they were one package.

Wrapping, Crating, or Boxing. Express companies, if requested, will crate, box, or rope articles at a charge representing the actual cost of the labor and material.

All packages containing jewelry or other valuables **must be sealed.**

The address of both the sender and the receiver should be written on a slip and enclosed in the package, for identification in case the outside addresses become effaced in transit.

Heavy paper wrapping, or cardboard or wooden containers, should be used in preparing articles for express shipment, according to the articles' need of protection.

Breakable articles should be thoroughly cushioned with packing material, and the packages marked FRAGILE.

Bottles containing liquids must be tightly sealed and surrounded with sufficient packing to absorb the entire contents of the bottles, should they break.

Animals (dogs, pets, etc.) may be sent by express and will receive special care. They should be crated, however, in order to be properly handled.

C.O.D. Shipments. There is no definite limit to the amount that may be collected on express C.O.D. shipments. A shipment valued at several thousand dollars may be sent by express, C.O.D.

Order bills of lading, securities, deeds, notes, and other papers on which there is to be a collection may be sent by express, C.O.D.

364

Typewritten or Handwritten Matter. Typewritten or handwritten matter of the nature of correspondence cannot be sent by express; it must be sent by first-class mail.

However, typewritten or handwritten matter that is **not of the nature of correspondence,** such as manuscripts to publishers, music manuscripts, blueprints and specifications, etc., and papers having a monetary value, such as securities, deeds, mortgages, checks, bills of lading, and other legal papers—especially those on which there is to be a collection—may be sent by express.

Refrigeration. Refrigeration is a separate and distinct service of express transportation, and is subject to a separate charge. Often this charge is included in the "commodity rate", as on fruit, etc.

Small shipments that are packed in ice will be re-iced without extra charge.

Special Express Rates

Express money order rates are: Up to $1.....5¢ $1.01 to $5.....10¢ $5.01 to $10.....15¢ $10.01 to $50.....25¢ $50.01 to $100.....30¢

Printed matter, books, etc., may be sent at a third-class express rate of 16¢ a pound. Minimum charge: $1.50. The value of each package is limited to $10.

Foodstuffs may be sent at a second-class rate (approximately 25% below regular rates).

Fruits and vegetables may be sent at a special "commodity rate". Minimum charge: $1.50.

All special-rate packages should have the nature of the contents written on the wrapper, as BOOKS, FOODSTUFFS, FRUITS, etc.

DOMESTIC AIR EXPRESS

Air express service has **door-to-door pickup** and **special delivery,** at no extra cost, in cities and principal towns.

Regular **express wrapping and packing** is acceptable on air express.

Shipments may be sent **prepaid, collect, or C.O.D.**

Practically **all types of merchandise** are accepted up to $25,000 in value, 200 pounds in weight, and 152 inches in length and girth combined. Larger and heavier shipments may be forwarded by special arrangement.

Space charges: 250 cu.in. to the pound, if that figure is greater than weight.

Live animals are not acceptable, with the exception of very small animals like hamsters. It is best to query the local express office on such shipments.

Not acceptable are explosives and highly inflammable or harmful materials, and (except by special arrangement) articles exceeding $25,000 in value.

Free insurance is given up to $50 on each 100 pounds or less; or 50¢ a pound over 100 pounds. Additional insurance may be carried for 11¢ per $100.

Air express rates may be obtained from the Railway Express Agency.

EXAMPLES OF AIR EXPRESS RATES
(All one class. Minimum charge $2.50)
(For air mileage, see table of distances, p. 568.)

Air Miles	2 lbs.	5 lbs.	10 lbs.	25 lbs.	40 lbs.	100 lbs.
249	$2.50	$2.50	$2.50	$ 3.25	$ 4.00	$ 7.00
549	2.50	2.73	3.46	5.65	7.84	16.60
1049	2.61	3.53	5.06	9.65	14.24	32.60
1549	2.93	4.33	6.66	13.65	20.64	48.60
2049	3.25	5.13	8.26	17.65	27.04	64.60
over 2350	3.51	5.77	9.54	20.85	32.16	77.40

Special commodity rates apply on newspapers, etc. Consult your local express office
Canada: Charges to and from points in Canada are somewhat higher than the above rates.

INTERNATIONAL EXPRESS (SURFACE CARRIERS)

International express shipments are handled by the large foreign express services, such as the American Express Company, Thos. Cook & Son, and others.

For small shipments, parcel post is cheaper than international express. However, there are certain shipments that cannot be sent by parcel post and must be sent by international express. **Insurance** is available, for an additional charge, on all international express shipments to all countries.

Packing. All international express packages should be in wooden containers. The packages may or may not be sealed; valuables are usually sealed, while merchandise is not sealed. The express companies will crate or box articles, if requested, at a charge representing the actual cost of labor and material.

Documents Necessary. The following papers or documents are necessary for all international express shipments:

1. Invoice (a regular commercial invoice on a billhead, showing an itemized list of the articles with their valuation, gross weights, and number of cases).
2. Shipper's export declaration, 2 to 13 copies (blanks obtainable from the express company).

Other papers or documents are required on shipments to certain countries. Before preparing an international shipment, call the express company and ascertain whether **consular documents** and **certificate of origin** will be required.

INTERNATIONAL AIR EXPRESS (AIR CARRIERS)

International air express is handled by the Railway Express Agency.

"Through" shipments may be made by domestic and international air express.

"Rail-and-air" shipments may be made by rail to the international airports at New York, Miami, New Orleans, Los Angeles, San Francisco, Seattle, Dallas, El Paso, Ft. Worth, San Antonio, Laredo, and Brownsville; thence by plane to the foreign destinations.

Check with the local express office for **weight** and **size limitations, valuation, insurance, minimum charges,** and **documents** required.

Space charges: 250 cu. in. to the pound, if that figure is greater than weight.

International air express rates per pound (rates decrease for 100 pounds and over):

From **New York** to Amsterdam, $1.17; Athens, $1.59; Bombay, $2.26; Copenhagen, $1.25; Frankfurt, $1.24; Geneva, $1.24; London, $1.10; Oslo, $1.25; Paris, $1.17; Rome, $1.39; Stockholm, $1.27. To Bermuda, 20¢.

From **Miami** to Balboa, C.Z., 39¢; Buenos Aires, $1.47; Havana, 8¢; Lima, 87¢; Maracaibo, 40¢; Montevideo, $1.43; Quito, 64¢; Recife, $1.16; Rio de Janeiro, $1.32; Santiago, Chile, $1.30.

From **New Orleans** to Guatemala, 34¢; Managua, 43¢; Mexico City 38¢ up to 100 lbs.—over 100 lbs., 21¢—over 3300 lbs., 18¢.

From **San Francisco** to Auckland, $1.76; Honolulu, 93¢; Sydney, $2.01.

From **Seattle** to Anchorage, 40¢; Fairbanks, 40¢; Juneau, 30¢; Nome, 55¢.

Minimum charges, in general, are: $2 to $5 to North and South America, Bermuda, and Hawaii; $5 to $10 to Europe, Africa, and the Far East.

MESSENGER SERVICES

Heavy packages or letters for local delivery can sometimes be sent as cheaply by messenger as by first-class mail. And with greater dispatch.

Messenger services are listed in the classified telephone directory under M.

Telegraph companies offer messenger service also, and will enter the charges therefor on the regular telegraph bill as "errand service".

Mark all packages or letters so sent "By Messenger".

Receipts. If a receipt is desired, write it out and clip it to the letter or package. This not only reminds the messenger to obtain the receipt, but is convenient for the receiver to sign.

366

TELEGRAPH

Preferred method of writing telegrams:

Telegram X Day Letter Night Letter	

Paid, Collect, or Charge

Date
Hour and Minute

Full Address

Body—double-spaced—in ordinary lettering,
not caps.

Signature (typed)

Initials
Name, Address, and Telephone Number of Sender (if not
printed elsewhere on the blank)

Note that: The time of day should always be given.
The body of the wire should be double-spaced, and not written in caps.
Initials should be used, as on letters.
The accounting information is placed in the space above the date.
The name, address, and telephone number of the sender should always be added, if it does not appear elsewhere on the blank, unless the sender is well known to the telegraph company.

Date

The time of day is as important as the date on a wire. The two questions most frequently asked concerning telegrams are "When was it sent?" and "When should it be received?"

The city need not be written above the date, unless the wire is uncommon and its point of origin might later be questioned.

April 9, 1952
11:15 a.m.

367

Address

Addresses on telegrams are not charged for—on cables they are. Give a complete address always. Include the **company name** whenever possible; this facilitates location of the addressee if the street or building number happens to be wrong. No charge is made for any number of words in a telegram's address, if they are solely to aid in locating the addressee.

Code addresses cannot be used on domestic messages.

An **"Attention"** line may be used below the company name in an address, and is not charged for. (If "Attention..." is written at the beginning of the message proper, it is charged for.)

> Northern Company, Inc.
> Attention John Baxter
> 2631 Woodward Ave.
> Detroit, Michigan (Postal zone is unnecessary in telegraphic addresses.)

"Personal" refers to the contents of a wire, not especially to delivery. **"Personal Delivery Only"** insures delivery to addressee, and no one else.

> Ralph James, Personal   Dan Lee, Personal Delivery Only

"Mr." should not be used before names in telegraphic addresses. It is not sent, because it is so often confused with **"Mrs."** by persons receiving messages. (**"Mr."** is sent if no first name or initial is given.)

"Mrs." or **"Miss"** may be used, and will be sent.

"Dr.", "Prof.", "Capt.", etc., may be used.

"Hold for Arrival" may be written after a name. **Or a time for delivery** may be specified. It is not charged for.

> Robert V. Mason, Hold for Arrival   or   Deliver 8 p.m.
> Biltmore Hotel
> New York City

"Will Call" should be written beneath the name in the address if a message is to be called for at the receiving telegraph office in a certain city. The message will be held at a central station and may be delivered at any branch office in that city.

> James T. Scott
> Will Call
> Louisville, Kentucky

"Care of" may be used in a telegraphic address without extra charge.

A telephone number may be given as an address on a wire. The message will be telephoned, and then mailed to the addressee if he so requests.

Building or street numbers may be used in addresses. Both are not necessary if the building is large or well known.

The room number, if known, should always be given when a building is named in the address.

Two addresses may be given for the same name, with the word "or" between them. The second address will be charged for.

Two names may be given for the same address; the last name is charged for.

Robert V. Mason, or James T. Scott
Room 5020
475 Commonwealth Ave.
Boston, Mass.

Two or more names and addresses may be given for a single message, with the following notation above them:

Please send same message to the following addresses:

Multiple-Addressed Telegrams. If copies of one wire are to be sent to many addresses, the addresses should be written on special perforated and sectioned sheets, obtainable from the telegraph company. Above the addresses should be written:

Please send attached message to the following addresses:

The message itself should be on a regular telegraph blank, only one copy being necessary for the telegraph company. Extra copies are made in the telegraph offices on a duplicating machine, and the addresses are cut and pasted on the copies.

Train Addresses. The following information should be given when a wire is addressed to a train:

Name of passenger	AS:	Thomas L. Meade
Care of conductor		Care of Conductor
Train name or number, and direction traveling		Santa Fe Train 19, Westbound
Car and berth number		Car 15, Room D
Station, and arrival time		Due Santa Fe Station, April 14, 6:25 a.m.
City, and state		La Junta, Colorado

If the car and berth numbers are not known, the name of the passenger will be sufficient; but always give as much information as is at hand—it is not charged for.

The arrival time is most important. This and the other train data may be secured from "Information" at the station of the railroad in question.

Travelers expecting messages should notify their conductors. The conductor is responsible for the delivery of messages to passengers on his train. If he is unable to locate a passenger on the train, he will return the message to the telegraph company at the next station. The telegraph company will then notify the sender that the message was undeliverable.

For Canadian and Mexican railroads, the addresses should be in the same form as given above; this train information may be secured from the American railroads whose lines make connections with the foreign routes.

Addresses to Airports. Messages may be dispatched to airports to be delivered to airplane passengers. They are addressed as follows:

Name of passenger	AS:	J. E. Macaulay, Passenger
Name of airline		United Air Lines
Trip or flight number, and direction traveling		Flight 645, Westbound Plane
Airport, and arrival time		Due Stapleton Airfield, June 10, 2:05 p.m.
City, and state		Denver, Colorado

Addresses to Sailing or Arriving Ships. Messages may be dispatched to sailing or arriving ships to be delivered to passengers as they embark or disembark. Such messages are addressed as follows:

Name of passenger	AS:	Robert V. Blair, Passenger
Name of steamship line		The American Line
Name of ship, and stateroom number*		SS. TRANSATLANTIC, Stateroom B 110
Pier, and sailing time		Sailing from Pier D, End West 55 St., August 20, 11 p.m.
Port of departure		New York City

* If the stateroom number is not definitely known, it may be omitted and will be supplied by the steamship officials from the passenger list.

Addresses to Ships at Sea. (See Radio to Ships at Sea, p. 384.)

Addresses to Isolated Places. A message may be addressed to any isolated place that has a telephone. Such an address might read:

William Granger
Mountain Creek Cabins—Telephone
150 miles above
Montpelier, Vermont

Words

The rule for counting words in the body of a wire is: If a word is given as one word in the dictionary, it is counted and charged for as one word.

An abbreviation representing more than one word may be written solid or with periods, but **without spacing,** and will be counted as one word (if not more than 5 letters), as "fob" or "f.o.b.", "pm" or "p.m.", etc. Single words should be written out rather than abbreviated.

Initials, if spaced, are each counted as a word in the text of a wire; a name such as "L. B. Towne" would be three words. If initials are written **without spacing,** or written solid, they are counted as one word, as "J.B.T. (or JBT) Parke" is but two words.

Single letters need not be written out, as "aitch" for H. They will be transmitted as letters and charged for as one word each.

Hyphens are now transmitted, and not charged for. However, words that are hyphened in the dictionary should be run together, and others written apart. Hyphened words are counted according to the number of words they contain. (For written-out numbers, see Figures, below.)

Proper names from any language are now counted (in the texts of domestic messages) according to the number of words they contain: United States (2 words), New Mexico (2), St. Louis (2), New York City (3), van Fleet (2), de la Fontaine (3), DeWitt (1). **Abbreviations** of proper names, if of not more than 5 letters each and written **without spacing,** are counted as one word each: N.Y. or NY, S.C., B&O, LOSA, NBC.

"Mr." and "Mrs." in the text of a wire are transmitted in abbreviated form. Do not spell them out.

Common coined 5-letter words are permissible in any wire.

> **relet** (re your letter); urlet (your letter); arlet (our); mylet (my)
> **retel** (re your telegram); urtel (your); artel (our); mytel (my)
> **refon** (re your phone call); urfon (your); arfon (our); myfon (my)
> **antel** (answer by telegram); anfon (by telephone); anlet (by letter)

Profane words are prohibited in all dispatches.

Code words are permissible in any domestic wire. They are counted at the rate of 5 letters to a word. All code words should be set in caps.

Foreign language words are permissible in any domestic wire.

Figures

Figures in the texts of **domestic messages** are now counted at the rate of one word for every 5 characters or fraction thereof.

A period or decimal point, comma, colon, hyphen or apostrophe, used with a figure group, is now considered **punctuation** and not counted.

The **affixes** -st, -d, -nd, -rd, and -th in ordinal numbers are counted as characters in the figure groups.

The **signs,** such as the dollar ($), pound (£), percent (%), fraction bar (/), number or pounds (#), ampersand (&), feet or minutes ('), inches or seconds ("), and "by" (x), are counted as one character each.†

Note that **each unbroken sequence** of figures, signs, and/or letters, is counted as one word for every 5 characters or fraction thereof.

One Word Each			Two Words Each		Three Words Each	
12,345	500th	$15.45	123456	110-hp. 8	and/or	100 37mm. guns
95–100	1500#	100%	33LC45	125DEGF	125 deg. F.	18,000-ton C-3
10&20.	4327′	PB4Y1	B/L196	2/10, n/30	$10 to $15	132-1/4:186-3/4
2-1/2*	5x12″	P-38's	$245.75	12:30 p.m.	6/15/45 50	1/20 14K $25

* If written "2½", it will be transmitted as "2 1/2" and counted as two words.
† The signs ¢, @, °, and * are not on the teleprinters; hence the corresponding words should be used.

If writing numbers out, observe the following:

Use **"zero"** or **"naught"** instead of "oh" in spelled-out numbers.

Compound numbers, such as "fifty-six", may now be hyphened, but will still be counted as two words. They should not be run together. (However, in cables they may be run together.)

Four-figure numbers may sometimes be grouped in their written-out forms to save words, as "nineteen thirty-nine" rather than "one nine three nine"; "eighty thirteen" instead of "eight naught one three", etc.

Body of Wire

Double-space all wires, regardless of the length.

Do not set them in caps. Use ordinary type and set only the code words in caps. All caps are difficult to write and difficult to read. Telegrams are received in caps because of the type on the telegraph machines.

Endeavor to make wires easy to read, both for later reference in the office and for the convenience of the telegraph operators. Do not run words incoherently together, thinking to avoid cost.

Do not eliminate words when transcribing a wire. Suggest words to be eliminated (by pencil check) and let the dictator cross out whatever he wishes. Small words are often necessary to make the meaning clear.

Paragraph if it seems advisable to separate different subjects. Paragraphing is valuable for office reference. If it is desired that paragraphs be transmitted, write SEND IN PARAGRAPHS at the top of the message. They will be sent but not charged for.

Verse may be sent in lines if SEND IN LINES is written at the top of the message. There is no extra charge for this.

Punctuation

Punctuation marks are now transmitted without charge in all domestic messages, and in messages to Canada and Mexico. But punctuation marks are still counted and charged for in cables.

The allowable free punctuation marks are the comma, period, colon, semicolon, question mark, dash, hyphen, quotation marks, parentheses, and apostrophe. There is no exclamation point on the teleprinters.

If punctuation marks are spelled out, such as "Stop", "Comma", etc., they will be counted, charged for, and transmitted as words. However, it is often advisable, around important quoted matter, to use **"Quote"** and **"Unquote"** instead of the quotation marks, which might be overlooked.

> Retel Collier wires Quote Will ship 612 partially conditioned XBLMC crates Monday 28th, and 312 W36LM (Carmen's) Thursday Unquote. We will dispatch these immediately. What is meaning "partially conditioned"?
>
> Dayton canceled 210 crates Tallmen's Best Saturday. No reason except wanted late Des Moines–Omaha f.o.b. delivery.

(The count for this message would be 46 words.)

Signatures

Single signatures on telegrams are not charged for. That is, a personal name may be signed; or a company name with "Inc." or "Ltd." as part of the name; or a company name and a personal name, considered as one, as

L. J. Ranger & Sons Co.—J. B. Henderson

Titles after names are not charged for, as "President", etc., unless a title is placed after a long compound signature, such as the above—then it is charged for.

If two personal names are used as a signature, one is charged for, unless the two represent a company name.

H. J. Bower and M. C. Lowe

An address immediately beneath a signature is sent and charged for.

A family signature (of two or three Christian names) is considered one signature, and no extra charge is made.

Gordon and Frances or Jack, Bill, and Bob

"Mrs." or "Miss" may be used before a woman's signature without extra charge.

Initials may be used as a signature.

Messages may be unsigned, in which case "Unsigned" should be written in the place for signature.

— — — —

Initials. The initials of both the dictator and the transcriber should appear on every wire. They are as important here as on a letter.

Place the initials in the lower left corner. The telegraph company disregards these notations.

Do not use only the transcriber's initials. This could indicate that the transcriber also composed the wire.

If two persons dictate a wire, use both sets of initials, or ask their preference regarding initials. If both dictators' initials are to be used, they may be written as—HJB-MCL:VM.

Paid, Charge, or Collect. If a message is sent prepaid (paid for at the time of sending), write PAID in the space above the date.

If a message is to be charged to an account, and the name of the account appears as the signature or is printed elsewhere on the telegraph blank, write simply CHARGE in the space above the date.

If a message is to be charged, and the name of the account does not appear elsewhere on the wire, write the name and address of the account under the words CHARGE TO THE ACCOUNT OF.

If a message is to be sent collect, write the one word COLLECT in the space above the date.

Address of Sender. The name, address, and telephone number of the sender should appear in the lower left corner of every wire, if it is not printed elsewhere on the blank, unless the sender is well known to the telegraph company. This provides a means of identification of the sender if it should be necessary to report an undelivery; and also provides a check for the telegraph company's accounting department in billing.

Second Pages. Use plain yellow or white paper for second and third pages of wires. It is unnecessary to use a second telegraph blank.

Head these pages as letter second-pages are headed.

<table>
<tr><td>James Scott</td><td>-2-</td><td>Oct. 24, 1952</td></tr>
</table>

Leave at least a two-inch space above the heading for "pasting space". The telegraph company usually pastes all pages of a wire together in one long strip.

Staple the pages of a wire together in the extreme upper left corner, before sending it out. The telegraph company can clip the corner to separate the pages and paste them. Pins or clips are not so satisfactory as staples for this purpose.

Extra Copies. Confirmation copies of wires are often mailed to the addressees. If a confirmation copy is to be mailed, and a confirmation blank is not at hand, use a regular telegraph blank for this copy, and write the word CONFIRMATION across the top.

An extra, "billing", copy of each wire should be made on cheaper paper, and these copies kept in a separate file for checking against the monthly telegraph bill. These copies may be destroyed each month after the bill has been checked.

Outgoing Wires. Every wire, no matter how short, should be shown to the dictator before it is sent. There may be some last-minute change necessary in the wording or method of dispatch.

Telephoning a Wire. Wires may be telephoned to the telegraph companies and charged to telephone numbers. It is unnecessary to ask for a special department or operator. When the telegraph company answers, simply say "I should like to send a message."

When telephoning confidential messages, **use a private telephone** so that no visitors will interrupt or overhear.

Give the telegraph company the information in the following manner:

1. This is (telephone number)
2. Sending a (paid or collect) (telegram, day letter, night letter, etc.) to (addressee)
3. The message reads:

....
Signed.......

If frequently spelling out words to a telegraph operator, memorize and use the following standard telegraph code for identifying letters:

A FOR:	Adams	J FOR:	John	S FOR:	Sugar
B	Boston	K	King	T	Thomas
C	Chicago	L	Lincoln	U	Union
D	Denver	M	Mary	V	Victor
E	Edward	N	New York	W	William
F	Frank	O	Ocean	X	X-ray
G	George	P	Peter	Y	Young
H	Henry	Q	Queen	Z	Zero
I	Ida	R	Robert		

Time Differences. Senders of wires should consider the time differences in the United States, and abroad, when calculating the delivery of messages. (See Standard Time, p. 571.)

Often savings can be effected by the use of the cheaper services; for instance, if a 23-word message is to be dispatched from New York at 9:30 in the morning to San Francisco, where it is 6:30, a day letter would

374

be as effective as a fast telegram; the day letter would arrive in sufficient time to be delivered at the beginning of the business day in San Francisco.

TELEGRAPH SERVICES
(For rates, see pp. 378 and 379.)
Straight or Fast Telegram*

Fifteen words at full rate.   Day and night delivery.
Transmission and delivery time: 15 to 30 minutes.
("Urgent" messages, marked "Rush", are often received, transmitted, and delivered within 7 minutes—across the United States.)

Code or foreign language—straight, or mixed with English—may be used without extra charge.

*There is no abbreviation or indicator for straight telegrams.   The absence of such an indicator on an incoming wire means that it is a straight telegram.

Day Letter (DL)

Fifty words or less at approximately $1\frac{1}{3}$ the 15-word telegram rate.
Each additional 5 words or less at reduced rates.
(A day letter should contain 23 words or more, because up to and including 22 words, straight telegrams are usually cheaper than day letters.)
Transmission and delivery time: 30 minutes to 1 hour.
(The transmission time depends on the number of straight telegrams filed ahead of the day letters.)

Day letters may be sent **at any time of the day or night,** and are delivered at any time of the day or night if the receiving offices are open.   To insure the delivery of a day letter at night put "Please phone" beside the name in the address, and the telephone number if it is available.   The receiving central telegraph office will reach the addressee by telephone if possible.   Day letters are delivered at night to hotels and all offices that are open.

Code or foreign language—straight, or mixed with English—may be used without extra charge.

Night Letter (NL)

Fifty words or less at minimum rates.
Each additional 5 words or less at reduced rates.

Note that in this single **domestic overnight service** the initial charge is for 50 words.   Reduced rates also apply; the maximum charge for 50 words for the greatest distance is $1.20.
Accepted until 2 a.m. for delivery on the morning, usually after 8 o'clock, of the following business day (in the business districts).   No deliveries on Sundays or **national** holidays to business offices, unless specifically requested.   Deliveries on any day in residential districts.   Night messages are not mailed unless an addressee resides in a district beyond the telegraph company's delivery radius, and unless all efforts to reach him by telephone have failed.
Code or foreign language—straight, or mixed with English—may be used without extra charge.

OTHER SERVICES

Serial Service has been discontinued.

Teleprinter Service (WUX) is a private wire connection from a business office to the telegraph office. Messages to companies having teleprinter connection do not require street addresses—just the name of the company, the symbol WUX, and the city and state.

Telemeter Service provides direct patron–to–patron written communication through connected teleprinters. Minimum charge is for 25,000 words a month.

Desk-Fax is an instrument that transmits typed or hand–written telegrams direct from a customer's desk to the telegraph operating room. This is done by a photo–electric process, called "facsimile", which reproduces messages between distant points exactly as written.

CND Service (Commercial News Department) furnishes reports of market quotations and sports events by ticker, private wire, or telegraph message.

Distribution Services. Telegraph companies will deliver samples or promotional advertising; set up counter displays; check display advertising; gather market data; purchase and pack products for tests; give health and weather reports; and collect and deliver merchandise parcels.

Marketing and Research Service. Surveys on particular subjects are conducted by the telegraph company. Interviews are held and data gathered, and the results are wired back to the customer.

Telegift Service. An available gift may be selected and paid for at a Western Union office, and the gift will be delivered in another city.

Credit Cards may be procured by persons having monthly charge accounts with the telegraph company; and messages may be "charged" with such credit cards anywhere in the United States.

Forwarding of messages is done only at the customer's expense.

Delivery Limits. Messages are delivered free within 2 miles of telegraph offices in cities of 5000 or more population (and $\frac{1}{2}$ mile in smaller towns).

Rural route deliveries, and those beyond free delivery limits, are made first by telephone and then by mail. If the sender wishes to pay for messenger delivery, however, the telegraph company will make the necessary arrangements at a reasonable charge, based on the distance.

Recall of Wires. A message may be recalled or "killed" by telephone, provided the request reaches the telegraph company before or while the message is being dispatched. No charge is made on a canceled message.

If the wire has been transmitted, the sender may send a paid message to the telegraph company at the point of destination, requesting the cancellation.

If he desires to know whether cancellation is effected or not, he may ask for a reply collect.

Report Delivery. If a report of delivery is desired, write REPORT DELIVERY beside the address. These two words are charged for.

The report (returned in the form of a collect message) will show the time and place of delivery and the person to whom delivery was made.

If any message is undeliverable, a free report will be given, whether a report of delivery has been requested or not.

Repeat Back. If it is desired that a message be checked or repeated over the wires, write REPEAT BACK above the message. These two words are charged for. All messages of a legal nature should be repeated.

Charge of $\frac{1}{2}$ the regular rate for repetition.

Telegraphing Money ("Telegraphic Transfer"). Money may be dispatched by telegraph and cable to all parts of the world. Payments in foreign countries are made in foreign currency—subject to fluctuations in exchange.

Night, Sunday, and holiday payment service is available at principal telegraph offices all over the world.

RATES FOR DOMESTIC MONEY ORDERS BY TELEGRAPH

An initial charge equal to the cost of a 15-word straight telegram, or a 50-word night letter, to the point of destination; plus a service charge as follows:

For $ 20.00 or less........	25¢	For $125.01 to 150.00.......	$1.45
20.01 to 25.00........	30	150.01 to 175.00.......	1.65
25.01 to 30.00........	35	175.01 to 200.00.......	1.85
30.01 to 35.00........	40	200.01 to 250.00......	2.15
35.01 to 40.00........	45	250.01 to 300.00.......	2.45
40.01 to 45.00........	50	300.01 to 350.00.......	2.75
45.01 to 50.00........	55	350.01 to 400.00.......	3.05
50.01 to 60.00........	65	400.01 to 450.00......	3.35
60.01 to 70.00........	75	450.01 to 500.00.......	3.65
70.01 to 80.00........	85	500.01 to 600.00.......	4.00
80.01 to 90.00........	95	600.01 to 700.00.......	4.35
90.01 to 100.00.......	$1.05	700.01 to 800.00.......	4.70
100.01 to 125.00.......	1.25	800.01 to 900.00.......	5.05
		900.01 to 1000.00......	5.40

For amounts from $1000.01 to $2000, the money order charge is $5.40 for the first $1000, plus 25¢ for each additional $100 or fraction thereof.

For amounts over $2000, the money order charge is $7.90 for the first $2000, plus 20¢ for each additional $100 or fraction thereof.

RATES FOR INTERNATIONAL MONEY ORDERS BY CABLE

The **charges for foreign money orders** by cable are:

2% of the first $500; then $\frac{1}{2}$ of 1% of the amount over $500; plus the cost of the full-rate cable transmitting the money order.

Thus, if $800 were being sent, the charge would be $11.50, plus the cost of the full-rate cable.

All foreign money orders are now paid in the currency of the country to which addressed, at the daily exchange rate.

Gift money orders are delivered on decorated checks and special blanks.

Messages of Greeting. Greeting messages of the senders' own composition may be dispatched as straight telegrams, day letters, or night letters, and will be delivered on attractive special greeting blanks in envelopes to match—for birthdays, weddings, anniversaries, and holidays.

Regular rates are now charged for all greeting messages.

Packages to Trains. A package may be dispatched by air mail to a telegraph company in a distant city for delivery to a passenger on a train. (See Envelopes, p. 330.)

Legality of Wires. Telegraphic messages may be considered as legal evidence in court, just as any other written correspondence; therefore, the necessity for correctness. All signatures on telegraphic messages given to authorized operators are valid at law. To disclaim a telegraphic signature, a person must prove that he had no knowledge of the sending of the message.

> **"A contract may be made and proved in court by telegraphic despatches."**
> —**Bouvier's Law Dictionary (Baldwin's Revision), p. 1168.**

WESTERN UNION RATES FOR

Rates between:	Atlanta, Ga.	Baltimore, Md.	Birmingham, Ala.	Boise, Idaho	Boston, Mass.	Buffalo, N.Y.	Charleston, W.Va.	Chicago, Ill.	Cincinnati, Ohio	Cleveland, Ohio	Columbia, S.C.	Dallas, Tex.	Denver, Colo.	Des Moines, Iowa	Detroit, Mich.	Hartford, Conn.	Houston, Tex.	Indianapolis, Ind.	Jacksonville, Fla.	Kansas City, Mo.
Atlanta, Ga.	50																			
Baltimore, Md.	100	50																		
Birmingham, Ala.	70	100	50																	
Boise, Idaho	145	160	145	50																
Boston, Mass.	115	85	115	160	50															
Buffalo, N.Y.	100	85	115	145	85	50														
Charleston, W.Va.	85	85	85	145	100	85	50													
Chicago, Ill.	100	100	100	130	115	100	85	50												
Cincinnati, Ohio	85	100	85	145	100	85	70	85	50											
Cleveland, Ohio	100	85	100	145	100	70	70	85	70	50										
Columbia, S.C.	70	100	85	145	115	100	85	100	85	100	50									
Dallas, Tex.	115	130	100	130	145	130	115	115	115	115	115	50								
Denver, Colo.	130	145	115	100	145	130	130	115	130	130	130	100	50							
Des Moines, Iowa	100	115	100	130	130	115	100	85	100	100	115	100	100	50						
Detroit, Mich.	100	85	100	145	100	70	85	85	70	60	100	115	130	100	50					
Hartford, Conn.	115	85	115	160	60	85	100	115	100	100	100	130	145	115	100	50				
Houston, Tex.	100	130	100	130	145	130	115	115	115	115	115	70	115	115	115	130	50			
Indianapolis, Ind.	100	100	85	145	115	100	85	70	60	85	100	115	115	85	85	100	115	50		
Jacksonville, Fla.	85	100	85	160	115	115	100	115	100	115	85	115	130	115	115	115	115	100	50	
Kansas City, Mo.	100	115	100	130	130	115	100	85	100	100	115	100	100	70	100	130	100	100	115	50
Little Rock, Ark.	100	115	85	130	130	115	100	100	100	100	100	85	115	100	100	130	85	100	100	85
Los Angeles, Calif.	145	160	145	100	160	160	145	145	145	145	160	130	115	130	145	160	130	145	160	130
Louisville, Ky.	85	100	85	145	115	100	85	85	70	85	85	100	115	100	85	115	115	60	100	100
Memphis, Tenn.	85	115	70	130	130	115	100	100	85	100	100	115	130	115	100	115	100	85	100	85
Miami, Fla.	100	115	100	160	130	130	115	130	115	115	100	115	145	130	130	130	115	115	85	130
Milwaukee, Wis.	100	100	100	130	115	100	100	60	85	85	100	115	115	85	85	115	115	85	115	100
Minneapolis, Minn.	115	115	115	130	130	115	115	85	100	100	115	115	100	85	100	115	115	100	130	85
Newark, N.J.	100	70	115	160	70	85	100	100	100	85	100	130	145	115	100	60	130	100	115	115
New Orleans, La.	100	115	85	145	130	130	115	115	115	115	100	100	115	115	115	130	85	100	100	100
New York, N.Y.	100	70	115	160	70	85	100	100	100	85	100	130	145	115	100	60	130	100	115	115
Oklahoma City, Okla.	115	130	100	130	130	130	115	100	115	115	115	70	100	100	115	130	100	100	115	85
Omaha, Nebr.	115	115	100	115	130	115	115	100	100	115	115	100	100	70	100	130	115	100	130	70
Philadelphia, Pa.	100	50	100	160	85	85	85	100	100	85	100	130	145	115	85	70	130	100	100	115
Phoenix, Ariz.	145	145	130	115	160	145	145	130	145	145	145	115	100	130	145	160	115	145	145	115
Pittsburgh, Pa.	100	85	100	145	100	70	70	100	70	60	100	115	130	100	70	85	130	85	100	115
Portland, Maine	115	100	130	160	60	100	100	115	115	100	115	145	145	130	100	70	145	115	130	130
Portland, Oreg.	160	160	160	85	160	160	160	145	145	160	160	145	115	130	145	160	145	145	160	130
Providence, R.I.	115	85	115	160	50	85	100	115	100	100	115	145	145	130	100	60	145	115	115	130
Raleigh, N.C.	85	85	100	145	100	100	85	100	85	85	70	115	130	115	100	100	115	100	85	115
Richmond, Va.	100	60	100	145	100	85	85	100	85	85	85	130	130	115	85	85	130	100	100	115
Salt Lake City, Utah	145	145	130	85	160	145	145	130	130	145	145	115	85	115	130	145	130	130	145	115
San Francisco, Calif.	160	160	145	100	160	160	160	145	145	160	160	130	115	145	160	160	145	145	160	130
Seattle, Wash.	160	160	160	85	160	160	160	145	145	145	160	145	115	130	145	160	145	145	160	130
St. Louis, Mo.	100	115	85	130	115	100	100	85	85	100	100	100	115	85	100	115	100	85	115	85
Washington, D.C.	100	50	100	145	85	85	85	100	85	85	100	130	130	115	85	85	130	100	100	115

—Reprinted by permission from

FIFTEEN-WORD FULL-RATE TELEGRAMS

Relationship of Rates

Where the Full-Rate Telegram Rate is:		The Night Letter Rate is:				The Day Letter Rate is:			
For 15 Words or Less	For Each Additional Word	For 50 Words or Less	For Each Additional 5 Words or Less			For 50 Words or Less	For Each Additional 5 Words or Less		
			51–100 Words	101–200 Words	Over 200 Words		51–100 Words	101–200 Words	Over 200 Words
50¢	2¢	35¢	2¢	2¢	1.5¢	65¢	4¢	3.5¢	2.5¢
60	2.5	45	2.5	2.5	2	80	5	4	3
70	3	50	3	2.5	2	90	5.5	4.5	3.5
85	3.5	65	4	3.5	2.5	110	6.5	5.5	4.5
100	4	75	4.5	4	3	130	8	6.5	5
115	4.5	85	5	4.5	3.5	150	9	7.5	6
130	5	95	5.5	5	4	170	10	8.5	7
145	6	105	6.5	5.5	4	190	11.5	9.5	7.5
160	6.5	120	7	6	5	210	12.5	10.5	8.5

City-to-city rate matrix (each row ends with its city; the diagonal value 50 marks the city's own column):

```
50                                                                                                  Little Rock, Ark.
130  50                                                                                             Los Angeles, Calif.
85  145  50                                                                                         Louisville, Ky.
70  145  85  50                                                                                     Memphis, Tenn.
115 160 115 115  50                                                                                 Miami, Fla.
100 145  85 100 130 | 50                                                                            Milwaukee, Wis.
100 130 100 100 130 | 85  50                                                                        Minneapolis, Minn.
115 160 100 115 115 |100 115  50                                                                    Newark, N.J.
85  145 100  85 100 |115 115 130  50                                                                New Orleans, La.
115 160 100 115 115 |100 115  50 130  50                                                            New York, N.Y.
85  130 100 100 130 |115 100 130 100 130 | 50                                                       Oklahoma City, Okla.
100 130 100 100 130 |100  85 130 115 130 | 85  50                                                   Omaha, Nebr.
115 160 100 115 115 |100 115  60 115  60 |130 115  50                                               Philadelphia, Pa.
130  85 130 130 145 |130 130 160 130 160 |115 115 160  50                                           Phoenix, Ariz.
115 160  85 100 115 |100 115  85 115  85 |115 115  85 145  50                                       Pittsburgh, Pa.
130 160 115 130 130 |115 130  85 130  85 |145 130  85 160 100 | 50                                  Portland, Maine
145 145 145 145 160 |145 130 160 145 160 |130 130  85 160 100 |160  50                              Portland, Oreg.
130 160 115 115 130 |115 130  70 130  70 |130 130  85 160 100 | 70 160  50                          Providence, R.I.
115 160 100 100 100 |100 115 100 115 100 |115 115  85 145  85 |100 160 100  50                      Raleigh, N.C.
115 160 100 100 115 |100 115  85 115  85 |130 115  70 145  85 |100 160 100  70  50                  Richmond, Va.
130 100 130 130 160 |130 115 145 130 145 |115 115 145 100 145 |160 100 160 145 145 | 50             Salt Lake City, Utah
145  85 145 145 160 |145 145 145 145 160 |130 130 160 100 160 |160 100 160 160 160 |100  50         San Francisco, Calif.
145 115 145 145 160 |145 130 160 130 160 |160  70 160 160 160 |160 100 100  50 130 |145 145  50     Seattle, Wash.
85  145  85  70 115 | 85 100 115 100 115 |130 145 115 100 100 |130 145 115 100 100 |130 145 145  50 St. Louis, Mo.
115 160 100 115 115 |100 115  70 115  70 |130 115  60 145  70 |100 160  85  85  60 |145 160 160 100  50 Washington, D.C.
```

The Western Union Telegraph Company.

CABLES AND RADIO

Cable Addresses.   Cable addresses are counted and charged for.

A code address is therefore preferable, and may be registered with the cable companies at a cost of $5.00 a year, or $3.00 for six months.   It must contain no more than ten letters.

Code addresses may be used on any class of cable, and should be set in caps to be identified immediately as code words.

The name of the country is necessary in a cable address, for the information of the telegraph company.   The name of the country should be enclosed in parentheses after the name of the city.   It is sent free.

If a traveler has no definite foreign address, cables or radio messages may be dispatched to him in care of the telegraph companies (to be held in the "Will Call" files); or wires may be sent in care of the large travel bureaus, such as Thos. Cook & Son, and the American Express Company. Special code addresses for such messages may be obtained from the telegraph companies or travel bureaus.   Cables sent in care of a registered code address should be clearly marked "Care".

LT	September 28, 1952
John Hamland	10:15 a.m.
Care AMEXCO	
Rome (Italy)	

Routing of Cables.   International messages to be dispatched by cable or radio may be sent from any telegraph office.   The sender may specify, without charge, the name of the international telegraph company he wishes to carry his message from the United States.   The routings available are:

Via All America	Via Mackay Radio
Via Commercial Cable	Via R C A
Via French Cable	Via Tropical
Via Globe Wireless	Via Western Union Cables

Cable Signatures.   Cable signatures are counted and charged for.

Cables may be sent unsigned, or signed with a code signature.

Cables Prepaid.   All cables must be prepaid, unless special arrangements are made for collect transmission.

Replies may be prepaid—the sender writing the letters RP (and the amount prepaid) above the address, and prepaying the reply when he sends the cable.

Coding Cables.   Numerous codes are in use, among the largest and best known being the Western Union Code, the A.B.C. Code, Bentley's Code, and the Acme Code.   Many codes are for special subjects, as for banking, securities, shipping, and commodities.   Many are printed in

380

different languages (each with an English text), as the Marconi Code, which is printed in nine languages.

Most countries will accept any type of code, provided the code words do not contain more than 5 letters each. However, some countries do not permit incoming cables to be coded in any but standard codes. If using a private code, check with the telegraph company to determine whether such code will be received in the country for which it is destined.

Double-check every word when coding or decoding a cable. One wrong letter can make the entire cable unintelligible.

If a code message is received in an unknown code, consult the telegraph company for assistance in determining the code if possible. If the code is unrecognizable to them, a regular cable code company must be consulted.

Numbering Cables. If a series of cables are being sent, they should be numbered consecutively, both for checking delivery and for future reference.

Make up a page of consecutive numbers on ruled paper. As each number is used on an outgoing cable, check it off and write opposite it the date sent, the addressee, and the initials of the sender.

Begin the cable message with the outgoing number followed by the incoming number, if any—in figures. (A plain-language letter message may include a check word or number as the first text word; but such check word or number is limited to 5 characters.)

STELDOT
Sydney (Australia)
    45/26   Compare prices with those cabled...
(This check number would be counted as one word and would mean "Our cable 45, your cable 26".)

Word Count

In cable texts, in plain or secret language, each word appearing in a standard dictionary of one of the admitted languages, or each word in common use in one of those languages, is counted at the rate of 15 letters to the word.

A proper name, such as the family name of one person, the full or abbreviated name of a place, square, boulevard, street or other public way, the name of a ship, or the designation of an aircraft or railway train, may be run together as one word, as "Vandekamp", "Newyork", "Stjamesstreet", and "Queenmary", and will be counted at the rate of 15 letters to the word.

Hyphened words are counted as separate words, unless they appear in a standard dictionary of one of the admitted languages, in which case they are joined and counted at 15 letters to the word.

381

Coined words, as "retel" and "relet", are now considered code words and, in full–rate messages, are counted at 5 letters to the word. Such coined words are not permitted in letter messages.

Common abbreviations when written solid, as "FOB", are counted at the rate of 5 letters to the word.

Groups composed of letters, figures, signs, or a mixture thereof, where authorized (such as commercial marks and trade-marks appearing in a published catalogue, price list, or the like), house numbers and ordinal numbers consisting of figures and letters—when written solid—are counted at the rate of 5 characters to the word. If spaced out, each separate letter or figure is counted as one word.

A whole number, fraction, decimal or fractional number, when written in words, may be run together as one word, as "sixfoursix", and will be counted at the rate of 15 letters to the word. When written in figures, numbers are counted at 5 characters to the word, as "12345".

Punctuation marks not essential to the meaning of a cable, such as hyphens and apostrophes, are not transmitted, except at the request of the sender, in which case they are counted and charged for as one word each. Punctuation marks essential to the meaning of the message, such as quotation marks and parentheses, are transmitted, counted and charged for as one word for each pair.

Dollar and cent signs ($ and ¢) and the pound sterling mark (£) are counted as one word each. The number sign (#) is counted as one word.

The percent sign (%) is counted as three characters in a figure group.

Decimal points, commas, fraction bars, colons, and dashes used in figure groups are counted as one character each.

Examples of Word Count in Cables

Airmail	1 word	GHF45 (commercial mark)	1 word
Air express	2	TD14's (trade term)	2
Parcel post	2	15–162 (6 characters)	2
Twentyfive tons	2	12-1/2 (5 characters)	1
*RECAB (for re cable)	1	133rd (ordinal number)	1
*RELET (re letter)	1	"Life" (punctuation)	2
*RETEL (re telegram)	1	$50.25 (dollar sign)	2
*REURTEL (re your telegram)	2	#80592 (number sign)	2
*RYCAB (re your cable)	1	10% (5 characters)	1
*MFIVE (my five)	1	12½% (8 characters)	2
*YLTWO (your letter two)	1	15x6 (dimension)	1
*YSIX (your six)	1	8' 9" (feet and inches)	4

* Not admitted in letter telegrams or press telegrams.

CABLE AND RADIO SERVICES

There are now only two classifications of international messages (INTL):

Full–Rate or Ordinary Messages,   and   Letter Messages

Full–Rate Messages

Any number of words at full rate per word (approximately 25¢ a word).
Minimum charge is for 5 words, counting address and signature.
Day and night service.   Straight, fast dispatch.

Plain language and secret language may both be used, alone or together in the same message, with the plain language (dictionary) words being counted at the rate of 15 letters to the word, and the code words at 5 letters to the word.

Any foreign language that can be expressed in letters of ordinary type may be used—straight, or mixed with English.

Cipher words are figure groups used as a code, as "46548".   A cipher message may be entirely in figures, or in plain language mixed with cipher.

A combination of figures and letters, figures or letters and signs with a secret meaning, within a single group, is not admitted.

Letter Messages (LT)

Any number of words at ½ the full rate (approximately 12¢ a word).
Minimum charge is for 22 words, counting address and signature.

Overnight service for delivery after 8 o'clock the next morning.   Accepted until midnight.   Delivery in the Far East, Australia, and South Africa is delayed because of time differences—delivery in some countries, such as India, being made at 2 p.m. the next day; and in countries like Australia at 9 a.m. on the second morning, or about 36 hours, after filing.   Delivery in the Hawaiian Islands (which are not across the date line) is made after 8 o'clock on the following morning.

Only plain language (English, or any foreign language that can be expressed in letters of ordinary type) may be used.

Secret language is not admitted in letter messages.

All words and figures must have a connected meaning, that is, each word, figure, or expression must have the meaning normally assigned to it in the language to which it belongs.

Code words cannot be used (with the exception of registered code addresses and signatures).   But a check word or number may be used as the first text word.

Coined words, such as "relet", are now considered code words and not permitted in letter messages.

Numbers written in figures (used in their natural sense), **commercial marks, trade terms, and abbreviations** are admitted—provided they present a connected meaning—and are counted at 5 characters to the word.

LT (meaning "letter telegram") **must be written above the address** on every letter message.   It is transmitted and charged for.

RADIO MARINE SERVICE

Radio to Ships at Sea.   One class of service.

Rate per word to vessels of American registry: 21¢ a word if dispatched from a near radio station, 29¢ a word from a far station.   (A higher rate— 5¢ a word more—is charged to vessels of foreign registry.)   If a ship cannot be reached from an American radio station, the message will be sent to a foreign station and relayed back to the ship, at an additional charge for the radiogram to the foreign station.

Radio messages to passengers on ships at sea will be dispatched by any telegraph company.

Write INTL (meaning "international message") above the address, and address as follows:

Radio indicator		INTL
Name of passenger	AS:	John McLane
Name of ship		SS BRITANNIA
Name of radio station		Newyorkradio

Note the brevity of the address.   It is not necessary to give the ship's destination or the name of the steamship company, unless there are two ships of the same name.

The passenger's stateroom number is unnecessary; that can be supplied from the passenger list when the message is received at sea.

The name of the radio station is run together as shown.

Addresses and signatures are counted and charged for.

Plain or code language may be used.

WIRES, GENERAL

Incoming Wires.   An understanding should be had in every office regarding the opening of incoming wires.

All wires should be either opened or delivered immediately to the addressees, whether they are engaged or not.   In the addressees' absence, business wires should be opened by some responsible person in the office, to determine whether any immediate action is required.

Personal wires should be held an agreed length of time for absent addressees, and after that time should be opened, or an effort should be made to reach the addressees by telephone.

No wire should lie unopened or unattended to for more than ten minutes, awaiting the return of the addressee.   The significance of a wire is "immediate attention".

If responsible for carrying out the orders or attending to the details mentioned in incoming wires, **mark off the sentences by diagonal lines, and check and double-check** to make sure that everything is complied with. It is very easy to overlook an important point because of the continuous and often blind phrasing of a wire.

If code words appear in an incoming wire, write the meaning above each code word. If a large number of the words are in code, write the decoded message on a separate page and attach it to the wire.

Garbled Words. If garbled or unintelligible words appear in an incoming wire, they will be "serviced" by the telegraph company for correction, without charge.

Copying Wires. When making copies of wires, copy in small, ordinary type, and not in capital letters.

Write at the top of all copies, as a means of identification:

(COPY OF WIRE RECEIVED)   or   (COPY OF WIRE SENT)

Copy the name of the telegraph company always. It is important for future reference.

Copy the class of message received or sent, as "Day Letter" (DL), "Night Letter" (NL), etc.

Copy the hour of receipt, as well as the date, and the name of the city of origin.

It is not customary to copy the various indicia—letters and numbers— that appear above the address on an incoming wire, unless the person who is to use the copy is likely to refer to the telegraph company concerning the wire. In that event the figures and letters would be necessary for identification of the wire.

Punctuate a copied wire with periods or spaces wherever stops are indicated. Paragraph it if several subjects are mentioned—this for convenience in reading.

Copy numbers, prices, dates, etc., in figures, and double-check to make sure that they correspond with the spelled-out numbers in the wire. But when copying a wire **for legal purposes,** copy it **exactly as it is written,** in the manner of punctuation, caps, spelled-out numbers, etc. (underlining any letter or mark that is obviously wrong).

Always write "(Sgd.)" before the signature on a copied wire.

❖

TELEPHONE

Listings in the telephone directories are sometimes difficult to find.

Government offices are under U, "United States Government".
Post Office is under "United States Government", if not under P.
State offices are under the name of the state.
County offices are under the name of the county.
City offices are under the name of the city.
Public libraries are under the name of the city, or under P.
Buildings are under "Office Buildings" or "Buildings" in the classified sections.
Company names beginning with letters are immediately under the alphabetizing letters (as "RCA Communications" would be among the first names under "R").
Radio stations are immediately under the alphabetizing letters, or under "Radio (or Television) Broadcasting" in the classified sections.
Consulates are under C, or under the names of nationalities or countries.
Weather forecast (if available) is in the front of the directory, or under W.
Time-of-day information (if available) is in the front of the directory, or may be listed under the name of the telephone company.
Information is in the front of the directory under "Service Calls".
Long Distance on dial telephones is 211 or 110 (or just "0" in smaller cities). It appears in the front of the directory.
Repair service for telephones usually appears in the front of the directory, or is listed under the name of the telephone company.
Business offices of the telephone company are listed in the front of the directory, or are to be found under the name of the telephone company.

Telephone List. In every office a special telephone list or small telephone book should be kept, in which are listed the numbers most frequently called. This list should always include the following numbers:

Nearest telegraph offices
Nearest post office station
Post office information
Home telephone number of every person in the office
Office of the manager of the building in which located
Hotel names most frequently called
Time-of-day information
Information (telephone)
Long Distance

New Numbers. Whenever an office telephone number is changed, all regular callers should be notified immediately. Especially should those be notified who might call over long distance.

Likewise, new telephone numbers should be noted in all office telephone books, and in the telephone directory itself.

Answering Telephone. The telephone companies spend money to advertise this request: "Please answer promptly." It is discourteous to the caller to permit a telephone to ring and ring.

386

When answering a business telephone, state the number or identity in a few words—not just say "Hello". For brevity, the secretary's name is not usually given, unless she has an executive position, when she may say such as "Mr. Lee's office, Miss Hunter speaking."

To soften "Who's calling, please?", preface the inquiry by an honest statement, such as "Mr. Lee is engaged at the moment, may I ask who's calling?"

Answer interoffice switchboard calls with "Yes?" rather than "Hello".

Do not let an incoming caller wait indefinitely for someone without asking him whether he prefers to hold the line, call back, or give a message.

Put the receiver down carefully when another is telephoning on an extension line. The sharp compact of a receiver being banged down can stop his conversation or hurt his ear.

Manner Over Telephone. Do not affect a detached air of speaking away from the mouthpiece, or over it. **Speak directly into it.**

Speak slowly and clearly, in an even tone of voice. Do not attempt to speak too low or in a muffled tone.

A telephone conversation should be in a rather deliberate, unhurried manner, which gives the hearer time to understand and the speaker time to think.

Be brief, but courteous. Every caller may be a prospective customer. Telephone insolence is almost always reported to an employer.

Never call a woman "Madam" over the telephone. It is not complimentary.

Taking Messages. On an incoming call—if the person called is not in, always offer to take a message.

Write down every message taken for another, and put it on his desk if he is absent; or keep a separate file of such messages for his immediate attention when he returns. Never attempt to "remember" telephone calls.

Date every message and give the hour of the call. This is most important.

Write down all of the pertinent and exact information that is given, not just a part of it. Vague messages are only confusing.

Telephone numbers and names must be absolutely correct. Ask the person to repeat them, or spell them, if necessary.

Instead of writing "called" on a telephone message, write "phoned". "Called" could mean that the caller came in person.

Printed slips are not always used for telephone messages; but all telephone memorandums are written in this approximate form:

1. Hour and date	3:45 p.m. May 18
2. Name and identity of caller	Mr. Meredith of the Lyons & Walsh Co. phoned.
3. Exact message	He would like to obtain a copy of our drawings on the Tower job so they can figure foundations.
4. Caller's telephone number	Phone – Cal. 5-7834, Ext. 8. L. M.

If a message has been difficult to take, repeat it to the caller, so he will know that it will be delivered correctly.

But if taking a difficult message when outsiders are present, do not repeat the information being received. Ask the telephoner to repeat it, and simply write it down.

Giving Messages. When calling a number for someone else, and the person called is not in, **find out when he will be in,** and do not hang up without first relaying this information to the person who is calling. Give the caller the privilege of leaving a message, always.

If telephoning about anything that will be particularly hard to explain, or about which something may be overlooked, make notes beforehand and talk from them; or have a file on the subject at hand. Do not trust to memory.

When telephoning a wire, or giving a message of any importance, use a private telephone if possible, so that visitors cannot overhear.

Giving Information. Never give any information voluntarily over the telephone unless authorized so to do. Speak rather in a general way.

Such a casual sentence as "He is in Chicago today" may be telling something very important to the listener. Business is a large game, and everything is information.

A friendly explanation, as "He's busy on another wire, talking long distance to Denver", may be to the listener definite information. All that need be said in such an instance is "He is talking on another wire. Will you hold the line?"

Note the difference in the following:

Definite information:	Indefinite yet sufficient:
"He hasn't come in yet."	"He isn't here just now."
"He's in Houston today."	"He is out of town today."
"He's playing golf this afternoon."	"He won't return to the office today."
"He's ill."	"He won't be in today."
"He has gone to California for a couple of months."	"He is on a trip and not expected back for several weeks."
"You can reach him at Los Angeles."	"I can get in touch with him and have him wire you."
	or
	"Is there anything that I can do?"

There are times, of course, when definite information should be given, but such information should be given only with the full knowledge of the person responsible for or affected by it. Transmit to him all incoming queries, and let him be the one to indicate the replies. Or have an understanding with him regarding information to be given out.

If, for example, a caller asks about an unfamiliar order or project, never say "I don't recall it", or "I haven't heard of it." Say rather, "I'll look it up"; and if after looking it up, it is found that a delay in delivery or some such bad news must be given to the inquirer, make sure that the person responsible knows that this information is being given out **before it is given out.**

Getting Information. When seeking information from a large organization, ask for a department or division under the name of the nature of the business in hand.

388

For instance, if desiring to order carbon paper from a large stationery store, and it is not known whether the order would be handled in the order department or the carbon paper department, phrase the request so as to cover the nature of the call:

"May I have the department that handles carbon paper orders?" Their operator will know immediately which department to call. Similar requests for departments may be phrased:

"May I have the typewriter repair department?"

"May I have the accounting department that handles accounts under the letter M?"

Never phrase an opening request like this: "We want to know something about our April bill." With such a beginning, the caller will probably be shifted from one department to another, telling his name over and over, until he strikes the right department.

If seemingly the wrong party has answered a telephone call, verify the number, as "Is this Capital 8892?" Never ask bluntly "Who is this?"

When Others are Telephoning. Stop typing when anyone is telephoning near the desk, or ascertain if it is all right to continue.

If the person telephoning appears to be having difficulty in hearing, or if he is talking over long distance, make the room as quiet as possible by closing doors and windows. Refrain from making the slightest unnecessary noise such as turning papers, pulling out desk drawers, etc.

If it is necessary to give a message to the person telephoning, write it on a slip of paper for him to read. He can read and listen, but he cannot listen to two people at once. If it is necessary to speak to him, let him break his conversation to listen.

If someone enters an adjoining room when an important telephone conversation is being held, close the connecting door.

If the conversation seems to be of a personal nature, find some excuse to leave the room quietly.

⋯

TELEPHONE SERVICES

Method of Placing Long Distance Calls. The preferred method of placing long distance calls is to give the Long Distance operator the information in the following order:

1. Name of city called.
2. Telephone number, or name and address of party called.
3. Name of particular person with whom caller desires to talk (if a person-to-person call); or state that caller will talk with anyone who answers (if a station-to-station call).
4. Telephone number and name of caller, when it is requested by the operator.
5. If the charges are to be reversed, the operator should be so notified.
6. If the caller desires to know the charges on the completed call, the operator should be so notified.

The reason for preference of the above method is that if the name of the city is given first, "Long Distance" can immediately make a connection to that city and practically complete the call while taking down the rest of the information.

On all long distance calls, give the telephone number of the person or company being called if possible. It expedites service.

Station-to-Station or Person-to-Person Calls. On a "station-to-station call", the caller agrees to talk with anyone who answers at the called number; while on a "person-to-person call", the caller may specify the particular person with whom he wishes to talk.

Because station-to-station calls are cheaper than person-to-person, always, when asked to place a long distance call, inquire regarding the method to be used.

Numbers 5 and 9 Confused. When placing a call, stress the difference between the numbers 5 and 9. An error in the telephone records may often be traced to a misunderstanding of 5 or 9. Notice that telephone operators usually sound these words very distinctly by elongating them into "fi-iv" and "ny-yen".

Long Distance Information. On most switchboards there is no Long Distance Information operator.

For information regarding telephone numbers in other cities, call the regular Information operator.

For information regarding rates, call the Long Distance Rate Operator.

For information regarding any other part of long distance service, call the Long Distance Chief Operator.

List of Calls Placed. Make a memorandum of every long distance call placed. Keep these memorandums in a file or an envelope and check them against the monthly long distance bill. If any errors have been made in the billing, they can be corrected by this checkup.

Charges. Long distance rates, including ship-to-shore and overseas rates, are given in the front and/or back of the telephone directory. Study these rate schedules carefully so as to be able to consult them intelligently and quickly when called upon to do so.

If any question exists regarding the actual charges, call the Long Distance Rate Operator for rates before placing the call. When the rate is received, write it in the address book beside the respective telephone number or address.

A partial charge, known as a "report charge", is made on a person-to-person call which cannot be completed for a certain reason, such as the called party's not being available. If the call is held and put through at a later hour, there is no report charge.

The toll charges on a completed call may be obtained from the Long Distance Rate Operator immediately after the call is completed.

If there has been trouble or dissatisfaction regarding the call, it should be reported immediately to the Long Distance Chief Operator. Adjustments are made for any unsatisfactory service.

Appointment Calls. A definite time for conversation may be specified when a long distance call is being placed, so that arrangements may be made in advance with the called station or person. Person-to-person rates apply.

Messenger Calls. A call may be placed to a person not having telephone service. A messenger is sent to summon the person to a telephone. A messenger charge, as well as a toll charge, is made for this service.

Reduced Night and Sunday Rates. Apply to both station-to-station and person-to-person calls, and, in general, go into effect at 6 p.m. (to England at 5 p.m.); the Sunday rates being effective from 6 o'clock Saturday evening to 4:30 Monday morning. The time at the calling station governs.

Reduced rates apply also to Canada, and certain overseas points; but do not apply to calls to ships at sea.

390

Ships at Sea. Telephone service is available only to certain of the larger ships equipped for such communications while at sea and within calling range. The names of such ships and the rates for this service are given in the front or back of the telephone directory.

Place the call through the regular Long Distance operator in the following manner:

1. Ask first for "Ship-to-Shore Service"; then give
2. Name of ship
3. Person called
4. Stateroom number (if available)
5. Person calling, and telephone number
6. And state whether the caller desires to know the charges on the completed call.

Ships in Harbor. Many of the larger ships have direct telephone service when in the New York harbor. Out-of-town calls direct to such ships can be made through long distance service. Local calls can be made through the steamship lines that operate such ships.

In other harbors, messages may be delivered to persons on ships by being telephoned to the steamship lines that operate the ships.

Train Service. In some of the large cities, telephone calls may be placed to certain trains within half an hour before their departure. These calls should be made through the offices of the railroads operating the trains.

Overseas Service. Overseas calls are placed through the regular Long Distance operators, in exactly the same manner as ordinary long distance calls, except that the caller should ask first for "Overseas Service".

If the foreign telephone number is available, it should be given.

There is but one class of overseas call (except to Cuba), that is, no differentiation between station-to-station and person-to-person calls.

"Collect" overseas calls can be made only to Cuba, Hawaii, and Puerto Rico.

Rates to different points may be found in the front or back of the telephone. directory, or obtained from the Long Distance Rate Operator.

Teletypewriter Service. The teletypewriter is a typewriterlike device that can be installed in any office for the sending and receiving of written messages, or for the carrying on of a written conversation, over telephone lines.

Teletypewriter service is divided into two classes:

1. **Private line teletypewriter service**—consisting of teletypewriters installed at two or more locations, either in the same city or in distant cities, and so connected that when copy is written on one machine it appears simultaneously on all other machines on the private line. It is possible to send and receive messages from any and all points on the circuit. This service is furnished on a daily basis for a fixed number of hours.

2. **Teletypewriter exchange service (TWX service)**—in which the teletypewriters are connected with an exchange or central office, and parties are called as they are in telephone service. There is no charge for the installation of this class of service; the charges are for the actual amount of use. Rates are based on a 3-minute period, as in long distance service.

Teletypewriter service is valuable for sending sales reports, orders, invoices, market quotations, news, company instructions, accounting records, summaries of stock, total day's business, or any other multiple business records.

The advantage in comparison with ordinary telephone service is that a written record of the message is available at both points of the conversation. Tabulated matter can be transferred easily; and special forms may be used.

The hectograph process of reproduction is available; or as many as six carbon copies can be made on each teletypewriter, if carbon-interleaved rolls are used.

Conference Service. Conferences may be arranged on the telephone, in the same city or in different cities. The several persons are simultaneously connected for discussion. Information and rates for this service may be obtained from the Long Distance Conference Operator.

Telephone Message Service. If an office telephone is to be left unattended for a considerable length of time, arrangements should be made with the telephone company to have the calls transferred to another number; or a telephone-answering service should be employed (if available) to take all messages.

Calls cannot be transferred for less than 24-hour periods, except in emergency instances.

Reduced Vacation or Suspension Rates. If a telephone is not to be used for a month or more, a special vacation or suspension rate may be had. For information consult the telephone company's business office.

Foreign and Domestic Telephone Books. Telephone books of domestic cities, and some foreign cities, may be consulted at the principal business offices of the telephone companies, or in large public libraries. Or they may be purchased at cost price through the business offices of the telephone companies.

❖

DICTATION

The following cautions may seem unimportant to some; but it is surprising how many shorthand writers sidestep these definite aids to efficiency.

Date the notebook every day. Much needless searching through notebooks has been caused by neglect to do this.

Have one place for the notebook on the desk, and keep it there when not in use, so as to be able to find it readily when called for dictation.

Save used notebooks for one year. Then discard the oldest when filing the latest. It is not unusual to be asked to retranscribe notes a year old.

Cross off dictation immediately after transcribing each page. This is an important safeguard against the possible omission of some part of the work.

Keep a rubber band around the notebook to mark the end of the finished notes, in order not to be constantly fluttering pages looking for a place to write when called for dictation.

If dictation, such as a telegram, is taken on a separate piece of paper, date that paper and file it away with the old notebooks. It may be necessary to refer to it again.

Do not be extravagant with notebooks by making large, careless notes. If it is difficult to keep the notes small, use a notebook with unglazed paper. The pencil will not glide so easily over this paper, and thus the strokes will be retarded, making smaller, neater notes.

Check the notebook at the end of each day to see that nothing important is left undone. Failure to do this has caused trips back to the office at night. Serious consequences might arise if, for instance, a wire is not dispatched as it should be.

Pencils. Keep three dictation pencils always in readiness in one certain place on the desk. Sharpen pencils **after** taking dictation, not after being called to take dictation.

The best shorthand pencil is the medium soft No. 2. The No. 1 is too soft to hold a point; and the No. 3, while hard and holding its point, tires the hand in pressing down to make the notes clear.

Sit Facing the Dictator. Always sit facing the dictator if possible— across the desk, or at one end of the desk. It is much easier to hear when facing the person who is speaking; and it is also much easier to write on the solidity of a desk than on the insecurity of a shelf or other device.

Taking Notes. In taking fast dictation, when it is almost impossible to follow the thought, **concentrate on each word.** Pronounce the words mentally as they are written. In transcribing, words will appear of which there is no recollection whatsoever, and the outlines must be depended upon. The memory will assist only if the words were mentally pronounced as written.

Interrupt a dictator, when the dictation is too fast, by repeating the last word written. Repeat any word not clearly understood or that seems incorrect.

Do not omit a single word in taking dictation, or write it indistinctly, thinking to remember it. Guesswork causes a high degree of inaccuracy.

If a sentence is not clear, check it, and read it back to the dictator at the end of the dictation. Do not attempt to "fix it up" in the transcription.

It is more experienced to ask than to be incorrect.

Longhand Notes. Write very little in longhand. Have distinctive outlines for all familiar names and write them in shorthand.

Unfamiliar names, initials, and addresses **should be written in longhand,** which will later serve to identify them in the notebook.

To Clarify Notes. Use the shorthand mark to indicate a period or a question mark after every sentence. Do not leave sentences open. It is difficult later to tell where one sentence ends and another begins.

If a shorthand character is written too long or too large, put two small marks through it; these will not cancel the character but will indicate that it was intended to be shorter or smaller.

If having difficulty reading the notes, make use of the accent marks to indicate long vowel sounds, etc.—if writing a shorthand that uses such marks. These facilitate transcribing.

Grammatical Errors. Grammatical errors should be corrected in transcribing not in taking dictation. Mention only the noticeable recurrence of a word or phrase to the dictator, who might want to correct it.

Extra-Copy Notations. When extra copies are to be made of a certain transcription, make this notation at the **beginning** of the notes, not at the end, so that it will act as a prompter at the start of the transcribing and not be discovered only at the finish.

Ask the dictator about making an extra copy of a letter when it seems obvious that a copy should be sent to someone besides the addressee.

Taking Telegrams. When a telegram is dictated, turn back a corner of the page to mark the place, and to serve as a reminder to write the wire first.

Interruptions. If interruptions occur while taking dictation, read over and correct the outlines of the notes already taken. This always aids in transcribing.

If a caller arrives, leave the room unless asked to remain.

If a telephone call interrupts, it is of course not necessary to leave unless the call is personal, in which case it is thoughtful to find some excuse to leave and close the door.

Reading Notes Back. In reading notes back, concentrate on the notes and not on the speed of the reading. Read in a clear, even tone.

394

Do not be embarrassed if it is necessary to pause over a shorthand note. It is better to pause than to read something incorrectly.

Receiving Papers. When papers are received with the dictation, keep them face up on the desk, and make very light shorthand notes (which can be erased later) on those that require special handling. It seems easy to remember what is to be done with a paper at the time of receiving it, but later, when many things have intervened, instructions sometimes will have vanished unless they have been written down.

Special Instructions. Make notes of all special instructions. These notes, whether pertaining to the dictation or not, may be written in the notebook, unless an extra pad of paper is handy. If they are written in the notebook, turn back corners of the pages to serve as reminders to attend to these outside details before beginning the transcribing.

Transcribing. Transcribing is an exacting job. Do not attempt to read notes too fast or indifferently, which invariably results in errors. Learn to follow and not anticipate the shorthand notes. Question things **before** writing them rather than afterward. Check dates, names, etc., against the papers handed with the dictation. Make sure that the dictator has answered all parts of incoming letters. No one is infallible in the matter of detail.

Grammatical Construction. Correct errors in grammar when transcribing. If the dictator questions a correction and desires that the sentence remain as dictated, comply with his wishes—"the dictator is always right".

Rearrange very little, if any, as the original manner of phrasing may mean more than the rearrangement

If small words, such as "so", "and", "but", "which", "that", and "the", have been noticeably repeated, some of them may be dropped or changed without impairing the meaning. But do not drop a word if without it the meaning will not be clear.

Do not be afraid to use the dictionary. Looking up words is not a sign of stupidity—it is a sign of care.

Mistakes. Never omit an unreadable word in the transcription. If a word is undecipherable, or if one has seemingly been left out of the notes, or if something looks obviously wrong, ask about it; or leave a blank space in the transcription with a pencil question mark after it.

Never hand in anything about which there is a question, thinking that it will "get by". Question-mark it in pencil on the margin, or write a note calling it to the attention of the dictator.

Errors that are discovered after material has been sent out are of much more consequence than those that are admitted and corrected at the start.

BUSINESS TERMS

Business terms are often not understood, or but vaguely understood, by those who encounter them in the course of their work.

DICTATION

Attempt to ascertain the exact meaning of all unusual phrasings that occur in business. Look them up, or as a final resort ask about them, rather than work with them for a period of time with only a hazy understanding of their meaning. The following are given merely to indicate that misconceptions might exist.

Nautical Terms

boxing the compass—not putting it away, but naming its 32 points in consecutive order.

charter party—not a person, nor a Magna Charta, but a lease of a ship.

dead reckoning—sailing by the use of instruments when observation of the heavenly bodies is impossible because of clouds. (Some laymen interpret "dead reckoning" as guessing, but it is far from that, unless the instruments fail.)

jettison—the casting overboard of a part of the cargo to save the rest.

jetsam and flotsam—are not the same. Jetsam is cargo cast overboard, or such cargo when washed ashore. Flotsam is cargo or wreckage found floating on the sea. (pron. flŏt'sam, not *float-sum*)

lighterage—not ballast thrown overboard, but a charge for conveying goods in a lighter.

log—means the speed-measuring instrument on a ship; the record of the log is entered in the "log book", which contains the complete record of the ship's journey. The log book is also called "the log".

lying in the harbor—not *"laying"*, but

lay days—the number of days allowed by a charter party for loading or unloading a ship.

Plimsoll mark—not a watermark on a ship, but a painted mark to indicate allowable depth a vessel may sink into the water, through loading.

ship chandler—a dealer who supplies provisions or accessories to ships.

ship's husband—an agent for a ship.

tramp steamer—not a derelict, but a ship legitimately engaged in independent trading.

Oil Terms

cracked gasoline—not undesirable gasoline, but that which is produced by cracking—breaking up petroleum products with intense heat and, usually, pressure.

fractionating—the breaking down of petroleum into its different fractions, such as gasoline, kerosene, lubricating oil, paraffin, etc.

spud in a well—does not mean clearing a piece of ground, but drilling in the first few hundred feet of hole.

wildcat well—does not imply rank speculation, but means a test well in an unproven area.

Newspaper Terms

fourth estate—not a mythical kingdom, but the press with its power, rank, and privileges. Historically, there were three estates or classes in Europe with distinct political powers. The press came to be known as the fourth estate.

The Gridiron Club—not a football association, but a newspapermen's club in Washington, D.C., which holds semiannual dinners, in December and April, and puts official Washington "on the fire".

the press—newspapers and periodicals collectively, as "the power of the press".

the Press—the persons working on or representing such publications.

BUSINESS TERMS

Railroad Terms

deadhead—to send a car or coach through empty.
rolling—shipment under way.
rolling stock—the wheeled equipment of a railroad.
shipped knocked down—shipped unassembled.
spot a car—place it at a certain spot on a siding.
spur track—a short sidetrack or branch track.
tariffs—not always import duties, but sometimes schedules of rates or carrying charges made by railroads, steamship lines, etc.

Political Terms

congressman—a member of Congress; may mean either a senator or a representative, but it is more frequently used to mean the latter.
congresswoman—may be used in the same manner as congressman.
filibuster—a blocking of legislative action, as by deliberately talking to consume time.
lame duck—an office holder who has been crippled politically, that is, he has not been re-elected to office.
omnibus bill—like a public vehicle, it carries many unrelated items.
pocket veto—A chief executive may cause a bill to fail by simply shelving ("pocketing") it until it automatically becomes void.
whip—an influential member of a political party who unofficially manages his fellow members or whips them into line, as the "Democratic Whip" in Congress.

Aviation Terms

airplane—a heavier-than-air craft.
airship—a lighter-than-air craft; a dirigible balloon, that is, one equipped with propelling and controlling devices.
avigation—the science of air navigation.
blind flying—flying by the use of instruments—"dead reckoning".
ceiling—the bottom or base of the cloud level. An airplane may fly through a ceiling and fly above it; or it may fly beneath the ceiling.
fuselage—the entire body (not just the engine space) of an airplane, including compartments for pilot, passengers, cargo, etc. (pron. fū′zě-lǐj; or Fr. fü′zě-läzh′)
meteorology—the science of the atmosphere and its variations or changes. Meteorology is not concerned merely with the common meteor or shooting star, but with winds, rain, snow, lightning, rainbows, auroras, etc., all of which are meteors of a sort. (pron. mē′tē-ēr-ŏl′ō-jy)

General Terms

backlog—unfilled orders, which give the security to a manufacturing company that a backlog gives to a fireplace.
bill of materials—not an invoice for materials, but a list of materials or parts that go into the fabricating of a piece of equipment; or a list of all equipment to be furnished on a job. Made up for the purpose of giving specifications or obtaining prices on the materials or equipment necessary.
bonded warehouse—a warehouse under bond to the Government for the storing and processing either of imported merchandise before the payment of duty thereon, or of domestic merchandise (such as liquors) before the payment of

397

taxes thereon. Such a warehouse operates under the supervision of a customs officer or a revenue officer, as the case may be. As the merchandise is removed for domestic consumption, the duty or taxes thereon are collected by the Government. Goods held thus are said to be "in bond".

cost-plus job—a job to be furnished at cost, plus a certain percentage of the cost as compensation to the contractor.

Diesel engine—an engine invented by Dr. Rudolf Diesel of Munich. The engine is economical in that it burns unrefined or crude oil. ("Diesel" is written with a capital, and pronounced dē′zĕl.)

ex dock
ex car
ex elevator
ex store
ex warehouse
} "Ex" is a preposition, not a prefix, in these phrases. It means "from" or "out of", as "from the dock", "out of the warehouse", etc. It is not hyphened to the word that follows, unless the two are used as a modifier.

firm price—a price that is unchangeable for a certain time.

nominal price—not necessarily a very low price (although sometimes it is), but often a price in name only—usually an approximate figure, or a reasonable figure.

Monel metal—a trade-mark for a rustproof alloy of high tensile strength, named after Ambrose Monell, an American manufacturer. ("Monel" is written with a capital, and pronounced mō-nĕl′.)

turn-key job—a job complete in every detail; the owner has simply to turn a key to start operations.

❖

TYPEWRITTEN WORK

Margins. An inch margin on all sides—slightly wider on the left—is a good standard margin for ordinary typewritten work. The margins on letters vary, of course, to permit centering.

Headings. **Main titles** should be centered and set in caps. They are not usually underlined, but often the letters are spaced.

Subheads are centered and underlined, with main words capitalized.

Sideheads are subordinate headings that are placed at the left and underlined, with main words capitalized. These headings may be set "flush" with the line of writing or extended two or three spaces beyond it. In the latter case, the typewriter left marginal stop should be set with the line of writing, not with the sideheads.

Paragraph ("run-in") heads, underlined, are used to save space.

To keep headings in line down the page, remember the starting position on the typewriter scale bar for each group of headings. This will save time when attempting to judge alinements.

Centering Headings. To center a heading, stop the carriage slightly to the right of the center of the page (because the center of the typewriting is a little past the center of the page) and then backspace slowly, spelling out the heading—one backspace for every two letters, or spaces, in the heading.

Punctuation of Headings. No period is necessary after a heading or title that stands alone (although occasionally a period is used after a segregated heading to make it conform to similar headings that are unsegregated). Usually the segregating space acts as sufficient punctuation. Question marks and exclamation points, however, are used after headings.

Underline headings with an unbroken line, not with a line under each word. Single words may be underlined in the text, but a heading is considered a single unit.

Long Headings. If a heading runs more than one line, do not break into the middle of a phrase when dividing the lines.

NOT: Labor, Materials, and Services to be
     Furnished by the Purchaser

BUT: Labor, Materials, and Services
     To be Furnished by the Purchaser

Never divide words at the ends of lines in headings.

Continued Headings. A heading may be carried over to the next page with the abbreviation "contd." after it—joined with a dash. The abbreviation "contd." need not be capitalized, enclosed in parentheses, or underlined. It is an unimportant word and should be unemphasized.

Building Materials—contd.

NOT: "(Cont'd)", which requires three needless liftings of the carriage.

Division of Headings. The order of importance in the subdivision of compositions is:

Volume	Article, or	MAIN TITLE
Book, or	Section	
Part	Clause, or	Centered Subheads
Chapter	Paragraph	
Section	Line	Sideheads
Paragraph		
Line		Paragraph Heads. ...

Numbered Headings and Items. The order of importance in numbered headings and items is as follows:

I. Roman Numerals (or Capital Letters)
  A. Capital Letters
    1. Arabic numerals (ordinary numerals)
      a. Small letters
      a-1. Small letters and figures   Small letters may be enclosed
      a-2. ....   in parentheses if being used to
      b. ....   number paragraphs; or if used
      b-1. ....   to number any other items
      c. ....   where they might blend with
    2. ....   the text.
  B. ....
II. ....

If only two divisions are involved, use:

I. ....   or   A. ....   or   1. ....
  1. ....   1. ....   a. ....
  2. ....   2. ....   b. ....
II. ....   B. ....   2. ....

The setup under the headings may be in indented, block, or hanging style, whichever best suits the text.

INDENTED: 1. ....
.... } for numbered paragraphs
....

BLOCK: 1. .... } for numbered sentences,
.... { separated by spaces

HANGING: 1. .... } for numbered items
....

Punctuation of Numbered Items. A period is sufficient punctuation to set off a numbering figure or letter. It is not necessary to go to the trouble of putting parentheses or dashes around each. Nor is it necessary to use -st, -d, or -th after the numbers.

WRITE SIMPLY:	RATHER THAN:
1. Cost of materials	–1– Cost of materials, or
2. Cost of transportation	(1) Cost of materials, or
3. Cost of production	1st. Cost of materials

If the items are short, it is not necessary to use periods after them—the spacing acts as punctuation. Even when such items end a sentence, often no period is used; yet a single period may be used (after the last item) if it is thought necessary.

If the items are long, a period may be used to close each item definitely.

If the items occur in a broken sentence, no punctuation is necessary after each item, unless the items run more than one line each and are closely connected; in that case a comma or semicolon may be used after each item, according to the need of segregation.

> We have investigated the questions involved in the divisions of
> 1. Shipping and related industries;
> 2. Construction and machinery, including lumber and metal products;
> 3. Chemicals, leather, and other manufactures;
> 4. Textiles and clothing;
> and we find that the points brought up by their attorney...

Capitalize only the first word of each item, unless a proper name occurs in the item.

Quantities are indicated by simple numbers before the words, or by dashes joining the numbers to the following items if the items begin with figures. The first word in each item need not be capitalized, since the number, not the word, begins the item.

> Included in the order are   The items necessary are:
>   2 telescopes   4 − 6″ frames
>   4 microscopes   20 − 2–5/8″ strips
>   8 thermometers   8 − 1″ pipes

Unnumbered Headings. Unnumbered subheadings should be indicated by underlinings and by unmistakable indention of margins.

Heading
>...
>...
>...

First Subhead
>...
>...
>...

First subdivision ....
>...

Second subdivision ....
>...

Second Subhead
>...
>...
>...

Heading
>...
>...
>...

Unsegregated Numberings. Parentheses are used to noticeably set off unsegregated numberings—except Roman numerals, which are distinctive enough in themselves, although not commonly used as numberings in texts.

No period or comma is necessary after the numbering in parentheses.

It is not necessary to capitalize unimportant items in an enumeration in the text. Capitalize only important divisions, or divisions that are sentences.

> The data required cover (a) weight, (b) dimensions, and (c) capacity.
> But if it is assumed (1) that the buyer is interested, and (2) that the price is right, an article may be...
> It is commonly used (1) to emphasize a point; (2) to separate a phrase; (3) to introduce an enumeration.
> It has these important assurances: (1) no adulteration of products; (2) supervision by experts; (3) constant analysis.
> They have three choices: (1) They can retrench. (2) They can consolidate. (3) They can liquidate.

First, Second, Third, etc.

first, second, third, last or final $\qquad$ are adjective forms.

first (or in the first place), secondly, thirdly, lastly (or last) or finally $\Big\}$ are adverbial forms.

"Firstly" is not commonly used with the adverbial forms; but it is predicted that it will some day return to favor.

1st, 2nd, 3rd, 4th, etc., are used in informal texts, without parentheses or periods.

These spelled-out numberings are usually introduced by a comma, dash, or colon (according to the pause indicated). They may be capitalized or not, according to the importance of the enumerations that they introduce.

> **As adjectives (describing nouns):**
> ...for the following **reasons:** first, that we ordered the goods; second, that they confirmed the order; and last, that shipment was made...
> They made three definite **proposals:** First, they will reduce the rent. Second, we can pay in quarterly installments. Third, the rent payments will apply on the purchase price if we exercise our option.
> **As adverbs (describing verbs):**
> It **represents,** first, a saving, secondly, an improvement, and last, a public benefit.
> Our discounts **are figured,** first, by the 15's; secondly, by the 10's; and thirdly, by the 5's; and it is our firm intention...
> The machines **were classified** carefully—first, by the speed, and secondly, by the power.

Paragraphing. Paragraph when the thought changes, or when it is necessary to emphasize a specific request or idea so that it will not be overlooked.

402

A paragraph need not cover an entire subject. One subject may extend over several paragraphs; but each paragraph should contain a certain phase or angle of the subject.

A paragraph should not run more than ten or fifteen lines. Paragraph rather frequently in single-spaced work so that the reader's eye can hold to the copy and his mind can retain the thought of the paragraph.

Avoid the constant use of short paragraphs of two or three lines each, unless information is being set down for quick reference. The staccato effect of short paragraphs gives great emphasis, but if the emphasis is not really intended, the value of the short paragraph is soon lost.

Indent the beginning of each main paragraph five or ten spaces, and each subordinate (set-in) paragraph enough spaces to keep the same indention as the main paragraph.

"Block" paragraphs and "hanging" paragraphs are not often used in ordinary letters. They are used chiefly in advertising and in various types of listings.

> This is a sample of block paragraphing.
> The first line is not indented, and all
> lines are set out to the same margin.

> This is a sample of a hanging paragraph.
> The first line is set out to the margin,
> and all others are indented.

Do not begin a paragraph within two lines of the bottom of a page. unless the paragraph is very short and can be finished on that page. Carry it over as a good beginning for the new page.

End of Page. Do not write too near the bottom of a page. On letters leave at least an inch margin always. Not only do papers slip at the bottom of a page (especially if it is necessary to erase), but some readers are particularly critical of and annoyed by seemingly careless writing too near the end of a page.

Do not crowd the signature almost off a page. This usually irritates the signer.

Learn to be a good judge of distances, or measure the page with a sheet of similar paper when nearing the bottom. The space concealed by the roller is often an optical illusion. There is a form of carbon paper that has a right marginal guide which is useful in determining the bottom margin of a page. Or a pencil dot may be used as a guide.

In some legal and governmental work, the first word on the next page is indicated in dropped position at the end of each page. But this is not done in general practice.

Page Numbering. To secure uniformity in the position of page numbers, select a number on the typewriter scale that is at approximately the center of the typewriting, and write all page numbers from that scale number. Place the page number at the extreme bottom of each page so that when the pages are turned all numbers will fall in an almost identical position.

Use a simple dash on each side of a page number. Do not surround it with fancy or unusual markings. It is unnecessary to write "Page" each time, or "#". Write simply –2–

NOT: *2*   NOR: =2=   NOR: #2   NOR: Page 2.

Inserted Page Numbers. When a page is inserted after the others are numbered, it should be numbered with a small letter, which is less conspicuous than, and therefore preferable to, a fraction or a capital letter.

	–18–a		–18–b		–18–c
RATHER THAN: –18½–	OR:	–18A–	OR:	–18–A–	

Avoid the insertion of extra pages if possible. It is often better to rewrite two pages than to insert a page with very little writing on it.

Canceled Page Numbers. (See Copy for the Press, p. 422.)

Appendix Page Numbers. Carry the regular page numbering straight through a composition, including the appendix, addenda, index, etc.

Prefaces are usually numbered with small Roman numerals.

Dating Papers. Date everything. Dates are one of the most important features on all business papers.

Write the month, the day, **and the year,** on every paper to be kept. Years change rapidly in business.

Date even notations, memorandum slips, and rough drafts.

The time of day is also most important on telegrams, memorandums of telephone calls, messages regarding callers, etc.

Place the date either at the beginning of a manuscript in the upper right corner (if it does not occur in the beginning of the text, as in legal papers), or at the end of the manuscript in the lower left corner (if it does not occur in the ending of the text).

If the date is not to appear on a manuscript—such as an article for publication—place a date on the file copy for future reference.

Charging for Piecework. In charging for occasional piecework, figure the time consumed, at a reasonable salary, and the cost of the material.

What may be considered "a day's work" depends upon the material being typed.

Fifteen to twenty pages of straight material, single-spaced, on letter-sized paper, with six or seven carbons, is considered a good day's work.

Thirty to thirty-six pages, double-spaced, on letter-sized paper, is a large day's work.

Tabulations

Timesavers. When setting up long tabulations, do not fail to make use of the tabulator key and stops. This saves time even though it takes time to set the stops.

Make a "practice line" first and set the stops accordingly. Guessing at the stops usually results in having to space twice or backspace once

404

after each stop, which not only causes loss of time but often results in misalinements.

Setup. **Put as much information as possible into the headings** of a tabulation and avoid the repetition of words or the use of ditto marks down the page.

It is not necessary to draw lines of dots or dashes ("leaders") in a tabulation unless the reading lines are hard to follow.

Note in the following illustration how many lost motions there may be in writing a simple tabulation. The second setup takes less time and effort, produces a better result, and is instantly clear.

Instead of this:		Use this form:		
	Price			Price/lb. in ¢
Oct. 25, 1935 Lead.......@ 4.0¢ lb.		1935		
" " " Zinc........@ 4.42¢ lb.		Oct. 25	Lead	4.0
" " " Tin........@ 52.5¢ lb.			Zinc	4.42
Nov. 1, " Copper.....@ 9.25¢ lb.			Tin	52.5
Jan. 17, 1936 Tin........@ 54.0¢ lb.		Nov. 1	Copper	9.25
		1936		
		Jan. 17	Tin	54.0

Dollars and Cents. The dollar sign ($) should be written but once at the beginning of a column and once under each main total line. It is in effect until broken by a main total line.

In long tabulations of dollars and cents, commas (after thousands) and decimal points are sometimes omitted and indicated by spaces. But the commas should not be omitted unless the spaces are used; unpunctuated numbers are most difficult to read.

$248 537 34	OR:	$248,537.34	BUT NOT:	$248537 34			
261 876 29		261,876.29		261876 29			
13 485 82		13,485.82		13485 82			
1 873 95		1,873.95		1873 95			

Signs and Abbreviations. Signs and abbreviations, such as %, #, @, lb., gals., and bbls., need to be written but once at the beginning of the column (or preferably included in the heading) if the entire column is of the same designation. It is unnecessary to repeat or ditto such designations unless they constantly change.

Ditto. **If an entire line is to be dittoed,** use "do." (not capitalized) instead of the repeated ditto marks.

Southern Lighting Corporation	8,970 shares
do.	10,260
Pennsylvania & Northern Co.	5,692

If only a few words are to be dittoed, use the ditto marks.

Willow Springs guide meridian
Yellowstone   "   "
Navajo meridian

MINUTES OF MEETINGS

Forms of minutes of meetings vary with different organizations. However, there is certain general information to be always included in minutes, as follows:

Title of meeting { Name of group, committee, or organization (in caps)
Regular or special meeting
Number of meeting, if numbered

Date and hour
Place
Presiding officer

Roll Call

Present   Absent
. . . .
. . . .

Statement of whether or not those present constitute a quorum.
Procedure:
        Reading of minutes of last meeting.
        Vote for approval or amendment of minutes.
        Reports.
        Unfinished business.
        Elections, if any.
        New business.
        Adjournment—hour.
Next meeting—date and place.

(Signed)_____
                         Secretary
(Minutes are sometimes signed also by the President or the Chairman.)

Corporation-meeting minutes follow the form outlined in the bylaws of each corporation, or in the printed instructions in corporation minute books.

Minutes are not usually recorded verbatim, with the exception of resolutions, which are usually recorded exactly as given.

Arrangement of Minutes. Arrange the minutes so that important matters, such as resolutions, votes, and decisions, can be instantly discerned.

If the minutes are long and involved, **sideheads** or **paragraph heads** may be used to advantage; or important words may be underlined.

Stock Issue
    . . . .
. . . .

New Building
    . . . .
. . . .

An **index** of the more important subjects discussed at the different meetings may be kept in the back of the minute book or on separate cards. An item in the index might read:

Louisiana Land Deal
Discussed in Minutes of   June 6, 1934
                          Sept. 5, 1934
                          Jan. 2, 1935
Survey and Report in Minutes of Feb. 6, 1936

Always make a rough draft of the minutes before copying them into the minute book. No erasures should appear in the minute book.

If minutes are amended or corrected at the meeting at which they are read, the corrections should be put in in red ink, or the amendments should be written on a separate page to be attached. No minutes should be rewritten after they have been read. They should stand as corrected.

If a certain paper is to be made a part of the minutes, it need not be actually written into the minutes unless it is very short. A notation may be made in the minutes to the effect that the paper is to be incorporated therein, and that it may be found in a certain file or other place of safekeeping.

Preparation for Meeting. The secretary of the meeting should see:

That notices of the meeting are sent to all concerned, in accordance with the rules or bylaws of the body that is to meet;

That the meeting-room is arranged for and is in readiness on the day of the meeting; and

That all papers pertaining to the meeting are at hand; also the corporation seal and other incidentals that may be necessary.

The secretary or recorder of the meeting should sit near the chairman, or in a position to hear every word that is said. If unable to hear, the recorder should, by a signal, so inform the chairman, who can interrupt the speaker and ask for a repetition of what has been said if he deems it of sufficient importance to do so.

Obtaining Information Beforehand. It simplifies the taking of minutes if information is obtained beforehand. Ascertain the purpose of the meeting, and if possible read copies of resolutions, reports, etc., to be presented.

Obtain a list of the persons to be present, and at the meeting simply check the names "p" or "a" (present or absent) on the list. Note late arrivals and early departures, as an important point may hinge on whether or not a certain person heard a certain discussion.

The more preknowledge that can be had of a meeting, the easier it will be to record the minutes.

Resolutions

Formal resolutions follow various forms. The following is an ordinary outline, with the word WHEREAS set in caps, the first word after it not capitalized unless it is a proper name, and no comma after WHEREAS unless punctuation is necessary for the sense of the sentence. The word RESOLVED is set in caps and followed by a comma and a capital letter. The "Therefore be it" is set on the line above RESOLVED.

WHEREAS it has become necessary......
.......................; and
WHEREAS conditions are such as to
warrant...............; and
WHEREAS, moreover, on the 16th of May,
1936, ...: Therefore be it
    RESOLVED, That ....
......................; and be it
    RESOLVED further, That...............
....

Informal resolutions dispense with WHEREAS and "Therefore be it", and simply state the facts or events leading up to the resolution.

......and the following resolution was unanimously adopted:
    RESOLVED, That...................
....
or
RESOLVED: First, that we........
    Secondly, that we.....
    Thirdly, that.........
    Finally, that.........

REPORTS

Reports are usually made in the following general form:

MAIN TITLE
Date*

To ....
    ....
    ....Introductory statement....................
....
Sidehead
    ....
....
Sidehead
    ....
....

– – – –

    CONCLUSION: (or RECOMMENDATION:)............
....
    Respectfully submitted,
Signature
Typed Signature
Initials

The "To" line and the "Respectfully submitted" line are often omitted if a "plain" report is being prepared.

* The date may be placed at the end beneath the initials, if preferred.

MEMORANDUMS

Ordinary form for memorandums:

Copies to . . . .
. . . .
. . . .

Date
(Hour is sometimes
necessary.)

MEMORANDUM to . . . . :

<u>Subject</u>

Body single-spaced or double-spaced, so that the writing will not
be too high on the page.

Signature
(typed on)

Initials
Notations

Note that: The word "Interoffice" is unnecessary before MEMORANDUM.
The "From" line is omitted, unless it is on a printed form.
No salutation is necessary.
No complimentary close is necessary.
Initials and other notations, such as "Attachments", and "Enc.",
are typed on.
The "Copies" notation may be at the top as indicated, or at the
bottom if preferred. Each person's name should be checked on
his copy.

Paper. Use plain paper for memorandums unless forms are provided. Memorandums to outsiders should be written on letterheads.

Signatures. Always submit a memorandum to the dictator to read
and sign or initial over his typed signature. Some dictators sign memorandums, and some do not.

Distributing Memorandums. If a memorandum is of a confidential
or personal nature, enclose it in a sealed envelope with the receiver's
name thereon.

Or if a memorandum has various attachments and will have to travel
through different hands, staple the attachments to the memorandum
and enclose it in an envelope with the first receiver's name thereon.

ROUGH DRAFTS

Write ROUGH DRAFT across the top of every rough draft. This
immediately identifies it and guards against any later confusion with the
finished copy.

Double-space all rough drafts so that corrections and interlineations
can be easily made.

Make only the number of copies to be actually used; otherwise copies
may get into the files and be mixed with the final copies.

Staple the pages of a rough draft together before submitting it, to preclude the possibility of later interchanging some of the pages with the corrected ones.

Destroying Rough Drafts or Handwritten Copy. Always return rough drafts or handwritten copies to the person responsible for them, for destruction. Clip a note thereto with the question "To be destroyed or filed?" It is his privilege then either to destroy the copies or mark them for the files.

A question often arises whether the final copy is as the original intended it to be; and if the dictator has the original he can compare the two.

TYPEWRITING

Touch. To acquire a very even touch, and produce typewriting that resembles printing—with carbon copies that are very clear—strike each key with the same force and with the same timing. To perfect this, practise occasionally following each word through mentally letter for letter as the keys are struck.

Speed. Adopt a steady pace when typing. Never hurry nervously even when working "against time". The time consumed in erasing invariably amounts to more in the long run than the time gained by hurrying. **It is the steady, even, errorless rate of speed that counts.**

Learn to follow and not anticipate what is to be written. The practice of following the first few words through mentally, until the mind and the fingers catch the rhythm, will eliminate errors in rush work Begin slowly, and a practically error-proof speed can be attained.

Concentrate also, word for word, on what is being read. Do not read a line ahead, except in shorthand. The moment the mind leaves the subject and does not follow word for word, the fingers are a little lost.

Do not be disturbed when given a large amount of work. Acquire the habit of arranging the most important work first. One who writes the most important papers or letters first will always seem speedier than another who attempts to do everything in routine order, although the first worker may even be the slower or more conservative typist.

Finger Discipline. When the fingers have a tendency invariably to miswrite or twist the letters of certain words, such as "expecially" for especially, "possible" for possibly, "enumberate" for enumerate, etc., practise writing such words at least twenty times, or until the fingers get the feel of the combination of the letters. Even experienced fingers slow down on some words such as the above.

Capital Shifts. Capital letters often "jump" or "drop" because the shift is made too quickly. Slow the fingers down a little on capitals, and this difficulty can be overcome. In nine cases out of ten it is the fault of the operator, not of the machine.

Never permit a piece of work to go out with the capitals all awry.

Be sparing in the use of capital letters. Unnecessary capitalization consumes time and effort in typing. To keep raising the carriage with the little fingers all day long is a tiresome job.

Spacing. Spacing with the right thumb is more satisfactory than alternate-thumb spacing. The left thumb is not generally strong enough to do all the spacing, unless the operator is left-handed. Alternate-thumb spacing is often productive of skipped spaces or of words run together.

Devices. Learn to make use of all the devices on a typewriter, especially the tabulator stops. The use of the stops saves much time in tabulated work, even though it takes a little time to set and reset them.

Learn to use the bell on the typewriter. This is an extra safeguard on margins. Particularly in rush work when the mind has other things to concentrate on besides margins, the bell will save many a line.

Always have the paper holders and paper guide working, and not pushed off to the sides. The holders prevent the paper from slipping when nearing the end of a page.

Do not attempt to maintain the left margin without the marginal stop. Reset the left marginal stop for every new setup in typing.

Make use of every mechanical device. The value of these mechanical assistants is fully appreciated only by the most efficient workers.

Typewriter Rollers. A hard or brass roller (platen) should be used on a machine **if more than four carbon copies** are usually being made.

It is almost impossible to make more than four clear copies with a soft roller; no matter how hard the keys are struck, the fifth and sixth copies blur.

Soft rollers are used for ordinary work—two to four carbon copies—because they produce less noise, and give the typewritten work an even effect.

When using a hard roller, if but one carbon copy is being made, run a piece of heavy paper behind the copy. This deadens the noise and gives the work an even appearance.

Ribbons. Use a black typewriter ribbon unless another color is specifically designated.

Change the ribbon frequently enough so that the work will be clear and black. A worker is judged by the appearance of his typewriting.

Never use a ribbon with holes in it, or one that is producing very uneven work. This is not economy of the right sort.

A red ribbon should be used conservatively. (As a substitute for a red ribbon, red carbon paper may be used.) Red may be used to indicate items of great importance, or to show deficits; but it should not be used for decorative purposes.

Accessories. Rubber caps on metal keys provide comfort for the fingers and for the eyes; they soften the finger contacts and eliminate the glare from the keys. They are unnecessary of course on the newer machines, which are equipped with dark composition keys.

411

A felt pad under the machine (or rubber caps on the feet) deadens the noise and steadies the typewriter; and if a typewriter is fastened down, it adds to the ease of writing.

Typewriter. Oil the typewriter about once a month; otherwise the carriage will become sluggish and "pull hard". Wipe the carriage tracks clean before applying new oil.

Keep the machine clean. Dust the typewriter every morning, and clean it thoroughly at least once a month—particularly the type. Clogged letters are a discredit to any typing.

Clean the roller with alcohol if it becomes slick and fails to grip the paper. A slick roller causes paper to slip, especially at the bottom of a page.

Cover the machine every night. The dampness of night air injures the delicate mechanism; and dust settling on a machine clogs it. A typewriter is a valuable piece of property.

Ordinary Typewriter Size. A 12-inch-gauge typewriter is the most practical size for ordinary purposes. Letter-sized paper may be inserted sidewise in this style of machine; and fairly long envelopes may be addressed on it.

Type Sizes and Styles. The two most popular sizes and styles of type are:

Elite	small
Pica	large

Specialized sizes and styles may be had on all standard makes of typewriters, in the following general classifications:

Microtype
Bank type
Econotype } very small, for use where space saving is desired, as in statistical work, on stencils, etc. A saving of from one-half to one-fourth of the ordinary amount of space and paper used may be effected by the use of these small types.
Miniature
Gothic

Italic—resembles italics.

Gothic—resembles printing; large or small sizes, for billing, labeling, card systems, etc.

Pin Point—for check-protection writing.

Boldface
or } very black, for distance reading, or for photographic reproduction.
Book type

Great Primer
Bulletin
Amplitype } very large, for use in schools.
Magnatype

Vogue
Vertical
Script } fancy or distinctive types for personal use.
Old English

Foreign languages—Type can be furnished for almost any foreign language desired.

ERASURES AND CORRECTIONS

Typographical Errors. Train the mind and hands to avoid these most frequent typographical errors:

Beginning to write without indenting paragraph.
Double-spacing when single-spacing should be used, or vice versa.
Leaving out a line.
Copying a line or paragraph twice.
Repeating a word, or leaving one out.
Repeating a word at the top of the second page.
Misspelling a word or name throughout a composition, because of not having taken the trouble to look it up at first.
Confusing words that sound alike, such as "cite" for "site", etc.
Copying from an old manuscript and not changing names, singulars and plurals, dates, etc., to conform to a new setup.
Punctuating hurriedly and incorrectly, and having to erase.
Beginning a tabulation too far to the right, and not having enough room to complete the tabulation.
Writing too near the bottom of a page.

And these annoying mistakes that show up only after the copy is out of the machine:

Carbons in backward.
Not enough carbons—one carbon paper having been overlooked.
Carbon corner folded over.
Under pages having gone around roller and printed twice.
Eraser protection slips having been left in, with blank spaces as a result.

Make a mechanical habit of thinking about and guarding against the above errors.

Question constructions **before** writing them, instead of afterward. It will save many erasures.

A few minutes extra time used in planning and careful typing on a page will save time and effort wasted in erasing or rewriting.

If the spelling of a word is doubtful, look it up **before** typing it, not afterward.

Decide upon the punctuation before putting it in, not afterward. Punctuation marks are very hard to erase.

Read shorthand notes a line in advance, and be sure of the meaning before writing anything down. Wrong words will be written if this is not done, and much time will be lost in erasing.

Erasures. Make clean erasures and replacements. No half erasures should be permitted.

Never be guilty of striking one letter over another.

Never permit a smudge or finger mark on any original paper; and keep the carbon copies as clean as possible. Cleanliness is of the utmost importance.

Write carefully when nearing the bottom of a page to avoid errors and to gauge distance. It is very difficult to erase low on a page and to have the machine hold the alinement.

413

Always move the carriage over when erasing so that the eraser refuse will not fall into the parts of the machine.

If a single letter is misstruck, it is necessary to erase on the original only. But if several letters are twisted, or a whole word garbled, it is necessary to erase on every carbon copy; otherwise letters will be piled on top of each other until a whole word is illegible.

If a figure is misstruck, it must be erased **on the original and every carbon copy.** A struck-over figure cannot be deciphered, and may cause a serious mistake by being misinterpreted.

Attempt never to erase in a price quotation or on a check. Sometimes one letter, but not a figure, may be erased. Verify sums of money before writing them, type carefully, and recheck after writing.

When to Erase and When to Rewrite. If it is necessary to remove two long words or several short ones (when five or six carbon copies are involved), it is easier to rewrite the page than to erase. The appearance of the page is of course improved, and time is sometimes gained by rewriting instead of making long and tiresome erasures.

To Make Clean Erasures. Use the round ink eraser with a brush for erasing on originals. But do not use this on carbons until they have first been erased with a pencil eraser. Keep the ink eraser clean for originals.

Always use an eraser shield (celluloid or steel) when erasing on copies that are out of the machine. The steel shield is the better—it has more perforations.

An eraser knife is an excellent aid in removing punctuation marks if the paper is heavy enough for such erasing. The point of the knife may be used to loosen deep impressions, and further erasing will be comparatively easy.

Artgum should be used with care. It is best suited to cleaning margins and large surfaces. See that the refuse from the artgum does not scatter through the papers. To remove it is a job in itself.

Erasing on Carbon Copies. Instead of using a scrap of paper as an eraser guard behind the next immediate carbon paper, use a regular steel guard (or a celluloid eraser shield). This sort of guard is thick enough to protect the under carbons; it is handy; and it is clean. And there is no danger of leaving it in the papers and writing over it as there is with the scrap of paper.

Corrections. Before putting in any corrections, proofread an entire letter or manuscript, noting errors with a light pencil check at the side. A page might require rewriting, and any erasures or corrections made thereon would be useless.

When putting in corrections on originals and carbon copies, do not erase and correct one copy at a time. Erase all copies, and then insert them, with carbons, in the machine and put in the corrections at one time. This can be done easily if the papers were properly alined when first written.

414

If copy is returned with pencil corrections thereon (they should never be in ink), do not erase the corrections until they have been typed into at least one copy of the manuscript. If they are erased first they may be forgotten.

Never put corrections in haphazardly. No one may see the letter or manuscript again before it is sent out, but the receiver will see it and judge it. Then too, letters are often returned with notations on them, and the employer can see the condition in which they were sent out.

Corrections in Bound Copies. Typewritten pages that are bound across the top may be reinserted in the typewriter for corrections. Run a blank piece of paper into the machine as a guide. As soon as it passes the paper holders in front, insert the bottom of the typewritten page behind it, and turn the roller backward, bringing the typewriting to the desired line.

Binding Copies. Bind the carbon copies first so that the original may have the benefit of the experience gained in putting the carbons together. Many things can go wrong in binding, such as holes being punched on the wrong side of the paper, improper spacing of holes, pages omitted, illustrations bound on the wrong side, etc.

❖

CARBON COPIES

Number of Carbon Copies. Check the number of carbon copies to be made before starting **each piece of work.** Failure to do this results, time and again, in insufficient copies. If any doubt exists regarding the number of copies, check with the person for whom the work is being done; or in his absence make one or two copies more than the number that seems logically necessary. It is not good practice, however, always to make more copies than are needed, unless it is on long or difficult jobs. Unnecessary copies waste time and material, and fill up the files.

Copies for Distribution. When making carbon copies for distribution to a number of persons, list the names, one below the other, at the top of the first page. This list is not only valuable for the files, but also valuable in that each person receiving a copy may know who else received copies.

Check each person's name on his copy.

Carbon Copies to be Mailed Out. Ordinary carbon copies being mailed to second and third persons are made on regular copy paper and do not usually bear original signatures. After the original has been signed, the signature is typed on the carbons, with "(Sgd.)" before it.

Special carbon copies (as of legal papers, etc.) should be made on paper similar to the original, and should bear original signatures. (See also Legal Papers, p. 460.)

Method of Handing in Contracts, Reports, etc. (Clipping Carbon Copies to Original). When preparing a long manuscript with several carbon copies, clip the original of each page and its carbon copies together upon removal from the machine. When the work is completed the manuscript may be handed in with the pages thus clipped together, in a manila folder bearing the title of the manuscript.

It is comparatively easy to read a manuscript in this form, and it makes the matter of correcting, rewriting, and destroying pages a very simple job.

If a page is to be rewritten, dispose of all the carbons of that page before starting to retype it, so that the old carbon copies will not be on the desk to get mixed with the new.

Segregating Carbon Copies. In segregating carbon copies and originals, lay out the last page of the manuscript first. This keeps the copies face up, and it is possible to watch the page numbers for error; whereas if the segregation is started with the first page, the copies must be placed face down and blindly put together.

Carbons and Papers. To make fast progress on a long piece of work that entails a number of carbon copies:

Clear the desk of all papers but the job on hand. Too many papers about are confusing.

Place the different kinds of paper to be used out on the desk, so there will be no constant pulling out of drawers to get new papers.

Count the number of sheets of carbon paper to be used, and do not have extra carbon paper loose on the desk—it soils other papers.

Count the number of white sheets to be used each time, before inserting the carbons. This will prevent the possibility of two carbon papers' sticking together, and of certain pages' being "one carbon short" in the final assembly.

Keep the carbon paper face up to prevent its smudging the desk, unless the carbon paper is curling from weather conditions. On these days, keep it face down on a clean sheet of paper or in a folder.

Even Edges. Have the top and left edges of each set of pages **absolutely even** before insertion into the machine; and then after insertion always restraighten the papers by use of the paper release. Pages that have been thus evened may be reinserted later, and corrections will fall in exactly the same place on every sheet.

To Prevent Carbon From Wrinkling. Crooked carbon papers will wrinkle and make unsightly lines. But carbon paper will not wrinkle or crease if the papers are even upon insertion into the machine, and if the **paper release is always used** to restraighten the papers after they are in the machine. The machine is not to blame for ugly "streak lightning" lines down carbon copies. This rests entirely with the operator.

If carbon paper becomes creased, do not throw it away unless it is old; place it face down on a piece of wastepaper and rub the creases out with the finger tips.

Legal-Sized Carbons With Letter-Sized Paper. Legal-sized carbon paper may be used to advantage with letter-sized paper. Clip off the upper left and lower right corners of the legal carbon. When carbons are to be removed, hold the white sheets in the upper left corner, and remove the carbons with one pull.

CARBON PAPER

Heavy and Light Carbon. Use heavy carbon with a hard finish if making but **one or two copies.** It wears longer than thin carbon.

Use light or thin carbon with a hard finish if making **six or seven copies.** Change light carbons about every ten pages, or discard the last carbon and renew the first every few pages, as the life of light carbon is very short.

"Hard finish" carbon produces clean copies and wears longer than "soft finish". The hard finish does not smear.

Do not be reluctant to discard used carbon paper, especially if copying figures. Never use carbon paper with holes in it. It is false thrift to use worn-out carbons and produce illegible copies.

Colored Carbon. Use black carbon paper unless another color is specifically designated.

Red Carbon. Red carbon paper may be used for inserting occasional red figures on the original and copies. Cut the red carbon into small pieces and insert one piece behind the ribbon (if it is all black) and one behind each carbon throughout the copy. Red figures or words may thus be imprinted without changing carbons.

But if a large part of the page is to be in red, whole sheets of red carbon paper should be used and the red parts filled in after the other typing is finished. The pages must be in perfect alinement at each insertion in order to have the red letters or figures fall in proper position on each copy.

Pencil Carbon. Use the special pencil carbon paper for making pencil copies or tracings. Ordinary carbon paper is unsatisfactory for this purpose.

Pencil carbon may be bought by the piece. Half-a-dozen sheets will usually last a long time.

Care of Carbon Paper. Carbon paper is expensive and deteriorates rapidly. Keep it in its original folders in the desk. This will prevent curling.

Heat injures carbon paper; therefore never put it on or near a hot radiator.

Do not permit an unsightly bunch of old carbons to accumulate on or in the desk. Discard them.

COPYING

Write the word "(COPY)" at the top of the first page of every manuscript copied. This identifies it immediately as a copy and guards against later confusion with the original.

In making a copy of a copy **write "(COPY OF A COPY)"** as the heading.

In copying a letterhead **always copy the address;** even if the company is well known, the address may not be known to the person using the copy.

Always write "(Sgd.)" before a signature when copying it, to show beyond a question that the original was signed, and that the name was not merely typed on.

Always copy initials—they may give a different meaning to a letter, for instance, if the letter has been dictated by someone other than the signer.

If a number of persons are to receive copies of the copy being made, write the list of names at the top of the first page, and opposite the list write the date the copies are made or are to be distributed. Check each person's name on his copy. It is sometimes necessary to note the disposition of the original, as shown in the following outline:

(Original in N.Y. Office)   :
July 14, 1937—Copies to RVL   :
                Lee ⩗   :
                Hunt   :
                Matthews :

- - - - - - - - - - - - - - - - - -

              (COPY OF A COPY)
        LETTERHEAD (including address)
                         Date

Full address
Salutation:
        (Copy everything just as it is written,
        unless it is an unmistakable typographical
        error.)
                Complimentary close,
                    (Sgd.) ....
Initials
Notations

Copying Guide. Always use a copying guide in the form of a ruler or a "line-a-time" device. **This is absolutely essential for accurate work.** It is very easy to leave out a line and cause great delay on urgent work.

Extra Copies. Make an extra copy for the files when copying anything of importance, or note on the original the date the copies were made, and the disposition of each copy.

Questions that recur in a business office are "Who got copies of this, and when were they sent?" or "Whose copy is this, and where is the original?"

Noting Errors and Copying Punctuation. If anything is omitted in the original, such as a figure or letter, make a short line beneath a space to note the omission in the copy.

If a letter or figure is obviously wrong, make a line beneath it. Do not, however, underline an entire word—put a pencil question mark after it.

The Latin word "sic", meaning "thus", is often inserted in brackets to indicate that the copy follows the original exactly.

> . . .to determine the new building cite [sic]; although it is. . .
> In the war of 1821 [sic] our merchantmen were. . .

Copy punctuation exactly as it is written, unless there is obviously a typographical error. In legal papers, copy punctuation exactly as it is written, right or wrong (underlining any mark that is plainly incorrect); a lawsuit can hinge on the punctuation of a contract.

Page-for-Page Copying. When copying legal papers, or papers of unusual importance, about which there is likely to be a discussion, copy "page for page" with the exact page number on each page. Later reference to a certain page number may be made, in a telegram, on the telephone, or in court.

Copying From Thin Paper. If copying from thin paper, place a piece of heavy white paper behind the page to bring out the letters.

Quoting Material. (See Quoted Matter, p. 242.)

Copying Wires. (See p. 385.)

Proofreading Copies. Do not neglect proofreading, nor attempt to escape it. It is a most important part of office work.

Proofread every copy carefully with the original. A wrong figure, for instance, may cost a company money or cause it embarrassment.

When two are proofreading, the one who typed the material should hold his own copy. The original copy should be held by the other reader, who might interpret it differently from the way in which it was copied.

Making a Number of Originals. When making a number of originals from a copy, copy carefully each time from the last copy written. When the copying is completed, compare the last copy made with the original; if it is correct, all the intermediate copies can be assumed to be correct.

❖

COPY FOR THE PRESS

Copy for the press should be prepared as follows:

Paper. Letter-sized (8½ by 11 inches), white, of good quality (not shiny or very thin).

Copies. In duplicate, or with as many extra copies as will be needed for the author's work. The printer or publisher usually requires but one copy—the original.

Nothing should be written on the backs of any of the pages.

Ribbon. Black, if available, and **very clear.**

Margins. One inch on each side, and at the top and bottom; one inch above a title. The margins should be uniform throughout the manuscript.

Spacing. Double-space all matter to be printed, to allow for proof-readers' and printers' interlineations. (For the spacing of quotations, see below.)

Divisions of Composition. In material intended primarily for study or reference, divisions of the subject matter should be clearly and uniformly indicated; that is, chapters, sections, topics, items, etc., should bear uniform headings.

In material intended for lighter reading, subdivisions, beyond chapters, are not often indicated.

Headings. The title of the manuscript and all chapter titles should be centered and set in caps. They need not be underlined.

Other subdivisions may be indicated by centered subheadings, or by sideheadings, or by paragraph titles.

By-Lines. On magazine articles and stories, two spaces below the title write "By" and the author's name on the same line.

Author's Address. On magazine articles and stories, the author's (or agent's) name and address should be typed above the title in the left corner. If the author is using a pen name, it should appear in the "by-line", and the author's real name (or the agent's name) should be given in the address. No explanation is necessary regarding the difference between the two names.

Number of Words. The number of words in a magazine article or story should be indicated on the title page in the upper right corner, for the convenience of those considering the manuscript in the editorial rooms.

It is not necessary to indicate the number of words in a book manuscript; the publisher usually makes his own estimate.

Numbering Pages. Number all pages, including the first or title page, in the upper right corner. Magazine articles and stories usually have lines of information and identification on the first page, as

421

R. L. Stevens
506 Sea Terrace
Monterey, California

Page 1
American Serial Rights
2000 words

THE VALUE OF GOLD
By George Lane

....

....

All succeeding pages bear the author's last name, an identifying word from the title, and the page number, in the upper right corner, as

Lane/Gold/2

This because the pages of manuscripts are often separated when being read or set in type in a printing establishment, and each page should bear some identification for reassembly.

Number every manuscript (even a book) with but one set of numbers from the beginning to the end. Do not start a new sequence of numbers for every chapter or for the appendix, addenda, glossary, bibliography, index, etc. The preface may, however, be numbered separately with small Roman numerals.

Inserted and Canceled Page Numbers. If extra pages are added, add letters to the number, as 12-a, 12-b, 12-c, etc. Make a note to the printer beneath the preceding page number that an inserted page follows, as "Page 12-a follows", or "Next 12-a".

If a page is canceled, mark the preceding page with both page numbers, its own and that of the canceled page, as 12 & 13; or if several pages are canceled, the preceding page should be marked to cover all the numbers, as 12–20, the following page number being 21.

Italics. Underline material to be set in italics. A printer's interpretation of an underline is *"italicize"*.

Underlining. If it is desired that underlinings show as underlinings, mark in ink on the margin opposite "Underscore as shown".

Boldface. If a heavy black type is desired instead of italics or underlining, write "bf" (meaning **boldface** type) in ink on the margin and draw a wavy line beneath the material to be set in boldface.

Spelling, Capitalization, Punctuation. Must be uniform throughout. Simplified or modernized forms of spelling are not generally used in printing—except in advertisements.

Abbreviations. Should not be used unless they are to be printed as written, in which case copy should be marked "Follow abbreviations".

Uniformity. To avoid extra charges for "author's corrections" in the proofs, the typewritten copy should be as consistent as it is possible to make it in the matter of spelling, hyphening, the use of figures or spelled-out numbers, abbreviations, etc.

Paragraphing. Copy should be paragraphed exactly as desired in the printed form. Paragraphs should be uniformly indented four typewriter spaces only.

To indicate a new paragraph where none has been shown in the typing, use the sign ¶. If material typed with paragraph indention is to be run in with the preceding paragraph, write "No ¶" on the margin, or draw a line to indicate the connection. (See p. 431.)

Each chapter or part should begin on a new page.

Number of Lines on a Page. For estimating purposes, the printer prefers the same number of lines on every page—about 27 typewritten lines.

End of Copy. Indicate the end of all copy, either by using the printer's mark (#) or by writing "The End".

Quotations. May be indented and single-spaced or double-spaced. If they are double-spaced they may be marked with a distinctive marginal line. Quotation marks may or may not be used if a quotation is to be set apart and distinguished by smaller type. But if the quotation is to have no particular distinction, quotation marks should always be used.

When making quotations, follow the original copy exactly in the matter of spelling, punctuation, etc. When quoting verse use the exact form, including indention, of the printed copy.

In quoting copyrighted work it is necessary to obtain permission from, and to give a credit line or permission line as approved by, the copyright holder.

Credit Lines. Put only as much information into a credit line as is necessary for the reader's purpose, or as is requested by the copyright holder. The usual forms are:

—Emerson.
—Emerson, "Behavior".
—Emerson, "Behavior", *Masterpieces of American Literature*, p. 289, Houghton Mifflin Company, Boston, 1891.
—Jespersen, "Essentials of English Grammar", p. 331.

With such a credit line as the last, a permission line might appear either as a footnote on the same page or with another reference to the book in the same publication, as

Excerpt reprinted by permission from Henry Holt and Company, New York.

Bibliographic References. The style of reference to books, and articles in periodicals and books, varies greatly with different publications and among different publishers. Many publishers and scientific and technical societies issue their own recommendations. If a manuscript is intended for a special publication, it is well for the author to ascertain that publication's practice and to secure, if available, a list of recommended abbreviations—if abbreviations are to be used.

One form of complete reference frequently adopted in bibliographies contains:

Name of Author: "Title of Book", edition, volume, or chapter (if any), page, publisher, city, year.
(In printing, the name of the author often appears in caps and small caps; and the title of the book is sometimes italicized instead of being quoted.)

For instance—

> MAETERLINCK: "The Life of the Bee", p. 68, Dodd, Mead and Company, New York, 1926.
> ROE, FREDERICK WILLIAM, and GEORGE ROY ELLIOTT (Editors): *English Prose*, "Selections from Ruskin", p. 327, Longmans, Green and Co., New York, 1913.   (showing manner of indicating a subdivision of a book)
> URQUHART, L. C., and C. E. O'ROURKE: "Steel Structures: Stresses in Simple Structures," 2d ed., p. 21, McGraw-Hill Book Company, Inc., New York, 1932.
> MORSHEAD, O. F. (Editor): "Everybody's Pepys: The Diary of Samuel Pepys, 1660–1669", p. 205, Harcourt, Brace & Company, New York, 1926. (showing manner of indicating a subtitle)

In extensive bibliographies the publishers' names are usually abbreviated, but in occasional bibliographic references the names are given as they appear in the publications, or as the publishers now write their names.

For a magazine article, the information is given in the following order:

> Name of Author: Title of Article, *Magazine*, volume, page, month, year.
> (In printing, the name of the author often appears in caps and small caps; and the title of the article is sometimes quoted.)

For instance—

> CRAVEN, THOMAS: "American Men of Art", *Scribner's*, vol. 92, pp. 262–7, November, 1932.
> CHAMBERLAIN, G. C.: Intensive Steel Testing, *Am. Jour. Sci.*, 3d ser., vol. 45, pp. 171–200, 1893.

The volume, page number, and date are often abbreviated thus:

> 92:262-7 N '32   45:171-200 (1893)

When a second reference is made to a work just cited, an abbreviation is used, as

> *Ibid.*, p. 529   (L. ibidem, in the same place [in the work **just above**])
> Scott, *op.cit.*, p. 250   (L. opere citato, in the work cited [**not just above**])
> *Loc.cit.*   (L. loco citato, in the place cited [in the exact **passage** just cited])
> *Idem* or *Id.*   (L. the same [the **author** just cited rather than his book])
> *Supra* (above); *Infra* (below); *Circa* (about); *Passim* (here and there)

Page and Illustration References. The page numbers of cross references may be left blank in the manuscript, to be filled in later in the page proofs. But numbers referring to illustrations should be filled in in the manuscript.

Footnotes. Avoid footnotes as much as possible—they are hindrances to smooth reading. Often it is better to place explanatory matter in parentheses in the text than to use footnotes. If footnotes are necessary, they may be written into the text immediately after the matter to which they refer, thus:

> ...as mentioned in a recent magazine article[1]...

---

[1] (Between two lines, give the footnote. See Bibliographic References, above.)

Or footnotes may be grouped at the foot of the page, or written all on one page, with proper references being made in the text. The printer will place each footnote at the bottom of the correct page.

If an added footnote is too long to be written at the foot of the page, it may be typed on a separate page, with an appropriate note to the printer, as "Footnote on page 12-a".

Tables or Tabulations. Should, as a rule, be written on separate pages, unless they are very short, as tabulated matter is usually set in smaller type and is therefore handled separately by the printer. Double-space all but very short tables, and indicate the desired alinement. Never put part of a short table or enumeration on one page and part on another. A long table, however, may require several pages. Footnotes should be written below the table.

If the tables do not bear page numbers, they should be numbered in a separate series, and the place for insertion of each table should be indicated both on the table and in the manuscript.

Illustrations. Photographs, drawings, charts, etc., should be submitted with the manuscript, but not inserted in it. They should be separated so that they may be sent to the engraver at the same time that the manuscript is sent to the printer. They should be properly titled on the back (very lightly) or at the bottom (often on a slip pasted to the bottom), and numbered (in separate series) consecutively from the beginning of the manuscript to the end.

The place for the insertion of each illustration may be indicated in the manuscript; but it is often more satisfactory to indicate these positions on the galley proofs.

Drawings, Charts, etc. Should be made with **india ink** on white backgrounds. However, since the size of drawing and lettering suitable for reduction is not easily determined except by experts, it is often better to submit pencil sketches, from which the engraver may make finished drawings. In case the author is required to make finished drawings, he should consult the publisher for specifications before entering upon the work.

Graphs. In plotting graphs, if the lines are not to show in the reproduction, use **blue** cross-section paper, and specify that the lines are not to show. (Blue ordinarily photographs white, but blue lines can be made to show if necessary.) If the lines are to show, use **green or red** cross-section paper. (These colors photograph black. Light green lines can be taken out, but it is rather a difficult process.)

Glossy Prints of Photographs. Are necessary for clear reproduction. Photostats and dull-finished pictures do not reproduce satisfactorily. Unmounted photographs should not be pasted on sheets of paper; they should be left unmounted. Photographs will not be returned unless a special request is made.

Never place numbers, letters, or other marks on the face of photographs or wash drawings. If numbers or letters are necessary, they should be indicated lightly in pencil at the proper point on the backs of

425

unmounted prints. This can be done by holding the print against a window facing a strong light. On mounted photographs, a flyleaf of thin paper pasted on the back of the photograph, at the top, and folded over the face of the photograph can be used for the numbers or letters.

Inserts. Type or paste all inserts on manuscript paper (8½ by 11 inches) to keep the copy uniform. Do not pin or clip an insert as a "flier" on any page; and do not write or paste on the reverse side of a manuscript page. Note both in the copy and on the insert where the insert is to go, as "Insert A—on page 25-a", and above the insert write "Insert A".

If both sides of a printed insert are to be copied, paste the insert along the left edge, and make a note to the printer below it.

Corrections in Manuscript. All corrections must be absolutely clear. No written-over words or struck-over figures are permitted. If it is necessary to make a longhand insertion in the manuscript, write it horizontally on the margin. Short typewritten corrections may be cut and pasted flat in the manuscript, but the page sizes should not be lengthened thereby; rather the inserts should be written on separate pages numbered as described above. If more than one-fourth of the number of lines on a page bear corrections, the page should be retyped.

Verification. All copy sent to a printer should be verified and **final.** Every correction thereafter, even a comma, costs money. Verify all figures, and the spelling, marking, and use of all proper names, foreign words, technical terms, quotations, references, etc. **The printer is not responsible for the authenticity of any part of the copy,** nor is he supposed to correct the copy.

Instructions to the Printer. Should be written in ink of a color different from that used in making corrections; and each instruction should be headed "Pr". Numbers and letters for the printer's guidance should be encircled.

Style of Printing. If a certain style of printing is desired, attempt to furnish a sample of similar printing as a guide for the printer. If a particular layout is desired, a plan of the arrangement should accompany the manuscript.

If dealing directly with a printer, **always obtain an estimate of the cost of printing.** Prices vary greatly when different specifications are made.

Copyrighting. A publisher regularly attends to the details of copyrighting material. A printer will also do this for a customer, but usually only upon request.

Indexing. A publisher usually suggests the style of index to be followed; but in the absence of any preferences, select from similar published works the most satisfactory index and use it as a guide in arranging items.

Indexes are usually made from page proofs. To make an index: First underline on one copy of the page proofs, in blue or red pencil, all words or titles to be indexed. Then list each subject and its page number on a 3- by 5-inch card. Arrange the cards alphabetically.

(Some publishers prefer to have indexes submitted on cards and others wish to have them typewritten on manuscript paper.) Check the completed index against the page proofs.

Numerous page references should not be given for a single item, as

Letter writing, 5, 12, 18, 26, 45, 87, 94, 106, 125, 187, 210, 251, 277, 389, 452, 548, 600

Such a reference often forces the reader to look up every page before he finds what he wants. There should be some indication of what phase of the subject is treated on every page; or at least the page numbers referring to each part of the subject should be grouped after a proper subhead.

Printed Office Forms. If making up a blank form to be printed, keep it as simple as possible. Too much information called for in a form is as confusing as too little. Many forms are too complicated; they are never entirely read or filled in.

See that the line spacing corresponds to that on the typewriter, so that spaces may be filled in without adjusting the machine. Leave enough space for the longest possible items under each heading. Cramped space on a form results in illegible entries.

Programs, Announcements, and Invitations. For correct forms for programs, announcements, invitations, etc., consult reliable stationers or printers. They will have the latest styles in paper, type, and composition.

Writing a Manuscript. When composing a business manuscript, speech, article, or advertisement, write in a concise, simple, and direct manner—**and state facts.**

A great newspaper office has across its editorial rooms, in large letters, the one word: FACTS.

> "There is no more convincing mark of a cultured speaker or writer than accuracy of statement."
> —House and Harman, "Handbook of Correct English",
> p. 120.

Fiction and Articles. In preparing fiction or articles for submission to publishers, follow the general rules for setup of any copy.

Estimate the number of words and compare with the number of words in similar printed material, so that the manuscript will not be too long. Great length bars consideration in many cases.

Submit the manuscript to a publication that uses similar material. Manuscripts are often returned because the type of material is not suited to the publication.

It is not ethical to send copies of a manuscript to more than one publication at a time. Allow each publisher the privilege of consideration or refusal before submitting the manuscript to another.

Prices are fixed by publishers, unless an author is well enough established to set prices on his work. It is unnecessary to write "Submitted at the usual rates"—that is understood.

Publication rates and royalties vary with different publications and publishers. An estimate of rates may be found in writers' magazines or magazines that cover the publishing field.

Dramatic Rights, etc. If an author desires to reserve all rights but the publication rights to a story or article, he may mark in the upper right corner of the title page "American Serial Rights", which shows that only the American serial rights are being offered, that is, the right to publish in an American serial (magazine, newspaper, or periodical). All other rights, including dramatic, photoplay, radio, British and other foreign rights, are then reserved.

If the manuscript of a book of fiction is being offered, it may be marked "American Book Rights", and all other rights are then reserved. Details of the various rights in connection with a book are included in the contract between the publisher and the author.

Mailing or Sending Copy to Printer or Publisher

1. Send the **original,** not a carbon copy; and send clear, clean copy. A duplicate copy should always be retained by the author.

2. Copy may be fastened together, but **not permanently bound.** (Printers separate the pages for setting up.) A brass fastener through the upper **left** corner is satisfactory and is easily removed.

3. The different parts or chapters of a manuscript may be separately fastened together for convenience in handling.

4. Send the **complete manuscript,** together with all illustrations, the latter being separated from the manuscript pages. Do not send the manuscript in installments.

5. Send all manuscripts **flat**—no matter what the number of pages. A flat page is more convenient to read than a page that has been creased in folds; and therefore, a flat manuscript has a better psychological effect on the reader. Never send a manuscript rolled. If a large illustration has to be rolled, it should be sent separately.

6. Send a **letter of transmittal** in connection with each manuscript. The letter should contain a brief summary of material sent, and the name and address of the sender; this for the printer's or publisher's records.

7. Address **unsolicited manuscripts** to the "Editorial Department" of a magazine or publishing house.

8. **Short manuscripts** should be sent as first-class mail; and if of unusual value, they should be registered. **Return postage** should be enclosed with all unsolicited manuscripts.

9. **Large manuscripts** should be shipped by express, insured for a proper value.

10. **Proofs** being returned to the printer or publisher should be sent special delivery or insured. (Proofs, together with the accompanying manuscript pages, may be sent as third-class mail or as parcel post.)

PROOFREADING

The proofreading of a printer's work must be done with the utmost care, to catch misplaced letters, missing punctuation marks, etc. Read every punctuation mark and spell out every unfamiliar word.

Corrections in Proof. Ink, not pencil, should be used in marking proof. The color of the ink should be different from that used by the printer's proofreader.

All corrections must be marked **on the margins,** first, to attract attention, and secondly, for clearness.

Do not attempt to make a correction by writing over the print or between the lines. Errors marked in this manner are in danger of being overlooked, and are usually illegible.

Before attempting to use proofreaders' marks, study and become familiar with them. If unfamiliar with them, write out the corrections horizontally on the margin and place a caret ($\wedge$) in the copy to indicate where each insertion or change is to be made.

All insertions of more than a line should be typed on separate pages, headed with the galley numbers; or, if there is room, inserts may be written or typed at the foot of the galleys. The inserts should be numbered consecutively; and on the margin of the galley proof should be indicated where each item is to be inserted, as "Insert A", etc.

Never cut and paste parts of galleys together, nor cut out any part of the material and paste it elsewhere; **leave the galleys intact.** Indicate transpositions of material by drawing lines around the parts to be moved and making marginal notations, as "tr to Gal. 58", and on Galley 58 draw an arrow to where the material is to be inserted and write opposite it "Insert from Gal. 24".

Most printers and publishers make a charge for "author's corrections" in the proof if the changes exceed a certain percentage of the cost of composition. Alterations are made on a time basis and are much more expensive than original composition. A change, if possible, should be confined to a single line; and adjustments in wording should be made wherever possible to avoid resetting a whole paragraph. The insertion of a single word at the beginning of a paragraph sometimes necessitates the resetting of the entire paragraph.

Changes in the page proofs that involve the re-makeup of pages are especially difficult and accordingly expensive.

Do not return blurred or indistinct markings on proof sheets. It is necessary for the printer to see every mark to make corrections.

Always return the original copy when returning the proofs.

Proofs. Two sets of proofs are usually sent to the author:

> **galley proofs**—the first proofs, in long strips, taken from the type on the galleys.
> **page proofs**—the second proofs, after the type has been made up into pages.
> **final or plate proofs**—made after the plates have been cast (not always submitted to the author).

COPY FOR THE PRESS

PROOFREADERS' MARKS

Punctuation	Write on margin	Mark in copy
Comma	,/	∧
Semicolon	;/	∧
Colon	:/	∧
Period	⊙	∧
Question mark	?/	∧
Exclamation point	!/	∧
Hyphen	=/	∧
Apostrophe	⌄/	⌄
Quotation marks	⌄/ ⌄/	⌄ ⌄
Parentheses	(/)	∧ ∧
Brackets	[/]	∧ ∧
Dash—long (one-em*)	$\frac{1}{em}$	∧
Dash—very long (3-em)	$\frac{3}{em}$	∧
Dash—short (en dash)	$\frac{1}{en}$	∧
Ligature (as æ)	*lig*	⌒ over the 2 letters to be run together
Asterisk	⋇	⌄
Footnote indicators: letters; superior figures, as mathematical indices; etc.	⌄/ or ⌄/	⌄
Chemical indices, inferior figures in mathematics, etc.	∧ or ∧	∧
Underscore	*underscore*	_____ beneath the words
End of copy		# Place this mark at the end of every piece of copy

Note: A diagonal line, caret, or circle is used with a punctuation mark on the margin to make the mark stand out. The diagonal line is also used to separate corrections. Two diagonal lines indicate that the same correction occurs twice in the same line.

Corrections on the margin should be small but very clear, made on the nearer margin in the order in which they are to be inserted, and exactly in line with the parts to be corrected.

* "Em" is derived from the letter m, the square of the body of which was used as a unit of measurement. "En" is derived from n, and is half the width of an em.

Wording and lettering	Write on margin	Mark in copy
Let it stand*	*stet*	. . . . . beneath material to remain as it was before being stricken
Delete—take out	ϑ or *kill*	—— or / through material to be stricken
Transpose	*tr*	∿ around letters, words, phrases or sentences, to be transposed
		⌐→ to where paragraph is to be moved
Take out letter, and close space	ϑ̂	/ through deleted letter
Spell out—if in figures	*spell*	○ around figures
Figures—if spelled out	*fig*	○ around words to be set in figures
Words missing, see copy	*Out, see copy*	∧ where words are missing
Letter omitted	(Write the letter with a diagonal line beside it)	∧ where letter belongs
Word omitted	(Write the word with a diagonal line beside it)	∧ where word belongs
Reset words in order indicated	*set* 1, 2, 3	①②③ Place small ringed numbers above words in order desired
Query from printer to author†	*Qy* or (?)	____ or (?)

* If a correction is to be disregarded, it should not be erased, but a line should be drawn through it and "stet" written beside it on the margin.

† If the copy is right, the author should run a line through the "Qy" or question mark, but not erase it, and write "OK".

PROOFREADERS' MARKS

Spacing	Write on margin	Mark in copy
Insert space	#	∧
Less space	∨	∨
More space	∧	∧
Equalize spacing	*eq* # or ∨ ∧	∧ ∨ ∧ ∨
Close up space	◡	◡
Straighten (a crooked part)	=	= above and below crooked material
Straighten end of lines	‖	‖ at end of lines to be straightened
Paragraph	¶	¶ or ∧
No paragraph	*No* ¶ or *run in*	⸣ Draw line from end of one paragraph to beginning of next
Insert lead (space between lines)	*ld* or #	> where more space is to be between lines
Delete lead (space)	⌿ *ld* or ⌿ #	> where less space is to be between lines
Lead shows—push it down ("Lead" used for spacing sometimes makes a blotch)	⌐	(beside the imprint being made by the lead
Move word to right or left	⌐ or L	⌐or L before or after word
Move up or down	⌐ or ⌐	over or under material to be raised or lowered
Set at margin indicated	[or]	[or] at place where margin is to be
Indent one em (for 2 ems, 2 squares or 2, etc.)	□	∧ where indention is to be
Reset type—so material, through respacing, will run a little longer and make a better line	*run over*	} around material to be reset
Reset—pulling the syllable, word, or line back to the preceding line or page	*run back*	} around material to be reset
Move word or letters	*move*	around material to be moved
Center	*ctr*	→ arrow from material to the center

Other changes in spacing, or other rearrangements in setup, may be indicated by lines and arrows showing the desired positions, with instructions written on the margins; but no such lines should cross each other. **"Full meas."** means that copy is to be set the full measure of the page—not indented.

Type	Write on margin	Mark in copy
Ordinary type (roman type)	*rom*	____ beneath words to be returned to regular type
Boldface type (fullface)	*bf*	∿∿ wavy underscore
Lightface type	*lf*	..... under words to be in lightface
CAPITALS	*caps*	≡ 3 straight underscores
BOLDFACE CAPITALS	*bf caps*	≡ 3 straight underscores and ∿ 1 wavy
SMALL CAPITALS	*sc*	= 2 straight underscores
SMALL CAPITALS, boldface (in only a few styles of type)	*bf sc*	= 2 straight underscores and ∿ 1 wavy
Italics	*ital*	___ 1 straight underscore
Italics, boldface	*bf ital*	___ 1 straight underscore and ∿ 1 wavy
ITALICS IN CAPITALS	*caps ital*	≣ 4 straight underscores
Capitals and Small Capitals	*c & sc*	≡ under letters or words to be in capitals, and = under letters or words to be in small capitals
Small type*	*small type* (or the type size)	│ single line before material to be set smaller
Very small type*	*very small* (or the type size)	‖ double line before material to be set in very small type
Lower case (reduce from capital to a small letter)	*lc*	/ through material to be reduced
Wrong font (letter or character of wrong size or style of type)	*wf*	/ through material of wrong type
Turn (type upside down)	*9* or *⌿*	( ) around upside-down material; or / through inverted letter
Broken letter or bad type	×	— under faulty type

* When two sizes of small type are to be used throughout a manuscript, a single opening note may explain them, as " 1st small type marked red on the margin, 2d small type marked blue on the margin."

TYPE SIZES AND STYLES

Type sizes are measured by "points" and are designated by the number of points in each type body.

FOR TABULATIONS AND EXAMPLES	ORDINARY BOOK SIZES
This is a sample of 5-point type	This is a sample of 9-point type
This is a sample of 5½-point type	This is a sample of 10-point type
This is a sample of 6-point type	This is a sample of 11-point type
This is a sample of 7-point type	This is a sample of 12-point type
This is a sample of 8-point type	

FOR HEADINGS

This is a sample of 14-point type

This is a sample of 18-point type

There are many styles of type, the following being some of the varieties:

BOOKMAN	Bookman
BODONI	Bodoni
BRUCE OLD STYLE	Bruce Old Style
CASLON	Caslon
CHELTENHAM	Cheltenham
KENNERLEY	Kennerley
SCRIPT	Script
TYPEWRITER	Typewriter
FRENCH OLD STYLE	French Old Style
GARAMOND	Garamond
BERNHARD GOTHIC	Bernhard Gothic
GOUDY BOLD	Goudy Bold
GOUDY OPEN	Goudy Open
SCOTCH FACE	Scotch Face
KENNERLEY ITALIC	Kennerley Italic
CENTURY	Century
Tudor Text	Old English	Goudy Text

432

STEPS IN PREPARING ART WORK AND COPY FOR THE PRESS

There are six steps in preparing art work and copy for the press:
1. Art work or photography—done by artist or photographer.
2. Zinc etching or copper or zinc halftone—made by a photoengraver.
3. Composition—done by a printer.
4. Electrotype ⎱
5. Matrix ⎰ made by an electrotyper.
6. Stereotype—made by a stereotyper.
All of these are entirely separate and distinct operations, each requiring an individual process.

A **line drawing**—is made in black and white, by an artist, from which a photoengraver makes a
> **line cut**—which is known as a
> **zinc etching** ("zinc")—being the drawing transferred to zinc by a photographic process, and then etched out with acid.

A **wash drawing, painting, or photograph**—which contains much fine detail is made into a
> **copper halftone or zinc halftone** ("halftone")—by a photoengraver. The picture is reproduced on copper or zinc by a photographic process through a screen, the fineness of the screen determining the density of the dots which bring out the lights and shadows or half tones of the illustration. Zinc halftones, made with a coarse screen, are used in newspaper work. They are less expensive than copper halftones, but do not wear so long.

If the zinc or halftone is to be used in an advertisement or printed form, the printer sets type around it, and from the type and the zinc or halftone, an

electrotype ("electro")—is made for the newspaper, magazine, or book. In this process a wax or lead mold is taken from the original, and copper is then electrically deposited in the mold. The shell of copper, bearing the impression of the original, is backed with heavy type metal, mounted on a wooden block, and is then ready to be printed from.

If the copy is an advertisement that is to run in many newspapers, the electrotyper makes ("pulls") a

matrix ("mat")—from the electro; the mat being a heavy papier-mâché formation which takes and retains the impression of the electro.

From the mat, the newspaper casts a

stereotype ("stereo")—which is made by pouring molten metal into the mat form. The stereo is printed from, but is not so perfect as an electro because it is of soft metal, and is also three steps away from the original type.

PRINTING TERMS

Ben Day—a process for shading line drawings and making color plates for photoengraving. (Named after the inventor, Benjamin Day.)

bleed edges—When a picture or advertisement runs to the edges of the paper, with no border (so that the ink "bleeds" over), it is said to "run to bleed"

433

or to have "bleed edges". "Cut to bleed" means trimmed too closely or into the printed matter.

board—heavy pasteboard used as the sides of book covers. Books so bound are said to be "bound in boards".

cut—the layman's term for either a zinc etching or a copper or zinc halftone. It comes from the old reference to a woodcut. It is often used to refer to any engraved block or plate for printing.

cut dummy—the form in which proof of illustrations is submitted.

deckle edges—untrimmed edges. (deckle-edged)

dummy—a sample of a proposed book, showing the format of the finished product.

dust cover—the paper jacket for a book.

end papers—the folds of paper that line the inside covers of a book; one half is pasted down, the other half acts as a flyleaf.

format—the form, size, and style of a book. (pron. fôr′măt; Fr. fôr′má′)

flyleaf—a blank page at either the beginning or end of a book; often half the end paper—so named because one side is pasted and the other flies.

pull a proof—to take a proof.

running head—a heading that is repeated on consecutive pages of a book.

running title—a title that is carried through a volume, usually on all left pages, but sometimes on all pages.

❖

FILING

There are but four systems of filing:

Alphabetic—the primary or foundation system; the most generally used for all types of filing. Names and subjects are simply filed in alphabetic order, either in the same file drawer or in separate drawers.

Geographic—used where location is important, as in sales work. The files are divided alphabetically, first by states, then each state by cities, then each city by individual names.

Numeric—used in scientific work. Names and subjects are given consecutive numbers and filed numerically. An alphabetic card index is necessary to show the number given each name or subject. (This system is difficult to keep up and has been replaced by the alphabetic system wherever possible.)

Dewey Decimal Classification—used in libraries. Books are numbered first by group, for instance, History is 900; then by class under each group, as 910, 920; then by subclass, 911, 912; and finally by subdivision, 911.1, 911.12, 911.2.

No two offices file in quite the same manner, although the fundamental principles may be the same. There are variations to be dealt with and understood, and the filing in each office is a study in itself. **The two general classifications** of filing are **name** and **subject**.

NAME FILING—by the names of persons or companies—is the simplest form of filing. The first question to be considered when starting new files or when revising old ones is "How much of this can be filed by name?" Name files may be divided into drawers or stacks labeled:

> **Correspondence**—in which is filed all general correspondence with customers, clients, and inquirers. Correspondence with salesmen or branch offices may be in separate drawers.
>
> **Order, Job, or Case**—in which are filed all papers pertaining to each actual order, job, or case, so that the whole story of each—from beginning to end—will be in one folder. In an order folder will be the purchase order, bill of lading, invoice, etc. When a shipment number is assigned, the folder is transferred to the "Shipped Orders" file; thence to the "Unpaid Orders" file, for collection; thence to the "Completed Orders" or dead files.
> These folders may be filed alphabetically by name of customer, with a numerical index of the order or job numbers. But in some offices it is more convenient to file the folders or papers numerically, by order or job number, and keep an alphabetical index of customers.

SUBJECT FILING is used when it is desired to group papers by subject. In this type of filing it is well to keep in mind that names of actual things are easier to remember and classify than names of abstract things like "Legal", "Financial", "Manufacturing", "Transportation", etc., which reach out into all transactions of a business. However, when files are extensive and kept in a central filing system, such divisions as those last mentioned may be used to segregate the files of different departments of a company; for instance, the Accounting Department files may be called "Finance and Accounts", the Traffic Department's, "Transportation", etc. But in an ordinary office, names of actual things are used as the main subjects and as subordinate subjects, for instance—

> Cement, Copper, White Pine, Wool, Rayon, Cacao Beans, Chemicals, Chemical Analyses, etc.
> Machinery, Engines, Pumps, Tools, Trucks, etc.
> Ships (by name), Books (by author), Motion Pictures (by name), etc.
> New Building, Factory, Private Rail Line, Drainage System, etc. (Name of project is main subject, with a folder for each important item, so that the whole story is together.)
> Advertising, Insurance, Supplies, Personnel (Applications, Office Staff, Shop Employees).
> Drawings, Maps, Charts, Blueprints, Photographs, Clippings, Samples, and Catalogues.

435

Subdividing Files. If any one folder or any one set of files becomes too large or bulky as one unit, it may be subdivided by date, month, or year; or by district or location; or by subordinate subjects.

A **"Miscellaneous" folder** should be kept for each letter of the alphabet and for each main subject, with the papers therein arranged first alphabetically, then chronologically. When six papers have accumulated for any one name—and the matter appears "active"—a separate folder should be made for that name.

Changes for the betterment of a filing system often suggest themselves, but they should be made only after their workability has been tested theoretically for a few days, and they have been approved by the person for whom the files are being kept.

Colored Tabs. When different sets of files are in use, it has been found an efficient measure to have all the folder tabs in a certain set of one color, with the main guides in the same color or in white. For instance, all the tabs in the "Subject" file may be blue; in the "Correspondence" file, pink; in the "Job" or "Case" file, green; in the "Data" file, yellow, etc. With this segregation, it is instantly apparent to which set of files a certain folder belongs when it is removed.

Colored gummed labels for labeling folders may be purchased in rolls, to be fed into the typewriter continuously as they are written.

Signals. If special meanings attach to certain folders, small colored metal "signals" may be procured to clip on such folders. For instance, a red signal on a folder may indicate a certain credit rating, a yellow signal may indicate some other standing, etc.

Out Cards. A colored cardboard "out" guide (of the height of the folder tabs) should be inserted whenever a file is to be removed for any length of time. Regular out guides have pockets for the insertion of out cards with notations on them identifying the missing files; but if plain colored cardboard is being used for out guides, light pencil notations may be made right on the guides, and erased for later use; or notations may be clipped to the out guides.

A supply of out guides should be kept handy in the front of each set of files.

Out Slips. When individual papers are removed from files, use for "out" slips a heavy paper of the same color as the out guides. Out slips should be wider than letter-sized paper so as to show well above the edges of other papers within a folder. It is then a comparatively easy matter to check through the files from time to time and follow up the out slips.

> **Caution:** Do not keep on the desk, notations of what is missing from the files, instead of putting out cards or out slips in the files. This "blanks" the files and invariably results in confusion regarding the whereabouts of certain papers.

Record of Files Taken out of Office. If a number of files are to be sent out of the office, make a list of them (besides putting in out cards) so that the files can be checked against the list when they are returned.

"Desk" Filing. If folders or papers are not returned promptly to the files but are kept "filed" in the various desks, it soon disrupts a

436

filing system. If such a condition exists, at some opportune time suggest to the executive in charge that a general memorandum be sent to the staff asking that all files or papers be returned promptly to the files. Usually an authoritative communication will induce more respect for the files than a filing clerk's continual asking for missing papers.

Do not be guilty of "filing" letters in your own desk and forgetting about them. If papers are temporarily placed in the desk, they should be put between the covers of a notebook, or with some article that is constantly used, so they will be automatically brought out when the book or article is removed.

Cross Index and Cross Reference. Cross index cards should be of a color different from the out cards; and cross reference slips should be different from out slips.

Head cross reference slips:

CROSS REFERENCE

(Name of file in which
cross reference slip
permanently belongs)

    Regarding ....
    Dated ....
    See ....(Name of file in which material is filed)....

While cross references are very necessary, there is such a thing as over-cross-referencing, which can make the files bewildering. Try always to have but one place to look for certain papers—never more than two places.

To avoid too much cross-referencing, excerpts from various letters may be filed under the appropriate heads. In making an excerpt, head it "Excerpt from..." and put rows of dots before and after each segregated item to show that it is incomplete. At the bottom of each page state where the entire letter or paper is to be found.

Card Indexes. The card index system is confined largely to extensive filing systems, but it may be used to advantage in small systems if numbered papers are being received or dealt with. Cards may be filed numerically, and the papers themselves filed alphabetically or according to subject.

Follow-up or Tickler Systems. The most compact and reliable form for follow-up work is the card tickler system in a small box.

Papers themselves should not be kept on or in the desk to act as ticklers or reminders. A futile search may be made for them if they are not in their proper places in the general files or in special follow-up files.

Daily or Reading File. If the correspondence is particularly heavy and on a variety of subjects, it is a good plan to make a thin extra copy of each outgoing letter, to be placed on a "Daily" or "Reading" file on the desk. These copies may be bound and filed each month.

As the regular copies are filed each day, their filing disposition should be noted on the corresponding Daily copies. Thereafter a missing letter may be traced in the files by reference to its copy in the bound Daily files.

Index of Files. Make an index for each set of files. Whenever a new folder is made, add its title to the index.

Indexes are necessary and valuable aids to the memory in filing or in searching for papers.

Accumulated Filing. Do not permit filing to accumulate on the desk. Keep it in temporary folders if necessary. This method will facilitate the finding of papers yet unfiled. The temporary folders should bear the five or ten principal classifications of the files; and papers can at least be segregated into these classifications each day.

Preparing Papers for Filing. Before filing anything (other than routine papers) be sure that the person for whom the files are being kept—or a designated superior—has seen or has a knowledge of every paper that is to be filed. Place all papers about which there can be any question on his desk in a folder marked "For Filing". He can then check them and mark certain ones for certain files if he desires.

Mark each paper for filing, that is, check or write on it the name of the file into which it is to be placed. Use a colored pencil and encircle the filing reference. Thereafter if the paper is removed from the file, it can be returned without question to its proper folder.

Make neat pencil notations on file copies regarding the disposition of other copies of the same material, or any other information which might be helpful later and which should be permanently a part of the file records.

Be very sure that whatever is noted on the papers **is correct,** not just a supposition. Make pencil notations concise, but clear.

If some temporary notation is necessary on a file copy, write it on a slip of paper attached to the copy. The slip can be easily removed when the notation is no longer pertinent. Thus the file papers will remain clean and not be covered with erasures or scratched-over notations.

Sorting and Arranging. Sort and arrange all filing before attempting to file it. Sort first alphabetically, then chronologically.

Never allow a clip to go into the files; not only are clips too bulky, but they too readily pick up other papers. Staple, with a permanent or temporary stapling machine, all papers that are to be held together. Pins may be used in the absence of a stapling device.

When stapling a letter and its answer together, **always put the answer on top.** Not only is this chronologically correct, but it immediately tells that the letter has been answered.

If papers are well arranged at the desk, much weary standing at the files will be done away with.

A sorter tray and base, on wheels, is a convenient contrivance for arranging filing. The tray is equipped with file guides, behind which the filing can be segregated as it accumulates.

Filing. Arrange the papers chronologically in each file—the **latest paper always on top.**

438

Try to attach some meaning to the filing of each paper, so that filing will not become a dull, monotonous task. If it is mechanically done, papers will get into the wrong files.

Much responsibility attaches to filing; but do not be dismayed if occasionally it is necessary to search for something in the files. No filing system is infallible, nor is any filer.

Filing Before or Behind Guides. Filing in front of the guides instead of behind them is recognized by many as an efficient practice. Filing in front of a guide permits its being always in full view; whereas filing behind a guide necessitates its being obscured when folders are being inserted or removed. Yet the latter is the more common method.

Neat Files. Form the habit of pushing the papers down evenly in all files, to give a neat appearance and to avoid frayed or torn edges.

Circulars, Catalogues, Timetables, etc. Some catalogues and circulars are kept in the files under company names; but generally they are too bulky for filing and should be kept in a separate cabinet or file drawer, under the company names. They should be discarded as new issues are received, and not allowed to accumulate and become obsolete and unreliable.

Timetables are often kept in the subject file in one folder under T. These especially should be kept up to date. (Everyone in an office should know how, or learn, to read timetables quickly and accurately.)

Filing Stool. A small stool on rollers is an available and very necessary adjunct to filing. It eliminates tiresome stooping to reach the lower files.

Inactive Files. Inactive or "dead" files should be kept in the bottom (or most inaccessible) drawers of the filing cases.

Old files should be transferred to storage at certain periods. Wooden cases and inexpensive guides are used for stored files.

Never destroy a dead file, no matter how old, unless specially authorized to do so.

Photographic Duplication. File records may be duplicated by a photographic process that is rapid and economical. It is especially valuable when records containing original signatures must be duplicated. Information regarding the process may be obtained from any file company.

·•+◄〓〓〓〓〓〓〓〓〓►+•·

ALPHABETIZING

There are two methods of alphabetizing: the dictionary method and the telephone directory method. (See note p. 443.)

The **dictionary method** follows strict alphabetic order, down to the last letter if necessary: first, according to surnames or first principal words; and second (when surnames are the same), according to Christian names, initials, or other words.

Rand, John	Randall Corporation (The)	Rhodes from Paris
Rand, J. P.	RCA Communications, Inc.	Rhodes of London
Rand, J. Ralph	Reade-Taylor Co.	Rockefeller Foundation
Rand, J., & Sons	R.E.M. Corporation	Rock Island Lines

The **telephone directory** method alphabetizes names in three steps:

1. According to the first unit.

L.	E. Q. Corporation*
L &	E Watch Co.*
L	Electrical Co.*
Lea &	Parker, Inc.
Leather	Trades Bureau
Le Baron,	John J.
Lee–	Thurston Co.
Leeds,	Barton & Hill
Lee's	Apartments
Leland	Stanford Assn.
Long	Island Club
New	York Central Syst.
Newark	Mercantile Co.
Ninety–	Nine Broadway
North	River Company
Northeast	Air Service
Pan	American Airways
Panama	Pacific Line
Rock	Island Lines
Rockefeller	Foundation
St.	Paul Flour Co.
San Juan	Trading Co.

2. When first unit is the same, then according to second unit.

Lee,	A.	W.
Lee	Air	Lines
Lee	Aircraft	Co.
Lee,	Art	J.
Lee,	Arthur	B.
Lee,	C.	R., & Co.
Lee &	Company	

3. When first and second units are the same, then according to third unit.

Lee, B.	
Lee, B.,	Co.†
Lee, B.,	Novelty Corp.†
Lee, B.,	& Sons, Inc.†
Lee, B.	A.
Lee, B.	Albert
Lee, B.	B.
Lee, B.	Ben
Lee, B.	Benjamin

* Company names made up of initials or letters are alphabetized before all other names beginning with the same letter.

† Company names beginning with a Christian name, or initial, and a surname are alphabetized before similar personal names with second initials or middle names—to keep like personal names grouped. (This is done in the New York telephone directory, but not in all others.)

Company Names. Company names are written with the initials or Christian names immediately after the surnames.

Harper, Geo., & Co.	NOT:	*Harper & Co., Geo.*
Haviland, L. J., & Sons	NOT:	*Haviland & Sons, L. J.*
Hawthorne, W. R., & Co., Ltd.		
Marshall, P. J., Company (The)		
Martin, J.,-Bernard Kennedy (firm name of two full names)		

Company names, familiar as trade names, are not broken down, even though the first name is a Christian name.

Marshall Field & Company   Montgomery Ward & Co.

Do not index a company name in an unfamiliar guise. For instance, Marshall Field & Company is not usually spoken of as "Field Company". Most company names are, however, more familiarly known by the last name, and are indexed accordingly, as

Wanamaker, John, New York

Test a company name to determine how it is commonly used.

Always cross-index a name under its familiar title if it is filed under a broken-down title. Telephone directories do this with certain names.

Smith, L. C., & Corona Typewriters, Inc. CROSS-INDEX UNDER L:
L. C. Smith Company—See Smith, L. C., & Corona Typewriters, Inc.

Small Words in Names. When "The" occurs before a name, it may be placed after the name in parentheses and disregarded in alphabetizing. If it occurs in a name, it is considered in alphabetizing.

440

Dalles (The) (Oregon)	Marx The Trader
Dalles Company (The)	Marx, Thomas J.
Hague (The) (Netherlands)	The Dalles (Oregon)—See Dalles (The)
Hague & Company	The Hague—See Hague (The)

Small words that form an indispensable part of a title must be considered in alphabetizing.

Marling's-by-the-Sea	To and From Library
Time O'Day Corporation	Troy's-at-the-Beach

Titles With Names. Disregard titles and designations, as "Dr.", "Capt.", "Jr.", "Mrs.", etc. Write them in parentheses after the names. (In book indexing they are written thus: Scott, Capt. Robert V.)

Gray, L. C. (Jr.)	Langford, Bruce (Col.)
(NOT: *Gray, Jr., L. C.*)	Scott, Robert V. (Capt.)
Gray, L. C. (Sr.)	Turnquist, David L. (Rev.)
Henderson, J. W. (Dr.)	Wilson, Thornwall (Prof.)
Henderson, J. W. (Mrs.)	or Henderson, Ruth T. (Mrs. J. W.)

BUT titles that begin trade names, as "Sir Walter Raleigh Tobacco", "Prince Edward Hotel", "Madame Cécile", "Dr. Day's Brushes", are not inverted and **are considered** in alphabetizing.

Mc and Mac. "Mc" and "Mac" are filed in their exact alphabetic order.

Mabury, C. J.	MacLane, Wm. F.
MacArthur, J. H.	Matson, M. J.
MacDonald, D. C.	McAdams, E. W.
Mack, Elliot	McDonald, Robert

Mt., Ft., St., Pt. Treat these abbreviations as if they were spelled out—"Mount", "Fort", "Saint", and "Point"—and cross-index them.

Fort Wayne (Indiana)	CROSS INDEX CARDS
Mount Shasta Ices	Ft.—See Fort
Point Pleasant (W.Va.)	Mt.—See Mount
Saint Francis Hospital	Pt.—See Point
Saint Paul Transport Co.	St.—See Saint

Foreign Names. When the "von", "de", "Le", "El", etc., in foreign names are parts of the last names, they should begin the names.

D'Antonio, Francis	La Fontaine, Jean de
De Forest, J. V.	Le Clair, Dennis J.
de la Rue, O. E.	van der Zee, B. T.
El Camino Club	von Griswold, Ernst

But if a foreign name is more commonly known without its prefix, it may be indexed in the familiar form, as

Beethoven, Ludwig van	Maupassant, Guy de

Usage differs in different languages, and if a problem in filing foreign names exists, consult a foreign dictionary.

Possessive Names.   File in strict alphabetic order.

Fuller, P. D.

Fullering, Frank

Fuller's Market

Fullers' Tavern

Fullerson Bros.

Fullerton & Son

Fullertons' Inn

Fullerton's Shop

Abbreviations.   Treat all abbreviations as if spelled out, except those that begin company names. "And" may be written "&" and disregarded.

Lee, Chas. V.

Lee Chart Co.

Lee, Cobb & Co.

Lee Co. (The)

Lee Mfg. Co.

Lee & Martin

Numerals as Names.   When numerals are used as names, spell out the names, and file under the spelled-out version.

450 Sutter   FILE UNDER: Four Fifty Sutter   CROSS-INDEX: Sutter, 450

308 Formula   FILE UNDER: Three Oh Eight Formula

The 220 Club   FILE UNDER: Two Twenty Club (The)

Common Phrases in Titles.   Titles beginning with phrases common to other titles, such as "Estate of", "Board of", etc., are inverted and the subjects filed under the principal names.

Lindon, Emerson S., Estate of

Universities, Schools, Colleges.   File under the principal part of the name (and cross-index under the full name, if only a few schools appear in the files).

FILE UNDER: California, University of

Notre Dame, College of (Baltimore)

Notre Dame, University of (Indiana)

Physicians and Surgeons, College of

Washington, University of

William and Mary, College of

CROSS-INDEX UNDER: University of California

College of Notre Dame (Baltimore)

University of Notre Dame (Indiana)

College of Physicians and Surgeons

University of Washington

College of William and Mary

Churches, Societies, Associations.   File under the full straight name.

Association of Voters

Astronomical Society

Church of Christ

Church of the Advent

Holy Trinity Church

Society of Pioneers

Bank names are similarly indexed:

Bank of New York

Chase National Bank

First National Bank of Chicago

Guaranty Trust Company of New York

National City Bank of New York

Government Departments.   Bureaus, boards, and departments of the different governments—Federal, state, county, and city—are filed under the name of the chief governing body.

442

California, State of
  Architecture, Division of
  Commerce, Bureau of
  Lincoln, County of
  Weights and Measures, Bureau of

San Francisco, City of
  Education, Board of
United States Government
  Commerce, Department of
  Census, Bureau of the

SUMMARY NOTE ON ALPHABETIZING. A study of indexes will disclose many variations in alphabetizing. The method used in each index is governed by the number of names being dealt with. The telephone directory method is particularly adaptable to voluminous lists; the dictionary method to shorter or less complicated lists. Good examples of the dictionary method may be found in the Congressional Directory (in the front and back indexes), in lists of advertisers in magazines, and in indexes in books and booklets.

Both methods are often used in the same book; for instance, in a telephone directory one will find all names beginning with "New" grouped before such names as "Newark", "Newcomb", etc.; but in the front of the same directory, in the shorter lists of out-of-town points, one will find in strict alphabetic order "Newark" before "New Bedford", etc.

The telephone directory method has undergone simplification from time to time. In strict alphabetic order according to surname now are to be found: all "Mc" and "Mac" names; all company names (except those noted on p. 440); all compound or hyphened names (both company and individual, according to the first surname); and all possessive names (no differentiation between singular and plural). And the word "The" within a name, as "John The Florist" is considered in alphabetizing. However, other small words, such as "of the", "for", and "from" are not yet considered as they are in the dictionary method, which latter method brings together all names beginning "Association of", "Association for", "Church of the", etc.

DIARY

A diary should be kept in every office, and in it should be noted the important happenings of each day.

Record should be made of the departure of persons on trips and their return; the signing of important documents or the closing of transactions; the arrival of persons from out of town, or of important callers, etc.

The desk calendar may be used as a diary, although a separate book is better if the notations are likely to be numerous.

SCRAPBOOK

When cutting out pages for a scrapbook, use a sharp knife, or a razor blade, and not scissors. Do not attempt to tear the pages out, or the reading matter may be destroyed.

The secret of neat pasting lies in using very little paste, especially on thin paper. Wet pages will wrinkle. In applying paste, start near the center of the page and work outward. Let the extreme edges remain dry until the paper has been pasted; then with the brush apply paste carefully beneath the edges and paste them down. Wipe away all surplus paste immediately so that no pages will stick together; and use a dry cloth or piece of tissue paper—not the palm of the hand—for smoothing down the pasted surface.

There is no excuse for a scrapbook's being kept in any condition but clean.

❖

DIPLOMACY AND EFFICIENCY

Punctuality. **Be on time in the morning**—even if working overtime at night. That is the company's gain. To make up the overtime, ask occasionally for time off—an afternoon or a day when the work is not heavy—but do not adopt the reasoning that overtime is being made up by being late in the morning.

Nothing signifies an interest in the work more than being on time both in the morning and at noon, and not "watching the clock" to get away in the evening.

If you are continually required to work overtime, ask for a later arrival hour in the morning. If there is an understanding in such matters no offense is created by arriving late.

Don't be habitually absent from the office for reasons other than illness. A worker may think his absences are not noticed, but usually, and generally very suddenly, some action is taken regarding them.

Make very few personal appointments that will consume office time. If it can be seen that something will cause an unusually late arrival at the office, telephone in, explaining the delay; or if an appointment is to be kept at noon which might cause a delay, explain that before leaving the office. Thus a better feeling is created than if a person simply turns up late and then explains the reason for his tardiness.

It is customary to say "Good morning" when first encountering anyone in the office, even though superiors do not sometimes speak first.

It is also usual to say "Good night", if it is reasonably convenient to do so. But do not go out of the way to say either.

Office Unattended. Arrange hours if possible so that the office will not be unattended at any time. If it is impossible for the office to be attended at the lunch hour, do not leave it open; lock the door and put a card on it giving the approximate time of return. It is discourteous to let people wait outside expecting someone to return momentarily.

Do not leave an office unattended and take time to shop. An important caller might be turned away or an important telephone call missed, and someone angered enough to report this to the employer.

Leaving at Night. When preparing to leave an office at night, do not rush about in a hurry to get away, banging up desks, etc. Learn to put a desk in order and close things quietly and carefully, and to take a deliberate rather than a hurried leave. It will consume only a few minutes more, will probably prevent some last minute error or oversight, and will create a much better impression.

If there is a possibility of further work, ask regarding it **before preparing to leave,** not afterward.

Mentally check over the work to see that all is in order before leaving at night.

444

Interest. Learn to work with a system. Do not be constantly confused. Improve as many conditions as can be improved, and have as many things as possible working mechanically each day, or performed as a habit under a well-thought-out system.

Be consistent in the work. Do not worry about small things and overlook large ones. Consider them all—the large ones first.

The more interest an employee takes in the business, the more he becomes an assistant and departs from being a servant. Do not sit back and read books or newspapers, and then feel hurt if asked to do some menial task that should have been done in the first place. A worker can be his own master in a great many respects. If it is unpleasant or embarrassing to be told to do things, think of things to do.

Understand that everything, **and anything,** is to be done willingly. If something gainful can be found in unpleasant tasks, they become easier.

If sometimes the disturbing thought occurs that perhaps someone else could do the job better—or perhaps the company thinks that someone else would be better—attempt to erase all points of doubt by methodically correcting one matter of inefficiency each day.

Cooperation. Attempt to see always from the other's viewpoint. Try once in a while to face the problems an employer is facing in his endeavor to make ends meet. If he seems annoyed at times, there might be a chance that he has a right to be.

When asking assistance from anyone, ask in the form of a question rather than a command; and do not be constantly disturbing another person by asking small favors. Respect his right to work in peace.

When leaving work for others to do—as when leaving on a vacation—make a list of things to be done, especially if someone unfamiliar with the work is to be assigned to it. Give the new person every assistance.

In explaining work to a new person, or in explaining anything to anyone, give the reasons for doing it in a certain manner, and it will be more easily remembered.

Never criticize one person's work in the presence of another.

Constructive Criticism. If something seems wrong about an office, find a constructive suggestion to offer instead of a criticism of present conditions.

If the suggestion does not meet with favor, try to see also how the other person could be right. If after analyzing the situation, it still seems that he is wrong, wait until he is proved wrong before making a further suggestion for a change.

Recognizing a Superior. Recognize the need for a head of every department—someone who carries the responsibility and knows the work that is being done.

Be tractable when working with a superior. Do not attempt to do things independently or fail to report things done, which really amounts to "going over a superior's head" by keeping him in ignorance of work or arrangements that are supposedly under his supervision.

445

When given instructions by someone higher in authority than an immediate superior, carry out the instructions, but let the immediate superior know of the arrangements. Then if anything goes wrong, responsibility rests where it should.

Make notes of all important things with which an immediate superior should be acquainted. Leave on his desk carbon copies of all outgoing letters that he has not seen.

If a mistake is made, admit it. Work as accurately and conscientiously as possible, apprising a superior of all things done—praise or blame.

Conferences With a Superior. Make notations of things to be taken up with a superior and choose a time for going over these details when he is not busy. Many things can be disposed of in this way, instead of every day asking something about the office or procedure.

It is necessary, of course, to ask a few questions that need immediate attention. But be very sure that they are urgent before disturbing a busy person. If they can be answered at any time throughout the day, and the person who can answer them is momentarily engaged with other things, simply put notations of the questions on his desk, or in the folder with his letters for signature.

When asking a question, mention the subject first so the person spoken to can grasp the matter and be able to answer immediately. Never preface a remark by saying "I wanted to ask you about..." Begin with the subject, as "The insurance papers that Mr. Barnes wanted—I could find but two..."

When asking for a personal favor or for time off, never say "I want to ask a favor..." or "There's something I'd like to ask you about..." This savors too much of unpleasantness. Simply say something like— "Wednesday, if it's convenient, I'd like to have the morning off..."

Poise. Poise is the manner of doing things in rather a deliberate way, with real thought behind every action. Speed is not nearly so important in a business office as calmness. There is no need for going about work in a constant hurry—entering and leaving rooms too quickly, and saying "Yes" to instructions before hearing half of what is being said.

Listen attentively—not nervously—to all instructions that are given, and act understandingly. Have a surety and firmness about everything that is done.

In a word—to have real poise, be calm, quiet, dignified, and very professional...and always immaculately groomed.

Accent and Speech. Tone down any definite accent and discard all affectations of speech. Many companies will not employ persons with noticeable accents; such voices are difficult to understand over the telephone. Assumed accents expose the speakers at the most awkward moments. Naturalness is in the best taste always.

Do not pitch the voice so low that it cannot be understood. If asked to repeat several times, be quick enough to understand that a

446

little louder or clearer speech is necessary. Particularly, speak clearly and distinctly when talking to a superior, whose time is valuable.

Manners. The correct thing in business manners is always the gracious thing. But business deportment should always remain slightly formal, no matter how long persons have been associated or have known each other. Informality generally leads to injured feelings through misunderstandings.

Have consideration for others in an office and do not cause unnecessary disturbances, by humming, whistling, or tapping with a pencil when people are trying to work.

Do not talk or laugh too much, or too loud. Don't be habitually amused. In every office there is an undercurrent of seriousness—have respect for that. If temporarily amused, be able to return immediately to the seriousness of the work. If an amusing incident happens in the presence of a superior, a good rule is not to laugh unless he laughs first. He may not think it funny at all—may even be annoyed to think that someone else is amused.

Callers. Treat every caller as a prospective customer.

If calling, be courteous to the receptionist or secretary. She is really an important person. Do not attempt to ignore her.

When meeting a caller, find out whom he wishes to see, and the purpose of his call if he is a stranger and has no appointment. Someone other than the person he asks for may be the person for him to see.

If it is not possible for a caller to see the person he is calling upon— because of previous appointments or conferences—ask him if he will not telephone for an appointment later. This overcomes much disappointment when people are being turned away.

If it is necessary for a caller to wait, see that he has something to read. Never attempt particularly to entertain him; many callers desire simply to wait and think. If talking to a caller, talk only about things in general—the chief item of commercial news in the paper that day, the weather, etc. If he inquires about anything pertaining to the business, be very courteous in answering, but reply in generalities, giving only such information as has been made public by the company.

Announcing Callers. It is much better to have an understanding with a superior regarding his wishes in the matter of announcing callers, the persons he wishes to see and does not wish to see, etc., than to guess at the proper procedure in each instance.

As a general rule, callers should be announced in the following manner, if the persons they are calling upon are engaged:

An ordinary caller without an appointment should be expected to wait until a conference is finished, or should see someone else in the organization.

A person with an appointment should be announced immediately, or if the person he is calling upon is only temporarily engaged, he should be expected to wait a few minutes before being announced.

An important visitor should be announced immediately, whether he has an appointment or not, unless the person he is calling upon is engaged with someone equally as important. In that event, he should be asked to wait a few minutes for the conference to be finished, before he is announced.

When announcing a caller to a person who is occupied with another, simply take the visitor's card in, or write his name on a slip of paper and hand it to the person whom he is calling to see.

If a message is being sent in, write it out on a slip of paper. It may be important that the other caller does not hear the message, or know that someone else is calling. Be extremely careful about presenting information to anyone when another (even someone from the same office) is present.

It is not customary for a secretary or stenographer to knock on a closed door when entering a conference room. It is her privilege to enter when she wills, but she should use that privilege with discretion. She should never enter hurriedly, always quietly and unobtrusively.

When a caller arrives, if it is known that certain papers will be used in connection with his call, obtain those papers from the files and hand them in when admitting the caller.

Introductions. It is not customary for an employer to introduce a caller to an employee, unless the employee is to work for or with the caller. Then they should be introduced.

A secretary often introduces a caller to her employer as she shows the caller in; although this is not always deemed necessary.

A woman's name should be mentioned first in an introduction, as "Miss Lawrence, Mr. James." When a group are being introduced in an office, the women should be named before the men.

When two men are being introduced to each other (or two women), it is complimentary for the one introducing them to mention the name of the older or more important person first. When the two persons are of almost equal age and importance, it is immaterial which name is mentioned first.

When a woman is being presented to an older person, it is complimentary for her to rise, especially if the older person is a member of the employer's family. In other introductions in business, it is usual for a woman to remain seated. She should always extend her hand if the other person offers his hand in greeting, saying simply "How do you do."

Information. Never give out any office information of any kind, especially financial or credit information, unless specifically authorized to do so. If necessary, obtain first an authorization by telephone or telegraph.

Never give information to anyone, even to someone in the same office, unless it is to be general news.

Never voluntarily give out any business information that might be "bad news", such as information about unstarted or unfinished orders, or about anything that does not comply with the customer's wishes.

448

For instance, if a customer telephones about an order, never say "We haven't started on that order yet." Let a superior do the explaining. Every effort should be made to remedy a situation before unpleasant news is given out.

If authorized to give out information, check carefully to see that it is all correct.

Memory Aids. The best method of remembering is by association of ideas. Analyze things and translate them into familiar terms.

Read a meaning into everything—a reason. **Meaningless things cannot be remembered.** Every paper that comes into or originates in an office has some importance. It is written for some purpose; it will bring about some result; it has some reason for existing.

If a real interest is created in the papers that pass through an office—in what they are doing to further or hinder the work—it will be easy to remember them, even though they have to be handled rapidly.

"Infallible Memory". The only way to have an infallible memory is to **write it down.** Make notes of everything: telephone calls, business appointments, supplies to be ordered, things to be done, messages taken—in fact, **everything.** Make a habit of making notes. It is the **only way** to avoid saying "I forgot."

Automatic Memory. To be reminded of something automatically, put the article in question (or a note regarding it) where it will be a reminder in itself. If, for instance, a book is to be returned to the library, or a letter is to be registered, put it with some automatic reminder, such as gloves, hat, or wraps.

If something is to be done at a certain time on a certain day, make a note of it on the desk calendar, and when that day arrives, circle the note in red and place the calendar in a forward position on the desk, to be a constant reminder until that duty is attended to.

Photographic Memory. Certain things may be remembered by "photographing" them on the mind. If, for instance, a mental picture is made of a telephone number the first time it is used, it rarely deserts thereafter. Or the image of the spelling of a word may be imprinted on the mind. Initials may also be remembered in this manner.

Odd Jobs and Dull Times. Dull time is inventory time. Make a list of things to do on dull days, **and do them.** The following are suggestions:

Rearrange parts of filing system.
Clean supply cabinet and check for restocking.
Clean desk and restock it with supplies.
Clean up the office generally, making it neater by clearing away any papers or other articles that have a tendency to accumulate uselessly.
Inaugurate newer and more efficient methods where needed.
Have repairs made to anything in need of them.
Do cataloguing, listing, or filing to improve later work or perfect office routine.
Practise shorthand, handwriting, or printing.
Address envelopes for routine work.

449

Create an interest in looking for things to improve when there is nothing else to do.

Practising Shorthand, Handwriting, etc. Practice is the one way to perfect shorthand. If mistakes occur in shorthand transcriptions, practise in every spare moment to overcome them. Write over and over the words that give trouble in dictation and the words common to the business. Take papers from the files and rewrite them in shorthand, or rewrite articles from technical magazines. Keep a shorthand dictionary handy to verify unusual words.

Also practise handwriting and printing in odd moments. A good handwriting and symmetrical printing show up to advantage in an office.

Reading. Read the newspaper every day—**but not in the office.**

Keep the morning paper throughout the day for reference, but read it only before arriving at work or at lunch time.

Do not read books or magazines unless everything pertaining to the office has been done. If reading becomes a last resort, read the technical magazines or papers of the office. If a better knowledge of the business is needed, read papers from the files. Also **read the dictionary.**

Reading fiction is a dulling distraction in an office. If an important telephone call comes in, it is difficult momentarily to get back to business and know what the caller is talking about. Also, when a reader becomes engrossed in a story, some important office detail is liable to be overlooked, and an employer more annoyed than if the office were busy.

Working Habits. Attempt to make a habit of every correct practice. Sooner or later they will all come under the head of "efficiency".

Analyze the reason for every habit, and avoid those that might have a reactive bad result. For instance, the habit of tearing papers in two before putting them in the wastebasket would seem to be efficient. On the other hand, papers are often wanted after being discarded, and if torn in two they are useless, or require time to be mended. Therefore, it would seem a better practice simply to throw papers in the wastebasket, without the added noise of tearing or crumpling them, and decide that once in the wastebasket they are to be considered discarded. (Sometimes, of course, it is necessary to destroy papers thoroughly, such as old or replaced legal documents, so that they cannot be used again.)

These are excellent habits to acquire:

> The habit of being punctual
> The habit of cooperating
> The habit of checking continually in order to be correct
> The habit of making notes of things
> The habit of being consistent
> The habit of being quiet
> The habit of being clean.

Mistakes. Accuracy heads the list of desirable qualifications for an office worker. Speed is far down on the list.

Standardize on everything to avoid errors. **System is a great aid.** When many of the little error-prevention devices are overlooked, the accuracy average is very low. If they are made use of, the reliability and accuracy average is usually high.

Avoid errors wherever possible by anticipating them. There is much truth in the old advice: think first and act afterward. Do not act first and think and regret it afterward. In deciding how to do anything, **think out the consequences of doing it in several ways.** Then choose the way that has the least possibility for criticism or error, **even though it is the hardest way.**

Never blankly or mechanically follow instructions. Think over the working out of all instructions before executing them.

Don't be uninterested when doing things. Attach some importance to every small task to be done. It is in the small things that the catch lies. They seem unimportant at the time, but if done incorrectly something of great importance may grow out of them.

If tired or ill, double-check the work, and work more slowly. Many errors creep in under these circumstances.

If an error of any consequence is made, never try to "fix it up" and say nothing. Serious outgrowths have come from so doing. Think out a way to remedy the situation if possible, and suggest the remedy along with confessing the error.

Be reasonably sure, but never too sure about anything. It is very easy to be wrong, which always proves embarrassing.

Everyone makes mistakes—and someone tells him about them— but the careful worker need never be told twice about the same thing.

Dismissal or Being "Fired". **Carelessness heads the list** of reasons for being discharged.

No matter who a person is, unless he is his own employer, there is always the possibility of being "fired".

Therefore the accuracy and interest averages should be kept high. Correct everything that can be corrected. Never depend on another to catch or correct small errors or inefficiencies that are known to exist. Correct them at their inception; there are always enough unavoidable mistakes to count against one.

Reasons for being "fired":
Being habitually late, leaving early, or taking long lunch hours.
Inability to cooperate with other people in the organization.
Long personal telephone calls, tying up the company lines.
Talking or laughing too much, or too loud.
Not taking messages correctly, or failing to write them down.
Insubordination (no task should be too small for any person to do if he is unoccupied).
Absence from the office on the slightest provocation.
Disloyalty or dishonesty.
Thoughts on being "fired":
Remember that many of the best people have been "fired";
That instead of being a calamity, it may be a start toward more satisfactory employment;

451

That something has been learned; and that mistakes in the long run are called "experience".

"Life is a long lesson in humility."—Barrie, "The Little Minister".

Money Matters

Increases in Salary. When asking for an increase in salary, state simply that it seems necessary and give the reasons. If you are not earning enough to live on, say so. Or if the work is very difficult or trying, perhaps the position warrants a higher salary. These are the main reasons for asking for an increase in salary.

If salaries come under the supervision of an immediate superior, discuss the matter with him first. It may be his position to recommend increases for those in his department.

Choose the opportunity for discussing an increase in salary when the person who might grant the request is in an unhurried mood. This discussion can always await an opportune time.

Discussing Money Matters. Money matters are the most private of all matters in a business office. **Never mention a money matter of any kind before a caller,** or before a third person in the same office, or even before members of an employer's family unless the employer mentions it first.

Do not refer to another person's insurance, income tax, your own pay check, or an IOU, except in privacy. If it is necessary to refer to any of these things before others, make a memorandum and hand it to the other person.

Never mention money that a superior owes for office expenses. Make an itemized slip and place it on his desk. Instead of writing "You owe..." suggest it in a businesslike way, as "Paid for messenger— $1.45", etc.

Borrowing Money. Do not borrow money from others in the office unless it is absolutely necessary. Much annoyance is caused by trivial borrowing.

Always make a note of money borrowed, even from friends. It is most embarrassing to forget to repay. And **always repay promptly.** Money matters are a very delicate subject—even between the best of friends.

Safeguarding Valuables. Never leave anything of value, money, purse, wraps, etc., in an unguarded place in an office. Many things have been lost or stolen in offices, which are more or less public places. See that all things of value, **especially stamps,** are put away at night in a locked drawer or in some other place of safekeeping.

Personal Matters

Personal Telephone Calls. Do not use the office telephone for long personal conversations. Personal calls at the office, both incoming and outgoing, should be very few and far between—and **very brief.**

452

Using the telephone for social purposes ties up the trunk lines, and a constant "busy" signal is usually reported to an employer. Even a good-natured employer resents the continued use of the office telephone for personal calls.

Personal Letters. Do not **write or read** personal letters in the office, except in privacy.

Do not use company stamps or send personal telegrams without paying for them.

Personal Engagements. Every social engagement should be made contingent upon and subordinate to business. In an office, **business comes first,** and social engagements last.

Ethics. A few of the little "unwritten laws" of business:

Absolute loyalty is expected at all times. Do not say uncomplimentary things about the company that pays your salary—in the office or out. Do not let dissatisfaction be known unless you are ready to resign; the company may request the resignation if rumors of dissension are heard.

Try by cooperation to work out all problems smoothly. If things remain unsatisfactory and irremediable after a thorough trial at betterment, do not resort to a condemnation of the company; simply resign, and attempt to find more congenial work.

Keep out of petty gossip. It is enticing sometimes, to be sure, but those who stay clear of it are always in the advantageous positions in the long run. If asked by a superior about another person under certain circumstances, make whatever is told as kindly as possible, but of course state the truth.

Guard office information carefully. Never tell anything outside the office—even in enthusiasm—that might be giving away valuable secrets. Whatever the company is working on should be kept confidential until it is ready to be released.

❖

OFFICE, GENERAL

Desk. Keep the desk clean.   It is a workbench, not a catchall.

Never allow a lot of old-fashioned relics to accumulate on a desk. File everything away in its natural place, and dispose of all obsolete things.   Keep current papers in a pending folder or basket, with explanatory notes clipped to them, and look them over **every day,** weeding out the ones that can be disposed of, or that someone else can dispose of.   Beware of piling papers in file boxes and forgetting them.

The more papers on a desk, the more to remember.

Keep the telephone book off the desk unless it is in constant use; keep it free from dust in a cabinet or drawer near the telephone.

Keep newspapers and magazines off the desk if they are not in actual use.   Save the morning newspaper for one day only, unless a regular file of newspapers is kept.

Do not have anything that might tip over and spill on a desk, such as a vase of flowers, an open ink bottle, sponge cup, etc.   Keep such things in safer places.

If near an open window, keep all papers weighted.   The wind has often carried valuable papers out the window.

Cover all papers or letters of a confidential nature when leaving the desk.   In extremely confidential work, place the papers inside the desk and lock it, thus further protecting responsibility.

Leave the desk clean at night.   Especially, put away carbon paper and close the inkwell.   Both supplies deteriorate rapidly.   See that the typewriter is covered or closed in a desk.   Never put an expensive piece of equipment, such as a "line-a-time", on the floor, where it may be injured by the cleaners.

Much waste comes from improper care of office equipment, and many an employer looks with discouragement upon his carelessly deserted offices at night.

The phrase "taking an interest in the business" means, in fact, "taking care of things".

Chair. An armchair is not a convenient chair for typing.   A swivel chair with a good **back rest** is the most practical and restful.

Chairs are often too high or too low for ease in typing.   Adjust the height until the chair seems comfortable.

Learn to lean back and rest against the chair.   If the back of the chair is too far away, fit a small cushion to it for the shoulders to rest against.   Pull the chair up close so that the body will be able to sit erect yet braced against the back rest.   This eliminates fatigue and the stinging neck and shoulder pains experienced by many who type all day without back support of any kind.

Keeping Supplies. Keep the supply cabinet in perfect order, even if time has to be taken to arrange it one day each week.

454

Have **only one opened package** of each different supply. Keep all others wrapped, and mark the contents on the outside in red or blue pencil, so there will be no tearing of corners of packages to see the contents, leaving the material to deteriorate. A **real loss of money is** involved in wasted supplies.

Group everything of one kind in one place. For instance, all the paper should be on one shelf, the envelopes on another, inks and bottled or tube supplies on another, erasers all in one box, carbon paper in one section, etc. Then if anyone wants a certain supply it is to be found in one place, or it is not in stock.

Keep the most used supplies in the handiest places on the most convenient shelves, not, for instance, the pencils on the bottom shelf, and the letterheads on the top shelf stacked behind seldom used papers.

Ordering Supplies. Keep a memorandum order list in the desk, and add a new item whenever a supply is getting low.

Order by number if possible, and state definitely the **size, quality,** and **quantity** desired. Unless this is done, many mistakes will occur.

Check prices and quantities on the invoices for goods, and write "Received by...", instead of "OK", on the bill. "OK" is used by the person passing upon payment.

Printed Supplies. Before reordering any supply of printed matter—letterheads, envelopes, forms, etc.—consult someone in authority about the order. A change in wording, lettering, size, or paper quality may be desired.

Always obtain an estimate from a printer before ordering any printing done. Prices vary greatly, according to the quality of paper used, etc.

When reordering printed forms, give the **printer's number** on the form, and send one form as a sample.

Also allow plenty of time for the printing to be done, by reordering at least **three weeks** before the supply will be actually needed.

Heating, Lighting, and Ventilating. Many discussions arise regarding the temperature of rooms, too much or too little air, and too much or too little light. In these matters attempt to see first from the others' viewpoint; but if their suggestions seem wrong after being given a trial, suggest an improvement of conditions.

Room temperatures should be approximately

> 70 degrees F. in summer, and
> 70 to 78 degrees F. in winter.
> (Air may be warmer in winter because of the cold air currents that carry the heat away.)

Windows should not be opened so wide in winter that the air cannot be slightly warmed before it is breathed. Health authorities state that the raw coldness of winter air is a great factor in producing the common cold.

Never place a desk in a draft; and arrange desks so that no one will sit facing a window. Light should come from the side or back.

Avoid glares on the metal of the typewriter from the morning or afternoon sun.

When using an electric fan, turn it so it will blow above the heads of workers, and not directly on them.

Dusting. An office should always have the appearance of being thoroughly clean.

Never permit it to become dusty or cluttered up. Such a condition looks old-fashioned. Modern desks are clean, files clean, rooms clean.

Every desk should be dusted every morning. If necessary, desks should be dusted again at noon.

Do not resent dusting—it's a part of the job.

Cabinets. Keep books and magazines or periodicals in a cabinet or bookcase if possible. Do not permit magazines to pile up and collect dust. The general rule is to save magazines for six months only. Ask the office's preference regarding this.

Arrange books alphabetically in the cabinets, according to the authors, as is done in libraries.

Arrange the issues of each magazine in a separate stack, chronologically, with the latest issue always on top.

Cleaning and Discarding. When cleaning an office, make a list of suggested things to be thrown away. Ask permission, from someone in charge, to dispose of such things. Never discard anything of possible value **without permission.**

Do not let things accumulate anywhere in an office, such as old newspapers or magazines, half-used carbon paper, addressed envelopes, old files and folders, etc.

Office Details. To keep an office in smooth running order, do not debate about doing small unwanted jobs; simply do them or see that they are done.

Analyze an office and anticipate its needs. If something seems to be necessary or called for a number of times, see if it cannot be procured. If there is a buzzer or bell system that is too loud, have it toned down. Do not permit harsh sounds or disturbing noises to irritate an office, if they are at all remediable.

Ordering Improvements. If contemplating any cleaning, redecorating, additions, or improvements in an office, **get an estimate** of the cost before ordering the work done. Submit this estimate to someone in authority for approval. Surprising charges have resulted from ordering without an idea of what the cost would be.

This advice extends even to personal matters; in fact, for any undertaking on which the final charges are unknown—**get an estimate.**

NEW POSITIONS

Letters of Application. Unsolicited letters of application rarely bring results. Attempt to ascertain whether a position exists before applying for it.

In answering an advertisement, comply with all its requirements. If the address given is a newspaper box number, use "Gentlemen:" or "Dear Sir:", whichever seems appropriate, as the salutation.

Begin with a simple statement, such as "I should like to submit my qualifications for the secretarial (or stenographic) position in your office." Then list the information, using sideheads such as:

Education, Experience, Age, Nationality and Religion (if requested), Salary expected or now earned (if requested), and References.

Close the letter with a short paragraph, such as "I shall be glad to call for an interview at any time you might wish to see me." Beneath "Sincerely yours," leave sufficient space for your signature, then type your name, address, and telephone number.

Copies, not the originals, of letters of recommendation may be enclosed if this is thought desirable. It is unnecessary to enclose a stamped, addressed envelope, unless you wish the copies returned.

Use good stationery, and be concise and businesslike in your reply—never artistic or "unusual" in an attempt to catch the interest.

Registering at an Agency. When registering for a position through an agency, state the exact facts about all accomplishments or experience. If these are exaggerated it will be discovered when the applicant is sent to a new position, and both applicant and agency will suffer thereby.

If sent to a position by an agency, keep the agency apprised of all dealings regarding the position. Do not disregard the agency after being sent out by it.

Advertising for a Position. If such advertising is done, it should be very dignified and very conservative.

Interviews. When calling in regard to a position, dress in business-like clothes. Be courteous to the secretary or girls in the outer office; that impression counts too. It is unnecessary, of course, to state the purpose of the call.

Wait to be asked to be seated in an interview. Do not talk too much. Let the other person do most of the interviewing.

Do not produce letters of recommendation unless asked to do so. Prospective employers usually write to the references given, if they are interested in the applicants.

Speak simply and clearly and use no unfamiliar words. Avoid pronouncing with a noticeable accent; it points toward affectation. Clear speech is immediately indicative of character and judgment.

Salary. Most positions are worth a certain salary. Attempt to arrange a salary commensurate with the position or the work.

A too low salaried person in an important position is not a good thing for the position, the person, or the company; and vice versa, a high-salaried person is misplaced in mediocre work.

A good method is to start at a reasonably satisfactory figure, and if able to fill the position competently and satisfactorily—and the work seems to warrant it—to ask then for an increase in salary.

Tests. Tests are often given in stenographic interviews. Therefore, do not be annoyed at a test. If asked to take dictation, do so graciously, and be careful to hear every word. Ask that a word be repeated if misunderstood; it is not unusual to misunderstand unfamiliar dictation.

In transcribing, do not attempt to hurry. Examine the machine for a few moments if unfamiliar with the style; arrange the setup of the typewriting carefully; and transcribe at an even pace to avoid errors. If erasures are necessary, see that they are especially neat; do not permit a struck-over letter on a sample page.

In anticipation of such a test, the resourceful applicant will have with him (in a pocket or purse) his own pen or pencils, an ink eraser, and a pocket-sized dictionary—and his own notebook if he prefers a special kind.

New Work. When accepting a new position, anticipate the hardest and heaviest work at first. Positions are usually created when work becomes heavy, or when someone has been absent and things have piled up. Then, too, unfamiliar work is almost always hard or trying.

Ask few questions as a beginner. Rather, see how many things will explain themselves; but of course ask about essential details. Do not attempt to learn everything in one day.

Make notes of the details to be remembered at first. Check the work against these notes to see that everything is being done correctly.

Obtain a list of the names, initials, and addresses of all persons connected with the company.

Make a small list of supplies necessary, if assigned to a new desk, and obtain them from the person in charge of the supply cabinet. Ask for only what is absolutely needed at first. An office regards with disfavor a newcomer who asks for numerous supplies or accessories, such as scissors, stapling machine, etc., before he knows whether his work is satisfactory and he is going to stay. Borrowed accessories will suffice for a few weeks, and the gradual stocking of a desk will allow time to consider what is definitely needed.

To become familiar with new work, read or copy papers from the files, and read the technical publications in the office containing articles pertaining to the business. These papers are the most valuable instructors, and give to the beginner an insight into the work that can be gained in no quicker way.

❖

LEGAL PAPERS

(The practice of law has, by the courts and respective legislatures, been delegated and restricted to members of the bar. Furthermore, because laws are complex and ever-changing, all legal documents—and especially wills—should be prepared by or under the supervision of competent lawyers.)

Some offices other than law offices routinely prepare or handle certain legal papers, under the general supervision of their own legal counsel. For papers such as the following, printed forms to be filled in or to act as guides may be purchased from any large stationery store:

Acknowledgments
Affidavits
Agreements
Articles of Incorporation
Articles of Partnership
Assignments
Bills of Sale
Builders' Contracts
Conditional Sales
   (Agreements for Sale)

Contracts
Deeds (of all kinds)
Leases
Liens
Mortgages (of all kinds)
Powers of Attorney
Proxies
Releases or Satisfactions of Mortgage
Wills

The following points should be observed in preparing legal papers.

Paper. White, legal-sized, or often letter-sized; of bond quality, and if thin it must be resistant to tearing.

Spacing. Double-spaced. Land descriptions and other descriptions may be single-spaced.

Wording. The primary purpose in the choice of words is to make the document clear—so that it has only one meaning.

The long, formal, ceremonious phrases of a generation ago are being discarded in favor of straightforward wording. For instance, instead of using "party of the first part", etc., many companies are employing "first party" and "second party", or but one word to designate each party, as "Buyer" and "Seller", or "Contractor" and "Purchaser".

Instead of:	Usage is favoring:
made and entered into	made
by and between	between
signed and executed	executed
day and year	date
understood and agreed	agreed
assign, transfer, and set over	assign
the title and ownership of the goods	the title to the goods
personally came and appeared	personally appeared
Know all men by these presents	(is being omitted)

459

Abbreviations. Should not be used in legal papers unless they are so common as to be understood without question. A personal name should never be abbreviated, as "Jas.", "Chas.", "Jno.", etc., unless the owner of the name uses the abbreviated form in his legal signature.

Figures. There is a general tendency toward the elimination of the repetition of numbers in legal papers, as "twenty-five (25) percent within thirty (30) days". The figure alone is now commonly used, even in land descriptions—except in papers that transfer title.

> The east fifty (50) feet of Lot Six (6) in Block Ten (10) of...
> East half (E½) of Section Two (2), Township Ten (10) North, Range Six (6) E.W.M.

(For further land descriptions, see Weights and Measures, p. 564.)

Prices in legal papers are still, however, written in words and repeated in figures. But a series or list of prices is written in figures only. (See Numbers, p. 267.)

Interlineations. Every interlineation in a legal paper must be initialed by all parties to the paper. It is better to rewrite a page than to permit an interlineation, if the insertion is noticed before the papers are signed. Nothing can be changed, however, after signatures are affixed.

Inserted Pages. Should be avoided in legal papers. But if extra pages are added they should be numbered a, b, c, etc., and initialed by the signers or by the notary public to show that all parties are aware of the insertions.

Date. Every legal paper should bear a date. If the date does not occur in the first or last paragraph, it may be added as a last line before the signature, simply as

> Dated April 20, 1951.

Dates are no longer written in words in legal documents, except sometimes in very formal papers such as wills; but even then it is not necessary that they be written out. (See also Numbers, p. 268.)

The End. Is often indicated by a closing mark after the signatures.

– – –o0o– – –

Carbon Copies. Copies that are to be signed should be made on the same quality of paper as the original. Copies that are not to be signed may be made on cheaper paper, and the signatures typed on (after the original has been signed), with "(Sgd.)" before each name.

Copying Legal Papers. (See Copying, p. 420.)

Quotations. (For quotations in legal papers, see Quoted Matter, p. 243.)

Signatures. Signatures cannot stand alone on the last page of a legal document. There must be at least one line of writing above them to bind them to the rest of the paper.

Names throughout a document should be written exactly as they are to be signed. If there is a difference between the typed names and the signatures, an affidavit will later have to be filed to correct this discrepancy.

Every person should decide upon the form of his legal signature and use it on all legal papers. If, for instance, a signer uses his initials at one time, his first name and middle initial at another, and his first and middle names at another, he will sooner or later be forced to file an affidavit certifying that the three signatures refer to one and the same person.

A good legal signature consists of the three full names—Christian name, middle name, and surname—without initials. There can be little question about the identity of a person who signs his three full names, as

James Earle Darmond

The name may be typed beneath the signature, as it is on letters, if the signature is illegible, and if the name does not appear elsewhere in the document.

"By" should be used instead of "Per" when a person is simply signing for a company, or as the representative of another person.

"Per", "Per Pro.", or "P.P.", is used when a lawful agent is signing, under special authorization, for a principal. The full term is "per procurationem" (L., by authorization, or by proxy).

If responsible for the signatures on a document, make sure that all persons sign exactly as their names appear in the document, and that corporation and notarial seals are imprinted beside the respective signatures.

Married Woman's Signature. A married woman's legal signature may be written in two ways:

1. The preferable form is a combination of her maiden name and her married name, as
Elizabeth Lee Snowden
2. Another form is a combination of her first and middle names and her married name, as
Elizabeth Marion Snowden

The first form more clearly identifies her; and in the text of the legal paper she may be further identified, if necessary, as " (formerly Elizabeth Marion Lee)".

If she signs her legal name in two different ways, as "Elizabeth M. Snowden" and "Elizabeth Lee Snowden", she will sooner or later be obliged to make an affidavit certifying that: "Elizabeth M. Snowden and Elizabeth Lee Snowden are one and the same person."

Seals After Signatures. Seals were once used in English law instead of signatures, and have been continued in present law as a part of the signatures on certain papers ("sealed instruments"). They authenticate the signatures, and in the eyes of the law add a greater dignity to the instruments. However, in some states seals no longer carry any significance.

A "seal" may be written or drawn by the signer after his signature, or it may be printed or typed there. Anything that a signer indicates as his seal will be accepted as a seal.

The letters "L.S." (L. locus sigilli—the place of the seal) are often used as a seal; or the word "Seal" enclosed in a scroll.

Cross for Signature. If a person is unable to write, he may make his "mark" or "hold" (touch) the pen while the mark is being traced for him; or he may make his thumb mark in ink.

Two disinterested witnesses are usually necessary to a mark signature.

Witnesses to mark: [or Attest:]
    Daniel Calvin Carter (Address)
    Albert John Maxon (Address)

His
Jonathan Henry ✕ Booth
Mark

Pencil Signatures. Although lead pencil signatures are valid in law, it is not safe to rely upon pencil writing, which not only is easy to erase, but often blurs and becomes illegible with handling. All signatures should be in ink or indelible pencil to insure their lasting qualities.

Papers Signed by Minors. Generally, persons under the age of 21 years should not sign legal papers. While in most jurisdictions papers signed by a "minor" are valid if the minor elects, and is able, to carry out his contracts, such papers can be made inoperative if the minor chooses to disregard them. However, contracts and bills for necessaries supplied to a minor are usually not voidable—necessaries being regarded as food, clothing, and other articles necessary to maintain the minor's station in life.

Parts of a Name. The following are the parts of personal names:

Full name	as	Thomas Victor Kirkpatrick
		Ellen Virginia Lane
Christian name Given name Baptismal name Forename	is the first name:	Thomas Ellen
Middle name	is the second given name:	Victor Virginia
Surname Family name	is the last name:	Kirkpatrick Lane
Maiden name	is a woman's surname before marriage: Lane	
	(Often a married woman's maiden name is indicated by the French word "née" [nā].)	
Married name	A woman's married name may be written in three ways:	
	Mrs. Thomas Victor Kirkpatrick	
	Mrs. Ellen Virginia Kirkpatrick	
	Mrs. Ellen Lane Kirkpatrick	
Legal name	is the full name (without abbreviations):	
	Thomas Victor Kirkpatrick	
Single legal name	Ellen Virginia Lane	
Married legal name	Ellen Lane Kirkpatrick	

Legal Age. If an adult does not care to state his true age in a legal paper, he may be referred to as "above the age of 21 years", or his age may be listed as "legal".

In all states the legal age, or "age of majority", for men is 21 years. In most states the age of majority for women is also 21 years, although a few states grant legal rights to women at 18 years of age.

In many states women become of age, or are "emancipated from minority", by marriage. For the laws of each state, consult the current Martindale–Hubbell Law Directory, Vol. III, in any public or law library.

Marriageable Age. The marriageable age in each state is given in the current almanacs, which are listed on p. 592.

Voting Age. The voting age in all states is 21 years for both men and women, except in Georgia, where it is now 18 years for both. For "Qualifications for Voting" in each state, see a current almanac, which will give the necessary periods of residence in state, county, and district.

Papers Signed on Sundays or Holidays. Although some papers may be legally signed and acknowledged on Sunday or a holiday in some states (if ratified on a business day), it is better practice to avoid the signing of any legal paper on a Sunday or holiday. The paper should be dated back to the previous business day. **Do not date it ahead,** as it may be made void by the sudden incapacity or death of a signer before the date shown.

Papers Maturing on Sundays or Holidays. If a paper matures on Sunday or a holiday, it is payable on the next succeeding business day. This extends to the payment of income taxes, life insurance policies, etc.

Payments on notes, drafts, contracts, etc., must be **in the hands of the payees,** and not "in the mails", on the last day for payment. Payments on certain papers, such as some insurance policies, etc., may be "in the mails" on the last day for payment; but this does not serve as a general rule for all papers.

Recording of Legal Papers. Legal papers, such as deeds, mortgages, chattel mortgages, liens, leases, bills of sale, etc., may be recorded in the county or city recorder's office upon payment of certain fees.

The papers are copied into the record books, compared, and then returned to the owners or to their attorneys. (In some jurisdictions certain papers, such as chattel mortgages, conditional sales, liens, etc., may remain on file in the recorder's office until they are satisfied or released.)

The recording of papers establishes a prior claim over similar papers that are unrecorded. To be recorded, most papers **must be acknowledged** before notaries public or other officers authorized to take acknowledgments.

Notary Public. A notary public was formerly one who drew up legal papers (a "scrivener"), but now is one who only certifies to the authenticity of papers or statements.

State laws differ regarding the age, qualifications, etc., for becoming a notary public. Definite information may be obtained from the Secretary of State at the capital in each state.

Laws. (For method of finding or obtaining copies of national or state laws, see Reference Books, p. 591.)

Agreement or Contract. Agreements and contracts may be made in simple form and with simple wording, but they should state fully the understanding and the obligations of each party.

The outline form of an ordinary selling agreement or contract is as follows:

CONTRACT

THIS AGREEMENT, made this .... day of ...., 19......, between ...., of .... (city) ...., ... (state) ...., first party (hereinafter called the SELLER), and ...., a corporation, incorporated under the laws of the State of ...., with principal place of business in .... (city) ...., ... (state) ...., second party (hereinafter called the PURCHASER),

WITNESSETH:

WHEREAS it is ....
....; and

WHEREAS the parties hereto ....
....; and

WHEREAS the conditions are ....
....:

NOW THEREFORE, it is agreed that ....
....

WITNESS the signatures of the parties hereto on the date aforesaid.

	_____
	Seller
	_____
(Corporate Seal)	Purchaser
	By _____
	President

The numberings 1, 2, 3, etc., or First, Second, Third, etc., may be used instead of the word WHEREAS, and the NOW THEREFORE may be omitted.

A contract or agreement does not usually require witnesses, but it does usually require acknowledgment before a notary public if it is to be recorded in the recorder's office.

Acknowledgment. An acknowledgment is the short certification that appears at the end of a legal paper showing that the paper was duly executed and acknowledged. A simple form of acknowledgment, according to the latest Uniform Acknowledgment Act, would read:

State of .... } ss.
County of ....

On this the .... day of ...., 19......, before me, ..., the undersigned officer, personally appeared ...., known to me (or satisfactorily proven) to be the person whose name .... subscribed to the within [or foregoing] instrument, and acknowledged that ....he.... executed the same for the purposes therein contained.

In witness whereof, I hereunto set my hand and official seal.

....
Title of Officer

If one person acts or signs as "attorney in fact" for another, the acknowledgment should read:

State of ....⎱
County of ....⎰ ss.
    On this the .... day of ...., 19......, before me, ..., the undersigned officer, personally appeared ...., known to me (or satisfactorily proven) to be the person whose name is subscribed [to the foregoing instrument] as attorney in fact for ...., and acknowledged that ......he executed the same as the act of h........ principal for the purposes therein contained.
    In witness whereof, I hereunto set my hand and official seal.

....

....
Title of Officer

For a corporation, the following is the form of acknowledgment:

State of ....⎱
County of ....⎰ ss.
    On this the .... day of ...., 19......, before me, ..., the undersigned officer, personally appeared ...., who acknowledged h........self to be the .... of ....,
                   (title of officer)
a corporation, and that ......he, as such ...., being authorized so to do, executed the foregoing instrument for the purposes therein contained, by signing the name of the corporation by h........self as ....
    In witness whereof, I hereunto set my hand and official seal.

....

....
Title of Officer

Affidavit. An affidavit differs from an acknowledgment in that the affidavit attests the truth or authenticity of the statements made in the paper, or in the affidavit itself; and the "affiant" signs the affidavit. A simple form of affidavit is as follows:

State of ....⎱
County of ....⎰ ss.
...., being duly sworn (or affirmed), say...... that ....is (or are) the .... named in the foregoing instrument, and that every statement or thing contained therein is true *to the best of .... knowledge and belief.

Subscribed and sworn to before me this .... day of ...., 19.....

                              †Notary Public in and for the State
      (Notarial   of ...., residing
        Seal)   in ....
                              My commission expires ....

* This phrase may be added if the affidavit is made upon information and belief.
† Or title of officer before whom affidavit is made.

Officers Who Take Acknowledgments. Acknowledgments may be taken by, and affidavits subscribed to before, notaries public, judges, justices of the peace, clerks of the court, mayors, and certain Government officials, including diplomatic representatives and consuls of the United States.

Power of Attorney. Is legal written authority to act for another. The word "attorney" in this sense does not mean an "attorney at law", but rather a "substitute", who can be any adult person empowered to act for another. **Attorney in Fact** is the person so empowered.

Proxy. A proxy is a short form of power of attorney, given by a first person to a second person, authorizing the second person to represent the first person in voting at a meeting. A sample is as follows:

PROXY

I, _____

_____, do hereby constitute and

appoint _____

attorney and agent for me, to vote as my proxy at _____

_____,

according to the number of votes I should be entitled to vote if personally present.

Dated _____

Witness: _____

(Notarial certification is not usually necessary.)

The person appointed to vote as proxy for another need not necessarily be a member of the organization, or a stockholder in the corporation, at whose meeting he is to vote. Some organizations, however, hold closed meetings to which nonmembers are not admitted as proxies.

Deeds

A deed is a written conveyance of real estate (or similar property).

Warranty Deed. A deed in which clear title to the property is guaranteed.

Quitclaim Deed. A deed in which the one giving the deed simply relinquishes his rights in the property, but makes no guarantee of the title to the property.

Grant Deed. The word "grant" implies a special warranty or security.

Joint Tenancy Deed. Implies joint ownership by two or more persons (usually husband and wife), under which holding, the survivor owns the entire property.

Trust Deed. Is given in trust to secure the payment of a debt; it is a conveyance to a trustee (an individual, bank, or trust company) for the benefit of creditors in case the debt is not paid. It is in reality a form of mortgage.

Tax Deed. A deed issued to one who buys property at a tax sale.

Mortgages

A mortgage is a written conveyance of property, intended by the party making it to be a security for the payment of money, or for the performance of some prescribed act. If the conditions are complied with, the conveyance is voided. The common mortgages are:

466

Real Estate Mortgage. A mortgage covering a certain piece of real estate and all permanent improvements thereon.

Chattel Mortgage. A mortgage covering personal property.

Crop Mortgage. A form of chattel mortgage, mortgaging a crop.

First Mortgage. A mortgage which represents the first claim on a property.

Second Mortgage. A mortgage that is subordinate to a first mortgage.

Underlying Mortgage. A mortgage representing a prior claim, having been given before a later "overlying mortgage".

Liens

There are many different names for liens, but a lien is primarily a legal right to claim or hold certain property for the payment of a debt. (pron. lē′ĕn, or lēn) "Filing a lien" is recording a legal claim against a property.

Wills

There are different names for wills, but the term most generally used is "Last Will and Testament".

Holographic Will. A will "entirely written, dated, and signed" in the handwriting of the maker. Such wills are not valid in certain states. (pron. hŏl′ō-grăf′ik)

Codicil. A later addition to, or modification of, a will. (pron. kŏd′ĭ-sĭl, not *kōd-*)

Testator
Testatrix (fem.) } The maker of a valid will.

Intestate. If a person dies without leaving a will (or a valid will), he is said to have died "intestate".

Bequeath. To give personal property by will (to make a bequest).

Devise. To give real property (lands, tenements, and hereditaments) by will; or a gift of real property by will. (pron. dē-vīz′)

Devisor. One who gives real property by will. (pron. dē-vī′zôr)

Devisee. One to whom real property is willed. (pron. dĕv′ĭ-zē′)

Legatee. One who is bequeathed a legacy (money or personal property).

Heirs. Technically, the persons entitled to receive real estate when there is no will. Now very generally used to mean any persons entitled (by will or otherwise) to receive the property of an estate.

Executor
Executrix (fem.) } The one named or appointed by the testator to execute his will.

Letters Testamentary. The authority and instructions given by a court to the person named as executor or executrix, to execute a will.

Letters of Administration. The authority and instructions given by a court to a person who has been appointed to administer the estate of one who has died without leaving a will (or a valid will), or if leaving a will, without naming an executor—or naming an executor who is unable to act.

Administrator
Administratrix (fem.) } The one appointed by the court to administer or settle an estate.

    Administrator, C.T.A. Administrator with the will annexed (L. cum testamento annexo).

Administrator, D.B.N. Administrator of the goods not [yet administered] (L. de bonis non); appointed when a vacancy occurs in the position of administrator or executor.

Administrator pendente lite. A special administrator appointed to act while a contest or litigation is pending. (pron. pĕn-dĕn′tē lī′tē)

Administrator ad colligendum. Administrator appointed temporarily to preserve an estate, especially to make collections. (pron. ăd kŏl-lĭ-jĕn′dŭm)

Probate. To "probate a will" is to prove it, that is, submit it to a court for approval; or to prove its validity to the court and secure authority to carry out its provisions.

COURT PAPERS

Courts

There are many kinds of courts, but the ones ordinarily referred to are:

Justice Court (a city or district court)
Cases involving small claims are tried, or preliminary hearings are had, before a justice of the peace.

Municipal Court (a city court)
Usually corresponds to a justice court.

Superior, Circuit, District, Chancery, or County Court (a county, circuit, or district court)
Cases involving large claims are tried before a judge or jury.

Supreme Court, or Court of Appeals (a state court)
The highest court in most states—the appellate court.

District Court of the United States
The trial court in each Federal district.

United States Circuit Court of Appeals
The intermediate Federal appellate court (one in each Federal judicial circuit).

Supreme Court of the United States (in Washington, D.C.)
The highest court of the land.

Besides these, there are courts pertaining to special matters, as the Police Courts, Military Courts, Juvenile Courts, Orphans' Courts, Probate Courts, Surrogate Courts, Bankruptcy Courts, Insolvency Courts, Common Pleas Courts, Small Claims Courts, United States Court of Customs and Patent Appeals, Court of Claims of the United States, United States Customs Court, The Tax Court of the United States (see p. 490), etc.

Juries

There are two kinds of juries:

Petit Jury. An ordinary jury: a body of, usually, twelve persons selected impartially to hear cases and render decisions (verdicts) under the direction of a judge. (pron. pĕt′ĭ)

Grand Jury. An investigating jury: a body of from twelve to twenty-three persons, called together for the purpose of investigating crimes committed within a certain territory, and bringing the offenders to justice by rendering indictments against them.

468

Papers in a Lawsuit

Papers in an ordinary lawsuit originate in the following order:

Complaint. Is made by the "plaintiff's" attorney, setting forth the cause of action, or in other words, the plaintiff's grievance. (Also called in some states a "declaration", in others a "petition"; in some actions "narr" [narratio], and in an equity action a "bill".)

Summons. Is attached to the complaint, summoning the "defendant" into court; and the two papers are served on the defendant by a United States marshal, the sheriff or a deputy, or a constable. (Also called a "subpoena" in an equity action.)

Demurrer. May be interposed by the defendant's attorney, asking that the court dismiss the action because of insufficient cause for complaint, or any other reason that would cause the court to dismiss the action. If the demurrer is overruled, the defendant must answer the complaint within a certain number of days. (A demurrer to any of the pleadings may be interposed later.) Instead of a demurrer, in some states a "motion for judgment" is interposed, which is in the nature of a general demurrer.

Motion to Quash. May be made to annul the proceedings because of illegality.

Motion to Dismiss. May be made to dismiss the proceedings. The defendant may admit all the facts, yet say that it is not a proper suit because no action lies against him.

Answer. Is made by the defendant through his attorney, setting forth the defendant's side of the story. (In some states called a "plea".)

Reply. Is the plaintiff's refutation of the defendant's answer or defense. (In some states called a "replication".)

The following pleadings may also be entered in some courts of law for the purpose of reducing the charges as much as possible before trial, in order that the points in issue may be clear and distinct:

Rejoinder. The defendant's answer to the plaintiff's reply.

Surrejoinder. The plaintiff's answer to the rejoinder.

Rebutter. The defendant's answer to the surrejoinder.

Surrebutter. The plaintiff's answer to the rebutter.

Bill of Particulars. If the claims of a plaintiff, or defendant, are not understood by the other party, the court may order the plaintiff, or defendant, to deliver a detailed pleading to the other party, which detailed pleading is called a "Bill of Particulars".

The action is then ready to be brought to trial before a judge or jury.

The clerk of the court (with whom the papers have been filed as they were issued) has a complete record of the case, and the court allots it a date for trial on the "trial docket", which is a register of cases to be tried.

Brief. May be prepared by either attorney, setting forth his client's case in brief, and giving the citations of law on which he makes his stand, in an endeavor to prove his case.

Subpoenas. Are served on witnesses, summoning them to court.

Subpoena Duces Tecum. Is a subpoena which orders a witness to bring certain papers or documents into court. (pron. sŭb-pē′nà dū′sēz tē′kŭm)

Deposition. May be made by a witness who is beyond reach by subpoena, or who is incapacitated. The witness's testimony is reduced to writing, signed, and sworn to before a legal authority. The one making the deposition is called the "deponent". (pron. dĕp'ō-zĭsh'on)

If the case is tried before a judge, an

Opinion, or Findings of Fact and Conclusions of Law. Are handed down by the judge, upon which a

Judgment, or Decree. Is later entered in favor of either the plaintiff or the defendant.

If the case is tried before a jury.

Instructions. Are given to the jury by the judge, citing the law applicable to the case, and directing a verdict for one party or the other if the jury finds that certain facts are true.

Verdict. The decision of the jury.

Motion in Arrest of Judgment. May be made by the defendant, for the stopping or arresting of judgment on the ground of errors, defects, or omissions apparent on the face of the record.

Judgment. Is the decree, or sentence, of the court based on the verdict.

Motion for New Trial. May be made by reason of newly discovered evidence, irregularity in the proceedings, etc.

Execution. A "writ of execution" may be given to execute the judgment, or enforce it.

Stay of Execution. May be granted to stay or withhold execution of the judgment.

Appeal. To a higher court (an appellate court) may be made from the judgment, or decree. The one taking the appeal is called the "appellant"; the other party is called the "appellee", or "respondent". The case may then be reviewed by the higher court and the judgment reversed or affirmed; or the case may be sent back for a retrial. (Certain cases cannot be appealed. Decision is final in some actions in the lower courts.)

Certiorari. A "writ of certiorari" may be issued to have the proceedings of a lower court reviewed by a higher court, on the ground that the lower court may have been without its jurisdiction, or that the proceedings may have been irregularly or improperly taken. (pron. sûr'shĭ-ō-rā'rī)

Bill of Exceptions. Is a list of the exceptions that either party takes to the ruling or decision of the judge.

Transcript of Record. Is the transcription of the record of the papers and proceedings of the trial, including testimony and other evidence offered.

– – – –

Court Testimony Style. The following is the general form for writing testimony. Note that "Q." and "A.", without dashes, are used for "Question" and "Answer", and that a question mark is used after every question. Quotation marks are not used; they are understood.

    Q. What is your address?
      A. Westport, Connecticut.
    Q. How long have you lived there?
      A. Since I was born. [Laughter.]

Q. Have you ever seen this paper? [Hands paper.]
  A. Not that I remember.
Mr. Martin—That is all.
The Witness—Am I excused?
Mr. Martin—Yes.
Mr. Hanover—May we suspend a few minutes?
The Court—Granted, for five minutes.
                    [Recess of five minutes.]

Heading for Court Papers. The form for court papers differs in the different states, but the following is the form generally used for superior court headings:

IN THE SUPERIOR COURT OF THE STATE OF ....
  IN AND FOR THE COUNTY OF ....
                              No. ....

```
                                    )
 .....................................)
                 Plaintiff          )
                                    )     (Name of Paper, as
        vs.                         )        COMPLAINT)
                                    )
                                    )
 .....................................)
                 Defendant    )
```

The fictitious names "John Doe", "Jane Doe", "Richard Roe", and "Jane Roe" (followed by an identification of the persons) are used in court papers if the real names are unknown.

The following phrases are often used after the names of plaintiffs and defendants, to signify the involvement of other persons.

  et al   and others (pron. ĕt awl; from Latin et alii—and others)
  et ux   and wife (pron. ĕt ŭks; from Latin et uxor—and wife)
  et vir and husband (pron. ĕt vĭr; Latin—and husband)

Miscellaneous Court Actions

Attachment. A "writ of attachment" is a court order authorizing a seizure or a taking into custody of property or moneys to satisfy a claim, usually pending a trial to determine the validity of the claim. A bank account may be "attached".

Garnishment. A proceeding wherein a party who owes money to, or holds personal property of, a defendant is ordered to withhold such money or personal property so that it may be applied to the payment of the defendant's debts. Wages may be "garnisheed".

Injunction. A court order to a party to enjoin him from doing some particular act that will be detrimental to another. Occasionally it is an order to do some act that will prevent injury to another, or repay for some injury already done.

Restraining Order. A court order temporarily restraining a party from committing a certain act until the court can decide whether or not an injunction should be issued.

Replevin. A "writ of replevin" is a court order authorizing the repossession of personal property that has been unlawfully taken or is being unlawfully held. To "replevy" property is to recover possession of it. (pron. rē-plĕv′in)

Mandamus. A "writ of mandamus" is a court order to compel a lower court, municipality, corporation, or person, to perform some public duty. (pron. măn-dā′mŭs, not *man-dăm′us*)

Quiet Title. A suit to "quiet title", or "quiet title proceedings", may be brought to perfect the title to property. If the suit is not answered and defended by anyone who may be interested, after due notice has been given, the title to the property is adjudged to be cleared.

Foreclosure Suit. A suit brought to foreclose a mortgage, that is, to close out a mortgagor's interest if he has defaulted in his payments on the mortgage.

Indictment. A formal charging with a crime by a grand jury. (pron. ĭn-dīt′-ment)

Arraignment. The formal calling of an accused person into court, reading the indictment to him, and asking him whether he is guilty or not guilty. If he pleads "guilty" he is sentenced. If he pleads "not guilty" his case is tried. (pron. ă-rān′ment)

Habeas Corpus. Concerns the right to personal liberty. A "writ of habeas corpus" may be issued by a court, ordering anyone holding or detaining another to bring the detained or imprisoned person into court for a hearing regarding the lawfulness of the detention. (pron. hā′bē-as kôr′pŭs; L., thou [shalt] have the body [in court])

LEGAL TERMS

abstract of title—a record of the title to a piece of land. It contains a brief summary of all deeds, mortgages, and other papers that have been recorded pertaining to the property. It shows how the title has passed from owner to owner, and whether or not the property is free and clear of encumbrances.

accessory before the fact—a person who instigates, or contributes to, but who does not actually take part in, the commission of a crime.
accessory after the fact—a person who knowingly aids or shelters a criminal after the commission of a crime.

appurtenances and hereditaments—things, rights, etc., that pertain to the land, and title to which goes with the land.
"Hereditaments" are particularly things that may be inherited. (pron. hĕr′e-dĭt′a-ments)

barrister (Br.)—a lawyer, admitted to the bar, and who may plead cases in the open court.
solicitor (Br.)—a law-agent who prepares cases for trial, but cannot plead in the superior courts.

beneficiary—the one who is benefited, as by a gift, the income from a trust estate, the proceeds of an insurance policy, etc. (pron. bĕn′ē-fĭsh′ĭ-er-y, or -fĭsh′er-y)

blanket—covering all in general, rather than one thing in particular, as a "blanket mortgage", "blanket bond", "blanket insurance", etc.

blue sky law—a law to protect the buyers of securities against fraud; so named because it was said that some promoters would "capitalize the blue skies" if not restricted.

{ **capital punishment**—death.

{ **corporal punishment**—bodily punishment.

certified copy—of an instrument is a copy made from the records in a recorder's (or county clerk's) office, and certified to by the recorder (or county clerk) as being an exact copy of the paper on file or of record.

covenant—a promise in a contract or other legal paper.

earnest money—a down payment given to "bind the bargain".

{ **-ee**—denotes the recipient of an action, as consignee, mortgagee, lessee, payee, vendee.

{ **-or**—denotes the doer of an action, as consignor, mortgagor, lessor, vendor. (In some words -er is used, as payer, adviser, etc.)

embezzlement—the misappropriation of funds, or other personal property, by the one to whom they have been entrusted.

larceny—the unlawful taking of personal property without the consent of the owner (stealing or theft).

    grand larceny—theft of a serious nature.

    petit larceny } theft of a trivial nature, as shoplifting. (pron. pĕt′ĭ)
    petty larceny

escrow—Papers may be executed and placed "in escrow"—in the hands of a disinterested party, usually a bank—which means that certain conditions are to be fulfilled before such papers can be delivered.

Exhibits A, B, C, etc.—documents attached to court papers as evidence in proof of the statements made in the case.

fee simple—an absolute title to property, with no limitations or restrictions. (Under the old feudal law, a "fee" was a piece of land held by a vassal on condition of service and homage to a superior lord. The word "simple" here means "absolute", indicating that title to the property has no restrictions or limitations regarding the persons who may inherit it as heirs.)

{ **felony**—a serious crime that is punishable by death or a sentence in a penitentiary.

{ **misdemeanor**—a minor crime for which the maximum punishment is less than imprisonment in a penitentiary. (pron. mĭs′dē-mēn′or)

fiduciary—held in "faith" or trust; or the one holding something in trust—a trustee. (pron. fĭ-dū′shĭ-er′y, or -shả-ry)

{ **franchise**—a special right or privilege granted by a city or a government; for instance, the right to operate a railroad or a public convenience.

{ **enfranchise**—to grant a special privilege to, as the privilege to women to vote.

husbandlike manner—a thrifty or economical manner.

indenture—a written agreement under seal, of which each party thereto holds a copy; so named because originally the paper was indented and cut apart in order that each party might have a copy and that the two parts should match.

leading question—not a main question nor one that "leads a witness on" to tell more than he means to, but a question so worded as to suggest the reply; in other words, a helpful question.

letters patent—may cover the rights to an invention; or may convey the title to public lands.

libel
slander } "Libel" is written, and "slander" is spoken, defamatory statements.

473

licenciado (Sp.)—an attorney. (pron. lē-thĕn-thē-ä′dō)

liquidated damages—those damages the amount of which is clear and certain; in contracts often fixed damages agreed upon before they occur, and in case they occur.

litigation—legal action, or a suit at law.

{ **malfeasance**—unlawful action; official misconduct. (mal-, evil [doing]) (pron. măl-fē′zans)

nonfeasance—failure to perform a definite duty. (non-, not [doing])

misfeasance—the improper performance of a lawful action, that is, in a manner which infringes upon the rights of others. (mis-, wrongful [doing])

malice aforethought—premeditated malice.

metes and bounds—used in describing the measurements (metes) and boundaries of a piece of property. (Incorrectly written "*meets* and bounds".)

opinion of title—an attorney's opinion or findings regarding the legality of a title to property, after an examination of the abstract of title.

premises—the matters involved or set forth, as "in the premises". Also property—lands or buildings.

prior art (patent law)—prior patents, publications, or public use.

statute of limitations—an enacted law (statute) fixing a definite time after which rights cannot be enforced.

ss.—an abbreviation for the Latin word "scilicet" meaning "to wit"; on legal documents, such as affidavits, it verifies the place of action.

time is the essence hereof—or "time is material and of the essence hereof", meaning that time is important and an essential factor in the contract.

venue—means "the place". "A change of venue" is a change in the place of trial, usually for the purpose of securing a fairer trial.

waiver—a voluntary relinquishment of a right or privilege.

with covenant of general warranty—with the promise that everything in the contract is warranted or guaranteed to be exactly as it is said, or proposed, to be.

without prejudice—without effect upon or detriment to any rights that existed prior to a certain act.

trust—an arrangement whereby property is transferred to one party, known as the "trustee", to hold for the benefit of another party, known as the "beneficiary" or "cestui que trust" (meaning "he who trusts"). (pron. sĕs′twē kē)

BUSINESS ORGANIZATIONS

Company. May be either a partnership, a corporation, an association, or a joint stock company.

Firm. Strictly, a partnership; often used loosely to refer to any business organization.

Partnership. Two or more persons associated in business under a contract to share profits and losses equally, or to prorate them according to the amount of capital invested. Some rules that are generally applicable to partnerships are:
Each partner is liable for the entire debt of the firm.
The business agreements or acts of any one partner bind the entire firm.

474

No new partner may be admitted, nor may the nature of the business be changed, without the consent of all partners.

The death, incapacity, retirement, or withdrawal of one partner may terminate the partnership.

A partnership may exist under a verbal agreement, but this is not a satisfactory arrangement. It is difficult to prove any verbal agreement. Every partnership agreement should be in writing, signed and acknowledged by all partners.

Limited Partnership. A partnership in which one or more partners may invest and be liable for only a limited amount. Such partners are known as "limited partners" (or "special partners" in some states) in distinction from the "general partners" who transact the business, share profit and loss, and generally are each liable for the entire debt of the firm.

Limited partners as a rule cannot actively engage in the transaction of partnership business, but may have a knowledge of, and give advice regarding, the affairs of the firm.

Corporation. A number of persons combined or "incorporated" into one body under the laws of the state. ("Corporation" comes from the Latin word "corpus" meaning "body".) A corporation acts as a single person; and its powers are limited to those set forth in its Certificate of Incorporation or Charter.

It is a legal being, separate and distinct from the persons who create, govern, or own it. Its members are not individually liable for its debts. Its owners, or stockholders, cannot act individually in making commitments for the corporation. It must act as one body, governed by its officers or board of directors.

When a company is to be incorporated, **Articles of Incorporation** are drawn up, setting forth the terms and conditions or "articles" under which the corporation is to operate. Such articles are sent, usually in triplicate, to a designated public office, such as the office of the Secretary of State, State Corporation Commission, or State Tax Commission, of the state in which the company is to be incorporated. If the articles conform to the state's corporation laws, they are approved by state officials, and a certificate of approval is issued; the articles being recorded and becoming known then as a **Certificate of Incorporation** or **Charter** under which the corporation operates.

Preliminary information regarding incorporation and corporation laws may be obtained from the Secretary of State, State Corporation Commission, or State Tax Commission, at the capital in each state.

A competent attorney should be engaged to handle the incorporation proceedings. The first meeting of the new corporation should be held in the attorney's presence.

Corporation books may be purchased from any reliable stationer. The corporation minute book may be in loose-leaf form. It usually bears printed instructions regarding the manner of conducting a corporation meeting.

Certificates of Stock are issued to owners of shares of stock in a corporation (each certificate representing a certain number of shares). If the stock is to be listed on a stock exchange, the stock certificates must be printed in a certain form. These requirements may be ascertained from the stock exchange.

Bylaws are private rules or laws drawn up by a corporation for its self-government.

Delaware Corporation is incorporated in the State of Delaware (to take advantage of the cheap incorporation rates and taxes in Delaware); but may be

475

licensed to do business in other states as well as in Delaware when it has complied with the laws of such other states.

Close Corporation is a corporation whose stock is all privately owned by a few persons. As a rule, one stockholder cannot dispose of his stock without the consent of the other stockholders.

Limited, or the abbreviation "Ltd.", after a company name is a British term signifying "limited-liability company", meaning that the financial responsibility or liability of the stockholders of the company is limited. (Like a corporation in America.) "Ltd." is sometimes used after the names of American corporations to signify that the liability of the stockholders is limited, but as a general rule this is unnecessary since the liability of stockholders in a corporation is understood to be limited by the corporation laws. In most states the law requires that the name of a corporation shall be such that an observer will know it is an incorporated company with limited liability.

Joint Stock Company. In fact, a large partnership, with some of the characteristics of a corporation (although not incorporated). Its members are as a rule individually liable for its debts; but the death or retirement of one member does not terminate the company; nor can any one member contract for the company—its acts must be governed by elected officers or directors.

It issues stock to represent shares of ownership, which stock may be transferred without the consent of the members of the company.

Public Utility. A company performing a public service, and devoting its property thereto, such as railroad and transportation companies, gas and electric companies, telephone companies, etc.

Holding Company. A company formed to buy and hold the stocks and bonds of other companies. It derives its income from the dividends or interest on the securities that it holds. It sometimes holds enough of the stocks of companies engaged in a certain industry to control that industry.

Operating Company. A company actually engaged in operating a business.

Subsidiary Company. A company the controlling stock of which is held by another company.

Association. A large number of people united for a common purpose. It is usually governed by rules or bylaws; and it may or may not be incorporated. If not incorporated its members are generally liable for its debts as in a partnership.

Syndicate. A group formed to finance a project. It may buy and resell new issues of securities (stocks and bonds); or it may "underwrite" them, that is, guarantee to take entire issues at certain discounts. In some states syndicates come under the corporation laws.

In journalism, a syndicate is a concern that contracts for and distributes authors' and artists' work to a group of newspapers or other publications.

❖

PATENTS, TRADE-MARKS, PRINTS AND LABELS

The United States Patent Office issues free "General Information" pamphlets on patents and trade-marks; and, for a small charge, booklets on "Patent Laws" (20¢), and "Rules of Practice" (Patents, 40¢; Trade-Marks, 35¢). These may be secured by addressing

The Commissioner of Patents
Washington 25, D.C.

PATENTS

The following general information applies to patents:

"A patent may be obtained by any person who has invented or discovered any new and useful art, machine, manufacture, or composition of matter, or any new and useful improvement thereof, or who has invented or discovered and asexually reproduced any distinct and new variety of plant, other than a tuber-propagated plant, not known or used by others in this country before his invention or discovery thereof, and not patented or described in any printed publication in this or any foreign country before his invention or discovery thereof..."

—Patent Office, "Rules of Practice", p. 7.

Medicines cannot be patented unless they are more distinctive than mere prescriptions. They must be actually "invented". Ordinary medicines may be marketed under trade-marks.

A model of the invention is not necessary, unless specifically requested by the Patent Office when examining the application. **A drawing is sufficient,** if it shows the complete arrangement. (Drawings must be made in accordance with certain specifications described in the Patent Office pamphlet "General Information Concerning Patents".) Models, if made to be submitted to patent attorneys, need not be elaborate or expensive. They may be made in any size and of any material desired. The **inventor's name and address** should be on every model, sketch, drawing, or photograph submitted to his attorney.

A detailed description or "specification" of the invention, including the manner of constructing and using it, must accompany the application.

The actual inventor, or joint inventors, must make the application for patent. Patents may be sold or assigned when issued.

"Patent Applied For", or **"Patent Pending",** may be used on articles only after the patent application has been filed in the Patent Office. No definite protection is afforded by law until a patent is actually issued, but "Patent Applied For" or "Patent Pending" is a warning that a patent may be issued which would immediately prohibit any unauthorized use of the patented device.

Term of Patent. The life or term of a patent is 17 years. It can be extended only by an act of Congress. After a patent expires the invention is public property.

Fees. On each original application for a patent, there is a filing fee of $30, and $1 for each claim in excess of twenty.

When the patent is issued there is a final fee of $30, and $1 for each claim in excess of twenty.

Any Inventor May Apply for Patent. Any actual inventor, or the executor or administrator of the estate of a deceased inventor, may apply for a United States patent.

Evidence of Date of Invention. To establish the date of disclosure of an invention, an inventor may make an affidavit before a notary public, or before two witnesses, describing his invention and giving a sketch or drawing thereof.

Such a "record of invention" may serve later as legal evidence of a definite date of disclosure.

Record Search. Before an inventor files an application for a patent, he should have a search made of the Patent Office records to determine whether any similar patents exist which would preclude his obtaining a patent.

The Patent Office does not make such searches; but any reliable patent attorney will conduct such an examination, and furnish a report and printed copies of all similar patents, usually for a small fee, in accordance with the time spent in making the search.

Copies of Existing Patents. Printed copies of patents may be obtained from the Commissioner of Patents for 25¢ each (design patents, 10¢ each). The date of the patent, title of invention, name of inventor, and the patent number if available, should be given when ordering a patent. Coupon books may be bought from the Patent Office for the regular ordering of patents.

Patent Attorney. Regarding an attorney, the Patent Office has this to say:

"An applicant . . . may prosecute his own case, but he is advised, unless familiar with such matters, to employ a competent registered attorney or registered agent, as the value of a patent depends largely upon the skillful preparation of the specification and claims. The Office cannot aid in the selection of an attorney or agent."

The Patent Office publishes and sells a "Roster of Registered Patent Attorneys and Agents"—$1 a copy. The Register in the Patent Office is open to public inspection. Also the names of registered patent attorneys may be found in local classified telephone directories; or in any law library.

Patents in Foreign Countries. American patent protection extends to all United States territories and possessions: Alaska, Hawaii, the Canal Zone, Puerto Rico, U.S. Virgin Islands, American Samoa, and Guam.

Patents may be applied for in various countries, usually within one year after the application has been filed in the United States. Annual taxes are imposed in many foreign countries; and further, in order to maintain the patent it is often necessary that the invention be used or "worked".

Information regarding the procedure to follow to secure a copy of a foreign patent may be obtained from the patent office of the government of the foreign country in question, at the capital city—or from the American Consul there. Copies of such foreign patents as are sent to the United States Patent Office are open to public inspection in the Scientific Library of the Patent Office.

The Canadian Patent and Copyright Office is at Ottawa, Canada. Printed copies of new (1949) Canadian patents are now available—price 25¢ or $1. Typewritten transcripts of older patents, and blueprinted or photostatic copies of the drawings, may be secured at cost. The amount of the fee required on any particular document may be obtained on application.

DESIGN PATENTS

A design patent may be obtained by any person who has invented any new, original, and ornamental design for an article of manufacture.

The Patent Office fees for a design patent for the following terms are:

3½ years......$10   7 years.......$15   14 years......$30

TRADE-MARKS

Trade-marks may be registered in the Patent Office.

The proof of ownership of a trade-mark lies in the mark's actually having been used in commerce. It must have been used on, or in connection with, goods sold in interstate or foreign commerce, or commerce with the Indian tribes, before it can be filed for registration in the Patent Office.

A trade-mark may be a **coined name; sign; symbol; emblem; device; monogram (initials); autograph; picture; or words or names written in a distinctive manner.** A personal or company name cannot be registered as a trade-mark unless it is written or printed in a distinctive manner. A **distinguishing package, bottle, or configuration of goods** may be registered. (Medicines, compounds, etc., are often marketed under trade-marks.)

No flag or insigne of any state or nation may be used in a trade-mark.

Other marks now registrable under trade-mark laws are:

> **Service mark**—a distinctive mark, name, title, symbol, or slogan, etc., used in the sale or advertising of the **services** of one person or one organization.
> **Certification mark**—a mark used by one or more persons to **certify** origin, material, mode of manufacture, quality, accuracy, etc., of goods or services.
> **Collective mark**—a mark used by members of a **collective group** or organization, to indicate membership, etc., as in a union or cooperative association.

Term of registration of a trade-mark is 20 years, with renewal privileges for like periods if the trade-mark is in bona fide use, and if application for renewal is made within the last six months of each term of registration.

A trade-mark, together with the goodwill connected with it, may be **assigned.**

Fees. The cost of filing an application for the registration of a trade-mark is $25. The cost of registering a renewal is $25.

Copies Necessary for Registration. Five specimens of the mark as used in commerce, together with a drawing of the mark, must be submitted with the application for registration. After registration, notice should be displayed with the mark, as **Registered U.S. Patent Office,** or **Reg. U.S. Pat. Off.,** or just ®.

Copies of Existing Trade-Marks. Printed copies of registered trade-marks may be procured for 10¢ each from the Commissioner of Patents. The number, registration date, and owner's name should be given, if possible, in the order.

Securing an Attorney. The employment of an authorized attorney or agent in the registration of a trade-mark is recommended by the Patent Office:

> "The owner of a trade-mark may prosecute his own application for registration of such trade-mark, but he is advised, unless familiar with such matters, to employ a competent attorney. The Patent Office cannot aid in the selection of an attorney."

Foreign Trade-Marks. Trade-marks should be registered in foreign countries, if possible, **before goods are sent into such countries.**

Foreign registered trade-marks may be registered in the United States if the countries in question grant reciprocal trade-mark registration rights.

American trade-mark protection extends to all United States possessions.

COMMERCIAL PRINTS AND LABELS

Commercial prints and labels, which are not trade-marks, may be registered under the Copyright Law, in the Copyright Office, Washington 25, D.C.

"**Commercial prints**" are artistic or pictorial works, with or without text matter, used in the **sale or advertisement** of commercial goods, but not actually placed on the goods. They may be published in newspapers, magazines, or on billboards; or distributed as circulars, leaflets, or folders.

"**Labels**" are artistic or pictorial works, and/or text matter, placed on, or attached to, commercial goods or the containers thereof. (Under the Federal Food, Drug, and Cosmetic Act, certain regulations regarding the marking of food, drugs, and cosmetics must be complied with before labels can be used.)

Notice of Copyright. Commercial prints and labels must be published (prior to the filing of the application for registration) with notice of copyright clearly legible thereon, as "Copyright", or "Copr.", or ©, with the true legal name of the copyright owner; or just © may be used with the copyrighter's initials, mark, or monogram near it, provided his full legal name appears on some accessible portion of the copies. The year date of publication is not necessary on this class of work, but it may be included.

If published without the copyright notice, commercial prints and labels are ordinarily considered "dedicated to the public", and cannot thereafter be copyrighted.

Term of Copyright. The term of copyright registration is 28 years, and may be renewed for an additional 28 years, if a renewal application is filed during the last year of the original term. The total term of copyright protection is 56 years. After that period the commercial print or label becomes public property—is "in the public domain".

Commercial prints and labels may be assigned, sold, or mortgaged; and may be bequeathed.

Fees. The fee for copyright registration of a commercial print or label is $6. The fee for copyright renewal is $2.

Copies Necessary for Registration. Two complete copies of each commercial print or label must accompany the application (Form KK) for copyright registration. If a commercial print is an advertisement in a periodical, two copies of the periodical may be sent, or one copy of the periodical with one tear sheet or proof copy of the print.

If the print or label is bulky, unwieldy, or of metallic character, an identifying photograph or photostat of it (not over 12″ × 18″) should be sent with the two copies. This, for use in the "specimen books" of the Copyright Office.

Trade-Marks not Copyrightable. A trade-mark as such cannot be copyrighted. A copyrighted commercial print or label may contain a trade-mark, but this does not give the trade-mark greater weight or eliminate the requirement for its registration in the Patent Office.

※

480

COPYRIGHTS

Information and application blanks for the securing of copyright may be obtained by addressing

The Register of Copyrights
Library of Congress
Washington 25, D.C.

and giving a short description of the nature of the work to be copyrighted. (Post offices are not prepared to distribute copyright information.)

Printed matter may be copyrighted if the following notice has been printed **on the title page,** or the next page: "Copyright (or Copr.), 19.., by (legal name of copyright owner)". The year in a copyright notice must be the year that the work is published, that is, the year it is issued to the public. Printers will attend to the details of securing copyrights if requested to do so.

If works are published without the copyright notice, they are ordinarily considered "dedicated to the public", and cannot thereafter be copyrighted.

Unpublished typewritten or handwritten matter cannot be copyrighted unless it is in the form of a lecture, sermon, radio script, or other oral address, or is a dramatic or musical composition, of which copies are not produced for sale.

Manuscripts of novels, stories, poems, words of songs without music, etc., cannot, under present law, be copyrighted in advance of publication.

The term "books" as used in the Copyright Law includes compilations, directories, catalogues, pamphlets, leaflets, cards, separate poems, and single pages.

Titles, names, slogans, mottoes, and like expressions, standing alone, are not in themselves copyrightable. (If such are used repeatedly in commerce, however—as a magazine title is—they may be registered in the Patent Office as trade-marks. Also, such words are often protectible under the general laws relating to unfair competition.)

Plays and dramatic scripts for radio or television may be copyrighted in typewritten form, if copies are not intended for public distribution.

Mimeographed matter, and other matter printed by processes other than typesetting, may be copyrighted if intended for public distribution. It must bear the copyright notice as described under Printed Matter.

Photographs, maps, prints, drawings, models, and works of art (paintings, sculpture, etc.), may be copyrighted if the copyright notice is inscribed thereon, clearly legible, in either of two ways: (1) the word "Copyright", or "Copr.", or ©, with the legal name of the copyright owner; or (2) just © with the initials, mark, or monogram of the copyright owner near it, provided his legal name appears elsewhere on some accessible portion of the work. The year date of publication is not necessary on this class of work, but it may be included.

Motion picture plays (in typewritten form) may be copyrighted if they can be fairly classed as "dramatic compositions", that is, if they are written in dramatic form, complete with dialogue, stage directions, etc. But motion picture plays in narrative ("story") form cannot be copyrighted in manuscript.

Motion picture films, "published" (reproduced in copies for sale or distribution), may be copyrighted upon deposit of a description of the action and two complete copies of each reel. These reels are returnable after registration. **"Unpublished" motion picture films** may be copyrighted upon deposit of a title and description, with a certain number of "frames" from different scenes.

Musical and dramatico-musical compositions may be copyrighted in either published or unpublished form—the latter if copies are not to be produced for sale.

Term of Copyright Protection. Copyright, under the Copyright Law, endures for a term of 28 years. It may be renewed for another 28 years—making 56 years in all—after which the work becomes public property (is "in the public domain"). Renewal application can be made only during the final year of the original term.

Copyrights may be sold, assigned, or mortgaged; and may be bequeathed.

Fees. The fee for copyright registration is $4, for any published or unpublished work. The fee for copyright renewal is $2.

For commercial prints and labels, the registration fee is $6. (See p. 480.)

Copies for Registration. Two copies of a published work, and one copy, photograph, or other identifying reproduction of an unpublished work, must accompany the application for copyright registration. These copies are not returned.

Foreign Countries. Foreign works are eligible for copyright registration in the United States, and American works are eligible for copyright registration in foreign countries, if reciprocal rights are granted by the countries in question.

American copyright protection extends throughout United States possessions and Canada; and on copyrighted **unpublished** works, throughout Great Britain.

The 1946 Inter-American Copyright Convention (when ratified by all 21 signatory Republics, including the United States) will give, to any work copyrighted in any one of the Republics, automatic copyright protection in all 21 Republics of the Western Hemisphere (in conformity with their respective copyright laws).

British Copyrights. Under British copyright law, copyright exists from the moment of creation of a work; hence British books are copyrighted although they bear no copyright notice. Copyright protection is given, during the life of the author and for 50 years after his death, throughout the [British] Commonwealth of Nations and in all countries belonging to the **International Copyright Union,** which includes all of Europe, except Turkey, Albania, and the U.S.S.R. (The United States is not a member.)

The British term of copyright for photographs, records, perforated rolls, etc., is 50 years from the making of the original negative or plate.

United States Copyright Laws. Copyright laws have been in effect in the United States for more than one hundred years, the first statute being passed in 1790. The present basic Act went into effect July 1, 1909. Copies of the 1947 Copyright Law may be obtained from the Superintendent of Documents, Government Printing Office, Washington 25, D.C., for 15¢ each.

Protection of Uncopyrightable Material. An author or owner of unpublished material has a common-law right to prevent the copying, publication, or use of such unpublished work without his consent, and to obtain damages therefor.

A method often used to protect unpublished manuscripts is this: The author sends one copy of the manuscript (in an envelope sealed with seals) by registered mail to himself. He retains this registered envelope unopened, as proof that the manuscript contained in the envelope was in existence in typewritten form on the day and year shown by the registration mark on the letter.

Writers' clubs often provide for registration of manuscripts in their organizations, by either members or nonmembers. Or a state may, as California does, provide for the filing of manuscripts with the Secretary of State. Fee—$5.

GOVERNMENT INFORMATION

Government Publications. The Government publishes through the Government Printing Office—the largest printing establishment in the world—a great number of informative and authoritative books and pamphlets, which are sold at a nominal price (5¢, 10¢, 20¢, etc.).

Free price lists describing each available book or pamphlet may be obtained by addressing the

> Superintendent of Documents
> Government Printing Office
> Washington 25, D.C.

Ask for price lists by name and number. The following are the official price list numbers:

10 **Laws.** Federal statutes and compilations of laws on various subjects.

11 **Foods and Cooking.** Home economics; household recipes; canning; refrigeration.

15 **Geological Survey.** Covers geology and water supply.

18 **Engineering and Surveying.** Leveling; tides; magnetism; triangulation; and earthquakes.

19 **Army.** Veterans' affairs. (See "Lists" at end of tabulation.)

20 **Public Domain.** Public lands; conservation; National Resources Planning Board.

21 **Fish and Wildlife Service,** and other publications relating to fish and wildlife.

25 **Transportation.** Shipping problems; postal service; Coast Guard.

28 **Finance.** Banking; securities; loans.

31 **United States Office of Education,** and other publications relating to education.

33 **Labor.** Child labor; women workers; wages.

33A **Occupations.** Professions and job descriptions.

35 **National Parks.** Historic sites; national monuments; geography and explorations.

36 **Government Periodicals,** for which subscriptions are taken.

37 **Tariff.** Compilation of acts, decisions, and regulations, relating to tariff and taxation.

38 **Animal Industry.** Farm animals; poultry; and dairying.

41 **Insects.** Bees; and insects harmful to man, animals, and plants.

42 **Irrigation, Drainage, Water Power.** Federal Power Commission; water resources.

43 **Forestry.** National forests; ranges; lumber and timber; American woods.

44 **Plants.** Culture of fruits, vegetables, cereals, grasses, grain.

45 **Roads.** Construction, improvement, and maintenance.

46 **Agricultural Chemistry, and Soils and Fertilizers.** Soil surveys; erosion; conservation.

48 **Weather, Astronomy, and Meteorology.** Climate; floods; aerology.

50 **American History and Biography.** Constitution of United States; Library of Congress.

51 **Health.** Hygiene; drugs; sanitation.

51A **Diseases.** Contagious and infectious diseases; sickness; vital statistics.

53 **Maps.** Maps for sale by Superintendent of Documents.

54 **Political Science.** Government; crime; liquors; District of Columbia; Supreme Court; un-American activities.

55 **National Museum;** Smithsonian Institution; Indians.

58 **Mines.** Explosives; fuel; gas; gasoline; petroleum; minerals.

59 **Interstate Commerce.** Steam railways; motor carriers; carriers by water.

60 **Territories and Insular Possessions.** Alaska; Guam; Hawaii; Puerto Rico; Samoa; and Virgin Islands.

62 **Commerce and Manufactures.** Foreign trade; patents; trusts; public utilities.

63 **Navy.** Publications relating to Navy and Marine Corps.

64 **Standards of Weight and Measure.** Tests of glass, leather, metals, paper.

64A **Masonry.** Brick; cement; clay; tile.

65 **Foreign Relations of United States.** International conferences; treaties; United Nations.

67 **Immigration.** Aliens; citizenship; naturalization; races.

68 **Farm Management.** Farm credit; farm products; marketing; rural electrification.

70 **Census.** Statistics of population; manufactures; agriculture; religious bodies.

71 **Children's Bureau,** and other publications relating to children.

72 **Suburbanites.** Publications of interest to suburbanites and home builders.

75 **Federal Specifications.** Federal standard stock catalogue.

78 **Industrial Workers.** Health; hygiene; safety; compensation.

List of Field Manuals and Technical Manuals.
List of Posters and Charts.
List of Radio Publications.
List of Army Regulations.
List of National Advisory Committee for Aeronautics Publications.

If the publication desired does not appear in the above price lists, ask the Superintendent of Documents for information regarding it. Many pamphlets are distributed free by various Government departments.

How to Order Government Publications. Orders should be sent direct to the Superintendent of Documents, and not to the Government bureaus.

If sending an order and making inquiry about other publications at the same time, write the **inquiry as a separate letter.** Different departments handle the orders and the inquiries.

Order by number if the number of the document is known; the price should also be stated after the title, as

N 29.13:41/S2	Diesel Engines	15¢
A 29.3:42	Weather Forecasting	15
		30¢

Orders are filled promptly, and usually reach their destinations in the United States within ten days after receipt.

484

Remittance must accompany the order; or if prices are not known, the order may be requested C.O.D. Make all remittances payable to the Superintendent of Documents.

> **Stamps** are not accepted. **Currency** is sent at the sender's risk.
> A **money order** is a good form of remittance.
> **Coupons** may be purchased—20 for $1—and used for small orders.
> An advance **deposit** of $5 or more may be made by regular customers.
> **Checks** are accepted; and no delay is caused by their collection.

Postage is free to addresses in the United States and its possessions; also to Canada, Mexico, and all of Central and South America, except as hereafter noted. Postage is charged to all other foreign countries, including Argentina, Brazil, British, French, and Dutch Guiana, and British Honduras.

One-third of the total amount of the order should be added to the remittance to cover foreign postage. Any excess will be returned. Foreign remittances should be by international money order or draft on an American bank.

Addressing United States Government Departments and Divisions. When seeking information from the Government, write to the division or bureau that should logically handle the matter in question.

> "When addressing letters to one of the Executive Departments of the Government, it is to the advantage of the writer to give the name of the department, the bureau therein, and, if possible, the particular division in which the letter will be handled, as this facilitates delivery of the matter, and, therefore, procures a more prompt response."
>
> —Post Office Department.

For instance, instead of addressing just "The Bureau of Reclamation, Washington, D.C.", address:

Information Division

Bureau of Reclamation
Department of the Interior
Washington 25, D.C.

Many of the departments and bureaus have offices in the various cities of the country. Consult the telephone book under "United States Government" to ascertain whether the office in question has a local branch, before writing to Washington, D.C.

United Nations. The address of the United Nations (UN) is just "United Nations, New York". The chief administrative officer is **The Secretary General.** Organs, commissions, and affiliated agencies are:

The General Assembly
Secretariat
Security Council
Trusteeship Council
International Court of Justice
Economic and Social Council (ESC)

Food and Agriculture Organization (FAO)
International Labor Organization (ILO)
International Civil Aviation Org. (ICAO)
World Health Organization (WHO)
International Telecommunication Union (ITU)
Universal Postal Union (UPU)

United Nations Educational, Scientific, and Cultural Organization (UNESCO)
United Nations Relief and Rehabilitation Administration (UNRRA)

International Bank for Reconstruction and Development
International Monetary Fund

485

THE GOVERNMENT OF THE UNITED STATES
(Compiled from the Congressional Directory.)

THE CONSTITUTION

LEGISLATIVE (Law Making) **The Congress** Senate House Washington 25, D.C.	EXECUTIVE (Administering) **The President** The White House Washington 25, D.C.	JUDICIAL (Judging) **Supreme Court of the United States** Washington 13, D.C.

Under the Executive Branch of the Government and, therefore, the President, are the following Departments and Agencies:

Executive Office of the President

The White House Office
Bureau of the Budget

National Security Council
Central Intelligence Agency (CIA)

Emergency Agencies

Office of Defense Mobilization (ODM)
Defense Production Administration
National Production Authority (NPA)
Emergency Procurement Service (EPS)

Economic Stabilization Agency (ESA)
Office of Price Stabilization (OPS)
Wage Stabilization Board (WSB)
Federal Civil Defense Administration

Department of State, Washington 25, D.C.   (The Secretary of State)

*Inter-American Affairs
*European Affairs
*German Affairs
*Far Eastern Affairs
*Near Eastern, South Asian,
   and African Affairs
†Personnel (incl. Foreign Service)
†Financial and Development Policy
†Transport and Communications Policy

*United Nations Affairs
†International Trade Policy
†International Information
†Educational Exchange
†Intelligence Research
†Public Affairs
†Consular Affairs
Passport, Visa, and
   Security Divisions

* Full title: "Bureau of . . . ."   †Full title: "Office of . . . ."

The Treasury Department, Washington 25, D.C.   (The Secretary of the Treasury)

Bureau of the Mint
Bureau of Customs
Bureau of Narcotics
Bureau of Accounts
U.S. Secret Service
U.S. Coast Guard

Bureau of Internal Revenue
Bureau of Engraving and
   Printing
Bureau of the Public Debt
Administrative Services, Office
International Finance, Office

U.S. Savings Bonds
   Division
Comptroller of the
   Currency
Treasurer of United
   States, Office of

Department of Justice, Washington 25, D.C.   (The Attorney General)

Antitrust Division
Claims Division
Federal Bureau of Investigation (FBI)
Immigration and Naturalization Service

Criminal Division
Customs Division

Lands Division
Tax Division
Bureau of Prisons
Office of Alien Property

Department of Commerce, Washington 25, D.C.   (The Secretary of Commerce)

Patent Office
Office of Technical Services
National Bureau of Standards
Weather Bureau
Bureau of the Census

Bureau of Foreign and Domestic Commerce
Bureau of Public Roads
Civil Aeronautics Administration
Coast and Geodetic Survey
Maritime Administration

486

DEPARTMENTS AND OFFICES IN WASHINGTON, D.C.

DEPARTMENT OF DEFENSE, Washington 25, D.C. (The Secretary of Defense)
Composed of three military departments: Army, Navy, and Air Force.

Joint Chiefs of Staff
Munitions Board

Research and Development Board
Office of Public Information

Department of the Army, Washington 25, D.C. (The Secretary of the Army)

GENERAL STAFF (Chief of Staff)
Personnel and Administration Division
   Women's Army Corps (WAC)
Intelligence Division
Logistics Division
Organization and Training Division
Plans and Operations Division
ADMINISTRATIVE SERVICES
The Adjutant General's Department
Provost Marshal General, Office of
Chaplains, Corps of
Special Services, Office of

SPECIAL STAFF
Reserve and ROTC Affairs
National Guard Bureau
Historical Division
Inspector General, Office of
Judge Advocate General, Office of
CHIEF OF INFORMATION
Public Information
Troop Information and Education

ARMY COMPTROLLER
Finance Department

TECHNICAL SERVICES

Chemical Corps	Ordnance Department	Quartermaster Corps	Corps of
Signal Corps	Medical Department	Transportation Corps	Engineers

Chief, Army Field Forces   Army Areas

Department of the Navy, Washington 25, D.C. (The Secretary of the Navy)

The EXECUTIVE OFFICE OF THE SECRETARY conducts the business management of
the Navy Department. Principal offices are:

Bureau of Aeronautics
Bureau of Medicine and Surgery
Bureau of Naval Personnel
Bureau of Ordnance
Bureau of Ships
Bureau of Yards and Docks

Chief of Naval Operations, Office of the
Office of Naval Research
Judge Advocate General, Office of the
Military Sea Transportation Service
Bureau of Supplies and Accounts
U.S. Marine Corps, Headquarters

Department of the Air Force, Washington 25, D.C. (The Secretary of the Air Force)

The Chief of Staff, UNITED STATES AIR FORCE (USAF), is head of the Air Staff,
and is the senior Air Force officer on active duty. Principal commands are:

Continental Air Command	Air Matériel Command	Headquarters Command
Alaskan Air Command	Air Training Command	Military Air Transport
Caribbean Air Command	Strategic Air Command	Service

Post Office Department, Washington 25, D.C. (The Postmaster General)

Office of the Chief Clerk and
   Director of Personnel
Bureau of the Chief Inspector

Office of Purchasing Agent
Bureau of Accounts
Office of the Solicitor

The following offices are each entitled "Division of..." –

Postmasters	Stamps and	Letter and Miscellaneous Mail
Post Office Personnel	Philately	Registered, Insured, & C.O.D. Mail
City Delivery Service	Money Orders	Newspaper and Periodical Mail
Rural Delivery Service	Parcel Post	International Postal Service
Surface Postal Transport	Postal Savings	Post Office Clerical Service
Air Mail Service	Postal Finance	Federal Building Operations
Motor Vehicle Service	Traffic	Equipment and Supplies
Post Office Quarters	Topography	Engineering and Research

487

Department of the Interior, Washington 25, D.C.   (The Secretary of the Interior)

Office of Land Utilization
Bureau of Land Management
Bureau of Indian Affairs
Bureau of Reclamation
Bureau of Mines
National Park Service
Fish and Wildlife Service

Geological Survey
Division of Geography
   U.S. Board on Geographic Names
Oil and Gas Division
Division of Power
Division of Territories
   and Island Possessions

Department of Agriculture, Washington 25, D.C.   (The Secretary of Agriculture)

Agricultural Research Administration
  Bureau of Agricultural and Industrial
    Chemistry
  Bureau of Animal Industry
  Bureau of Dairy Industry
  Bureau of Entomology and Plant
    Quarantine
  Bureau of Human Nutrition and
    Home Economics
  Bureau of Plant Industry, Soils, and
    Agricultural Engineering
  Office of Experiment Stations
Forest Service

Farmers Home Administration
Commodity Credit Corporation
Commodity Exchange Authority
Extension Service
Federal Crop Insurance Corporation
Soil Conservation Service
Farm Credit Administration
Rural Electrification Administration
Bureau of Agricultural Economics
Office of Foreign Agricultural Relations
Production and Marketing Administration
  Commodity Branches
  Price Support and Foreign Supply, etc.

Department of Labor, Washington 25, D.C.   (The Secretary of Labor)

Bureau of Labor Standards
Bureau of Labor Statistics
Bureau of Apprenticeship
Women's Bureau
Office of the Solicitor
Office of International Labor Affairs
Bureau of Employees' Compensation

Wage and Hour and Public Contracts
  Divisions
  Child Labor Branch
Bureau of Veterans' Reemployment Rights
Bureau of Employment Security
  Unemployment Insurance Service
  U.S. Employment Service (USES)
  Veterans' Employment Service

Federal Security Agency, Washington 25, D.C.   (Administrator)

Public Health Service
  Office of the Surgeon General
  National Institutes of Health
  Bureau of Medical Services
  Bureau of State Services
Food and Drug Administration
Office of Education

Social Security Administration
  Bureau of Old-Age and Survivors Insurance
  Bureau of Public Assistance
  Children's Bureau
  Bureau of Federal Credit Unions
Office of Vocational Rehabilitation

Housing and Home Finance Agency, Washington 25, D.C.   (Administrator)

Federal Housing Administration (FHA)   Public Housing Administration (PHA)
Home Loan Bank Board
Federal Home Loan Bank System   Federal Savings and Loan Insurance
Home Owners' Loan Corp. (HOLC)   Corporation

General Services Administration (GSA), Washington 25, D.C.   (Administrator)

Public Buildings Service
Federal Supply Service
Community Facilities Service

Contract Settlement
National Archives and Records
  Service

INDEPENDENT OFFICES AND ESTABLISHMENTS

American National Red Cross, The, Washington 13, D.C. Organized to succor the wounded and sick in war, and to aid distressed people in times of great emergency.

Atomic Energy Commission, United States (AEC), Washington 25, D.C. Created for the civilian control of atomic energy. Supervises atomic research and development projects; guards the making of atomic weapons; and forbids transfer of fissionable materials and divulgence of atomic secrets.

Civil Aeronautics Board (CAB), Washington 25, D.C. Prescribes safety rules, regulations, and operational standards for civil aircraft. Investigates certain classes of accidents and takes steps to prevent their recurrence. Fosters the development of an adequate and economically stable air transportation system. Cooperates in the development of international civil aviation.

Civil Service Commission, Washington 25, D.C. Conducts examinations for Government positions; makes appointments; maintains service records; and supervises health requirements and retirement. Also regulates political activity in the service and conducts the loyalty program. (See p. 490.)

Export-Import Bank of Washington (EIB), Washington 25, D.C. Makes loans and guaranties that serve to promote the export-import trade of the United States.

Federal Communications Commission (FCC), Washington 25, D.C. Regulates interstate and foreign commerce in communication by wire and radio.

Federal Deposit Insurance Corporation (FDIC), Washington 25, D.C. Created to insure deposits (now up to $10,000) in banks entitled to such insurance benefits.

Federal Mediation and Conciliation Service, Washington 25, D.C. Acts to prevent, or settle, labor disputes that interrupt the free flow of commerce.

Federal Power Commission (FPC), Washington 25, D.C. Has jurisdiction over all power projects on the navigable waters, public lands, and reservations of the United States, and also over interstate movement of electric energy and natural gas.

Federal Reserve System (F.R., FRS, FRB [Board or Bank]), Washington 25, D.C. Organized under the Federal Reserve Act—"to provide for the establishment of Federal Reserve banks, to furnish an elastic currency, to afford means of rediscounting commercial paper, to establish a more effective supervision of banking..."

Federal Trade Commission (FTC), Washington 25, D.C. Investigates and prevents unfair methods of competition and deceptive practices in commerce. Conducts investigations of broad economic problems; and collects industrial financial reports.

Interstate Commerce Commission (ICC), Washington 25, D.C. Regulates carriers, brokers, and freight forwarders engaged in interstate commerce. Requires all rates to be just and reasonable, and safety measures to be taken. Fixes standard time zones. Acts to develop and preserve a national transportation system.

Library of Congress, Washington 25, D.C. "Established to serve the Congress, the Library of Congress has expanded its activities to include the entire Government and the public at large, so that it has become, in effect, the national library. The Copyright Office is a part of the Library."

Maritime Commission, United States, Washington 25, D.C. Created "to further the development and maintenance of an adequate and well-balanced American merchant marine, to promote the commerce of the United States, to aid in the national defense..." It investigates and regulates ocean services, routes, rates, practices, employment conditions, ship sales and charters, ship mortgage insurance, terminal facilities, and ocean mail contracts. It conducts a Merchant Marine training program. In a national emergency, the Commission may have new vessels constructed and old ones reconditioned, and may grant aid to citizens for the construction and operation of vessels. (Maritime Commission has been transferred to Commerce Department.)

National Advisory Committee for Aeronautics (NACA), Washington 25, D.C. Supervises and directs the scientific study of the problems of flight, with a view to their practical solution; and also conducts research and experiment in aeronautics.

National Labor Relations Board (NLRB), Washington 25, D.C. Created to investigate unfair labor practices, and to maintain employees' rights of self-organization and collective bargaining in the settling of labor controversies.

489

National Mediation Board, Washington 25, D.C. Organized under the Railway Labor Act—"an act to provide for the prompt disposition of disputes between carriers [railroad and air] and their employees, and for other purposes".

Organization of American States, The, Washington 6, D.C. The official international organization of the 21 Republics of the Western Hemisphere. **The Pan American Union** is the central and permanent organ, and the General Secretariat, of the Organization. ("Pan" means "All".)

Panama Canal, The, Washington 25, D.C. The Governor of the Panama Canal, under supervision of the Secretary of the Army, is charged with the defense, maintenance, and operation of the Canal, and with the administration of the Canal Zone.

Railroad Retirement Board (RRB), Washington 25, D.C. Provides for the payment of annuities and pensions to aged and disabled railroad employees; unemployment insurance to those unemployed; and death benefits to survivors.

Reconstruction Finance Corporation (RFC), Washington 25, D.C. Makes loans to, and purchases the securities of, United States business enterprises, financial institutions, public agencies, and government projects.

Securities and Exchange Commission (SEC), Washington 25, D.C. Supervises the registration of security issues, and suppresses fraud in the sale of securities; qualifies certain trust indentures; regulates trading in securities, both on the stock exchanges and in the over-the-counter markets; regulates gas and electric public utility holding companies; submits to the courts advisory reports on corporate reorganizations; and registers and regulates investment companies and advisers.

Selective Service System (SSS), Washington 25, D.C. Conducts the drafting of men for limited military training and service.

Smithsonian Institution, The, Washington 25, D.C. "Created by act of Congress in 1846, under the terms of the will of James Smithson, an Englishman, who in 1826 bequeathed his fortune to the United States to found, at Washington, under the name of the 'Smithsonian Institution', an establishment for the 'increase and diffusion of knowledge among men'."

Branches under the direction of the Smithsonian Institution are:

United States National Museum	Bureau of American Ethnology
National Collection of Fine Arts	National Zoological Park
National Gallery of Art	Astrophysical Observatory
National Air Museum	International Exchange Service

Tariff Commission, United States, Washington 25, D.C. Investigates customs laws; tariff relations; competition between domestic and imported articles; unfair practices in import trade; and discrimination against United States trade. Supplies facts for the working out of **trade agreements.**

Tax Court of the United States, The, Washington 4, D.C. Adjudicates controversies between taxpayers and the Commissioner of Internal Revenue; also, controversies relating to excess profits on war, Navy, or Army aircraft contracts; and reviews refund cases under excess profits and processing tax laws. (For names of other United States Courts, see p. 468.)

Tennessee Valley Authority (TVA), Washington 25, D.C. Organized to maintain the Muscle Shoals project, and to develop the water resources of the Tennessee Valley by constructing dams to provide navigation, control floods, and produce power—the power to be distributed to measure the cost of power production. Also to develop the natural resources and provide for the general welfare of the Valley; to effect erosion control; to promote forestation; to maintain a nitrate plant; to manufacture and experiment with fertilizers, etc.

Veterans' Administration (VA), Washington 25, D.C. Administers the laws providing relief and other benefits for former members of the U.S. Armed Forces.

CIVIL SERVICE

Civil Service examinations are announced through notices posted in Federal buildings (post offices, customhouses, etc.). Newspapers sometimes publish the notices, but not always. The closing date for acceptance of applications is stated in each examination announcement.

The announcements also give full information on such matters as salaries, age limits, experience and education necessary, the application form to be used, and the duties and location of the positions. No information concerning an examination other than that given in the public announcement can be given by the Civil Service Commission.

Examinations are held only as the needs of the service require, not regularly on definite dates throughout the year. Some examinations are held for positions in a particular agency; but most examinations are held for positions in the Federal service generally. Preference may be stated regarding the locality in which an applicant desires employment, but there is no assurance that a position will be available in that location.

Written Examinations. Sample questions for "open" (announced) written examinations (such as stenographic, clerical, etc.) may be obtained from the local Civil Service offices. For examinations held in the past, sample questions are sometimes, but not always, available.

The United States Civil Service Commission has published a booklet, "Specimen Questions from U.S. Civil Service Examinations", which is valuable to those planning to take written Civil Service examinations. This booklet may be obtained from the Superintendent of Documents, Government Printing Office, Washington 25, D.C., for 15¢.

Unwritten Examinations. A large number of Civil Service examinations (such as those for statisticians, etc.) are not written tests. These are called "unassembled examinations"; and competitors are rated on education or experience, or both.

Overseas Positions. Some Federal positions overseas are filled under Civil Service requirements, but many are not. Persons interested in overseas employment should write to the U.S. Civil Service Commission, Washington 25, D.C., for a free copy of the pamphlet, "Federal Jobs Outside the Continental United States".

AMERICAN FOREIGN SERVICE
(Requirements are subject to change.)

Information and application blanks for positions in the Foreign Service may be obtained by addressing the Recruitment Section, Division of Foreign Service Personnel, Department of State, Washington 25, D.C.

Qualifications for "clerks" (which includes secretaries, stenographers, typists, accounting clerks, and code clerks) are, in general: the candidate must be at least 21 and not over 35 years of age; must be in excellent health; unmarried and without dependents; a high school graduate or the equivalent; and, if sent from the United States, must have been an American citizen for at least 5 years. (Foreigners are employed locally at the posts abroad.) A knowledge of a foreign language is desirable, but not essential. Women are equally eligible with men for clerkships in the Foreign Service.

At the present time, written examinations for clerical positions are given in Washington, D.C., on a continuous basis—and at intervals in the field. Clerical aptitude tests are given, in addition to performance tests in shorthand and typing.

A Foreign Service Officer candidate—for appointment in the diplomatic or consular service—must be over 21 and under 31 years of age, and in excellent health; must have been an American citizen for at least 10 years; if married, must be married to an American citizen; and must pass rigid written and oral examinations. A knowledge of one foreign language is essential. Sample questions may be obtained from the Board of Examiners for the Foreign Service, Department of State, Washington 25, D.C.

"Applicants for appointment to the Foreign Service must be willing to accept assignment to any foreign post. Persons who limit their availability to specific locations cannot be considered unless qualified candidates prepared to accept assignment to any post are not available."—The State Department.

BUSINESS AND BANKING PAPERS

The fundamental purpose of business papers is to "keep track of things". They are the written record of what is bought and sold, transported, and paid for.

Every business paper should be dated; and most of them are numbered.

Papers usually originate in the following order:

A Requisition is made within a company, asking permission to purchase something.

An Inquiry is sent out for prices.

Quotations,
Bids, or } are sent in return.
Proposals

A Purchase Order,
Formal Order, or } is sent to the successful bidder.
Contract

A Confirmation, or } is returned from the bidder.
Contract

When the goods are ready for delivery, if they are to be shipped, a

Space Permit may be obtained from a steamship company (if it is an ocean shipment), reserving space for the shipment; or

Car-Order Forms may be used to order space for freight shipments. Some shippers order space or empty cars direct, through their traffic departments, and some order through trucking or drayage companies.

When the goods are delivered to the transportation company, a

Bill of Lading (B/L) is made up and signed by the transportation company. The bill of lading enumerates the materials being shipped and acts as a receipt and contract for the shipment of the goods loaded (laded) on the carrier. The transportation company (called "agent" or "carrier" in the bill of lading) may be a railroad, a steamship line, or a trucking line.

In order to save time, the bill of lading is often prepared by the shipper on his own forms, or on the transportation company's forms—procured in advance—and simply handed to the transportation company to sign.

Bills of lading are made up **in triplicate.** The first copy is called the **"Original Bill of Lading"**, and is given to the shipper to be sent to the receiver for presentation when the latter claims the goods.

The second copy is called the **"Shipping Order"**, and is retained by the transportation company for its records.

The third copy is called the **"Shipper's Memorandum"**, or **"Shipping Receipt"**, and is given to the shipper for his files.

492

The transportation company may make additional copies for different purposes. For instance, one copy may be given to the freight conductor as a "waybill"; another copy may accompany the shipment as a part of the "manifest" to be delivered to the agent at the receiving end of the line; another copy may be sent to the receiving agent to serve as a "freight bill"; and still another copy to serve as a "delivery receipt" or "delivery order" when the receiver takes delivery of the goods. (See description of these papers below.)

Bills of lading are of two kinds: "Straight Bills of Lading", and "Order Bills of Lading".

Straight Bill of Lading. Is used when title to the goods passes immediately to the consignee; that is, when the goods are to be delivered to a certain person or company, without any conditions.

A straight bill of lading is not negotiable; that is, it cannot be endorsed and transferred. The goods must and will be delivered to the consignee named in the straight bill of lading (sometimes even without the presentation of the original bill of lading—if the consignee is known to the transportation company). (A straight bill of lading may be transferred only by a written assignment or agreement.)

Order Bill of Lading. Is used when title to the goods is retained by the shipper until certain conditions are fulfilled. Under an order bill of lading, the goods are "Consigned to ORDER of" the shipper, which makes this form of bill of lading negotiable; that is, title to the goods may be transferred by the shipper's endorsing the original order bill of lading. (The original order bill of lading, properly endorsed by the shipper, **must be presented** to the transportation company before the goods will be delivered.)

Order bills of lading are usually used for the purpose of making collections; or they may be used when goods are shipped and sold while "rolling" or en route, because the names of the consignees are not known at the time of shipment; or they may be used when goods are consigned to brokers or agents.

If a collection is to be made before the goods are delivered, the shipper endorses the original order bill of lading, and through his bank sends it, together with an invoice, insurance papers, and a sight draft, to a bank in the purchaser's city. This bank will notify the purchaser when the papers have arrived; and the purchaser must then call at the bank and pay the sight draft before the order bill of lading will be delivered to him, and he must present this original order bill of lading to the transportation company before the goods will be released to him.

Different Ways of Collecting on Order Bills of Lading. Instead of being sent through a bank for collection, an original order bill of lading may be mailed C.O.D. to the purchaser, if the amount of the collection does not exceed $200; or an original order bill of lading may be sent by express C.O.D. for any amount.

C.O.D. truck shipments are made on straight bills of lading, the collections being made by the drivers as the goods are delivered.

493

Through Export Bill of Lading. Is used when a shipment is made from an interior point to a foreign destination, and a transshipment of goods is necessary at the port of exportation. A through bill of lading may be either a straight or an order bill of lading.

Shipping Receipt. Is signed by the transportation company when the goods are delivered to it. It is a detailed list of the goods being shipped, and is usually made up by the shipper on his own short form of bill of lading. This short form is replaced by the transportation company's regular form when the goods are all ready for shipment. On some "short hauls"—and in some coastwise shipping—this short form of bill of lading will suffice and is not replaced by the longer form.

Dock Receipt. Is signed by the steamship company when goods are delivered to the docks. This may be on the shipper's short bill-of-lading form, which is later exchanged for the steamship company's regular ocean bill of lading.

Waybill. Is made up by the transportation company for its own use. Waybills are the freight conductor's records (giving shipping instructions, description, and destination) of all goods that are being shipped on his train.

The driver of a truck may carry a waybill covering the goods on his truck.

Manifest. Is made up by the transportation company for its own use. It is the list and description of all the freight for a certain destination. The transportation company's representative at the receiving end of the line receives the manifest and checks all incoming goods against it.

Freight Bill. Is prepared by the transportation company and presented to either the shipper or the receiver—whichever is to pay the freight. Usually the receiver pays the freight; but on certain shipments the freight must be prepaid.

Tracer. Is sometimes sent by the transportation company to check up on goods in transit. A tracer may be put on a shipment when it starts, by the shipper's simply asking the transportation company to "Trace this shipment and notify". There is usually no extra charge for tracing a shipment through.

Arrival Notice. Is sent by the transportation company to the consignee when the shipment arrives at destination.

Delivery Order (D.O.). Is primarily an order for the delivery of certain goods to a certain person. There are several forms of delivery order.

A shipping "delivery order" or **"delivery receipt"** is made up by the transportation company, to be signed by the receiver when he takes delivery of the goods. He may order the goods delivered to himself or to a third party. The delivery order is made up from the incoming manifest, and the items on the order must check with the invoice or the original bill of lading presented by the receiver. Any shortages or damage must be noted on the delivery order.

494

Freight Claim. If goods are damaged or lost in transit, or if there is an overcharge in freight, a freight claim is prepared by the transportation company and signed by the shipper or receiver. Such a claim may be called a "Loss and Damage Claim" or an "Overcharge Claim".

If a shipment arrives in bad condition, the receiver—before touching the shipment—should notify the transportation company, so that a transportation inspector can examine the goods; and thus it will be established that a pre-notice was given to the transportation company that the shipment was faulty.

Demurrage. Is a charge assessed by the transportation company for detention of a carload shipment beyond the "free time" allowance for loading or unloading goods.

On water shipments, demurrage is charged if a vessel is delayed beyond the "lay days" allowed in the charter party for loading or unloading.

Storage. Is charged on goods shipped in less than carload lots, after a certain "free time" for unloading or removing has elapsed.

Warehouse Receipt (W.R.). Is issued if the goods are stored in a warehouse.

The receipt may be made out for redelivery of the goods to one certain person (nonnegotiable form), or for redelivery of the goods to "bearer" or "to order of" some certain person (negotiable form). Most warehouse receipts are made out in the negotiable form. Banks often lend money on goods in a warehouse—or "on a warehouse receipt".

Pickup Order. Is a local form of delivery order. It is an order given by an owner to a holder of goods to deliver all or certain parts of the goods to the bearer of the order.

Withdrawal Order. Is another form of delivery order. It is an order given by an owner of goods to a warehouse to deliver certain goods to the holder of the order, or to the person named in the order.

Consignment. When goods are "shipped on consignment" they are consigned to a broker or agent to sell for the shipper's account.

Order Notify. When goods are shipped "Order Notify" they are shipped on an order bill of lading, and the receiver is notified by the transportation company when the goods arrive.

Store-Door Service. Is a collection of goods from the shipper's door and delivery to the receiver's door, by the transportation company.

Insurance. Should be carried on every shipment. The shipper may insure his shipments separately (the transportation company often arranging or placing the insurance for him); or he may insure his shipments collectively under an "open policy" with an insurance company. If insuring under an open policy, he notifies the insurance company of his shipments periodically—usually each day.

Caution: If responsible for the insuring of a shipment, make sure that but one form of insurance is being carried. Through a misunderstanding, separate insurance may be written and charged for when the shipment is already insured under an open policy.

Export Shipping Papers. Various papers are required for export shipments—different papers for different countries—but for all foreign destinations a U.S. Shipper's Export Declaration and some form of invoice must be prepared. Names of the papers are:

Shipper's Export Declaration	Certificate of Origin
Consular Invoice	Certificate of Registration
Commercial Invoice	(for medicines, etc.)
Ocean Bill of Lading	Inspection Certificate
Marine Insurance Policy	Weight Certificate, etc.

Information regarding the preparation of a foreign shipment and the papers required may be obtained from any railroad, steamship line, or large transportation company. In a seaport city, information and papers may be obtained from the customhouse, or from the consulate of the country to which shipment is to be made; or a customhouse broker and forwarding agent may be engaged to arrange the entire shipment.

Invoice. Is an itemized list of goods and prices or valuations. It is usually in the form of a statement or "bill", prepared by the seller and mailed to the buyer, listing the goods sold and showing the amount due and the terms of payment. The invoice accompanies the original bill of lading.

Paying Invoices. If an invoice reads "net 60 days" it is commonly considered to be payable 2 months from its date. For instance, if it were dated July 5 it would be payable September 5. Payment, theoretically, should be mailed so as to be in the hands of the payee on the 60th day, but in actual practice payment is usually "in the mails" on the 60th day.

Account Sales (A.S.). Is an accounting by a broker or commission merchant to the owner of goods shipped on consignment, showing how the goods were sold and for what prices, and what deductions were made for freight, commission, advertising, etc.

Trade Discounts. Are discounts from wholesale price lists. Different discounts are allowed different customers, according to the amount of goods bought, the standing of the customer, etc.

Discounts. Ordinary discounts are allowances for cash or prompt payment. In taking discounts, strictly speaking, payment should be made so that the money, or evidence of money, will be in the hands of the payee within the period allowed for discount. But as ordinarily interpreted, discount can be taken if payment is "in the mails" within the time, or on the last day, allowed for discount.

Some companies are strict about enforcing discount rules. Others will allow the discount to be taken several days after the period has elapsed. But it is not well to assume that any concern is of the latter type. Many are of the first type, and allow no exceptions to their rules.

496

Discount days are figured from the **date of the invoice,** not from the date of receipt of the invoice or merchandise, unless a special clause follows the discount rate, as "1% 10 days arrival of merchandise", which means that the discount period may be figured as 10 days from the date of arrival of the merchandise.

Calendar days are figured rather than "business" days. The date of the invoice is not counted. If, for instance, an invoice is dated February 15, and the discount is "1% 10 days", the discount must be taken by February 25. If the final discount day falls on Sunday or a holiday, the next succeeding business day is considered the last day.

Debit and Credit Memoranda. Errors and allowances are adjusted by the issuance of debit and credit memoranda between companies who do a large amount of business.

Credit Reports. (See p. 589.)

Financial Ratings. (See p. 590.)

Drafts. A draft is an order drawn by one party (usually a seller) directing a second party (usually a purchaser) to pay a certain sum to a third party (usually a bank), to be credited to the first party.

The purpose of drafts:

To obtain assurance of payment of accounts. When delivering goods, a seller requires assurance that his account will be paid; or he sometimes requires a cash payment. A draft serves this purpose by bringing back the immediate payment (if it is a sight draft), or a promise to pay (if a time draft), thus giving a tangible form of payment. The seller may borrow money on accepted drafts to finance further business transactions; but it is difficult to borrow money on open accounts because of the uncertainty of collection involved.

To obtain payment of old accounts. Drafts are sometimes used to obtain payment of old accounts or debts. Such drafts are called "dunning drafts". A purchaser or debtor may be "slow" in sending a check or in signing a note, but if a draft is drawn on him and presented by a bank for collection, he must take some action regarding it. If he refuses or "dishonors" the draft, the bank makes a report, which is written into his credit rating.

To make collection on papers. Drafts may be drawn to accompany any papers on which there are to be collections, such as bills of lading, warehouse receipts, stocks, bonds, deeds, etc. The one upon whom the draft is drawn must, usually, pay the draft before the bank will deliver the papers to him.

Form of Drafts. Drafts are made up in rather an unnatural order; that is, the name of the party upon whom a draft is drawn is placed at the bottom of the draft, instead of at the top. If drafts were arranged in the simplest possible form, they would read, for example, as follows:

497

No. **892** Springfield, Illinois May 11, 1937

To James Thomas & Sons Co.
  San Antonio, Texas
On June 15, 1937 Pay to the order of ourselves
Five hundred fifty and no/100 – – – – – – – – – – – – – – – – DOLLARS ($550.00)

ACCEPTED: May 14, 1937
Payable at Pioneer Bank
  San Antonio, Texas HAYWARD & RANDOLPH, INC.
JAMES THOMAS & SONS CO. By G. C. Hayward
By James Thomas, Jr.
  President

Instead, drafts may read something like this:

HAYWARD & RANDOLPH, INC. No. **892**
$550.00 Springfield, Illinois May 11, 1937
  At thirty days' sight Pay to the Order of
Pioneer Bank of San Antonio, Texas for collection
Five hundred fifty and no/100 – DOLLARS
Value received and charge to the account of
To James Thomas & Sons Co. } HAYWARD & RANDOLPH, INC.
  San Antonio, Texas } By G. C. Hayward

The acceptance on the above draft would be written across the face.
Drafts are drawn payable to banks in order that they may be handed to the banks for collection. Banks in one city send drafts to their representatives in other cities for presentment and collection.

The words "Value received and charge to the account of" make the draft, when it is finally paid, a receipt from the drawer to the payer.

Any certain time may be specified for the payment of a draft. It may be payable "At sight", or "At thirty days' sight", or "Three months after date", or on any definite date, etc.

Drafts may bear interest if it is specified. Such interest is computed as it would be on a promissory note.

Sight Draft. Orders payment "At sight" or "On demand". If honored, a check is given in payment; or the one upon whom it is drawn may write directions to his bank across the face of the draft, asking the bank to pay the draft and charge the amount to his account.

Demand Draft. Is a sight draft, ordering payment "On demand".

Time Draft. Orders payment at a certain time after receipt or acceptance, or after date. The one upon whom the draft is drawn writes ACCEPTED, the date, the place payable, and his signature on the face of the draft. It is then known as an

Acceptance and is practically the same as a promissory note. Twenty-four hours are usually given the party upon whom the draft is drawn to examine the goods purchased and the papers attached to the draft, and to decide whether or not to accept the draft. If acceptance is refused, the draft is **"dishonored"**.

D/A ("documents upon acceptance"). Means that documents

498

are to be delivered upon acceptance of the draft.

D/P ("documents upon payment"). Means that documents are to be delivered only upon payment of the draft.

Bank Draft. Is a draft drawn by one bank on another bank, and payable to a third party. Banks have deposits, or "carry balances", in other banks much the same as individuals do, and in reality a bank draft is a check drawn by a bank on its own account in another bank.

Bank drafts are regarded as cash; and many business men send remittances by bank draft rather than by check, so that the payee may have cash immediately and not have to wait the necessary number of days for a check to be returned to its bank before it is paid. Even a cashier's check must go through a process of "clearing" before it is paid. Charges for a bank draft are from 15¢ to $1.

Arrival Draft. Is so called because it represents the payment to be made upon the arrival of goods bought.

Clean Draft. Is a draft with no papers attached.

Trade Acceptance. Is an accepted time draft, but it differs from an ordinary time draft in that it states definitely that the debt represents merchandise purchased.

An ordinary draft shows no acknowledgment of merchandise received —in fact, it might represent an old debt—and therefore is not so valuable as a trade acceptance which acknowledges that the acceptor has received goods, with the proceeds from which he should be able to pay the trade acceptance.

A trade acceptance may be sent direct to a customer with the invoice and original bill of lading; or it may be sent to a bank, to be presented to the customer for his acceptance.

An accepted trade acceptance is regarded as a note receivable by the holder thereof. Usually it can be discounted at a bank if the holder is in need of immediate funds.

Banker's Acceptance. Is often used instead of a trade acceptance. A purchaser establishes credit at his bank in an amount sufficient to pay for certain goods ordered. His bank then notifies a bank in the seller's city (by a letter of credit) that the credit has been established.

When the goods are shipped, the seller draws a draft on the purchaser's bank (or payable through the bank), and sends the draft to the bank together with the original bill of lading, invoice, insurance papers, etc.

When the goods are received, the bank makes an examination of them, and if satisfactory, accepts the draft or guarantees its payment; thus lending the bank's credit instead of money to the purchaser. The purchaser must pay the bank when the draft is due; and the bank charges the purchaser a commission instead of interest for this accommodation of credit.

Bill of Exchange. Is a draft. But the term is now usually applied to foreign drafts, that is, drafts drawn in one country and payable in another country. International bills of exchange are sometimes drawn in duplicate.

"With Exchange" written on a draft means that the difference in exchange and all collection charges are to be paid by the one who pays the draft.

Letter of Credit. Is a letter from a bank to another bank, or from a business house to its bank or business associates, stating that a certain amount of credit has been established by a certain person or company.

Commercial Letter of Credit. Is largely used by exporting and importing concerns. A purchaser arranges at his bank for a sufficient amount of credit to meet his obligations on a certain purchase of goods. His bank then notifies a bank in the seller's city that the credit has been established. Drafts may then be drawn against, and in conformity with, this letter of credit, and the bank will honor the drafts. The seller is thus assured of receiving his money before he ships the goods. (See Banker's Acceptance, above.)

Traveler's Letter of Credit, or Circular Letter of Credit. Is issued by a bank to a traveler—the traveler either paying cash therefor or establishing credit at the bank in the amount named in the letter of credit.

This letter of credit may be presented to any one of a number of listed foreign banks, and the traveler may draw checks or drafts against the credit. The amount of each check or draft is entered on the letter of credit until the full amount of the credit is used.

Letter of Advice (often called "Advice"). Is a letter of acknowledgment or understanding of a certain transaction; or advice regarding the issuance of a certain paper, etc. Letters of advice are often written regarding the issuance of drafts, bills of exchange, letters of credit, etc.

Trust Receipt. Is a receipt for shipping documents delivered upon trust. If a bank holds title to imported goods because of having accepted a draft drawn by the seller of the goods, the bank may permit the importer, or buyer, to take the bill of lading and other documents necessary to obtain possession of the goods, upon his signing a trust receipt. In the trust receipt the importer acknowledges that the title to the goods is vested in the bank, and that the proceeds from the sale of the goods shall be first applied to the payment of the bank's accepted draft.

Days of Grace. On "notes and bills", no grace is now allowed in any state in the United States, and in most foreign countries. But England, Ireland, and Canada still grant three days of grace. (On sight drafts, Massachusetts, Mississippi, New Hampshire, and Rhode Island grant grace.)

Date of Payment. A note or draft must be paid at the place of payment specified and **on the due date.** Payment cannot be "in the mails" but must be in the hands of the payee on the due date.

To determine the date of payment of a draft or note, count the exact number of days, **excluding the first day.** A draft payable "Sixty days after sight" would be payable 60 calendar days after acceptance (not

500

including the day of acceptance). If accepted September 10, it would be payable November 9.

If a draft is payable "Two months after date", it is payable on the same day of the month, two months later. If dated March 15, it would be payable May 15.

Note that there is sometimes a wide difference between the date of the draft and the date of acceptance, and whichever date is named in the draft should be figured.

Paper Maturing on Sunday or a Holiday. Is payable on the next succeeding business day.

Negotiable Instrument. Is a paper that may be endorsed and transferred from one person to another.

A prime requisite for the negotiability of an instrument is that it be made out **"to bearer"** or **"to the order of"** some person. If these words do not appear, a paper is nonnegotiable; that is, it cannot be endorsed—the proceeds must be paid to the person named in the instrument, and to no one else, unless a separate assignment of the paper is made. It is for this reason that so many papers bear the line "Pay to the order of". If they should read simply "Pay to", they would be nonnegotiable.

Promissory Note. Is a written, unconditional promise to pay a certain sum at a certain time and place.

Notes bear interest only after maturity unless a definite rate is specified in the note. Some notes do not bear interest even after maturity, if such is the agreement between the maker and the holder of the note.

Secured Note. Is one whose payment is guaranteed by the maker, by his either "putting up" collateral or giving a chattel mortgage as security.

Joint and Several Note. Is a note signed by several persons who agree to pay it jointly or severally—that is, separately—each to be liable for the full amount if the others fail.

Collateral. Is salable security pledged to guarantee the payment of a note, or an obligation.

Hypothecation. Is the actual pledging ("hypothecating") of the collateral. A "Hypothecation Agreement" is signed when the collateral is "put up", that is, when it is delivered and assigned to the creditor with full power to sell it if the debt that it secures is not paid.

Future revenues or taxes may be "hypothecated" or pledged by a government as the security for a loan.

"Hypothecation" has still another and older meaning, namely, the pledging of an undelivered property for the payment of a debt. The pledged property (as a ship) remains in the possession of the debtor, so that with the earnings therefrom he may pay the debt. If he defaults, the creditor has the right to have the property sold to satisfy the debt.

"Without Recourse" or "Not Holden". These words, appearing in an endorsement, relieve the endorser of any future liability on the instrument so endorsed.

Protest. If payment is not made on a note, draft, or other paper when it becomes due, or if a draft is not accepted when presented, a notary public formally presents the paper again for payment or acceptance. If payment or acceptance is still refused, the notary makes up a statement or "Protest" giving the facts in the case. A copy of this protest is served on all parties whose names appear on the instrument, in order that they may be apprised of their liability.

"**Protest Waived**" written above an endorser's signature, means that the protest notice need not be served if the instrument is not paid, and that the endorser will assume his responsibility if simply notified that the maker has defaulted.

"**No Protest**" written on or attached to a note or draft, signifies that no formal protest is to be made if the instrument is not paid— that is, that no protest fee will be paid thereon.

Commercial Paper. Promissory notes made by large companies in good financial standing, and issued to finance certain commodities, are called "commercial paper". These notes are sold by "note brokers" to banks that have funds to invest, in different parts of the country. The notes bear no interest; the interest is collected by the banks when they "discount" the notes in buying them.

Accommodation Paper. Is negotiable paper that has been endorsed by a disinterested party, simply as a means of lending his credit to the maker of the paper.

Trade Paper. Notes, acceptances, etc., bearing two or more names, given as payment for merchandise in the ordinary transaction of business, are called "trade paper".

Two-Name Paper. Paper bearing two names (representing separate interests) as makers, or one as maker and one as endorser, is called "two-name paper".

An acceptance (accepted draft) is considered two-name paper because both the acceptor and the drawer are liable for the payment if a bank buys or "discounts" the acceptance.

Single-Name Paper. Paper bearing a single name as maker. The maker may be a corporation, and its subsidiary corporation may endorse the note to lend credit, but the note is still regarded as "single-name paper" because of the close connection between the two companies— if one fails the other might fail.

Cattle Paper. Notes secured by chattel mortgages on cattle are called "cattle paper". They are dealt in extensively in cattle-raising regions.

Bank Discount. Is interest deducted in advance.

Rediscount. Notes or trade acceptances that have been sold to and discounted by a bank, may be resold—usually to a Federal Reserve bank—and rediscounted by the buying bank.

Voucher. There are many forms of voucher, but a voucher is primarily a receipt for, or proof of, money paid. It vouches for the authenticity of a business transaction.

Voucher Check. Is a check that has an invoice attached, showing for what the payment is being made.

Warrant. There are also many forms of warrant, but a warrant in banking is primarily a written order to pay money.

States and counties often make disbursements (pay salaries, etc.) by issuing warrants drawn on their own treasuries. These warrants may bear interest, if registered, and may be cashed at certain banks at face value, after arrangements have been made for their acceptance. (See also Warrants, p. 512.)

Debenture. Is an evidence of indebtedness. The term is variously used as a synonym for "debt", generally in connection with bonds or stock. In British usage, "debenture" is the general term for "bond".

CHECKS

Making out a check is a simple matter, yet many checks are incorrectly written.

Date. Never omit the date on a check. If a check is received without a date, date it the day of receipt, not any earlier or later date.

Antedating is dating a check back to some past date (to a date which has gone before).

Postdating is dating a check forward to some future date (to a date which is to come after).

Money will not be paid on a postdated check, nor can it be deposited, until the day of its date. If money is inadvertently paid on a postdated check, it may be recovered. In fact, a postdated check should not be presented to a bank until the day of its date; such a pre-presentment may reflect unfavorably not only upon the maker of the check but also upon the one presenting it for payment.

Checks dated on **Sundays or holidays** are accepted at banks.

Old or "Stale" Checks. All checks should be presented for payment promptly or within a reasonable time after their dates. A bank will question any check that may be considered "old"; and if a check bears a date more than six months old, the bank may refuse to honor it on the ground that it is a "stale" check.

Payee. Attempt always to write the name of the payee correctly and as he writes his name; for he is forced to endorse the check exactly as his name appears on the face.

Draw a line **before and after** the name of the payee.

If the payee is a "Receiver", "Treasurer", or "Secretary" of an organization, use that title after his name on the check. He then accepts the money in his official capacity when endorsing the check.

503

Pay to the order of – – Robert May, Treasurer – – $54.06
Fifty-four and 06/100 – – – – – – – – – – – – Dollars

Personal titles, like "Dr.", "Capt.", "Judge", "Miss", should, theoretically, not be used before the names of payees on checks, because such titles are not used in endorsements. However, American banks disregard these titles now. But in some foreign countries, personal titles cannot be used; hence are never on travelers' checks or letters of credit.

Lead Pencil. Should not be used in the writing of a check. While lead pencil checks are not entirely prohibited, some banks refuse to accept them because they are easily altered and because pencil writing so often blurs in handling.

Erasures. Checks should be typed slowly and carefully so that no erasures whatsoever will be necessary. A bank has the right to return a check if "altered" in any manner. Checks are usually printed on a sensitized paper that makes erasures noticeable and sometimes glaring.

Amounts. If there is a discrepancy between the amount written in words and the amount in figures, the words are considered correct; but the bank may, if convenient, return the check for verification.

After even amounts of dollars, it is customary to write "and no/100". **A line should always be drawn to the word "Dollars".**

Checks may be written for cents; but banks do not encourage this practice, because of the cost of handling. If, however, it is occasionally necessary to write a check for cents, put parentheses around the figures, and write "Only" before the words. Do not write "$0.65".

Pay to the order of – – James Scott – – $ – (65¢)
Only sixty-five cents – – – – – – – – – – Dollars

Changing the Name of the Bank. One bank's check should not be changed to direct its payment at another bank. This is sometimes done, but it is a practice that is not approved by banks, because the changing of a name makes an "altered check", and in some states a check may be returned if it bears the slightest alteration.

Blank checks should be kept in every office; but if a blank check is not at hand, a check may be made up on a piece of heavy white paper cut to the size of a check.

When filling in the name of a bank on a blank check, **fill in the address** also, and the bank number if it is known. One bank may have several branches in the same city, and the address is important.

Notations on a Check. Any information that the signer desires by way of a receipt may be written in the lower left corner of a check, or on the back above the place for endorsement.

Signatures. A signature should be written in exactly the same manner on every check, and with the same style of pen.

A signer should not use his full name on one check, his abbreviated first name on another, and his initials on a third, as "James F. Scott", "Jas. F. Scott", and "J. F. Scott".

He should sign always as he signed his name when he opened the account. He may add his address below his signature for identification.

Endorsements. Checks may be endorsed in several ways: (1) with just the **payee's name**—which makes the check payable to bearer; (2) with **"Pay to the order of..."** above the payee's name—the check then requires the designated person's endorsement; (3) with **"For deposit only"** above the payee's name; and (4) **"Without recourse"** below it.

Endorse a check across the reverse **left** end, never across the right end. And endorse it exactly as the name appears on the face, even though incorrect. If incorrect, write the correct signature immediately below. It is not necessary to write an explanation of the two signatures; they will be understood by the bank. Do not write the correct signature first and the incorrect one below in parentheses. This violates the banking rule that **the last endorser must be the person to whom the money is paid.** (For deposit endorsements, see p. 506.)

Identification. If the payee is unknown at the maker's bank, where a check is to be cashed, he should ask the maker of the check to guarantee his signature. The check should be endorsed by the payee, and the maker should write below, "Signature guaranteed", and sign his name.

If the maker of the check is not present, the payee should, if possible, obtain a similar signature guarantee from someone who is a depositor at the bank in question.

Stop Payment. Payment of a check may be stopped upon application of the maker by telegraph or telephone, if confirmed by letter.

Payment must be stopped before the check reaches the bookkeeper of the bank upon which it is drawn, or it will be paid.

The death of a depositor immediately stops payment on all outstanding checks (in most states).

Certified Check (usually accompanies a bid). It is an ordinary check that has been "certified" or guaranteed by the bank. Funds in the amount of the check are immediately set aside from the maker's account to meet the check when it is returned. Charges: none or 25¢.

Payment can be stopped on a certified check only by court order.

Cashier's Check (used for payments above $100). It is a bank's check drawn on its own funds by its cashier. The charge is 15¢ to 25¢.

Bank Money Order (used for payments below $100). The charge is 15¢. (Some banks issue cashier's checks instead.)

Bank Draft (transfers "cash"). Charges: 15¢ to $1. (See p. 499.)

Travelers' Checks or Cheques. Sold (for 75¢ per $100) by banks, Western Union, and large travel agencies like Thos. Cook & Son, and the American Express Company. The spelling "cheques" is British.

Mailing Money. Currency should never be sent in a letter unless such a course is absolutely necessary, and unless the letter is registered.

Ways in which money may be transmitted are by

Personal check	Bank draft	Money order—Postal, Bank,
Certified check	Savings stamps	Telegraph, or Express
Cashier's check		Stamps (for small amounts)

Torn Money. Currency that has been torn in two may be pasted and deposited or exchanged for new money at the bank. (If a portion of a bill is missing, but if more than one-half remains, it may be redeemed at a bank.)

Torn checks may also be pasted together and deposited or cashed.

Transparent tape, if available, should be used to mend torn money or checks, so that no writing will be covered.

Deposits. The following may be deposited in banks:

Cash	Warrants
Checks	Interest coupons that are due
Money orders	(with which Ownership Certificates
Bank drafts	are required)

Accepted drafts, on or after their due dates, may be deposited in some banks, but generally they are "handled for collection" and credited when paid.

Notes that are due are not deposited, but may be handled through a bank for collection.

Deposit Slips. Checks should be listed on deposit slips **by bank numbers** instead of by bank names.

Banks have adopted a universal numbering system to save labor in their clearing and transit departments. Every bank in the United States has been given a number. These numbers are printed immediately after the names of the banks on all checks and on other papers. The number consists of two parts, as 11-8, the first part designating the state or city, and the second part the number of the individual bank. For instance, banks in San Francisco, California, are in city Number 11, and their numbers are 11-8, 11-9, 11-10, etc.; while banks in Los Angeles, California, are in city Number 16, and their numbers are 16-1, 16-5, etc. Banks in the smaller cities of California take the state number, 90, as 90-4, 90-15, etc.

Often a routing symbol, containing the Federal Reserve district number, is given below the bank number, as $\frac{1\text{-}23}{210}$, which means bank Number 23, in city Number 1, Federal Reserve district Number 2.

Listings on a deposit slip should appear as

11-8	$345.90
16-1	60.80
90-4	38.65

Checks for deposit by a business house are, preferably, endorsed with a rubber stamp that reads like this: "Pay to the order of the Bank of New York, 1077, The Westland Company". The "1077" is a customer's number assigned by the bank. The date is also carried on some rubber stamps.

In the absence of a rubber stamp, the payee's name may be **typed** on the checks with just "**For deposit only**" above it, like this: "For deposit only, John T. Lee". No other name or wording needs to appear.

All checks for deposit should be so endorsed to safeguard them in case they are lost while being taken or mailed to the bank.

A carbon copy of all deposit slips should be kept by the depositor for future reference.

Duplicate Deposit Slip. If the passbook is not at hand for making a deposit, make an extra copy of the deposit slip to be stamped by the bank as a "duplicate deposit slip". The bank will enter this deposit in the passbook later.

Certificate of Deposit. Is a receipt given by a bank for a special deposit. Checks cannot be drawn against moneys held under a certificate of deposit. A certificate of deposit may be transferable or nontransferable.

The money held under a certificate of deposit cannot be released unless the certificate is returned to the bank.

If the money is to be held a certain length of time, the certificate of deposit may draw interest.

BANKS AND FINANCIAL HOUSES

There are various kinds of banks and financial houses, organized and operating under different laws. One bank may fall under several classifications; for instance, a "Commercial Bank" may be also a "National Bank", and it may have "Trust" and "Savings" departments. The ordinary classifications are:

National Bank. Organized under the National Bank Act; acts as a commercial bank, often having savings and trust departments. All national banks must have the words "National Bank" in their titles.

State Bank. Organized under state laws; acts as a commercial bank, often having savings and trust departments.

Commercial Bank. Does a general banking business, primarily in financing industries on short-term or seasonal loans. National and state banks are commercial banks, and may have savings departments as well as trust departments, depending on the laws of the various states.

Savings Bank. Organized primarily for the deposit of savings; but may do a general banking business, depending on the laws of the state in which organized.

Trust Company. Acts in a fiduciary capacity, either for individuals or for corporations. It may be a part of a commercial bank, but the trust funds are separate from the banking funds.

Federal Reserve Bank. Organized under the Federal Reserve Act. It acts as agent of the United States in dealing with other banks; in other words, the Federal Reserve banks are the bankers' banks.

Land Bank. Organized under the Federal Farm Loan Act; lends money on real estate mortgages.

Investment Banker. Deals in securities and finances business by supplying it with capital through the sale of securities, chiefly bonds; and may act further in an advisory capacity on investment matters.

Private Banker. A type of investment banker, often lending money on a large scale to finance international projects. Some private bankers engage in commercial banking.

Investment Trust. Invests in securities and issues and sells its own securities against such investments.

Morris Plan Company. Engages in industrial banking, that is, makes small loans to employed persons, who repay the loans on the installment plan.

Finance Company. Finances industries, such as the automobile industry, by discounting (buying) dealers' and manufacturers' open accounts, sales contracts, installment paper, acceptances (drafts), and/or notes receivable. (Also sometimes called a **Credit Company**, an **Acceptance Corporation**, or a **Discount Corporation** or **Company**.)

Building and Loan Association. An organization in which the members buy shares on the installment plan by depositing their savings. These accumulated savings are loaned by the association to finance the building of homes; they are also loaned on improved real estate.

Clearing House. An establishment where banks exchange checks and adjust balances. It is maintained and regulated by the association of banks that "clear" through it.

❖

SECURITIES

Stocks and bonds are called **"securities"**.

Stocks are shares of ownership in corporations. A stockholder is entitled to share in the assets and profits of the corporation.

Bonds represent money loaned to corporations, municipalities, or governments. **They do not represent ownership.** Bonds are in reality formal, long-term notes, bearing interest, and issued in series.

STOCKS

Stocks are variously designated, according to the manner in which they are issued, or according to the manner in which they share with other stocks in the profits of the corporations.

Capital Stock. The total amount of stock that a corporation is authorized to issue under its certificate of incorporation or charter. (This includes common and preferred stock.)

Common Stock. Ordinary stock, without any special preferences.

Preferred Stock. Receives preference in the distribution of dividends or assets. Preferred stock may claim a dividend of a specified percentage before the common stock is paid anything. But if the earnings of a corporation are large, the common stock may receive a larger dividend than the preferred stock, in which case the common stock would probably sell at a higher price than the preferred.

Prior Preference Stock. Stock that receives a dividend before any other preferred stock. (Also called "First Preferred", or "Prior Preferred".)

Participating Preferred Stock. Stock that is preferred as to certain first dividends, beyond which it participates with the common stock in the division of other dividends—after the common stock has been paid a certain dividend.

Cumulative Preferred Stock. If dividends are passed (not paid), this stock is entitled to receive accumulated dividends (when they are finally paid), before dividends are paid on the common stock.

Convertible Preferred Stock. Can be exchanged for common stock on or after a certain date, and on a specified basis of exchange.

Guaranteed Stock. Has its dividends guaranteed by another company.

Floating Stock. The amount of a company's stock that is on the market, or that can be dealt in for speculation.

Treasury Stock. A company's own stock (originally issued as full-paid stock) bought back and held in the company's treasury. (Unissued stock is not treasury stock.) Dividends are not paid on treasury stock.

Debenture Stock. Of the nature of preferred stock in America; and of the nature of a bond in England.

Scrip. A certificate showing ownership of a part of a share of stock; or a certificate showing installment payments on a share of stock.

Voting Pool Stock. Capital stock with restricted voting power.

Voting Trust Certificates. Certificates issued instead of stock certificates when the voting privileges of a stock are lodged in a voting trust (composed of voting trustees).

Watered Stock. Stock that is issued, or stock dividends that are declared, against inflated or padded assets.

BONDS

Bonds bear many different designations—the variety is large, and the names unlimited.

Bonds may be designated or classified according to the corporation, municipality, or government that issues them, as

Government bonds   issued by the United States Government.
Industrial bonds   issued by various industries.
Insular bonds   issued by United States island possessions.
Irrigation bonds   issued by irrigation districts.
Municipal bonds   issued by city and county governments.
Public Utility bonds   issued by public service companies, such as gas, light, power, water, telephone, and street railway companies.
Rail bonds   issued by railroads.
State bonds   issued by states.
Territorial bonds   issued by United States territories.

– – – –

Foreign bonds   issued in foreign countries and sold in the United States.
External bonds   issued in one country and sold externally in other countries; usually payable in the currency of the country or countries in which they are sold.

Bonds may be designated according to the purpose for which they are issued, as

Bridge bonds   for building bridges.
Construction bonds   for making constructions.
Equipment bonds   for buying equipment.
Improvement bonds   for making improvements.
Liberty bonds   for financing the war.
Purchase Money bonds   for acquiring money with which to purchase property or a business.
Reclamation bonds   for reclaiming land.
School bonds   for building schools.
Water bonds   for furnishing water supplies.

Bonds may be named for some particular characteristic, as

Adjustment bonds   issued in a readjustment or reorganization of a company.
Assumed bonds   assumed by a company that purchases or merges with another.
Consolidated bonds   issued for the purpose of consolidating previous bond issues.
Convertible bonds   may be converted into stock under certain conditions and at specified times. If the earnings of a company are large, a bondholder may desire to convert his bonds into stock so that he may share in the profits.
Funding bonds   issued to convert a floating debt into a funded debt.
Refunding bonds   issued to cover, or "re-fund", mortgages or bonds about to mature. A refunding bond is a second mortgage bond, until all of the original mortgages or bonds are paid.
Unifying bonds   issued to replace previous forms of indebtedness and to make them uniform.

510

MISCELLANEOUS SECURITIES

Bonds may be designated according to the manner of payment, as

Annuity bonds payable in equal annual installments.
Callable bonds may be called for payment before maturity.
Called bonds called in for payment.
Currency bonds payable in currency rather than in gold.
Extended bonds on which the maturity date has been extended.
Gold bonds payable in gold.
Income bonds interest to be paid out of earnings or income of company.
Participating bonds besides drawing interest they participate in the excess profits of the issuing company.
Perpetual bonds the principal has no definite maturity date, and the interest is to be paid perpetually.
Serial bonds redeemable in series.
Short-Term bonds issued for short periods of time.

Bonds may be designated according to the manner in which they are secured, as

Collateral Trust bonds secured by collateral deposited with a trustee.
Debenture bonds usually unsecured other than by the name and reputation of the issuing company.
Equipment Trust bonds (See Equipment Trust Certificates, p. 512.)
General Mortgage bonds secured by a blanket mortgage on properties.
Guaranteed bonds payment guaranteed by a third party.
Joint bonds for the payment of which two or more parties are jointly responsible.
Mortgage bonds secured by a mortgage on property.
Prior Lien bonds represent a prior claim against property.
Real Estate bonds secured by a mortgage on real estate.
Sinking Fund bonds secured by a sinking fund.

General classifications of bonds are:

Coupon bonds those to which are attached coupons representing the interest payments. As the interest becomes due the coupons are clipped and presented for payment.
Registered bonds those that are registered on the books of the issuing companies in the names of the bondholders. Interest is paid only to the registered holders; and the bonds may be transferred only by assignment. Bonds are registered as a protection against loss or theft.
Registered coupon bonds are registered as to principal, but not as to interest, which is evidenced by coupons payable to bearer.

Bonds not Securities in the Usual Sense. Another use of the word "bond" is its application to the form of pledge or surety given by an individual to guarantee his faithful performance of certain duties or his carrying out of a certain trust. The names of these bonds are self-descriptive:

surety bond	attachment bond	trustee's bond
fidelity bond	injunction bond	executor's bond
indemnity bond	bail bond	receiver's bond

MISCELLANEOUS SECURITIES

Various general terms applied to securities are:

Assented Securities. Securities deposited with a trustee for a readjustment of values or some other change in status. Such securities are called or stamped "assented" indicating that the owners thereof have agreed or assented to the change.

Certificates of Deposit. Are given for securities so placed in trust. These "certificates" are bought and sold on the stock exchanges.

Consols or Annuities {
British Government bonds or forms of indebtedness. (pron. kŏn-sŏlz′, note accent) (The full term is "consolidated annuities".)

Equipment Trust Certificates.   Bonds issued against an equipment trust mortgage —a chattel mortgage on railroad equipment, held in trust for the repayment of borrowed money.   Or bonds issued against a lease of railroad equipment ("Philadelphia Plan"), the railroad leasing the equipment from a trustee that holds absolute title for the benefit of the bondholders, until the railroad pays the last installment of its obligation and takes title to the property.

Deferred Securities.   Securities on which the payment of dividends or interest is deferred for a specified length of time.

Definitive Securities.   When stocks or bonds are announced and sold but are not actually ready for delivery, receipts, called **"interim certificates"**, are issued therefor by a trustee.   These interim certificates are bought and sold as the securities would be, and are later exchanged for the final or complete (definitive) stocks or bonds.

Investment Securities.   Securities issued by sound corporations or governments, and purchased by investors who desire safe investments, to provide reliable incomes.

Listed Securities.   Securities listed for trading on a stock exchange.   Requirements for "listing" involve the furnishing of facts and financial data regarding a corporation, and registration with the Securities and Exchange Commission.   **Unlisted securities** are those not listed for trading on a stock exchange (although they are sometimes dealt in on the smaller exchanges, at the request of exchange members).

Mortgage Certificates.   Certificates for small amounts issued and sold by mortgage companies against large first mortgages or first mortgage bonds which they hold or own.   (Also called "mortgage participation certificates", meaning that the holder participates in the large first mortgage or first mortgage bond.)

Receipts.   American depositary receipts for foreign shares; also receipts for bonds or stocks deposited in trust under a plan of exchange or reorganization.

Rentes.   French Government bonds or forms of indebtedness. (pron. räṅt; Fr., income)

Rights or Privileges {
Certain rights or privileges are often given to the holders of stocks or bonds in the matter of the purchase of new stocks or bonds.   These rights or privileges are bought and sold on the stock exchanges.

Stamped Securities.   Stocks or bonds on which some guarantee, extension, privilege, or changed condition has been stamped.

Tenders.   Sealed bids or offers for securities.

Treasury Bills.   Short-term Government obligations, which do not bear interest, but which are sold at a discount to provide the buyers with interest for the use of their money.

Treasury Certificates.   The Government, instead of issuing short-term bonds to finance its current debts, issues certificates of indebtedness, which bear interest.

Warrants.   Are primarily orders to pay money or to deliver goods or papers. They may be issued by companies for the payment of dividends on stocks, as **"dividend warrants"**; or they may be issued for the payment of interest on bonds or notes, as **"interest warrants"**; or they may be issued to give options, or the privilege of buying stock, as **"subscription warrants"** or **"purchase warrants"**. (See also Warrant, p. 503.)

STOCK MARKET TERMS

arbitrage—buying stocks, bonds, or exchange in one market and selling in another market to make a profit.

backwardation—a charge paid by a seller, to a buyer, for delaying delivery of securities; and
contango—a charge paid by a buyer to a seller for withholding delivery of securities or demand for payment. (British)

Big Board—a term for the New York Stock Exchange, derived from its original title of "The New York Stock and Exchange Board". It was once referred to as the "Regular Board" to distinguish it from its competitor the "Open Board". In current usage it is popularly referred to as the "Big Board".

Boerse—the Berlin stock exchange. (Ger. Börse; pron. bûr′zĕ)

Bourse—the Paris stock exchange. (pron. bŏŏrs; Fr., purse)

bucket shop—a place where illegal betting on security prices is done. A "bucket shop" operation is one in which a broker takes the opposite side of the market from his customer. A customer may order him to buy a certain amount of stock, and he may take the customer's money without actually purchasing the stock, gambling on the market's declining before he is forced to buy and deliver the stock.

bulls—those who buy on the expectation that the market will advance; and by their transactions tend to, or attempt to, advance the market.
bears—those who sell "short" on the expectation that the market will decline; and by their transactions tend to, or attempt to, depress the market.

buyer four (or **buyer ten,** etc.)—a term meaning that the buyer has four days within which to receive purchased stock. He may demand delivery of the stock at any time within the four days, upon one day's notice. But he must take delivery and pay for the stock on the final day.

call—see "put", below.

call money—borrowed money that is returnable on call or demand.

Change—means "exchange" in the phrase "on Change". (In British usage no apostrophe is placed before "Change"—it is not considered a contraction.)

Chicago Board of Trade—the world's largest grain market. It furnishes also a market for cotton, provisions, and securities. "Memberships" correspond to "seats" on stock exchanges.

cornering the market—gaining control of enough stock to force those who have sold "short" to pay high prices to "cover".

cover—to buy stocks to cover "short" sales.

cum div.—with, or including, the dividend that has been declared or is due. (L. cum dividendo)

Curb Market—generally refers to the New York Curb Exchange, which was formerly a stock market on the curb in Broad Street; now in a building. It is the second largest stock market in the United States. In the matter of rules and regulations, standards, etc., it does not differ essentially from the New York Stock Exchange.

cutting a melon—distributing surplus earnings to stockholders.

due bill—a form of IOU for undelivered stocks, dividends, or rights. For instance, if certain stocks are not actually available for delivery when sold, a broker may give a due bill for them. The due bill lists the stocks and promises a later delivery.

equity—a buyer's equity in a stock bought "on margin" is the difference between the market value of the stock and what is still owed on it, in other words, the "excess of the market value of a customer's securities over his debit balance" on the broker's books. (The cost of the stock includes all charges, such as broker's commission, financing costs, taxes, etc.)

ex bonus—without or not including the bonus.

ex coupon—without or not including the current interest coupon.

ex dividend—without or not including the declared dividend.

ex interest—without or not including the interest due.

ex privileges ⎫ without or not including the right to subscribe for new stock, or
ex rights ⎬ any other granted rights or privileges.
("Ex" in these phrases, meaning "without", is a preposition, not a prefix. Therefore no hyphen is necessary.)

floating a loan—launching a loan for the financing of a project.

flotation—the marketing of securities.

futures—contracts for future deliveries (chiefly a commodity exchange term).

hedge—a buying to offset a sale, or a selling to offset a purchase, as a fortification against loss. Trading in "puts and calls" is often called "hedging".

hypothecation—the pledging and depositing of security for the payment of a loan.

Lombard Street—the financial center of London; the commercial district of London is commonly called "the City".

London Stock Exchange—known in London as "the House".

long—If a trader owns or holds certain stocks, he is "long" of those stocks.
short—If a trader sells stocks that he does not own, hoping to secure them at a lower price on a falling market, he is "short" of those stocks. His broker borrows the stocks to make delivery, if immediate delivery is necessary. If the market rises, the trader must buy at a higher price when he "covers" his short sales.

margin—If stocks are not bought outright, they may be held "on margin"; that is, a trader may deposit a certain amount of money or security with a broker to cover the financing of the transactions, and to act as a "margin of safety" in case the market reverses quickly. "Margin" is generally used to mean the "amount of excess that a broker requires a customer to maintain".

melon—surplus earnings distributed in the form of an extra dividend or stock.

odd lots—see "round lots", below.

Orders:

market order—an order to buy or sell at the market price (for one day only).

limit order—an order to buy at or below a certain price; or to sell at or above a certain price.

514

one-day order—an order to be executed on a specified day. If not accomplished on that day, it is automatically canceled.

open order } an order that is to stand until it is withdrawn. Also called a GTC—
GTC order } "good till canceled" order.

stop-loss order {
stop order } an order to sell and stop the loss at a certain figure if a stock is declining; or an order to buy to cover "short" sales and stop the loss at a certain figure if a stock is advancing.

over-the-counter trading—Many securities that are not listed on the exchanges are sold privately by dealers. These tradings are known as "over-the-counter sales".

passing a dividend—failing to pay a dividend, or not declaring a dividend when one is expected.

pegged—fixed or maintained at a certain price.

pit—(a commodity exchange term) a special section, in the Chicago Board of Trade building, that trades in a certain commodity, as the "Wheat Pit".

point—the unit of fluctuation on the market. If the price of a stock usually changes in dollars, then one dollar is a "point". If the price of another stock usually changes in cents, then one cent is a "point". Or $\frac{1}{100}$ of a cent may be a "point", as in foreign exchange.

pool—a group of interests combined to control the price of certain securities.

premium—If the market value of a stock exceeds the par value, such stock is said to be selling "at a premium". The premium, or the amount above par, is referred to as a percentage of the par value; for instance, "a premium of 5%" means 5% of the par value. "Premium" is also used to mean the amount paid for an option.

privilege—a contract giving one party the privilege of exercising an option to buy or sell certain securities on certain terms.

{ **put**—an agreement in which a first party agrees **to receive** from a second party certain stock at a certain price, if the second party chooses to deliver (put) it within a certain time. The second party pays a fee for this privilege and may sell it.

{ **call**—an agreement in which a first party agrees **to deliver** to a second party certain stock at a certain price, if the second party chooses to receive (call for) it within a certain time. The second party pays a fee for this privilege and may sell it.

pyramiding—building on profits, that is, using the profits realized on an advancing or declining market as the "margin" on which to buy or sell more stock.

rehypothecation—repledging stock that is held as security. For instance, a customer pledges stock to a broker as security for payment for the stock, and the broker repledges the stock to a bank to finance the transaction.

rigged market—a manipulated market—one that does not represent true values.

{ **round lots**—are sales of a round number of shares, usually 100.
{ **odd lots**—are sales of less than 100 shares. (There are also occasions when sales of less than 100 shares are called "round lot" sales.)

seat on the stock exchange { a membership in a stock exchange, that is, a share in the assets of the exchange and the privilege of trading on the floor of the exchange.

515

seller four (or **seller ten,** etc.)—a term meaning that the seller has four days in which to deliver stock, but that he can deliver it on any day within the four days by giving one day's notice.

short—see "long", above.

spread—a combined "put and call".

squeeze—A "squeeze" is effected when those who have sold "short" are forced to pay high prices to "cover" (usually in the cornering of a stock or commodity).

The Street—Wall Street in New York, or the financial district of any city. In London, the district near the stock exchange.

wash sale—a maneuver in which two traders engage in fictitious trading to make a stock appear active and to establish artificial prices, with no real intention of exchanging money or goods.

❖

FOREIGN EXCHANGE

For a study of foreign exchange, how to figure it, etc., consult **"Tate's Cambist"**, or any recent book on foreign exchange at the public library.

The Treasury Department, Office of the Director of the Mint, Washington 25, D.C., publishes quarterly, on January 1, April 1, July 1, and October 1, a free circular sheet entitled **"Values of Foreign Moneys"**, giving the par values of foreign monetary units.

The Department of Commerce, Bureau of Foreign and Domestic Commerce, Office of International Trade, Washington 25, D.C., publishes the **"Foreign Commerce Weekly"**, which gives news by countries, and by commodities. Foreign exchange rates are given regularly.

> Annual subscription: domestic, $9; foreign, $12. Single copy, 20¢.
> Order from the Superintendent of Documents,
> Government Printing Office, Washington 25, D.C.

The Federal Reserve Board issues monthly the **"Federal Reserve Bulletin"**, which, besides giving financial, industrial, and commercial statistics for the United States, gives financial statistics for foreign countries, including foreign exchange rates. The Bulletin may be secured from the Federal Reserve Board in Washington, D.C., or from any Federal Reserve bank—yearly subscription $2, single copies 20¢.

Methods of Writing Foreign Moneys. In many foreign countries sums of money are written in much the same manner as they are in the United States; that is, the abbreviation for the monetary unit is written before the figures, or often the dollar sign ($) is used to designate the currency.

The principal difference in the manner of writing moneys is that in many countries a point is used instead of a comma to indicate thousands, and a comma instead of a decimal point, as in

> France   Frs 46.859,20 means 46,859 francs and 20 centimes.
> Germany   DM 4.560.348,50 means 4,560,348 Deutsche marks and 50 pfennige.

In some countries the decimal point is raised, as in

> Austria   S 8·—   S 3·90   S—·95   S 1,456.872·50
> (Note the use of the period to separate thousands, and the comma, millions.)

In a few countries a space is used instead of a decimal point.

In some countries the symbol $ is placed where ordinarily the decimal point would be placed—between the unit and its fractional part, as in

Portugal	46$15 means 46 escudos and 15 centavos.
	$15 means just 15 centavos.
French Indo-China	5$25 means 5 piasters and 25 centimes.

The conto sign (:) is used in Portugal to designate the higher sums of money; the conto representing 1000 escudos, as

Portugal   6.519:218$85 means 6,519 contos 218 escudos and 85 centavos.

In British India, commas are used to indicate the number of lacs (of 100,000 rupees) and crores (of 10,000,000 rupees), as

Rs 2,56,76,874 means 2 crores 56 lacs and 76,874 rupees.

Several countries, besides the British countries, use the pound as a monetary unit; it is designated by the symbol £ and the initial of the country, as

£   English pound or "pound sterling"
£E   Egyptian pound
£P   Palestine pound
£T   Turkish pound
£S   Syrian pound

If in doubt about the proper method of writing any item of foreign money, write simply the figures followed by the name, as

89 pesos and 65 centavos   24 francs and 80 centimes

as one might write in American money "89 dollars and 65 cents".
British Money.   British money is written in three parts:

£8 4s. 6d.   or   £8 4 6   or   £8:4:6   or   £8.4.6   or   8/4/6
meaning 8 pounds 4 shillings and 6 pence.

£ represents the Latin word "librae" meaning "pounds".
The diagonal line, derived from the old-fashioned S (ʃ) meaning "shillings", is used to divide shillings and pence.

6/10 means 6 shillings and 10 pence ("six and ten").
10/— or 10'— means 10 shillings even.

"Guinea" is a term used to express "1 pound 1 shilling"—or 21 shillings (about $5). A "crown" is 5 shillings (about $1.25).
"Sterling" is standard British money—it may be gold or silver. The "pound sterling" is often called simply "sterling".
The term "sterling silver" is derived from the amount of silver in former British standard silver, which had a "fineness" of .925, that is, 925 parts of silver to 75 parts of alloy. British standard silver now has a "fineness" of .500, that is, 500 parts of silver to 500 parts of alloy.

518

Monetary Terms

legal standard—means the standard measure of value, in gold or silver, adopted by the government of a country, by which all forms of its money are rated.

gold standard—means that gold is the measure of value; that paper money is redeemable in gold; and that exchange is stabilized at a fixed ratio with gold.

silver standard—means that silver is the measure of value; that paper money is redeemable in silver; and that silver is the principal circulating medium.

legal tender—lawful money that may be tendered in payment of debts.

specie—hard money or metal money as distinguished from paper money. "Specie payments" are payments made in coin; but "in specie" payments specified in legal papers are usually understood to mean payments "in United States currency".

bullion—uncoined gold or silver in bars, etc.

FOREIGN MONEYS

(For values of gold and silver, see page 562.)

Standard values only are given in the following table. Exchange rates fluctuate from day to day; for such changes in value, consult the foreign exchange tables in the financial sections of daily newspapers (in which tables some rates will be found to be based on the new par values, and some on the old).

Country	Monetary unit (plurals are indicated)*	Abbreviation or symbol	Par value (of gold unit) in U.S. money (nongold has no par)		Small coin (number in one monetary unit)
			Before U.S. revalued gold†	After U.S. revalued gold‡	
Argentina	peso -s	★	$0.9648‖	$1.6335‖	100 centavos
Australia	Australian pound -s	£	4.8665	8.2397¶	20 shillings of 12 pence each
Austria	schilling -s	S	.1407	.2382	100 groschen
Belgium	franc -s	Fr. or Frs	.0278	.0339	100 centimes
	belga -s(old)		.1390	.1695	5 francs
Bolivia	boliviano -s	B. or Bs.	.3650	.6180	100 centavos
Brazil	cruzeiro -s	Cr$ as Cr$1.348,50	......	.0533	100 centavos
British Honduras	dollar	$	1.0000	1.6931	100 cents
Bulgaria	lev -a	L	.0072	.0122	100 stotinki
Canada	dollar	$	1.0000	1.0000	100 cents
Chile	peso -s	$	.1217	.2060	100 centavos
China	yuan (pl. same)	$	.3159**	.2950	100 fen
	Hong Kong or British dollar	$	.3262**	.3280**	100 cents
	Mexican dollar	$	.3286**	......	††
Colombia	peso -s	$	.9733	.5714	100 centavos
Costa Rica	colon -es	₡	.2500	.4233	100 centimos
Cuba	peso -s	$	1.0000	1.0000	100 centavos
Czecho-Slovakia	koruna -ny	Kč	.0296	.0351	100 haleru (heller)
Denmark	krone -r	Kr.	.2680	.4537	100 øre
Dominican Republic	dollar	$	1.0000	1.0000	100 cents
Ecuador	sucre -s	S/ or $	.2000	.3386	100 centavos
Egypt	Egyptian pound	£E	4.9431	8.3692	100 piasters or 1000 millièmes
El Salvador	colon -es	C. or ₡	.5000	.8466	100 centavos
England (See Great Britain)					
Estonia	kroon -i	Ekr.	.2680	.4537	100 senti
Finland	markka -a	Fmk. or mk.	.0252	.0426	100 penniä
France	franc -s	Fr. or Frs	.0392	.0286	100 centimes
Germany	Deutsche mark	DM	.2382	.4033	100 pfennige
Great Britain	pound sterling	£	4.8665	8.2397¶	20 shillings of 12 pence each
Greece	drachma -i	Dr.	.0130	.0220	100 lepta
Guatemala	quetzal -es	Q. or Qs.	1.0000	1.0000	100 centavos
Haiti	gourde -s	G. or Gde.	.2000	.2000	100 centimes
Hawaiian Islands	(U.S.)				
Holland (See Netherlands)					

FOREIGN MONEYS—contd.

Country	Monetary unit (plurals are indicated)*	Abbreviation or symbol	Par value (of gold unit) in U.S. money (nongold has no par)		Small coin (number in one monetary unit)
			Before U.S. revalued gold†	After U.S. revalued gold‡	
Honduras	lempira -s	L or $	$0.5000	$0.8466	100 centavos
Hungary	forint (pl. same)	F	.....	.0852	100 fillér
India	rupee -s	R or Rs	.3650	.6180	16 annas
					1 anna = 12 pies
Indo-China, French	piastre -s	$ as 1$00	.3918	.2857	100 centimes
Iran (Persia)	rial -s	....	.2433	.0824	100 dinars
	pahlavi	... .	4.8665	8.2397	100 rials
Ireland, Northern (British)					
Ireland (Eire)	Irish pound -s	£	4.8665	8.2397¶	20 shillings of 12 pence each
Italy	lira -re	L	.0526	.0526	100 centesimi
Japan	yen (pl. same)	¥	.4985	.8440	100 sen
Latvia	lat -i	L	.1930	.1983	100 santimi
Liberia	dollar (U.S.)	$	1.0000	1.6931	100 cents
Lithuania	litas -tu	Lt.	.1000	.1693	100 cents
Mexico	peso -s	$	.4985	.8440†‡	100 centavos
Netherlands	guilder -s (florin)	f, fl., gld.	.4020	.6806	100 cents
Newfoundland	dollar	$	1.0000	1.6931	100 cents
New Zealand	New Zealand pound -s	£	4.8665	8.2397¶	20 shillings of 12 pence each
Nicaragua	cordoba -s	C.	1.0000	1.6931	100 centavos
Norway	krone -r	Kr.	.2680	.4537	100 øre
Panama	balboa -s	B.	1.0000	1.0000	100 centesimos
Paraguay	guarani -s	G	.....	.3000	100 centimos
Persia (See Iran)					
Peru	sol -es	S/	.2800	.4740	100 centavos
Philippines	peso -s	₱	.5000	.5000	100 centavos
Poland	zloty -te	Zl.	.1122	.1899	100 grosze
Portugal	escudo -s	$ as 1$00	.0442	.0748	100 centavos
Rumania	leu (pl. lei)	L	.0060	.0101	100 bani
Russia (See U.S.S.R.)					
Salvador (See El Salvador)					
Siam (now Thailand)	baht (pl. same)	....	.4424	.7491	100 satang
South Africa, Union of	South African pound -s	£	4.8665	8.2397¶	20 shillings of 12 pence each
Spain	peseta -s	P. or Pta.	.1930	.3267	100 céntimos
Straits Settlements	Straits dollar	$	.5678	.9613	100 cents
Sweden	krona -nor	Kr.	.2680	.4537	100 öre
Switzerland	franc -s	Fr. or Frs	.1930	.2243	100 centimes
Turkey	piaster -s	Pst.	.0440	.0744	40 paras
	Turkish pound	£T	4.3966	7.4438	100 piasters
Uruguay	peso -s	$	1.0342	.6583	100 centesimos
U.S.S.R. (Russia)	ruble -s	Rs.	.5146	.1981	100 kopecks
	chervonets (pl. chervontsy)	Ch.	5.1457	1.9810	10 rubles
Venezuela	bolivar -es	B.	.1930	.3267	100 centimos
Yugoslavia	dinar -i	D. or Din.	.0176	.0298	100 paras

* English plurals (ending in -s or -es) are often used for all currencies, as "kroons" instead of "krooni", "lats" instead of "lati", etc.
† Prior to January 31, 1934, when the United States revalued gold.
‡ After January 31, 1934. (Many of these values are theoretical.)
★ Gold peso is called "oro sellado" and abbreviated "o/s" or "o$s". Paper peso is called "moneda nacional" and abbreviated "m/n", "M$n", or simply "$".
‖ Values are for gold peso. The paper peso is normally worth 44% of the gold peso, making the old value of the paper peso $0.4245, and the new value $0.7187.
¶ Market values of the various pounds fluctuate between $4 and $5; different rates being quoted for the Australian pound, the South African pound, etc.
** Estimated market value of silver content.
†† "Mex." refers to the Mexican "dollar" or peso which was formerly exported to China.
‡‡ Gold peso value. The exchange value of the silver peso is maintained at approximately $0.2015.

FINANCIAL STATEMENTS

No one system of accounting can be applied to every business, because no two businesses are exactly alike. But there are two accounting statements that are generally prepared by all companies. Since these statements are often used in the different departments of organizations, they are considered here.

> **Balance Sheet.** A statement of the financial condition—assets and liabilities—of a business on a certain date. (It may also be formally designated "Statement of Financial Condition", or "Statement of Resources and Liabilities".)
>
> The statement of financial condition of a company is often issued or made public for the purpose of giving information to the stockholders and to persons expecting to trade with, invest in, or lend money to the company.
>
> **Profit and Loss Statement.** An operating statement, or summary of income and expense. (It is also called an "Income Statement", "Income Account", "Income Sheet", or "Operating Statement".) It shows how much was made or lost over a certain period of time—a month or a year.
>
> A **Manufacturing Statement** is sometimes submitted as a supporting schedule to the statement of profit and loss, to show more details with respect to the cost of goods produced. The manufacturing statement contains three main captions: Cost of Raw Materials, Direct Labor, and Manufacturing or Overhead Expense.

(Forms for either of these statements may be purchased at stationery stores.)

The forms for balance sheets vary, as do the forms for profit and loss statements; but the general outlines of all balance sheets and of all profit and loss statements are much the same. The amount of detail to be included in the headings and the grouping of the headings must be governed by individual preference and the purpose for which the statement is being made.

In the preparation of statements, a company should follow the same general form year after year, if possible, not only for uniformity but in order to facilitate the study of trends.

The American Institute of Accountants publishes a pamphlet entitled "Examination of Financial Statements by Independent Public Accountants", in which is set forth the best modern practice in the preparation of financial statements. This pamphlet may be procured direct from the American Institute of Accountants, 13 East 41st Street, New York 17, N.Y.—15¢ a copy.

Moody's Manuals and Poor's Manuals (to be found in most public libraries) give financial statements of most of the large corporations of the United States, and Canada and other foreign countries, whose stock is bought by the public or in which there is a public interest. (See also Financial Ratings, p. 590.)

Example of a Profit and Loss Statement or "Income Sheet":

THE CORTLAND COMPANY, INC.
(A Maryland Corporation)
STATEMENT OF PROFIT AND LOSS
Period January 1–December 31, 1936

Sales			
Gross sales		$230,424.00	
Less: Returns and allowances		1,319.00	
Net sales			$229,105.00
Cost of Goods Sold			
Inventory, December 31, 1935		$ 26,550.00	
Purchases	$102,860.00		
Freight and storage	1,480.00	104,340.00	
Total		$130,890.00	
Less: Inventory, December 31, 1936		26,970.00	
Cost of goods sold			103,920.00
Gross profit on sales			$125,185.00
Expenses of Operation			
Office expense and salaries		$ 9,580.00	
Selling expense and salaries		14,800.00	
Advertising		9,500.00	
Store and workroom expense and salaries		64,280.00	
Delivery		2,000.00	
Rent, light, heat, repair, telephone, etc.		5,200.00	
Taxes, miscellaneous		790.00	
Insurance		610.00	
Depreciation		3,000.00	
Bad debts		1,486.00	
Miscellaneous expenses		200.00	
Total expenses of operation			111,446.00
Net profit from operation			$ 13,739.00
Other Income			
Discounts received		$ 2,290.00	
Interest and dividends		2,540.00	
Rentals		2,590.00	
Total miscellaneous income			7,420.00
Total			$ 21,159.00
Deductions from Income			
Interest		$ 590.00	
Loss on sale of fixed assets		400.00	
Total deductions from income			990.00
Net income before income taxes			$ 20,169.00
Income Taxes—Current Year			
Federal income tax		$ 3,256.00	
State income tax (none)		—	3,256.00
Net income after income taxes			$ 16,913.00
Earned Surplus, January 1, 1936			17,843.00
			$ 34,756.00
Less: Surplus charges (attributable to prior periods)		$ 1,250.00	
Dividends paid		7,500.00	8,750.00
EARNED SURPLUS, December 31, 1936			$ 26,006.00

FINANCIAL STATEMENTS

Example of a Balance Sheet:

THE CORTLAND COMPANY, INC.
(A Maryland Corporation)
STATEMENT OF FINANCIAL CONDITION—December 31, 1936

ASSETS

Current Assets

Cash in banks and on hand	$33,468.00	
Marketable securities (at market—cost $24,000)	20,000.00	
Accrued interest receivable	450.00	
Notes receivable	3,960.00	
Accounts receivable (net after allowance of $2,000 for doubtful accounts)	20,980.00	
Merchandise inventory (at cost—lower than market)	26,970.00	
Total current assets		$105,828.00

Prepaid Expenses

Rent paid in advance	$ 390.00	
Deposit on lease	500.00	
Prepaid insurance	305.00	
Advertising contract advances	4,000.00	
Office supplies on hand	100.00	
Total prepaid expenses		5,295.00

Fixed Assets (at cost)

Land		$12,000.00	
Buildings	$27,000.00		
Furniture and fixtures	5,000.00		
Machinery and equipment	25,000.00		
Automobiles and trucks	4,400.00		
	$61,400.00		
Less: Allowance for depreciation	20,000.00	41,400.00	
Net fixed assets			53,400.00

Intangible Assets

Patents }	
Trade-mark } Not valued	
Goodwill }	

Investments

In capital stock of affiliated company	$10,000.00	
In other companies (not readily marketable)	4,300.00	
Total investments		14,300.00
		$178,823.00

LIABILITIES AND NET WORTH

Current Liabilities

Accounts payable	$15,900.00	
Notes and drafts payable	4,460.00	
Advances received on orders	5,556.00	
Provision for income taxes	3,500.00	
Sundry accrued payables	1,500.00	
Total current liabilities		$ 30,916.00

Fixed Liabilities

Mortgage—due January 1, 1938		8,000.00
Total liabilities		$ 38,916.00

Net Worth

Capital Stock

Preferred stock, 7 % cumulative			
Authorized 6,000 shares, par value $5 each			
Issued	5,800 shares		
Less repurchased and held in treasury	800		
Outstanding	5,000 shares	$25,000.00	
Common stock			
Authorized 14,000 shares, no par value			
Issued and outstanding 10,000 shares (at declared value)		50,000.00	
Total capital stock		$75,000.00	

Surplus and Reserves

Capital (paid-in) surplus	$28,901.00	
Earned surplus	26,006.00	
Total surplus		54,907.00
Reserves for general contingencies		10,000.00
NET WORTH		139,907.00
		$178,823.00

ACCOUNTING TERMS

Assets or Resources. What is owned.

Current Assets. Cash and those assets that will be converted into cash in the ordinary course of operations and in a relatively short time—usually within a year—such as notes and accounts receivable, inventories, and marketable securities. (Often called **"Liquid Assets".**)

Quick Assets. Cash, receivables, and marketable securities, or any asset that can be quickly converted into cash.

Working Assets. Inventories, or any other assets that must be handled or "worked" before money can be realized on them.

Deferred Assets. Assets whose benefit is deferred until a future time. They may be subdivided into:

Prepaid Expenses. Prepayments that have some liquidating value, such as advance payments on contracts, deposits on leases, office supplies on hand, etc.

Deferred Charges. Development costs incurred in one period but whose benefits extend over succeeding periods; such charges are deferred and prorated over the entire period of benefit.

Fixed Assets. The assets used in conducting the business which have a relatively long life, such as land, buildings, machinery, furniture and fixtures, and automotive equipment.

Intangible Assets. A term ordinarily applied to such assets as patent rights, copyrights, trade-marks, trade names, franchises, etc. Because it is sometimes difficult to determine the real value of these assets, they are often omitted in a financial statement, or are given only a nominal valuation (usually based on unamortized cost).

Goodwill. An intangible asset that represents the value of a company's earning power over what it would ordinarily be expected to earn. The extra earning power may be created by advertising, by the manner of doing business, by advantageous location, or by the company's standing or good name in the business world. While of definite value, goodwill is often not valued in a financial statement, or given only a nominal valuation (calculated from excess profits, or based on unamortized cost).

Liabilities. What is owed.

Current Liabilities. Short-term liabilities—usually to be paid within one year. Examples: accounts payable, short-term notes payable, taxes, etc.

Deferred Liabilities. Also are called "deferred credits", and represent income received and not yet earned, such as rents or interest received in advance.

Fixed Liabilities. Long-term liabilities, such as mortgages, bonds, contracts, etc., for terms longer than one year. They are usually incurred in the acquisition of fixed assets.

Miscellaneous Terms:

Fund. Is made up of specific assets, usually cash or securities, set aside for a definite purpose.

524

Reserve. A part of the profits or surplus set aside (or simply designated on the books) for specific purposes, or for general purposes and contingencies.

Funded Reserve. A reserve for which a fund has been established and invested so that it will bring in interest or earnings.

Funded Debt. Long-term indebtedness, for the payment of which a fund has been established. (See "sinking fund", below.)

Bonded Debt. Indebtedness represented by bonds.

Floating Debt. Unfunded debt, that is, current debt.

Sinking Fund. Usually a fund that is started when bonds are issued, or other long-term indebtedness is incurred. The sinking fund is increased and invested so that it will completely pay the debt as the bonds or other forms of indebtedness mature.

Amortization. The gradual payment of a debt; or the writing off of intangible assets over a period of time as they expire.

Surplus. The amount by which the assets exceed the liabilities and capital. Surplus may be divided into two main classifications:

Capital Surplus. Accumulations which add to the net worth of a company, as

Paid-in Surplus—from the sale of capital stock at a premium, or other profits on capital stock transactions.

Revaluation Surplus—from revaluation of assets.

Donated Surplus—from donated stock, etc.

Earned Surplus. Net income from the operation of a business (after deduction of dividends and other appropriations).

Equity. The difference between what is owed on a property and what the property is worth; or the amount by which the assets exceed the liabilities.

"Window Dressing". The manipulation of items on a financial statement to make them appear more favorable than they really are.

Contra. Means "against" or "opposite". A "contra asset" is an opposite or offsetting asset. A "contra credit" is an opposite or offsetting credit.

Book Value. The value at which an asset is carried on the books of a company. A piece of property or equipment may be worth more or less to a "going concern" than it would be worth if it were sold in the open market. "Book value" may be far above "scrap value". Likewise, the book value of stock may be above or below its market value, because on the books it represents the net assets (excess of assets over liabilities) divided by the shares outstanding.

Bad Debts. Accounts or notes receivable that are uncollectible. They are written off usually by a direct charge to operations. If an "allowance for doubtful accounts" is carried, it signifies that the company has made a provision for probable losses.

Liquidation. The payment of debts. A business is "in liquidation" when its assets are being sold and its affairs are being closed.

Liquidating may also mean voluntarily turning securities, goods, or properties into cash to take profits or prevent losses.

Insolvency. A company is "insolvent" if it cannot meet its debts as they become due. It may have assets in excess of its liabilities, but if it is

525

unable to convert its assets into ready money with which to meet its current liabilities, it is "insolvent".

Receivership. A receiver may be appointed by the court to conduct the business of an insolvent company in an attempt to pay its debts. If the operation of the business is successful under the receivership, the company may be returned to its owners when its debts are discharged; if unsuccessful, it may be liquidated.

Reorganization. Under the Corporate Reorganization Act, an insolvent company may reorganize with the consent of a majority of the creditors and under court supervision. Reorganization is undergone to effect financial compromises on debts, and to avoid the expenses of a receivership or the sale of the property through regular bankruptcy proceedings.

Bankruptcy. A company is bankrupt if it is unable to meet its debts, and if its assets do not cover its liabilities.

Voluntary Bankruptcy. A company may voluntarily declare, in writing, its inability to pay its debts and petition the court to be declared a bankrupt.

Involuntary Bankruptcy. The creditors of an insolvent company may "throw it into bankruptcy" by petitioning the court to declare it a bankrupt.

A Trustee is elected or appointed in bankruptcy proceedings to take charge of the assets and wind up the affairs of the bankrupt.

Referee in Bankruptcy. An officer, usually an attorney, appointed by the court to assist in a judicial capacity in investigating and hearing bankruptcy cases.

Defunct. A defunct concern is one that is dead or extinct.

INTEREST

In computing interest:

> 360 days to the year are used in ordinary interest calculations—12 months of 30 days each.
>
> 365 days to the year (366 in leap year) are used in exact interest calculations. The Government uses this figure.

In ordinary business transactions, a month's interest (on small amounts) is considered to be 1/12 of a year's interest. On large amounts, the exact number of days is figured.

In banking, all interest is figured by the day, whether the amount is large or small, and whether the term is in months or days. For instance, a note dated May 12 and payable 2 months after date would be payable July 12, and the interest would be figured for 61 days.

> A day's interest is 1/360 (approximate) or 1/365 (exact) of a year's interest.

For sums less than $1500, the basis of a 360-day year will give the interest to within a few cents of the exact figure; and for convenience this basis is ordinarily used.

If the basis of a 360-day year is used, it permits many shortcuts. For instance, 90 days becomes 1/4 of a year; 60 days, 1/6 of a year; 30 days, 1/12 of a year, etc.

But if the days are uneven, as 77, the process is, of course, to find the interest for one day and multiply by 77.

To find the interest for an uneven number of days:

Find the interest for one year. Divide by 365 (or 360) to find the interest for one day. Multiply the interest for one day by the exact number of days.

Count the exact number of days on the calendar, excluding the first day, which is not counted. (It is reasoned that part of the first day and part of the last day are not covered in the transaction; therefore, one whole day is not counted, and it is usually the first.)

> For instance, from the 10th to the 28th of a month would be 18 days, not 19. A note dated April 15, payable 60 days after date, would be due June 14, not June 15.
>
> If a note dated April 15 is payable 3 months after date, 3 calendar months are figured, and the note is payable July 15. But if the same note is payable 90 days after date, the exact number of days is figured (excluding the first), and the note is payable July 14.

Banks use interest tables to make rapid calculations, but for one unfamiliar with these tables, the better method is to figure the interest exactly by the number of days.

To figure 6% interest: (For 3% interest, take 1/2 the 6% amount.)

A quick method of finding 6% interest for 60 days (2 months) is simply to point off two decimal places. Thus the interest for 60 days at 6% on $1,078 would be $10.78.

For 30 days (1 month) at 6%, divide the above result by 2, which gives $5.39.

For 90 days (3 months) at 6%, find the amounts for 60 and 30 days and add them, as $10.78 plus $5.39, which gives $16.17.

For 1 day at 6%, find the amount for 6 days (by pointing off three decimal places) and divide by 6, as $1.078 divided by 6, which gives 18¢.

To figure compound interest:

Add the interest to the principal each year to form a new principal for the next year, for example:

> $100 at 5% compound interest will give a principal of
> $105 for the second year,
> $110.25 for the third year, and
> $115.76 for the fourth year; or a total compound interest of $15.76 for 3 years.
> Simple interest at 5% on $100 for 3 years would be $15.

It is understood that interest is to be compounded annually (if compounded) unless otherwise specifically stated.

527

Compound interest is not collectible by law in many states, even when agreed to.

Legal Rate of Interest.

The "legal rate of interest" is a rate fixed by law in each state to apply to papers that do not specify any certain rates of interest, but on which interest may legally be charged. Banks often charge the legal rate of interest. The legal rate is not, in most states, "the highest rate that can be charged by written agreement".

The legal rates of interest and the highest rates that can be charged by written contract in the different states may be found in the current Martindale-Hubbell Law Directory, Vol. III, in any public or law library; or in the Rand McNally Bankers Directory (The Bankers Blue Book) in any public library or at any bank.

The **statute of limitations** on open accounts, notes, written contracts, sealed instruments, and judgments, in each state may also be found in the above publications.

◆◆◆═══════════◆◆◆

INVENTORIES

Merchandise is inventoried usually "at cost price or at market value, whichever is lower". The lower figure should always be used. To mark goods up to a market price is to assume a profit that may never be realized.

Depreciation. Depreciation on buildings and equipment such as furniture, machinery, etc., may be calculated as follows:

> **Straight-Line Basis** (presuming the depreciation to be practically the same each year)—Estimate the life of the equipment and the scrap value; subtract the scrap value from the cost; and write off an equal amount of the depreciation each year.
>
> **Sum-of-the-Life-Digits Basis** (presuming the depreciation to be heavier in the first years)—Subtract the scrap value from the cost, and figure the depreciation on a fractional basis. The fractional basis is arrived at by adding the digits in the number of years calculated. For instance, if the life of a piece of machinery is estimated to be 5 years, add the digits 1, 2, 3, 4, and 5, which gives 15. Since the depreciation is to be considered heavier in the first years than it is in later years, the depreciation for the first year should be figured as the largest fraction, 5/15 of the total depreciation; the second year 4/15; the third year 3/15, etc.

The following is an example:

Cost $2000 Scrap value $200 after 5 years Depreciation $1800

LIFE OF EQUIPMENT		YEARLY CHARGE-OFF
1 year	5/15 of $1800	$ 600
2	4/15	480
3	3/15	360
4	2/15	240
5	1/15	120
15 fractional basis	15/15	$1800 total depreciation

PETTY CASH ACCOUNT

A petty cash account may be kept separately from the general books, but it should be so kept that entries may be prepared from it for the general books of account.

Debit petty cash when a check is received putting money into it. (This will show as a credit in the general cashbook.)

Credit petty cash when something is paid for out of its funds.

For example:

PETTY CASH

	DEBIT				CREDIT		
1937				1937			
Mar. 2	Check for cash	$25	00	Mar. 5	Stationery	$ 4	65
				11	Stamps	5	00
				17	Express	11	89
				25	Messenger	1	50
				26	To balance	1	96
26		$25	00			$25	00
26	Balance	$ 1	96	30	Stationery	$ 2	35
26	Revolving check	23	04	31	Stamps	5	00

When the petty cash fund is "revolved" or renewed, with a check issued on the general bank account for the amount of petty cash expenditures, the petty cash account should be ruled off and the balance of cash actually in the fund brought down as shown in the foregoing illustration.

A receipt, often called a "voucher", should be obtained for every disbursement of petty cash. These vouchers should be kept in the petty cash box, and when their total is sufficiently high—as shown from the entries in the petty cash account—they should be sent to the cashier with a request, on a "revolving voucher", for a check to cover their amount.

Whenever cash is borrowed from the petty cash box, an IOU for the amount should be placed in the box. Unless this is done, it is difficult to remember what is due the cash box, and the keeper of the box is often obliged to pay for someone else's negligence.

❖

INSURANCE

The general classifications of insurance are:

Accident Insurance
Agricultural Insurance
Annuities
Automobile Insurance
Aviation Insurance
Boiler Insurance
Burglary Insurance
Casualty Insurance
Common Carriers' Insurance
Compensation Insurance
  (Workmen's Compensation Insurance)
Credit Insurance
Disability Insurance
Earthquake Insurance
Endowment Insurance
Explosion Insurance
Fidelity Bonds
Fire Insurance
Forgery and Alteration Insurance
Health Insurance
Judicial Bonds
Liability Insurance
  Employers' Liability
  Public Liability
Life Insurance
Livestock Insurance
Machinery Insurance
Malpractice Insurance
Marine Insurance
Plate Glass Insurance
Rain Insurance
Rent Insurance
Riot, Strike, and Civil Commotion Insurance
Robbery Insurance
Sprinkler Leakage Insurance
Surety Bonds
Title Insurance
Transportation Insurance
Use and Occupancy Insurance
Water Damage Insurance
Weather Insurance
Windstorm, Cyclone, and Tornado Insurance

All insurance policies held by one company or one person should be listed on a schedule so that no policies will be allowed to lapse because of nonpayment of premiums.

List the policies in the following form, and enter all premium-payment dates on the desk calendar as reminders of the dates on which checks should be mailed.

SCHEDULE OF INSURANCE POLICIES

Company	Policy No.	Kind or Plan	Property or Risk Covered	Date Issued	Term Ends	Amount	Beneficiary	Yearly Prems.	Prems. Payable

The time for payment of premiums is specified in each insurance policy. Many, but not all, insurance premiums may be paid within one month after their due dates. Payments should be sent early enough to reach the insurance companies well within the prescribed time. Some companies will accept payment, without canceling policies, if checks or money orders are "in the mails" on the last days for payment of the premiums. But it is not wise to follow the procedure of mailing a check on the last day for a payment of any kind.

All insurance policies should be kept in a place of safekeeping, preferably in a safe deposit vault.

INSURANCE TERMS

actuary—the official statistician of an insurance company, who calculates or computes insurance risks, premiums, surrender values, etc.

adjuster—one appointed to determine and make adjustment of loss or damage under insurance policies.

all risk—does not mean any and every possible risk, but only certain common risks; there are certain excluded risks under "all risk" policies.

annuity—provides an annual or periodic income to the annuitant for life, or for a specified term.

arson—the malicious burning of the dwelling house of another. Under some state laws, the crime covers the willful and malicious burning of any property.

binder or cover note { a note or memorandum given to the insured before the insurance policy is actually issued. The note certifies that insurance is in effect (provided all conditions are fulfilled) and will be paid if loss or damage is sustained prior to the issuance of the policy.

blanket policy—a policy that covers property collectively, rather than by specific items.

casualty insurance—This term covers a large field. It is primarily an insurance against accidental injury to persons or property. But it also includes health insurance, burglary insurance, fidelity bonds, etc.

coinsurance or average clause { a type of fire insurance wherein the property is insured for a certain percentage of the cash value in case of loss—for instance, 80%. If the owner of the property fails to, or does not care to, keep the insurance up to this value, he becomes his own insurer, or "coinsurer", for the difference.

common carriers' insurance—covers transportation companies' liability for loss of, or damage to, cargo or property being transported by them.

credit insurance—insures wholesalers, manufacturers, and jobbers against **excess or abnormal loss** from purchasers' failure to pay for merchandise.

declaration policy—(See "reporting policy", below.)

deficiency insurance—a type of insurance written to cover loss in case the payment under a coinsurance policy is not adequate.

endowment policy—an investment or saving policy—a certain sum or "endowment" is paid to the insured at the end of a specified period of time; or paid to his heirs in case of his death prior to the expiration of the period.

fidelity bond—given to insure an employer against loss through dishonesty (or sometimes neglect of duty) of an employee in a position of trust.

floater policy—a policy that covers property which is changeable in its quantity, value, and/or location.

general average—in marine insurance, is a general charge made against all parties interested when a certain part of the cargo or ship has been sacrificed for the common safety.

incendiary—pertaining to the willful or malicious burning of property; also one who sets fire to property—a "firebug", or pyromaniac. (pron. in-sĕn'dĭ-ĕr'y)

Inchmaree clause—in marine insurance, a specific clause covering damage to ships' hulls or machinery. Named from the famous SS. Inchmaree case, in which no damage was awarded by reason of the bursting of a boiler.

insured
assured
These terms are interchangeable; but in life insurance the "insured" is usually the person whose life is insured, and the "assured" is the beneficiary or person who is assured of a benefit payment. Likewise, in other types of insurance "insured" may refer to the property that is insured, and "assured" to the person who is assured of indemnity.

merchandise floater—a floater policy covering merchandise that changes in quantity, value, and/or location.

moral hazard—signifies the personal hazard in insurance. It refers to the financial circumstances of the insured, his habits, and his history. It concerns dishonesty, carelessness, "rapacity in claims", "willful neglect", "arson", etc.

open policy—a policy in which the value of the property insured is not fixed but left open, and must be proved in case of loss or damage. A type of open policy very generally used by shippers is one in which the property to be insured is left open—the shipper reporting his shipments periodically to the insurance company.

premium—the amount paid for an insurance policy; it is paid in advance, in one sum or in installments. (See also "premium", p. 515.)

public liability insurance—insures against damages from accidents suffered by members of the general public.

reinsurance—An insurance company, as a protection against possible large or "shock" losses under a policy, may reinsure its own risk (or a part of it) with another insurance company. The first company is called the "direct-writing company", the second the "reinsurer".

reporting policy
or
declaration policy
a policy written to cover moving stock or merchandise, the value of which fluctuates. Shipments or mailings are reported to the insurance company periodically, as daily or monthly, and at the end of the period the premium is determined.

riders—separate clauses or agreements (in printed form) attached to policies. Sometimes written endorsements are called "riders", and often printed riders are called "endorsements".

surety bond—given to guarantee the proper performance of certain acts on the part of another, such as the carrying out of a contract, execution of an instrument, honest handling of funds, etc.

title insurance—insures against loss by reason of a defective title to real estate; and may further insure a mortgagee against loss by reason of a mortgagor's nonpayment of principal and interest on a mortgage.

transportation insurance—covers loss to shippers by reason of accident to goods in transit.

underwriting—means literally "subscribing the name beneath", which in turn means that the underwriter guarantees whatever he "underwrites" or signs his name to. "Underwriting" in insurance involves the whole procedure of the business of making rates and accepting risks.

use and occupancy insurance—covers loss of net profits, and loss by reason of a proprietor's being obliged to pay fixed expenses, such as salaries, taxes, etc., when an establishment is shut down because of fire or other casualty.

valued policy—a policy in which the value of the property insured is fixed, and not left to appraisal and adjustment in case of total loss.

ITINERARY

Some travelers, on extended trips, carry itineraries or schedules of their journeys; others, on less complicated trips, do not. The railroads and airlines have itinerary forms (with very useful maps on the backs thereof) that are given, completely filled out, to prospective travelers along with their tickets. To such a prepared itinerary should be added the names of hotels at which reservations have been made, and any other necessary names and addresses. A separate schedule of appointments is often carried with this itinerary.

Copies of both the itinerary and the appointment schedule should be kept in the home office.

If an itinerary is prepared in an office—from the traveler's ticket and timetables—it is usually a combination of both the traveling and the appointment schedules, as follows:

ITINERARY—Seattle to Houston
For Mr. J. T. Davis, 1910 Smith Tower, Seattle 4, Wash.

Day	Date	Time	City	Via
Wed.	Feb. 22	PST 1:00 p.m.	Lv. Seattle	Southern Pacific Car 62, Lower 8
Thurs.	23	1:30 p.m.	Ar. San Francisco Res. Mark Hopkins Hotel	
		2:30 p.m.	Appt. Western Lumber Co. 1456 Monadnock Bldg. Phone—Douglas 5690	
Fri.	24	10:00 a.m. 12:00 noon 9:00 p.m.	Factory tour Club luncheon—Palace Hotel Lv. San Francisco	Southern Pacific Car 25, Lower 6
Sat.	25	9:00 a.m.	Ar. Los Angeles	

(And so on, with similar notations for the entire trip.)

An itinerary should be typed on strong, wear-resistant paper.

All folders containing papers to be used on the trip should be labeled to show the nature of the contents of each; and an extra folder containing supplies, such as letterheads, second pages, plain paper, carbon paper, envelopes, stamps, pencils, binders, clips or fasteners, etc., should be included if such material is likely to be needed.

An understanding should also be had regarding the forwarding of letters or copies thereof, the attending to business matters during the traveler's absence, and the sending of a periodic report of office happenings.

❖

533

ABBREVIATIONS

Use of Abbreviations. The nature of the manuscript governs the use of abbreviations.

Abbreviations are generally reserved for use in technical or scientific work, statistical writings, tabulations, and routine or informal work.

Very few abbreviations should be used in letters.

The month of the year should not be abbreviated in a letter, unless it occurs in a tabulation, or in a second-page heading.

The name of a state should not be abbreviated when standing alone in a letter. It may be abbreviated in an address on a letter, but it should be written out on the envelope. (See Envelopes, p. 324.)

The name of a city should never be abbreviated, unless it occurs in a tabulation, or in routine work.

Units of measurement should not be abbreviated unless they are preceded by numerals, or occur in headings.

Manuscripts to be printed should contain no abbreviations unless the abbreviations are to be printed as written, in which case the copy should be marked "Follow abbreviations".

Attempt to be consistent in the use of abbreviations. Do not abbreviate a word in one place in a manuscript and in another place write it out, when it is used similarly. Decide at the beginning of the paper which form is to be employed throughout.

Do not switch back and forth between two forms for the same abbreviation in the text of one manuscript, as between

    lb. and #   No. and #   sq. feet and sq.ft.

When using unusual abbreviations, give an explanation of them in footnotes, headings, or in parentheses the first time each is used.

Capitalization of Abbreviations. Do not capitalize abbreviations unless the word or words represented would ordinarily be capitalized, or unless the abbreviation itself has become established as a capital, as

    A. for acre   NE. for northeast

The capitalizing of any and every abbreviation gives too much importance to unimportant words.

Note that "p.m." and "a.m." are now commonly written in small letters.

Periods After Abbreviations. In ordinary writings, a period usually follows each part of an abbreviation that represents a single word. This aids in the quick interpretation of an abbreviation.

    f.o.b. RATHER THAN: fob.   i.e. NOT: *ie.*   a.m. NOT: *am.*

An abbreviation period is retained in a sentence, even though other marks of punctuation immediately follow it.

...from noon to 2:30 p.m.; from then until midnight.
Was the temperature recorded as 230° F.?

An abbreviation period at the end of a sentence serves also as a final period, unless the abbreviation is enclosed in parentheses.

It will reach a temperature of 230° F.
They are shipping fruits, etc.
That is their price to us (f.o.b.).

When Periods are not Used

Certain symbols and letters do not take periods.

Metric System. The official National Bureau of Standards abbreviations for the metric system are shown in the following list of abbreviations, and also in the tables of weights and measures herein.

The same form is used for both singular and plural.

Periods are not used.

Chemical Symbols. Do not take periods, as

H for hydrogen   O for oxygen   Au for gold

The symbols are used in chemical formulas, with inferior figures to show the number of parts (atoms) of each element in each compound, as

H_2O—water—2 parts of hydrogen to 1 part of oxygen
H_2SO_4—sulfuric acid—2 parts hydrogen, 1 part sulfur, and 4 parts oxygen
CO_2—carbon dioxide—1 part carbon to 2 parts of oxygen

Two compounds may be combined to form another compound, in which case an ordinary figure may be used to denote the number of parts (molecules) of either compound; and a period may separate the compounds, as

$$ZnSO_4.7H_2O$$

which means that zinc sulfate crystals are composed of zinc sulfate and 7 parts of water. No other periods are used in chemical formulas.

In routine work, the inferior figures are sometimes written as ordinary figures, as H2SO4, CO2, etc.; but this should not be done if there is the slightest danger of misinterpretation.

Contractions. Contractions, such as "Int'l", "Sam'l", etc., are not abbreviations, but simply contracted words like "don't" and "doesn't", and need a period no more than these words do. To place a period after a contraction is double punctuation.

Abbreviations, because of their compactness, are generally preferred to contractions; and also because it is considered that the apostrophe has enough work to do without being used promiscuously for contractions. Furthermore, in typewritten work, the ease of writing an abbreviation is to be preferred to the effort of using the shift key to write a contraction. Therefore:

Dept.		Dep't
Corp.	IS PREFERRED TO:	Corp'n
contd.		cont'd, etc.

1st, 2nd, 3rd, 4th, etc. Do not take periods. They are considered shortened forms rather than abbreviations.

Letters. Letters used as letters or as words do not take periods.

A to Z   IOU   SOS   A-1   an x and a y   a "b"
(Note that letters need not be quoted unless quotation marks are needed for emphasis or clarity.)

If a letter is chosen to designate someone or something, it does not require a period, as

Miss A   the B stock   JB type   C grade   Class A

But if a letter represents an actual name, it takes a period, as

Mr. G. for Mr. Glenn   J.B. for J. B. Towne, etc.

Radio Stations. No periods should follow the letter designations of radio stations, as

WABC   KPO   XEB   CFCF

But if a radio station's letters are the abbreviations of a real name, periods may be used, as

N.B.C. for National Broadcasting Company
C.B.S. for Columbia Broadcasting System

However, for uniformity with other station designations, the periods are often dispensed with, as

NBC   CBS

Diagonal Lines. Are properly used to signify the omission of words (the word "per" in technical abbreviations); and when so employed, no periods are necessary, as

| bbls/day   barrels per day | D/A   documents upon acceptance |
| B/L   bill of lading | A/P   authority to pay |

(The periods are sometimes retained in three- or four-word combinations, as "lb./sq.in.", although they may be omitted if the writer is dropping all periods, as "oz/sq yd", etc.)

Some writers use the diagonal line to divide any abbreviation of two words; but the line is more useful if reserved to indicate omitted words. Also, in typewriting, less effort is required to write periods than to shift the carriage down from capitals and back again to write the diagonal line; hence the desirability of restricting its use.

Technical Work. If abbreviations occur frequently in technical work, the periods are usually dropped. But in ordinary work, the periods are usually retained.

Temperatures	75° F	85° C	295° A	235° K	25° R
Shipping	SS	RR	fob	fas	cod	cif
Telegraph	CDE	DL	NL	NLT	SER
Military	GHQ	AWOL	USN	USA	USMC
Engineering	rpm	fbm	mph	bhp	kva

Percent. Although "percent" is the abbreviation of "per centum", it is now written as one word with no period. (U.S. Government usage.)

French Abbreviations. No period is used after French abbreviations if the last letter of the abbreviation is the last letter of the word, as

Mme for Madame   St for Saint   Cie for Compagnie

But if the last letter of the abbreviation is not the last letter of the word, the period is used, as

Fr. for francs   M. for Monsieur

⋅⋅▪▰▮═════════════▮▰▪⋅⋅

Spacing Abbreviations. Since one of the chief purposes of abbreviations is to save space, no spaces are left in most abbreviations containing periods.

Ph.D.   A.S.T.M.   at.wt.   cu.ft.

Abbreviations of state names may also be written without spaces, as

N.H.   N.Y.   Washington, D.C.   N.Mex.   W.Va.

But spaces are usually left between parts of abbreviated titles, unless an abbreviated title appears after a name.

Lt. Comdr. Roger Brooke   Paul Wayland, M.D.
Maj. Gen. Victor Grant   Spencer Winthrop, V.P.
Lt. Gov. Calvin Hughes   The Very Rev. Leo Camden, V.G.

A space is also left between initials, unless there are three initials; then the spaces are commonly omitted.

J. R. Park   J.M.E. Sutherland

Forming New Abbreviations. To form a new abbreviation, use only the first three letters of the word, as "sim." for "similar"; or use the three letters that will best represent the sound of the word, as "mfg." for "manufacturing".

If a word could have several endings, add the last letter to the simple abbreviation, as

rec. for receive   recd. for received
recr. for receiver   recg. for receiving

Attempt to limit all abbreviations to three or four letters. Longer abbreviations defeat the purpose of abbreviating.

If an unfamiliar two-word expression is to be abbreviated, use a three-letter abbreviation for each word, or at least a three-letter abbreviation for the first word, as

whs.stk. for warehouse stock   bal.s. for balance sheet

537

instead of the mere initial of each word; for it is sometimes difficult to remember what unfamiliar initials stand for.

If an abbreviation for a group of three or four words is desired, use the first letter of each important word, as

S.P.C.A. for Society for the Prevention of Cruelty to Animals

Small words are not usually represented in abbreviations, or else they are written in in full, as

A.F. of L. for American Federation of Labor
C. of S. for Chief of Staff

Plurals of Abbreviations. The plurals of most abbreviations are formed by simply adding -s.

gals.   yds.   bbls.   lbs.   Bs/L   Drs.   Cos.

Some are the same in both singular and plural, as

in. for inch or inches   mi. for mile or miles
deg. for degree or degrees   oz. for ounce or ounces

> **"The use of the same abbreviation for both singular and plural is recommended."**
>
> **—National Bureau of Standards, Circular 47, "Units of Weight and Measure", p. 12.**

Doubled single letters serve as the plurals of some abbreviations.

pp. for pages   JJ. for Justices   LL.D. for Doctor of Laws
pp. 220 ff. means page 220 and the following pages

Plurals of capitalized abbreviations may be formed by simply adding a small s. (An 's is hardly necessary, since the difference between the caps and the small letter is a sufficient division.)

C.P.A.s   Y.M.C.A.s   C.O.D.s   A.M.s   NLs   EMFs

Plurals of uncapitalized abbreviations may be formed by adding an 's.

p.m.'s and a.m.'s   Btu's   emf's   f.o.b.'s

Plurals of letters, signs, and symbols are usually formed by adding an 's; although capitalized letters, and some signs and symbols, may be pluralized by the addition of a simple s.

ABC's   IOU's   OK's   L's   the three R's   o's   s's $'s   ¢'s
or: ABCs   IOUs   Ls   OKs $s   ¢s

Possessives of Abbreviations. Are formed in the same manner as other possessives. If the abbreviation is **singular,** an 's is added—now usually outside the final period, in order to retain the original form of the abbreviation, and to keep all such possessives uniform. If the abbreviation is **plural** (ending in -s), only an apostrophe is added.

Since three clear forms are needed, the apostrophe is being largely reserved for possessives, and a simple s used for plurals wherever possible.

538

Singular Possessive	Plural	Plural Possessive
Jr.'s	Jrs.	Jrs.'
Dr.'s	Drs.	Drs.'
Co.'s	Cos.	Cos.'
Bro.'s	Bros.	Bros.'
R.R.'s	RRs.	RRs.'
M.D.'s	M.D.s	M.D.s'
C.P.A.'s	C.P.A.s	C.P.A.s'
SOS's	SOSs	SOSs'
B/L's (Bill of Lading's)	Bs/L (Bills of Lading)	Bs/L's (Bills of Lading's)

This method leaves company names undisturbed when possessives are added. Note that no comma follows "Inc." and "Ltd." when the possessive is employed.

Bell & Barnhart Co.'s prices
Barker Bros.' sale
Galt & Bro.'s window display
General Electric Supply Corp.'s report
Hamilton, Inc.'s statement
London Travel, Ltd.'s guide

Hyphens in Abbreviations. Hyphens may be used in abbreviations of hyphened words. If used, they may replace the periods that would otherwise be used.

ft-lb. for foot-pound   h-p.cyl. for high-pressure cylinder

Quoting Abbreviations. Do not quote abbreviations, unless they are slang, or unless the words abbreviated would be quoted if spelled out.

That will be OK.
He always used the title "Dr."
The workmanship looked "n.g." to us.
Prices seemed to have the "D.T.s".
He became T.R.'s close friend.

Letters or Abbreviations Used as Verbs. The -s, -d, or -ing is added with an apostrophe.

SOS'd   X'd out   OK'd   OK'ing   OK's (NOT: *O.K.-es*)
...if he "n.g.'s" it.
They are c.o.d.'ing the shipment.

Letters as Descriptive Words. When letters are being used as descriptive words, it is not necessary to spell them out. The simple letter is more readily understood, and therefore preferable.

T-rail   RATHER THAN: tee rail
T-shaped   tee-shaped
I-beam   eye beam
an L   an ell
It makes a V in the road.
It fits to a T.

"Tee" is used in derived constructions, as

golf tee   curling tee   wind tee or landing tee

Compass Points. Since the names of the compass points are practically all single or compound words, the abbreviations require only a final period.

N. north   NE. northeast   NNE. north-northeast
NbE. north by east   NEbE. northeast by east

In technical writings, and on compasses, the periods are not used, as

N   NbE   NNE   NEbN   NE   NEbE   ENE   EbN   E

Single Words. An older practice has been to cut into the abbreviations of various single words with a period, as

S.S.   R.R.   H.Q.   P.S.

evidently a holdover from the time they were two words.

The newer and more logical practice is to write solid abbreviations of all solid words, as

SS.   RR.   Hq.   PS.

This method is followed herein.

Degree Letters. The three academic degrees, in the order in which they are earned or conferred, are:

B. Bachelor   AS: B.S. Bachelor of Science
M. Master   M.S. Master of Science
D. Doctor   D.S. Doctor of Science

Various letters are combined with each of these three degree letters to signify the particular branch of learning in which the degree was earned or awarded.

B.S. in Ae.E.   Bachelor of Science in Aeronautical Engineering.
B.A. in Ed.   Bachelor of Arts in Education.
A.B. in B. & B.   Bachelor of Arts in Business Administration and Banking.
M.S. in Arch.E.   Master of Science in Architectural Engineering.

Since the combinations are unlimited—the number of degrees having increased very rapidly in recent years—only the ordinary degrees are given in the list of abbreviations herein.

Note that the letters are often reversed, as

A.B. for Bachelor of Arts
Sc.D. for Doctor of Science
S.T.P. for Professor of Sacred Theology, etc.

Other letters that are often seen in combinations after names are:

A. Associate   an associate member of an institution; or a person who has
                completed a course shorter than the ordinary degree course.
F. Fellow   a member of an incorporated academic society or institution; or a
             graduate elected to a fellowship.
G. Graduate   one who has completed a prescribed course of study.
L. { Licentiate   one licensed to practise a profession.
     { Lector   a reader, or lecturer.

Letters signifying college degrees, fellowships, etc., are used chiefly in published works and in formal writings. They are not commonly used in letters and other commercial papers. (See Degree Letters. p. 301.)

ABBREVIATIONS

A

a   are (metric)
@   at; to
A   angstrom unit (of light)
A.   Army; acre; absolute (temperature); answer (in court writings)
A-1   first-class
A.A.   Associate in Arts
AAA   Agricultural Adjustment Administration
AAA.   Alaska (officially spelled out); sometimes **Alas.**
A.A.A.   American Automobile Association
A.A.A.S.   American Association for the Advancement of Science
A.A.S.   Fellow of the American Academy (Academiae Americanae Socius)
A.A.U.   Amateur Athletic Union
ab.   about; absent
A.B.   Bachelor of Arts (Am.); **B.A.** (Br.)
A.B.A.   American Bankers Association; American Bar Association
abbr.   abbreviation; abbreviated
ab ex.   from without (L. ab extra)
ab init.   from the beginning (L. ab initio)
abr.   abridged; abridgment
abs.   absolute; abstract; absent
Abs., A.   absolute (temperature)
abs.re.   the defendant being absent (L. absente reo)
abst.   abstract
abt., ab.   about
a.c.   alternating current (elec.); **a-c.** (adj.)
A.C.   Air Corps; account current
a/c, acct.   account
accum.   accumulative
acre-ft.   acre-foot
act.   active
Actg.   Acting [officer]
ad   advertisement (pl. ads) (usually written without period)
a.d.   before the day (L. ante diem)
A.D.   in the year of our Lord (L. anno Domini) (A.D. does not mean "after death" as it is often interpreted; it is written before the year, with no separating comma, as "A.D. 1920"; or it may appear after the year, as "about 1450 A.D.")
A-D-C.   Aide-de-Camp
add., addl.   additional
ad fin.   to the end (L. ad finem)
ad h.l., a.h.l.   at this place (L. ad hunc locum)
ad inf.   to infinity (L. ad infinitum)
ad init.   at the beginning (L. ad initium)
ad int., a.i.   in the meantime (L. ad interim)
adj.   adjective; adjustment (bonds)
Adj.   Adjutant
Adj.Gen., A.G.   Adjutant General
ad lib.   at pleasure (L. ad libitum)
ad loc.   at the place (L. ad locum)
Adm.   Admiral, -ty; administration, -tive
Admr.   Administrator
Admx.   Administratrix
adrm.   airdrome
ads.   address
ad us.   according to custom (L. ad usum)
adv.   adverb

ad val., adv., a/v   according to the value (L. ad valorem)
adv.chgs.   advance charges
advt., ad   advertisement
advtg.   advertising
ae., aet.   aged; of age (L. aetatis)
A.E.   Agricultural Engineer
A.E.F.   American Expeditionary Forces
a.f.   audio frequency; **a-f.** (adj.)
Af., Afr.   African; Africa
aff.   affirmative
AFL, A.F. of L.   American Federation of Labor
A.G., Adj.Gen.   Adjutant General
agcy., agy.   agency
agr., ag., agri.   agriculture; agricultural
agt.   agent; against; agreement
a.i.   (See ad int.)
A.I.   American Institute
A.I.B.   American Institute of Banking
A.I.E.E.   American Institute of Electrical Engineers
aj., adj.   adjustment (bonds)
Ala.   Alabama (official)
A.L.A.   American Library Association
Alas.   Alaska (officially spelled out); commonly **AAA.**
alt.   altitude; alternate
Alta.   Alberta, Canada
Am.   American; America
a.m.   before noon (L. ante meridiem)
A.M.   in the year of the world (L. anno mundi); Master of Arts (Am.); **M.A.** (Br.)
A.M.A.   American Medical Association
Amb.   Ambassador
amp.   ampere (elec.)
amp-hr.   ampere-hour (elec.)
amt.   amount
A.N.   arrival notice (shipping)
anal.   analysis; analytic; analogy
anon.   anonymous
ANPA   American Newspaper Publishers Association
ans.   answer; **A.** in court writings
antilog   antilogarithm (math.)
ap.   according to (L. apud); apothecaries'; approximately; airplane
a.p.   additional premium
AP   Associated Press
A.P.   accounts payable
A/P   authority to pay or purchase
A.P.I.   American Petroleum Institute
app.   appendix; appointed; apparatus
approx., ap.   approximately
Apr.   April (usually spelled out)
Apt.   Apartment
aq.   water (L. aqua); aqueous
ar.   arrive
Ar.   Arabian; Arabic; Arabia
A.R.   Army Regulations; accounts receivable; all risks (ins.)
A.R.A.   Associate of the Royal Academy; American Railway Association
A.R.A.M.   Associate of the Royal Academy of Music
A.R.C., ARC   American National Red Cross
arch.   architect; architecture
Arch.E.   Architectural Engineer

541

A.R.I.B.A. Associate of the Royal Institute of British Architects
Ariz. Arizona (official)
Ark. Arkansas (official)
arr. arranged
art. article (pl. arts.); artist
as., asst., ast. assented (securities)
A.S. Academy of Science; Apprentice Seaman; account sales
ASA American Standards Association
A.Sc. Associate in Science (Br.)
A.S.C.E. American Society of Civil Engineers
asd. assumed
asgd. assigned
asgmt. assignment
ash. airship
Asle., A.S. account sales
A.S.M.E. The American Society of Mechanical Engineers
asmt. assortment; assessment
assd. assessed; assigned
Assn. Association
asso., assoc. associate; associated
asst., ast. assented; assessment
Asst. Assistant
astd. assorted
A.S.T.M. American Society for Testing Materials
astr. astronomy; astronomical
AT American terms (grain)
Atl. Atlantic
atm. atmosphere; atmospheric
att. attached
Attn., Atten. Attention
Atty. Attorney
Atty.Gen. Attorney General
at.wt. atomic weight
au. author
Aug. August
AUS Army of the United States (p. 323)
Austral. Australian; Australia
aux. auxiliary
av., avdp. avoirdupois
a/v (See ad val.)
Ave. Avenue
avg. average
avn. aviation
A.W.G., AWG American wire gauge
AWOL absent without leave (military)

B

b. base; bay; bond; battery; born
b7d, b10d, b15d buyer 7 days to take up, etc. (stock market)
B., Bé., Be. Baumé (hydrometer)
B.A. Bachelor of Arts (Br.); **A.B.** (Am.); British Academy; British Association [for the Advancement of Science]
bal. balance
bar. barometer; barometric
bat., b. battery
bbl. barrel (pl. bbls.)
bbls/day, b/d barrels per day (See b.p.d.)
B.C. British Columbia, Canada; before Christ (written after the year, with no separating comma, as "80 B.C.")
bchs. bunches
bd. board; bond; bound
bd.ft. board foot or feet (See f.b.m.)
bdl. bundle (pl. bdls.)
bd.rts. bond rights (securities)
bds. [bound in] boards (bookbinding)

Bé., Be., B. Baumé (hydrometer)
Benj. Benjamin
bet. between
b.f., brt.fwd. brought forward
bg. bag (pl. bgs.)
Bhn Brinell hardness number (metals)
b.hp., bhp brake horsepower
bk. bank; book (pl. bks.)
bkg. banking
bkt., bsk. basket
bl. bale (pl. bls.); block
B/L, b/l bill of lading (pl. Bs/L, bs/l)
B/L Att. bill of lading attached
Bldg. Building
bldr. builder
blk. block; bulk
B.L.S. Bachelor of Library Science
Blvd. Boulevard
b.o. buyer's option; back order
B.O. branch office
Boh. Bohemian
Bor. Borough
B.O.T. Board of Trade
b.p., bp boiling point; boiler pressure
B.P., b.p., b.pay. bills payable
b.p.d., bpd, b/d, bbls/day barrels per day
B.Pd. Bachelor of Pedagogy
br. branch
Br. British
B.R., b.r., b.rec. bills receivable
Brig. Gen. Brigadier General
Bro. brother (pl. Bros.)
brt.fwd., b.f. brought forward
B.S. Bachelor of Science; balance sheet
B. & S., B&S Brown and Sharpe wire gauge
bsk., bkt. basket
B.S. & W. basic sediment and water [deductions from crude oil]
bt. bought; boat
btl. bottle (pl. btls.)
B.t.u., Btu British thermal unit (pl. B.t.u., Btu, B.t.u.'s, or Btu's)
bu. bushel (pl. bu. or bus.)
bul., bull. bulletin
Bur. Bureau
bus. business; bushels
b.v. book value
B.W.G., BWG Birmingham wire gauge
B.W.I. British West Indies
bx., x box (pl. bxs.)

C

c carat (metric); cycle (elec.); candle
c. coupon; cent; cash; cost; carat; chapter
c., ca. about (L. circa)
C 100 (L. centum); gallon, apothecaries' (L. Congius)
C. Centigrade; Congress
©, Copr. copyright
ca centare (metric)
C.A. Chief Accountant; capital, credit, or current account; Central America
CAA Civil Aeronautics Administration
CAB Civil Aeronautics Board
c.a.f., caf cost and freight
cal. small calorie (See g-cal. and kg-cal.); calendar; caliber
Calif. California (official); sometimes **Cal.**
Can. Canadian; Canada
canc. canceled; cancellation
Cantab. of Cambridge University (L. Cantabrigiensis)

cap. capital
caps capital letters
Capt. Captain
car., c. carat (metric carat, c)
Cash. Cashier
'at. catalogue
c.b. currency bond
C.B. Companion of the Bath (Br.); Cape Breton Island
C.B.S., CBS Columbia Broadcasting System
c.c., cc., cc older form of abbreviation for cubic centimeter (official [NBS] abbreviation, cm^3); carbon copy
CCC Civilian Conservation Corps; Commodity Credit Corporation
cd. cord
CDE code (cables)
cd.ft. cord foot or feet
c.e. at buyer's risk (L. caveat emptor)
C.E. Civil Engineer; Canada East
cen. center; central; century
Cen.Am., C.A. Central America
cert., ct., ctf. certificate, -tion; certified
cf. compare (L. confer); certificate
c. & f. cost and freight
C.F.C. Consolidated Freight Classification
c.f.s., cfs cubic feet per second
cg centigram (metric)
c.g. center of gravity
C.G. Consul General; Commanding General; Coast Guard
C.G.S., c.g.s., c-g-s., cgs centimeter-gram-second [system]
ch. chain (pl. chs.); choice; chests; check
Ch. Chinese; China; Chaplain; Church
CH. Customhouse; Courthouse
c.h. candle hours
C.H. Clearing House
chap., ch. chapter (pl. chaps. or chs.)
Chas. Charles
Ch.Clk. Chief Clerk
Ch.E., Chem.E. Chemical Engineer
chem. chemical; chemistry
chf. chief
chg. charge (pl. chgs.)
chge. change
Chin., Ch. Chinese
Chm. Chairman
chron. chronological
Cía. company (Sp. Compañía)
Cie company (Fr. Compagnie)
c.i.f. cost, insurance, and freight
C.I.O., CIO Congress of Industrial Organizations
cir. circular; circumference
cir. mils, c.m. circular mils (wire measure)
cit. citation; citizen
civ. civil; civilian
ck. cask; check (pl. cks.)
cl centiliter (metric)
cl. class, -ification; carload; clause
cld. colored; cleared; called (bonds)
clk. clerk
clr. color
clt collateral trust (bonds)
cm centimeter (metric)
cm^2 square centimeter
cm^3 cubic centimeter (For liquids, milliliter, ml)
c.m., cir.mils circular mils (wire measure)
cml. commercial; chemical (Army)
cm.pf. cumulative preferred (stocks)

C.M.T.C. Citizens' Military Training Camp
cn. consolidated (bonds)
CN compass north
C.N., c.n. cover note (ins.)
c/o, % care of
C.O. Commanding Officer; cash order
Co. Company; County (pl. Cos.)
c.o.d. certificates of deposit (securities)
C.O.D., c.o.d. collect·or cash on delivery
coef. coefficient (math.)
C. of C. Chamber of Commerce
C. of S. Chief of Staff
col. column; colony
Col. Colonel; College
coll. collection; collateral
colloq. colloquial
coll.tr., clt collateral trust (bonds)
Colo. Colorado (official); sometimes Col.
colog cologarithm (math.)
com. commerce; commission; committee common; communication
Comdr. Commander
Comdg. Commanding
Comdt. Commandant
coml., cml. commercial
Commo. Commodore
con., cons., consol. consolidated
Con. Consul
conc. concentrate
cond. conductivity (elec.)
Cong., C. Congress
Conn. Connecticut (official); often Ct.
cons. consolidated; consigned; consignment
const. constant; construction
cont. contract; contents; continent
contd., cont. continued
contl. continental
conv. convertible (See cv.)
co-op co-operative
Copr., © copyright
cor. corner; correct, -ed
Corp. Corporation; Corporal (now Cpl.)
corr. corrected; corresponding, -ence
Cor.Sec. Corresponding Secretary
cos cosine (trigonometry)
cp. compare; coupon; candlepower
CP Central Press; Canadian Press (news)
c.p., cp chemically pure; center of pressure
C.P.A. Certified Public Accountant
Cpl. Corporal
cpn., cp. coupon
C.P.O. Chief Petty Officer (Navy)
cp.off coupon off (bonds)
cp.on coupon on (bonds)
cr. credit; creditor (pl. crs.)
C.R., c.r. company's risk (ins.)
crt. crate (pl. crts.)
cs centistere (metric)
cs. cases
CSB Central Statistical Board
csc cosecant (trigonometry)
csk., ck. cask
C.S.T. Central standard time
ct. cent; count; certificate (pl. cts.)
Ct. Connecticut (Conn., official); Court
C.T. Central time
C.T.A. with the will annexed (L. cum testamento annexo)
ctf., ct., cf. certificate (pl. ctfs.)
ctg. cartage
ctn cotangent (trigonometry)
ctn. carton

c. to c.   center to center
ct.stp.   certificate stamped (securities)
cu.   cubic; cumulus (clouds)
cu.ft., ft³   cubic foot or feet
cu.in., in³   cubic inch or inches
cum.   cumulative
cum   with (L.)
cum d., cum div.   with dividend (L. cum dividendo)
cum.pref., cu.pf.   cumulative preferred (stocks)
cur.   current; currency
cu.yd.   cubic yard or yards
cv., cvt.   convertible (securities)
cv.db.   convertible debentures (securities)
cv.pf.   convertible preferred (securities)
C.W.   Canada West
C.W.O.   Chief Warrant Officer (military)
cwt.   hundredweight (c for centum [100] and wt. for weight)
cy.   currency; copy
cyl.   cylinder
C.Z.   Canal Zone (officially spelled out)

D

d.   date; died; dose; density; distance; penny (L. denarius); pence
D.   Democrat; diameter
D/A   documents upon acceptance [of draft]
dal   (See dkl)
Dan., Da.   Danish
Dan'l   Daniel
db   decibel (unit of sound)
D.B.N.   of the goods not [yet administered] (L. de bonis non)
db.rts.   debenture rights (securities)
d.c.   direct current (elec.); d-c. (adj.)
D.C.   District of Columbia
dcg   (See dkg)
dcl   (See dkl)
D.C.L. ·   Doctor of Civil Law
dcm   (See dkm)
D.Cn.L.   Doctor of Canon Law
dd.   delivered
D.D.   Doctor of Divinity (honorary); delayed delivery
d.d. in d.   from day to day (L. de die in diem)
D.D.S.   Doctor of Dental Surgery
D.D.Sc.   Doctor of Dental Science
D.E., D.Eng.   Doctor of Engineering
deb.   debenture
dec.   decrease; deceased
Dec.   December
def.   defense; definition; deferred (securities)
deg., °   degree or degrees
D.E.I.   Dutch East Indies
del.   deliver; delegate; he, or she, drew it (L. delineavit)
Del.   Delaware (official)
Dem., D.   Democrat
dep.   deposit; deputy; depot
dep.ctfs.   deposit certificates (securities)
Dept.   Department (pl. Depts.)
der.   derived
det.   detached; detachment
dev.   deviation
D.F.   Distrito Federal (Mexico City is now a Federal District, like Washington, D.C.)
dft.   draft

Dft.   Defendant
dg   decigram (metric)
D.G.   by the grace of God (L. Dei gratia)
DH.   deadhead (freight)
DHQ   Division Headquarters (Army)
dia., diam., D.   diameter
diag.   diagram
dict.   dictionary
Dir.   Director
dis.   discount; discharge
disch.   discharge
dist.   district; distance; distributed, -tion, -tor
dit   called (Fr., said)
div.   dividend; division
D.J.S.   Doctor of Juridical Science (Science of Law) (See J.S.D.)
dk.   dock; deck
dkg   dekagram (metric)
dkl   dekaliter (metric)
dkm   dekameter (metric); dkm²; dkm³
dks   dekastere (metric)
dl   deciliter (metric)
DL   day letter
dld.   delivered
D.Lit., D.Litt.   Doctor of Literature or Letters
dls/shr   dollars per share
dlvy., dly., dy.   delivery
dm   decimeter (metric)
dm²   square decimeter
dm³   cubic decimeter
D.M.D.   Doctor of Dental Medicine
D.Mus., D.M.   Doctor of Music
do.   ditto (It., the same)
D.O.   Doctor of Osteopathy; delivery order
doc.   document
dol., dl.   dollar (pl. dols. or dls.)
dom.   domestic; dominion
doz.   dozen
D/P   documents upon payment [of draft]
D.P.H.   Doctor of Public Health
D.P.Hy.   Doctor of Public Hygiene
D.Q.   direct question
dr.   dram; drum; debtor; debit (pl. drs.)
Dr.   doctor (pl. Drs.); Drive
dram.pers.   characters of a play (L. dramatis personae)
dr.ap., ℥   dram apothecaries'
dr.av.   dram avoirdupois
D.R.E.   Doctor of Religious Education
ds   decistere (metric)
D.Sc., D.S.   Doctor of Science
D.S.C.   Distinguished Service Cross
D.S.M.   Distinguished Service Medal
D.S.O.   Distinguished Service Order (Br.)
d.s.p.   died without issue (L. decessit sine prole)
D.S.T.   Doctor of Sacred Theology; daylight saving time
dstn.   destination
D.T.   daylight time
Du.   Dutch
D.V.   God willing (L. Deo volente)
D.V.M.   Doctor of Veterinary Medicine
D.W.   dock warrant
dwt.   pennyweight (d for penny, and wt. for weight)
d.w.t.f.   daily and weekly till forbidden (advtg.)
dy   penny (as 10dy nails)
dy.   delivery
D.Z.   Doctor of Zoology

E

e erg
E. East; Engineer, -ing; English
ea. each
EB eastbound
ECA Economic Cooperation Adm.
Ed. Editor; Edition (pl. Eds.); Education
Ed.D. Doctor of Education
E.D.T., EDT Eastern daylight time
educ. educated; education, -al
Edw. Edward
E.E. Electrical Engineer
E.E. & M.P. Envoy Extraordinary and Minister Plenipotentiary
eff. efficiency
e.g. for example (L. exempli gratia)
E.I. East Indies; East Indian
el. elevation
elec. electric, -al, -ian, -ity
E.long. east longitude
E.M. Engineer of Mines (Mining Engineer)
e.m.f., emf, E.M.F. electromotive force (pl. e.m.f.'s, e.m.fs., emf's, E.M.F.s)
enc. enclosure or enclosures
end. endorsed; endorsement
ENE. east-northeast
Eng. English; England; Engineer, -ing
Engg. Engineering
Engr. Engineer; Engraver, -ing
Ens. Ensign
entd. entered
Env.Ext. Envoy Extraordinary
e.o.d. every other day (advtg.)
E. & O.E. errors and omissions excepted
e.o.m. end of month
e.p., ep end point (distillation)
eps envelopes
eq. equal; equivalent; equalize; equipment; equation
eq.tr. equipment trust (bonds)
ESE. east-southeast
esp. especially
Esq. Esquire (pl. Esqs.)
est. established, -ment; estimate; estate
E.S.T., EST Eastern standard time
E.T., ET Eastern time
ETA estimated time of arrival
et al and others (L. et alii)
etc., &c and so forth (L. et cetera)
et seq., seq., sq. and the following (L. et sequens) (pls. et seqq., seqq., sqq.)
et ux and wife (L. et uxor)
et vir and husband (L.)
Eur. European; Europe
ex out of, or from, as: ex dock, ex car, ex elevator, ex warehouse, ex store
ex without, or not including, as: ex coupon, ex dividend, ex interest, ex privileges, ex rights, ex warrant (See x)
ex. example; exchange; exchange rate; exception; extra; executive
exam. examined; examination
exc., exch. exchange
Exec. Executive
ex.fcy. extra fancy
exp. express; expense; export; expiration
Exr. Executor
Exrx. Executrix

ext. exterior; extended; extension; extract; external; extinct
exx. examples

F

f farad
f. and the following [page] (pl. ff.); folio (or f°); feminine; female
F., Fahr. Fahrenheit
f.a.a. free of all average (ins.)
F.A.A.A.S. Fellow of the American Association for the Advancement of Science
F.A.C.S. Fellow of the American College of Surgeons
F.A.G.S. Fellow of the American Geographical Society
F.A.I.A. Fellow of the American Institute of Architects
f.a.s. free alongside ship
fath., fm. fathom
FBI Federal Bureau of Investigation
f.b.m., fbm feet board measure
FCA Farm Credit Administration
FCC Federal Communications Commission
fcp. foolscap
f.c. & s. free of capture and seizure (ins.)
fcy.pks. fancy packs
fd. fund; funding
fdg. funding (bonds)
FDIC Federal Deposit Insurance Corporation
Feb. February
fec. he, or she, made it (L. fecit)
Fed. Federal; Federated; Federation
fem., f. feminine
ff. and the following [pages]; folios
FHA Federal Housing Administration
Fid. Fidelity; Fiduciary
fig. figure (pl. figs.)
fin. financial; finance
Fin.Sec. Financial Secretary
first 1st (no period)
first class A-1, 1 cl., 1C, 1c
fl. fluid; floor
Fla. Florida (official)
fl.dr., f $\mathfrak{z}$ fluid dram, apothecaries'
fl.oz., f $\mathfrak{z}$ fluid ounce, apothecaries'
Flt. fleet; flight; filing time
flts., fts. flats
fm. fathom; from
FM, f.m. frequency modulation (radio)
fn.p., fnp fusion point
fo., f°, fol., f. folio (pl. ff.)
F.O. Foreign Office
f.o.b. free on board
fol. folio; follow, -ing
for. foreign; forestry
fourth 4th (no period)
f.p., fp freezing point
f.p.a. free of particular average (ins.)
FPC Federal Power Commission
f.pd. full paid
f.p.m., fpm, f/m feet per minute
f.p.s., fps, f/s feet per second
F.P.S., f.p.s., f-p-s., fps foot-pound-second [system]
fr. from
Fr. French; France; francs; Father (Catholic); Frau (Ger., Mrs.)
F.R., FR, FRS Federal Reserve System
FRB Federal Reserve Board or Bank

F.R.C.P. Fellow of the Royal College of Physicians
F.R.C.S. Fellow of the Royal College of Surgeons
F R.G.S. Fellow of the Royal Geographical Society
Fri. Friday; F. in tabulations
F.R.I.B.A. Fellow of the Royal Institute of British Architects
Frl. Fräulein (Ger., Miss)
F.R.S. Fellow of the Royal Society
frt. freight
Ft. Fort
ft. foot or feet
ft², sq.ft. square foot or feet
ft³, cu.ft. cubic foot or feet
FTC Federal Trade Commission
ft-c foot-candle
ft-L foot-lambert
ft-lb. foot-pound
ft/s, fps feet per second
ft-sec. foot-second
ft-tn. foot-ton
fur. furlong
furn. furnished; furniture
fut. futures (exchange)
fwd. forward
FX foreign exchange

G

g gram (metric)
g. gold; gauge; gulf; gravity
g.a. general average (ins.)
Ga. Georgia (official)
G.A., GA General Agent; General Assembly
gal. gallon (pl. gals.)
G.B. Great Britain
g-cal. gram-calorie (small calorie)
GCD, gcd greatest common divisor
GCT, G.C.T. Greenwich civil time
gen. general; generator; genus or kind
Gen. General
Geo. George
geog. geography, -ic, -ical, -er
geol. geology, -ic, -ical, -ist
Ger. German; Germany
g.gr. great gross (144 dozen)
GHQ General Headquarters (Army)
gi. gill or gills
GI Government Issue (Army) (pl. GIs)
gm general mortgage (bonds)
gm. old abbreviation for gram (See g)
G.m.b.H. company or corporation with limited liability (Ger. Gesellschaft mit beschränkter Haftung)
G.M.T., GMT Greenwich mean time
gn., gen. general
G.N. Graduate Nurse
GNT Government land grant (bonds)
G.O., GO general orders
G.O.P. Grand Old Party (Republican)
Gov. Governor
govt. government
G.P. Graduate in Pharmacy
g.p.d., gpd, g/d gallons per day
g.p.m., gpm, g/m gallons per minute, or mile
g.p.s., gps, g/s gallons per second
gr. gross; grade; grain (spelled out for weight); gravity
Gr. Greek; Greece; Grecian
grad. graduate; graduated

grain spelled out (for weight)
gr.wt. gross weight
g.s. ground speed (aviation)
gt. drop (L. gutta) (pl. gtt.)
GTC good till canceled (brokerage order)
gtd. guaranteed
gu., guar. guarantee; guaranteed

H

h henry (elec.); hours, as 12ʰ or 12h
ha hectare (metric)
h.a. this year (L. hoc anno)
Hawaii officially spelled out; sometimes T.H.
hdbk. handbook
hdwe. hardware
hf. half
h-f.c. high-frequency current
hg hectogram (metric)
hhd. hogshead
H.I. Hawaiian Islands
hist. history, -ical, -ian
hl hectoliter (metric)
hm hectometer (metric); hm²; hm³
H.M.S. His, or Her, Majesty's Ship, or Service
HOLC Home Owners' Loan Corporation
Hon. Honorable
hp., hp, HP horsepower
h.p. high pressure; h-p. (adj.)
h-p.cyl. high-pressure cylinder
hp-hr. horsepower-hour
Hq. Headquarters
hr. hour (pl. hrs.)
H.R. House of Representatives
H.R.H. His, or Her, Royal Highness
H.S.S. Fellow of the Historical Society (L. Historiae Societatis Socius)
ht. height; heat; Hts. Heights
h.t. in, or under, this title (L. hoc titulo); at this time (L. hoc tempore)
HT Hawaiian time
hund., C hundred (hundredweight cwt.)
Hung. Hungarian; Hungary
Hwy., Hy. Highway

I

I. Island(s); Isle(s)
Ia. Iowa (officially spelled out)
ib., ibid. in the same place (L. ibidem)
i.b.p., ibp initial boiling point
i.bu. imperial bushel
I.C.C., ICC Interstate Commerce Commission
id. the same (L. idem)
i.d., ID inside diameter
Ida. Idaho (officially spelled out)
i.e. that is (L. id est)
I.E.S. Illuminating Engineering Society
i.gal. imperial gallon
ign. unknown (L. ignotus); ignition
i.hp., ihp, IHP indicated horsepower
IHS monogram for the Greek word for Jesus
ill., illus. illustration; illustrated
Ill. Illinois (official)
imp. improvement; implement; imperial; import, -ing, -ed, -er
in. inch or inches; income
in², sq.in. square inch or inches
in³, cu.in. cubic inch or inches
Inc. Incorporated

incl.   inclusive (For "enclosure", see enc.)
incog. in secret; unknown (It. incognito); unofficially
ind.   industrial; industry; independent
Ind.   Indiana (official); Indian; India
Ind.E. Industrial Engineer
inf.   inferior; below (L. infra)
init.   initial
in-lb. inch-pound
in lim. at the outset (L. in limine)
in loc. in the proper place (L. in loco)
INP   International News Photos
INS   International News Service
ins.   insurance; inspector
inst.   instant (present month); instrument; installment
Inst.   Institute; Institution
int.   interest; interior; international; interstate; internal; intermediate
Intl.   International
inv.   invoice; investment; inventor, -tion
invt.   investment; inventory
IOU   I owe you (no periods)
Iowa   officially spelled out; sometimes Ia.
i.p.   intermediate pressure; i-p. (adj.)
i.p.s., ips   inches per second
i.q.   the same as (L. idem quod)
I.Q.   intelligence quotient
Ir.   Irish
I.R.   Internal Revenue
Ire.   Ireland
is., isl.   island (pl. is. or isls.)
iss.   issue
It.   Italian; Italy
I.W.W.   Industrial Workers of the World

J

j   joule (elec.)
J.   Judge; Justice (pl. JJ.)
J.A.   Judge Advocate
Jan.   January
Jap.   Japanese; Japan
Jas.   James
J.C.D.   Doctor of Canon or Civil Law (L. Juris Canonici Doctor, or Juris Civilis Doctor)
J.C.L.   Licentiate in Canon Law (L. Juris Canonici Licentiatus)
J.D.   Doctor of Laws (L. Jurum Doctor)
JJ.   Justices
Jno.   John
jnt.stk.   joint stock
Jos.   Joseph
J.P.   Justice of the Peace
Jr.   Junior (pl. Jrs.); journal
J.S.D.   Doctor of Juristic Science (Law)
jt.   joint
J.U.D.   Doctor of both Canon and Civil Laws (L. Juris Utriusque Doctor)
J.U.L.   Licentiate in both Canon and Civil Laws (L. Juris Utriusque Licentiatus)
July   spelled out; Jul. in tabulations
junc.   junction
June   spelled out; Jun. in tabulations

K

k.   knot
K   karat (gold measure)
K.   Kelvin (absolute scale of temperature)
Kans.   Kansas (official); sometimes Kan.
kc   kilocycle (radio)

K.C.   King's Counsel (Br.)
K.C.B.   Knight Commander of the Bath (Br.)
K.D.   knocked down (freight)
kg   kilogram (metric)
kg.   keg or kegs
K.G.   Knight of the Garter (Br.)
kg-cal.   kilogram-calorie or kilocalorie (large calorie); sometimes Cal.
K.G.F.   Knight of the Golden Fleece (Austrian and Spanish)
kg-m   kilogram-meter
kg/m^3 kilograms per cubic meter
kg/s, kgps   kilograms per second
K.K.K.   Ku Klux Klan
kl   kiloliter (metric)
K.L.H.   Knight of the Legion of Honor (Fr.)
km   kilometer (metric)
km^2 square kilometer
km^3 cubic kilometer
km/s, kmps   kilometers per second
K.O.   keep off (bad risk, ins.)
Kr.   krone (a foreign coin)
Kt.   Knight Bachelor (Br.)
kv   kilovolt
kv-a, kva   kilovolt-ampere
kvar   kilovar (reactive kilovolt-ampere)
kvarh   kilovarhour (reactive kilovolt-ampere-hour)
kw   kilowatt
kw-hr., kwh   kilowatt-hour
Ky.   Kentucky (official)

L

1   liter (metric); lumen (unit of light)
l.   line; left; league; leaf; length
L   listed (securities); lire (Italian money); elevated railway; lambert (unit of brightness)
L.   Latin; law; ledger
£   pound sterling (L. libra)
la., lge.   large
La.   Louisiana (official)
L.A.   Literate in Arts
lab.   laboratory; labor
lang.   language
lat.   latitude
lb.   pound (L. libra) (pl. lbs.)
lb.ap., lb   pound, apothecaries'
lb.av.   pound, avoirdupois
lb/ft^2 pounds per square foot
lb-in.   pound-inch
lb/in^2 pounds per square inch
lbr.   lumber
lb.t.   pound, troy
l.c., loc.cit.   in the place cited (L. loco citato)
LC   deferred cable (letter cable)
L/C   letter of credit (pl. Ls/C)
L.C.L., LCL   less than carload lots (pl. L.C.L.s or LCLs)
LCM, lcm   least common multiple
L.D.S.   Licentiate in Dental Surgery
lea.   league
Leg.   Legislature
l-f.c.   low-frequency current
lge., la.   large
l.h.   left hand
L.H.D.   Doctor of the Humanities, or Doctor of Humane Letters (L. Litterarum Humaniorum Doctor)
l-hr.   lumen-hour

547

ABBREVIATIONS

li.   link
L.I.   Long Island
lib.   library; book (L. liber)
Lic.   Licenciado (Sp., attorney)
Lieut., Lt.   Lieutenant
Lieut. (jg), Lt. (jg)   Lieutenant (junior grade) (Navy)
lin.   linear; lin.ft.   linear foot
liq.   liquid
lit.   literature; literally
lter   spelled out (a metric unit)
Litt.D.   Doctor of Letters (L. Litterarum Doctor)
ll.   lines; leaves
l.l.   in the place quoted (L. loco laudato); leased line (railroad)
L.L.A.   Lady Literate in Arts
LL.D.   Doctor of Laws (often honorary)
ln.   lien; loan
loc.   location; local
loc.cit.   in the place cited (L. loco citato)
log   logarithm (common)
log_e, ln   logarithm (natural)
long.   longitude
l.p.   low pressure; 1-p. (adj.)
l.s.   left side
L.S.   place of the seal (L. locus sigilli)
£ s. d.   pounds, shillings, pence
lsd.li., l.l.   leased line (railroad)
lt.   light
Lt., Lieut.   Lieutenant
Lt. Col.   Lieutenant Colonel
Lt. Comdr.   Lieutenant Commander
Ltd.   limited [liability] (not *Lt'd.*)
Lt. Gen.   Lieutenant General
Lt. Gov.   Lieutenant Governor
Lt. (jg)   Lieutenant (junior grade) (Navy)
l.tn.   long ton
lv.   leave
l/w, lpw   lumens per watt

M

m   meter (metric); minutes, as 10^m or 10m
m²   square meter
m³   cubic meter
m.   mass; mile; noon (L. meridies)
M   1000 (L. mille); **2M, 3M,** etc., are used in commercial work, rather than the Roman numerals MM, MMM, etc.
m, m, **min.**   minim or drop, apothecaries'
M.   Monsieur (Fr., Mr.) (pl. MM. or Messrs.—Messieurs); Master
ma   milliampere (elec.)
M.A.   Master of Arts (Br.); **A.M.** (Am.)
mach.   machine; machinery
mag.   magazine; magnitude
Maine   officially spelled out; sometimes **Me.**
Maj.   Major
Maj. Gen.   Major General
Man.   Manitoba, Canada; Manhattan
mar.   market; maritime
Mar.   March (usually spelled out)
mas.   masculine
Mass.   Massachusetts (official)
mat.   maturity (bonds)
math.   mathematics, -cian, -ical
max.   maximum
May   spelled out
M.B.M., MBM, Mbm   thousand [feet] board measure (lumber)
M.C.   Member of Congress; Military Cross
Md.   Maryland (official)

M.D.   Doctor of Medicine
Mdm.   Madam (Anglicized from **Fr.** Madame)
mdnt., **mid.**   midnight
mdse.   merchandise
Me.   Maine (officially spelled out)
M.E.   Mechanical Engineer; Military Engineer; Mining Engineer (See E.M.); Managing Editor
meas.   measure
mech.   mechanic, -ics, -al
med.   medium; medicine; medical
memo   memorandum
m.e.p., **mep**   mean effective pressure
mer.   mercantile
Messrs.   Messieurs (Fr., Misters); **MM.** (Fr.)
met.   metropolitan; meteorological
metal.   metallurgy
Met.E.   Metallurgical Engineer
Mex.   Mexican; Mexico
mf   millifarad (elec.) (See mu f)
mf.   manufacture (pl. mfs.)
mfd.   manufactured
mfg.   manufacturing
mfr.   manufacturer (pl. mfrs.)
mfst.   manifest
mg   milligram (metric); modified guaranteed (securities)
m.g.d., **mgd**   million gallons per day
Mgr.   Manager (See also Msgr.)
mh   millihenry (elec.)
M.H.   Medal of Honor
m.h.cp., **mhcp**   mean horizontal candlepower
mi.   mile or miles; mill
Mich.   Michigan (official)
mid., mdnt.   midnight
Mid'n   Midshipman
mil.   military; mileage
min.   minute; minimum; mineral; mining; minim or drop, apothecaries'
Minn.   Minnesota (official)
misc.   miscellaneous
Miss.   Mississippi (official)
M.I.T.   Massachusetts Institute of Technology
mk.   mark
m-kg   meter-kilogram
mkt., **mar.**   market
ml   milliliter (metric)
mL   millilambert
Mlle   Mademoiselle (Fr., Miss) (pl. Mlles)
mm   millimeter (metric)
mm²   square millimeter
mm³   cubic millimeter
m.m.   the necessary changes having been made (L. mutatis mutandis)
MM.   Messieurs (Fr., Misters)
Mme   Madame (Fr., Mrs.)
Mmes   Mesdames (Fr.); **Mmes.** (Eng.)
m.m.f., **mmf, M.M.F.**   magnetomotive force
m mu, mμ   millimicron
Mn   House (Fr. Maison)
MN   magnetic north
M.N.A.S.   Member of the National Academy of Sciences
mo.   month (pl. mos.)
m.o.   money order; mail order
Mo.   Missouri (official)
mod.   modified (securities); moderate
mol.   molecule
mol.wt.   molecular weight

ABBREVIATIONS

Mon. Monday; **M.** in tabulations
Mont. Montana (official)
mot. motor
m.p., mp melting point
M.P. Member of Parliament; mounted police; military police
M.P.C. Member of Parliament, Canada
m.p.g., mpg miles per gallon
m.p.h., mph miles per hour
mphps miles per hour per second
Mr. Mister (pl. Messrs.)
Mrs. Mistress or Madam (pl. Mmes.—Mesdames)
ms. manuscript (pl. mss.)
m/s meters per second
MS. motorship
M.S. Master of Science
m.s.cp., mscp mean spherical candlepower
Msgr. Monsignor (It., my lord); messenger
m.s.l. mean sea level
M.S.T. Mountain standard time
Mt. mount; mountain (pl. Mts.)
M.T. Mountain time
mt.ct.cp. mortgage certificate coupon (securities)
mtg. mortgage; mounting
mu, μ micron
mu a, μa microampere
mu f, μf microfarad
mu mu, μμ micromicron
mun. municipal
mus. music, -al, -ian
Mus.D. Doctor of Music
mu w, μw microwatt
mv millivolt (elec.)
m.v. market value
M.V. motor vessel

N

n. note; net; new; noon; noun
n/30 net in 30 days
N. north; Navy
N.A. no account
N.A., N.Am. North America
NACA National Advisory Committee for Aeronautics
NANA North American Newspaper Alliance, Inc.
Narr a declaration or complaint (law) (L. narratio)
N.A.S. National Academy of Sciences
Nat., Natl. national
naut. nautical
nav. naval; navigation
nb. nimbus (clouds)
n.b. note well (L. nota bene)
NB northbound
N.B. New Brunswick, Canada
N.B.C., NBC National Broadcasting Company
N.B.S., NBS National Bureau of Standards
N.C. North Carolina (official)
n.d. no date [of publication]; next day's delivery
N.Dak. North Dakota (official); sometimes **N.D.**
NE. northeast
N.E. New England
NEA Newspaper Enterprise Association
N.E.A. National Education Association; National Editorial Association

Nebr. Nebraska (official); sometimes **Neb.**
NEC National Electrical Code; National Emergency Council
NED New English Dictionary (the Oxford English Dictionary)
neg. negative
nem.con. no one contradicting; unanimously (L. nemine contradicente)
Nev. Nevada (official)
NF. Newfoundland
n.g. no good, or "out"
N.G. National Guard
N.H. New Hampshire (official)
N.J. New Jersey (official)
n.l. it is not permitted (L. non licet); it is not clear (L. non liquet)
NL night letter
N.lat. north latitude
NLRB National Labor Relations Board
NLT night letter cable
NM night message
NMB National Mediation Board
N.Mex. New Mexico (official); sometimes **N.M.**
NNE. north-northeast
NNW. north-northwest
no. number (L. numero) (pl. nos.)
N.O.I.B.N. not otherwise indexed by name (freight)
nol.pros. to be unwilling to prosecute (L. nolle prosequi)
non pros. he does not prosecute (L. non prosequitur)
non seq. it does not follow (L. non sequitur)
noon spelled out; sometimes **n.** or **m.**
Nor. Norwegian; Norway
nos. numbers
N.O.S. not otherwise specified (freight)
Nov. November
np nonparticipating (stocks)
n.p. no place [of publication]
N.P. Notary Public; no protest
NRA National Recovery Administration
N.S. Nova Scotia
N.S.F. not sufficient funds (banking)
N.S.W. New South Wales, Australia
N.T. Northern Territory, Australia
nth indefinite, as "nth degree"
N.T.O. not taken out (insurance policy)
n.t.p. no title page (cataloguing)
n.u. name unknown
number no. (pl. nos.)
nv nonvoting (stocks)
NW. northwest
n.wt. net weight
NW.T. Northwest Territories, Canada
N.Y. New York (official)
NYA National Youth Administration
N.Y.C. New York City

O

o. order
O pint, apothecaries' (L. Octarius)
O. Ohio (officially spelled out)
o/a on account
ob. he, or she, died (L. obiit)
O.B/L, ob/l order bill of lading
obs. obsolete; observatory
ob.s.p. died without issue (L. obiit sine prole)
oc. overcharge

549

Oct.   October
o.d.   outside diameter
o.e.   omissions excepted
OED   Oxford English Dictionary
ofc., off.   office; official; officer
OGPU   (See GPU)
Ohio   officially spelled out; sometimes O.
ohm-cm   ohm-centimeter
OK   correct (no periods); OK'd, OK'ing, OK's—verb forms (pl. OKs or OK's)
Okla.   Oklahoma (official)
Ont.   Ontario, Canada
op.   opera; work (L. opus); overproof
o.p.   out of print
op.cit.   in the work cited (L. opere citato)
OPM   Office of Production Management
opp.   opposite
opt.   optional
optg.   operating
optns.   operations
o.r.   owner's risk (shipping)
Or.   Oriental
O.R.C.   Officers' Reserve Corps
ord.   ordinance; order; ordinary
Oreg.   Oregon (official); sometimes Ore.
orig.   original, -ly
o/s   out of stock
ow.   one way [fare]
Oxon.   Oxford University; of Oxford (L. Oxonia, Oxoniensis)
oz.   ounce or ounces
oz.ap., ℥   ounce, apothecaries'
oz.av.   ounce, avoirdupois
oz-ft.   ounce-foot
oz-in.   ounce-inch
oz.t.   ounce, troy

P

p.   page (pl. pp.); per; pressure; population; power; pole
¶   paragraph (or ⁋)
pa.   paper
p.a., per an.   per annum (by the year)
Pa.   Pennsylvania (official); sometimes Penn.
P.A.   Purchasing Agent; Press Agent; private account
Pac.   Pacific
P.a.C.   put and call (stock market)
p.ae.   equal parts (L. partes aequales)
pam.   pamphlet
par.   paragraph, also ¶ (pl. pars.); parallel; parenthesis
part.   participating (securities)
pat.   patent, -ed
Pat.Off.   Patent Office
payt.   payment
PBX   private branch exchange (telephone)
pc.   piece (pl. pcs.)
pc., pct., %   percent
pcl.   parcel
pd.   paid
Pd.D.   Doctor of Pedagogy
P.E.I.   Prince Edward Island, Canada
Penn.   Pennsylvania (Pa. is official)
penny   d. (L. denarius)
pennyweight   dwt.
per an., p.a.   per annum (by the year)
perp.   perpetual (bonds)
Per Pro., P.P.   by authorization; by proxy (L. per procurationem)
pet.   petroleum
petn.   petition

pf., pfd.   preferred (securities)
p.f., P.F.   power factor (elec.)
Pg.   Portuguese; Portugal
Phar.D.   Doctor of Pharmacy
Ph.C.   Pharmaceutical Chemist
Ph.D.   Doctor of Philosophy
Ph.G.   Graduate in Pharmacy
P.I.   Philippine Islands (official)
pinx.   he, or she, painted it (L. pinxit)
pk.   peck; pack; park (pl. pks.)
pkg.   package (pl. pkgs.)
pkt.   packet
pl.   place; plural; plate (pl. pls.)
P. & L.   profit and loss
Plf.   Plaintiff
P.L. & R.   Postal Laws and Regulations
pm., prem.   premium
p.m.   after noon (L. post meridiem)
PM.   postmaster
p.n.   promissory note
P.O.   post office; Petty Officer (Navy)
P.O.D.   Post Office Department; pay on delivery
pol.   politics, -cal, -cian
Pol.   Polish; Poland
pop.   population
P.O.R., p.o.r.   pay on return (express)
pos.   positive
pot.   potential
pound   lb. (L. libra) (pl. lbs.); pound sterling, £
pow.   power; powder
pp.   pages; prepaid
p.p.   parcel post; postage paid
P.P., Per Pro.   by authorization; by proxy (L. per procurationem)
P.P.C.   to take leave (Fr. pour prendre congé)
p.p.i.   parcel post, insured
p.p.m., ppm   parts per million
P-PS.   post-postscript
P.Q.   Province of Quebec, Canada
pr.   price; present; pair; prior; province; printed; printer
PR   payroll
P.R.   Puerto Rico (official)
pref.   preferred; preference; preface
prem., pm.   premium
prep.   preposition; preparation
Pres.   President
prim.   primary
prin.   principal
p.r.n.   as the occasion arises (L. pro re nata)
prob.   problem
prod.   product; produce; produced
Prof.   Professor
pron.   pronunciation; pronounced; pronoun
prop.   property; proposition
Prot.   Protestant
pro tem.   for the time being (L. pro tempore)
prov.   province; provision, -al
prox.   of the next month (L. proximo)
pr.pf.   prior preferred (stocks)
prs.   pairs
Prus.   Prussian; Prussia
Ps.   Psalm (pl. Pss.)
PS.   postscript (pl. PSs.) (See p. 540)
P.S.T.   Pacific standard time
pt.   part; payment; pint; point; port (pl. pts.)
p.t.   private terms

550

P.T., PT Pacific time
P.T.A., PTA, P-TA Parent-Teacher Association (pl. P.T.A.s, PTAs, P-TAs)
ptg. printing
pt.pf. participating preferred (stocks)
Ptr. printer (proofreading)
pub. public, -ation; published, -ing, -er
pur. purchaser; purchasing
Pvt. Private (Army)
pwr., pow. power
pwt. pennyweight; usually **dwt.**
PX Post Exchange (mil.) (pl. PXs)

Q

q quintal (metric)
Q. question; query (pl. QQ.); Queensland, Australia
Q.E.D. which was to be proved or demonstrated (L. quod erat demonstrandum)
Q.E.F. which was to be done (L. quod erat faciendum)
QM. Quartermaster
qr. quarter; quarterly; quire (pl. qrs.)
q.s. quarter section; a sufficient quantity (L. quantum sufficit)
qt. quart (pl. qts.)
qty. quantity
qu., Q., ques. question
quad. quadrant
Que. Quebec, Canada
q.v. which see (L. quod vide)
Qy., Q. query

R

r. right; road
R. Range (pl. Rs.); Republican; reports; registered; river; rule; Republic; radius; Réaumur (thermometric scale)
Ⓡ Registered in U.S. Patent Office
R.A. Rear Admiral; Royal Academy
rad. radio; radiant
R.A.F. Royal Air Force
R.A.M. Royal Academy of Music
R.C. Red Cross; Roman Catholic
rcd., recd. received
rct., rec. receipt (pl. rcts., rec.)
rd. rod; road; round
R.D. rural delivery (See R.R.)
re in regard to
R.E. real estate
REA Rural Electrification Administration
Rear Adm. Rear Admiral
rec. record, -ed, -er; recipe; receipt; reclamation (bonds)
recd., rcd. received
Rec.Sec. Recording Secretary
ref. reference; referee; refining; refrigerating; refunding (bonds)
reg. registered; regulation; regular
R.E.O. real estate owned (banking)
rep. repeat; report; repair
Rep. Republican; Republic; Representative
req. requisition
res. reserve; residence; resort; resolution
ret. retired; return
retd. returned
rev. revised; revolution; revenue; reverse
Rev. Reverend
Rev.Stat., R.S. Revised Statutes
rf., rfg. refunding (bonds)

r.f. radio frequency; **r-f.** (adj.)
R.F. French Republic
RFC Reconstruction Finance Corporation
R.F.D. rural free delivery (See R.R.)
rg., reg. registered (bonds)
r.h. right hand
R.I. Rhode Island (official)
R.I.P. may he, or she, rest in peace (L. requiescat in pace)
rm. ream; room (pl. rms.)
Rm. reichsmarks (German money)
r.m.s., rms root mean square
R.N. Registered Nurse; Royal Navy
R.N.R. Royal Naval Reserve
Robt. Robert
r.o.p. run of paper (advtg.)
R.O.T.C. Reserve Officers' Training Corps
RP reply paid (cables)
R.P.D. Doctor of Political Science (L. Rerum Politicarum Doctor)
r.p.m., rpm revolutions per minute
r.p.s., rps revolutions per second
rpt. report
RR., railroad (pl. RRs.) (See p. 540)
R.R. rural route
r.s. right side
R.S. Revised Statutes; Recording Secretary
R.S.V.P. Please answer; Reply, if you please (Fr. Répondez, s'il vous plaît)
rt. right (pl. rts.); round trip
Rt. Hon. Right Honourable (Br.)
Rt. Rev. Right Reverend
Rus. Russian; Russia
rva reactive volt-ampere (See var)
R.V.O. Royal Victorian Order
Ry. railway (pl. Rys.)

S

s stere (metric); seconds, as 15ˢ or 15s
s7d, s10d, s15d seller 7 days to deliver, etc. (stock market)
s. silver; stock; steamer; shillings
S. south; science; Senate; mark a prescription (L. signa)
S.A. South America; South Africa; South Australia; an incorporated company (Fr. Société Anonyme); stock company (Sp. Sociedad Anónima)
S.Afr. South Africa
S.A.I. an incorporated company (It. Società Anonima Italiana)
S.Am. South America
Sam'l Samuel
San.D. Doctor of Sanitation
s.ap., sc., ℈ scruple, apothecaries'
Sask. Saskatchewan, Canada
Sat. Saturday; **St.** in tabulations
Sav. Savings
SB southbound
S.B. Bachelor of Science
sc., sci. science
sc., scil., sct., ss., s. namely or to wit (L. scilicet) (See ss.)
sc., sculp. he, or she, carved or engraved it (L. sculpsit); sculptor
S.C. South Carolina (official)
Sc.D. Doctor of Science
sch. school; schooner
Scot. Scottish; Scotch; Scotland
s.cp., scp spherical candlepower

s.d. without a day [being named] (L. sine die)
S.Dak. South Dakota (official); sometimes **S.D.**
SE. southeast
Sea. Seaman (Navy)
Sea. 1c. Seaman, first class
sec secant (trigonometry)
sec. section; second; security; secured
Sec., Secy. Secretary
SEC Securities and Exchange Commission
second **2d** (no period); **2nd,** older form
sel. selected, -tion
Sen. Senate; Senator
sep. separate
Sept. September; **Sep.** in tabulations
seq. the following (L. sequens) (pl. seqq.)
ser. series; serial; service
SER serial service (telegraph)
serv. service
sess. session
s.f. sinking fund; near the end (L. sub finem)
sg., sig. signature
S.G. Surgeon General
sgd. signed
Sgt. Sergeant
sh. share (pl. shs.)
s.hp., shp shaft horsepower
shpt. shipment
sh.tn. short ton
sic so; thus (L.) (inserted to confirm a word, statement, or quotation that might be questioned)
sig. signature; write [on medicine container]
sin sine (trigonometry)
sing. singular
sinh hyperbolic sine (math.)
S.J. Society of Jesus (the Jesuits)
S.J.D. Doctor of Juridical Science (Law) (See J.S.D.)
sk. sack (pl. sx)
S.lat. south latitude
sld. sailed
sm. small
S.M. Master of Science
s.o. seller's option
Soc. Society
sol. solution; soluble
SOS distress signal (no periods). The U.S. Naval Communications office states that these letters do not represent words—the group is simply a signal which, because of its distinctive character, was adopted after the International Radiotelegraph Conference in London in 1912. The SOS signal is . . .– – –. . . (three dots, three dashes, three dots). In radiotelephony the distress signal is the spoken expression **MAYDAY** (corresponding to the French pronunciation of "m'aider").
S.O.S. Service of Supply (military)
s.p. without issue (L. sine prole); single phase (elec.)
Sp. Spanish; Spain
spec., spl., sp. special
spg. spring (pl. spgs.)
sp.gr. specific gravity
sp.ht. specific heat
s.p.s. without surviving issue (L. sine prole superstite)
spt. seaport

sq. square, as sq.in., sq.ft., sq.yd., sq.rd., sq.ch., sq.mi.
sq. the following (L. sequens) (pl. sqq.)
Sr. Senior; Sir; Señor (Sp., Mr.)
S.R. star route
Sra. Señora (Sp., Mrs.)
Sres. Señores (Sp., Messrs.)
S.R.O. standing room only
Srta. Señorita (Sp., Miss)
ss. namely or to wit (L. scilicet) (On legal documents, such as affidavits, it verifies the place of action.)
SS. steamship (pl. SSs.) (See p. 540)
SSA Social Security Administration
SSE. south-southeast
SSR, S.S.R. Soviet Socialist Republic
SSS Selective Service System
SSW. south-southwest
St. Street; State; Saint; Store; Strait (pl. Sts.); Statute –s
Sta. Station; Santa; stamped (securities)
stat. statistics; statutes
std. standard
S.T.D. Doctor of Sacred Theology
Ste Sainte (Fr., feminine of Saint)
stet let it stand (from L. stare, to stand)
stg. sterling; storage
stk. stock
Stk.Ex. Stock Exchange
Stk.Mkt. Stock Market
S.T.L. Licentiate, or Lector, in Sacred Theology
stp., st., sta. stamped (securities)
S.T.P. Professor of Sacred Theology
str. steamer
S.U. set up (freight)
sub. substitute; suburb; subscriber
subj. subject
subs. subsidiary; subscription
Sun. Sunday; **Su.** in tabulations
sup. superior; supply; above (L. supra)
supp. supplement
Supt. Superintendent
surg. surgeon; surgery; surgical
s.v. under the word (L. sub verbo)
s.v.p. if you please (Fr. s'il vous plaît)
Sw., Swed. Swedish; Sweden
SW. southwest
S.W.G., SWG Standard wire gauge (Br.)
sx sacks
syl. syllable or syllables
synd. syndicate
syst. system

T

t metric ton (ordinary ton is **tn.**)
t. temperature; town; troy; time
T., Tp. township (pl. Tps.)
T.A.G. The Adjutant General
tan tangent (trigonometry)
t.a.w. twice a week (advtg.)
T.B. trial balance
T.D. trust deed (See p. 466)
T.E. Topographical Engineer
tech. technical
tel. telephone; telegraph; telegram
temp. temperature; temporary
Tenn. Tennessee (official)
Ter. Territory; territorial
Tex. Texas (official)
t.f. till forbidden (advtg.)
tg., tel. telegraph; telegram

T.H. Territory of Hawaii (officially spelled out—**Hawaii**)
third **3rd** or **3d** (no period)
Thos. Thomas
thou. thousand; **M** in lumber, etc.
Thurs., Thu. Thursday; **Th.** in tabulations
tkr. tanker
t.l.o. total loss only (ins.)
t.m. true mean; trade-mark
tn. ton (metric ton is **t**); town
TN true north
tonn. tonnage
tp., tel. telephone
Tp., T. township (pl. Tps.)
tr. trust; trustee; transit; transfer; transpose; translated, -tion, -tor
T.R. tons registered (shipping)
Treas. Treasurer; Treasury
t.s., ts tensile strength
T.T.s telegraphic transfers (of money)
Tues., Tue. Tuesday; **Tu.** in tabulations
Turk. Turkish; Turkey
TV television; terminal velocity
TVA Tennessee Valley Authority
Twad. Twaddell (hydrometer)
Twp. township (See T.)
tx. tax or taxes

U

u.d., ut dict. as directed (L. ut dictum)
u.i. as below (L. ut infra)
U.K. United Kingdom
ult. of the last month (L. ultimo)
un. unifying or unified (bonds)
Un., Union; United
U.N., UN United Nations
Univ. University; Universal
unl. unlimited
up. underproof (alcohols)
UP United Press
US Universal Service (news)
u.s. as above (L. ut supra)
U.S. United States
U.S.A. United States of America; United States Army; Union of South Africa
U.S.A.F., USAF United States Air Force
U.S.C. United States Code
U.S.C.G. United States Coast Guard
U.S.M.C. United States Marine Corps
U.S.N. United States Navy
U.S.N.R. United States Naval Reserve
U.S.P. United States Pharmacopoeia
U.S.R.S. United States Reclamation Service
U.S.S. United States Ship (also used for dirigibles); United States Senate
U.S.S.R. Union of Soviet Socialist Republics
ut. utilities
Utah officially spelled out; sometimes **Ut.**
ut dict., u.d. as directed (L. ut dictum)

V

v volt (elec.)
v. verse (pl. vv.); verb; volume; versus
V. valve; Victoria, Australia
v-a, va volt-ampere (elec.)
Va. Virginia (official)
vac. vacuum
val. value; valuation
var reactive volt-amper

var. variety; various; variant; variation
V.C. Victoria Cross (Br.); Vice Consul
V.D.M. Minister of the Word of God (L. Verbi Dei Minister)
Ven. Venerable
V.G. Vicar General
v.i. see below (L. vide infra)
V.I. Virgin Islands; Vancouver Island
Vice Adm. Vice Admiral
Vice Pres., V.P. Vice President
vid. see (L. vide)
VIP very important person (pl. VIPs)
vis. visibility (aviation)
viz namely (L. videlicet)
V.M.D. Doctor of Veterinary Medicine
vol. volume (pl. vols.)
vou. voucher
voy. voyage
v.p., vt.pl. voting pool (stocks)
V.P., Vice Pres. Vice President
vs., v. against (L. versus)
v.s. see above (L. vide supra); volumetric solution
V.S. Veterinary Surgeon
vt. voting (stocks)
Vt. Vermont (official)
v.t.c., vtc voting trust certificates (stocks)
vv. verses
v.v. vice versa

W

w watt (elec.)
W. west
w.a. with average (ins.)
W.A. Western Australia
WAC Women's Army Corps (pl. WACs)
war., wt., w. warrant (securities)
Wash. Washington (official); often **Wn.**
wb. wheelbase (length of car between axles)
WB waybill; westbound
w/c, wpc watts per candle
Wed. Wednesday; **W.** in tabulations
w.g. wire gauge
whf. wharf
whge. wharfage
whs. warehouse
whsle. wholesale
whs.rec., W.R. warehouse receipt
w.i., wi when issued (securities)
W.I. West Indies
Wis. Wisconsin (official)
wk. work; week (pl. wks.)
w.l. wave length (elec.)
W.long. west longitude
Wm. William
Wn. Washington (**Wash.** is official)
WNW. west-northwest
W.O. Warrant Officer (military)
w.r., wr with rights (securities)
W.R., whs.rec. warehouse receipt
WSW. west-southwest
wt. weight; warrant (pl. wts.)
W.Va. West Virginia (official)
w.w., ww with warrants (securities)
Wyo. Wyoming (official)

X

x box or boxes
xc, xcp. ex or without coupon (bonds)
xd, xdiv. ex or without dividend (stocks)
x in. ex or without interest (securities)

553

XP monogram for the Greek word for Christ
x pr. ex or without privileges (securities)
xr, x rts. ex or without rights (securities)
xw ex or without warrants (securities)
XQ. cross-question

Y

yb. yearbook
yd. yard (pl. yds.)
yd², sq.yd. square yard or yards
yr., y. year (pl. yrs.)
Y.T. Yukon Territory, Canada

Z

z. zone; zero
Z.S. Zoological Society

SIGNS AND SYMBOLS

$+$ plus, or more than; north, in astronomy
$-$ minus, or less than; south, in astronomy
$-$ over last figure of a decimal indicates that it is approximate $(0.12\bar{5})$
$\pm$ plus or minus; more or less
$\times$ by, in dimensions, as $3' \times 10''$
: is to; compared with
:: as, or equals, as $1:3::6:18$
∴ therefore; hence
∵ since; because
$\parallel$ parallel to
$\perp$ perpendicular to
$\equiv$ identical with
$\doteq$ approaches
$\fallingdotseq$ is approximately equal to
$\neq$ is unequal to
$\sim$ difference
$\int$ integral of
! the factorial of a number, as $5! = 5 \times 4 \times 3 \times 2 \times 1$
∞ infinity; indefinitely great
0 infinitesimal; indefinitely small
$\propto$ varies as; is proportional to
$'$ feet, as $10'$; minutes of arc
$''$ inches, as $10''$; seconds of arc; ditto
$>$ is greater than
$\geqq$ is either equal to or greater than
$\not>$ is not greater than
$<$ is less than
$\leqq$ is either equal to or less than
$\not<$ is not less than
$\rightarrow$ approaches as a limit
$\checkmark\!\!\!\!\!\checkmark$ double check ($\checkmark$ check)
$\#$ number, if before a figure; pounds, if after a figure
$/$ per, as bbls/day; of; by; after; shilling, -s; proportion, as $a/b = c/d$
2/10, n/30 means 2 % discount in 10 days, net in 30 days

° degrees
□ square; square miles
□′ or □ft square feet
′□ foot or feet square
□″ square inches
#/□″ pounds per square inch
$\sqrt{}$ root or radical sign; square root
$\sqrt[3]{}$ cube root
(To make these signs on the typewriter, use the diagonal line with the underline above it. Draw in only the first short lines.)
′ ″ ‴ accents used to distinguish several things of the same general designation, as A′, A″, A‴—read "A prime, A second, A third", etc.
¹²³⁴⁵ superior figures used as footnote indicators; a superior figure may also indicate the power to which a given number is to be raised, as 12^2 (squared), 10^3 (cubed)
ʰ ᵐ ˢ hours, minutes, seconds, in scientific work, as $4^h 30^m 10^s$
° ′ ″ degrees, minutes, seconds of an arc
Longitude 30° 08′ 14″ W.
Latitude 40° 19′ 12″ N.
°F degrees Fahrenheit
°C degrees Centigrade
% percent; in care of
@ at, as @ 10¢ each; to, as $10 @ $16
&c and so forth; etc.
& ampersand (a corruption of the words "and per se and"; the symbol comes from the Latin Et [&] meaning "and")
§ section
℔ per
¶ paragraph (or ⁋)
HP horsepower
Yᵉ an old printing symbol for "the" (pron. thē)
℞ take (L. Recipe); response
ℨ dram, apothecaries'
℥ ounce, apothecaries'
℈ scruple, apothecaries'
℔ pound, apothecaries'
♏ minim or drop, apothecaries'
f° folio
4to, 4° quarto (folded in 4—a book size)
8vo, 8° octavo (folded in 8—a book size)
12mo, 12° duodecimo (folded in 12—a book size)
© copyright
10dy tenpenny nails (dy means penny)
1st first
2d second; 2nd is the older form
3d third; 3rd is the older form
4th fourth
3s, 4s interest rates on bonds
* asterisk; capital cities in geographic work; correct quotations on ticker tape
☞ "fist" or index (pointer)

Greek Letters. The Greek letters are used by different engineers and scientists to mean different things. For instance:

Δ distance, in astronomy; finite difference
Δp pressure drop, or difference in pressure
δ variation; declination, in astronomy
ϕ phase, in electricity; angle of roll, in aviation; angle of eccentricity, in astronomy
Φ magnetic flux
Σ sum, in algebra
π pi, or 3.14159265+ (generally 3.1416)

GREEK ALPHABET

ε   2.7182818+ in logarithms; eccentricity; dielectric constant; angle of downwash, in aviation
μ   micron; permeability; coefficient of viscosity; mean angular motion in unit of time, in astronomy
μ^2 square micron
μ^3 cubic micron
mμ   millimicron (1/1000 of a micron)
μμ   micromicron (1/1,000,000 of a micron)
μa   microampere
μf   microfarad
μw   microwatt

GREEK ALPHABET

CHARACTER		GREEK NAME	PRONUNCIATION
CAPITAL	SMALL		
A	α α	Alpha	ăl′fá
B	β ϐ	Beta	bā′tá, or bē′tá
Γ	γ	Gamma	găm′á
Δ	δ	Delta	dĕl′tá
E	ε	Epsilon	ĕp′sĭ-lŏn (Br. ĕp-sī′lon)
Z	ζ	Zeta	zā′tá, or zē′tá
H	η	Eta	ā′tá, or ē′tá
Θ	θ ϑ	Theta	thā′tá, or thē′tá
I	ι	Iota	I-ō′tá
K	κ	Kappa	kăp′á
Λ	λ	Lambda	lăm′dá
M	μ	Mu	mū, or mōō
N	ν	Nu	nū, or nōō
Ξ	ξ	Xi	zī, or ksē
O	ο	Omicron	ŏm′ĭ-krŏn (Br. ō-mī′krŭn)
Π	π	Pi	pī
P	ρ	Rho	rō
Σ	σ s	Sigma	sĭg′má
T	τ	Tau	ta, or tou
Υ	υ	Upsilon	ūp′sĭ-lŏn (Br. ūp-sī′lon)
Φ	φ φ	Phi	fī
X	χ	Chi	kī, or kē
Ψ	ψ	Psi	sī, or psē
Ω	ω	Omega	ō-mē′gá, or ō-mĕg′á

❖

WEIGHTS AND MEASURES

Checked by the Division of Weights and Measures, National Bureau of Standards,
Washington, D.C.

THE METRIC SYSTEM

The metric system is the international system of weights and measures. It is commonly used throughout the world, and is accepted as standard in all scientific work.

It was legalized by Congress in the United States in 1866.

The principal units are:

meter	m	for length
gram	g	for weight
liter	l	for capacity
are	a	for area
stere	s	for volume

All other units in the system are the decimal subdivisions or multiples of the above units:

micro-	μ	1/1,000,000
milli-	m	1/1000
centi-	c	1/100
deci-	d	1/10
Unit	one	
deka-	dk	10
hecto-	h	100
kilo-	k	1000
myria-	my	10,000
mega-		1,000,000 (not commonly used)

The main units are interrelated as follows:

meter	the unit of length—the basic unit
kilogram	the unit of mass—the weight of approximately 1 cubic decimeter of water* (actually 1.000027 dm³)
gram	the weight of approximately 1 cubic centimeter of water* (actually 1.000027 cm³)
liter	the cubic space occupied by 1 kilogram of water*
stere	the volume of 1 cubic meter
are	the area of 100 square meters

* See Water Volumes, p. 563.

Metric Abbreviations. The metric abbreviations here given are those adopted by the National Bureau of Standards.

Note that no periods are used after metric abbreviations.

"Square" and "cubic" are indicated by the exponents [2] and [3], as

cm³   instead of c.c.   or c.cm.

THE METRIC SYSTEM

All metric abbreviations are written in small letters; and the same abbreviation is used for both singular and plural in each instance.

LENGTH
Unit—Meter

Name	Abbreviation	Metric equivalent	No. of meters	Common equivalent
1 millimeter...................	mm	....	1/1000	0.03937 inch
1 centimeter...................	cm	10 millimeters	1/100	0.3937 inch
1 decimeter....................	dm	10 centimeters	1/10	3.937 inches
1 METER.....................	m	10 decimeters	......	39.37 inches
				3.2808 feet
				1.0936 yards
1 dekameter...................	dkm	....	10	393.7 inches
				32.8083 feet
1 hectometer..................	hm	10 dekameters	100	328.0833 feet, or
				328 feet 1 inch
1 kilometer....................	km	10 hectometers	1000	0.62137 mile
				3280.833 feet
1 myriameter..................	mym	10 kilometers	10,000	6.2137 miles

Small subdivisions:

Name	Abbreviation	Metric equivalent	No. of meters	Common equivalent
1 micron.....................	μ	1/1000 millimeter	1/1,000,000	0.03937 mil
1 millimicron.................	mμ	1/1000 of a micron	....	0.00003937 mil
1 micromillimeter.............	μmm	1/1,000,000 millimeter		
1 micromicron................	$\mu\mu$	1/1,000,000 micron		

To convert meters into feet, and vice versa:

$$\text{Meters} = \text{feet} \div 3.28$$
$$\text{Feet} = \text{meters} \times 3.28$$

Relation to liter:

$$1 \text{ liter} = 1.000027 \text{ cubic decimeters}$$
$$1 \text{ milliliter} = 1.000027 \text{ cubic centimeters}$$

(For most practical purposes the liter is considered equal to 1 cubic decimeter, and the milliliter equal to 1 cubic centimeter; although in the actual standards the above differences exist.)

WEIGHT
Unit—Gram

Name	Abbreviation	Metric equivalent	No. of grams	Avoirdupois equivalent
1 milligram.......................	mg	....	1/1000	0.0154 grain
1 centigram.......................	cg	10 milligrams	1/100	0.1543 grain
1 decigram........................	dg	10 centigrams	1/10	1.5432 grains
1 GRAM..........................	g	10 decigrams	....	15.4323 grains
1 dekagram.......................	dkg	....	10	0.3527 ounce
				0.3215 troy ounce
1 hectogram......................	hg	10 dekagrams	100	3.5274 ounces
				3.2151 troy ounces
1 kilogram........................	kg	10 hectograms	1000	2.2046 pounds
				2.6792 troy pounds
1 myriagram......................	...	10 kilograms	10,000	22.046 pounds
1 quintal.........................	q	10 myriagrams	100,000	220.46 pounds
1 metric ton (millier, or tonneau).......	t	10 quintals	1,000,000	2204.62 pounds

WEIGHTS AND MEASURES

CAPACITY
Unit—Liter

Name	Abbreviation	Metric equivalent	No. of liters	Dry measure	Liquid measure
1 milliliter...........	ml	....	1/1000	0.061 cubic inch	0.2705 fluid dram
1 centiliter...........	cl	10 milliliters	1/100	0.6102 cubic inch	0.3381 fluid ounce
1 deciliter...........	dl	10 centiliters	1/10	6.1025 cubic inches	0.8454 gill
1 LITER.............	l	10 deciliters	......	0.9081 quart	1.0567 quarts
1 dekaliter...........	dkl	....	10	1.1351 pecks	2.6418 gallons
1 hectoliter...........	hl	10 dekaliters	100	2.8378 bushels	26.4178 gallons
1 kiloliter...........	kl	1 stere	1000	1.308 cubic yards	264.178 gallons

SURFACE
Unit—Are

Name	Abbreviation	Metric equivalent	No. of ares	Common equivalent
1 square centimeter.............	cm²	1/10,000 square meter	......	0.1550 square inch
1 centare....................	ca	1 square meter	1/100	1550 square inches
1 ARE......................	a	100 square meters	......	1.1960 square yards 119.6 square yards
1 hectare...................	ha	10,000 square meters	100	2.4710 acres
1 square kilometer.............	km²	1,000,000 square meters	10,000	247.104 acres 0.3861 square mile

VOLUME
Unit—Stere

Name	Abbreviation	Metric equivalent	No. of steres	Common equivalent
1 centistere............................	cs	....	1/100	0.3531 cubic foot
1 decistere............................	ds	10 centisteres	1/10	3.5314 cubic feet
1 STERE..............................	s	10 decisteres 1 cubic meter	.....	1.3079 cubic yards 0.2759 cord
1 dekastere...........................	dks	....	10	13.079 cubic yards

LONG MEASURE

Name	Abbreviation	Common equivalent	Metric equivalent
1 inch..............................	in.	....	2.54 cm
1 foot.............................	ft.	12 inches	0.3048 m 30.48 cm
1 yard.............................	yd.	3 feet; 36 inches	0.9144 m
1 rod.............................	rd. }		
1 pole.............................	p. }	5½ yards; 16½ feet	5.0292 m
1 furlong...........................	fur.	40 rods; 220 yards	201.168 m
1 mile.............................	mi.	8 furlongs; 1760 yards; 5280 feet	1.6093 km
1 geographical mile (see Mariners' Measure)			

558

WEIGHTS AND MEASURES

SQUARE MEASURE

Name	Abbreviation	Common equivalent	Metric equivalent
1 square inch	sq.in.	....	6.4516 cm²
1 square foot	sq.ft.	144 square inches	0.0929 m²
1 square yard	sq.yd.	9 square feet	0.8361 m²
1 square rod	sq.rd.	30¼ square yards; 272¼ square feet	25.2930 m²
1 square chain	sq.ch.	16 square rods	404.6873 m²
1 acre	A.	160 square rods; 43,560 square feet (approximately 69.57 yd. or 208 ft. 8½ in. on each side)	0.4047 ha
1 square mile	sq.mi. }	640 acres	258.9998 ha
1 section	sec. }		2.5900 km²
1 township	T. or Tp.	36 square miles (6 miles square)	

CUBIC MEASURE

Name	Abbreviation	Common equivalent	Metric equivalent
1 cubic inch	cu.in.	....	16.3872 cm³
1 cubic foot	cu.ft.	1728 cubic inches	0.0283 m³
1 cubic yard	cu.yd.	27 cubic feet	0.7646 m³

WOOD MEASURE

Name	Abbreviation	Common equivalent	Metric equivalent
1 board foot	f.b.m.	144 cubic inches (1' × 1' × 1'')	0.00236 m³
1 cord	cd.	128 cubic feet (4' × 4' × 8'); 8 cord feet	3.625 s or m³
1 cord foot	cd.ft.	16 cubic feet (4' × 4' × 1')	

SHIPPING MEASURE

Name	Common equivalent	Metric equivalent
1 register ton	100 cubic feet	2.8317 m³
1 displacement ton	35 cubic feet	
1 barrel bulk	5 cubic feet; ⅛ ton	141.58 l
1 shipping ton	40 cubic feet; 2240 pounds	

SURVEYORS' MEASURE
(Gunter's Chain)

Name	Abbreviation	Common equivalent	Metric equivalent
1 link	li.	7.92 inches	0.2012 m
1 chain	ch.	100 links; 4 rods; 66 feet; 22 yards	20.1168 m
1 furlong	fur.	10 chains; 40 rods	201.168 m
1 mile	mi.	80 chains; 5280 feet	1.6093 km

WEIGHTS AND MEASURES

Surveyors' Area Measure
(Gunter's Chain)

Name	Abbreviation	Common equivalent	Metric equivalent
1 square link	sq.li.	....	0.0405 m²
1 square rod	sq.rd. ⎫	625 square links	25.2930 m²
1 [square] pole	p. ⎬		
1 square chain	sq.ch.	16 square rods; 16 [square] poles	404.6873 m°
1 acre	A.	10 square chains; 160 square rods	0.4047 ha
1 square mile	sq.mi.	640 acres	2.59 km²
1 township	T. or Tp.	36 square miles (6 miles square)	

Engineers' Measure

Name	Abbreviation	Common equivalent	Metric equivalent
1 link	li.	1 foot; 12 inches	0.3048 m
1 chain	ch.	100 links; 100 feet	30.4801 m
1 mile	mi.	52.8 chains	1.6093 km

Mariners' Measure

Name	Abbreviation	Common equivalent	Metric equivalent
1 fathom	fath.	6 feet	1.8288 m
1 cable	....	100 to 120 fathoms; 200 to 240 yards	
1 nautical mile ⎫		⎰ 6080.20 feet; 1.1515 ordinary miles	⎱ 1853.248 m
1 sea mile ⎬	....	⎱ (British Admiralty mile, 6080 feet)	⎰ 1.8532 km
1 geographical mile ⎭			
1 league	l.	approximately 3 nautical miles	5.5597 km
1 degree	deg.	60 nautical miles	111.1949 km
1 knot	k.	1 nautical mile in 1 hour	

(Note that a knot is a measure of speed, not of distance; therefore it is incorrect to say "23 knots *per hour*" when meaning "a speed of 23 knots".)

Liquid Measure

Name	Abbreviation	Common equivalent	Metric equivalent
1 gill	gi.	....	0.1183 l
1 pint	pt.	4 gills	0.4732 l
1 quart	qt.	2 pints	0.9463 l
1 gallon	gal.	4 quarts; 231 cubic inches; 0.83267 Br. imperial gallon	3.7853 l
1 barrel*	bbl.	31½ gallons (32 gallons in some states)	119.238 l
1 barrel of oil	....	42 gallons (U.S.)	
1 hogshead	hhd.	2 barrels; 63 gallons	238.476 l

(British measures differ from the above.)

1 imperial gallon (Br. standard)	i.gal.	1.20094 U.S. gallons; 277.42 cubic inches	4.5460 l

* Sizes of barrels differ for different commodities.

WEIGHTS AND MEASURES

DRY MEASURE

Name	Abbreviation	Common equivalent	Metric equivalent
1 quart............................	qt.	2 pints; 67.2 cubic inches	1.1012 l
1 peck.............................	pk.	8 quarts	8.8096 l
1 bushel...........................	bu.	4 pecks; 2150.42 cubic inches	35.2383 l
1 barrel*..........................	bbl.	105 dry quarts; 7056 cubic inches	115.6260 l

(British measures differ from the above.)

1 imperial bushel (Br. standard)........	i.bu.	1.0320 U.S. bushels; 2219.36 cubic inches	36.3677 l

* Sizes of barrels differ for different commodities.

ORDINARY WEIGHT
(Avoirdupois)

Name	Abbreviation	Common equivalent	Metric equivalent
1 grain*............	(spelled out)	....	0.0648 g
1 dram..............	dr.	27.34375 grains	1.7718 g
1 ounce.............	oz.	16 drams; 437.5 grains	28.3495 g
1 pound.............	lb.	16 ounces; 7000 grains	453.5924 g
1 hundredweight......	cwt.	100 pounds (U.S.); 4 quarters	0.4536 kg / 45.3592 kg
1 ton { short ton......	sh.tn.	112 pounds† (Br.); 4 quarters of 28 pounds each	50.8023 kg
{ long ton†......	l.tn.	2000 pounds (U.S. ton)	0.9072 metric t
1 metric ton.........	t	2240 pounds (British ton)	1.0160 metric t
		2204.62 pounds	

* The grain is the same in all weights—avoirdupois, troy, and apothecaries'. It was derived from the weight of a grain of wheat.

† The "gross ton" and "long hundredweight" are sometimes used in the United States, but their use appears to be decreasing.

TROY WEIGHT
(For Precious Metals and Jewels)

Name	Abbreviation	Common equivalent	Metric equivalent
1 grain*......................	(spelled out)	....	0.0648 g
1 pennyweight.................	dwt.	24 grains	1.5552 g
1 ounce†......................	oz.t.	20 pennyweights; 480 grains	31.1035 g
1 pound†......................	lb.t.	12 ounces; 5760 grains	0.3732 kg
1 carat.......................	c.	3⅙ grains—"International carat" (old)	205.3 mg
1 carat grain.................	....	¼ carat	
1 metric carat................	c	200 milligrams (standard); 3.0865 grains	0.2 g

* See Ordinary Weight table, above.

† The ounce and the pound are the same in troy and apothecaries' weights.

WEIGHTS AND MEASURES

GOLD MEASURE
(The "fineness" of gold is the purity of it. "Karat" is a measure of the fineness of gold.)

Name	Abbreviation	Common equivalent
1 troy ounce..............	....	$35, as fixed January 31, 1934; formerly $20.67
24 karats fine.............	24K	pure gold
18 karats fine.............	18K	18/24 pure gold—18 parts gold, 6 parts alloy
1 karat...................	K	1/24 pure gold (by weight)

A 14.2-inch cube of pure gold bullion (999.99 fine) weighs approximately a ton.

SILVER MEASURE

(The "fineness" of silver is the purity of it. "Sterling" is a measure of the fineness of silver.)

1 troy ounce......value fluctuates above and below 70¢; formerly approximately 60¢ (expected some day to reach $1.29, the monetary value fixed by law)

Sterling silver.....has a fineness of .925; that is, 925 parts of silver to 75 parts of alloy. (Silver is commonly alloyed with copper to give it hardness.) (See also British Money, p. 518.)

APOTHECARIES' WEIGHT
(For Compounding Medicines)

Name	Abbreviation	Common equivalent	Metric equivalent
1 grain*.......................................	(spelled out)	....	0.0648 g
1 scruple......................................	s.ap. (Э)	20 grains	1.2960 g
1 dram..	dr.ap. (ʒ)	3 scruples	3.8879 g
1 ounce†......................................	oz.ap. (℥)	8 drams; 480 grains	31.1035 g
1 pound†......................................	lb.ap. (℔)	12 ounces; 5760 grains	0.3732 kg

* See Ordinary Weight table, above.
† See Troy Weight table, above.

APOTHECARIES' FLUID MEASURE
(For Compounding Medicines)

Name	Abbreviation	Common equivalent	Metric equivalent
1 minim................................	min. or ♏ (♏)	1 drop	0.0616 ml
1 fluid dram...........................	fl.dr. (f ʒ)	60 minims	3.6966 ml
1 fluid ounce..........................	fl.oz. (f ℥)	8 fluid drams	2.9573 cl
1 pint*................................	O (L. Octarius)	16 fluid ounces	0.4732 l
1 gallon*..............................	C (L. Congius)	8 pints; 231 cubic inches	3.7853 l

(British measures differ from the above.)
* The apothecaries' fluid pint and gallon are the same as the ordinary liquid pint and gallon.

WATER VOLUMES

Weight of pure water under specified conditions of temperature and pressure:

Volumes of water	Weight, avoirdupois	Metric equivalent
1 U.S. gallon..........................	8.3452 lb. at 4° C (in vacuum)	3.7853 kg
1 U.S. gallon..........................	8.3358 " " " (in air)	3.7811 kg
1 U.S. gallon..........................	8.3216 " " 20° C (in air)	3.7746 kg
1 imperial gallon......................	10 " " 62° F (in air)	4.5359 kg
1 liter...............................	2.2046 " " 4° C (in vacuum)	1 kg
1 cubic inch..........................	0.03609 " " " (in air)	0.0164 kg
1 cubic foot..........................	62.3565 " " " (in air)	28.284 kg
1 milliliter equals 1.000027 cubic centimeters		1 g

CIRCULAR OR ANGULAR MEASURE

Name	Abbreviation	Common equivalent
1 minute.........................		60 seconds (″)
1 degree.........................	°	60 minutes
1 sign (zodiac)..................	......	30 degrees
1 radian.........................	......	57.2958 degrees; $180/\pi$
1 quadrant.......................	quad. }	90 degrees
1 right angle....................	L }	
1 circle }		360 degrees; 12 signs; 4 quadrants
1 circumference }	O	
1 circular mil...................	cir.mil	0.7854 square mil (a circular mil is the area of a circle 1 mil in diameter)

Calculations:

Circumference	= diameter × 3.1416
Diameter	= circumference ÷ 3.1416
Area of circle	= diameter squared × 0.7854
Radius	= circumference × 0.15915
Surface of sphere	= diameter squared × 3.1416
Solidity, or cubic contents, of sphere	= diameter cubed × 0.5236
Surface of cylinder	= (diameter × 3.1416) × length
Cubic contents of cylinder	= (diameter squared × 0.7854) × length
Gallons in cylinder	= cubic contents (in cubic inches) ÷ 231 (number of cubic inches in U.S. gallon)

PAPER MEASURE

Measure for papers put up in cases, bundles, or frames:

Name	Abbreviation	Common equivalent
1 quire.........................	qr.	25 sheets
1 standard ream.................	rm.	20 quires; 500 sheets
1 printers' ream................	....	516 sheets
1 bundle........................	bdl.	2 reams

Old measure, which is still used for small papers:

Name	Abbreviation	Common equivalent
1 quire.........................	qr.	24 sheets
1 ream..........................	rm.	20 quires; 480 sheets

WEIGHTS AND MEASURES

LAND MEASURE

Name	Abbreviation	Common equivalent
1 lot, or plot.........................	....	a small area of ground (sizes vary)
1 block.............................	blk.	a city block (sizes vary)
1 acre..............................	A.	160 square rods
1 section...........................	sec.	640 acres; 1 square mile
1 township.........................	T. or Tp.	36 square miles (6 miles square); 36 sections
1 range............................	R.	6-mile strip of land—a row of townships—running north and south, laid out from a principal meridian

Ranges are numbered east and west of chosen meridians.

Townships are numbered north and south of designated base lines.

County is the largest subdivision in all states in the Union, except Louisiana, where "parish" is used instead of "county".

Some subdivisions of a section of land:

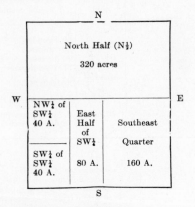

Legal land descriptions are written in abbreviated form:

NE¼ of Sec. 4, T. 6 S., R. 15 EBM

E½ of SE¼ of NE¼ of Sec. 6, T. 8 N., R. 40 EWM

Written out, these land descriptions would read:

The northeast quarter of Section 4, Township 6 south, Range 15 east of the Boise meridian.

The east half of the southeast quarter of the northeast quarter of Section 6, Township 8 north, Range 40 east of the Willamette meridian.

LATITUDE AND LONGITUDE

Longitude lines—the lines of measurement (meridians) running north and south from pole to pole, at right angles to the equator. Longitude is measured east or west of the prime meridian, which is the meridian of Greenwich, England, known as Longitude 0°. There are 180° in east longitude, and 180° in west longitude—360° making the complete globe.

Latitude lines—the lines of measurement (parallels of latitude) running east and west around the earth, parallel to the equator—north and south of the equator, which is 0°. There are 90° in north latitude, and 90° in south latitude—reaching to each pole.

Latitude and longitude are figured in degrees, minutes, and seconds (in circular measurement).

Longitude 30° 08′ 14″ W.

Latitude 40° 19′ 12″ N.

means that this place is located on the line which is 30 degrees 8 minutes and 14 seconds west of the meridian through Greenwich, England, and at a point on that line 40 degrees 19 minutes and 12 seconds north of the equator.

Latitude and longitude are also expressed in degrees alone, as

Latitude 10.2 N., longitude 167.43 W.

564

WEIGHTS AND MEASURES

COUNTING MEASURE

Name	Abbreviation	Common equivalent
1 dozen....................................	doz.	12 units
1 gross....................................	gr.	12 dozen; 144 units
1 great gross..............................	g.gr.	12 gross; 1728 units
1 score...................................	....	20 units

MISCELLANEOUS MEASURES

1 hand (a hand's breadth)	4 inches
1 line	button measure, $\frac{1}{40}$ inch
1 load (of earth, etc.)	1 cubic yard
1 mil (wire measure)	$\frac{1}{1000}$ inch; 0.0254 millimeter
1 pace (ordinary)	2.5 feet
1 pace (for measuring distances)	{ 3 feet; 1 yard; sometimes 3.3 feet ($\frac{1}{2}$ rod)
1 pace (military)	{ 30 inches—quick time; 36 inches—double time
1 pace (geometrical, or "great pace")	5 feet; sometimes 4.4 feet
1 palm (a hand's breadth)	3 or 4 inches
1 perch (linear)	$5\frac{1}{2}$ yards; 1 rod
1 perch (land)	1 square rod
1 perch (stonework)	$24\frac{3}{4}$ cubic feet (ordinarily)
1 point (type)	0.0138 inch, or about $\frac{1}{72}$ inch
1 pole (linear)	$5\frac{1}{2}$ yards; 1 rod
1 pole (surface)	1 square rod
1 quarter	25 pounds (U.S.); 28 pounds (Br.)
1 rood	40 square rods; $\frac{1}{4}$ acre
1 span	9 inches
1 square (flooring, or roofing)	100 square feet
1 stone (British)	14 pounds
1 tierce	42 gallons

❖

RAILROAD MILEAGE

Distances compiled from Rand McNally & Company's "Commercial Atlas", and the War Department's "Official Table of Distances".

Data used by permission.

Note: These distances are for the shortest generally traveled routes.

From: \ To:	Atlanta, Ga.	Boston, Mass.	Chicago, Ill.	Cincinnati, Ohio	Cleveland, Ohio	Denver, Colo.	Detroit, Mich.	El Paso, Tex.	Jacksonville, Fla.	Kansas City, Mo.	Los Angeles, Calif.	Memphis, Tenn.	Minneapolis and St. Paul, Minn.	New Orleans, La.	New York City	Omaha, Nebr.	Pittsburgh, Pa.	Portland, Oreg.	Salt Lake City, Utah	San Francisco, Calif.	Seattle, Wash.	St. Louis, Mo.
Atlanta, Ga.																						
Boston, Mass.	1105																					
Chicago, Ill.	733	1011																				
Cincinnati, Ohio	488	916	298																			
Cleveland, Ohio	723	681	339	235																		
Denver, Colo.	1525	2037	1026	1256	1365																	
Detroit, Mich.	749	739	272	261	171	1298																
El Paso, Tex.	1479	2411	1400	1566	1739	714	1672															
Jacksonville, Fla.	335	1212	1068	823	1053	1860	1084	1803														
Kansas City, Mo.	889	1462	451	617	790	636	723	949	1184													
Los Angeles, Calif.	2282	3242	2231	2397	2570	1404	2503	812	2615	1780												
Memphis, Tenn.	419	1387	527	494	729	1120	755	1209	700	484	1972											
Minneapolis and St. Paul, Minn. (10 mi. between)	1141	1419	408	706	747	895	680	1439	1476	490	2168	886										
New Orleans, La.	493	1574	923	835	1070	1330	1096	1191	612	867	2003	396	1282									
New York City	876	229	910	751	571	1936	637	2280	983	1331	3111	1158	1318	1345								
Omaha, Nebr.	1025	1499	488	718	827	538	760	1145	1360	194	1811	678	357	1061	1398							
Pittsburgh, Pa.	799	669	468	311	131	1494	302	1840	922	891	2671	805	876	1146	440	956						
Portland, Oreg.	2800	3274	2222	2520	2561	1374	2494	1945	3135	1969	1130	2453	1814	2732	3132	1775	2690					
Salt Lake City, Utah	2052	2526	1515	1745	1854	570	1787	1334	2387	1221	784	1705	1384	1950	2425	1027	1983	887				
San Francisco, Calif.	2755	3318	2307	2537	2646	1372	2579	1285	3088	1969	473	2415	2176	2441	3217	1819	2775	772	792			
Seattle, Wash.	2906	3184	2173	2471	2512	1467	2445	2128	3227	2061	1313	2545	1765	2928	3083	1867	2641	183	980	955		
St. Louis, Mo.	611	1206	284	339	525	914	488	1227	946	278	2058	305	581	701	1053	414	613	2189	1441	2233	2281	
Washington, D.C.	649	456	770	562	433	1805	604	2128	756	1169	2903	931	1178	1118	227	1258	302	2992	2285	3077	2943	891

AUTOMOBILE MILEAGE

Distances from the "Shell Transcontinental Mileage Chart". Reprinted by permission from The H. M. Gousha Company, Chicago, Copyright Owners.

From: \ To:	Atlanta, Ga.	Boston, Mass.	Chicago, Ill.	Cincinnati, Ohio	Cleveland, Ohio	Dallas, Tex.	Denver, Colo.	Detroit, Mich.	El Paso, Tex.	Houston, Tex.	Jacksonville, Fla.	Kansas City, Mo.	Los Angeles, Calif.	Memphis, Tenn.	Miami, Fla.	Minneapolis and St. Paul, Minn.	Montreal, Canada	New Orleans, La.	New York City	Omaha, Nebr.	Pittsburgh, Pa.	Portland, Oreg.	Salt Lake City, Utah	San Francisco, Calif.	Seattle, Wash.	St. Louis, Mo.	Tulsa, Okla.
Atlanta, Ga.																											
Boston, Mass.	1126																										
Chicago, Ill.	744	1004																									
Cincinnati, Ohio	473	886	305																								
Cleveland, Ohio	717	640	360	244																							
Dallas, Tex.	892	1875	990	1026	1232																						
Denver, Colo.	1567	2057	1087	1262	1442	843																					
Detroit, Mich.	726	727	277	257	172	1198	1364																				
El Paso, Tex.	1555	2465	1525	1628	1831	663	655	1362																			
Houston, Tex.	930	2027	1143	1159	1398	262	1101	1772	820																		
Jacksonville, Fla.	328	1240	1072	801	1011	1065	1860	1060	1728	1009																	
Kansas City, Mo.	861	1457	514	621	817	517	658	758	1014	755	1189																
Los Angeles, Calif.	2401	3186	2243	2350	2546	1509	1271	2487	846	1649	2658	1729															
Memphis, Tenn.	452	1410	552	560	784	481	1115	750	1144	614	712	490	1967														
Miami, Fla.	682	1594	1426	1155	1365	1378	2160	1414	2041	1363	354	1543	3012	1066													
Minneapolis and St. Paul, Minn.	1179	1420	420	725	780	1013	984	697	1466	1323	1492	496	2059	885	1846												
Montreal, Canada	1266	332	859	803	568	1798	1960	602	2374	1969	1397	1360	3089	1355	1738	1215											
New Orleans, La.	567	1653	972	885	1129	544	1387	1142	1189	386	623	838	2035	420	977	1333	1762										
New York City	903	218	859	636	506	1655	1837	652	2245	1807	1023	1238	2967	1193	1377	1279	386	1371									
Omaha, Nebr.	1071	1475	496	717	837	705	615	769	1097	967	1399	210	1812	700	1753	369	1371	1094	1328								
Pittsburgh, Pa.	766	593	477	291	124	1313	1463	288	1895	1443	977	864	2541	836	1331	897	602	1176	375	946							
Portland, Oreg.	2894	3294	2294	2577	2654	2223	1416	2571	1811	2485	3222	2033	1010	2523	3540	1874	2995	3153	2764	1874	2771						
Salt Lake City, Utah	2037	2408	1516	1720	1870	1362	555	1792	950	1574	2365	1176	756	1666	2683	1358	2394	1906	2349	1023	1967	861					
San Francisco, Calif.	2821	3342	2372	2505	2655	1929	1340	2563	1285	2089	2994	1961	420	2320	3307	2088	3179	2453	3122	1808	2748	708	785				
Seattle, Wash.	2921	3255	2206	2511	2566	2298	1459	2507	1953	2560	3249	2060	1202	2550	3567	1786	2907	2842	3065	1907	2683	192	1003	900			
St. Louis, Mo.	599	1199	297	351	558	682	911	522	1296	846	927	267	2007	305	1273	588	1116	745	979	489	597	2300	1443	2228	2327		
Tulsa, Okla.	893	1628	736	789	994	286	707	953	837	1153	1628	260	1575	441	1406	780	1555	756	1408	419	1034	2123	1256	1951	2166	437	
Washington, D.C.	674	446	708	501	367	1443	1672	531	2080	1676	792	1073	2802	962	1146	1128	592	1205	228	1169	230	3002	2172	2957	2914	806	1244

AIRWAY MILEAGE

Distances from the table "Air-Line Distances in Statute Miles", issued by the Department of Commerce, Washington, D. C. Reprinted by permission.

From: \ To:	Atlanta, Ga.	Boston, Mass.	Chicago, Ill.	Cincinnati, Ohio	Cleveland, Ohio	Denver, Colo.	Detroit, Mich.	El Paso, Tex.	Fort Worth, Tex.	Galveston, Tex.	Jacksonville, Fla.	Kansas City, Mo.	Los Angeles, Calif.	Memphis, Tenn.	Miami, Fla.	Minneapolis and St. Paul, Minn.	Missoula, Mont.	New Orleans, La.	New York City	Oklahoma City, Okla.	Omaha, Nebr.	Pittsburgh, Pa.	Portland, Oreg.	Salt Lake City, Utah	San Francisco, Calif.	Seattle, Wash.	St. Louis, Mo.
Atlanta, Ga.																											
Boston, Mass.	933																										
Chicago, Ill.	583	849																									
Cincinnati, Ohio	368	737	249																								
Cleveland, Ohio	550	550	307	218																							
Denver, Colo.	1208	1766	918	1090	1223																						
Detroit, Mich.	595	613	236	234	94	1153																					
El Paso, Tex.	1293	2067	1249	1333	1521	554	1475																				
Fort Worth, Tex.	750	1574	820	839	1046	643	1018	543																			
Galveston, Tex.	688	1598	954	897	1116	925	1111	723	283																		
Jacksonville, Fla.	286	1015	861	628	768	1468	832	1481	943	799																	
Kansas City, Mo.	675	1250	413	541	700	555	643	836	460	677	952																
Los Angeles, Calif.	1935	2590	1741	1892	2044	831	1976	702	1212	1423	2153	1352															
Memphis, Tenn.	335	1133	481	410	627	878	621	978	448	492	591	370	1602														
Miami, Fla.	610	1258	1190	957	1088	1732	1156	1662	1150	941	328	1247	2355	878													
Minneapolis and St. Paul, Minn.	905	1125	356	603	632	699	542	1156	870	1087	1192	413	1522	700	1516												
Missoula, Mont.	1790	2124	1348	1578	1640	670	1552	1115	1312	1595	2070	910	1675	1483	2359	1010											
New Orleans, La.	427	1359	831	708	922	1079	938	986	470	288	511	678	1675	358	681	1050	1733										
New York City	747	188	711	568	404	1628	483	1902	1398	1415	838	1097	2446	953	1095	1019	2030	1173									
Oklahoma City, Okla.	753	1490	689	755	946	503	905	578	188	456	1150	293	988	422	1233	692	1162	575	1324								
Omaha, Nebr.	815	1280	432	620	738	485	666	875	590	828	1098	165	1312	529	1402	291	978	845	1144	405							
Pittsburgh, Pa.	520	478	411	258	115	1320	208	1592	1097	1286	703	784	2135	660	1014	745	1754	923	313	1013	837						
Portland, Oreg.	2172	2553	1765	1987	2063	985	1975	1286	1612	1885	2442	1397	825	1852	2716	1435	430	2063	2455	1488	1373	2174					
Salt Lake City, Utah	1580	2099	1260	1450	1567	372	1490	689	977	1249	1840	922	577	1250	2098	988	435	1433	1972	862	833	561	636				
San Francisco, Calif.	2133	2696	1855	2037	2163	946	2087	993	1454	1693	2375	1500	345	1923	2603	1585	762	1923	2568	1386	1425	2264	636	592			
Seattle, Wash.	2180	2508	1743	1974	2035	1020	1945	1373	1658	1938	2450	1505	956	1867	2740	1403	395	2098	2419	1523	1372	2145	143	697	680		
St. Louis, Mo.	467	1036	259	308	490	793	452	1033	568	697	755	238	1585	242	1067	464	1331	599	873	456	352	561	1723	833	1738	1722	
Washington, D.C.	542	392	594	403	303	1490	397	1726	1210	1214	647	943	2295	763	927	936	1940	968	204	1150	1012	188	2360	1845	2437	2335	710

TIME

CLOCK TIME

Writing Clock Time. A colon is used in ordinary work to separate hours and minutes; but a period is often employed in tabulations and in statistical work to save the effort of continually using the shift key on the typewriter.

5:40   or   5.40

Write "a.m." and "p.m." in small letters, with a period after each letter. In telegraphic usage they are written A and P, without periods. In tabulations the periods are omitted.

Use "a.m." and "p.m." with figures, not with words, as

at 10 a.m.   NOT: at *ten a.m.*

Never use "a.m." for "morning", nor "p.m." for "afternoon", in sentences unless figures are used before the abbreviations.

> NOT: Referring to our phone conversation of this *a.m.* ... (USE: morning)
> NOT: They work from nine *a.m.* to five *p.m.* (USE: from nine to five OR: from 9 a.m. to 5 p.m.)
> NOT: He is expected to arrive tomorrow *p.m.* at 3. (USE: afternoon)

Caution: Do not use "a.m." and "morning" together, nor "p.m." and "afternoon"; one is simply a repetition of the other.

> NOT: ...this afternoon at 4 *p.m.* (OMIT: p.m.)
> NOT: ...at 8 *a.m.* on the morning of April 26. (USE: 8 o'clock)
> NOT: ...broadcast at 8:30 *p.m.* each evening. (OMIT: p.m.)

"O'clock" is preferably not used with "a.m." or "p.m.", because of the rather ungainly construction.

> NOT: at 3 o'clock p.m.
> BUT: at 3 p.m.   or   at 3 o'clock in the afternoon

Even Hours. It is unnecessary to carry the ciphers after even hours, unless it is done for a specific purpose, as in tabulations.

> at 11 a.m.   RATHER THAN: at 11:00 a.m.
> at 3 in the afternoon   at 3:00 in the...

Figures or Words. Figures should be used if the time of day is inserted for the purpose of ready calculation. Otherwise words or figures may be used, according to the formality of the text.

Manners of writing time are:

Figures:

at 4:30 p.m.
at 4:30 in the afternoon
at 4 in the afternoon
at 10 a.m. and 6 p.m.

on the 8-o'clock train

at 4:30 o'clock
this afternoon at 4:30
in the morning at 10
at 10 o'clock in the morning
and 6 in the evening
on the 8:30 train

Words:

at four o'clock
at four-thirty
a quarter to three (or "of")
on the four-o'clock train

at four in the afternoon
at half past four
a quarter past three
on the four-thirty train

Noon and Midnight. To designate exact noon or exact midnight, write out the words, or use the abbreviations "n." for noon, and "mid." for midnight. Noon is sometimes designated by "m." (L. meridies), but this abbreviation is not recommended because it may be confused with midnight. In railroad timetables, noon is "n'n" or just "nn".

WRITE: at 12 noon or
at 12 n. or 12 nn.
at 12 midnight or
at 12 mid. or mdnt.

RATHER THAN: at 12 m. (noon)

at 12 p.m. (midnight)

European Clock Time. Many foreign countries have the 24-hour system of telling time in railroad and telegraph stations, and clocks are arranged accordingly. The following tabulation will show the difference between the Continental system and the American.

AMERICAN SYSTEM (12 HOURS)	CONTINENTAL SYSTEM (24 HOURS)
12 midnight	0 hours 0 minutes
1 a.m.	1 o'clock
2	2
3	3
4	4
5	5
6	6
7	7
8	8
9	9
10	10
11	11
12 noon	12
1 p.m.	13
2	14
3	15
4	16
5	17
6	18
7	19
8	20
9	21
10	22
11	23
11:59 p.m.	23^{59}
12 midnight	24 or 0^{00}
12:15 a.m.	0^{15}

ARMED FORCES TIME		
The **Army** and **Navy** use the 24-hour clock system in official communications, and express time in four figures always—from midnight to midnight.		
THUS: 12 midnight	IS	2400
12:01 a.m.		0001
12:30 a.m.		0030
1:00 a.m.		0100
6:35 a.m.		0635
12:00 noon		1200
12:40 p.m.		1240
1:30 p.m.		1330
5:15 p.m.		1715
11:50 p.m.		2359
12 midnight		2400

Continental timetables are marked accordingly. For instance, a train departing at 14^{45} would be leaving at 2:45 by a 12-hour watch.

Periods of Time. For ready calculation of periods of time, figures instead of words are commonly used. Commas are not necessary between the different parts of one period of time, which is considered a single unit.

5 hours 8 minutes 15 seconds   5 years 10 months 20 days

(For ages, see Numbers, p. 270.)

STANDARD TIME

Standard time in the United States is divided into four zones, with one hour's time difference between each zone and the next.

	Comparison with others *Later (L) or earlier (E) than			
	EST	CST	MST	PST
Eastern standard time (E.S.T.) is............		1 hr. L	2 hr. L	3 hr. L
Central standard time (C.S.T.) is............	1 hr. E		1 hr. L	2 hr. L
Mountain standard time (M.S.T.) is.........	2 hr. E	1 hr. E		1 hr. L
Pacific standard time (P.S.T.) is.............	3 hr. E	2 hr. E	1 hr. E	

* "Later" as used in the tables in this section means later in the day, or having a time that is so many hours faster than the time in question. "Earlier" means earlier in the day, or having a time that is so many hours slower than the time in question.

Daylight saving time (D.S.T.) is observed in certain cities, states, and foreign countries, from approximately May 1 to October 1 each year. It advances standard time one hour.

World Date Line. The date line in the Pacific Ocean between Hawaii and the Orient marks the ending of one day and the beginning of the next.

In calculating standard time around the world, consider the path of the sun. When the sun rises on Japan and China a new day is begun. The sun carries that day across Siberia, Russia, Germany, France, England, the Atlantic Ocean, the United States, and on to the Hawaiian Islands. When it sets on the Hawaiian Islands that day is finished, and as it rises again on Japan, China, the Philippines, and Australia, the next day is begun, while the United States is still in the darkness of the night before. Thus it is that a radio broadcast from the Orient on Wednesday morning can be received in the United States on Tuesday evening.

Greenwich Mean Time (G.M.T.). Greenwich time is simply the correct **hour** time by which other times are set. The meridian passing through the observatory at Greenwich, England, was chosen as a standard; and other times are reckoned as so many hours earlier or later (slower or faster) than Greenwich time. (pron. grĭn´ĭj)

571

TIME

Standard Time in the United States

(Note: Some states on the time border lines have small corners or tips running into other time zones. Such parts have not been here considered, as they are thinly populated desert or mountainous regions.)

State	Standard Time Used
Alabama	Central
Arizona	Mountain
Arkansas	Central
California	Pacific
Colorado	Mountain
Connecticut	Eastern
Delaware	Eastern
District of Columbia	Eastern
Florida	Eastern—except part west of Apalachicola River, which uses Central
Georgia	Eastern (adopted by state law)
Idaho	{ Mountain—below the Salmon River { Pacific—above the Salmon River
Illinois	Central
Indiana	Central
Iowa	Central
Kansas	{ Central—in most of state { Mountain—in northwestern quarter
Kentucky	Central
Louisiana	Central
Maine	Eastern
Maryland	Eastern
Massachusetts	Eastern
Michigan	{ Eastern—on lower peninsula { Central—on upper peninsula { Sault Ste. Marie uses Eastern
Minnesota	Central
Mississippi	Central
Missouri	Central
Montana	Mountain
Nebraska	{ Central—in eastern part { Mountain—in western part { Ainsworth uses Mountain time { North Platte uses Central
Nevada	Pacific
New Hampshire	Eastern
New Jersey	Eastern
New Mexico	Mountain
New York	Eastern
North Carolina	Eastern
North Dakota	{ Central—in most of state { Mountain—in southwestern quarter { Bismarck uses Central
Ohio	Eastern
Oklahoma	Central
Oregon	Pacific
Pennsylvania	Eastern
Rhode Island	Eastern
South Carolina	Eastern
South Dakota	{ Central—in eastern half of state { Mountain—in western half of state { Pierre uses Central time
Tennessee	Central
Texas	Central (El Paso uses Mountain)
Utah	Mountain
Vermont	Eastern
Virginia	Eastern
Washington	Pacific
West Virginia	Eastern
Wisconsin	Central
Wyoming	Mountain

STANDARD TIME IN FOREIGN COUNTRIES

STANDARD TIME IN FOREIGN COUNTRIES
Compiled from the National Bureau of Standards Circular C406,
"Standard Time Throughout the World".

Country	Hours later (L) or earlier (E) than United States Standard Time			
	EST	CST	MST	PST
Abyssinia (See Ethiopia)				
Aden, Arabia	8 L	9 L	10 L	11 L
Afghanistan	(*9 L)	(*10 L)	(*11 L)	(*12 L)
Africa, South-West; and Union of South Africa	7 L	8 L	9 L	10 L
Alaska				
Extreme western coast	6 E	5 E	4 E	3 E
Central portion	5 E	4 E	3 E	2 E
Southern point, except Ketchikan	4 E	3 E	2 E	1 E
Ketchikan	3 E	2 E	1 E	same†
Albania	6 L	7 L	8 L	9 L
Algeria	5 L	6 L	7 L	8 L
Anglo-Egyptian Sudan	7 L	8 L	9 L	10 L
Angola	6 L	7 L	8 L	9 L
Arabia	(*8 L)	(*9 L)	(*10 L)	(*11 L)
Argentina	1 L	2 L	3 L	4 L
Ascension	4 L	5 L	6 L	7 L
Australia				
Western Australia	13 L	14 L	15 L	16 L
Northern Territory } South Australia }	14½L	15½L	16½L	17½L
New South Wales } Queensland } Victoria }	15 L	16 L	17 L	18 L
Austria	6 L	7 L	8 L	9 L
Azores	3 L	4 L	5 L	6 L
Bahamas	same†	1 L	2 L	3 L
Balearic Islands	5 L	6 L	7 L	8 L
Barbados	1 L	2 L	3 L	4 L
Batavia, Dutch East Indies	12½L	13½L	14½L	15½L
Bechuanaland	7 L	8 L	9 L	10 L
Belgian Congo	6 L	7 L	8 L	9 L
Belgium	5 L	6 L	7 L	8 L
Bermuda	1 L	2 L	3 L	4 L
Bolivia	*½L	*1½L	*2½L	*3½L
Borneo, North	13 L	14 L	15 L	16 L
Brazil				
Eastern coast	2 L	3 L	4 L	5 L
Western part	1 L	2 L	3 L	4 L
Extreme western point	same†	1 L	2 L	3 L
Islands	3 L	4 L	5 L	6 L
British Honduras	1 E	same†	1 L	2 L
Bulgaria	7 L	8 L	9 L	10 L
Burma	11½L	12½L	13½L	14½L
Cameroons—British, and French	6 L	7 L	8 L	9 L
Canada				
Alberta	2 E	1 E	same†	1 L
British Columbia	3 E	2 E	1 E	same†
Manitoba	1 E	same†	1 L	2 L
New Brunswick	1 L	2 L	3 L	4 L
Nova Scotia	1 L	2 L	3 L	4 L
Ontario				
Eastern and central part	same†	1 L	2 L	3 L
Western part	1 E	same†	1 L	2 L
Quebec				
Eastern part	1 L	2 L	3 L	4 L
Western part	same†	1 L	2 L	3 L
Saskatchewan	2 E	1 E	same†	1 L
Yukon	4 E	3 E	2 E	1 E
Canal Zone	same†	1 L	2 L	3 L
Canary Islands	4 L	5 L	6 L	7 L

Standard Time in Foreign Countries—contd.

Country	Hours later (L) or earlier (E) than United States Standard Time			
	EST	CST	MST	PST
Cape Colony (Cape of Good Hope)	7 L	8 L	9 L	10 L
Cape Verde Islands	3 L	4 L	5 L	6 L
Caroline Islands				
Western	15 L	16 L	17 L	18 L
Eastern	16 L	17 L	18 L	19 L
Celebes	13 L	14 L	15 L	16 L
Ceylon	10½L	11½L	12½L	13½L
Chile	1 L	2 L	3 L	4 L
China				
Hong Kong, and east coast	13 L	14 L	15 L	16 L
Interior	(*11½L)	(*12½L)	(*13½L)	(*14½L)
Chosen (Korea)	14 L	15 L	16 L	17 L
Colombia	same†	1 L	2 L	3 L
Corsica	5 L	6 L	7 L	8 L
Costa Rica	1 E	same†	1 L	2 L
Crete	7 L	8 L	9 L	10 L
Cuba	same†	1 L	2 L	3 L
Cyprus	7 L	8 L	9 L	10 L
Czecho-Slovakia	6 L	7 L	8 L	9 L
Dahomey	5 L	6 L	7 L	8 L
Denmark	6 L	7 L	8 L	9 L
Dominican Republic	⅓L	1⅓L	2⅓L	3⅓L
Dutch East Indies (Indonesia)	*13 L	*14 L	*15 L	*16 L
Ecuador	*¼E	*¾L	*1¾L	*2¾L
Egypt	7 L	8 L	9 L	10 L
El Salvador	1 E	same†	1 L	2 L
England	5 L	6 L	7 L	8 L
Eritrea	8 L	9 L	10 L	11 L
Estonia	7 L	8 L	9 L	10 L
Ethiopia (Abyssinia)	(*8 L)	(*9 L)	(*10 L)	(*11 L)
Falkland Islands	1 L	2 L	3 L	4 L
Faroe Islands (Faeroes)	5 L	6 L	7 L	8 L
Fernando Po	5 L	6 L	7 L	8 L
Fiji Islands	17 L	18 L	19 L	20 L
Finland	7 L	8 L	9 L	10 L
Formosa (Taiwan)	14 L	15 L	16 L	17 L
France	5 L	6 L	7 L	8 L
French Equatorial Africa (French Congo)	6 L	7 L	8 L	9 L
French Indo-China	12 L	13 L	14 L	15 L
French Sudan				
Eastern part	5 L	6 L	7 L	8 L
Western part	4 L	5 L	6 L	7 L
Friendly Islands (See Tonga Islands)				
Gambia	4 L	5 L	6 L	7 L
Germany	6 L	7 L	8 L	9 L
Gibraltar	5 L	6 L	7 L	8 L
Gilbert and Ellice Islands	17 L	18 L	19 L	20 L
Gold Coast	5 L	6 L	7 L	8 L
Great Britain	5 L	6 L	7 L	8 L
Greece	7 L	8 L	9 L	10 L
Greenland, western coast	2 L	3 L	4 L	5 L
Guadeloupe	1 L	2 L	3 L	4 L
Guam	15 L	16 L	17 L	18 L
Guatemala	1 E	same†	1 L	2 L
Guiana—British, French, and Dutch (Surinam)	*1 L	*2 L	*3 L	*4 L
Guinea—French, and Portuguese	4 L	5 L	6 L	7 L
Guinea, Spanish	5 L	6 L	7 L	8 L
Haiti	same†	1 L	2 L	3 L
Hawaiian Islands	5½E	4½E	3½E	2½E
Holland (See Netherlands)				
Honduras	1 E	same†	1 L	2 L

574

STANDARD TIME IN FOREIGN COUNTRIES—contd.

Country	Hours later (L) or earlier (E) than United States Standard Time			
	EST	CST	MST	PST
Hong Kong Colony	13 L	14 L	15 L	16 L
Hungary	6 L	7 L	8 L	9 L
Iceland	4 L	5 L	6 L	7 L
India	*10½L	*11½L	*12½L	*13½L
Indo-China	12 L	13 L	14 L	15 L
Iran (Persia)	(*9 L)	(*10 L)	(*11 L)	(*12 L)
Iraq (Mesopotamia)	8 L	9 L	10 L	11 L
Ireland	5 L	6 L	7 L	8 L
Italy	6 L	7 L	8 L	9 L
Ivory Coast	5 L	6 L	7 L	8 L
Jamaica	same†	1 L	2 L	3 L
Japan	14 L	15 L	16 L	17 L
Java	12½L	13½L	14½L	15½L
Jugoslavia (See Yugoslavia)				
Kenya	7½L	8½L	9½L	10½L
Korea (See Chosen)				
Labrador (coast)	1½L	2½L	3½L	4½L
Labuan	13 L	14 L	15 L	16 L
Latvia	7 L	8 L	9 L	10 L
Lebanon (See Syria)				
Liberia	4¼L	5¼L	6¼L	7¼L
Libya	6 L	7 L	8 L	9 L
Liechtenstein	6 L	7 L	8 L	9 L
Lithuania	6 L	7 L	8 L	9 L
Luxemburg	6 L	7 L	8 L	9 L
Macao	13 L	14 L	15 L	16 L
Madagascar	8 L	9 L	10 L	11 L
Madeira Islands	4 L	5 L	6 L	7 L
Malay States	12 L	13 L	14 L	15 L
Malta	6 L	7 L	8 L	9 L
Manchukuo	(*13½L)	(*14½L)	(*15½L)	(*16½L)
Martinique	1 L	2 L	3 L	4 L
Mauritania	4 L	5 L	6 L	7 L
Mauritius	9 L	10 L	11 L	12 L
Mesopotamia (See Iraq)				
Mexico (except upper part of Lower California)	1 E	same†	1 L	2 L
Upper part of Lower California	3 E	2 E	1 E	same†
Monaco	5 L	6 L	7 L	8 L
Morocco	5 L	6 L	7 L	8 L
Mozambique	7 L	8 L	9 L	10 L
Nauru Island	16 L	17 L	18 L	19 L
Netherlands	5⅓L	6⅓L	7⅓L	8⅓L
New Caledonia Island	16 L	17 L	18 L	19 L
Newfoundland	1½L	2½L	3½L	4½L
New Guinea, eastern part	15 L	16 L	17 L	18 L
New Hebrides	16 L	17 L	18 L	19 L
New Zealand	16½L	17½ L	18½L	19½L
Nicaragua	1 E	same †	1 L	2 L
Niger				
Western part	5 L	6 L	7 L	8 L
Eastern part	6 L	7 L	8 L	9 L
Nigeria	6 L	7 L	8 L	9 L
Norway	6 L	7 L	8 L	9 L
Nova Scotia	1 L	2 L	3 L	4 L
Nyasaland	7 L	8 L	9 L	10 L
Oceania, French	5 E	4 E	3 E	2 E
Palestine	7 L	8 L	9 L	10 L
Panama, and Canal Zone	same †	1 L	2 L	3 L
Paraguay	1 L	2 L	3 L	4 L
Persia (See Iran)				
Peru	same†	1 L	2 L	3 L
Philippines	13 L	14 L	15 L	16 L

STANDARD TIME IN FOREIGN COUNTRIES—contd.

Country	Hours later (L) or earlier (E) than United States Standard Time			
	EST	CST	MST	PST
Poland	6 L	7 L	8 L	9 L
Portugal	5 L	6 L	7 L	8 L
Puerto Rico	1 L	2 L	3 L	4 L
Réunion Island	9 L	10 L	11 L	12 L
Rhodesia	7 L	8 L	9 L	10 L
Río de Oro	4 L	5 L	6 L	7 L
Rumania	7 L	8 L	9 L	10 L
Russia (See U.S.S.R.)				
Saint Helena Island	*4½L	*5½L	*6½L	*7½L
Salvador, El	1 E	same†	1 L	2 L
Samoa Islands				
Eastern	6 E	5 E	4 E	3 E
Western	6½E	5½E	4½E	3½E
Santo Domingo, Distrito de (See Dominican Republic)				
Sarawak	12½L	13½L	14½L	15½L
Sardinia	6 L	7 L	8 L	9 L
Saudi Arabia	(*8 L)	(*9 L)	(*10 L)	(*11 L)
Scotland	5 L	6 L	7 L	8 L
Senegal	4 L	5 L	6 L	7 L
Seychelles	9 L	10 L	11 L	12 L
Siam (now Thailand)	12 L	13 L	14 L	15 L
Siberia (See U.S.S.R.)				
Sicily	6 L	7 L	8 L	9 L
Sierra Leone	4 L	5 L	6 L	7 L
Somaliland—British, French, and Italian	8 L	9 L	10 L	11 L
South Africa, Union of; and South-West Africa	7 L	8 L	9 L	10 L
Spain	5 L	6 L	7 L	8 L
Straits Settlements	12 L	13 L	14 L	15 L
Sumatra	*12 L	*13 L	*14 L	*15 L
Surinam (See Guiana, Dutch)				
Sweden	6 L	7 L	8 L	9 L
Switzerland	6 L	7 L	8 L	9 L
Syria	7 L	8 L	9 L	10 L
Tahiti	5 E	4 E	3 E	2 E
Tanganyika Territory	8 L	9 L	10 L	11 L
Tasmania	15 L	16 L	17 L	18 L
Timor Island	13 L	14 L	15 L	16 L
Togoland—British, and French	5 L	6 L	7 L	8 L
Tonga (Friendly) Islands	17⅓L	18⅓L	19⅓L	20⅓L
Trinidad and Tobago	1 L	2 L	3 L	4 L
Tunisia (Tunis)	6 L	7 L	8 L	9 L
Turkey	7 L	8 L	9 L	10 L
Turks Islands	same†	1 L	2 L	3 L
Uganda	7½L	8½L	9½L	10½L
Union of South Africa	7 L	8 L	9 L	10 L
Uruguay	1½L	2½L	3½L	4½L
U.S.S.R. (Russia)				
Western part	8 L	9 L	10 L	11 L
(There are 11 divisions of time across Russia and Siberia.)				
Venezuela	½L	1½L	2½L	3½L
Virgin Islands	1 L	2 L	3 L	4 L
Windward Islands (Grenada, St. Lucia, and St. Vincent)	1 L	2 L	3 L	4 L
Yugoslavia	6 L	7 L	8 L	9 L
Zanzibar	8 L	9 L	10 L	11 L

EST Eastern standard time   L Later (faster) than
CST Central standard time   E Earlier (slower) than
MST Mountain standard time   ( ) No standard time, but an approximate time is indicated
PST Pacific standard time   * Approximately
same† Same as standard time indicated at head of column

STANDARD TIME ZONES OF THE WORLD

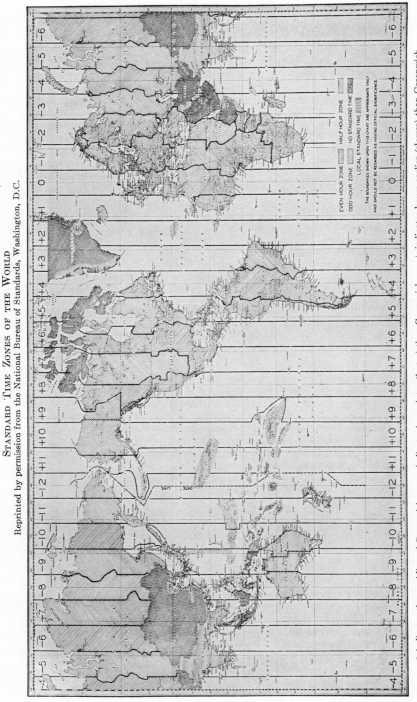

Standard Time Zones of the World
Reprinted by permission from the National Bureau of Standards, Washington, D.C.

0 indicates the meridian of Greenwich   − indicates hours later (faster) than Greenwich   + indicates hours earlier (slower) than Greenwich
The date line in the Pacific Ocean indicates where one day ends and a new one begins.

DIVISIONS OF TIME

Minute   60 seconds
Hour   60 minutes
Day   24 hours
Week   7 days
Fortnight   14 days; 2 weeks
Month   30 days (for general calculations)
> (For exact calculations, the exact number of days in the given months must be figured.)

Months with 30 days—April, June, September, November.
Months with 31 days—All the rest, except February, which has 28, and in leap year, 29.
The old rhyme (slightly modernized) is still an effective aid in remembering the number of days in each month:

> Thirty days hath September,
> April, June, and November;
> All the rest have thirty-one,
> Save February, which alone
> Hath but twenty-eight in time,
> Till leap year gives it twenty-nine.

Lunar month   period of a complete revolution of the moon, approximately 28 days
Lunar day   a day reckoned by the moon
Solar month   average time taken by the sun to pass through a sign of the zodiac
Solar day   a day reckoned by the sun
Sidereal month   average time of the moon's revolution from any star back to the same star, approximately $27\frac{1}{3}$ days
Sidereal day   a day reckoned by a star

Year   365 days (360 days for general calculations); 52 weeks; 12 months
Calendar year   the civil or legal year—from January 1 to December 31
Fiscal year   a financial year—an accounting period of 12 months. The end of a fiscal year implies a closing of the books. (Financial statements may be issued without a closing of the books.) The Government fiscal year ends on June 30; but a business fiscal year may end on the last day of any month.
> Under the Income Tax Law, a fiscal year may be "established" as ending on the last day of any month except December (for computation of rates and dates for tax payment). Fiscal years ending on December 31 are already established under the Law—as calendar years.

Leap year   366 days
> Leap year occurs every 4 years, in the years that are exactly divisible by 4, as 1936. The even century years, as 1900, must be divisible by 400 to be leap years. Hence, 1900 was not a leap year; but the year 2000 will be.

Decade   10 years (pron. dĕk'ād)
Fourscore   80 years
Century   100 years
> Twentieth Century—The years 1901 to 2000 are called the "Twentieth Century" because nineteen centuries have passed, and it is in fact the twentieth century that is elapsing. The first century covered the years 1 to 100; the second century, the years 101 to 200. Thus the year 114 was in the second century; and the years 19— are in the twentieth century, which will have elapsed when the numbers reach 2001.

Olympiad   the 4 years between Olympic Games; or the year of the celebration of the Olympic Games

DIVISIONS OF TIME

WORDS RELATING TO PERIODS OF TIME

diurnal	daily; of a day
semidiurnal	occurring twice a day; pertaining to half a day
semiweekly	occurring twice a week
biweekly*	occurring every 2 weeks
triweekly*	occurring every 3 weeks
thrice-weekly	occurring 3 times a week
semimonthly	occurring twice a month
bimonthly*	occurring every 2 months
trimonthly*	occurring every 3 months
thrice-monthly	occurring 3 times a month
semiannual	occurring twice a year
annual	yearly; pertaining to a period of 1 year
perennial	occurring year after year
{ biennium	a period of 2 years
{ biennial	pertaining to a period of 2 years
{ triennium	a period of 3 years
{ triennial	pertaining to a period of 3 years
{ quadrennium	a period of 4 years
{ quadrennial	pertaining to a period of 4 years
{ quinquennium	a period of 5 years
{ quinquennial	pertaining to a period of 5 years
{ sexennium	a period of 6 years
{ sexennial	pertaining to a period of 6 years
{ septennium	a period of 7 years
{ septennial	pertaining to a period of 7 years
octennial	pertaining to a period of 8 years
novennial	pertaining to a period of 9 years
{ decennium	a period of 10 years
{ decennial	pertaining to a period of 10 years
{ decennary	a 10th anniversary
{ undecennial	pertaining to a period of 11 years
{ undecennary	an 11th anniversary
duodecennial	pertaining to a period of 12 years
vicennial	pertaining to a period of 20 years
tricennial	pertaining to a period of 30 years
{ semicentennial	pertaining to half a century or a period of 50 years
{ semicentenary	a 50th anniversary
septuagenarian	pertaining to the 70s, in age
octogenarian	pertaining to the 80s, in age
nonagenarian	pertaining to the 90s, in age
centenarian	pertaining to 100 years, in age
{ centennium	a period of 100 years; a century
{ centennial	pertaining to a period of 100 years
{ centenary	a 100th anniversary
sesquicentennial	pertaining to a period of 150 years
{ bicentennial	pertaining to a period of 200 years
{ bicentenary	a 200th anniversary
{ tercentennial	pertaining to a period of 300 years
{ tercentenary	a 300th anniversary
quadricentennial	pertaining to a period of 400 years
{ quincentennial	pertaining to a period of 500 years
{ quincentenary	a 500th anniversary
{ millennium	a period of 1000 years
{ millennial	pertaining to a period of 1000 years
{ millenary	a 1000th anniversary

The Millennium—the thousand years of Christ's kingdom on earth; also an imaginary period of perfection—a Utopia.

(Note: A useful distinction in the above words is the application of the -ium endings to nouns denoting periods of time; the -ial endings to adjectives; and the -ary endings to anniversaries.)

---

* "Biweekly" is used to mean either "twice a week" or "every two weeks". To avoid this ambiguity, use "semiweekly" for "twice a week", and "biweekly" for "every two weeks". "Triweekly" is similarly interchanged; to avoid confusion, use "thrice-weekly" for "three times a week", and "triweekly" for "every three weeks". The same remarks apply to "bimonthly" and "trimonthly".

❖

HOLIDAYS

National holidays are eight:,

> New Year's Day
> Washington's Birthday
> Memorial Day
> Independence Day
> Labor Day
> Armistice Day
> Thanksgiving Day
> Christmas Day

"National" is here used to mean holidays that are legalized in all states in the Union. The "legalizing" of holidays by Congress pertains only to holidays for Federal Government employees, who are thus authorized to observe the eight national holidays (in some instances they observe also the holidays of the states in which employed). Thanksgiving Day is proclaimed by the President each year, but it is legalized in each state.

State holidays are the various other holidays observed by the different states.

Post office holidays, in all states, are the eight national holidays. (Postmasters have discretionary authority to reduce, but not suspend, postal service on state or local holidays.)

Bank holidays are the national holidays, and the respective state holidays.

Stock exchange holidays follow the holidays observed by the New York Stock Exchange. Good Friday is a stock exchange holiday. Stock exchanges are often closed on the Saturday after, or the Saturday before, a holiday.

When a holiday falls on Sunday, the following Monday is observed.

– – – –

Calendar for 200 Years. In the current World Almanac may be found a ready-reference calendar for 248 years, from which may be ascertained the day of the week on which any given date fell or will fall, from 1753 to 2000, inclusive.

Rules for Display of the Flag. The rules for display and use of the flag, as established by the Congress, and approved by the President, may be found in the current World Almanac.

Or the complete flag circular may be obtained free by addressing The Adjutant General's Office, Army Department, Washington 25, D.C.

LEGAL HOLIDAYS IN THE UNITED STATES

LEGAL HOLIDAYS IN THE UNITED STATES

Holiday	Date	Observance
New Year's Day	January 1	**National**
Battle of New Orleans	January 8	Louisiana
Lee's Birthday	January 19	Ala., Ark., Fla., Ga., Ky., La., Miss., N.C., S.C., Tenn., Tex., Va.
Inauguration Day	January 20	District of Columbia, every four years
Roosevelt's Birthday (F.D.R.)	January 30	Kentucky, Hawaii
Lincoln's Birthday	February 12	General, except in Ala., Ark., D.C., Fla., Ga., Idaho, La., Maine, Mass., Miss., N.H., N.Mex., N.C., Okla., R.I., S.C., Va.
Admission Day	February 14	Arizona
Mardi Gras	Shrove Tuesday	Ala., Fla. (in some towns), La. (in some parishes)
Washington's Birthday	February 22	**National**
Texas Independence Day	March 2	Texas
Arbor Day	between March 1 & April 15	Utah
Andrew Jackson's Birthday	March 15	Tennessee
Maryland Day	March 25	Maryland
Seward Day	March 30	Alaska
Good Friday	before Easter	Conn., Del., Fla., Hawaii, Ill., Ind., La., Md., Minn., N.J., N. Dak., Pa., Tenn.
Halifax Independence Day	April 12	North Carolina
Jefferson's Birthday	April 13	Ala., Mo., Okla., Va.
Patriots' Day	April 19	Maine, Massachusetts
Battle of San Jacinto	April 21	Texas
Arbor Day	April 22	Nebraska
Oklahoma Day	April 22	Oklahoma
Confederate Memorial Day	April 26	Ala., Fla., Ga., Miss.
Fast Day	4th Monday in April	New Hampshire
Arbor Day	usually 1st Monday in May	Wyoming
R.I. Independence Day	May 4	Rhode Island
Confederate Memorial Day	May 10	North Carolina, South Carolina
Mecklenburg Declaration Day	May 20	North Carolina
Memorial Day (Decoration Day)	May 30	**National**, except in a few states in South: Ala., Ga., Miss., S.C. (This is a post office holiday in all states.)
Jefferson Davis's Birthday	June 3	Ala., Fla., Ga., Miss., S.C., Tex., Va.
Confederate Memorial Day	June 3	Ky., La., Tenn.
Kamehameha Day	June 11	Hawaii
Flag Day	June 14	Pennsylvania
West Virginia Day	June 20	West Virginia
Independence Day	July 4	**National**
Forrest's Birthday	July 13	Tennessee
Pioneer Day	July 24	Utah
Colorado Day	August 1	Colorado
Victory Day	August 14	Rhode Island
Bennington Battle Day	August 16	Vermont
Huey P. Long's Birthday	August 30	Louisiana
Labor Day	1st Monday in September	**National**
Admission Day	September 9	California
Defenders' Day	September 12	Maryland
Regatta Day	3d Saturday in September	Hawaii
Columbus Day	October 12	General, except in Alaska, Ark., D.C., Hawaii, Idaho, Iowa, Maine, Mich., Miss., N.C., S.C., S.Dak., Tenn.
Alaska Day	October 18	Alaska
Nevada (Admission) Day	October 31	Nevada
All Saints' Day	November 1	Louisiana
General Election Day	1st Tuesday after 1st Monday in November in even years	In most states
Armistice Day	November 11	**National**
Thanksgiving Day	4th Thursday in November	**National**
Christmas Day	December 25	**National**
Christmas holiday	December 26	South Carolina

MISCELLANEOUS DAYS

Arbor Day. Observed on different days in different states—usually by proclamation. It is a legal holiday now only in Nebraska, Utah, and Wyoming.

Armed Forces Day. Third Saturday in May. Army, Navy, and Air Force day.

Children's Day. The second Sunday in June.

Father's Day. The third Sunday in June.

Flag Day. June 14—by proclamation. Not a legal holiday, but nationally observed.

Groundhog Day. February 2—a weather-forecasting day. The legend is that the groundhog, or woodchuck, comes out for the first time on this day after his winter's sleep. If he sees his shadow he is frightened into his retreat again for another six weeks—which portends bad weather. If the day is cloudy and he does not see his shadow, he stays out unafraid—which means that spring is at hand.

Halloween. The evening of October 31. The legend of Halloween, or "Allhallow-e'en", is that wicked spirits roamed the earth the night before All Saints' Day (Allhallows), November 1. To ward off these evil spirits, various antics were indulged in. Thus the evening has developed into a maskers' revel.

Leap year. Occurs every 4 years. (See Divisions of Time, p. 578.)

Mother's Day. The second Sunday in May. It is nationally observed.

Olympic Games. Held every 4 years, in years divisible by 4—1948, 1952, etc.

Presidential Election Day. The first Tuesday after the first Monday in November, every 4 years—in years that can be divided by 4, as 1948, 1952, 1956, 1960, etc.

St. Patrick's Day. March 17; named in honor of St. Patrick, patron saint of Ireland.

United Nations Day. October 24—anniversary of founding of United Nations (1945).

Valentine's Day. February 14; named in honor of St. Valentine, a Christian martyr.

Victory Day. August 14—by proclamation. Anniversary of Japan's surrender, 1945.

CANADIAN HOLIDAYS

The following are the holidays observed in Canada:

New Year's Day
Good Friday
Easter Monday
Victoria Day—May 24

Dominion Day—July 1
Labour Day—1st Monday in September
Thanksgiving Day—usually in October
Remembrance Day—November 11
Christmas Day

Anniversary of the birth of the Sovereign (day in June fixed by proclamation) (The birthday of the present Sovereign, George VI, is December 14 [1895]; the birthday of The Princess Elizabeth is April 21 [1926].)

And any other day appointed by proclamation as a holiday.

⋅⋅✦✚═══════════════✚✦⋅⋅

NAMES OF THE MONTHS IN SIX LANGUAGES

English	French	German	Spanish	Italian	Portuguese
January	janvier	Januar	enero	gennaio	janeiro
February	février	Februar	febrero	febbraio	fevereiro
March	mars	März	marzo	marzo	março
April	avril	April	abril	aprile	abril
May	mai	Mai	mayo	maggio	maio
June	juin	Juni	junio	giugno	junho
July	juillet	Juli	julio	luglio	julho
August	août	August	agosto	agosto	agosto
September	septembre	September	septiembre	settembre	setembro
October	octobre	Oktober	octubre	ottobre	outubro
November	novembre	November	noviembre	novembre	novembro
December	décembre	Dezember	diciembre	dicembre	dezembro

Compiled from a table in the Style Manual of the United States Government Printing Office.

Note that the names of the months are capitalized in English and German, but are not capitalized in French, Spanish, Italian, and Portuguese.

EASTER

Easter Sunday. Is fixed as the first Sunday following the Paschal Full Moon, which happens on or next after the 21st of March. The date was so determined in ancient times, it is said, because of the pilgrims' need of moonlight to travel yearly to the great Easter festivals.

Lent. A 40-day period of fasting, beginning on **Ash Wednesday,** which is 40 weekdays before Easter. Sundays are not counted in Lent, because Sunday is always a feast day.

Shrove Tuesday. The day before Ash Wednesday. The Mardi Gras carnival on Shrove Tuesday marks the final festivities before Lent.

Good Friday. The Friday before Easter. Devotions are held on this day in memory of the Crucifixion of Christ.

Palm Sunday. The Sunday before Easter, in commemoration of Christ's entry into Jerusalem, when palm branches were strewn in his path.

DATES ON WHICH ASH WEDNESDAY AND EASTER SUNDAY FALL

Year	Ash Wednesday	Easter Sunday
1936	February 26	April 12
1937	February 10	March 28
1938	March 2	April 17
1939	February 22	April 9
1940	February 7	March 24
1941	February 26	April 13
1942	February 18	April 5
1943	March 10	April 25
1944	February 23	April 9
1945	February 14	April 1
1946	March 6	April 21
1947	February 19	April 6
1948	February 11	March 28
1949	March 2	April 17
1950	February 22	April 9
1951	February 7	March 25
1952	February 27	April 13
1953	February 18	April 5
1954	March 3	April 18
1955	February 23	April 10
1956	February 15	April 1
1957	March 6	April 21
1958	February 19	April 6
1959	February 11	March 29
1960	March 2	April 17

Excerpt from the World Almanac table which gives the dates of Ash Wednesday and Easter Sunday for 200 years—from 1801 to 2000. Reprinted by permission from The World Almanac.

WEDDING ANNIVERSARIES

1st	paper	10th	tin	30th	pearl
2nd	cotton, or straw	12th	linen	40th	emerald
3rd	silk	15th	crystal	45th	ruby
4th	leather	20th	china	50th	golden
5th	wooden	25th	silver	60th	diamond

Wedding anniversary lists differ. See also dictionaries and latest books on "Etiquette".

Birthstones. January, garnet; February, amethyst; March, bloodstone; April, diamond; May, emerald; June, pearl; July, ruby; August, moonstone or sardonyx; September, sapphire; October, opal; November, topaz; December, turquoise.

STATES, COUNTIES, AND CITIES

The United States

State	Official abbreviation*	Capital	State flower
Alabama	Ala.	Montgomery	Goldenrod
Arizona	Ariz.	Phoenix	Saguaro (Giant Cactus)
Arkansas	Ark.	Little Rock	Apple Blossom
California	Calif.	Sacramento	Golden Poppy
Colorado	Colo.	Denver	Blue Columbine
Connecticut	Conn.	Hartford	Mountain Laurel
Delaware	Del.	Dover	Peach Blossom
District of Columbia	D.C.	Washington	American Beauty Rose
Florida	Fla.	Tallahassee	Orange Blossom
Georgia	Ga.	Atlanta	Cherokee Rose
Idaho	spelled out	Boise	Syringa
Illinois	Ill.	Springfield	Wood Violet
Indiana	Ind.	Indianapolis	Zinnia
Iowa	spelled out	Des Moines	Wild Rose
Kansas	Kans.	Topeka	Sunflower
Kentucky	Ky.	Frankfort	Goldenrod
Louisiana	La.	Baton Rouge	Magnolia
Maine	spelled out	Augusta	Pine Cone and Tassel
Maryland	Md.	Annapolis	Black-eyed Susan
Massachusetts	Mass.	Boston	Mayflower (Trailing Arbutus)
Michigan	Mich.	Lansing	Apple Blossom
Minnesota	Minn.	St. Paul	Moccasin Flower
Mississippi	Miss.	Jackson	Magnolia
Missouri	Mo.	Jefferson City	Hawthorn
Montana	Mont.	Helena	Bitter Root
Nebraska	Nebr.	Lincoln	Goldenrod
Nevada	Nev.	Carson City	Sagebrush
New Hampshire	N.H.	Concord	Purple Lilac
New Jersey	N.J.	Trenton	Violet
New Mexico	N.Mex.	Santa Fe	Yucca
New York	N.Y.	Albany	Rose
North Carolina	N.C.	Raleigh	Dogwood
North Dakota	N.Dak.	Bismarck	Wild Prairie Rose
Ohio	spelled out	Columbus	Scarlet Carnation
Oklahoma	Okla.	Oklahoma City	Mistletoe
Oregon	Oreg.	Salem	Oregon Grape
Pennsylvania	Pa.	Harrisburg	Mountain Laurel
Rhode Island	R.I.	Providence	Violet
South Carolina	S.C.	Columbia	Carolina Jessamine
South Dakota	S.Dak.	Pierre	Pasque Flower
Tennessee	Tenn.	Nashville	Iris
Texas	Tex.	Austin	Bluebonnet
Utah	spelled out	Salt Lake City	Sego Lily
Vermont	Vt.	Montpelier	Red Clover
Virginia	Va.	Richmond	American Dogwood
Washington	Wash.	Olympia	Rhododendron
West Virginia	W.Va.	Charleston	Rhododendron (Big Laurel)
Wisconsin	Wis.	Madison	Violet
Wyoming	Wyo.	Cheyenne	Indian Paintbrush

Territories, Dependencies, and Possessions

Alaska, Territory of	Alaska	Juneau	Forget-me-not
Canal Zone	spelled out	Balboa Heights	
Guam	spelled out	Agana	
Hawaii, Territory of	Hawaii	Honolulu	{ Hibiscus
Midway Islands	spelled out	Honolulu	{ Lehua, flower of isl. of Hawaii
Puerto Rico	P.R.	San Juan	Royal Palm
Tutuila (and 4 other Samoan Islands)	spelled out	Pago Pago	
Virgin Islands	spelled out	Charlotte Amalie	
Wake Island	spelled out		

* The "official abbreviations" are those in Government usage. Several shorter abbreviations are commonly used, as

AAA. } Alas. }	Alaska	Ida.	Idaho	O.	Ohio
Cal.	California	Kan.	Kansas	Ore.	Oregon
Col.	Colorado	Me.	Maine	S.D.	South Dakota
Ct.	Connecticut	N.D.	North Dakota	T.H.	Territory of Hawaii
C.Z.	Canal Zone	Neb.	Nebraska	Ut.	Utah
Ia.	Iowa	N.M.	New Mexico	Wn.	Washington

POPULATION OF CITIES

The Largest Cities in the United States—With Names of Counties

106 Cities Having 100,000 Inhabitants or More in 1950
Data from the Bureau of the Census; counties from the Official Postal Guide.
(Alphabetic list on the following page)

1950 population (tentative)*	City, County, State	1950 population (tentative)*	City, County, State
7,835,099	New York†, N.Y.	176,954	Des Moines, Polk, Iowa
3,606,436	Chicago, Cook, Ill.	175,647	Grand Rapids, Kent, Mich.
2,064,794	Philadelphia, Philadelphia, Pa.	173,359	Nashville, Davidson, Tenn.
1,957,692	Los Angeles, Los Angeles, Calif.	167,643	Youngstown, Mahoning, Ohio
1,838,517	Detroit, Wayne, Mich.	166,306	Wichita, Sedgwick, Kans.
940,205	Baltimore (Independent City), Md.	163,344	New Haven, New Haven, Conn.
905,636	Cleveland, Cuyahoga, Ohio	162,800	Flint, Genesee, Mich.
852,623	St. Louis (Independent City), Mo.	162,601	Springfield, Hampden, Mass.
802,178	Washington, D.C.	160,484	Spokane, Spokane, Wash.
790,863	Boston, Suffolk, Mass.	159,352	Bridgeport, Fairfield, Conn.
760,753	San Francisco, San Francisco, Calif.	152,533	Yonkers, Westchester, N.Y.
673,763	Pittsburgh, Allegheny, Pa.	142,975	Tacoma, Pierce, Wash.
632,651	Milwaukee, Milwaukee, Wis.	139,423	Paterson, Passaic, N.J.
594,321	Houston, Harris, Tex.	135,761	Sacramento, Sacramento, Calif.
577,393	Buffalo, Erie, N.Y.	134,382	Albany, Albany, N.Y.
567,257	New Orleans, Orleans Parish‡, La.	133,219	Charlotte, Mecklenburg, N.C.
517,277	Minneapolis, Hennepin, Minn.	132,840	Fort Wayne, Allen, Ind.
500,510	Cincinnati, Hamilton, Ohio	132,496	Gary, Lake, Ind.
462,440	Seattle, King, Wash.	131,964	Austin, Travis, Tex.
453,290	Kansas City, Jackson, Mo.	130,333	Chattanooga, Hamilton, Tenn.
437,857	Newark, Essex, N.J.	130,125	Erie, Erie, Pa.
432,927	Dallas, Dallas, Tex.	130,003	El Paso, El Paso, Tex.
424,683	Indianapolis, Marion, Ind.	129,583	Kansas City, Wyandotte, Kans.
412,856	Denver, Denver, Colo.	127,867	Trenton, Mercer, N.J.
406,811	San Antonio, Bexar, Tex.	127,151	Mobile, Mobile, Ala.
394,012	Memphis, Shelby, Tenn.	125,426	Shreveport, Caddo‡, La.
380,576	Oakland, Alameda, Calif.	124,747	Scranton, Lackawanna, Pa.
374,770	Columbus, Franklin, Ohio	124,543	Camden, Camden, N.J.
371,011	Portland, Multnomah, Oreg.	124,183	Knoxville, Knox, Tenn.
367,359	Louisville, Jefferson, Ky.	124,073	Tampa, Hillsborough, Fla.
331,262	Rochester, Monroe, N.Y.	123,957	Baton Rouge, East Baton Rouge‡, La.
327,090	Atlanta, Fulton, Ga.	120,676	Cambridge, Middlesex, Mass.
321,485	San Diego, San Diego, Calif.	119,689	Savannah, Chatham, Ga.
309,474	St. Paul, Ramsey, Minn.	116,312	Canton, Stark, Ohio
301,358	Toledo, Lucas, Ohio	115,698	South Bend, Saint Joseph, Ind.
300,447	Jersey City, Hudson, N.J.	113,217	Berkeley, Alameda, Calif.
298,720	Birmingham, Jefferson, Ala.	112,675	Elizabeth, Union, N.J.
277,047	Fort Worth, Tarrant, Tex.	111,759	Fall River, Bristol, Mass.
273,189	Akron, Summit, Ohio	111,523	Peoria, Peoria, Ill.
247,700	Providence, Providence, R.I.	109,907	Wilmington, New Castle, Del.
247,408	Omaha, Douglas, Nebr.	109,869	Evansville, Vanderburgh, Ind.
246,983	Miami, Dade, Fla.	109,062	Reading, Berks, Pa.
244,072	Long Beach, Los Angeles, Calif.	109,033	New Bedford, Bristol, Mass.
243,108	Dayton, Montgomery, Ohio	108,053	Corpus Christi, Nueces, Tex.
242,450	Oklahoma City, Oklahoma, Okla.	106,233	Allentown, Lehigh, Pa.
229,906	Richmond, Henrico, Va.	105,442	Phoenix, Maricopa, Ariz.
220,067	Syracuse, Onondaga, N.Y.	105,098	Montgomery, Montgomery, Ala.
203,404	Jacksonville, Duval, Fla.	104,242	Waterbury, New Haven, Conn.
201,885	Worcester, Worcester, Mass.	104,087	Pasadena, Los Angeles, Calif.
188,601	Norfolk, Norfolk, Va.	104,066	Duluth, Saint Louis, Minn.
181,718	Salt Lake City, Salt Lake, Utah	102,254	Somerville, Middlesex, Mass.
180,586	Tulsa, Tulsa, Okla.	101,479	Utica, Oneida, N.Y.
177,073	Hartford, Hartford, Conn.	101,387	Little Rock, Pulaski, Ark.

* Preliminary figures.   The **final population count** of any city or town in the United States (having more than 1000 inhabitants) may be ascertained from the Population Bulletin, "United States Summary", published by the Bureau of the Census, and for sale by the Superintendent of Documents, Government Printing Office, Washington 25, D.C.

† **New York City** ("Greater New York") comprises five boroughs, coextensive with counties: Manhattan (New York County); Brooklyn (Kings County); Bronx; Queens; and Richmond.

‡ **"Parish"** is used in Louisiana, only, instead of "county".

The **county** in which any city or town in the United States is located may be found in the Official Postal Guide under the list of post offices by states.   (See p. 331 for description of Postal Guide.)

POPULATION OF CITIES AND STATES

ALPHABETIC LIST OF THE LARGEST CITIES IN THE UNITED STATES
(On the preceding page, arranged according to rank)

City	1950 population (tentative)	City	1950 population (tentative)	City	1950 population (tentative)
Total, 106 cities...	43,954,910	Fort Wayne, Ind....	132,840	Phoenix, Ariz.......	105,442
		Fort Worth, Tex....	277,047	Pittsburgh, Pa......	673,763
Akron, Ohio........	273,189	Gary, Ind..........	132,496	Portland, Oreg......	371,011
Albany, N.Y........	134,382	Grand Rapids, Mich.	175,647	Providence, R.I....	247,700
Allentown, Pa.......	106,233	Hartford, Conn.....	177,073	Reading, Pa........	109,062
Atlanta, Ga........	327,090	Houston, Tex.......	594,321	Richmond, Va.......	229,906
Austin, Tex........	131,964	Indianapolis, Ind....	424,683	Rochester, N.Y.....	331,252
Baltimore, Md.....	940,205	Jacksonville, Fla...	203,404	Sacramento, Calif...	135,761
Baton Rouge, La....	123,957	Jersey City, N.J....	300,447	St. Louis, Mo.	852,623
Berkeley, Calif.....	113,217	Kansas City, Kans..	129,583	St. Paul, Minn.....	309,474
Birmingham, Ala....	298,720	Kansas City, Mo...	453,290	Salt Lake City, Utah.	181,718
Boston, Mass.......	790,863	Knoxville, Tenn....	124,183	San Antonio, Tex...	406,811
Bridgeport, Conn....	159,352	Little Rock, Ark....	101,387	San Diego, Calif....	321,485
Buffalo, N.Y.......	577,393	Long Beach, Calif...	244,072	San Francisco, Calif.	760,753
Cambridge, Mass....	120,676	Los Angeles, Calif..	1,957,692	Savannah, Ga.......	119,689
Camden, N.J.......	124,543	Louisville, Ky......	367,359	Scranton, Pa.......	124,747
Canton, Ohio.......	116,312	Memphis, Tenn.....	394,012	Seattle, Wash......	462,440
Charlotte, N.C.....	133,219	Miami, Fla.........	246,983	Shreveport, La.....	125,426
Chattanooga, Tenn..	130,333	Milwaukee, Wis....	632,651	Somerville, Mass....	102,254
Chicago, Ill........	3,606,436	Minneapolis, Minn..	517,277	South Bend, Ind....	115,698
Cincinnati, Ohio....	500,510	Mobile, Ala........	127,151	Spokane, Wash.....	160,484
Cleveland, Ohio....	905,636	Montgomery, Ala....	105,098	Springfield, Mass....	162,601
Columbus, Ohio.....	374,770	Nashville, Tenn....	173,359	Syracuse, N.Y......	220,067
Corpus Christi, Tex..	108,053	Newark, N.J.......	437,857	Tacoma, Wash......	142,975
Dallas, Tex........	432,927	New Bedford, Mass.	109,033	Tampa, Fla........	124,073
Dayton, Ohio.......	243,108	New Haven, Conn...	163,344	Toledo, Ohio.......	301,358
Denver, Colo.......	412,856	New Orleans, La....	567,257	Trenton, N.J.......	127,867
Des Moines, Iowa...	176,954	New York, N.Y.....	7,835,099	Tulsa, Okla........	180,586
Detroit, Mich......	1,838,517	Norfolk, Va........	188,601	Utica, N.Y........	101,479
Duluth, Minn.......	104,066	Oakland, Calif......	380,576	Washington, D.C....	802,178
Elizabeth, N.J......	112,675	Oklahoma City, Okla.	242,450	Waterbury, Conn....	104,242
El Paso, Tex.......	130,003	Omaha, Nebr.......	247,408	Wichita, Kans......	166,306
Erie, Pa...........	130,125	Pasadena, Calif.....	104,087	Wilmington, Del....	109,907
Evansville, Ind.....	109,869	Paterson, N.J.......	139,423	Worcester, Mass....	201,885
Fall River, Mass....	111,759	Peoria, Ill.........	111,523	Yonkers, N.Y......	152,533
Flint, Mich........	162,800	Philadelphia, Pa....	2,064,794	Youngstown, Ohio..	167,643

1950 POPULATION OF THE UNITED STATES
Continental United States = 150,697,361 (final figures)

State	1950 population (final)	State	1950 population (final)	State	1950 population (final)
Alabama..........	3,061,743	Kentucky.........	2,944,806	North Dakota......	619,636
Alaska............	128,643	Louisiana.........	2,683,516	Ohio.............	7,946,627
Arizona..........	749,587	Maine............	913,774	Oklahoma.........	2,233,351
Arkansas.........	1,909,511	Maryland.........	2,343,001	Oregon...........	1,521,341
California.........	10,586,223	Massachusetts.....	4,690,514	Pennsylvania......	10,498,012
Colorado.........	1,325,089	Michigan..........	6,371,766	Rhode Island......	791,896
Connecticut.......	2,007,280	Minnesota.........	2,982,483	South Carolina....	2,117,027
Delaware.........	318,085	Mississippi........	2,178,914	South Dakota.....	652,740
District of Columbia.	802,178	Missouri..........	3,954,653	Tennessee........	3,291,718
Florida...........	2,771,305	Montana..........	591,024	Texas............	7,711,194
Georgia..........	3,444,578	Nebraska.........	1,325,510	Utah.............	688,862
Hawaii...........	499,794	Nevada...........	160,083	Vermont..........	377,747
Idaho............	588,637	New Hampshire....	533,242	Virginia..........	3,318,680
Illinois...........	8,712,176	New Jersey.......	4,835,329	Washington.......	2,378,963
Indiana..........	3,934,224	New Mexico.......	681,187	West Virginia......	2,005,552
Iowa.............	2,621,073	New York.........	14,830,192	Wisconsin........	3,434,575
Kansas...........	1,905,299	North Carolina....	4,061,929	Wyoming..........	290,529

REFERENCE BOOKS

An office worker is not expected always to have information at his finger tips, but he is expected to know where to turn to find it.

Every office should have:

> An unabridged dictionary
> A good atlas, and a map of the city
> A statistical almanac for the current year.

Dictionaries. The outstanding American dictionaries are:

> Webster's New International Dictionary (the Merriam-Webster)
> DESK: Merriam-Webster's New Collegiate Dictionary
> Funk & Wagnalls New Standard Dictionary of the English Language
> DESK: Funk & Wagnalls New College Standard Dictionary
> The American College Dictionary, Random House (a desk dictionary)

Every person should own one or all of these desk dictionaries. Each has some words that the others have not.

A pocket edition of a good dictionary should also be kept near the typewriter as a handy spelling reference.

Buy a new and up-to-date dictionary every five or six years—it is a most valuable personal investment.

Technical Dictionaries. Various technical dictionaries are available, such as chemical dictionaries, law dictionaries, medical dictionaries, and financial dictionaries.

If an office has no technical dictionary, an alphabetic list of words peculiar to the business should be compiled and kept in the front of a small dictionary. Many technical words recur infrequently enough to present a spelling problem unless they can be verified; and they are often difficult to relocate in the files. (See also Spelling, p. 143.)

Quotations. For the verification of quotations, both classical and modern, the following books are authoritative:

> Bartlett's **Familiar Quotations,** arranged according to author.
> Stevenson's **Home Book of Quotations,** arranged according to subject.

WHERE TO FIND INFORMATION

Statistical information on various subjects may be found in standard reference books. The following are examples:

ADVERTISING RATES

Standard Rate & Data Service (Chicago: Standard Rate & Data Service, Inc.)

> Advertising rates and circulation figures of daily and weekly newspapers in the United States and Canada; and of all important magazines, business publications, and radio and television stations.

ASSOCIATIONS AND SOCIETIES

Handbook of Scientific and Technical Societies and Institutions of the United States and Canada (Washington, D.C.: The National Research Council of The National Academy of Sciences)

The American **almanacs**, listed on p. 592, contain lists of prominent associations and societies in the United States (alphabetized under the principal word in the name).

BANKS

Rand McNally Bankers Directory (The Bankers Blue Book) (Chicago: Rand McNally & Company)

Data regarding banks in the United States and its possessions, Canada, Mexico, West Indies, Central and South America, Australia, and Asia. Maps.
A selected list of foreign banks and bankers.
List of the directors of national and state banks, savings banks, and trust companies. Names of bankers' associations; state bank officials and examiners; national bank examiners and districts.
Federal Reserve Bank information, and Government banking agencies.
Investment Bankers Association membership; stock exchange members.
Clearing houses in the United States.
Bank numbering system. Accessible banking points.
Digest of banking and commercial laws of the United States, Canada, and Cuba. Uniform Negotiable Instruments Act.
Interest rates; grace on sight drafts, notes, and bills; and statutes of limitations.

BOOKS

The United States Catalog (New York: The H. W. Wilson Company)

List of books published in the United States, indexed by author, subject, and title, with the name of publisher, price, etc.
Supplemented by the Cumulative Book Index, which contains a world list of books in the English language.

CHURCHES

Yearbook of American Churches (New York: Federal Council of the Churches of Christ in America)

Directories of religious bodies in the United States.
Cooperative organizations; service agencies.
State and city councils; ecumenical agencies.
Theological seminaries; colleges and universities.
Religious periodicals; statistics of organized religion.

The Official Catholic Directory (New York: P. J. Kenedy & Sons)

Ecclesiastical statistics of the United States, Alaska, Hawaii, Puerto Rico, Virgin Islands, Canal Zone, Guam; Canada, Ireland, England, Scotland, Wales, Australia, New Zealand, Jamaica, B.W.I.; Cuba, Mexico; Philippines.

The Living Church Annual—The Yearbook of the Episcopal Church (New York: Morehouse–Gorham Co.)

Statistics of the church; names of the clergy; and church almanac.
Statistics and officials of each diocese. Religious orders and institutions.

The annual **almanacs**, listed on p. 592, give various church statistics, the names of bishops, etc., and the headquarters of the various religious denominations.

CITY OFFICIALS

A **directory** or list of city officials is usually for sale in each city, or may be consulted at the public library. Names of city officials may also be obtained from the city hall.

CONGRESS

Congressional Directory (Washington, D.C.: Congressional Committee on Printing)

> Names, addresses, and brief biographies of all congressmen and chief executives in Washington, D.C. Senate and House committee members.
> Departments, agencies, and offices of the Government, with executive personnel.
> List of diplomatic representatives and consular officers here and abroad.
> Members of the press and radio galleries, and news photographers' association.
> Maps of congressional districts.

The Congressional Directory may be consulted at public libraries; or a copy may be obtained from the Superintendent of Documents, Government Printing Office, Washington 25, D.C.—$1.50 a copy.

The **American almanacs,** listed on p. 592, give the names and terms of the members of Congress.

CREDIT RATINGS

Dun & Bradstreet Ratings and Reports (Local offices, or New York: Dun & Bradstreet, Inc.)

> These reports are obtained through subscription; they are not in public libraries.

Credit information may be obtained through arrangement with **credit-reporting bureaus or associations,** listed in the telephone directory under "Credit".

> Credit information may also be obtained through a company's bank. A small charge is made therefor, if a special investigation is necessary.

CUSTOMS INFORMATION

United States Customs Hints for Persons Entering the United States (Washington, D.C.: United States Treasury Department, Bureau of Customs)

> A folder designed to furnish travelers with general information regarding U.S. customs laws and regulations.
> A Spanish version is issued for the information of persons entering the United States from Mexico and other Spanish-speaking countries.
> Copies of these folders may be obtained (without charge)—
> In the United States: from district offices of the Bureau of Foreign and Domestic Commerce; collectors of customs; or the Bureau of Customs, Washington 25, D.C.
> In foreign countries: from United States diplomatic and consular officers; commercial attachés and trade commissioners of the Bureau of Foreign and Domestic Commerce; or Treasury attachés and representatives.
> On passenger vessels: from pursers or other ships' officers.

Passport regulations are given in The World Almanac.
Copies of the **Tariff Act of 1930** may be obtained from the Superintendent of Documents, Government Printing Office, Washington 25, D.C.—20¢ a copy.

Custom House Guide (New York: Import Publications, Inc.)

> U.S. customs ports; customs tariff; customs, shipping, and commerce regulations; internal revenue code; and trade agreements.

589

Exporters' Encyclopaedia (New York: Thomas Ashwell & Co., Inc.)

Consular, shipping, and general information relative to shipments for every country in the world. Ports and trade centers, shipping routes, steamship companies, freight forwarders; communications; foreign trade organizations.

DENTAL DIRECTORY

American Dental Directory (Chicago: American Dental Association)

List of dentists of the United States and its possessions; dental manufacturers; accredited dental schools; state and district societies; foreign associations.

FINANCIAL RATINGS

Moody's Manuals (New York: Moody's Investors Service)
Standard Corporation Records (New York: Standard & Poor's Corporation)

Financial ratings, balance sheets, and income accounts of all the large corporations in the United States, Canada, and foreign countries, in which there is a public interest.
Information for investors in bonds and stocks, including a brief history of each company, with names of officers and directors.

FRATERNITIES AND SORORITIES

Baird's Manual of American College Fraternities (Menasha, Wisconsin: The Collegiate Press)

Description of all American fraternities, sororities, and honor societies.

The World Almanac contains a list of American college fraternities and sororities; also professional fraternities, and honor and recognition societies.

FREIGHT AND EXPRESS

Bullinger's Postal and Shippers Guide (New York: Bullinger's Guides, Inc.)

A shippers' guide for the United States and Canada, containing:
Every post office and railroad station, with the railroad or steamer line on which every place, or the nearest communicating point, is located; and the delivering expresses for every place; also whether or not each place has a post office and a telegraph office.
List of railroads and water lines, with their terminal points.
County for each place, and county seats in the United States.
Steamship lines and foreign ports. Warehouse and transfer section.

GOVERNMENT OFFICIALS

The American **almanacs**, listed on p. 592 (See also Congress, and City Officials, above, and State Officials, below; also Government Departments, p. 486.)

The almanacs give the names, with brief biographies, of the presidents of the United States and their wives. Also a list of their cabinet members.
The names of the following present officials are given in The World Almanac:
President, vice president, and cabinet members.
Executive officers of the departments in Washington, D.C.
Justices of the Supreme Court of the United States; Federal court judges and clerks.
Members of Congress, and their terms.
Rulers or heads of the governments of the world.
Diplomatic representatives here and abroad.
Governors, and other government officials, of the states and territories.
Mayors and city managers of principal American cities.

HOTELS

Hotel Red Book and Directory   (New York: American Hotel Association)

List of hotels, with plan of operation, rates, and name of proprietor or manager. Covers United States, Alaska, Hawaii, West Indies, Bermuda, Mexico, Central and South America, Canada, Australia, and New Zealand.

Hotels in the various cities will supply the names of reliable hotels in other cities.

LAWS AND LAWYERS

The Martindale-Hubbell Law Directory (Summit, N.J.: Martindale-Hubbell, Inc.)

Vols. I & II—Complete roster of the bar of the United States and its posses-
sions, and Canada.   Biographical data and ratings.
Roster of lawyers registered with U.S. Patent Office.
Selected list of lawyers in principal foreign cities.
Vol. III—Digests of the laws of every state in the United States and of its
possessions, Canada, and foreign countries.
Digests of U.S. copyright, patent, tax, and trade–mark laws.
Court calendars; uniform acts; bank collection code.

National Laws—Copies of the various national laws, such as the copyright laws, may be purchased for a nominal sum from the Superintendent of Documents, Government Printing Office, Washington 25, D.C.   (See p. 483 for price list.)

Salient points of certain **national laws,** such as the **Federal income tax, social security, selective service, immigration, and naturalization laws,** may be found in the current American **almanacs,** listed on p. 592.
Public law libraries have copies or synopses of almost all the laws of the land.

The Declaration of Independence⎫
Constitution of the United States⎬ may be found in the current American alma-
Charter of the United Nations⎭   nacs, listed on p. 592.

State Laws—Copies of the different state laws are printed in most of the states, and may be purchased for a nominal sum through the Secretary of State, or the State Librarian, at the capital in each state.   State laws may also be found in inexpensive law books at stationery and book stores in the cities of the various states; and in law books at public libraries (see Martindale-Hubbell Law Directory, above).

Salient points of **state laws** regarding **inheritance taxes, motor vehicles, labor relations, marriage and divorce, interest rates, and taxes,** may be found in the current American **almanacs,** listed on p. 592.

MAPS, MILEAGE, AND STATISTICS

Rand McNally Commercial Atlas and Marketing Guide   (Chicago: Rand McNally & Company)

Part I—United States and Possessions:
Standard map of the United States.
Principal U.S. cities, according to population.
Marketing data; retail sales map and analysis by counties.
Transportation and communication section.
U.S. economic maps; harvesting season maps; manufacturing map
data for manufactures.
U.S. population maps; and population analysis of counties.
State maps and statistics.
Maps and indexes of U.S. possessions.
Highway map; railroad map and distance table.
Air transportation map; air distance table.

Part II—Foreign Countries:
    Maps of continents and foreign countries.
    Principal foreign cities and towns.
    Polar region maps.
    Airline distances between 45 world cities.
    Steamship lines and distances between American and foreign ports.
    World time zone map; world time chart.
    Products, exports, and imports of principal foreign countries.

Road maps may be obtained from gasoline service stations.

MEDICAL DIRECTORY

American Medical Directory (Chicago: American Medical Association)

A register of legally qualified physicians in the United States and its possessions, and Canada.

Information regarding hospitals, medical schools, colleges, and institutions, and medical societies, in the United States and its possessions, and Canada.

Medical officers of Government service.

Examining and licensing boards; medical libraries and journals.

MERCHANTS, MANUFACTURERS, AND SHIPPERS

Thomas' Register of American Manufacturers (New York: Thomas Publishing Company)

Vols. I & II—Classified products list.
Vol. III—Leading manufacturers of the United States.
    Leading trade names and trade–marks. Leading trade papers.
    Boards of trade, chambers of commerce, and similar organizations.
    International section.

MacRae's Blue Book (Chicago: MacRae's Blue Book Company)

An American buyers' guide, giving names and addresses of all important manufacturers, producers, and wholesalers in the United States.

Local distributors; classified material section; trade name section.

Kelly's Directory of Merchants, Manufacturers, and Shippers (London: Kelly's Directories, Ltd.)

Names and addresses of companies throughout the world who are engaged in the exporting and importing, shipping, and manufacturing industries.

General trades classification.

MISCELLANEOUS INFORMATION

The World Almanac (annual) (New York: New York World–Telegram)
Information Please Almanac (annual) (New York: Information Please Almanac)
Whitaker's Almanack (annual) (London: J. Whitaker and Sons, Ltd.)

NEWSPAPERS AND MAGAZINES

N. W. Ayer & Son's Directory of Newspapers and Periodicals (Philadelphia: N. W. Ayer & Son, Inc.)

Names of publications printed in the United States, Alaska, Hawaii, Puerto Rico, Philippines, Canada, Bermuda, and Cuba. Numerous maps.

Description of each publication, telling whether daily, weekly, or monthly, and in what language printed (if foreign); also circulation, and subscription rates; and the salient facts of the town where published, including population.

Classified lists, according to issuance and/or fields.

REFERENCE BOOKS

Newspaper Articles and Stories

The New York Times Index   (New York: The New York Times Company)

All news items and reports are indexed under a name or subject. Following the name or subject, a brief summary or outline of the news report is given with date, page, and column of publication in The New York Times.

Other newspapers keep indexes of their own publications in their own libraries, and will assist in locating articles or stories that have appeared in their papers.

Magazine Articles and Stories

Readers' Guide to Periodical Literature   (New York: The H. W. Wilson Company)

Author and subject index of articles and fiction in a selected list of periodicals, including scientific, technical, and business publications.

POSTAL INFORMATION

United States Official Postal Guide—U.S. Post Office Department (Washington, D. C.: Government Printing Office) (For description and price, see p. 331.)

Postal information may also be obtained by telephone, from "Information" at main post offices.

SCHOOLS

Education Directory—U.S. Office of Education   (Washington, D.C.: Government Printing Office)   (Issued annually in four parts, approximately 25¢ each)

Principal school officers and school governing officials in the United States:
Part 1.   Federal Government and states.
Part 2.   Counties and cities.
Part 3.   Higher education.
Part 4.   Education associations.

Patterson's American Educational Directory   (Chicago: American Educational Company)

Complete list and description of all public, private, and endowed schools, colleges, higher and secondary institutions of learning in the United States.
List of educational officials; library directory.
State and national educational associations and societies.
University and college colors.

American Universities and Colleges   (Washington, D.C.: American Council on Education)

Comprehensive descriptions of various aspects of American higher education.
Pertinent information about 820 accredited institutions of higher learning.

The World Almanac and **Information Please Almanac** give lists of American colleges and universities, including the location of each, year founded, governing official, number of students, number of teachers, and endowment.

Sargent's Handbook of Private Schools for American Boys and Girls   (Boston: Porter Sargent)

American private schools; schools to meet special needs.
Associations, and educational directories.
Private schools in Latin America.

SHIPS

Lloyd's Register of Shipping   (London: Lloyd's Register of Shipping)

> Names, classes, and information about all seagoing merchant ships in the world.
> List of fast merchant steamers and motorships; trading ships on North American lakes; particulars of ships fitted with refrigerating appliances.
> Details of docks and harbors; weight of water at various places.
> List of shipowners, managers, and shipbuilders; marine insurance companies.
> Telegraphic addresses of companies connected with shipping.

Lloyd's Register of Yachts, and **Lloyd's Register of American Yachts**

> Names and classification of yachts; yacht clubs; and yacht owners

STATE OFFICIALS

The state directory, containing a list of state officials and legislators at the state capital (and sometimes officials throughout the state), may be consulted at the public libraries in each state.   Some states have printed directories for free distribution; others make a small charge; while still others have privately printed directories that are sold by the copy.   A few have no printed directories.   Write the Office of the Secretary of State, or the State Librarian, in each state capital for information.

STATISTICS

Statistical Abstract of the United States—U.S. Bureau of the Census   (Washington, D.C.: Government Printing Office)

> Annual summary statistics on the industrial, social, political, and economic organization of the United States.

The American Year Book   (New York: The American Year Book Corporation)
The New International Year Book   (New York: Funk & Wagnalls Company)
The almanacs for the current year   (Listed on p. 592)

> Annual compendium of the world's progress in the scientific, political, business, social, and cultural fields.   Statistics; maps; diagrams; chronology.

TELEPHONE DIRECTORIES

(For directories of American and foreign cities, see Telephone, p. 392.)

TRAVEL

Baedeker's Guide Books (pron. bā'dĕ-ker)   (New York: Charles Scribner's Sons)
The Blue Guides—edited by Muirhead   (New York: Rand McNally & Company)
A Satchel Guide to Europe   (Boston: Houghton Mifflin Company)

> Travelers' handbooks of the different countries of the world; maps and plans.

Guide to America—edited by Jenkins   (Washington, D.C.: Public Affairs Press)

> Historical background, salient facts, and points of interest of each state. Numerous cities and towns, parks, and recreation areas are described.

The American Guide—edited by Alsberg   (New York: Hastings House)

> Tour maps and interesting trips for each region of the United States.

Travel Agencies—**Thos. Cook & Son,** and the **American Express Company**

> These agencies have offices in all of the principal cities of the world.

Travel information may also be obtained from railroads, airlines, bus lines, automobile associations, hotels, banks, and the various travel agencies.

❖

INDEX

600

Envelopes, dark-colored, objectionable in mails, 347
  dispatch methods, 326
  forwarding or holding directions, 327
  full addresses, importance of, 326
  hotel names, 325
  incoming, 363
  letters, preparing for, 327
    method of folding, 328
  mailing, 329
  official form of address, 324
  "Personal", 327
  preferred positions on, 324
  return addresses, 326
  room, apartment, and box numbers, 325
  sealing, 328
  slitting open, 363
  small-sized, objectionable in mails, 332, 347
  stamping, 328; stamped, 347
  street numbers, 325
  trains, mailing on, 329
    packages for, how to address, 330
  weighing, 329
  when to address, 294
"equally as good as", 34
Equipment trust certificates, 512
Equity, in accounting, 525
  in a brokerage account, 514
-er, -est, 42
Erasures and corrections, 413–415
  binding copies, 415
  carbon copies, erasing on, 414
  on checks, 504
  clean erasures, how to make, 414
  in copy for the press, 426
  corrections, putting in, 414
    in bound copies, 415
  errors, typographical, most frequent, 413
  when to erase and when to rewrite, 414
"err is human..., To", 36
Errors, in dictation, 394, 395
  in English, fifteen most common, 3
Escrow, 473
especial, special, 208, 209
"Esquire", in addresses, 296
"essence, time is the", 474
-est, -er, 42
Estimates, obtaining, 426, 455, 456
"et al", "et ux", "et vir", 471
etc., commas around, 224
  not capitalized in headings, 136
  does not pluralize subject, 75
  quoted and not quoted, 237
European clock time, 570
European telephone calls, 391
even, placement of, 11
ever so often, 11
every, singular, 71
every now and again, every now and then, 11
every once in a while, 11
every place for everywhere, 24
every so often, 11
everybody, singular, 71
  occasionally plural, 72
everybody's, 123
everyone, every one, singular, 71
  occasionally plural, 72
everything, singular, 71
except listen, except to listen, 91
Exclamation point, 246–248
  ejaculations or commands, 247
  exclamations in question form, 247
  expressions of emotion, 247
  irony or doubt, expressed by, 247
  mild exclamations, 247
  "O" and "Oh", 247
  placement of, 248
"ex dividend", "ex coupon", "ex rights", 514
"ex dock", "ex warehouse", etc., 398
Execution, in a lawsuit, 470
Executor, executrix, 467
Exhibits A, B, C, etc., 473
expect, for suppose, 31, 210
"Exporters' Encyclopaedia", 590
Export-Import Bank, 489
Export shipping papers, 496

"Exprès" (special delivery), 353
Express services, 364–366
  air express, domestic, 365; foreign, 366
  charges and insurance, 364
  C.O.D. shipments, 364
  foreign express, 366
  grouping of packages, 364
  pickup and delivery, 364
  refrigeration, 365
  special rates, 365
  typewritten or handwritten matter, 365
  wrapping, crating, and boxing, 364
extrapolate, interpolate, 194

F

-faced, etc., 48
Facts, assumed, not subjunctive, 104
  stating, in manuscripts, 427
Familiar phrases, 35–37
"Fan mail", forwarding, 344
Farm Credit Administration, 488
Fashions in words, 27–35
fast, adverb, 47
Father's Day, 582
favor, for letter, 291
Federal Communications Commission, 489
Federal Deposit Insurance Corporation, 489
Federal Housing Administration, 488
Federal Mediation and Conciliation Service, 489
Federal Power Commission, 489
Federal Reserve Bank, 489, 507
"Federal Reserve Bulletin", 517
Federal Reserve System, 489
Federal Security Agency, 488
Federal Trade Commission, 489
Fee simple, 473
Felony, 473
fewer, less, 43
Fiction, writing and marketing, 427
Fidelity bond, 531
Fiduciary, 473
Figures, 265–277 (See also Numbers)
  in cables, 382, 383
  in legal papers, 460
  in telegrams, 371
  in writing clock time, 569, 571
File references, placement of, on letters, 279
Filibuster, 397
Filing, 435–443
  accumulated, 438
  alphabetizing, 439–443
  before or behind guides, 439
  card indexes, 437
  circulars, catalogues, timetables, 439
  classifications, 435
  colored tabs, 436
  cross index and cross reference, 437
  daily or reading file, 437
  "desk" filing, 436
  files taken out of office, 436
  filing stool, 439
  follow-up or tickler systems, 437
  four systems of, 435
  how to file, 438
  inactive files, 439
  index of files, 438
  out cards, 436
  out slips, 436
  photographic duplication, 439
  preparing papers for, 438
  signals, 436
  sorting and arranging, 438
  starting a system, 435
Finance company, 508
Financial papers, 492–516
Financial ratings, where to find, 590
Financial statements, 521–529 (See also Statements)
"Financial Statements, Verification of", 521
Findings of fact, in a lawsuit, 470
fine, for well, 31
finish off, 34
"Fired", reasons for being, 451
Firm, a partnership, 474

609

613

INDEX

The, capitalization of, 134
thence, 12
There is . . . , There are . . . , 76
"Thesaurus, Roget's", 175, 587
they say, 19
they who, or **them who,** 56
think *for,* 34
"Third" ("3d" or "III"), after names, 296
Third-class mail, 333–336
    bulk mailings, 335
    forwarding, 344
    insurance, 339
this, for **thus** or **so,** 30
"Thomas' Register of American Manufacturers",
    592
Thos. Cook & Son, 594
those **kind of,** 13
those *ones,* 34
thousand, singular or plural, 277
    by the thousand, by thousands, 276
"three R's, the", 36
"three sheets in the wind", 36
thrive, principal parts of, 102
through, for **finished,** 32
thusly, 49
Tickler system, 437
Time, 569–579
    clock, 569
    differences in, in telegraphing, 374
    divisions of, 578
    European clock, 570
    Greenwich mean, 571
    periods of, how to write, 571
    periods of years, words relating to, 579
    standard, 571–577
Time expressed, by verbs, 93–96
"time is the essence", 474
Timetables, catalogues, etc., 439
Title insurance, 532
Titles, abbreviations of, 300
    business, in addresses, 299
    capitalization of, 133
    in signatures, 283–284
    on telegrams, 373
    foreign, for "Mr.", "Mrs.", etc., 307
    pluralized with names, 115
    possessive of, with names, 118
    possessives in, 122
    unhyphened, 255
"to" omitted, 30, 91
to be, to have been, time expressed by, 94
to be he, him, I, or **me,** 51
to do, or **to doing,** 92
to her and them, 49
too, for **too much,** 22
to use, or **to using,** 92
"To Whom It May Concern:", 289
Township, division of land, 564
Tracer, on shipments, 494
"track, on the wrong", 36
trade-mark, trademark, 253n.
Trade-marks, term of, fees, etc., 479
Trade paper, 502
Train mail time (table), 348
Trains, addresses to, 369
    mail for, 329–330
    telephone calls to, 391
Tramp steamer, 396
Transcript of record, 470
Translation bureaus, 307
transmission, transmittal, transmittance, 212
Transmittal, letters of, 289
Transportation insurance, 532
Travel, information about, 594
Travel agencies, 594
Travelers' checks, 505
Treasury bills, treasury certificates, 512
Treasury Department, the, 486
Troy weight (table), 561
Trust, property held in, 474
Trust company, 507
Trust deed, 466
Trustee, in bankruptcy, 526
Trust receipt, 500
try and come, 92
Turn-key job, 398

Twentieth century, defined, 578
two first, two last, 11
Two-name paper, 502
Type, kinds of, 431
    sizes and styles of, 432
type of, 13; "of" omitted, 49
Typewriter, 411, 412
    ribbons, rollers, etc., 411
    type sizes and styles, 412
Typewriting, touch, speed, etc., 410–412
    capital shifts, 410
    errors, typographical, 413
    to make fast progress on long job, 416
Typewritten matter, mailing, 331
    not by express, 365
Typewritten work, 399–415
    dating papers, 404
    end of page, 403
    headings, 399
        indenting unnumbered, 401
    margins, 399
    numbered items, 400
        "first", "second", etc., 402
        quantities, 401
        unsegregated numberings, 402
    page numbering, 403, 404
    paragraphing, 402
    piecework, charging for, 404
    tabulations, 404

U

un-, 23
Underlying mortgage, 467
Underscore, 263
    in copy for the press, 422
"under way", 37
Underwriting, 532
Unfinished sentences, punctuation of, 262
United Nations, 485
United Nations Day, 582
United States, the (table), 584
"United States Catalog, The", 588
"United States Customs Information for Pas-
    sengers from Overseas", 589
United States Government departments, 485–490
    (See also Government information)
"United States Government Printing Office Style
    Manual", vi
    on not hyphening titles, 255
    on spelling, 140
United States Maritime Commission, 489
Universities, pronunciation of names of, 173
unless, without, 22
"unless and until", 35
unlike, 22
Unlisted securities, 512
Unmailable matter, 347
Unprintable words, how indicated, 262
up, superfluous after some verbs, 35
up **above,** 35
upon, on, up on, 65
up **until,** 35
upward of, 69
use, no use in, of **no use to,** 16
Use and occupancy insurance, 532
use **to, used to,** 93
us workers, 50

V

Valentine's Day, 582
Valued policy, 532
"Vanity of vanities . . .", 37
vary from, 69
Vegetables, special express rate on, 365
Vegetation, pronunciation of terms pertaining to,
    174
Venue, 474
verbal, oral, 200
Verbs, 79–103
    old forms of, 98
    principal parts of, 98
    proper relation of tenses, 97
    time expressed by, 93–96
    wrong forms as modifiers, 102
Verb understood, in inverted construction, 79

615

INDEX